THE
JEWISH PARENTS'
ALMANAC

THE
JEWISH PARENTS'
ALMANAC

JULIE HILTON DANAN

JASON ARONSON INC.
Northvale, New Jersey
London

Grateful acknowledgment is made to the following for permission to reprint material copyrighted or controlled by them:

Translation of the *berachah* formulation is taken from *Vetaher Libenu,* copyright © 1980 Congregation Beth El of the Sudbury River Valley, and is used with their permission.

"The Dalai Lama Speaks to the Jews," by Jeffrey K. Salkin, copyright © April 1990, *Moment* magazine. Reprinted by permission of *Moment* magazine.

Recipes from *Love and Best Dishes* copyright © 1977 by Agudas Achim Sisterhood. Reprinted by permission of Agudas Achim Sisterhood.

"The Enchanted Broccoli Forest," from *The Enchanted Broccoli Forest . . . and other timeless delicacies,* by Mollie Katzen, copyright © 1982 by Mollie Katzen. Reprinted by permission of Ten Speed Press.

"Hutzpah Hamantaschen," from *The Kosher Cajun Cookbook,* by Mildred L. Covert and Sylvia P. Gerson, copyright © 1987 by Mildred L. Covert and Sylvia P. Gerson. Reprinted by permission of Pelican Publishing Company, Inc.

Material by Arlene Rossen Cardozo and Danny Siegel is used with their permission.

Design by Pamela Roth.

This book was set in 10 pt. Palacio by Lind Graphics of Upper Saddle River, New Jersey, and printed and bound by Haddon Craftsmen of Scranton, Pennsylvania.

Library of Congress Cataloging-in-Publication Data

Danan, Julie Hilton.
    The Jewish parents' almanac / by Julie Hilton Danan.
       p. cm.
    Includes bibliographical references and index.
    ISBN 0-87668-474-6
    1. Jewish families—Religious life. 2. Jewish way of life.
  3. Judaism—Customs and practices. 4. Fasts and feasts—Judaism.
  5. Parenting—Religious aspects—Judaism. I. Title.
  BM723.D37 1993
  296.7'4—dc20   91-45181

Manufactured in the United States of America. Jason Aronson Inc. offers books and cassettes. For information and catalog write to Jason Aronson Inc., 230 Livingston Street, Northvale, New Jersey 07647.

TO MY PARENTS

In loving memory of my father
Dr. Charles Bernard Hilton

אבי מורי גדליה ברוך בר ישעיהו וציפורה ז״ל

A man who was larger than life,
who taught me to have a passion for life
and showed me how to learn from everyone.

להתב׳לח׳א

In honor of my mother
Betty Lindheim Hilton

אמי מורתי יפה בתיה בת חיה ומיכאל
who has given me a love for the written word
and a lifelong commitment
to the spiritual journey.

לדור ודור נגיד גדלך

"From generation to generation
we will proclaim Your greatness,
And to all eternity
we will tell of Your holiness."

CONTENTS

CONTENTS

PART II   LEARNING, LEARNING, LEARNING

PART III JEWISH INTERPERSONAL VALUES: TRANSMITTING A GOODLY HERITAGE

CONTENTS

PART IV   ISRAEL: THE JEWISH HOME AND THE JEWISH HOMELAND

PART V   THE JEWISH WEEK, MONTH, AND YEAR

CONTENTS

CONTENTS

PART VI SPECIAL TIMES IN THE LIFE OF A YOUNG JEWISH FAMILY

CONTENTS

ACKNOWLEDGMENTS

Many people generously contributed of their time and knowledge to help me complete this book. There are two individuals without whom the present volume would not be what it is. Dr. Wendy Drezek read much of the book at various stages, contributed numerous ideas and family anecdotes, and gave many helpful suggestions based on both her expertise as a child-development specialist and her experiences as a mother of three Jewish teenagers. In addition, she generously gave many hours of her time to discussing the book and its progress.

I am very grateful to Arthur Kurzweil for his part in making this book a reality. Not only did Arthur have faith in a first-time author with an interesting idea, but he helped to shape the direction of this project from just another "activity book" to something that I hope will prove more meaningful and enduring.

Likewise, I am indebted to my copy editors, Sanford Robinson and Marlys Lehmann, to Jason Aronson's editorial director, Muriel Jorgensen, and to production editor Janet Warner, for their excellent and thoughtful work.

I met Arthur Kurzweil at a conference of the Coalition for the Advancement of Jewish Education (CAJE), and it is CAJE that I must acknowledge next. It was through CAJE that I was able to meet leaders in Jewish education and Jewish thought and to learn about the many resources listed in this volume. Special thanks to Eliot Spack, CAJE's executive director, and Betsy Dolgin Katz, general chairperson at the time this book was in progress.

Appreciation is due to Dr. Jonathan Woocher, executive vice-president of JESNA, the Jewish Educational Service of North America. His lectures on the American Jewish family were very helpful, and he also took the time to discuss this book and its potential audience with me.

It would be impossible to list all of the CAJE members who have helped me in some way, but I would particularly like to acknowledge how much I have learned from several individuals. Danny Siegel contributed to this book and was generous with materials and ideas. The content of the "Jewish values" section is largely due to his inspiration. Seymour Rossel, who has taught me much

about Jewish education, took the time to speak to me at length about a number of issues. He also chaired the CAJE Israel Conference, which proved important to many parts of this book. Peninnah Schram provided many insights and materials on Jewish storytelling, as well as her friendship.

Many other CAJE members have helped with the development of this book. Carolyn Starman Hessel has been a friend to me during the "long haul" of preparing this manuscript. I thank her for all the long-distance phone calls, bibliographic material, and networking suggestions. She put me in touch with Vicky Kellman, who taught me about Jewish family education and persuaded me to attend the Whizin Institute. Rabbi Stuart Kellman guided me to resources about Jewish prayer. Rivka Behar, of the Board of Jewish Education of Greater New York, was most helpful with ideas and materials on Jewish early-childhood education. Cherie Koller Fox offered valuable ideas about Jewish family education and its significance. Lyn Fine provided material on peace education and conflict resolution. Thanks also to singer Debbie Friedman and to the members of *Beged Kefet* and *Hallel* for their wonderful music, which inspired me during many long hours at my desk.

The Whizin Institute Seminar on Jewish Family Education, which I attended while I was completing this book, enhanced my work greatly. Thanks to Dr. Ron Wolfson, Gail Dorph, and all the teachers. The late Prof. Perry London, in particular, took time to speak with me about Jewish identity, society, and history. Dr. Kathy Chesto offered insights into the spirituality of family life. Thanks to the Whizin family for making it possible.

A number of parents contributed anecdotes from their personal experiences for this book. I am most grateful to author Arlene Rossen Cardozo for generously contributing her family story to the current volume. I would also like to thank my friends Wendy and Stan Drezek, Saul and Cindy Rosenthal, Joel and Hedy Rutman, and Jody and Hal Crane, who contributed "family snapshots." Thanks to my "Israel correspondents," Sue Rosenstein Reiss and Charley Levine, and to Rukhl Schaechter-Ejdelman for her piece about Yiddish in the home.

ACKNOWLEDGMENTS

A number of individuals and organizations provided me with research and background materials for this book. Dr. Steven Bayme, director of Jewish Communal Affairs for the American Jewish Committee, provided me with AJC Institute of Human Relations publications about research on contemporary trends in Jewish life. The American Friends of the Shalom Hartman Institute, particularly Rabbi Donniel Hartman and Ms. Dorothy Minchin, generously sent me Hartman Institute publications of Jewish source materials. Ellen Bernstein, executive director of *Shomrei Adamah*, provided materials on conservation.

I want to thank several other individuals who offered spiritual and educational ideas that enhanced this book: Dr. Yehudah Wurtzel, Rabbi Naomi Levy, Rabbi David Nelson, Dr. Barry Holtz, Joel Lurie Grishaver, and Hanoch Teller. I am especially grateful that I was able to interview Rabbi Harold Kushner about contemporary Jews and their relationships to God.

Thanks to all the San Antonio friends who helped to make this work possible. It would be impossible to mention everyone by name, but I am particularly indebted to Rabbi Aryeh and Judy Scheinberg for their continued encouragement and support, particularly to Rabbi Scheinberg for use of his library and for his interest in this project. Thanks to Hilton and Sylvia Goldman for their help at Temple Beth El's Bendiner library and Jewish resource center, to Gerry Phillips of the L'Chayim Gift Shop for providing me with many addresses of Judaica suppliers, to Caela Kaplowitz (since moved to Seattle), who let me rummage through her library, and to Ruthie Premack for enabling me to attend CAJE by providing child care. Gary Stillman helped with the initial research into resource materials, and Barbara Ganz (since moved to Arizona) contributed her research into Holocaust literature for young people. Thanks to Aviva Bass for sharing her famous *hallah* and *sufganiot* recipes. Lenell Thomas and Jody Tucker typed the early proposals and query letters that led to this book.

My deepest appreciation and affection goes to all the members of Congregation Beth Am. Particular thanks to Gary Kates for his assistance with my research at Trinity University and to everyone who has learned about and worked on Jewish education with me, especially Judith Lipsett and Gayle Fish.

And thank you, John Boswell, for writing *The Awful Truth About Publishing* (Warner Books), without which I may have given up after my first fifteen tries at finding a publisher.

Aharon, aharon, haviv—finally, and dearest, the people without whom there wouldn't be any *Jewish Parents' Almanac*—because without them I wouldn't be a Jewish parent! To my wonderful children, Liora, Elisheva, Shira, Charles Haviv, and Arielle: thank you for putting up with having a mother who spent all those hours in front of the word processor, writing about things you'd rather be *doing*. Thank you to my beloved husband, Avraham, for learning with me, parenting with me, and in many, many ways enabling me to write this book.

All thanks are ultimately due to the One:

"*Open my lips, that my mouth may declare Your praise.*"

INTRODUCTION

This book is designed to give Jewish parents the knowledge, creative ideas, and resources to create an exciting and stimulating Jewish environment in their own homes. A decade of work in Jewish education has shown me that today's Jewish parents care deeply about creating happy and beautiful Jewish memories for their children. Parents instinctively know that raising their children is a sacred task; for many, the most spiritually intense endeavor of their lives. At the same time, many parents feel that they themselves lack the Jewish education to teach and guide their children. Other parents have a strong and committed Jewish background, but are looking for new activities and materials to share with their families. This book was written to give Jewish parents of all backgrounds the tools they need to create a rich Jewish life-style.

This book is the book that I found myself looking for ten years ago as a young parent: a volume that would provide Jewish family activities, guidelines, and resources, along with spiritual, psychological, and intellectual Judaic perspectives. Writing this book has been a long and exciting journey, both as a parent and as an educator. I have read hundreds of publications and attended dozens of lectures and workshops by leaders in Jewish education, and now I want to share my discoveries with the most important educators of all, Jewish parents.

My journey started as a Jewish teen in Texas. Like many of my generation, I wanted to learn more about my heritage. As a teenager, I began to learn Hebrew, to read Jewish philosophy, and to study Jewish sources. I continued my quest in college, where I concentrated in Hebrew and Judaic studies at the University of Texas. After a year there, I moved to Israel and studied for another year in the Combined Jewish Studies program (for Israeli students) at Bar-Ilan University, before receiving a degree in literature from Tel Aviv University.

My career in Jewish education began back in the United States. Much of my motivation stemmed from my concerns as a parent as well as a teacher. I wanted my young children to enjoy stimulating and creative early-childhood programs in Jewish education as well as in secular education. Gradu-

ally, I began to work all around my local Jewish community: teaching in religious schools and adult education programs, speaking for a community lecture bureau, getting involved in informal education such as day camps, and writing for and helping to edit the local *Jewish Journal*.

As I got more deeply involved in Jewish education, I read many books and periodicals on both Judaism and education and attended numerous lectures and in-service programs, as well as the Conference on Alternatives in Jewish Education, which is sponsored annually by the Coalition for the Advancement in Jewish Education. At these conferences, I was able to learn from leading Jewish thinkers, authors, and educators and to see the latest developments in Jewish publications, music, the arts, and informal educational tools. In this book, I hope to bring much of what I have learned home to you, the Jewish parent.

I became the director of the San Antonio Association for Jewish Education, where I coordinated communitywide educational programs and organized in-service programs for teachers from Reform, Conservative, and Orthodox schools, as well as a community day school and early childhood program. I also created home-study guides for the local Jewish newspaper, on subjects such as the Jewish holidays, Shabbat, and Jewish values. Families responded warmly to these resources, and I was encouraged to circulate my articles on Jewish living more widely. I self-syndicated my column, "BaBayit: The Jewish Home," and it appeared in a couple of dozen Jewish publications around the country. In many communities, parents wanted to learn more about how to celebrate, teach, and inspire their children in Jewish living. What started as individual columns and study guides soon began to grow into a book.

When I became religious program director of Congregation Beth Am in San Antonio, I also became involved in the exciting new field of Jewish Family Education. Our congregation became a grant recipient and test site for family-education programs disseminated by the Whizin Institute for Jewish Family Life at the University of Judaism in Los Angeles, where I attended an intensive seminar on the subject. Jewish Family Education views the entire family, parents as well as children, as the clients of Jewish education. Through publications and programs for the family, it aims to empower parents as the primary educators of their own children. The current volume is one example of a family-education tool.

Many friends have shared with me in my journey of discovery of Jewish education. In particular, Dr. Wendy Drezek, a special-education teacher and child-development specialist and the mother of three Jewish teenagers, has spent long hours sharing her perspectives on developmentally appropriate Jewish education with me. She and her husband, Stan, who also holds a doctorate in education, provided their children's Jewish educations almost completely at home, even though that sometimes meant teaching themselves one step ahead of their own children. Their children became proficient in Hebrew, liturgy, Bible, Midrash, and even studied Mishnah. They helped to found a local *havurah* and congregation and often held popular holiday programs at their own home. At the same time, they have lived their values by infusing their everyday lives with *tzedakah* and deeds of social action. The fact that Stan is a Jew-by-choice and that two of their children are adopted African-Americans, combined with Wendy's educational specialty, has made the Drezeks into real-life experts on the multifaceted reality of today's Jewish community. Wendy frequently reviewed my growing manuscript and provided it with the dual perspectives of a master educator and the parent of older children.

My husband, Avraham Raphael Danan, has been my closest companion on the journey of Jewish education and parenting. He has given me a completely new Jewish perspective, since he is a Sephardic Jew born in Morocco and educated in traditional settings in Morocco and later in Israel. Most American Jews, like myself, are the descendents of Ashkenazic Jews from Central and Eastern Europe. Sephardic Jews trace their roots back to Spain, the Middle East, and the Balkans. Avraham has taught me a great deal about Judaism and has introduced me and our children to the special customs and approaches of Sephardic Jewry, which I have integrated throughout this book. These Sephardic Jewish practices provide a Jewish dimension that is artistic, spiritual, mystical, and sometimes even humorous.

The great Jewish sage Rabbi Yehudah HaNasi said, "I have learned most of all from my students." That is true for me as a parent and educator as well. My pupils of all ages, and especially my own five children, have taught me the most about education and family life. They have shown me what works, and sometimes what doesn't work. The ideas in this book are not only the result of study and research, but also of practical experience, both as an educator and as a parent.

One crucial thing that I have learned over the years is that we as parents can teach our children to love and appreciate something only when we value and cherish it for ourselves. That's why this book is designed to help parents discover or rediscover the treasures of Judaism for themselves first. Resources for adults are listed before resources for children. When you know what your Jewish heritage means to you, conveying it to your children can become a natural process.

This book, like raising my children, is a labor of love. May it be one of the guidebooks for Jewish parents on the journey of discovery that leads back home.

A NOTE ON THE TRANSLITERATIONS AND TRANSLATIONS OF THE *BERACHOT*

The *Berachah* formula with which traditional Jewish blessings begin, *Baruch Atah Adonai, Eloheinu Melech HaOlam*, is commonly translated as "Blessed are You, Lord our God, Ruler of the Universe."

In this volume, I have used an alternate translation: "Holy One of Blessing, Your Presence fills creation."

The phrasing of this alternate translation is contemporary and poetic, yet deeply rooted in Jewish spiritual and mystical tradition. It is used in *VeTaher Libenu* (Purify Our Hearts), the prayer book of Congregation Beth El of the Sudbury River Valley (Sudbury, MA, 1989), and I appreciate their permission to adopt it for the present volume.

Throughout the book, English and transliterations have been provided for blessings, prayers, and services. Readers wishing to have the Hebrew should refer to a prayer book.

THE SECRET

One of the most important, and one of the most unusual moments in interreligious dialogue occurred in a mountain retreat in New Jersey. The Dalai Lama, the major spiritual leader of Tibetan Buddhism, held a meeting with a small group of Jewish thinkers. It is possible that this was the first time in history that a Buddhist leader has ever talked with Jews.

Even more unusual than this was the purpose of the meeting. The Dalai Lama wanted advice. The Dalai Lama is in exile from his land. He wanted to know how we did it . . . how it is that we survived exile from our land over the centuries.

The men in the group had their own answers. One said that it was the study of Torah that has kept us alive. Another said that it was the study of Talmud that kept us alive. A third said that it was the doing of *mitzvot* and the pursuit of justice that has kept us alive. A fourth said that it was our inability to agree on what has kept us alive that has kept us alive.

Blu Greenberg, the Orthodox feminist, told the Dalai Lama: "The secret of our survival is the Jewish family. For it is the family where the physical existence of the people and the values of Judaism intersect."

And the Dalai Lama looked at Blu Greenberg and said, almost in a whisper: "That is the secret."

—"The Dalai Lama Speaks to Jews"
Jeffrey K. Salkin
"Sermon Excerpts"
Moment magazine, April 1990

I

HOME AND HERITAGE

1

JUDAISM AND STRONG FAMILIES

THE INHERITANCE UNDER OUR OWN FLOORBOARDS

A story:

A poor but starry-eyed hasidic Jew—we'll call him Yankel—dreamed repeatedly of a faraway treasure buried near a royal palace and finally decided to seek that treasure, whatever the effort. He journeyed many days over rough terrain until he reached the great city and the royal palace. But when at last poor Yankel reached his destination, a palace guard laughed at his dreams of grandeur. The guard mockingly told Yankel that he, too, had dreamed of a buried treasure—hidden under the floor of a humble home whose description, it so happened, exactly matched the poor Jew's home.

Yankel quickly returned home, pried up part of the floor, and discovered that, lo and behold, the treasure of his dreams had been hidden there all the while, left as an inheritance from generations past.[1]

Like Yankel, who journeyed far in search of riches, contemporary parents will go to great lengths to seek the best for their children. Never before have parents, particularly those who are well educated (as so many American Jews are), analyzed the process of raising a child to the degree we do today. The very neologism "parenting" is not only significant as a nonsexist term for "mothering" and "fathering" but also represents a new self-consciousness about what was once considered a nearly instinctive role. There are many

new volumes on every conceivable aspect of parenting and family life. Parents spend millions each year on books about children's nutrition, fitness, academic achievement, behavior, self-esteem, moral development, and much more. There are many conflicting theories on the "right" way to raise children in a changing and sometimes threatening world.

Yet when it comes to being a good parent or creating a warm and nurturing family environment, the treasure "under our own floorboards" may provide the greatest resource of all. The great riches of the Jewish heritage are our inheritance, waiting to be discovered no matter how far away we may have journeyed. This treasure known as Judaism includes a way of life that fosters family strengths and intimacy, that adds an extra measure of stability and nurturance in an insecure time.

Contemporary theories of child development and child psychology can provide us with many useful guidelines and techniques. But Judaism can go beyond the "how," toward the "why." Judaism can help our families develop a sense of meaning and purpose.

This treasure called Judaism is not for ourselves alone, but for generations to come. Most of us take great care in planning how to provide for our children financially, how to pay for their higher education, and even for the inheritance we will someday leave for our children. But there is another legacy besides the financial and another "higher" education besides the academic. Parents today are rediscovering the importance of plan-

3

ning for their children to receive a legacy of faith and an education in values. Along with an inheritance, our children deserve a heritage.

For the fortunate, the Jewish way of life is a treasure they grew up with. Others begin to recover its riches on their own as adults. Still other Jews rediscover the potential in a Jewish way of life when they have children and realize that they want to give them a sense of meaning and belonging beyond what a secular society can offer.

"STRONG FAMILY" RESEARCH

There are many new challenges and stresses facing the modern family. American Jewish families are subject to the same changes and strains as the rest of society, including high mobility (and the concurrent lack of stability, roots, and close extended family), divorce and single-parent or blended households, two-career families with limited time and energy to spare, as well as the general stresses of raising children in a complex society burdened with such problems as environmental hazards, substance abuse, moral failings, and violence.[2]

Despite these stresses, many families today not only survive, but also thrive; somehow these families find the inner resources necessary to flourish amid the pressures of modern society. Although much research has focused on what makes families dysfunctional, some recent studies have examined what makes them "work." Researchers found that certain qualities and traits, expressed in concrete behaviors and actions, foster family strength and health.[3] Among these traits and qualities vital to healthy family functioning are a strong commitment to the family unit and a strong sense of family (including special family traditions); effective and frequent communication; appreciation, affirmation, and support for one another; large quantities of quality time together—including lots of shared "table time" and leisure time; a shared religious core that includes family-centered rituals and traditions and that fosters spiritual wellness; strong values about things such as right and wrong and service to others; and, of course, mutual respect, trust, and other manifestations of emotional wellness.

"Strong" and "healthy," of course, do not mean "perfect" or "stress free." The researchers were quick to point out that possessing these desirable characteristics cannot guarantee that families will never face problems. Rather, the ability to recog-

nize problems, to seek help in solving them, and to grow stronger as a result of life's challenges are key traits of a successful family unit.

THE JEWISH DIMENSION

It's striking how many of these general qualities and specific traits of "strong, healthy" families are fostered by a Jewish way of life. Clearly, Judaism offers a family a shared religious core and a spiritual orientation with many beloved rituals and traditions that center in the home. Moreover, the Jewish way of life values and emphasizes commitment, appreciation, quantities of shared family time (especially around the Shabbat and holiday table), the teaching of values and morals, service to others, participation in a community that gives psychological support in difficult times, and other traits of emotional health and stability.

Many contemporary Jewish families are rediscovering that Judaism is a healthy and nurturing framework for raising a family. Parenting books and courses can help us to be good parents, but Judaism can offer our families even more—opportunities for closeness, communication, and commitment.

As already noted, possessing certain traits or qualities does not guarantee that a family's life will be perfect. Similarly, choosing a Jewish life-style, even a deeply committed one, does not promise that our family life will be an ideal one. But Judaism itself, and the Jewish communities we connect with and create, can help us to deal with many of life's difficulties and challenges.

And Judaism adds yet another dimension. For as sacred and precious as our families are to most of us, it would be a mistake to look to the family unit as a world unto itself or as the ultimate source of meaning in our lives. Hard as it is to believe in the child-centered early years of a family, there is no guarantee that the family alone will continue to satisfy our hunger for meaning and validation over an entire life span. The nuclear family is much more than a certain household configuration; it is a mentality that sees the family as a closed unit, an island. But the family needs to be much more than a drifting island, no matter how lovely and peaceful that island may be. Rather, the family needs to be part of a network that links it to a past heritage, a present community, and a future vision. Such is the case for a family life based on Judaism.

BRINGING JUDAISM BACK HOME

Just as if Judaism is good for the Jewish family, enhancing family life is good for the future of Judaism. Without overromanticizing the "traditional" Jewish family, it is clear that the home has been a primary building block of Jewish life and has helped to sustain the Jewish people through the ages. Many (although certainly not all) important Jewish observances take place in the home rather than in the synagogue or public domain. Home, as well as synagogue, is called *mikdash me'at*, a "miniature Holy Temple."

A striking change in Jewish life in contemporary times has been its dramatic shift from the personal to the public realm. Few Jews these days feel a need to hide or deny that they are Jewish, but for many, *Judaism itself* has become the province of big synagogues, professionals, organizations, and institutions—"out there." Of course, this is a tendency in modern life in general: increasing specialization and professionalization accompanied by decreasing self-sufficiency.

When many contemporary American Jews go home, their homes are just like the homes of other secularly oriented, middle- or upper-middle-class families. For many Jews, being Jewish has been emptied of spiritual content and has become, as writer and Jewish thinker Leonard Fein puts it so well, "essentially about patterns of affiliation and association rather than values and beliefs and ideas."[4] Where Enlightenment thinkers had urged Jews to "be a Jew in your home and a man on the street," now most of us can confidently wear our Jewish identities in public, but often have little use for Judaism itself in the privacy of our homes.[5]

Just as a body without a soul cannot survive, so our Jewish community cannot really flourish without the personal dimension. The most sophisticated and magnificent institutions may become empty facades when our homes lose the radiance of Jewish learning, spirituality, and practice. Conversely, a revitalized Jewish home life can breathe new life into all facets of the Jewish enterprise in our day.

This revitalization of Judaism is happening—at least among a significant minority. Now that Jews of Eastern European descent in America have very successfully Americanized themselves, many among the younger generations have begun to make a real effort to *re-judaize* their lives.[6] Where this hasn't occurred, often the problem is not a lack of desire but a lack of confidence. Many fourth- and fifth-generation American Jews really want to "know more about Judaism" or to "do more Jewish things at home with their families," but they feel ignorant and hence, "inferior." Someone who is extremely sophisticated and educated in secular life, yet virtually illiterate when it comes to Judaism, would often rather stay uninvolved than suffer the awkwardness of exposing this vulnerability.

The Talmud tells of an illiterate shepherd who lived in the land of Israel in Roman times. At the age of 40, he sat down with his children and studied the Hebrew alphabet, then the Torah, then the Oral Law. He chose to study a little each day, rather than to despair over his lack of knowledge. Soon he became a teacher, then a leader of hundreds and thousands.

Thus goes the story of Rabbi Akiba, one of the greatest sages, Jewish leaders, and moral heroes who ever lived. Whenever an adult puts aside discomfort and apprehension to seek again the wisdom of Torah, Rabbi Akiba is there, learning by his or her side.

2

MAKING LIFE MORE MEANINGFUL

BACK TO THE CENTER

... It is indeed a return to Judaism, but not to the external framework, not to the religious norms that man seeks to understand or to integrate into, with their clear-cut formulae, directives, actions, rituals; it is a return to one's own paradigm, to the prototype of the Jewish person.

—Adin Steinsaltz[1]

There is no one today who is not alienated, or who does not contain within himself some small fraction of alienation. All of us to whom Judaism, to whom being a Jew, has again become the pivot of our lives—and I know that in saying this here I am not speaking for myself alone—we all know that in being Jews we must not give up anything, not renounce anything, but lead everything back to Judaism. From the periphery back to the center; from the outside, in.

—Franz Rosenzweig[2]

I learned an important concept for Jewish parenting in an unlikely setting: a large public lecture given by author Chaim Potok. Potok spoke of the unseen trail of ideas through civilization, of how ideas transcend their originators, overcoming time and space to shape the course of history. Without realizing it, most of us see the world through the concepts of thinkers whose names and lives we are scarcely aware of.

We may live at the core or on the periphery of a civilization, explained Potok. We may be infused

with its most profound ideas or have commerce only with its most trivial ideas. In terms of education, many young people today grow up on the periphery of American culture. If they go to a fine university or a liberal arts college and there encounter the core ideas, concepts, and literature of Western civilization, their whole way of thinking and seeing life may be profoundly transformed. (Too often, of course, their education lacks even this dimension.)

Potok remembered walking through a hasidic section of Brooklyn. Approaching him were a father and son, in traditional dress, conversing in Yiddish about some subject from the Torah. These were obviously people steeped in the core ideas and practices of traditional Judaism. They managed to live in the midst of American society, yet remain aloof from most of its culture. Suddenly, the boy saw a collie (if memory fails me not, it was Potok who was walking the dog for a friend). The boy began to call to his father, "Look, *Tatte*, it's Lassie!" Despite his insulation from much of contemporary American culture, this hasidic child couldn't avoid some contact with its periphery. For him and his family, such peripheral trivia as "Lassie" was probably considered the essence of modern American society.

But what if that boy, like Potok's hasidic character in *The Chosen*,[3] went to a top university and encountered some of the more central elements of Western culture: philosophy, psychology, literature? Of course there would be the danger that he would turn away completely from his past, or that he would withdraw even more from the threat

7

of the outside world. But there would also be a unique opportunity for synergistic growth. The situation would, in Potok's analysis, contain the potential for tremendous creativity. When someone infused with the core of one culture encounters the core of another, the creative results can be awesome, such as Maimonides' meeting with Greek philosophy or Picasso's "discovery" of African art.

All this, of course, has a great deal of bearing on our experiences as Jewish parents today. Many Jewish Americans grow up today on the periphery of Jewish culture, experiencing an isolated ritual here or there, having only a passing familiarity with some of the more obvious outward forms and norms of their heritage. The core of the Jewish experience—the sources and texts, the Hebrew language, the spirituality, philosophies, and creative expressions—are almost unknown to many American Jews. Yet these same people may at the same time be quite immersed in the core of secular Western culture. American Jews are among the highest academic achievers in secular fields, with a percentage all out of proportion to our numbers graduating from college and going on to earn advanced degrees, yet in Jewish studies our educational enrollment peaks at age thirteen! Jews who know literature, philosophy, music, and science may know little of their Jewish heritage.

When a person is on the periphery of a culture, he or she tends to think that the peripheral elements *are* the core, as the hasidic boy and his family probably thought that Lassie-type *narishkeit* (nonsense) was pretty much what the secular world had to offer. Conversely, those Jews on the periphery of Jewish culture can easily mistake the *Jewish* periphery for the core of Judaism. They might suppose that the core of the Jewish experience lies in things that actually constitute the fringe phenomena of a four-thousand-year-old religious civilization. Perhaps *Judaism* to them is represented by their materialistic neighbors in the suburbs or expensive High Holiday tickets, or ethnic self-stereotyping, or the boring junior congregation services they had to go to sometimes (or a lot) as a kid, or the smattering of a Jewish education they received as a child, or by "I Have a Little *Dreidl*." It's like reducing Western civilization to "The Flintstones" or the Avon lady.

Many American Jews, secure now in their place as thoroughly enculturated Americans, have a greater desire to rediscover their heritage. What many are still afraid of is to become "too Jewish."

There seems to be a feeling that cores can never meet; that somehow if we become "too" immersed in the core of Jewish learning and culture, we'll be "ghettoized." The source of this prejudice dates back to the not-so-distant past, when there was indeed a choice between one's Jewish identity and professional success or social acceptance. Meanwhile, other Jews, such as the more extreme *baalei teshuvah* (returnees to tradition), argue that we *should* reject and insulate ourselves from non-Jewish culture and learning—whether from "Lassie" or a college education. This xenophobia seems to me to betray a lack of confidence in Judaism's ability to thrive in a free world.

It's limiting to continue to view "Jewishness" in a linear fashion, a kind of continuum from the least observant on the left to the most observant on the right. A more helpful image could be that of a circle or circles with central hubs (the bagel paradigm?). In some ways a Jew could be close to one or more "cores" of Judaism (such as observance, learning, Israel, Hebrew, or values), while in other areas the same person may still be only peripherally involved.

Jewish authenticity is not a matter of renunciation, but of relating the seemingly "secular" and "foreign" back to the Jewish pivot of our lives, back to the core. Today, as in centuries past, tremendous creativity is coming from individuals—in every denomination from Orthodox to Reconstructionist—who have either grown up in a Jewish core and later encountered authentic ideas of various other cultures or philosophies, or who encountered a Jewish core after having been immersed in the "essence" of another cultural or intellectual experience. Sometimes the encounter has resulted in retreat or rejection, but often, it has resulted in an outpouring of creativity, whether the previously unheard of core-to-core meeting was between Orthodoxy and feminism or youth counterculture and traditional Jewish sources.

Judaism has grown through the ages by its meetings with other civilizations, cultures, and ideas. Other civilizations, cultures, and religions have also benefited greatly from Judaic contributions. Raising our children within the core of Jewish life gives them an identity and ethos within which they can and should encounter other substantive ideas and philosophies and with which they can and should contribute both to Jewish life and to universalistic concerns. Conversely, raising them only on the periphery of Jewish culture and learning impoverishes them. Our children will decide for themselves about their own identities, no matter what we do. The real question is: Based on what Jewish and secular knowledge and experiences will they make their choices? Core or periphery? "Hamlet" or "Lassie"? The Talmud or "I Have a Little *Dreidl*"?

But what if we feel ourselves on the periphery of Judaism? The most basic step is to begin or to intensify our own encounter with the core ideas and texts of Judaism. In classic Jewish thought, ignorance is incompatible with spirituality (*Pirke Avot* 2:6). It's hard to think of any religion or culture to which learning and understanding, the life of the mind, is more essential. Indeed, the very idea of religion per se is fairly foreign to Judaism; classically, our religion itself would be called Torah, or teaching. Likewise, our rabbi is, classically speaking, not a cleric but a master-teacher.

Jewish learning is meant to lead to action. Not ritual alone, but sanctification of daily life and relationships, interpersonal activism, and intellectual discovery, are all part of this approach to drawing closer to the core of Judaism. Each holiday or Shabbat—and eventually, every day—brings opportunities or entrances to intensify and expand our Jewish observance.[4] The present volume is also designed to present these various paths toward the Jewish core.

A core experience also implies an immersion experience, that is, being in the center rather than on the fringe. Some surveys and a lot of anecdotal evidence indicate the crucial importance to Jewish commitment of various sorts of immersion in a total Jewish environment, whether an intense and extended experience in Israel (the center of Jewish life in so many ways), Jewish camping (at a camp that stresses Jewish learning and living, not just bunking with other Jewish kids), or intensive experiences involving Jewish learning. Connecting with a close-knit Jewish community, such as a *havurah* or a dynamic *minyan* or congregation, is another way of taking our family from periphery to center. There are also more accessible, micro-immersion experiences by which we facilitate the creation of such a holistic Jewish environment in our own homes—surrounding ourselves with Shabbat, eating in a family *sukkah*, filling the house with Jewish music, learning together.

There is a tendency in Jewish life today to evaluate Jews and their chosen life-styles as Jewishly good, authentic, or real. (Being Jewish, to my mind, is not a matter of good or bad, but, like being pregnant, you either are or you aren't.) A better goal is to discover which types of Jewish options are potentially more meaningful and satisfying (and therefore probably more effective, too).

In a free society, educating Jewish children to become Jewishly involved adults almost surely needs to involve core experiences of Judaism in the form of serious learning, meaningful observance, distinctive values, and as many opportunities as possible for macro- or micro-immersion.

One can hardly teach a child to appreciate classical music if the family never gets beyond playing cutesie kiddie selections. Likewise, limiting a child's Jewish education to peripheral encounters with Judaism or watered-down juvenile versions of a few holidays is like putting one foot in the *sukkah*—not a very inspiring experience.

Kind of like endless reruns of "Lassie." . . .

KAVANAH: A JEWISH WORD FOR THE MEANING OF LIFE

My iconoclastic philosophy professor at Tel Aviv University, Dr. Asa Kasher, gave the following question on our final exam: "What is the meaning of life?" I no longer remember what I said, but I guess it wasn't half bad, because I got a C+.

Contemporary existentialist philosophies have shifted the search (to put it rather simplistically) from discovering "the meaning of life" to finding a meaning *in* life. Dr. Viktor E. Frankl,[5] an eminent psychiatrist who survived the Holocaust, developed a school of "Logotherapy." Frankl taught that, more than we are motivated by the desire for pleasure or power, we are driven by a search for meaning to our existence.

Part of the way in which the Jewish tradition views life's meaning can be discovered through the language of faith. One Hebrew word for meaning is *mashma'ut*, as in "*Mah mashma'ut hahayim?*"—"What is the meaning of life?" But there is another Hebrew word for meaning, an even plainer and simpler word: *kavanah*. *Kavanah* generally indicates meaning in the sense of *intention*, as in "what did you mean by that"?

Kavanah comes from the same Hebrew root as *kivun*, direction. In one sense, *Kavanah* implies a direction, purpose, or goal, something we "take aim at" (*lechaven*, in Hebrew). Our "meaning" in life would then imply that our existence has some sort of goal, some vision we are aiming for, some mission to accomplish. *Bechavanah* means "on purpose," doing something intentionally, with a purpose in mind.

But *kavanah* has another meaning, too. It is the word used to describe the inner, meditative intention of a prayer, ritual, or deed. In this sense, *kavanah* means awareness, concentration, the internalization of an experience. Doing something "with *kavanah*" means doing it consciously and attentively.

The Western paradigm of finding meaning in life is the first definition of *kavanah*—purposefulness, achievement, movement toward a goal. This sense of meaning in life could be realized through activism, redemptive work, striving toward a vision of a better world. The Eastern paradigm of finding meaning in life is the second definition of *kavanah*—awareness, consciousness, peace of mind. This meaning in life could be discovered by turning inward, by spirituality, contemplation, and meditation. The one might be called the "left-brain" meaning, the other the "right-brain" meaning.

Judaism rejects neither aspect of life, but bridges these two worlds of meaning, as the corpus callosum links the two hemispheres of our brains. In Judaism, the two "meanings" of life are inseparable. Judaism means living with direction: working toward redemption, *tikkun olam*, a "messianic era" as some call it. Each deed, each small step on the path in that direction is meaningful. Yet Judaism also means living with a conscious awareness of life's holiness and wonder, of the sanctity of each moment and each encounter with another. As Abraham Joshua Heschel says, "Just to be is a blessing. Just to live is holy."[6]

As parents, what more can we do than to instill in our children these twin meanings of *kavanah*: a sense of purpose in life, along with awareness, appreciation, and reverence? At the ultimate level, there are no mere formulas. Heschel wrote that the roots of religion lie in the depths of thought, in reflection that surpasses our power of expression, in awe and amazement before the wonder and the mystery beyond all comprehension or utterance. Together with our children, we can stand in awe at the wonder of God's creations, relate to one another with love, engage in the challenge of righteous living. As Heschel put it, we as parents have the privilege and duty of educating for reverence.

Yet we continually struggle to communicate what words cannot say. We call out in prayer. We express in art. We sing. We tell stories that allude to a greater meaning in the everyday. We use ritual to tie our personal experiences to transcendent meanings. The Jewish heritage is rich with opportunities for such communications of meaning. Our "*kavanah* as direction" Jewish meanings may be expressed in learning, in the activism of *tzedakah* and *hesed* (justice and lovingkindness); our "*kavanah* as awareness" Jewish meanings may be expressed in prayer, blessing, meditation, ritual and symbol, *midrash*, musical and artistic expression—and again, learning and teaching. The Judaic way of life could be characterized as a veritable *curriculum of meaning*.

Unless we transmit a sense of meaning in life to our children, we labor in vain. All the achievements we could want for our children and for ourselves—education, success, wealth, fame—in and of themselves may add up to emptiness, to a bunch of zeros, unless we can put one single digit before all the zeros. That one single digit is meaning. A sense of meaning gives everything else in life its worth.[7]

NAASEH VENISHMA: LEARNING AND DOING GO HAND IN HAND

The heart and soul of the Judaic tradition, the Sabbath, cannot be described: it can only be experienced.

—Jacob Neusner[8]

Naaseh VeNishma, "we will do and we will hear" (Exodus 24:7), were the words of the Israelites when they accepted the Torah. Traditionally, this has been interpreted to mean that the people of Israel merited receipt of the Torah because they were willing to fulfill it without preconditions, before they even heard or understood it.

I think that there can be another interpretation for those words. To be even more precise, they could mean: "We will do, and *then* we will understand." There are many experiences in Jewish life that can only be fully understood and appreciated by participating in them. "Judaism is permeated by a mystique of action. The archetypal concept for the Jew is *mitzvah*."[9] Any Hebrew school teacher who has tried to teach about Shabbat or the holidays to children of families without Jewish home observance knows this. Shabbat, the holidays, and other observances have to be experienced before they can really be understood.

But *nishma*—we'll learn, we'll understand—is

important, too. I've heard two complaints from adults who thought they were shortchanged in their Jewish upbringing. The first complaint came from those who simply had no significant or meaningful Jewish experiences—no *naaseh*, so to speak.

The second complaint came from Jews who were expected to participate in Jewish customs by rote alone, with no understanding, no appreciation of the magnificent intellectual content of Judaism, of the deep meanings behind the actions. As Rabbi Abraham Joshua Heschel taught, Judaism is not mere "religious behaviorism," but a profoundly spiritual way of living, for "the *mitzvoth* [religious commandments] demanding the heart are more numerous even than the *mitzvoth* demanding external performance. . . . In Jewish tradition we exalt the deed, but we do not idolize external performance."[10]

Judaism has a rich intellectual and spiritual tradition, and each observance can best be appreciated only when one has an understanding of the meaning behind it. *Kavanah*, the inner understanding and meditative quality of the observance, is the soul of the Jewish deed.

Study itself is one of the preeminent religious activities in Judaism. In the analysis of historian Arthur Hertzberg, American Jews, in general the descendants of the least educated European Jews and also influenced by American pragmatism, have emphasized behavior, organization, and ethnicity over the intellectual and spiritual sources of the faith. Any lasting renewal of Judaism must spring from a renewed commitment to serious Jewish learning.[11] An encounter with Judaism needs to involve a respectable commitment to learning and serious exploration, not just a sampling of random experiences.

That's another reason that book lists and other resource guides are an integral part of this volume. Understanding the why (*nishma*) of Judaism is as important as the how and the how to (*naaseh*).

Action or activity cannot be separated from learning and understanding when it comes to creating a Jewish way of life in the home. Jewish parents must pursue both goals in order to make Judaism meaningful for themselves and their children.

THE IMPORTANCE OF RITUALS

Recently, the media and psychological literature have begun to pay more attention to the impor-

tance of rituals for the emotional well-being of the individual, the family, and the community. There is a new appreciation of the ways in which symbolic rituals can satisfy deep inner needs to celebrate, to mourn, to mark transitions, and to bond with others. The "strong family" research previously described has highlighted the importance of home-centered rituals and traditions in fostering spiritual and emotional wellness as well as family cohesion.

Rituals have gained so much popularity that there are now books that suggest ways to create new ones, just for the family unit. Such individualized family customs can be fun and meaningful. But when a family shares Jewish rituals as well, they forge links, not only among themselves but also to a larger community and to an ancient and ongoing heritage.

Jewish customs and rituals have yet another function. They give concrete form to profound spiritual teachings and help us to discover and honor the holiness of everyday life. And they serve as vessels in which to transmit these lessons to our children.

Jewish tradition teaches that it is a mistake to divide life into religious and mundane realms. If we but open our eyes, we perceive that all of God's creation is miraculous, awe-inspiring. Every aspect of ordinary, secular life should really be considered holy. How absurd, from this perspective, to hear some Jews call themselves secular Jews . . . for how can a person, created in God's image, be secular, devoid of holiness?

But if everyday life can be holy, then why do we have a *Havdalah* ceremony each week to praise God "who separates between the holy and the mundane," at the end of each Sabbath? Why call one day *kadosh*, holy, leaving another *hol*, mundane?

When we look at the Hebrew word for "holy" or "sacred," *kadosh*, we find that it means nothing more mysterious than "set apart," or "set aside." Something sacred in Hebrew is something set aside. When we "make *kiddush*," we are proclaiming, over a cup of wine, that this day is set aside for God as a sacred day of rest. Likewise marriage, *kiddushin*, is the setting aside of two people for each other alone.

Sometimes loving one person awakens in us a greater love for life. Or becoming a parent and loving a child may make us realize the preciousness of all life and care for the suffering of all children. Such is the way of *kedushah*, holiness. We set aside one day as the Sabbath and call it "holy."

We devote our *kavanah*, direct our thoughts and feelings to focus on the holiness of this one particular day. But many find that (as Rabbi Samson Raphael Hirsch taught a century ago) such a focus on Shabbat begins to extend to the "secular" weekdays as well. By focusing on the holiness of one day, set aside and in particular, we have raised our awareness of every day, of the preciousness of time as the essence of life.

All of creation is awe-inspiring to the receptive heart and mind. Yet a blessing focuses our thoughts onto the miracle of one small part of creation: this piece of fruit, that tree in bloom, this scent of fragrant herbs. When we set aside a part of creation and direct (*kavanah*) our awareness toward its holiness, we may be sensitized to the wonder in all that is around us. (And blessings are not just for the beauties of creation; there are also blessings that help us to acknowledge the divine in what we don't take delight in seeing or encountering.)

By setting aside a part, seeing its *kedushah*, distinctive holiness, we more fully appreciate the holiness of the whole.

When God told the Israelites to build a tabernacle, God said: "They will make me a holy place, that I may dwell among them" (Exodus 25:8). The commentators point out that God did not say, "that I will dwell in it." Why, "The earth is the Lord's and the fullness thereof"! But the one small holy place became a focus for the Israelites of service to God, so that the Divine would dwell within their hearts and souls wherever they stood.

Just as water needs a vessel to keep it from being lost, spirituality (for most people) needs structured methods of focusing—"vessels," such as holy days, blessings, rituals, prayers, and observances—in which to transmit its powerful messages from generation to generation.

Look back to your childhood, to your earliest Jewish memories. Chances are that they include sensory experiences, which were also emotional experiences, in a family or intergenerational context. You enjoyed chicken soup and candlelight long before you understood what peace and holiness meant. You tasted the crunchy *matzah* and the horseradish *maror* before you could understand words like freedom and redemption. You marveled at the odd call of the *shofar* long before you could have understood the concepts of repentance and community. Presumably, by the time you were ready to grasp the abstract concepts, your Jewish identity was already firmly established on a deep emotional level.[12]

If we try to convey abstract concepts to the next generation without the regular use of concrete symbols or emotional and sensory experiences, our chance of transmitting the loftiest ideals is gravely endangered. Jewish movements that have tried to transmit Judaism in a purely idealistic form, without concrete rituals and observances, have either failed or had to drastically reevaluate their methods. A soul must have a body to survive in this world.

Rabbi Herbert Weiner, in his perceptive book *The Wild Goats of Ein Gedi—A Journal of Religious Encounters in the Holy Land*, describes Zionist pioneer A. D. Gordon as a mystic for whom tilling the soil of Israel was a profoundly religious experience. But Weiner also acknowledges the failure of Gordon and others of the pioneering generation to transmit their deep spirituality and idealism to later generations on the *kibbutz*: " . . . this type of mystic experience, central in Gordon's life, had not been transmitted to others in Dagania. Lacking were what the Hassidim of Meah Shearim would call the 'vessels' of such transmission. The old religious vessels had been thrown away, and the new ones . . . were empty of emotional content and historical depth."[13]

Rituals, blessings, observances—these are the vessels by which we convey our ideals, our Jewish spirituality, and even our Jewish identity itself to our children—and strengthen them within ourselves as well.

The home, like the synagogue, is called a small holy place, *mikdash me'at*. If our home life is lived with a *kavanah*, a focus on the holiness of our one small part of society, we may hope to raise our children with a heightened sensitivity to the holiness that can be found everywhere.

KEVA: THE MEDITATIVE MODEL OF SPIRITUALITY

Together with *kavanah*, Jewish spirituality requires *keva*, a certain amount of regularity, discipline, and repetition.

Americans tend to view spiritual experiences using what I call an epiphanic model, that is, as authentic and meaningful only if they appear spontaneously. Regular, habitual religious practice is seen as stifling, and this is often one of the complaints about Jewish observance.

Yet, by way of comparison, we are used to

thinking in terms of discipline and regularity in the area of physical development. Those of us who are weight lifters or athletes know that we have to maintain a schedule of workouts to improve our abilities or just to maintain fitness. We can't wait for the mood to strike before exercising but have to get in those regular "reps." Still, a common experience is that we go to a workout out of discipline or habit but soon find ourselves infused with new energy, really high, involved in the exercise for the experience itself.

Jews have been called "ethical athletes." The regular practice of *mitzvot* (whether prayers, rituals, study, or good deeds) forms our spiritual workouts. Abraham Joshua Heschel said that the *tzaddik*, or truly righteous person, is not merely one who does good deeds, but one who is in the habit of doing them.[14] Rather than waiting for the mood to strike, the Jewish way of life provides a training regime for moral fitness and spiritual sensitivity. Again, feeling often follows form.

Many Jews also follow what might be called the meditative model of spirituality. Researchers of the mind-body connection have explained the physiological, psychological, and—in certain contexts—spiritual benefits of regular, daily meditation. The habitual nature of the practice is what makes it work. Likewise, those who are disciplined to fulfill the Judaic regimen have more opportunities to achieve those seemingly illusive spiritual highs.

In Jewish tradition, *keva*, or regularity of behavior, is considered essential to personal growth, whether spiritual, moral, or intellectual (*Pirke Avot* 1:15). We need our spiritual "reps" to develop moral muscle. *Keva* is also considered essential to the ongoing life of the community from generation to generation. It has been said that Judaism did not find eternity in monuments meant to last a millenium, but in the regular and dependable re-creation of moments of holiness.

Of course, *keva* alone is not enough. Mere habit or lifeless form is not the Jewish goal (*Pirke Avot* 2:18). However, just as the magnificence of an Olympic performance comes as much from expertise as from inborn talent, from endless hours of daily practice ("genius is 98 percent perspiration"), so many of life's spiritual peaks may emerge with most faithfulness from regular daily and weekly religious practice.

from an imperfectly prepared instrument? Some people say that the whole of what Judaism is about is a way of preparing body and soul for having this ability.
—Adin Steinsaltz[15]

FAMILY SNAPSHOTS

A PROGRESS REPORT

[Arlene Rossen Cardozo is the author of *Jewish Family Celebrations*[16] and several other books on family living.]

Twenty-one years ago, when our daughters Miriam and Rachel were six and three, and Rebecca not even a gleam in the eye, my husband Dick and I decided the family would "become" Jewish. Both of us were born to Jewish parents, but were raised with very little Jewish practice (though always strong Jewish values of *tzedakah*—helping others not only monetarily but through the giving of self). Practice in our homes had consisted primarily of High Holidays and Passover *seders*, and this was where we began when we decided to "become" Jewish.

There were no books at that time from which to glean what we wanted—a firm intellectual grasp of the foundations of both our Jewish heritage and Jewish practice and ideas on how to make practice fun, not ponderous—a definite prerequisite for applicability to our family life. We learned through taking university courses, talking with Jewish educators, and most of all through the role models of several young Jewish families who came from strong Jewish backgrounds and who were transmitting those practices in their own homes.

Within a couple of years, as I have shown in *Jewish Family Celebrations*, we looked and felt like longtime Jewish practitioners. Shabbat dinner Friday nights and special family activities the next day became the framework for our Jewish family. The Shabbat rhythm is complemented by the full cycle of festivals—Rosh HaShanah, Yom Kippur, Sukkot complete with *sukkah*-building and open *sukkah* parties all week long, a week of Hanukkah festivities, Purim with costumes and plays, wonderful Passover *seders*, and Shavuot.

Another called it becoming a violin that can be played upon. I have to do all the tuning of the violin and only then will it be fit to play. What can one get

The girls attended Hebrew School after school and religious school on Sundays, celebrated their *benot mitzvah*, and we took them to Israel half a dozen times between 1978 and 1988. On one occasion, we all lived there for several months, with the girls attending public school and ulpan.

With what result? As I look back over two decades of a radically altered, greatly enriched life-style for myself and Dick, I tally what our three daughters are taking of Jewish practice as they move into their own lives and, in the case of Miriam and Rachel, establish their own homes.

"Shabbat," they chorused, when at this year's Passover seder I asked what is most important to them Jewishly. Shabbat is indeed the guiding framework for each of them, with Miriam seeking a *havurah* of friends with whom to share Shabbat in Boston, Philadelphia, and New York, where she has lived, Rachel proudly taking prized possessions—candlesticks, *hallah* cover, and *kiddush* cup—into her new marriage, and Rebecca never too busy with her myriad university activities to be home for Shabbat dinner. The cycle of festivals is equally important to them, with each actively involved in making each festival a memorable family-centered activity.

Miriam and Rachel are synagogue Torah readers, frequently reading at High Holiday services, and all of them tutor (or have tutored) *bar/bat mitzvah* children. They now are either teaching, or have taught, religious school and Hebrew classes. Our time spent in Israel, coupled with their university-level Hebrew coursework, has contributed greatly to the fluency that all three have with the Hebrew language.

So the progress report is definitely encouraging! In but one generation it's possible to go from highly assimilated to thoroughly committed, practicing Jews—and, further, to share that Judaism through teaching it to others, as our daughters have done and are doing.

The example of our family leads me to the certainty that many more Jewish families have the potential to "become" more Jewish by enriching their lives with Jewish practice; by visiting Israel and understanding firsthand our grounding in over 5,000 years of history, as well as the problems facing contemporary Jewish survival; and by teaching the language, the practice, and the culture to others.

—*Arlene Rossen Cardozo*

3
PARENTING AS A SPIRITUAL PATH

While being a parent often seems the most mundane of enterprises, in Jewish thought it is one of the most exalted. Parenting with awareness, with *kavanah*, can be a spiritual path because it causes us to draw closer to God through emulating Godly qualities, actions, and relationships.

QUALITIES IN GOD'S IMAGE

One of the greatest Jewish teachers of this century, the late Rabbi Abraham Joshua Heschel, described the great challenge for parents of all faiths when he wrote: "The mainspring of tenderness and compassion lies in reverence. It is our supreme educational duty to enable the child to revere . . . without profound reverence for father and mother, our ability to observe the other commandments is dangerously impaired. The problem we face, the problem I as a father face, is why my child should revere me. Unless my child will sense in my personal existence acts and attitudes that evoke reverence—the ability to delay satisfactions, to overcome prejudices, to sense the holy, to strive for the noble—why should she revere me?

"Reverence for parents is the fundamental form of reverence, for in the parent is incarnated the mystery of man's coming into being. Rejection of the parent is a repudiation of the mystery. Only a person who lives in a way which is compatible with the mystery of human existence is capable of evoking reverence in the child. The basic problem is the parent, not the child."[1]

The primary task for parents is the development of the godly in our own characters, priorities, and deeds, to strive to be worthy of our children's reverence, and, it is hoped, to inspire them and ourselves to reverence for God. We must ask ourselves if we truly embody qualities such as patience, compassion, mercy, justice, truth, and holiness in our lives. *Imitatio Dei*, or emulation of divine *midot* (qualities), is considered in Jewish ethical tradition to be one of the ways for a person to draw closer to God.

Striving to be worthy of the role of father or mother is one way in which parenting is indeed a spiritual path.

ACTIONS IN GOD'S IMAGE

Our tradition stresses that the parent-child relationship is an allusion to the divine–human relationship. Dr. Kathy Chesto, a gifted innovator in religious education within the family, teaches that every action we take as loving, caring, devoted parents teaches our children about God.[2]

When we pick up a crying baby, she says, we are teaching our children: When you cry out, someone answers.

When we play peek-a-boo with our toddlers, we are teaching them: Hiddenness does not mean that no one is there.

15

When we prepare our children's things for the beginning of school—all the little gestures of concern such as taping milk money in lunch boxes so it won't fall out—we're teaching them about Providence, that God prepares a way for us in life (called *hashgahah* in the Jewish tradition).

Religious tradition, Torah, is greatly diminished if we think of it as one compartment of life or relegate it to the care of professionals. It is diminished when it is not intimately connected to everyday experience, offering expanded ways of seeing and acting upon the world. Religious tradition validates what we as parents already know in our hearts—that there must be a source for the love, devotion, and selflessness that goes beyond what we ever thought we had within us.

Those who build a family with loving dedication are already engaged in a sacred service. Religion is what recognizes that and calls it by name.

RELATIONSHIPS IN GOD'S IMAGE

The third way in which parenting can be a spiritual path is in the development of Godly relationships between parent and child. In classical Jewish thought, the parent-child relationship alludes to the Divine-human relationship.[3] The Bible and prayer book are replete with metaphorical language in which we describe God in a parental role, ourselves as God's children.[4] Human parents are viewed as God's "partners" in creating a life, and the Talmud describes honor for parents as a way of honoring God (*Kiddushin* 30b).

What could it mean to be "images of God" in our role as parents? Perhaps the analogy of parent to divine can inspire the philosophies and methods we employ in raising and educating our children.

In his book *The Star of Redemption*, the great twentieth-century German Jewish philosopher Franz Rosenzweig described the meeting points of God, humanity, and the world as taking three forms: Creation, Revelation, and Redemption.[5] These central themes of Creation, Revelation, and Redemption are expressed repeatedly in Jewish texts, liturgy, and observance. If the parent-child relationship can somehow allude to the God-humanity relationship, then a Jewish philosophy of parenting might be outlined by referring to these three metathemes of the human encounter with divinity.

The role of parents in creating the child is the most obvious of the three. The conception, gestation, and birth of a child is a process during which even those who feel out of touch with religion are struck by a sense of awe and wonder at the miraculous creation of a new life (should anything go wrong at this critical nexus, religious faith—or doubt—will also play a heightened role). We are engaged in one of the most creative moments of life, and yet we realize our creatureliness most fully; despite all the modern medical techniques, the formation of a unique person is still fundamentally outside our control. And yet we are privileged to be partners with God in this miracle. In creating a new life, we realize the simultaneous limitation and exaltation of our humanity.

But physically creating the baby—the biological dimension of parenthood—is only the beginning; raising and educating the child is of even greater importance (Talmud, *Sanhedrin* 19b). And of course, it is not biological parents alone who may engage in this holy task.

Redemption is the other end of the process of parenting: We enable a child to become independent, free, to function on her or his own as an adult. The classical talmudic demands on parents (described in *Kiddushin* 29a in the masculine idiom of the period, but today applicable to both sexes) concern this necessity of freeing the child from dependency on his or her parents: "circumcise him" (that is, enter him or her into the covenant independent of his parents); "redeem him" (i.e., through the traditional *pidyon haben* ceremony that symbolically freed each firstborn son from dedication to service in the sanctuary); "teach him Torah" (ensure that he or she can think and function independently as a Jew); find the child a spouse, teach the child a trade; "and some say to teach him to swim" (ensure that the child can look out for his or her self-preservation and safety). In other words, bring him or her to independent and self-reliant functioning in the religious, intellectual, emotional, financial, and physical spheres.

The parent must gradually step back and "withdraw from power," allowing the child to develop into independence, even though that involves a process of making personal mistakes and learning from experience (which also alludes to the pitfalls of human free will vis-à-vis God). Just as our covenant with God involves both obligation and autonomy, so the parent-child relationship allows room for both expectations and individuality.

Seymour Rossel, a noted Jewish educator, draws on philosopher Eugene Borowitz's interpretation of the Lurianic Kabbalah, a Jewish mystical teaching, in providing a model of the teacher-pupil relationship. Just as the Kabbalah portrayed God as performing an act of "contraction" (*tzimtzum*), in order to make room for an independent creation and human free will, so too, writes Rossel, "The teacher who wishes to initiate learning must first withdraw from power to make space for the student." He emphasizes that, "this approach does not call for a complete shift from dominance to abandonment," but is a constant and delicate balance of leadership and letting go.[6]

Inasmuch as Judaism views the parental role as the primary teaching role, this model of *tzimtzum* is appropriate for parents as well. The task of the parent-educator is a graduated withdrawal from power as the years go by, a constant and delicate balance of leadership and letting go, but steadily directed toward growing autonomy for the child. Again, this mirrors the Jewish view of the divine-human dynamic, in which God is pleased to find humanity assuming "adulthood" and independent choice (Talmud, *Baba Metzia* 59b).

Mediating between these two stages, creating a baby and redeeming the child into adulthood, is revelation. And it is here that the ongoing task of parenting is most illumined.

The connection between revelation and relationship is integral to Judaism. The prayer *Ahavah Rabbah*, "With a great love," which directly precedes the *Shema*, describes God's transmission of the Torah to us as an action of relating to us with the greatest love and mercy. The Shavout holiday, which centers on Revelation (giving the Torah at Sinai) and Covenant, is also thematically linked to love. The Hebrew verb *ledaat*, to know, can signify both knowledge and intimacy. In English, too, we can reveal knowledge and reveal ourselves.

Revelation could thus be described as loving instruction, or instruction flowing from a loving relationship. For the parent's role to best imitate God, our primary, ongoing mode of child rearing (and revelation is perceived as a dynamic, ongoing event in Jewish tradition) would reflect this paradigm of loving instruction.

Both aspects are crucial: instruction and love. We are charged with the *hinuch*, or education of our children: "teach them unto your children." Parenting, in Judaism, is the quintessential teaching relationship. Jewish children are not simply to be raised, but to be educated. The Hebrew word for parent, *horeh*, is related to the word *moreh* or teacher and to the word Torah or "instruction." Now, teaching is a most exalted

calling in classical Judaism: the word *rabbi* means "my (master) teacher," the greatest Jew was "Moses our teacher," and even God is portrayed as teaching us Torah. We are to call our parents, "my father, my teacher" and "my mother, my teacher," as indications of the great reverence due them. *Hinuch*, or education, is also related to the word for dedication; Jewish education signifies not simply the transmission of knowledge, but the holy and holistic process of dedicating the next generation for a sacred task, a life imbued with purpose.

But the inseparable and complementary aspect of revelation is that of love and relationship. Another outstanding twentieth-century Jewish thinker, Martin Buber, contributed an important philosophical perspective here: the concept of the "I-Thou" mode of relationship. Buber taught that we encounter humanity, and by extension divinity, only in the context of dialogue. The "I-Thou" interaction is one of wholly relating to another's essential being without exploitation or objectification. Rossel also employs Buber's concept of the "I-Thou" in his philosophy of Jewish education: "True education is in the meeting of teacher and pupil that aims toward the meeting between the human being and the Divine."[7] Again, his insights are most relevant to parenting as well: True parenting, one could say, is in the meeting of parent and child that aims toward the meeting between the human being and the divine.

The ongoing essence of Jewish parenting as it unfolds over the years is this revelatory relationship, this "instruction in love." The Jewish view of parenthood is that of a continuous devotion to the education of the whole child, in the context of a personal and loving relationship.

The child is not an extension of us, but an image of God in his or her own right. Although parents usually have tremendous influence on their children, each child has inner resources and qualities of his or her own. A classic Jewish legend tells that the child learns the entire Torah while still in the womb, then an angel strikes the babe on the mouth, making the child forget everything that has been learned (Talmud, *Niddah* 30b). All of learning throughout life, then, is seen essentially as a revelation of the child's inner potential (the English word *educate* likewise signifies bringing out or drawing forth). Parenting, then, involves not only guiding and influencing, but creating the environment (in the fullest sense of the word) in which the "divine image" of each family member can most fully blossom and be revealed.

A relationship or dialogue can never be reduced

to a mere formula but is a matter of human sensitivity that grows with the parent's experience and maturity. How often I have to wake myself from the habit of objectifying my children and focus instead on really relating to them, really listening, touching, looking them in the eyes, seeing the divine image of their being. Living with true *kavanah*, or meditative awareness, is a lifelong challenge. "Methods" and techniques of various sorts are at best only useful tools when needed, and they must always be in harmony with these overarching Jewish values (thereby excluding theories that either objectify the child into an animal to be trained, or abdicate parental responsibility to educate and lead).

In Judaism, spirituality is never separated from real life. Raising children, dedicating a new generation who will teach and discover and pursue justice and heal and love and create and reveal and redeem is an exalted and holy task in itself.

At the same time, parenting, the greatest teaching (revelation) opportunity, is one of the greatest learning (self-revelation) opportunities. The Jewish concept of education—a sacred endeavor—always involves the education of the teacher as well: "I have learned . . . most from my pupils" (Judah HaNasi, Talmud, *Taanit* 7a). We can learn from our efforts to imitate God by striving to be parents worthy of reverence and emulation. We can learn by living creatively, instructing in love, revealing ourselves to our loved ones—and by fostering the revelation of our children's fullest selves. We can learn by leading, but also by gently withdrawing, so that our children can grow to reach the redemption and autonomy of adulthood. And we can learn perhaps most wonderfully of all from our children as people, from the ongoing revelation of their beings.

In this way, too, parenting may truly become a spiritual path.

4
THE ART OF JEWISH PARENTING

Thus to be a Jew is an act of art: that is, of imagination and creation; of making ourselves out of ourselves. . . . To be a Jew is, therefore, an act of will; and will wells up from within: an act of imagination. Words make worlds within—and then we change the world.

—Jacob Neusner[1]

HOMEMAKING AS ART

Parenting can be an exciting creative endeavor. There is a lot of artistry involved in making a home—a Jewish home in particular.

Dr. Yehudah Wurtzel, film maker and Jewish educator, reminds us that the word *art* carries such a mystique today that it may be easy to forget that it is essentially a type of communication.[2] We are frequently engaged in communicating with others, but communication is not limited to verbal interactions. Communications may be direct and informational, in which case their form is perhaps incidental to their content. Yet there are things that we wish to communicate that cannot simply be confined to linear informational data. If we wish to convey something more experiential and holistic, words alone may be inadequate. We may use music, movement, image, ritual—words, too, but broken out of their strictly linguistic contexts to become metaphor, allusion, poetry.

This kind of communication is called art. In artistic communication, the form of the communication is integral to the content. Artistic forms of communication allow us to simulate experiences we have never known, to try on feelings we don't yet have, to become what we are not.

Art in one form or another plays a central role in the content of any culture. All major human social groups use some form of storytelling, of communicating through symbols and ritualized behaviors. Artful communications that ensure the assimilation of affective cultural messages are necessary to the continuity of any society or culture.

Judaism cannot be conveyed through information alone, but also needs to be experienced in these artful, affective ways. As noted previously, *naaseh*, "we will do," comes before *nishma*, "we will understand." A child or an adult is motivated to learn more about Judaism if he or she loves the experience of Jewish living.

Consider the Passover *seder*—an artful, holistic, nonlinear learning experience if ever there was one! Many modalities are involved. We learn through taste, tasting the bitterness of slavery. The Hallel prayer praising God is in the form of musical poems (Psalms). In some Sephardic traditions, actual dramatization has been essential to the *seder*; individuals play-acted scenes from the Exodus and the expected ultimate redemption. Even in the most staid Ashkenazic rite there is a required amount of dramatic movement: leaning on pillows to experience the luxury of freedom, opening the door for Elijah, searching for the *afikoman* (not to mention all the dramatic build-up in the search for *hametz* and burning the *hametz*).

Imagine that the *seder* were simply a matter of straightforward verbal communication. ("Once we were slaves; now we are free. Good night, everyone.") It's quite doubtful that the communication of redemption would then have had the same amazing staying power. We are trying to communicate much more than words can say: I was a slave—I taste the bitterness and the tears! Now I'm free—I taste, feel, sing the drama of my redemption! As Wurtzel says: "Talking about *matzah* is about as awful as eating a record."[3]

In the past, the vibrant community context of life provided Jews with holistic, emotional experiences of Jewishness. Three or four generations ago in Europe, two or three generations ago in immigrant neighborhoods, the sights, sounds, and even smells of everyday living centered around Jewish observances. Most young parents today have hardly any memories of such environments, and our children have even fewer. Today in Israel, even nonreligious Jews live in an atmosphere in which the rhythms of life emanate from the Jewish calendar. But outside a few traditional enclaves, most Jewish families in the United States today, even if they live in areas with many Jews, no longer live in intensely Jewish environments.

Because the communal setting no longer provides a Jewish ambiance, and contemporary communal structures are at best still groping for artistic forms of expression,[4] more and more of the burden of Jewish art has fallen to the home environment. Not that the home hasn't traditionally been a center stage of Jewish expression, but the difference today is that the artistry for most of us is a conscious choice rather than an inherited cultural pattern. I use the *seder* as an illustration because the power of the *seder* has withstood even the toughest ravages of assimilation, but every holiday, every Sabbath, and even every weekday has its own subtle artistic communications. By use of symbolic actions such as ritual hand washing, reciting blessings, and dipping bread in salt, the Jewish sages elevated a simple meal to an artistic expression in which each person became what he or she was not: a priest of the Temple. Neusner has described Jewish ritual as an artistic "enchantment," in which one's intimate personal experience alludes to great mythological events and ideas.[5]

Let this be quite clear: The home and the life we create in it, *not the child*, are our canvas (and soon enough the children will assert their creativity upon it, too!). To say that the parent is an artist is not to imply that the children are waiting to be molded like clay in the hands of the potter.

Anyone with a two-week-old baby already knows the limits of such parental influence. (For that matter, any writer or artist knows that an artistic creation—even one on paper—is not totally under its creator's power.) But the direction that children take does depend to a great degree on the quality of the home environment in which they grow up.

To create a Jewish home environment may seem not only artful, but, initially at least, artificial for many contemporary Jewish parents. But not to decide is to decide. Parents can choose to create a Jewish, humanistic home environment and way of life with awareness and artistry, or they can abdicate the opportunity and let outside social, cultural, or economic forces speak through them. But have no doubt: *something* is always being communicated. I find it useful to ask myself frequently, and for my husband and me to ask each other, "What are we communicating to our children right now with our words, style, actions, choices, priorities?"

There are many ways that we as parents may be artists. The home is our stage in which we create settings and enact scenes such as celebrations, rituals, and traditions. For the richest experiences, all the senses will be engaged: seeing symbols, artwork, or decorations; hearing music and liturgy; tasting and smelling special foods; feeling the emotions and moods each event or holiday evokes; and sensing the movement of our bodies in dance, ceremonial action, and clasped hands.

Likewise, the words we speak at home may be limited to strictly informational communications ("Do your homework," "Have you cleaned your room?"), or they may include expressions of wonder or love, stimulating conversation, stories, *midrash* (in the broad sense: drawing meaning from source materials and life experiences), the prayers and blessings that accompany everyday Jewish life. Everything from our decor to what we discuss around the dinner table (and how we discuss it) is a form of communication that may become an art. (Not all artistic expression is high seriousness either; it frequently includes humor, playfulness, and fun.)

Neither is artful living some sort of expendable indulgence for people without real problems. Anyone who reads the Bible knows otherwise! Artistic communication often arises from struggle and suffering. Some of the most profound, artistic Jewish communications have emerged from our greatest sorrows, and some of our most joyful communications have been celebrated triumphantly despite danger and intimidation.

The book of Exodus describes in painstaking detail the artistic efforts that went into building the Tabernacle in the wilderness, the archetypical Jewish "Holy Place." The Jewish home is called a "small holy place." It should also be established and maintained with the artistic care and consciousness of building a tabernacle or a temple. Just as the Tabernacle, or *mishkan*, created a focus for the Israelites to realize that God dwelt among and in them, our Jewish homes create a focus for family members and others to realize the wonder and divinity both within the self and between people.

THE JEWISH HOME: A SMALL HOLY TEMPLE

Rabbi Yossi says: It is not the place that honors the person, but the person that honors the place.
— Talmud, *Taanit* 21b

Set aside a special place in your home for meditation. Remember the mind learns by association. . . . The place where you habitually meditate takes on the energy of that activity.
— Joan Borysenko, Ph.D.[6]

But how is it that some things and places seem to be holy while others seem hopelessly profane. . . . This comes about not because of anything intrinsic to the things or the places but rather because of people and memories . . . some things and places carry within them more memories of ascent than others.
— Lawrence Kushner[7]

What do we think of when we envision our ideal home? One person sees a stunning estate with fancy decor, another dreams of an efficient apartment in the city, still another of a cozy little cottage with a big garden.

When I was a teenager growing up in a comfortable Texas suburb, many of my friends from high school or my Jewish youth group lived in homes that could simply be described as . . . well, gorgeous. Some of them, in fact, were veritable mansions, replete with fancy decor and large swimming pools. They were filled with fine furniture and original art, fully equipped game rooms, and deluxe kitchens. Parked out front were Cadillac convertibles or Lincolns. No doubt about it—

these were the kinds of places that could easily inspire a teenage girl's daydreams.

Now, just because they could afford impressive homes didn't mean that the owners were materialistic or shallow. A lot of them cared about us young people, and many devoted their time and efforts to worthy causes in general. No, there was certainly nothing overtly *wrong* with these lovely homes or the people who lived in them. They were very good. But for Jews, there is something beyond "good" toward which we must aspire.

There was a certain house in a more modest area of town that meant more to me than any of the showier houses. It had an extra something about it, and I often thought, "This is what I want *my* home to be like when I have a family of my own." It was no mansion. Neat and clean, if a bit seedy around the edges, it had a tiny backyard, no swimming pool, and an old station wagon parked in the driveway near the basketball hoop.

But this house was different. As soon as you walked in the door there was a special atmosphere. It was an intensely Jewish atmosphere, yet more than the mezuzah on each door, the artwork from Israel, and the shelves of Jewish books in the study. More than the poster with Hebrew blessings in the kitchen or the smell of traditional kosher dishes cooking there for the holidays.

This house was cozy—you could say it was a little on the crowded side—but there was always room for lots of guests around the *Shabbat* table and space for an out-of-town visitor to sleep. And around that *Shabbat* table there were always songs, jokes, and words of Torah along with the food.

The only way I can describe that house adequately is to say that it felt like a holy place—every day and especially on Shabbat. Stepping inside it was like stepping into a temple. The other homes were good, but this house was a world apart, a higher plane. You could almost touch the holiness in the air.

Although I might daydream about having one of those fancy houses with the swimming pools, I knew, of course, that I could be happy with something a bit more modest. But I made up my mind that, no matter what, I would have a home that felt like the little holy place.

It was only later that I found out that the traditional Jewish name for a home, just as for a synagogue, is *mikdash me'at*, meaning "temple in miniature," or simply: "little holy place."

In Jewish tradition, God is The Holy One. A primary way for us to draw closer to God is by emulating that holiness in our personalities ("As

God is merciful, you be merciful; as God is gracious, you be gracious" [Talmud, *Shabbat* 133b]) and in our spiritual disciplines and ethical deeds ("You shall be holy, for I the Eternal your God am Holy" [Leviticus 19:2]).

Human habitations from the micro (rooms) to the macro (cities) exude atmospheres only partly dependent on their physical makeup. They also have an energy about them, an atmosphere that clings to them from the collective memory of the types of experiences that have taken place, or habitually take place, therein. Consider how different you feel in a bustling restaurant, a suburban shopping mall, a university library, a museum, and various houses of worship. Consider how some places, like beautiful natural places, can evoke reverence, while other places feel cold, frightening, or merely vacuous.

What about our homes? What kind of atmosphere do they have? The decor has its role to play, but it is secondary to the deeds and relationships that take place in the home. Home atmospheres are primarily created—consciously or unconsciously—by the nonverbal communications and life-styles of their inhabitants. It is who we are and what we *do* in our homes that creates the atmosphere we live in and that our children will remember for the rest of their lives.

The role of the parent is manifold. Often we feel that being a parent is just being cook and chauffeur, cruise director and referee. But the parent may be, our tradition tells us, a Torah teacher, a holy priest.

The home may be a furniture showroom or a sanctuary. It may be a dormitory or a "miniature temple." The choices are ours.

SETTING THE STAGE

Advertisers know that the images and messages we are exposed to daily, even when not consciously acknowledged, can significantly affect our priorities and choices. Teachers know that room decorations and bulletin boards can serve as educational vehicles, even when little attention is deliberately drawn to them.

Likewise, parents ought to know that the decor of the home, meaning, in the broadest sense, all of the sensory atmosphere of the home, can play a subtle but profound role in the education of children. When a home is filled with high-quality books, music, and artwork, for example, children are exposed to rich cultural influences in a natural way.

There is a Jewish dimension to this, of course. The decor of the home can play its role in Jewish enculturation, just as the stage set plays an important, although background, role in a play. Just as the stage set does not make the play, so pictures of *hasidim* on the walls don't make the family more Jewish any more than a Rembrandt print makes them more Dutch. It is when the stage action is meaningful that the setting can further enhance the whole effect.

Here are some basics to consider in setting the stage of the Jewish home.

MEZUZAH

Jewish law requires (Deuteronomy 6:9, 11:20) one sign of the Israelite covenant with God on the doorposts of every Jewish home—the *mezuzah* (plural *mezuzot*; the word means "doorpost"). The *mezuzah* consists of a small parchment scroll (*klaf*) with the text of the *Shema* (Deuteronomy 6:4–9, 11: 13–21) inscribed upon it. The scroll is rolled from left to right, so that it unrolls to reveal the beginning of the text, and is placed in a container.

The *mezuzah* is not an amulet, but a symbolic reminder to let God dwell within us, in all our comings and goings. The scroll itself is the important aspect of the *mezuzah*, but in the interest of *hidur mitzvah* (beautifying the *mitzvah*), many people buy artistic *mezuzah* cases. A wide range of cases is available today—metal, ceramic, glass, wood, Jerusalem stone, even paper cases decorated with paper cuts for indoor use. The case often has a Hebrew letter *shin* written on it, or the name *Shaddai*, which means Almighty God. This is also written on the outside of the scroll itself. The Hebrew letters of the name *Shaddai* form an acronym, "Guardian of the doors of Israel."

Many Jewish families are returning to the traditional practice of placing *mezuzot* on every door in the home (except for such utilitarian areas as bathrooms or closets), on the right side of the door as one enters the room. The *mezuzah* is securely affixed, slanting slightly inward, within the top third of the door, but more than a handbreadth from the top (usually more like one quarter of the way down; give it the old touch-and-kiss test for comfort). Some people hang the *mezuzah* lower for children's rooms or for individuals in wheelchairs.

The *mezuzah* should be affixed within thirty days of moving into a house, apartment, or dorm (the same day, in Israel). A *mezuzah* is holy writing, like a Torah or *tefillin*; only a handwritten parchment scroll, made according to ancient traditions by a scribe, is considered kosher (proper). In these days of high-tech word processing, that constitutes *real* high touch! Traditionally, the scroll is checked every few years to be sure it hasn't faded, so if you make your own, allow some provision to remove the scroll. When Jewish families move, they take down the *mezuzot* if non-Jews will live in the home after them (lest they be thrown away), but leave them up if Jews will live in the house. The protective cases may be changed if the family wants to keep their own.

Just before affixing a *mezuzah*, one says the blessing:

Baruch Atah Adonai, Eloheinu Melech HaOlam, asher kidshanu bemitzvotav vetzivanu likbo'a mezuzah.

Holy One of Blessing, Your Presence fills creation; You have made us holy with commandments and bid us to affix the *mezuzah*.

One blessing suffices for putting up a number of *mezuzot* at once. This may be the occasion for a *Hanukkat HaBayit* or "home dedication," if one has just moved in.

Mezuzah Ideas

● You can make your own *mezuzah* cases as a family project. I know of people who have used clay (try bake-at-home, self-glazing clay available from craft and fine toy stores), natural objects, or even a decorated plastic toothbrush case!

● Special *mezuzot* designed for children's decor are available from Jewish gift shops and catalogs. Children could help affix the *mezuzot* in their own rooms or elsewhere in the house.

● When you buy a new *klaf*, look at it with your children. Treat the parchment gently and avoid rubbing the writing. Explain how it is written reverently by a scribe, in the old-fashioned way, with a feather pen. If the children read Hebrew, try to read it together (there are no vowel markings); they will probably be able to decipher the first line of the *Shema* if they can read a little.

● With school-aged children, look up the commandment to affix the *mezuzah* as well as the meaning of the verses in the *mezuzah* (see above).

● We glued a *mezuzah* case (a *mezuzah* pendant from a necklace, without any scroll) on our dollhouse door!

One of my most profound impressions of life in Israel was that there are *mezuzot* on every door: dormitories, cafeterias, stores, and classrooms. I can truly say that one of my most emotional moments in Israel was not at any holy shrine, but at the grimy Ford garage in Tel Aviv—discovering, even there, a *mezuzah* on the door! The subconscious mind begins to anticipate them on every threshold; it's striking to be back in the Diaspora and look for those "missing" *mezuzot*.

The *mezuzah* is the only "required" symbol of a Jewish home. However, there are a number of other decorative and ritual items that can enhance the Jewish atmosphere of a home.

THE *MIZRAH*

The *mizrah*, meaning "east," is a wall hanging traditionally hung on the eastern wall in a Jewish home to indicate the direction of Jerusalem, the direction a Jew is to face in prayer. Of course, the symbol hangs on the western wall if you live in Hong Kong. The word *mizrah* is written in Hebrew letters.

Mizrah Ideas

● Purchase a *mizrah* for your living room or you can make your own, using any of the techniques for making a *hallah* cover (pp. 151–152), such as felt applique, embroidery, batik, fabric decoration (paints and glue-ons are available at crafts shops). Use a longish piece of cloth or felt; drape one end over a dowel (later attach a ribbon to hang) or even over a nice clothes hanger; then glue or sew to hold in place.

● For a faster *mizrah*, use a long piece of parchmentlike paper, which can then be decorated like a collage or painted. Just be sure that your creation includes the word *mizrah* (מזרח), which can be written on in paint-pen or permanent marker (a stencil is helpful).

● A stylized Old City skyline with the *Kotel* (Western Wall) can be constructed on your *mizrah* from geometric shapes (rectangles, squares, arches, semicircles, triangles) cut from wallpaper scraps with appropriate textures (wallpaper and home decorating stores often give away old samples).

● The easiest way to make a *mizrah* may be to use a large photograph of Israel or a collage of Israel photos (from sources such as brochures or your own photos) or artwork or greeting cards from Israel. These can be framed with enough space beneath to reveal a piece of paper on which is written the word *mizrah* (מזרח). Cover it with clear plastic adhesive paper.

● A modern-day *mizrah*—The modern-day *mizrach* takes the traditional idea a step further: it's a big bulletin board devoted to visual and verbal images of contemporary Israel. Hang your bulletin board on the eastern wall of a room the family uses a lot—you can even use an entire wall of a den or playroom. The word *mizrah* can go in the middle of the board or wall, if desired. Then, let your imaginations loose. Use the modern-day *mizrah* to display clippings of articles about Israel, brochures for travel or programs in Israel, literature from organizations in Israel, letters and picture postcards and family or friend's photos from Israel, your own family's artwork about Israeli/seasonal subjects, photographic greeting cards and other "smaller than poster" photos of Israel, and perhaps your own photographs from your stays in Israel. It is a kind of fluid collage of Israel ideas and images.

● This modern-day *mizrah* concretizes faraway, "abstract" Israel for our children. When they learn about Israel or, it is hoped, visit there, this will help them understand and remember. Like the traditional *mizrah*, it's also a quiet, but ever-present, reminder of our ties to Israel as a Jewish family.

● A more permanent version of the modern-day *mizrah* can be made by collecting photos and clippings about Israel, then arranging and gluing them in collage-fashion on a large poster board (this can also serve as a *mizrah*; in that case, include the word). Finally, cover with clear plastic adhesive paper to preserve. Hang it where you will all be able to see it.

TZEDAKAH BOXES

Containers to collect *tzedakah*, money known in Yiddish as *pushkes*, should be found in every Jewish home to concretize the importance of *tzedakah*, the Jewish imperative of righteous giving. See pp. 109–110 for ideas on making your own and using them.

JEWISH CALENDARS

Every Jewish home needs a Jewish calendar, and it's nice for children to have their own as well. You can purchase one at most Jewish bookstores or gift shops (see Resource Guide, pp. 307–308).

JUDAIC ARTWORK AND RITUAL ITEMS

Artwork with Judaic themes is widely available from galleries and gift shops (see Resource Guide, p. 308, for starters). Artists and craftspeople in America and Israel produce beautiful and meaningful art items in many media as well as highly aesthetic ritual items. Today there is certainly something for every taste and decor.

Creating your own artwork is especially meaningful. See p. 67 for ideas on visual arts, and the holiday and Shabbat sections (Part V) for various suggestions on making ritual objects.

Basic ritual items for the Jewish home include Shabbat/holiday candlesticks, *kiddush* cups, *hallah* covers and trays, *Havdalah* sets (wine cups, spice boxes, candle holders with braided candles, and trays), *hanukkiyot* (or *menorahs*), Passover *seder* plates and *matzah* covers. These make wonderful gifts for many occasions. Other items, such as *etrog* containers or *shofars*, may also be added.

The main purpose of ritual items, of course, is not to display them but to use them. We saw a large display of Jewish ritual items in the anthropology section of the Smithsonian Institution's Museum of Natural History. How sad it seemed to see items languishing behind glass, never to be used again. But it is not much better to display such items at home as if they were museum pieces.

As long as the items are to be used, however, there is a point in purchasing (or lovingly making) beautiful, quality items. First, there is the Jewish value of *hidur* or *noy mitzvah*, or beautifying the *mitzvah*, derived from the biblical verse, "This is my God, whom I will glorify" (Exodus 15:2). Second, there is the unspoken message to our children of what we consider worth spending money on and selecting or making with care. What do we spend the most on: sports equipment, electronic gadgets, clothes—or maybe also Jewish ritual items, Jewish books? It all says something to our children about our values.

Young children might enjoy an actual "Jewish tour" of the home, starting with the *mezuzah* on the front door.

FAMILY HEIRLOOMS

Family photos and albums (which will also include Jewish life-cycle events), heirlooms, and other memorabilia help our children to relate to their personal heritage. Take the time to show such items to your children and to discuss their history and significance. See pp. 39–40 for more ideas on family records.

JEWISH BOOKS

Jewish books, particularly primary sources (in English or dual-language, if Hebrew skills are lacking), are essential to the intellectual and spiritual atmosphere of a Jewish home. The basics would include a complete Jewish Bible, *Humash* (book of the Torah readings, including *haftarahs*, prophetic readings), *siddur* (prayer book), and Passover *Haggadah*(s). A collection of rabbinic works (such as the Mishnah, Gemarah [Talmud], various Codes of Law) could be begun with a translation of the mishnaic *Pirke Avot* ("Ethics of the Fathers") and gradually expanded to include individual volumes of and about other rabbinic materials. Some books on contemporary Jewish practices should be handy for use as reference guides in everyday situations. Children should have age-appropriate Jewish books, but should also observe that parents have and read their own.

CHILDREN'S ROOMS

Children's rooms are important to them, and here, too, are many opportunities for Jewish decor. The more traditional decorations are an *alef-bet* chart or a *Modeh Ani* morning prayer in calligraphy. These are available commercially, or you can make your own. Many gift shops and Judaica catalogs carry *mezuzot* with designs appropriate to a child's room and door plaques that can be personalized with a child's Hebrew name. For babies there are naming certificates, mobiles, music boxes, and even amulets! The child can have his or her own *tzedakah* box in the room. Other possibilities are pictures with

Judaic themes or posters of Israel, a Jewish calendar or a bulletin board with photos and mementoes of Israel, the extended family, or Jewish celebrations.

I made an *alef-bet* chart by tracing foam-rubber letters from a Hebrew alphabet puzzle. Stencils can also be used. First I laid out the letters on a large construction-paper page and penciled them in, then I traced over them with colored markers. For each letter I drew and colored a picture of a Hebrew word that started with that letter (use a picture dictionary for suggestions). I chose to emphasize Jewish symbols wherever possible (Torah for *tav*, *tzedakah* box for *tzade*, *shofar* for *shin*, and so forth). I tried to integrate the pictures with the letters, such as drawing a *kippah* on the *kaf*, a *yonah* (dove) perched on the *yud*, a *tallit* spread over the *tet*, the *ayin* made into an *eitz* (tree) with roots and branches. I matted the chart on a colored oak-tag board and laminated it. Be careful with laminating crayoned pictures. You can frame them instead.

Those talented with a needle and thread could embroider such a picture. A Hebrew alphabet chart of felt with little pockets to hold an object for each letter is now available commercially (see Resource Guide, p. 314).

JEWISH CLOTHING

Certain items of clothing are symbolic expressions of Jewish belief. The Midrash tells that one reason the Jews kept their identities alive while they were slaves in Egypt was that they maintained a distinctively Jewish style of dress. We feel one way in a business suit and another way in a pair of torn cut-offs. Likewise, each element of "Jewish dress" is intended to heighten our awareness of holiness and can function to increase the sense of a distinctive Jewish identity in our homes.

Symbolic Jewish religious garments include a *kippah* (scull cap) or other head covering worn as a sign of reverence for God, at least for study and prayer, holidays and Shabbat (many observant Jews cover the head at all times). The *tallit*, a prayer shawl with ritual fringes, is worn for morning prayer by men and in liberal Jewish circles is increasingly worn by women as well. Orthodox men and boys often wear the *tzittzit* (ritual fringes) attached to a four-cornered garment worn under their clothing all day. On weekdays, *tefillin*, small black leather cubes bound on arm and forehead and containing biblical verses are traditionally donned for morning prayer.

The Torah prohibits the wearing of *shaatnez*, any garment that contains a mixture of wool and linen. Like *kashrut*, this is a *hok*, a religious discipline that is said to be observed not for rational reasons, but to practice obedience to God in a basic area of life.

Dignified and modest dress and the practice of wearing especially nice clothing for Shabbat and holidays can function as additional reminders of the Jewish role as "a kingdom of priests and a holy nation." We can also connect the subject of clothing to our worship and awareness of God by teaching children the blessing to say upon wearing a new garment for the first time, praising God, "who clothes the naked" (see Blessings, p. 89).

HANUKKAT HABAYIT: THE JEWISH HOUSEWARMING

Hanukkat HaBayit, "dedicating the house," the same phrase used for dedicating the Holy Temple in Jerusalem, is used for dedicating our private homes, our "miniature temples." All that is required is putting up the *mezuzot* along with the blessing (see p. 23), but a small creative ceremony can be composed by selecting readings (for example from the Psalms) or simply by sharing words of Torah. Some people say the *sheheheyanu* (p. 89). Friends and relatives can be invited to participate, and of course be sure that the children actively participate in the ceremony if they wish. Play Jewish music and serve refreshments. For Moroccan Jews like my husband's family, a housewarming requires couscous. And of course—a tour of the house!

If you are invited to a housewarming for another Jewish family, consider giving a gift that will enhance the Jewish life in their home, such as a book or subscription, a musical recording, a ritual item, or an additional *mezuzah*.

KITCHEN JUDAISM

LEARNING BY COOKING

"Gastronomic Judaism" is a disdainful term sometimes used to describe a predilection for bagels as one's chief manifestation of Jewish identity. Nonetheless, the kitchen can be a wonderful learning center for Jewish families. Children often learn best from concrete, multisensory experiences, and getting one's hands full of tasty *hallah* dough or *matzah* ball mix is memorable fun. The Shabbat and holiday foods also often contain symbolism of Jewish ideas: fried foods for Hanukkah to remind us of the miracle of the oil and honey on Rosh HaShanah for a sweet year, for example. (Dietary deconstructionists are apt to point out that often the symbolism came after the food was popular, not the other way around.)

Preparing Jewish dishes from around the world can also be interwoven with learning and talking about various Jewish traditions. There are many cookbooks that offer background materials on different Jewish customs and cultures (and, of course, one can learn from cooking foods of other cultures).

Parents who have the patience to involve young children in cooking will often be rewarded later when teens can take over making some of the family meals. Preparing food together is a natural "quality time" activity. With most people's schedules as crowded as they are, this is a convenient time to be together with our kids; after all, we still have to eat! Sunday bake-and-freeze sessions are useful for busy families. Or let the children take turns helping parents cook so that each child gets individual attention and cooking is a privilege rather than a chore.

The Shabbat section (see p. 149) offers suggestions on the kinds of jobs children can do, but of course common sense is the best guide in selecting jobs for children to perform at various ages. Kneading, grating (carefully), peeling, stirring, spreading, and presenting food aesthetically ("decorating it") are all activities that most children enjoy. And kids should learn from the start that cleaning up is part of cooking! You can find selected recipes in the holiday and Shabbat sections of this book.

B'teyavon! (Bon apetit!)

KASHRUT: JEWISH SOUL FOOD

Keeping kosher—observing the Jewish dietary laws—has fallen out of favor with American Jews. It is estimated that only 28 percent of American Jews keep kosher and that the figure drops to a mere 8 percent among Jews whose parents or grandparents were born in this country.[8] On the other hand, the kosher-food industry, the variety and number of certified-kosher products available, has grown by incredible leaps in the past few years alone, and is now said to have a $1.5 billion market, with most of the products being bought by non-Jews.[9] Rather than a general cultural norm for the many, *kashrut* has become a matter of strict observance for the few. Some Jewish leaders have noted that while today there are more Jews who observe a punctiliously correct *kashrut*, a generation ago there were many more Jews who kept the practice in some moderate form.

Why? Social scientists might note that *kashrut* doesn't fit the mold of popular Jewish observances in the United States. The classic theory of sociologist Marshall Sklare[10] is that American Jews tend toward observances that, among other criteria, are infrequent and require little social isolation. Keeping kosher, obviously, affects people every day and, depending on the degree of observance, can impair their social interaction (around food at least) with non-Jews (and these days seems just as likely to impair their social interaction with other Jews). Unlike some more popular observances, *kashrut* hasn't found a trendy new interpretation that makes "kitchen Judaism" (as Israeli scholar Gershom Scholem[11] called it) compelling enough for large numbers of Jews to give up their Big Macs. It's ironic that in an age of diets—Pritikin, "natural hygiene," vegetarian, macrobiotic—the Jewish diet is one of the less popular observances among contemporary American Jews.

Kashrut is considered one of the *hukkim*, those *mitzvot*, or Torah commandments, that have no rational explanation (unlike, for example, "thou shalt not steal"), but are simply done in the service of God. To overrationalize it might invite excuses about why the reasons no longer stand. Yet, as usual, various interpretations (or at least observations of the benefits resulting from the practice) have been offered over the ages, and here are some of the major ones: (1) *kashrut* is physically healthy (an explanation that has fallen into disfavor today because it is often dismissed in these days of refrigeration and sanitation); (2) *kashrut* is spiritually healthy—not eating birds of prey or scavenger fish and such reminds us to be gentler and more wholesome (the "you are what you eat" approach); (3) *kashrut* heightens sensitivity and curbs cruelty, since it mandates more humane slaughter techniques, forbids consumption of blood, and disallows combinations of milk (life) and flesh (death); (4) *kashrut* reinforces the unity of the Jewish people because wherever they go, it forces them to seek out Jewish community in order to eat; (5) *kashrut* does not deny pleasure, but trains a person to be more disciplined and to

sublimate some of his or her appetites and desires; and (6) *kashrut* is part of an overall holy way of life, because—along with blessings, hand-washing, and so forth—it elevates the physical act of eating to a spiritual discipline in which "the table is an altar." (God's command after describing the permitted and forbidden species is to "be holy, for I am holy" [Leviticus 11:45]).

Many Jews who have made the effort to find the level of *kashrut* with which they can live comfortably discover that this observance can provide important lessons for them and for their children. Every culture says something about food and about human appetites of all kinds. Judaism neither denies nor glorifies physical appetites but seeks to elevate and sanctify them, creating a way of life that focuses on serving God. Some Jewish educators tell me that *kashrut* seems to be a positive identity-building discipline for many young Jews. The cases where it sometimes seems to have a negative effect are where the children perceive their parents' observance as hypocritical, particularly where the home is strictly kosher, but the family eats anything outside. Although I can well understand why people would choose to keep kosher at home only (say, to accommodate the needs of relatives or to be able to host more observant Jews), to children's straightforward perception it usually seems sanctimonious.

I have found that *kashrut* (even in the rather moderate version in which we keep it) has heightened my children's Jewish identity. My daughter's non-Jewish Brownie leader was impressed, for example, that a seven-year-old would turn down Oreo cookies because her religion didn't allow them (they previously contained beef tallow). The children also know that they have certain Jewish observances every time they sit down to eat. (And when Christmas comes along, it's no shock suddenly to be different.)

Today many people are beginning to heighten their consciousness about what is being "fed" to them by the government, the media, the corporate world, the majority culture, the trend-setters in clothing or relationships or religion. They're waking up and starting to question not only what's in their drinking water and the air they breathe, but also with what subliminal messages and propaganda this or that "establishment" is trying to "satisfy" them. The consumer society promotes unconscious ingestion, for its main priority is to consume more and "better." One message of *kashrut* is to be aware of what one takes in, of where it comes from, what the moral implications are. *Kashrut* reminds us, for example, that eating meat means taking a life. *Kashrut* makes us stop and pay attention every time we crack an egg. What do we choose to absorb into our bodies—and our minds? Not to choose with awareness is to let someone else do the choosing for us. To teach our children to think before consuming could be a most meaningful contemporary *midrash* on the classical pillar of Jewish life.

Kosher, in addition to meaning "ritually fit," or "conforming to the dietary laws," literally means proper or decent. A number of contemporary Jewish leaders have suggested that the spirit of *kashrut* requires more than the mechanics of meat processing and dish separation. If Jews really wanted to keep kosher, they would avoid consuming products that are not proper and decent. Truly kosher consumers would boycott food items that involve exploitation of workers, destruction of the environment, or cruelty to animals. Jewish families could discuss how this meaning of *kashrut* might affect their food purchases and eating habits.

Kashrut Basics

The Jewish dietary laws come from the Torah and the oral tradition later embodied in the Talmud and Codes of Law. Here are the bare basics:

1. All fruits and vegetables are permitted, but only certain animals (those with a cleft hoof that chew their cud), domestic game, and fish that have both fins and scales (no shellfish, and—sorry, Texans— no catfish) (Leviticus 11).

2. Meat must be slaughtered in a carefully regulated, quick, and pain-minimizing way by a *shohet* (ritual slaughterer), who must be a person of excellent character, learning, and piety. Certain parts of the animal are not allowed and the meat must be salted and soaked to remove the blood (in the United States this is usually done before the meat reaches the consumer). Liver must be broiled to remove the blood (other cuts of meat may be "*kashered*" this way, too, if not previously soaked and salted), and even egg yolks must be checked to be sure they contain no blood spots.

3. Meat and milk products may not be eaten together, but a waiting period of several hours must elapse between eating meat and eating milk.

After eating milk, one may generally have meat right away, although there are varying customs. Meat and milk are of course not cooked together, and separate dishes are maintained for preparing and serving them. Fish, eggs, and nonanimal foods are considered *parve* and may be served with either meat (*fleishig*—Yiddish, *basari*—Hebrew) or dairy (*milchig*—Yiddish, *halavi*—Hebrew) foods.

4. Many prepared foods today are certified kosher by various rabbis and organizations, which is indicated by a sign such as ⓤ or Ⓚ. Not everything with just a K on it has actual *kashrut* supervision.

JEWISH VEGETARIANISM: KEEPING KOSHER WITH ONE SET OF DISHES

It is said that when Nobel laureate Isaac Bashevis Singer was asked in an interview if his vegetarian practices were motivated by health consideration, he replied in the affirmative.

"Yes," Singer is said to have responded, "I do it for the health of the chickens."

Singer is just one of a number of notable Jews in the arts, philosophy, and religion who have adopted a vegetarian diet for a variety of humanitarian and moral reasons. The Israeli writer S. Y. Agnon, another Nobel-prize winner, the visionary Zionist A. D. Gordon, and novelist Franz Kafka were all vegetarians. Modern Jewish religious leaders who espoused vegetarianism include Rabbi Abraham Isaac Kook, philosopher and first Ashkenazic chief rabbi of pre-state Palestine; Rabbi David Rosen, chief rabbi of Ireland; and Rabbi Shlomo Goren, a chief rabbi of Israel who was first to conduct a service at the Western Wall in 1967.

Many Jews find that observing *kashrut*, combined with other Jewish values, leads them closer to vegetarianism. *Kashrut*, which requires a more humane form of animal slaughter and forbids eating blood or mixing meat and milk, fosters a heightened sensitivity to the issue of taking life for food. In addition, traditional Judaism is keenly sensitive to *tzaar baalei hayyim*, concern for the suffering of animals. Rabbi Kook[12] pointed out that the original human diet in Genesis was a vegetarian one, meat eating being only a later concession to people's baser nature. *Kashrut*, in his view, was a compromise with total vegetarianism, and everyone will become vegetarians when the Messiah arrives!

In recent years vegetarianism has grown in popularity for various reasons. Vegetarianism sup ports many Jewish and humanitarian values: It is less of a burden on the environment than meat eating, it can lead to a more equitable sharing of food, and it alleviates *tzaar baalei hayim*, not only in respect to slaughtering animals but to the inhumane conditions in which many farm animals are raised today. Vegetarianism is also generally healthier and more economical than meat eating.

For *kashrut* observers, a vegetarian diet is generally easier because it requires fewer sets of dishes and eliminates the possibility of mix-ups and the wait between meat and milk meals. Passover can be a bit spare if one observes the Ashkenazic practice of refraining from legumes and rice. Some vegetarians I know have switched to the Sephardic customs of eating rice and beans on Passover, while others prefer to fill up on vegetables. Many vegetarians substitute a beet for the traditional shank bone. Strictly kosher vegetarians will still be on the lookout for kosher labels, which also guarantee that a product (if *parve* or dairy) contains no animal additives.

Vegetarianism is also a nice way to raise children. For many Jews today, it has become a very special kind of *kashrut*.

5

CHILD DEVELOPMENT AND JEWISH PARENTING

Long before twentieth-century researchers charted the stages of child development, long before European society had much of a notion of a distinctive period of childhood, the rabbis perceived childhood and adolescence as "a period of evolution . . . (part of) a process of development that begins in the earliest years and apparently never ceases."[1] They realized, in particular, that children were ready for more abstract and sophisticated learning experiences at certain ages (*Pirke Avot* 5:24).

Modern researchers have emphasized that children's intellectual, emotional, and moral development is qualitatively different at different stages of maturity. A school-aged child doesn't need just more of what a preschooler needs; she or he needs quite different educational approaches.

When it comes to Jewish education in the home, it's vital that the experiences we provide and the parental role we take are developmentally appro-priate for our children. One needn't be an expert to realize that a "birthday cake for the world" approach to Rosh HaShanah makes about as much sense for adolescents as a discussion of "particularism versus universalism" would for preschoolers. But too often these developmental changes aren't taken into account. Many kids get nearly identical approaches and information year after year.

The following table provides examples of Jewish educational activities that parents might employ (and might look for in school settings, where applicable) at their children's different developmental stages. This is not a curriculum or a check-list of skills to be achieved by children at certain ages. The four stages given here are based on the major developmental theories and research avail-able today.[2] *Exact ages for stages will of course vary with the individual child.*

A DEVELOPMENTAL APPROACH TO JEWISH PARENTING

INFANT—TODDLER (BIRTH TO APPROXIMATELY 2 1/2 YEARS)

General traits

Learns by hands-on and sensory experience of objects, rather than by looking at symbols or thinking about processes

Needs to be active

Centered on self and body

Sees and imitates

Good time for language input

Objects experienced as specific and separate, lacks categories

Needs emotional security, secure bonds with care-givers

31

Parental role in Jewish education

Structure the home environment as a Jewish one — in both time and space — concrete Jewish experiences natural part of daily life

Foster secure, trusting attachments to parents and reliable caregivers

Stress physical action and sensory experience: concrete experiences now create rich associations for representational or symbolic learning to develop

Know your child's unique style and match experiences to it (active and stimulating versus low-key and gentle, and so forth)

Shabbat and holidays

Experience through all five senses: see and feel ritual objects, taste foods, see lights, hear and move to melodies, sing very simple songs (2–5 words)

Torah learning

Soft-sculpture Jewish toys (such as huggable Torah)

Simple stories and talks about holidays and Jewish life can focus on actual objects, homemade picture books, felt boards, dolls and puppets, finger plays or movement

Prayer and synagogue

Experience prayer routines, melodies, movements as part of home life; involve all senses

Hebrew prayers and biblical songs as lullabies, music to move to, bring child to communal prayer and celebration settings for short times (as appropriate for individual child)

Values and morals

Secure daily interaction with parents and caregivers helps create basis for future trusting relationships and empathy for others

Encourage independence in daily-living skills and expect thoughtful behavior within developmental limits

Israel

Israeli music, art, and photos as part of home environment

Hebrew

Hebrew expressions, songs, and Jewish terms in Hebrew as part of daily life

Hebrew graphics as part of visual art in the home, evident in children's toys and room decor (without attempts to teach child formally)

(Bilingual parents: begin speaking Hebrew at home from birth and *persist*)

Current events and history

Bring child to participate in appropriate community activities

Life-cycle and daily life

Participate in daily routines and life-cycle events

PRESCHOOL (AGES APPROXIMATELY 2 TO 6)

General traits

Initiative, curiosity, exploration

Asserts independence in daily routine

Learns with language

Concepts differ from those of adults — more physical

Prime time for verbalization and language learning

Can represent things with symbols (words and pictures), but categorizations still limited

Learns through play

Deals with anxieties and guilt through story and fantasy

Judges morality of behavior by outcome (seeks to avoid punishment)

Parental role

Model Jewish adult life while providing real and playtime opportunities for child's active involvement

Provide material to facilitate Jewish play and hands-on experiences in various media

Child's natural drive toward autonomy and discovery can be channeled toward learning opportunities

Form scaffold of Jewish life experiences on which to build future learning

Make Jewish stories and imaginative play a regular facet of childhood

Encourage caring behavior from early age; both demonstrate and describe

Shabbat and holidays

Tell simple versions of holiday stories, make picture books, make books for children about their holiday experiences

Basic mood of holiday or Holy Days perceived through family observance

Demonstrate basic holiday *mitzvot* and home customs

Cooking, arts and crafts (creative, process-oriented), simple games involving holiday symbols

Dress-up and dramatic play, puppets

Simple songs, move and dance to music, rhythm instruments, finger plays, whole-body dramatics (act out melting candle, growing tree)

Imagination (the Shabbat queen, Elijah coming to the *seder*)

Torah learning

Create a Jewishly literate home environment: reading Jewish stories from Torah, Bible, *Midrash*, folk tales (variations: oral telling, puppets, felt boards, and so forth)

Simple Jewish storybooks with pictures

As appropriate, relate stories to simple conduct rules such as hospitality and kindness to animals

Prayer and synagogue

Reciting (and understanding general concepts of) home prayers for daily life: morning and bedtime prayers (for example, *Modeh Ani*, *Shema*), food blessings

Frequently heard songs and refrains in synagogue, key prayer vocabulary words

Learning objects in the sanctuary, places, and people at synagogue

Participation with parents in "tot Shabbat" or other early childhood services

Blessings for Shabbat, holidays, special life experiences (such as new clothes, thunder, sweet smells, rainbow)

Experience and discuss the wonders of nature, family love, the beauty of Torah, and the joys of Jewish life as gifts from God

Cultivating inner stillness and serenity, using guided imagery with Jewish content

Values and morals

Concern and empathy for others modeled in family and preschool or day-care interactions

Describe empathetic behavior: "That was very thoughtful." Also use *specifically Jewish terms*: "You did a mitzvah," "That's *derech eretz* (manners)," "What lovely *shelom bayit* (peaceful home)"

Point out opportunities for compassionate actions ("Shoshanah looks as if she could use some help with the door; let's open it for her.")

Illustrate values through traditional and contemporary stories

Giving *tzedakah* as part of home routine; child helps set aside items to donate

Israel

Books with simple stories of everyday life of Israeli children, books of photographs, recordings, songs, and circle dances

Videos (such as "Shalom Sesame"), posters

Yom HaAtzma'ut (Israel Independence Day) celebrations

Hebrew

Preschool to kindergarten: use age-appropriate language materials for early childhood, with a focus on spoken language along with simple Hebrew songs, stories, games, and toys

(*Bilingual*: Parent reads child stories in Hebrew, Israeli preschool songs and tapes, continues to speak Hebrew even when child answers in English)

Pre-kindergarten to first grade: letter and sound recognition for children who are ready, experience letters in various media and activities, sight-word recognition

Kindergarten to second grade (as developmentally ready): begin reading and printing in context of a whole-language approach (including stories and prayers)

Current events and history

Relate preschool magazines to Jewish concepts, explain holidays as re-creations of Jewish history

Daily life, life-cycle

Observances integrated into household routines (shopping for kosher food, cleaning for Shabbat)

Family albums, stories, videos

Jewish enrichment: puzzles, toys, picture books, art projects, songs and melodies

ELEMENTARY-SCHOOL AGE (6/7 TO 11/12)

General traits

General acceptance of authority in the early years, changing to questioning later

Fact orientation, learning to operate by rules (in academic subjects as well as socially)

Comprehends physical relationships, generalization

Mental problem solving with some symbols (letters, numbers)

Can categorize and perceive hierarchical categories, if concrete referents are the base

Close same-sex friendships may be important to emotional development

Prime time for developing sense of accomplishment and industry unless continual failure and criticism undermine self-image

Morality of behavior judged by intention, rules, fairness (a major concern)

Parental role

Personal embodiment of desired traits and behaviors—prayer, study, interest in Hebrew and Israel, *tzedakah*, values—on adult level

Let them be children—avoid precocious involvement in teen interests

Natural inclination toward accomplishment and pleasing adults makes this a prime time to teach facts, skills, routines, and rules

Provide concrete, active base of Jewish knowledge on which more abstract concepts can be built in adolescence and adulthood

Maintain parental authority while relating to child with unconditional love and individual attention

Culturally rich Jewish home environment makes formal education far more effective

Use child's individual interests, learning styles, and personality as guides to appropriate home activities

Shabbat and holidays

Holiday histories with greater chronological and geographical detail, key concepts (awe, dedication, freedom), characters as people making choices

More detailed laws and customs

Hands-on making or assembly of holiday items

Enrich with more complex stories, texts, songs, crafts, dramatics, or games; try recipes and customs from other countries or time periods

Torah learning

Moving from story to text, noting details, repetitions, vocabulary

Introduction of commentaries as search for meaning of texts

Values and morals

Parental and other adult models of ethical, caring, involved behavior; not sporadic lessons, but an entire life-context of compassion, morality

Values taught as fairly straightforward rules with reasons

Illustrate values with contemporary stories as well as classic Jewish ones

Guided use of *teshuvah* process (regret, restitution, resolution to change—in gradual stages if needed) to facilitate behavioral changes

Concept of people as partners of God working toward *tikkun olam*

Hebrew names for values, behaviors; phrases from Torah, *Pirke Avot*, and so on, in daily speech (reinforce with informal artistic activities)

Frequent family *tzedakah* projects as volunteers, *tzedakah* co-ops

Stress responsibilities of daily life (chores, study) as base for later moral responsibility

Israel

Meanings and origin of the word *Israel*: people, land, beliefs; concept that various meanings of "Israel" link all Jews

Basic facts, national symbols, simple geography, broad outline of history (idea of exile and return), how life in Israel is similar to and different from life in North America

Stories about history, places, and leaders in Israel, past and present

Zionist-oriented youth group and camping experiences: songs, cultural events

Pen pals, *mizrah* bulletin board, hobbies and collections

Family-oriented trips to Israel

Hebrew

Hebrew as a top priority in formal Jewish education from early grades, ideally as language of instruction, emphasis on acquisition of spoken language, with graduated reading and writing (script)—emphasis on *comprehension and communication*

Enrich formal instruction with Hebrew songs and simplified Hebrew stories, games and clubs, Hebrew-speaking camp, and so forth

(Bilingual: Provide books and media in Hebrew, creative writing and journals or letters, conversation)

Current events and history

Discuss current events from news, relate to Jewish values

Children's magazines: Jewish and general

Visit places in Jewish community, meet community workers, participate in communal events

Civic education: family meetings, school activities

Pictorial histories, historical fiction, and adventure stories, visit Jewish museums and historic sites as part of family vacations, personal oral histories of older Jews, creative projects (models, collections)

Gradual exposure to Holocaust period through age-appropriate books, meeting survivors, Yom HaShoah programs

Life-cycle and daily life

Learning daily rules of Jewish life as your family observes it (*kashrut* and so forth)

Discuss meanings behind the rules (for example, blessings show appreciation)

Appropriate participation in life-cycle events and other family celebrations

Family albums of parents and older generations, oral histories, family trees

Jewish enrichment: arts, books, games, music, cooking, collections

Youth groups and other informal Jewish experiences, day and overnight camps with Jewish content (versus merely Jewish auspices), family *shabbatons* (Sabbath retreats)

ADOLESCENCE (AGES 11/12 TO 17/18)

General traits

Resists or reacts to authority

Behavior judged by principles, tendency toward absolutist stance

Developing personal identity, deciding what kind of adult to be

Identity related to perceptions of personal competency, sex role, relationships to adults and peer group

Self-centered, projects personal thoughts onto others ("imaginary audience")

May lack sense of personal vulnerability

Still in transition from childhood, emotional vacillations in maturity level

Developing concepts of social contract, universal values

Can deal with abstractions, can think about thinking

Applies general rules and systems to particular situations

Can manipulate symbols with higher-order symbols

Parental role

Maintain, even amplify expressions of love and personal interest; important not to withdraw touch, focused attention

Be available and an active listener

Allow for gradual development of autonomy, trustworthiness, and responsibility

Foster and guide gradual growth of self-control and appropriate emotional expression

Be flexible in relating to frequent fluctuations in level of maturity, while maintaining and reinforcing positive expectations for behavior and responsibility

Love and value youngster unconditionally, maintain lines of communication

Provide positive models of Jewish adulthood (not only parents, but other adults very important now)

Provide Jewish peer frameworks (youth movements, and the like) with Jewish content (versus merely Jewish auspices)

Mandate service to others (for example, use of family car contingent on certain time it is used for *tzedakah*, volunteer work)

CRUCIAL period to continue and deepen *structured* Jewish education

Shabbat and holidays

Deeper philosophical meanings and themes, thematic relationships in yearly cycle

Historical development of holidays and holiday cycle

Biblical and rabbinic text study related to holidays

Contemporary interpretations (ecological, feminist, political, and so on)

Ethical implications of activities

Torah learning

Biblical and major rabbinic texts: broad concepts of content and methodology but emphasize detailed study of selections, guided topical study

Use of study aids (encyclopedias, concordances, dictionaries, commentaries) to enable independent learning

Traditional and modern Torah commentaries; contemporary scholarship

Traditional *Midrash* and contemporary expressions of "*Midrash*" (including personal)

Text study through more sophisticated inquiry, commentary, debate; various aspects including historical, psychological, philosophical

Relating Jewish texts to current ethical issues; explore issues raised by texts themselves: *halachic*, ethical

Relating personal concerns, finding personal meaning in Jewish sources

If possible, identify a mentor

Prayer and synagogue

Personal commitment to prayer realized in context of home, school, youth group, synagogue adult service (*tefillin*, *tallit*, as applicable)

Structure of service well internalized

Ability to lead all or parts of service

Metathemes of *siddur* (such as creation, revelation, redemption)

History of major prayers and *siddur*; historical development of Jewish prayer

Psalms—study, creative expression

Meditation and prayer, Jewish spirituality and mysticism in daily life and in prayer

More sophisticated personal definitions of Jewish spiritual concepts, for example, *kedushah* (holiness, distinctiveness); balance of *keva* (regularity) and *kavanah* (intention, meaningfulness)

Why pray, types of prayer

Individual concepts (metaphoric understanding) of God

Comparative Judaism and comparative religion

Ethical dimension of prayers and observances: learn and practice

Compose personal prayers, personal interpretations of traditional liturgy

Values and morals

Jewish concepts of set and situational ethics

Musar (ethical development) text selections, working toward emotional maturity

Complex ethical issues with many sides: learn how to explore from a Jewish perspective

Contemporary moral and ethical issues—Jewish values perspectives

Jewish perspectives and support on challenges facing adolescents: self-esteem, friendship, peer pressures, sexual activity, drugs and alcohol, cults, pressures to achieve, interdating and intermarriage

Relate contemporary ethical issues to personal identity and actions

Personal and group involvement in *tzedakah*, activism

Israel

History—more detailed, formative ideologies, archeology

Geography—maps, historical, political, geological, nature

Social and political issues—historical background and various perspectives

Zionist-oriented youth groups and camps; teen study and service programs in Israel, exchange programs with Israeli peers

Hebrew

Emphasize programs in Hebrew as living language, Hebrew for high-school accreditation and advanced college placement, Hebrew spoken in camp settings and Israel programs

More formal study of grammar, syntax

Various possible study emphases:

Traditional: Learn Rashi script, tropes, Aramaic and rabbinic terminology, advanced texts

Contemporary: Simplified Hebrew literature, Israeli poetry and songs, regular newspapers, unvocalized Hebrew, letter and essay writing

(*Bilingual*: Reinforce areas of greatest need, spend time in Israel, in Hebrew-speaking environment)

Current events and history

Teen and adult level general and Jewish periodicals

Issues, conflicts, multiple viewpoints, debates

Civic education: student and youth movement government, volunteer involvement in political issues

More sophisticated study of Jewish history through texts, media, role playing

Sensitively taught study of Holocaust period, anti-Semitism, racism—and contemporary responses (important to bring to high-school–aged students of all religions)

Life-cycle and daily life

Halachah—personal orientation to Jewish law as system with both stability and flexibility, life path

Design own ceremonies as appropriate

Relate life-cycle events and everyday practices to values and social issues

Research family history (documents, and the like); keep journals and albums

Jewish society outside the family: youth movements, camps, peers, retreats, nonparental models of Jewish adulthood

Look into Jewish life and learning at college level; relate career and study aspirations (including secular) to Jewish values

Jewish enrichment possibilities: advanced folk arts and handicrafts, artistic expressions (dance, video, drama, creative writing, poetry); enjoy Jewish music, literature, journalism, hobbies, and individual interests (such as sports—Maccabiah games, and so forth)

6

FAMILY HERITAGE: JEWISH HISTORY BEGINS WITH GRANDMA AND GRANDPA

The world of the family has shrunk beyond all measure. Where once it stretched horizontally into extended networks of relationship and vertically back into generations of history, today's family is often cut off from both kinds of associations. While a few of my friends grew up with family reunions and cousins' clubs or have family trees in their possession, most of my Jewish friends of my generation barely know which countries their great-grandparents hailed from; many don't know their original family names.

The majority of Jews in today's world have been in the same countries for only a few generations at most, and many have little knowledge of their genealogies and family histories. With the destruction of most of European Jewry, we are even more cut off from our roots. Looking back only a couple of generations, all seems dark and silent. How many of us feel that we sprang up mysteriously in some American suburb, rootless as tumbleweeds?

Rediscovering Jewish traditions ties us to generations past in a most important way by awakening us to the cycles of sacred time, while rediscovering our Jewish family makes us realize that there are also real human links to that Jewish past. We begin to want to learn more about our ancestors' worlds, to understand what was lost so that the future may be based on something more profound than our own brief experiences.

And what of our children? Jewish history may be abstract to them, but Grandma and Grandpa are people they can relate to, and family stories can be as compelling to children as any fairy tale or legend because they are *their* stories. Maurice

Samuel called a knowledge of one's grandparents "an excellent introduction to history."[1] Connection to the family's past and to extended family members also helps to satisfy our children's important human need for belonging.

To a Jew, the ultimate destruction is not death itself, but the erasure of a name, the blotting out of memory. Every time we uncover someone from our family's past, a redemption takes place, both of them and of a forgotten part of us. And finding our living relatives wherever they are scattered, picking up the fragments of our shattered families, as Jewish genealogist Arthur Kurzweil[2] describes it, reverberates for me with an almost kabbalistic metaphor of redemption.

IDEAS FOR EXPLORING YOUR FAMILY HERITAGE

Note: This section is not intended to exclude families in which all or part of the family has chosen Judaism through conversion. Each family's unique mixture of heritage is part of the Jewish saga and should be celebrated as such. Likewise, families with adopted children and blended families should adapt these ideas to affirm the way their family was created.

(The first three ideas are adapted from a lecture by Arthur Kurzweil):[3]

● Oral histories: Speak to the older members of your family about their memories. Let your children ask some of the questions. Make notes, tape record, and if at all possible, videotape.

● Obtain documents about the family's immigrant generation. These are available from the U.S. Immigration and Naturalization Service, as well as from ship's records in the National Archives. Kurzweil's books (see Resource Guide, p. 310), give details. Even elementary-school–age children can benefit from seeing and discussing such records. Suddenly Bubbie isn't an old lady in a nursing home, but a plucky fifteen-year-old, arriving at Ellis Island with ten dollars in her pocket.

● Together with older relatives, preserve, restore, and label the backs of old family photographs. If they go unlabeled, the names may be lost forever. One way to duplicate old photos safely is simply to photograph them with a tripod-held camera with slow exposure. (My sister has done this with several old photos that relatives were reluctant to send through the mail.) Display old family photographs in the home rather than keeping them hidden away. Talk about the people in them with your children.

● Today's family albums are tomorrow's historical treasures, so create them with care. Be sure to label the backs of photos clearly—and don't wait too long. Sticky-backed album pages allow for the creative display of pictures, captions, and mementos, but find the kind that are free of any damaging chemicals. Likewise, family videotapes may serve as tomorrow's historical documents. It's advisable to give some copies of photos and videos to other relatives, in case of the rare event of loss in a fire (God forbid).

● Together with your children, make a family tree. Photos can be used to enhance it.

● Establish a bulletin board to display photos of relatives, especially those who live far away. Discuss the people in the pictures with your children.

● Set aside a shelf or drawer as your family archives, to collect and organize copies of photos, clippings, mementos, and other family memorabilia. Be sure to take these things out on certain occasions and to talk about them.

● Display a world map. Put in color-coded pins to indicate where the various branches of your family live today and where they came from. Refer to the map when your children study these places in school and relate their studies to your own family history.

● Hold a family reunion. Family research (see Resource Guide p. 310) can help you to turn up more family members. Keep up the ties year round by publishing a cousins' newsletter.

● When you visit Israel, go prepared with family names and origins to check out at the computer of Beit Hatefutzot, The Diaspora Museum in Ramat Aviv, Tel Aviv.

● Make a cookbook of family recipes and indicate sources. Or make a community cookbook of family recipes from your synagogue, *havurah*, or Jewish school. Include introductions about the family origins of each recipe.

● Use family heirlooms wherever possible, particularly if you have inherited Jewish ritual items. Create heirlooms of the future by purchasing fine ritual items for family members and having them engraved with names, place, date, occasion.

And you will see your children's children; peace upon Israel!

—Psalm 128:6

IN PRAISE OF GRANDPARENTS

No one needs a book to tell them what grandparents mean to children. Grandparents give children a different perspective, a deeper history—and so much love. Grandparents can bypass many of the conflicts that often seem inherent in the parent-child dynamic. Grandparents often have a lot of good advice, too, when we get ready to listen! And besides, a little spoiling never hurt anyone. Families with grandparents nearby are really blessed.

When grandparents are far away or the child has no grandparents, it's helpful to build relationships with other older adults who can relate to the child in grandparently ways. But there is still nothing like the real grandparents, even if they are far away. Cards and letters, phone calls, photos (not just of the children to the grandparents, but the other way around, too), and even cassettes and videotapes can help to bridge the gaps between visits. Children can and should participate actively in these communications from a very young age.

Grandparents can add an extra dimension to children's Jewish lives in many ways. They can share family memories, traditions, mementos, and recipes. They can bless the grandchildren at

Shabbat gatherings. And the memories they can discuss of the significant Jewish history they have witnessed in their own lifetimes can often be a key factor in making that history come alive for the grandchildren. The different sets of grandparents (and often, great-grandparents, too) can offer different perspectives to the child. Some children call their grandparents *Saba* and *Savta* (Grandpa and Grandma in Hebrew) or *Zadie* and *Bubbie* (in Yiddish).

7

THE CHANGING JEWISH FAMILY

Jewish families have faced many challenges in the past—challenges which were usually evoked by adversity rather than prosperity. Today, however, Jewish families face the challenge of retaining their vitality and cohesion while responding to the opportunities of an open society.

— Dr. Sylvia Barack Fishman[1]

We talked, when they got divorced how lots of things were going to change. They have to whether you want them to or not. But the Jewish stuff doesn't change at all. It's like all that is much more important than any one of us, than any family, no matter who they are. And that's really good for people to know.

— Esther Golleb, age 13[2]

LIKE OTHER AMERICANS, ONLY MORE SO

"Jews are like other people, only more so," goes the old saw, and apparently this is more so than ever in contemporary America. In three to five generations, the majority of American Jews who have roots in Eastern Europe have succeeded in transforming themselves from outsiders with a different language and culture to complete Americans, only more so.[3] As a whole, American Jews have become extraordinarily competent and acculturated in the secular arena. (For many Jews this secular competency stands in striking contrast to their overall lack of *Jewish* literacy, knowledge, and skills.)[4]

Yes, there are impoverished Jews, and yes, there are many "middle-class squeezed" Jews trying to cope with the high cost of living and the high cost of Jewish affiliation, but Jews as a group are among the more affluent, educated, and highly mobile of the American population. Over 85 percent of Jews attend college, and 50 percent or more obtain advanced degrees.

Concurrent with our cultural changes have come changes in our family structure. In most, although not all, areas of recent family evolution, Jews reflect the larger American community in which we live—often more so. If Ozzie and Harriet and their two-parent, mom-at-home nuclear family have become the decided minority, so too have their Jewish counterparts Izzie and Chanah, with their large brood, extended family, and traditional division of roles.

The American trend is toward later marriage and childbearing; in general, Jews tend to marry even later and delay childbearing even longer than other groups. The long years in college and professional training are also frequently a period of relative uninvolvement in Jewish life. Outside the Orthodox community (who are estimated to make up about 6–9 percent of the American Jewish population), Jews frequently delay childbearing until their thirties and tend to have fewer children than other American religious groups. Meanwhile, the high mobility of many Jews tends to fragment extended families and to reduce Jewish affiliations.

The most dramatic change in the Jewish family

in the past few decades has been the rise in intermarriage between Jews and non-Jews. Some studies show that more than half of Jewish marriages today involve a partner who was not born Jewish. If, as happens in a minority of cases, the Gentile spouse converts to Judaism, the family is likely to be actively involved in Jewish life. In intermarriages where the spouse does not convert to Judaism, however, the children are statistically much less likely to grow up to be practicing Jews.[5] (Still, statistics can never tell the whole story. As a Jewish educator, I know of many families in which a non-Jewish spouse participates actively in a Jewish way of life. In some cases, a nonconversionary intermarriage has led to a home in which religion is explored seriously and in which the family eventually develops a strong Jewish identity and involvement.)

One area where Jews are "behind" the general population is in somewhat lower divorce rates. Yet Jews, like other groups, have seen a rise in divorce in the past couple of decades. Divorce rates are still much lower among more traditional and Orthodox Jews, although even there they have risen in recent years. Remarriage rates are very high among divorced Jews, a fact that somewhat masks the real divorce rate. These second or third marriages also have a higher rate of intermarriage. Blended families experience many challenges even if they do share the same religious practices, and more so if they don't.

Feminism has changed all of our lives dramatically, and the Jewish community is no exception. The traditional religious roles for male and female are undergoing far-reaching changes in the synagogue, home, and community. These changes are most obvious in the more liberal Jewish branches, but are substantial, if more subtle, in much of Orthodoxy as well. Again, change can be simultaneously positive and stressful. In the secular arena, "baby-boomer" American Jewish women along the entire religious spectrum are likely to be comparatively well educated and to pursue careers along with motherhood. In many ways the Jewish community has yet to catch up with the now-prevalent two-career life-style.

In general, the more religiously traditional Jewish families present more traditional patterns of family life and are also more affiliated with Jewish institutions. The traditional Jewish life-style, bulwarked by the norms of a traditional Conservative or Orthodox community, does seem to be linked to patterns of greater family stability (likewise, more traditional family patterns and

values are seen among Israeli Jews than among those in the United States). Traditional family values lead to greater affiliation with Jewish institutions, which reinforce traditional family values, which further foster Jewish affiliation, and so on.

On the other side, some experts point to a kind of vicious cycle in which nontraditional family patterns, such as divorce, lead to more tenuous Jewish affiliation, which leads to further nontraditional patterns (such as an interfaith remarriage), propelling the family even farther from any Jewish identification or affiliation. Yet at other times, family crises and changes lead the family to more intensive Jewish involvement.

CREATIVE RESPONSES TO CHANGES IN THE JEWISH FAMILY

Obviously, these changes are complex, and complete volumes have been—or ought to be—devoted to each. If the experts continue to search for methods and approaches for dealing with the waves of change, an exhaustive discussion of these issues is beyond the scope of this book. I do believe, however, that there are significant ways for individual families to deal with these culture shocks as they experience them in their own families. These involve five basic components, which can be headed as Jewish communal responses, the family's Jewish self-image, the power of networking, discovering practical strategies, and the role of Jewish tradition itself, which may provide stability.

JEWISH COMMUNAL RESPONSES

The first component is the obvious one. The Jewish community, from the national policies of large organizations down to the daily procedures of the smallest congregation, needs to respond more fully to the changing needs of its constituent families. Sometimes the needs are financial and may include dues and tuition reductions and discounted services for economically squeezed single parents, for example. At other times they are emotional and social and may include support groups for parents in blended or intermarried families, synagogue *havurot* that incorporate different kinds of families, Jewish "big brothers and sisters," rabbinical outreach to couples going through divorce, Shabbat retreats for single-parent families, and "*mitzvah* committees" in synagogues to match families for holiday time support and comradeship. Elsewhere, the needs are logistical and may need expanded Jewish day care for children of two-career households and Jewish education programs that take parents' work schedules or visitation schedules into account (note that conflict between different constituencies may result). And often, simple sensitivity is needed: space for stepparents on Hebrew-school-application forms, teacher awareness that not all grandparents are Jewish and not all daddies are home to make *kiddush*, personal attitudes of acceptance and inclusion rather than rejection toward those with different types of families and life-styles.

For a long time, there was a feeling in much of the Jewish community that outreach toward groups such as the divorced or intermarried would be seen as a way of encouraging these patterns, which are often perceived as major threats to Jewish stability and continuity. Today, more and more organizations realize that the "head in the sand" approach serves only to alienate more Jews from Jewish life. There is much that can be done to promote traditional family values while at the same time enhancing and supporting the Jewish lives of those in nontraditional situations.

All of us who are involved in Jewish community and synagogue life, whether as professionals, lay-leaders, or volunteers, need to take into account the changing nature of our constituency as we formulate policies and programs. Sociologist Chaim Waxman points out that it is important to *include* people from different family configurations (single parents, two-career couples) in the decision making of Jewish institutions, lest programs "be planned paternalistically, with no input from those to be served."[6]

For families in nontraditional patterns who feel uncomfortable or unsatisfied with current policies, there are different options: (1) get involved in leadership positions where they can affect policy and programming more directly (obviously, many are not in a position to do this); (2) ask for what they need, join together (see the following) with others in similar circumstances to lobby for what they need; and (3) if sincere efforts fail, look elsewhere in their Jewish communities. In many areas, there are marked differences between synagogues and other institutions in regard to such items as financial adjustments, comfort level for nontraditional families of various sorts, and social groupings. Obviously, all of this is easier said than done in some places and for some families. But the point is not to rush to reject the entire Jewish world because one rabbi seemed insensitive or one synagogue appeared cliqueish.

THE FAMILY'S JEWISH SELF-IMAGE

Several writers have pointed out that what pushes many Jews in nontraditional family configurations away from Jewish life is not as much the attitude of the institutions as it is their own internalized feelings of failure or illegitimacy as Jews, which they project onto representatives of the religious tradition.[7] One study showed that Jews are more inclined to tie their marital stability to their overall sense of self-esteem than are other ethnic groups.[8] Our heritage is family oriented and our ideal of the Jewish family continues to resemble *Fiddler on the Roof*, but our families are more likely to resemble *thirtysomething*. This can lead to a lot of emotional dissonance.

Those who do succeed in creating a meaningful Jewish home life within a nontraditional family structure generally have in common a view of themselves and their families as *Jewishly legitimate*. They consider themselves both deserving and capable of making a vital Jewish life for their families, rather than as having failed in some way (although in some situations they have had to work through normal feelings of failure). They acknowledge areas where they need help and support but are not passively waiting and hoping for the synagogue or Jewish professionals to recognize their needs. Rather, they take the initiative to create a Jewish home environment, to get involved in some aspect of Jewish community, to link up with other families.

For example, in intermarried families (whether conversionary or mixed marriages), "the strongest factor determining the degree of Jewishness . . . appears to be the strength of the Jewish commitment of the Jewish-born spouse."[9] In single-parent families, success in creating a positive Jewish life is often achieved by recognizing that, as one study put it, "the responsibility for outreach works both ways."[10]

Another aspect of the legitimacy issue is the growth of individuals into new and different roles, particularly into changed gender roles. Even traditional perspectives emphasize that in a Jewish home Shabbat should be celebrated regardless of who lights the candles. So a single mother can and should learn to feel comfortable saying kiddush, and a single father can light candles, while a husband whose wife is employed outside the home can know that it's a *mitzvah* to take on more of the pre-Shabbat cooking and cleaning.

One writer described her sense of family legitimacy with the traditional Jewish concept of *shelom bayit*, peace in the home. *Shalom*, the word for peace, also means wholeness, and she decided that her children needed to know that the family was not broken, but would experience a whole and complete Jewish home environment whether she was single or, later, remarried. "We interacted with the community in the same way as any other family. We were not ashamed of who we were, nor did we feel ourselves incomplete. Every Shabbat we made *Shabbos* in a very traditional way. . . ."[11] Note, too, how the Jewish traditions are inextricably linked with that sense of wholeness and stability.

THE POWER OF NETWORKING

The Torah records that in ancient times when one family was too small to need an entire Paschal lamb, small families would get together to share the holiday's sacrificial meal. A lesson to be drawn from this is that modern families also can join together to create new extended-family-style networks where they can help one another live fuller Jewish lives. These support systems, ranging from two families who regularly celebrate Shabbat together to a full-fledged *havurah*, can help create a sense of tradition and belonging. A warm and nurturant synagogue environment (for those who find the right kind of place) can also function this way. A single parent wrote that "synagogue-focused Judaism" helped to make up for the solitariness of her home situation by providing a community for worship and celebration, as well as by presenting enlarged perspectives on the varieties of family interaction.[12]

Synagogues, Jewish Family Services, and Jewish resource or parenting centers can be the settings for seminars and support groups that deal with a range of family issues. If your institutions don't provide the services you need—ask, push, take the initiative. Once groups of parents with similar concerns get together, they can often continue to work together in seeking appropriate services and programs from their local Jewish community, as well as organizing programs for themselves and their families.

Networking with others in similar family configurations can help parents to share ideas and common experiences, but connecting with different kinds of families can be important, too. Our community is fragmented enough as it is, and it can be rewarding for us and for our children to be with and learn from different kinds of families from our own.

DISCOVERING PRACTICAL STRATEGIES

Finally, there are specific strategies that families learn which can make their particular families thrive. A blended family finds compromises for dealing with the mixed emotions of life-cycle events, a two-career family figures out how to get ready for Shabbat despite its members' full schedules, an intermarried family deals with intergenerational holiday dilemmas. As with many other aspects of family life, strategy development is a gradual process of networking with other families, reading articles and books (see Resource Guide, pp. 306–307, for books and articles with specific ideas), and using common sense and trial and error to find one's own way.

JEWISH TRADITION MAY PROVIDE STABILITY

A number of studies have pointed out that for many families the Jewish tradition has provided stability and rootedness in times of family crisis or new and more stressful life-styles.

For example, a study of nearly a hundred working mothers showed that "Jewish beliefs and attitudes helped them juggle their multiple obligations. They also view their willingness to 'work through' their problems as an expression of Jewish family values. Several stated that the religion and tradition 'held them together' when a child came down with a debilitating illness, a husband walked out, both husband and wife lost their job, or in some other major crisis."[13] Interestingly, this held true even though the women felt that the Jewish community itself was seriously lacking in the programs or services that would help them to deal more successfully with their daily lives!

Another study pointed to the many children in family crisis (in this case divorce) who attach great importance to their religious lives, Jewish schools, and Jewish religious ceremonies.[14] Having "something bigger" than their immediate problems can help children as well as adults to cope with family changes.

In a different context, I look at my own family. When my mother was suddenly and devastatingly widowed at the age of 46 (and one daughter was still at home, so my mother was also a single parent), Judaism and the Jewish community were tremendously important to her as she rebuilt her life. I want to emphasize that she was not a conventionally traditional Jew (although she was interested in the spiritual and intellectual aspects of life), nor did she live in a major Jewish community at the time. Yet her life crisis, rather than alienating her, brought her closer to Judaism. Her rabbi, Samuel Stahl, was very supportive, and Temple Beth El helped my sisters get scholarships to Jewish study programs in Israel. My mother and my youngest sisters spent summers together at a Jewish camp (Mom worked, one of my sisters was a counselor, and the other was a camper and later a counselor-in-training). My mother remained involved with a *havurah*, and even studied for a year in Israel, where she was accompanied by my teenage sister. Today Mom has moved to a city with a much larger Jewish community, continues to be active in a congregation and to study Torah regularly, and has worked for a major Jewish organization. (She has also remarried.)

This is not to say that other widows, widowers, or single parents are going to want or be able to do exactly what my mother did. But it is an example of the powerful role that Jewish tradition, Torah, and the Jewish community (even though it still has a lot of catching up to do to meet contemporary families' needs) can play in providing stability and continuity in situations where individual lives have become anything but stable or traditional.

FAMILY SNAPSHOTS

DISCOVERY AND REDISCOVERY

[Saul and Cindy Rosenthal live in San Antonio, Texas. Saul is a psychiatrist; Cindy is an artist and businessperson. They are the parents of a toddler, Sadie, and Saul also has two grown sons from a previous marriage. Cindy had been learning about Judaism for a number of years and formally converted to Judaism while she was pregnant with Sadie.]

Cindy said: "For years, Saul and I had had a Jewish home, but I had never officially converted. Then I became pregnant with my first child, a daughter, and our whole lives and perspectives changed. Fortunately, this event coincided with our discovery of and joining a rather small but warm and friendly Jewish congregation, with a wonderful Conservative woman rabbi then serving as the part-time rabbi. There were many leadership roles for lay women, from being president of the congregation to leading services. Actually, women and men worked together in harmony, unlike the male-dominated congregations we had attended in the past. All of these factors provided the impetus for me not only to learn more about Judaism, but to convert as well.

"The preeminent issue for me has become to learn more in order to teach my daughter. My husband and I realize that we are a link (no longer dangling) in an historical chain and we have to pass knowledge of Judaism along to our child."

Saul said, "My wife, Cindy, had undertaken to go to the *mikveh* as part of her conversion and we were to meet the assistant rabbi at the community *mikveh* at another congregation. I came from a background in which I knew nothing about the *mikveh* and had a moderate amount of anxiety about whether it would be a positive emotional experience for Cindy or whether it would turn her off. At first everything seemed to be going wrong; we were even locked out of the building. I was picturing an emotional letdown and a disaster, but eventually everything was straightened out. . . .

"Cindy emerged very happy. Floating totally immersed and suspended in the *mikveh* had been a transcendental experience for her. She thought it must have felt like being in the womb. The floating in warmth was very comforting. She also identified with her daughter, who was at that time in Cindy's womb, three months from being born. Cindy, who had thought of the *mikveh* just as a step toward her conversion, found herself appreciating that she was participating in a very ancient ritual.

"[As for me] relearning about Judaism as an

adult was an eye-opening experience. My prior Jewish education ended when I was 13. This left me with both a child's understanding of the religion and a feeling that the religion was primarily for children. When my wife was going through conversion preparation, and since, I have read a great deal about Judaism, the Jewish holidays, and Jewish history. This has allowed me to see Judaism through adult eyes and to discover it as a mature, healthy, and sophisticated philosophy that is humane, flexible, adaptable, and eminently sensible, with a full, colorful, and useful tradition that I am proud to practice with my family and to pass on to my children."

—*Saul and Cindy Rosenthal*

8

THE IMPORTANCE OF COMMUNITY

Through all of our work, no single conclusion registers so strongly as our sense that there is, among the people we have come to know, a powerful, perhaps even desperate, longing for community, a longing that is, apparently, not adequately addressed by any of the relevant institutions in most people's lives.

—Leonard J. Fein

A great debate has been raging of late in a number of Jewish publications: What is more important to the Jewish future, an emphasis on the individual Jewish family and home, or the building of cohesive and dynamic Jewish communities?[1]

It seems abundantly clear that this is yet another classic case of "and the *rebbe* said: 'You're both right!' " The vitality of the Jewish future depends on strong and active Jewish homes *as well* as on strong and active Jewish communities. What's more, the family and the community are interdependent. Each needs the other in order to be complete.

But what does one mean by "Jewish community"? There are several levels of communal involvement. When Jews refer to "community," they often mean all of the Jews in a given city, or organizations such as Jewish federations and community centers. This is one valid definition. Participation in local and national organizations and institutions, including raising funds for communal needs and *tzedakah*, is clearly important. The "body," as it were, must be maintained in order to preserve the soul.

But the type of community I am referring to goes beyond secular communal institutions, even beyond maintaining a synagogue membership. My definition of Jewish community is the Jewish fellowship experience that can be found in a close-knit congregation or *havurah* devoted to mutual spiritual, emotional, and educational support. Intensive personal involvement and interpersonal support is what makes the difference between membership in an institution and participation in a community. One of the best ways to grow Jewishly and to strengthen the family in the process is to get involved with a Jewish community that encourages active participation.

The need for community is gaining recognition in general American society. The emotional benefits of communal support are increasingly realized. Thousands of Americans are reaching out from the prevalent life-style of emotional isolation to form communal groups that range from informal fellowships to co-housing villages and intentional communities of various ideological outlooks.

Judaism traditionally finds spiritual meaning, as well as emotional support, in community. Much of Jewish ritual practice takes place in community, and God's presence is said to be felt when people study or worship together in a group. By finding and getting involved in the appropriate kind of Jewish community for your family, you can gain a great deal of support for your family's emotional, spiritual, and intellectual growth and well-being.

49

FINDING THE RIGHT COMMUNITY FOR YOUR FAMILY

How do you find the right kind of community for your family? The answers are as individual as each family itself. The ideal, I would think, is to be involved in a warm and intimate congregation. In such a setting, the physical place of the synagogue is combined with the emotional security of the community. It has both "body" and "soul," both the stability of an institution and the dynamism of a growing, active group of people. There are groups of Jews all over the world who have formed their own congregations or revitalized older institutions.

If your synagogue per se is too large to be considered "warm and intimate," a *havurah* or other fellowship group within or outside the synagogue is often a meaningful alternative. These fellowships, which have blossomed throughout the country in the past couple of decades, may be independent of a synagogue, or they may take place under synagogue auspices. Such a fellowship may be called a *havurah* (fellowship) or a *minyan* (worship group). You may be able to join an existing group or form your own with friends. Ideally, the *havurah* is a group that will last for years, offering a meaningful emotional base for the individuals involved. There are *havurot* as simple as groups that meet once every month for an informal evening arranged by the members to those as elaborate as small congregations that run study and worship programs and schools for their children. In some areas several *havurot* join forces for educational programs and holiday services. *Havurot* are now found across the Jewish ideological spectrum, although the independent variety have been particularly prominent in the Reconstructionist movement.

Meaningful Jewish fellowship, as defined by Jacob Neusner in his landmark book *Contemporary Judaic Fellowship in Theory and Practice*,[2] may have a variety of goals but will probably include five central activities: prayer, study, service, celebration, and record-keeping. Prayer may take the form of traditional services or other forms the group develops, but will aim for meaningful religious experiences. Study of Jewish texts, books, and source materials will be done in a way that emphasizes discussion and new ideas. The fellowship will serve others by performing acts of compassion (*gemilut hasadim*), will celebrate the many facets of the Jewish sacred calendar, and will preserve the history of the communal experience through records of prayers, writings, and the like.

The experience of Jewish community can take other forms besides the congregation or *havurah*. Ideally, the Jewish way of life includes a support network of extended family. Increased mobility has resulted in many Jewish children growing up far from relatives. Families may be able to partially fill this gap by creating substitute extended families in the form of friendship with individuals of various ages and stages in life. Synagogues and Jewish organizations can work to foster such intergenerational connections.

Many Jewish families seek out a Jewish neighborhood in which to make their home. But a high proportion of Jewish surnames in the local phone book is not enough to create a community, unless there are institutions such as a synagogue or school to help link the residents. The Jewish neighborhood formed around a congregation is a more common form of community pattern among Orthodox and traditional Jews, where the need to live within walking distance of a synagogue fosters more cohesive Jewish enclaves. Besides the thriving Jewish neighborhoods in and near major cities on the Eastern seaboard, there are also traditional and not-so-traditional, closely knit Jewish communities in the Rockies, New England, the West coast and the Pacific Northwest, and other areas of the country.

Other, more experimental, forms of Jewish community have been tried and continue to be developed. In Israel, of course, there are *kibbutzim*, *moshavim*, and other group settlements of various types and ideologies. A very few such groups have also been tried in the United States. Although it seems unlikely that there will be much of this type of settlement in North America, there are probably many ways in which Jewish groups could join in community and cooperative living arrangements, such as co-housing, especially in these troubled economic times.

It's ironic that for all of our "organization" the achievement of genuine community remains such a great challenge for contemporary Jews. It is challenging, but it is not impossible. New congregations, *havurot*, neighborhoods, and other forms of community continue to be developed by Jewish individuals and families. Become involved with a group of Jews who are creating a community, and your family is likely to reap benefits for years to come.

There is much more to say about the importance and meaning of Jewish community than can be said here. However, I urge all Jewish families to listen to their hearts, to put forth the effort to join with others in much more than membership in an institution. Judaism is a religion of community. Jewish families, wherever they live, have an urgent need to find or create fellowships that foster mutual emotional, intellectual, and spiritual growth.

FAMILY SNAPSHOTS

[Jody and Hal Crane live in Denver, Colorado, with their four children: Alex, Molly, Milton, and Hannah. Hal is an orthopedic surgeon and Jody is a homemaker. They have chosen an Orthodox way of life as adults.]

My husband and I first became observant when we were both around thirty. We were living in a community that had only a handful of Orthodox people. It was very difficult to convince a six-year-old son to suddenly stop watching Saturday morning cartoons and to keep kosher. But in a community where there are no other families keeping *Shabbos*, it is a monumental task—particularly with children.

When we moved to another city, which had a much larger *frum* (Orthodox) population, we were overwhelmed by the sense of community. I gave birth a few months after moving, and our new friends made a beautiful *sholom zochar* (Friday-evening party to welcome a newborn son), to which 75 people came, and *bris milah*, and brought meals for a week. It seemed to me that having an external support system was essential to the whole enterprise of practicing Judaism.

In our community in Denver, which is fairly closely knit, we usually spend *Shabbos* with other families. It enhances the Sabbath experience, but it also provides a time for exchange of ideas. It also provides a forum for people to vent their anger and frustration with perceived communal shortcomings.

Over time I have begun to see, with increasing clarity, the importance of communal life in Judaism. Sometimes I find that it takes a lot of personal strength to cope with intracommunal conflicts. Jews are an incredibly opinionated group of people; everyone is a *maven* (expert). Sometimes this characteristic seems like a deficiency, but in truth it is a strength. Being forced to share communal institutions with those whose views differ brings the opportunity to learn to share and to get along.

I have also come to appreciate the wisdom of Judaism in making communal life imperative. The *shul*, day school, *mikveh*, and other institutions of the traditional community are like threads that become woven into a fabric that is Jewish life. Without some compelling reasons to remain interwoven, the fabric disintegrates.

—*Jody Crane*

II

LEARNING, LEARNING, LEARNING

9

JEWISH EDUCATION BEGINS AT HOME: THE IMPORTANCE OF INFORMAL LEARNING

And these words, which I command you today, shall be upon your heart. And you shall teach them faithfully to your children, and shall talk of them when you sit in your home. . . .

—Deuteronomy 6:6, 7

It is wrong to define education as *preparation* for life. Learning *is* life, a supreme experience of living, a climax of existence.

—Abraham Joshua Heschel[1]

Learning, learning, learning: that is the secret of Jewish survival.

—Ahad HaAm[2]

LEARNING, LEARNING, LEARNING

For the Jew, learning is life's very essence. Although various Jewish sources stress that learning alone, without the accompaniment of good deeds and ethical behavior, or teaching others, may be bankrupt; still, in Jewish tradition the intellectual and spiritual dimensions of life are tightly interwoven. Learning—apprehending God's teachings and creations—is itself a primary spiritual path for the Jew. "Learning Torah equals all (the other commandments)" (Talmud, *Shabbat* 127a) said the sages, and "An ignorant person cannot be pious" (*Pirke Avot* 2:6). The study of Torah (Jewish teaching) is perceived as one of the primary ways to "the apprehension of God and the attainment of the sacred."[3] Our holidays, customs, and ceremonies highlight affective learning, our liturgy and services center around public readings and textual study. Education, in the Judaic ethos, is far more than the narrow sense of preparing young people for a career, but is considered a supreme experience of living at every stage of life.

The Torah instructs parents, not to hire a teacher or send their children to a religious school, but to "teach them [the commandments] unto your children." Although formal schooling has been a characteristic of Jewish communities from early times, it is only in the recent past that the Jewish school was expected to instruct without the emotional and informal cultural and religious support of the home.

Some contend that it is the Jewish home environment and the family, as much as the school, that traditionally played "a central, if not the central, role in defining and transmitting Jewish identity and identification."[4] Whereas most textual instruction took place at the *heder* (schoolhouse) or the *yeshivah*, the home has traditionally been the locus of a holistic Jewish education in which religion, values, culture, language, folklore, and tradition have been passed on as a natural part of life. Jewish law and tradition—learning experiences every day, week, and season of the year. Formal education, as a complement to the informal enculturation taking place at home, could focus almost exclusively on textual instruction.

Now educators are increasingly pointing out that the Jewish home and social grouping are no longer providing the type of informal Jewish cultural education common in the past.[5] Many Jewish parents feel themselves Judaically ignorant. The vast majority of contemporary Jews have taken their heritage of scholarship and transferred it to secular fields, achieving "the perfect and continuing viability of the intellectual tradition, along with its absolute de-Judaization."[6] And although American Jewish parents are generally eager to provide their children with a broad range of cultural and educational experiences outside of school, the problem for many is how few of these experiences are Jewish ones. Jewish children, by and large, are among the most intellectually and culturally advantaged in public and private schools and among the most culturally deprived vis-à-vis their supplementary Jewish educations.[7]

There is an increasing recognition that Jewish educational approaches have to change to accommodate this lack of home involvement. Many educators are urging the schools and institutions to take on the activities of informal education and enculturation formerly provided by the home or neighborhood. Some attempt to provide the students with more emotional, rather than strictly cognitive and instructional experiences, within the school context or through retreats and summer camping experiences. A related approach is Jewish Family Education, which focuses on involving parents as well as children in the educational process.

The best result for the Jewish community would be for individual families to take advantage of all these new approaches, not as a way to subcontract yet another aspect of their lives to the public and professional sector, but rather, as Jewish family educator Victoria Kelman[8] says, to provide a scaffolding on which to build their own more intensely Judaic life-style at home. Plugging into educational programs, reading books such as this one, and learning from and with other families or fellowship groups are other ways for the individual Jewish family to make the home a richer educational environment.

Does this mean that we are to adopt a formal Jewish curriculum at home, perhaps beginning with flash cards of the *Shema* at two months of age? Those of us who are concerned with a nonhurried, developmentally appropriate education know that this is not the case. (Although there are families who carry out Jewish home schooling with success, most of us will choose to enroll our children in formal Jewish schools as well.) The problem lies in the confusion of education with instruction.[9] Formal instruction is but one component of the education of a whole person. Although in a tradi-

tional Jewish model some kinds of formal instruction do take place at home (for example, reviewing a Torah portion or studying *Pirke Avot* at home with one's children), the informal component of a child's education is equally crucial.

Dr. David Elkind, noted child psychologist and author of *The Hurried Child—Growing Up Too Fast Too Soon*, points out that "a love of learning," on the parents' part, rather than formal home instruction, was the influential factor in the childhood homes of very successful, intelligent adults. Elkind writes that "parents who love learning will create a stimulating environment for children, which is far more beneficial to them than specific instruction. Parents who fill the house with books, paintings, and music, who have interesting friends and discussions, who are curious and ask questions provide young children with all the intellectual stimulation they need. In such an environment, formal instruction would be like ordering a hamburger at a four-star restaurant."[10] Certainly the kind of home environment Elkind describes is precisely the kind that educated Jewish parents aspire to.

To see how his insight applies specifically to the Jewish life of the family, one can translate it into Judaic terms. Thus, the best way to create an educational Jewish home environment would be for the *parents themselves to love Jewish learning*. The parents would model a dedication to Jewish learning by reading books on Judaic topics, studying as a couple or with friends, or regularly attending classes at their *havurah*, synagogue, J.C.C., or other adult study program. They would seek the best possible Jewish schools for their children as a reflection of their own dedication to Jewish learning. The home library would include many Jewish books and periodicals; Judaic art would be represented in the decor; Jewish music would be heard frequently. Interesting discussions on Jewish topics and texts would be heard at Shabbat meals, while the Jewish perspective would be raised in everyday conversations about current events and family concerns. The family's friends would include other families and individuals committed to Jewish life, including fellow members of a congregation or *havurah* in which the family is actively involved. (Notice that this is not to say that they read *only* Jewish books, listen to Jewish music, or hang out with committed Jews!)

The Book of Proverbs states, "Teach a child *bed'arko*," which is usually translated, "in the way he should go," but could just as well be translated, "in his or her particular way." Children learn in different ways. Some are more visual, some more aural, and some more kinesthetic (they learn best when movement and touch are involved)—and most, of course, combine the three modalities for optimal learning. Even taste and scent can be drawn into many holistic learning experiences. Parents, of course, don't need a book to tell them that children learn and remember best of all through active involvement and doing. Jewish learning—especially the informal variety—includes not only linear, methodical, left-brain experiences, but holistic, experiential, right-brain experiences as well. Learning that is hands-on, involving various media (that is, materials of all natures) and a range of modalities, allows the child more opportunity to internalize the subject. (For example, a young child might learn the Hebrew letters, not only with pencil on paper or from a book, but by sculpting them in modeling clay, drawing them in wet sand, acting them out physically, and so forth.)

The following section on Jewish learning presents several types of informal learning experiences for the Jewish home, such as storytelling, music, and play. More formal home learning experiences, such as the study of texts, Hebrew, prayers, and history are included as well. Parents are invited to begin thinking of themselves as Jewish educators, and suggestions and resources for further involvement are offered. (See also Resource Guide, pp. 311–334.) Finally, there is a brief examination of current trends in Jewish education and some ideas about choosing both informal learning programs and Jewish schools outside the home.

"Teaching them unto our children" can be a pleasure and a delight.

Teach them diligently . . .

"You shall teach them diligently unto your children" is a basic *mitzvah*, an ancient and primary imperative of Jewish life (Deuteronomy 6:7—the continuation of the *Shema Yisrael*).

Veshinantam, teach them diligently, connotes *oral repetition*: in other words, you shall transmit the Jewish heritage by word of mouth, talk to your child about Jewish ideas, discuss important issues within a framework of Judaic values. You shall tell Jewish stories and relate Jewish anecdotes to create a rich storehouse of memories that can nourish your child for life.

Levanecha, to your own child, means that you shall take back the responsibility for your child's Jewish education. Don't leave everything up to the school. Rather, choose the best Jewish school you can find, but remember that the school is simply your partner. As a parent, you have the privilege of being your child's primary Jewish teacher.

And the Torah continues: "and speak of them when you sit in your home, when you walk by the way, in your lying down and in your rising up." Don't limit Jewish education to a school setting, or even just to Shabbat or holidays at home. Make it a part of your every day: Say a *berachah* when you see something beautiful in nature, read Jewish stories at bedtime, discuss current events from a Jewish perspective at dinner, discuss how Jewish values apply to personal issues while on a walk, talk about a Torah portion at a Shabbat meal.

But before all this is "these words [of Torah] shall be upon your heart" (Deuteronomy 6:6). They must mean something to *you*. In the Hebraic tradition, the heart connotes not only emotion, but understanding as well. In order to transmit this tradition, parents must first learn and care passionately about Judaism for themselves, at an adult level.

"Teach them diligently unto your children" is an educational method that's worked for over 3,000 years. And it's as powerful as ever today.

10

JEWISH STORIES, MUSIC, PLAY, AND IMAGINATION

JEWISH STORIES AT HOME: THE AGGADIC TRADITION

The Jewish people has always been the People of the Book and the Word. We are a storytelling people. . . . We have relied on the oral tradition for interpretation, communication, laws, customs and shared experiences. Whether it was King David's psalms or the rhythmic recitation of the *badchen* (jester) at a wedding or a mother telling her child a bedtime story or a *rebbe* teaching with a parable, all of these stories and folktales became woven into the fabric of Jewish life. The stories became the link between generations. . . . Sharing a story creates a bond between teller and listener. The listener trusts the teller, enjoys the direct, personal contact between them—regardless of how many listeners there are, and feels the teller is offering a gift—a gift of self, of time, of heritage.

—Peninnah Schram[1]

Reading aloud is the contemporary parent's "quality time" dream-come-true. The nightly bedtime ritual, or a story read aloud at any other time or place, is one of the simplest, easiest ways to encourage family closeness and bonding while developing children's imaginations, listening skills, vocabularies, and knowledge of the world. The attachment of children to an adult who spends time reading to or with them has been found to be a crucial factor in motivating children to begin reading, and later to develop a continued interest in books.[2]

Telling and reading Jewish stories to our chil-

dren has the additional dimension of being double quality time. Reading Jewish books to our children has all the benefits of reading aloud *plus* exposure to Jewish values and practices and the opportunity to experience Jewish life in settings far removed from our children's everyday places. Jewish stories may include classic motifs repeated in cultures around the world, but they may also contain elements of Jewish holidays, biblical and talmudic characters, and Jewish culture. These elements, according to famous Jewish storyteller Peninnah Schram, "gradually fill the [child's mental] storehouse of images and memories"[3] and are there for the child to draw on as she or he grows and learns more about Judaism. Moreover, Jewish tales often convey Jewish values such as kindness, learning, and *tzedakah*.

The books children hear and read weave the fabrics of their imaginations; including Jewish books helps to ensure that there are many Jewish threads sparkling in that cloth. Parents can make sure that their children's imaginations hold not only "Care Bears" and "The Little Mermaid" but Elijah the Prophet and the Shabbat Queen as well.

Passing on the stories of our tradition: Bible, *Midrash*, *Aggadah*, the moral and the mystical, is a prime way of joining the generations while linking them to generations long past and those that are still to come. As Schram has written, facts and figures may be lost, but stories are not soon forgotten: "the stories we hear remain in our memories for easy recall when we need to extract the necessary wisdom and knowledge from them."[4] Jewish stories remain with us and our children, offering enduring psychological and ethical insights as well as a scaffold on which to build more complex Jewish learning and textual study. Jewish storytelling, then, is not only a simple recipe for quality time, closeness, and enjoyable family activity, but is one of the primary factors in transmitting Judaism as a living heritage. How could such a simple activity be that important?

The rabbinic writings at the core of classical Judaism contain both *Halachah*—"law"—and *Aggadah*—"lore." These two categories can be perceived as complementary archetypes of Jewish religious and cultural expression: *Aggadah*—lore, stories, myths, legends, literature, imagination, mysticism—is the inseparable partner of *Halachah*—law, ethics, procedure, path, action, deed. Metaphorically speaking, *Halachah* might be called the logical, methodical, left brain of Judaism, whereas *Aggadah* would be the imaginative, associative, right brain.

Increasingly, a wide range of influential thinkers in the fields of psychology and anthropology have emphasized the importance of cultural and personal myth, stories, dreams, and symbols (*Aggadah*) to psychological and spiritual wholeness and well-being.

Earlier, I wrote of the importance of connecting with the core of our own culture. Stories, literature, and imagination are vital components of that core culture. American Jewish children grow up with Santa Claus, the Easter bunny, and the tooth fairy—the visions of American culture. Hopefully, they get "good, liberal educations" that include learning more of the core of Western culture, including Greek mythology, philosophy, and a little Bible according to Christian "midrash." Because we are living in a time of social ferment in which challenges to old cultural myths are increasing (frequently focused on attacks on a so-called Judeo-Christian worldview), it is crucial for Jews to know their own *Aggadah*. (For example, is the Jewish Eden myth of the archetypical man as nature's caretaker, molded of the earth, really consistent with purported "Judeo-Christian" myth of man as egocentric exploiter of nature? I would say no.)

Today there is a conscious revival of the aggadic tradition in Jewish life. There are scores of new books that contain collections of everything from classic stories to Jewish fairy tales to modern *midrash*. There are professional Jewish storytellers who have networks and conferences. There are Ph.D.'s in *Midrash*! The resources are there to infuse a new generation with the great aggadic

traditions—while they are sitting cozily on our laps.

In Judaism, *Halachah* and *Aggadah* are inseparable, just as the two hemispheres of the brain are conjoined. With either side missing, Judaism becomes diminished. Ironically, a master of *Aggadah*, the poet laureate of the Hebrew renaissance, Chayim Nachman Bialik, wrote an essay in which he deplored the ascendency of *Aggadah* over *Halachah*: "The whole world is but *Aggadah*, of *Halachah* there is not a trace . . . A generation is growing up in an atmosphere of mere phrases and catchwords, and a kind of go-as-you-please Judaism is being created out of the breath of empty words. Our cries are nationalism, revival, literature, creation, Hebrew education, Hebrew thought . . . and these things hang by the gossamer thread of some kind of love—love of the land, love of the language, love of the literature. But what is this love-in-the-air worth? Love? But where is duty? Whence can it come? . . . if you wish to build: 'make ordinances for you' (Nehemiah 10:1). That is how our ancestors began to build . . . more *Halachah* than *Aggadah*."[5]

Yet Rabbi Abraham Isaac Kook, first chief rabbi of Israel, one who certainly studied and lived by *Halachah* for years, devoted "perhaps the largest bulk of his intellectual and practical energy" to a new *yeshivah* curriculum that would expand from the realm of *Halachah* to "the entire range of *Aggadah*. Jewish thought, speculation, history, poetry, exegesis, mysticism, in all its depth, variety, richness, and plurality."[6]

Halachah and *Aggadah* should nourish and inspire each other. Our lives need to be filled with Jewish deeds, our imaginations with Jewish stories. If our homes combine Jewish stories with Jewish living, how rich and vibrant they will be.

READING AND STORYTELLING: ACTIVITY IDEAS

Some extol the benefits of reading aloud in fostering a love of books; others insist that there's nothing like telling a story with drama and involvement. Most parents will probably want to do some of both. Reading aloud proves the main form of story telling for most families. The important thing to remember is that reading aloud should be dramatic and exciting, just like a good oral rendition. Put some feeling into it. Glance at your listeners. Invite their comments where appropriate. Pause for drama. Reading aloud can be nearly as involving as telling.

At other times telling stories without a book makes the best sense. There are excellent story collections (such as Ginzberg's classic *Legends of the Jews*)[7] whose language doesn't lend itself to reading aloud. Parents can still learn the stories and tell them to children. Or you may find several versions of a classic tale that you want to retell with your own emphasis. The more stories you read and hear, the more stories you will have stored up for those spontaneous, "tellable moments" with your children.

● Telling a story needn't mean word-for-word memorization. For the purposes of telling a story to family or friends, simply outline the story in your own mind (you might want to write down the outline if it's complicated) and then retell it in your own words. For very young children, a simple description of an everyday experience is exciting enough. For more sophisticated listeners, the general formulation would include introducing the protagonist and setting and describing a conflict and the denouement in which the conflict is resolved. Imagine the details of your scenes and characters, then paint pictures with your words. Relax, the idea is to enjoy yourself.

● For young children, stories that cast them in the role of the hero can help them deal with common childhood anxieties such as trying new skills, separation anxiety, new situations. Stories can function as fantasy versions of real dilemmas ("The princess was worried that the queen would not find her way back home from the fair," and so on).

● Family stories and personal stories from your life should be included. I grew up with more tales of my eccentric extended family than I did with fairy tales. It helped to give me a sense of family, although I grew up far away from most of my relatives.

● Children often like to hear stories from their parents' younger days ("the olden days"), including stories that show that the parent was once a child, too. A child's sense of historical perspective, of course, is not the same as an adult's. One Shabbat, my husband told our children some stories about his days in the War of Attrition and the Yom Kippur War, fighting the Egyptians, and finished his story by saying that Israel later signed a peace treaty with Egypt. Afterward one of the

girls urged him, "Abba, tell us more about how you fought Pharaoh in Egypt!"

● Despite the current popularity of myths and legends, my own preference and my children's has usually been for true stories which are often stranger and more wonderful, tragic, moving, and amazing than fiction. True stories about brave or noble deeds can provide inspiration and moral guidance. There are books that contain true stories (see the Resource Guide on pp. 311, 341), or transform a news item or current event into a story by changing the form: "Once there was a . . . ." The possibilities are virtually endless. My children found the love story of Natan and Avital Scharansky, retold in this way, more fascinating than any fairy tale and more meaningful for its veracity.

Another of our favorite stories came from a television documentary I saw in which a crew member from the ship *Exodus* told how the babies of refugees had been born on board during a clandestine journey. Years later, when he was speaking in front of a group, a young woman approached him afterwards and told him that she had been one of those babies! She showed him her handwritten birth certificate, which the crew had improvised. My children were awed by this story: "Is that really a true story, Mommy?" I could answer that, indeed, it was a true story.

● Add interest to stories by including songs or tunes, repeated rhythms, sounds, or phrases. As appropriate, ask questions that involve the listeners. Or ask young children to act out various elements in the story (for example, "Let's all make noise like the rain falling on Noah's ark").

● Enrich storytelling with show and tell. For example, let young children hold, feel, and smell the *lulav* and the *etrog* while telling stories about them (see p. 200), or show a souvenir from Israel as the basis for a personal story or a link to a story from a book.

● Make reading aloud each night your family tradition. It's a good way to unwind and to be together at the end of a long and hectic day. Obviously, not all the stories need to have, or should have, Jewish content. But by including Jewish stories often we ensure that they will become a natural part of our children's lives. Children may want to hear a story from a Jewish anthology each night for a long time, then they may want to switch to something completely different for a while. Or you might want to make Shabbat bedtime the special time for Jewish stories. We have read one section aloud from a Bible anthology each evening before the children turned to their own reading in bed or listened to me read a chapter from their current choice.

● Reading aloud isn't only for prereaders. Preschoolers also enjoy picture books and simple stories. As children grow, many still enjoy being read to. By age four or five the child may be ready for a nightly selection from a story anthology or children's novel. Beginning readers will often enjoy hearing one chapter each night from such an ongoing "chapter book," as the kids call them. (This often leads the child to continue reading the book on her or his own, which leads to greater reading involvement.) Children can also read aloud to each other and to their parents. One family we know enjoys "reading parties" with their older children, with each family member selecting favorites to read to the others. Afterwards they all share refreshments.

● Don't feel limited to juvenile storybooks. Most volumes of folk tales and *midrash* can be read to almost any child from age five or six. Don't be afraid to use a few words that are a bit advanced for the listener; that's how they learn. Many stories directed at adults can be told to mid-elementary-school-aged children with just a little vocabulary simplification.

● What about scary stories? I still remember my childhood fear on hearing stories such as Babar and Bambi in which the animal protagonists' mothers are shot by hunters—the most frightening idea for any child. Some early-childhood educators advise modifying or skipping such scary stories. But as children grow older and can distinguish fantasy from reality, scary situations in stories may serve a useful psychological function. Storyteller Peninnah Schram says that stories need to be "frightening, sad, beautiful, happy, powerful and tragic"[8] if there is a purpose and meaning to the tragedy. While one wouldn't select a scary story for bedtime, hearing the classic and powerful tales is actually a cathartic experience for children by which they vicariously work through their fears and discover "healing, empowering and creative options," explains Schram.

All this is one thing in the realm of fantasy, but what about frightening true stories? From my own childhood experience, I think that one should be very careful and gradual about introducing such stories to young children. One otherwise good book of Sephardic stories for children contains a story about children during the Inquisition going to be burned at the stake (I didn't read it to my young children). This ties in very much with the issue of telling children about the Holocaust, which is discussed on pp. 79–81.

● Check out of a library or purchase literary selections and other books of Jewish interest to read aloud or for eager readers to read to themselves. The true cereal box reader, the child who can't resist reading *anything* placed before her or him, can enjoy an enriched Jewish education by being generously supplied with books.

● Parents can also enjoy literary selections of Jewish interest. The scope of this book does not allow a bibliography of literature with Jewish themes, but libraries and bookstores will provide an ample range of selections by the many notable contemporary Jewish authors. Whereas some authors shun being categorized as "Jewish writers," they are indeed heirs to a long and vibrant tradition of Jewish literature, and many consciously draw upon classical Jewish themes and motifs.

● Poetry, from the Psalms to modern English and Hebrew anthologies, can also be enjoyable to read and may inspire creative writing endeavors by parents and children. Poetry selections, read aloud or recited, can enrich family celebrations and ceremonies. Try writing some poetry about your own children as a personalized gift of love.

● Many children enjoy acting out stories. This can be a great way to learn a Torah portion or holiday narrative.

● Puppets are another dramatic expression that afford not only entertainment, but also educational and even therapeutic value. Use them year round to act out Jewish stories and to role play various everyday situations and conflicts. Using puppets often enables children to express themselves unselfconsciously and freely.

● Make your own storybooks with your children. (See the next section for a variety of ideas for topics and formats.)

● Make a "Shabbat Story Journal" for your family. Collect favorite stories of all types: family, news or current events, *midrashim* on Torah portions, and others, and record them on pages in a blank book, looseleaf notebook, or folder. You can also illustrate your stories. Your family's story journal can then be used as a source for Shabbat and holiday story sessions.

● Start a personal library of Jewish story anthologies, literature, and other books of Jewish interest.

● Treat your synagogue library as a family resource.

● Join a Jewish book club.

● Visit book fairs at your local Jewish Community Center, synagogue, or school during Jewish Book Month (the month prior to Hanukkah).

● Organize a storytelling evening for your *havurah* or synagogue. Incorporate storytelling into retreats and holiday celebrations.

● Take advantage of local opportunities to take children to professional storytelling presentations, puppet shows, library reading sessions, or plays and films with Jewish content.

● Children enjoy dramatics. Performing in plays with Jewish content can be educational and fun for children.

MAKE YOUR OWN BOOKS

Be a *sofer* (scribe, author)! Making your own Jewish books at home can be an enhancement of informal Jewish learning. Making your own storybooks can concretize Jewish memories and show that Jewish themes and stories are a personal part of your family experience. Bookmaking also encourages creativity and interest in reading and writing and is a shared family activity. With very young children, parents can make the book for the child. As the children grow, they can be more and more involved in the project, perhaps coauthoring books with a parent. Often, children will make their own books as an extension of their love of writing and stories.

There are two parts to making your own books: the medium and the message. Mix and match the following suggestions for the message and the medium to create your own personalized Jewish books. As always, tailor the subject matter and level of sophistication to the child's development. Tots enjoy simple pictures of people and objects, whereas preschoolers need a simple story line, and older children are interested in more elaborate adventures.

Ideas for the Message

1. Your ancestors and extended family ("How the Weinsteins Came to America," "The Cohen Cousins on the Kibbutz," or "When Grandma Was a Little Girl"). Illustrate with copies of family photos if possible (old and fragile photos should not be used but can be photographed themselves).

2. Your immediate family experiences: holidays, life-cycle events, trips, the synagogue, doing mitzvot, and others ("Jewish Things I Like to Do," "I Can Do *Mitzvot*," "The Story of Our *Sukkah*," "The Stern Family's Purim Adventure").

3. Adventures of an imaginary family not unlike your own. This can be highly imaginative ("Shabbat in Outer Space") or realistic.

4. Make up your own *midrash* (interpretive story based on a biblical episode) or simply retell a story from the Bible or another Jewish source.

5. Anthropomorphisms: the adventures of a little *Sefer*-Torah, a *siddur*, a *shofar*, a *kiddush* cup, or what have you—even a classical item such as "Joseph's Coat of Many Colors." Examples of this genre are *K'tonton* and *Achbar the Mouse*—you can invent your own *Jewish* fantasy character with a very different perspective.

6. For older children, the fictional diary of a real or imagined Jewish character from history or contemporary life.

7. Take a Jewish story you have found in an anthology and create an illustrated version of it.

8. Make a Hebrew picture dictionary. Use cutouts, photos, or hand drawn pictures to illustrate it. If your Hebrew is more advanced, write your own Hebrew stories.

9. Make your own home prayer book, Jewish song book, Shabbat story journal, children's *Haggadah*, Torah portion synopsis, or children's *megillah* (can be made on a long roll of paper to simulate a real *megillah*).

10. Illustrate your favorite Jewish sayings, such as verses from the Torah, *siddur*, Book of Proverbs (*Mishle*), or *Pirke Avot* ("Sayings of the Fathers").

Ideas for the Medium

1. *Album book*: Simply purchase a photo album, the kind that has sticky-backed pages. Arrange cutouts, photographs (taken especially for the book if desired), pictures, and cards with a text on

a page, even small flatish objects, then cover with the plastic page cover. *Voilà*—instant book!

2. *Folder book*: Purchase a folder that holds pages in with brads. Make the story and illustration on other pieces of paper, then punch holes in them and place them in the folder (of course, you can also make a construction-paper cover held on with staples or brads, but it's more trouble and flimsier).

3. *Cassette story*: Make one of the above book ideas and also record a soundtrack for it. Read the text (with sound effects, if desired) and be sure to include a bell or other signal to indicate when to turn the pages.

4. *Simple ring book*: For young children, a simple picture book can be made from holiday greeting cards, 5" × 7" photo enlargements, or postcards of Israel. Laminate or cover the book with clear adhesive paper for sturdiness. Punch a hole in one corner of each card, then hold the cards together with a metal ring, which can be found at stationery stores. Older children may also enjoy a book such as this as a keepsake of a holiday or trip. They can write a short text on the back of the cards.

5. *Texture book*: Make a folder book as above, but add textures to the illustrations. This is especially good for a homemade *Haggadah* for small children. Glue in items to represent each of the different *seder* objects. Parents who sew can make cloth books with textured items sewn on or attached with Velcro.

6. *Felt stick-on book*: Make a story in which a central object appears on each page (see "anthropomorphisms," p. 63). Make the object itself out of felt. On each page of the story, glue a small piece of felt over part of the illustration where the central object should appear. As you read the story, move the object from page to page and attach to the felt piece on that page. It will stick to the page as you read. For even more impressive results, use Velcro.

7. *With older children*: Write a book together, taking turns writing alternate chapters. This can be done in a purchased blank book with elegant results.

MUSIC: THE SOUL OF A JEWISH HOME

I will sing unto the Eternal as long as I live,
I will make music to my God while I exist.
— Psalm 104:33

Jews are a *singing* people. Since the earliest times, long before King David, the sweet singer of Israel, a love for music—perhaps it may even be called a deep need for expression in music—has existed in the people.

—Edith Samuel[9]

Nature, God's creation, is the greatest artistry, which no human being can match. The closest that human beings can come to pure creation is making music.
—My father, of blessed memory

We fall in love and marry not only because of logical considerations, but because of a certain mysterious, emotional "chemistry" with the beloved. In raising children to love the Jewish way of life, there are elements beyond words, beyond the rational. Music in particular is an important way of adding to the emotional and spiritual dimensions of our families' Jewish lives.

Of course, music is important to all cultures, and we should enjoy a variety of musical expressions, from folk to classical to country and western. But much as I love many beautiful voices and have heard many glorious ones indeed, there is no voice quite like my mother's. The musical expressions of one's own people evoke a special response.

Music is integral to Jewish spirituality. Since biblical times, music has been one of the most highly valued expressions of Jewish culture. Music has been known for its profound effect on our emotions and on our very souls. Great figures of the Bible expressed themselves in songs, psalms, and even dances. The Torah and prophetic readings in our synagogues are not only read but also chanted, and our prayers are traditionally expressed in musical form (notice how many Jews prefer a congregation where there is a lot of communal singing). Music has been particularly central to the mystical strains of Judaism. The *hasidim* taught that a song without words was even more spiritual than one with lyrics. Yiddish songs have inspired Jewish humanists and sustained our people in their darkest hours. Folk songs and dances have enlivened the spirit of the Jewish national renaissance in Israel. Jewish music, then, encompasses a vast range of genres, many diverse expressions of the Jewish spirit in its core-to-core interaction with surrounding cultures.

Personally, Jewish music has had a profound impact on my life, despite the fact that I haven't considered myself a very musical person, especially compared with some of the other members of my family. Yet Jewish American songs at summer camps and youth groups inspired me spiritually and helped me to learn Hebrew, college song sessions and recordings of Israeli music fueled my desire to make *aliyah*. The first time I met my husband, I heard him singing—chanting the *haftarah* to the Sephardic cantillation. Avraham introduced me to other Jewish musical traditions, including his own Sephardic melodies and contemporary Israeli religious, folk, and popular songs. I introduced him to American Jewish tunes. Together we've enjoyed classical, country and western, and Middle Eastern music. A wide range of music has continued to be central to our lives, especially our Jewish lives; we enjoy Shabbat and holiday song sessions, the melodies of prayer and liturgy, concerts, and recordings.

Music has a tremendous, often subliminal, influence on our psyche. Try listening to various songs while driving down a highway. The road may look different as the background music changes from classical to pop to new age to Israeli folk music. Or try cleaning the house, paying bills, dining, or exercising without music, then with different types of music. The experiences can be very different, depending on the use and type of music.

We can create different atmospheres in our homes by our choice of music. Simply playing Jewish music (of any type) at home changes the most secular atmosphere into a Jewish one. Going a bit further and singing Jewish songs at a Shabbat meal helps to bring the observance to life. Music isn't the only informal educational activity that should take place at home, but it is certainly one of the easiest to carry out. Torah study, and even storytelling, may seem a bit forced at first, but musical recordings can create moods like magic for many families.

Music can make our Jewish souls dance.

Suggestions for Enjoying Jewish Music at Home

● Cultivate a sensitivity to sound. Sit quietly and listen to sounds: What do you hear? Try this in the country as well as in the city. Ecologists tell us that the very landscape, the wind against the hills, has a distinctive sound that is quickly obliterated by human interference. Divers can hear the myriad sounds of sea creatures in the deep. Sit quietly with your children and listen to the sounds of

dawn, day, evening, night. The *hasidic* rebbe, Nahman of Breslov, taught that each blade of grass sings in constant praise of God. Jewish tradition from the Bible on tells us that everything in creation is engaged in endless songs of praise to the Creator, and we can help our children learn to be still and to be receptive to the song of creation, the primal music.

● Sing Jewish songs together as a family: on a hike, in the car, at a Shabbat or holiday meal, with a *havurah* or with a group of friends, to wake everyone up, while cleaning for Shabbat or Passover, while sitting by the fire—anytime. Many music educators insist that singing with children (no matter what your talent or lack thereof) is *the* primary way to encourage in them an affinity for music. Besides, song is an essential element of Jewish living.

● Sing Hebrew or Yiddish songs to your children as lullabies. Any soft, comforting tunes can be used; they don't have to be lullabies per se. Babies and tots are most interested in the soothing tune and the comfort of your arms, anyway. Some say to begin singing to your baby while he or she is still in the womb.

● What if you know hardly any Jewish songs? Books and tapes (see the Resource Guide, p. 313) are one of the easier ways to learn. If you can't read music, purchase recordings with the songs you are trying to learn from the books. (Some books and recordings come as sets.)

● More ways to learn songs: Invite over friends who know lots of songs and ask them to teach you. Visit synagogues where there is a lot of singing. Organize a *havurah* or synagogue sing-along to learn new songs for Shabbat or the holidays. Ask your synagogue's cantor or music director, or the music teacher at your Jewish school, to lead such song-learning sessions. Get the youth group song leader to teach Hebrew songs to the adults, or the seniors to teach Yiddish songs. Ask your Jewish Community Center, Bureau of Jewish Education, Jewish Resource Center, or adult education institute to offer singing sessions for families, or even to start a Jewish folk-singing club.

● Begin collecting records, tapes, or CD's of a wide variety of Jewish music. Sample all kinds of music with Jewish themes or inspirations, such as classical, cantorial, *klezmer*, Yiddish, Sephardic, Yemenite, Israeli folk and pop, and Jewish-American folk music. (There is also Jewish baroque, jazz, rock, Middle Eastern, and even country and western music.) Soon you will find the kinds of music your family enjoys the most. Or you may like everything!

● Fill your house with the sound of music. Playing music frequently at home not only helps to set a mood but also instills in children a love of music and is an influence on their musical taste. The family can enjoy a wide range of musical experiences at home from their own collection of recordings and those of friends, from broadcasts, and even from recordings checked out of libraries. Including a generous selection of Jewish music adds the element of Jewish identity to your listening.

● Play quiet music at bedtime and naptime. Many children like to listen through earphones. They can also listen to commercial tapes of Jewish stories. Or, you can record a Jewish story (of your own invention or from a book—see previous section), augmented by sound effects and musical selections from various recordings.

● Make your Jewish holidays come alive with music. *Halachically* observant Jews will not play recordings on Shabbat and major holidays (*Yom Tov*), but will find plenty of opportunities to play them while preparing for the holiday, on the intermediate days of festivals such as Sukkot and Passover and during minor holidays such as Hanukkah and Purim, for example. Singing, of course, is an important part of the experience of Shabbat and every holiday (as stated earlier).

● Music to go: Play Jewish tapes on your car's stereo system, take a portable cassette player on an outing and a Walkman with earphones on a plane trip.

● If you play instruments, learn some Jewish music to add to your repertoire. If you're strictly singers, cajole some friends who play instruments to participate in a Saturday night or holiday Jewish play-and-sing session. The recorder is an ideal instrument for children to learn and lends itself to many folk tunes and Israeli songs.

● Active listening and multisensory experiences: Combine your listening sessions with movement, artwork, or just concentrating on hearing something special. Paint or draw what the music triggers in your imagination. Finger paint to music: What color does it sound like?

● Dance as the melody inspires you, adding props such as scarves or streamers if desired. Most young kids don't have to be encouraged to move to music!

● Act out the song or musical selection, with or without costumes or props.

● Feel the beat: Clap your hands, tap your feet, use simple rhythm instruments. The beat of our own hearts, always with us, is the elemental basis for all musical rhythm. Anita Goldberg, a friend of mine who has run early childhood music schools in Mexico City and San Antonio, stresses following rhythms as the primary step in learning about music. Goldberg recommends patting a baby's body gently to the beat of the music.

● Encourage your Jewish school to make music and singing a priority. Not only is music an important affective element in Jewish education, but many educators stress Hebrew songs as an important way to gain fluency in Hebrew prayers and increase Hebrew vocabulary.

● Take your children to children's and family concerts, including those with Jewish themes.

● Israeli folk dancing is a wonderful way to experience Jewish folk music and is also good exercise! Enroll in a class, attend a folk dance club, or take the family to a performance.

PLAY, IMAGINATION, AND ART EXPERIENCES

It is important for a growing child to be given things [s/he] can break: Rabbah often bought imperfect earthenware for his little ones to smash, should they want to.

—Talmud, *Yoma* 78b

A person will be called to account in the hereafter for each enjoyment [s/he] declined here without sufficient cause.

—Jerusalem Talmud, *Kiddushin* 4:12

Imagination is more important than knowledge.

—Albert Einstein[10]

Play can be serious business for children. The youngest learn mainly through play: manipulating objects and discovering their properties, then later acting out grown-up roles. Play can also have important psychological purposes, and even therapeutic value. As children grow, play—whether formal games or imaginative, dramatic play—provides opportunities for them to try on new experiences and emotions, and imagine situations far removed from their everyday experience. A well-developed imagination enables children to create, empathize, and envision new possibilities.

Play is important to adults, too. One of the joys of raising children is that it often enables us, the parents, to get in touch with the imaginative, sensual, pleasurable world of play—to let the child within us all have some fun. The capacity for love and work may be the key to a mature adult psychology, but an ability to play enables adults to remain healthy, happy, and creative.

Judaism contains elements of play, humor, and the lighter side of life. Holiday celebrations incorporate games and play for the children: flags and sweets on Simhat Torah, *dreidl* contests on Hanukkah, masquerading and jokes on Purim, hunting for the *afikoman* on Passover, archery on Lag BaOmer, the Sephardic custom of water play on Shavuot. Humor—sometimes as an antidote to the darkest situations—is a salient feature of Jewish culture. Even in reading the rabbinic literature one is struck by delightful expressions of intellectual playfulness. The Judaism in our homes, likewise, should not be all solemnity and earnestness, but needs elements of fun.

A certain amount of playfulness and humor within Judaism indicates familiarity and comfort. Jewish play ought not to become a chore! The idea isn't to artificially foist Jewish play experiences on our young ones, but simply to foster and encourage them as we do any other good play experiences.

Judaic art projects are another wonderful way to use our imaginations and our hands in Jewish ways. Rabbi Howard Bogot suggests that artistic experiences can be used to make abstract Judaic themes more concrete (such as making and wearing crowns to symbolize the Shabbat as a queen) and conversely to represent concrete observances in a more abstract way (such as making a fabric collage to convey the feeling of Shabbat). Art can result in the production of useful items such as ritual objects for the home and can provide creative new ways to experience Jewish prayers, texts, and observances.[11] Browsing through books on Jewish art and modeling your own artwork on Jewish folk art or the styles of famous artists can provide an enjoyable family activity. Try some of the art projects suggested throughout this book and see the Resource Guide, p. 316, for books on Jewish arts and crafts.

Ideas

● Kinesthetic capers: Young children enjoy, and learn from, acting out various Jewish objects through whole-body movement. "Let's pretend that we're . . ." are the magic words to start this activity. You can pretend to be Shabbat or holiday candles melting (one person lights them, the others melt), a shaking *lulav*, a seedling growing into a tall tree for Tu-Bishvat, a noisemaker for Purim. Young children enjoy playing the *hallah* dough, which is kneaded (child is massaged by parent) and then puffs up. Appropriate holiday background music makes these dramatics even more fun.

● Instead of being the object, act as if you are doing the activity: pretend to be cleaning for Shabbat, hunting for *hametz*, building a *sukkah*, and so forth.

● Encourage Jewish elements in young children's dramatic play by providing costumes and materials. Those mismatched *kippahs* from various *simhas*, an old shawl for a *tallit*, and kerchiefs or Jewish ethnic costumes from a trip to Israel can go in the dress-up drawer. Old candle holders, an extra *hallah* cover you don't use, and odds and ends of ceremonial objects (such as model *seder* plates), can all be used for dramatic play. (Organizing toys into categories in boxes on open shelves is more conducive to order than a jumble of junk in a toy chest.)

● Holidays provide opportunities for dramatic play: a toy Torah, flags, and music make for a Simhat Torah reenactment; my friend's children used aluminum cookware of various sizes for Maccabean armor for Hanukkah games; our children enjoyed a play *seder* with extra Passover paraphernalia. Crowns and royal robes are good for acting out the Purim story and other biblical episodes.

● Make puppets to act out various biblical and holiday stories.

● Include Judaic puzzles, toys, and games among the toys you buy your children (see the Resource Guide).

● Make your own Jewish dollhouse objects, toys, and games.

● In creating or adapting new Jewish ceremonies, consider the tradition of including play elements for the children. For example, some of my friends had a walnut hunt (like hunting the *afikoman*) at a Tu BiShvat *seder*.

● Jewish children deserve to imagine the classic mythical figures of their own heritage. How many Jewish children know all about Santa Claus (and his representation of the spirit of giving), but have barely heard of the Shabbat Queen? Develop your children's Jewish imaginations by describing mythical figures to them at the appropriate moments. Here are some suggestions:

— On Friday night, imagine the beautiful Shabbat Queen coming to your home. What does she look like? Sound like? Smell like?

— Imagine the two angels coming home with family members from Friday night services (p. 155).

— Imagine the four angels surrounding your bed at night: Michael, Gavriel, Uriel, and Raphael. Each angel gives you a different blessing: love, strength, wisdom, and health. Over your bed is the light of the *Shechinah*, God's presence. Or picture a *sukkah* of peace overhead. These images are taken from the traditional bedtime prayers in the *siddur*.[12]

— Imagine *ushpizin* (biblical guests) visiting your *sukkah* (see p. 197).

— Tell lots of stories about Elijah the Prophet. Imagine the many guises he could take as the Jewish spirit of giving. Imagine him coming to your *seder*. Did you see a sip missing from his cup? Imagine him at your weekly *Havdalah* service.

● Guided imagery: This is an extensive exercise in imagination that is often used in art classes and for other affective educational experiences. It's a good way to relax and encourage peaceful thoughts at bedtime or naptime. You can play soft background music if desired. Encourage your children to lie back, close their eyes gently, and relax one part of the body at a time (relaxation can be facilitated by first tensing then relaxing parts of the body). Their breathing should be natural, the diaphragm rising with each inhalation.

Once children are relaxed, tell a story in which their imaginations take them to any setting you wish: the Garden of Eden in all its beauty, a magic *sukkah* that flies through time and space, a magic carpet that takes them to a Mediterranean beach. Holidays and Jewish story anthologies can provide ideas for such "imagination trips." To make the experience more effective, refer to the different senses: "smell the beautiful flower," "feel the warm sun on your arms." Afterward, verbally lead your children through a gradual awakening ("you are starting to hear the sounds in this room," "slowly move your arms and legs and begin to open your eyes"). Then let the children share what they imagined.

Many young children enjoy this type of story (some, however, are resistant to it), although their perceptions may not be what one expects. I once led a class of preschoolers on an imagination trip to the ancient land of Israel at Sukkot time. When the time came to share experiences, one young fellow joyfully announced that he had seen "a great big grizzly bear!"

MAKE YOUR OWN TOYS AND GAMES WITH JEWISH THEMES

Although there are a variety of Jewish toys available commercially (see Resource Guide, pp. 314–315), the family may wish to make some of their own at home for several reasons: to save money, to produce a greater variety of toys than they can buy, to personalize the toy or game to family interests, and to enjoy a shared family activity. Parents can do the making for the youngest (or for very complex projects and hazardous steps such as applying hot glue); as children grow the toy and game making can become a family affair. The following are a few suggestions to get you started.

Toys

● *Toy Torah scrolls*: For descriptions of how to make model Torah scrolls see the section on Simchat Torah, pp. 203–204. You could make a toy ark to hold the Torah scrolls out of a cardboard box.

● *Puppets*: Act out a favorite Jewish story with puppets made from paper bags or socks. There are more puppet ideas in the chapter on Purim, p. 223.

● *Accessories for imaginative play*: Include Jewish objects along with your child's usual dress-up paraphernalia.

● *Tzedakah box*: For a toy *tzedakah* box for tots still at the oral stage, cover a coffee can with adhesive paper. Cut a large slit in the lid. Save the smooth-edged metal lids that come off juice-concentrate cans to use as toy coins. Baby can now be in on the *tzedakah* action without the danger of swallowing coins in the process (pennies especially are highly toxic).

● *Felt toys*: Make toy ritual objects from double pieces of colored felt cut into the desired shapes. Sew the felt pieces together securely and stuff them. Details can be cut from smaller pieces of cloth and sewn on (or glued on with a hot-glue gun).

● *Noah's ark*: For *Parashat Noah*, a Noah's ark can be made from a shoe box. Paint it brown or cover it with wood-patterned adhesive paper. Cut a hole in the side for the window, or glue on a construction paper window. Make toy animals from modeling clay or poster board (fold over a piece of poster board and cut the animal out so that you have a double animal that stands alone) or use toy animals purchased from a dime store.

● *Felt board*: Glue a large piece of felt onto a piece of sanded plywood or sturdy cardboard. Shapes and pictures can be cut from felt (details can be cut from other fabrics and glued on or drawn on with permanent markers), which will adhere to the felt on the board. Alternately, figures or pictures can be cut from paper to which you glue some small pieces of felt in the back to make the picture adhere to the felt on the board.

You can use a felt board to illustrate Jewish symbols and ceremonies, for example, a Shabbat table: cloth, *kiddush* cup and wine bottle, candlesticks, candles, and flames to attach to it, and a *hallah*—for which a cover can be made from a bit of velvet. Or you can make the characters and objects from a Bible or holiday story and tell the story with the aid of the board. A felt board is a good *"Shabbosdik"* toy because a child can make a picture without drawing.

● *Vinyl board*: You can make a vinyl board (similar to "Colorforms") with colored vinyl sheeting (look in the yellow pages under plastics). Stretch a sheet of black vinyl over a thin piece of composition board and tape it down in the back with duct tape or another sturdy tape or strong glue. Cut shapes and pictures from various other colors of vinyl sheeting, and use these in the same way felt is used on the felt board (as described here). You can make a jumbo-sized board, even taller than your child, for making enormous pictures.

● *Paper dolls*: For your paper dolls' costumes, research Jewish costumes of various periods and countries in Jewish history books, travelogues of Israel, or encyclopedias. Paper dolls can be cut

from posterboard or thin cardboard. Draw free hand or trace commercial paper dolls if you're unsure of yourself. Trace around the doll to get the correct silhouette for the clothes, then draw and color in the details, adding tabs to attach the clothing. You can even make houses or backdrops from old boxes or posters. A felt-board doll can be made using the same principle as that used for the felt board above: Cut a doll from posterboard, decorate it using crayons and glue on felt underwear, and make other clothes from felt and cloth that will adhere to felt.

● *Doll house objects*: Use your imagination to make Jewish dollhouse accessories such as holiday and ritual miniatures. For the most elegant results, use a clay that self-glazes in a home oven, such as Fimo or Cernit (available from craft shops and finer toy stores), to make tiny objects. Or just use modeling clay and various odds and ends to reproduce the objects in a Jewish home on a miniature scale. These items can also be made for larger dolls. "Barbie" has enjoyed a fulfilling Jewish life at our home, including her own Rosh HaShanah dinner with Ken—I guess it beats her night at the prom!

● *Dolls*: If you are talented with a needle and thread, you can make rag dolls and teddy bears with head coverings, *tallit*, and various Jewish costumes. Soft sculpture dolls with stuffed stocking faces can be charming *alte bubbies* and *zaydies* (grannies and grandpas).

Sample Games

● *Memory (preschooler version)*: Place several objects (Jewish holiday objects such as various colored *dreidls* or Hanukkah candles) on a table. The child closes his or her eyes or turns around while one object is removed, then guesses which object is missing.

● *Touchie-feelie*: A young child tries to identify the objects in a bag by touch alone.

● *Memory (more advanced version)*: Picture cards in identical pairs are used. Players overturn two cards at a time; if they get a pair they keep it and continue playing. The player with the most cards left at the end of the game wins. To make identical pairs of picture cards, use note cards, or cut construction or colored stationery paper (which can be bought from stationery shops by weight) as backings for the pictures, which might be drawings (free hand, photocopied, or stenciled), real photographs, postcards (duplicate copies), or identical greeting cards. The subject of the memory game can be Jewish holidays (using greeting cards), scenes of Israel (using postcards), or family events (using photos—kids love the personal pictures). Obviously, the more pairs of cards involved, the harder the game. You can also play *alef-bet* memory with stencils or photocopies of the Hebrew letters. Use of any of the games described here can be prolonged by laminating them or covering them with clear adhesive paper.

● *Lotto*: Make a lotto board with any number of squares. Color or paste in pictures of Jewish symbols, scenes, or objects, with or without titles (in Hebrew or English). Again, make duplicates, but this time the duplicates are left as separate cards to be drawn one by one by a caller. Players cover called pictures with a button or other token. The first one to make a row or black out (cover the entire board) wins. For a Hebrew challenge: put Hebrew words on the board, or call out the name of the pictures on the board in Hebrew. For variety, make a cassette tape in which you randomly call out the items, then let the tape be the caller, starting it at a different place each time you play.

● *Quiz games*: Make up the questions and answers, then write the questions on note cards and the answers in a notebook. Players take turns drawing the cards and trying to answer them. When they answer correctly, they get to keep the card.

● *Board games*: Board games on various Jewish topics can be made at home with a little effort. Use a poster board for the game board. There are many possible formats; here is but one possibility: Use labels to mark off the spaces (mark them first with a pencil for best results). Every four to six spaces or so, place a special space marker with a decorated label that instructs the player to take an action such as drawing a card from a specific pile. The cards, which can be made from note cards, will give messages related to the theme of the game and be accompanied by instructions such as "go forward two spaces," "miss a turn," or "draw again." The spaces can meander toward the destination (the first player to reach it wins) or form a circle (in which case the player to collect the most points or other tokens wins). Use dice and playing pieces

from a commercial game or purchased at a crafts store, or make your own. Give the game a trial run so that you can make changes before you try it out on your friends. There are generally little glitches and questions about rules that will arise the first time you play.

Before you can make a game, of course, you need to think about what the game is going to teach. You can make up board games about the holidays, historical periods or locations, the Bible, or Jewish values. Books may be translated into games. Tailor the illustrations as well as the messages and instructions to the subject matter.

VIDEO PROGRAMS OF JEWISH INTEREST

Videos of Jewish interest can be an effective tool for enriching Jewish education in the home. They can provide entertainment and bring the art form of film into the home, offering viewers the opportunity to try on experiences, emotions, and ideas far removed from their everyday lives. Videos can also instruct; they can bring in teachers and learning environments that would ordinarily be impossible to re-create in the home. In addition, video recordings of films in Hebrew or Yiddish provide an opportunity to improve language skills along with cultural exposure.

Today's children are often visual learners. High-quality videos of Jewish interest can turn their television viewing into a worthwhile educational experience. See the Resource Guide, pp. 313–314, for sources for videocassettes.

JEWISH SOFTWARE FOR THE FAMILY

Because so many families today have personal computers, there is a wide array of software available for the Jewish home and school. Judaic software ranges from a vast array of educational Jewish games to Hebrew-teaching programs, from Judaic graphics and Hebrew word processing to data bases involving the Jewish calendar or talmudic law.

A computer program can never take the place of live teaching (although the interactive videos now in development are coming pretty close!), but it is yet another way to enhance our children's Jewish education—in a medium they know and love. (See Resource Guide, p. 314.)

11

JEWISH CULTURAL LITERACY

Rabbi Hananyah ben Teradion says: "When two sit and do not exchange between them words of Torah, this is 'the seat of the scornful' [Psalm 1] . . . . But when two sit and do exchange between them words of Torah, the Divine presence (*Shechinah*) rests between them."

—*Pirke Avot* 3:3

In the mediating model, the family . . . mediates or fosters interaction . . . between tradition and modernity, between memories of the religious past and the experience of the secular present. . . . The mediating family struggles to apply the richness of the past to the experiences of the present in order to anticipate the uncertainties of the future.

—Norman Linzer[1]

The study of Torah equals all (the other commandments).

—*Mishnah, Pe'ah* 1:1

If a parent wished to study Torah, and he has a child who must also learn—the parent takes precedence. However, if the child is more insightful or quicker to grasp what there is to be learned, the child takes precedence. Even though the child gains priority thereby, the parent must not ignore his own study, for just as it is a *mitzvah* to educate the child, so, too, is the parent commanded to teach himself.

—Maimonides, *Mishneh Torah*
Laws of Torah Study 1:4

Don't say: I will study when I find the leisure: perhaps you will never have the leisure.

—Hillel, *Pirke Avot* 2:5

Cultural literacy can be described as a basic familiarity with the core texts, ideas, and experiences of a culture or cultures. The development of greater cultural literacy among American young people has become a growing concern of contemporary educators.

A parallel concern exists in the Jewish community. Jewish social scientists, historians, and educators all caution that Jewish life in this country cannot continue for many more generations on the basis of shared sentiments, or even of organizational and institutional life alone. For Judaism to survive and thrive, Jews need to confront anew the sources of our heritage. Feeling Jewish and even acting Jewish may not be enough; we need to begin to "think Jewish" as well, to approach life through a Jewish ethos.

As American Jews, we can give our children and ourselves the unparalleled richness of immersion in more than one cultural core. Our families can become culturally literate as Jews as well as Americans or members of other Western societies. While the tendency of so much of education today is to narrow a person's horizons, a quality Judaic education can broaden our perspective.

The profound intellectual heritage of Judaism belongs to all of us. *Torah tzivah lanu Moshe, morashah kihalat Yaakov* (The Torah encharged to us by Moses is the inheritance of the Community of

Jacob) is intended to be the first phrase Jewish parents teach their children when they have just begun to talk! Torah, Jewish learning, is not supposed to belong only to rabbis or academicians, but to every Jew from the articulation of his or her first word.

The study of Jewish sources, language, and history may be pursued primarily in a school setting, but it should be part of our home experience, too. Jewish cultural literacy can begin at home, with caring parents who are avidly interested in the sources of their Jewish heritage and who create an environment in which Judaism is learned, loved, and discussed as a natural part of life.

This chapter will examine some of the elements of Jewish cultural literacy and some ways in which they can be integrated into modern family life, both at home and in the educational settings we choose for ourselves and our children.

LEARNING TORAH

In Judaism, it is learning Torah, even more than prayer, that is the classic religious act. "To occupy oneself with words of Torah," "to learn and to teach," and "to teach them diligently to your children," are but a sampling of the phrases from the sources and liturgy to remind us that the study and transmission of Torah is to be a primary Jewish occupation and preoccupation.

Torah, in classic Jewish parlance, indicates more than the Torah scroll read in the synagogue, more than the Five Books of Moses recorded therein, even more than the entire Hebrew Bible of Torah, Prophets, and Writings. The word *Torah* literally means, "teaching." Over the centuries, the word *Torah* grew to mean all of Jewish learning: *Torah Shebichtav*, the Written Torah or Pentateuch, and *Torah Shebe'al Peh*, the Oral Tradition (which expanded upon the Written Torah and came to be recorded in the rabbinic writings, particularly the Talmud); even beyond this essential core, Torah also means the entire range of Jewish texts, teaching, and sacred literature.

Many adult Jews are reclaiming this vast heritage. Time and again, I have met Jews with extensive secular educations who have kindled their passion for Judaism only as adults when they began to encounter the Jewish sources for the first time. They simply hadn't realized what they were

missing. It was in the study of Torah that these Jews gradually realized the meaning and depth that Judaism could add to their daily lives.

THE JEWISH WAY OF LEARNING: A DISCOVERY OF MEANING

There is a difference between conventional reading and traditional Jewish textual study, often called *lernen* (Yiddish). The latter is similar to literary interpretation in its close attention to detail; even more so, it is distinguished by a "hyperliteral" attention to each word, turn of a phrase, or repetition. Because Scripture is traditionally considered the Divine word, every seeming contradiction or superfluity demands explanation (*derashah*). Four levels of textual analysis are classically employed in Jewish study: *peshat*, the simple meaning; *derash*, interpretation; *remez*, allusion; and *sod*, the hidden or mystical meaning. Together these make the Hebrew acronym *PaRDeS*, meaning Orchard. The classic rabbinical method of Torah interpretation focused intensely on individual words, often to the extent of actually decontextualizing language in a nonfundamentalist way in the relentless pursuit of the Divine meaning.[2]

The Sages used *midrash*, "the reading of Scripture as parable or allegory," to transform the biblical history of Israel into a present, meta-historical, mythical reality.[3] The term *midrash* can refer to certain classic collections of such homiletical interpretation, the genre of such interpretation, and more broadly to Jewish literature that draws on classical Jewish motifs. It can also refer to the way Jews of every generation "seek out" (*lidrosh*) and generate meaning from our classical sources: "The purpose of *derashah* is not to interpret Scripture on the basis of objective, verifiable data, but rather to *generate meaning* from the text of the Scripture . . ." (my emphasis).[4]

Just as Torah has brought meaning to the lives of countless generations, so it can help us in our search for "meanings in life" today. We may learn Torah with the traditional methods of study, as well as by employing scholarly, historical, and literary approaches. Finding new allusions, we will make our own modern *midrashim*. Some of our questions will be timeless, others will address contemporary problems. Some will involve perennial human issues, others matters of particular Jewish concern. In the language of Heschel, "The word of God never comes to an end. No word is God's last word."[5]

In the Family: Teaching Torah as an Act of Love

Jewish study is more than occupation; it is a veritable love affair with Torah. Revelation is linked to love in the Jewish tradition. We don't merely study Torah, we encounter it, we dialogue with it. And by extension, this dialogue is with the ultimate Source of Understanding, with God.

The Jewish ideal is for the parent to be occupied with Torah on the adult level and gradually initiate the child into the lifelong pursuit of Jewish education. With love, the parent welcomes the child as the newest generation in this ongoing Jewish dialogue. Torah learning—much like enjoying classical music or fine literature—is not a juvenile activity that the parent indulges in "for the children's sake." It is an adult activity that children can begin to experience at a child's level in the family setting as well as in school and can aspire to advance into as they grow up. As *Torah With Love* authors David Epstein and Suzanne Singer Stutman explain, a simple discussion of the weekly Torah portion or other Biblical text at Shabbat dinner can provide a primary method of teaching values, ethics, and proper behavior.[6]

Divrei Torah, words of Torah or Torah talk, are the uniquely Jewish speech priority. It's not for nothing that talk is considered a Jewish passion. According to myriad Jewish sources, we and our families are to speak about matters of Torah as part of daily life, sitting at table or walking on our way. It's a beautiful way to impart the undivided attention and verbal interaction children long for, while continuing the ongoing dialogue with Jewish tradition from generation to generation.

The Stages of Learning Torah

Noted Jewish educator Joel Lurie Grishaver has developed a "Torah Taxonomy" of the developmentally appropriate stages for learning Torah from preschool through adulthood.[7] In Phase One, at ages two to eight, "Bedtime Stories," the loving context of the parent–child relationship provides an opportunity to familiarize the youngster with key biblical personalities, settings, situations, and phrases. Phase Two, "Biblical Texts," at about ages seven to eleven, is the stage when the child is ready to learn careful reading skills to discover patterns, repetitions, and the importance of minor variants in the Torah text (whether in the original Hebrew or in a good translation). In Phase Three, "Attack Skills," at about ages twelve to

fifteen, the learner is ready to learn the more complicated and abstract skills needed to interpret Jewish sources. The reader learns to identify problems and issues presented in the text and to "think like a commentator" in responding to them.

Finally, in Phase Four, "Meta-Bible," at ages fourteen to adult, the learner becomes "interdependent," continuing to learn from teachers and study with others, but able to draw a personal "working meaning from a passage." The learner is able to identify broader, overarching themes in the Jewish sources. Torah study for the mature learner involves a deeply personal and examined Jewish ideology that enables the learner to apply the lessons of Jewish sources to her or his personal experience.

Today, we are privileged to witness a flowering of Jewish publications for the lay reader, particularly in books designed to make the traditional sources accessible to all. Consequently, riches abound for the Jewish learner. With the many translations and study guides available for the English reader today, adults can begin to learn from Jewish sources even if they have had little Jewish education. The expertly developed study materials for young people and families can help us to teach our children, too. Gradually, the members of almost any Jewish family or microcommunity can learn to become independent and interdependent Torah learners. Our Jewish ethos can evolve from serious and thoughtful encounter with the sources of our tradition.

Ideas for Family Torah Learning

● Read aloud from the Bible or a collection of Bible stories as either a nightly or a weekly bedtime story.

● Hold a weekly family Torah discussion on the Torah portion of the week (or other biblical selections of your choice) at Shabbat dinner or lunch. See the Resource Guide, p. 316, for several books that will be helpful in this endeavor. You might employ one or more of the following techniques:

— Summarize the portion and read selections aloud in English or Hebrew.

— Ask questions about the portion at your family's level of understanding (multiple-choice-type questions for the youngest, values-oriented questions for older children and adults).

— Discuss a values dilemma in the portion;

hold a debate or use creative dramatics to relate to the problems of characters in the portion.

— Read aloud from a *midrash* on the portion of the week. Make up your own *midrash* about some event for which the text omits details.

— Discuss how themes in the portion relate to current events.

— Prior to Shabbat, select inspirational or instructive verses from the Torah portion and Haftarah (weekly reading from the Prophets). Write them down inside folded slips of paper. Let each person at the table select one from a container and discuss and keep it for week-long inspiration.[8]

• During the summer, it is traditional to learn a chapter from the *mishnaic* tractate *Pirke Avot* (generally translated as "Sayings of the Fathers"), which is a collection of Jewish ethical teachings from around the third century of the Common Era. Several good translations are available, including a couple oriented toward young people that lend themselves to family study (see Resource Guide, p. 318). *Pirke Avot* text provides a traditional discussion topic for the third Shabbat meal.

• Experience the joy of learning Torah for yourself at the adult level by enrolling in a synagogue or adult education class on the Hebrew Bible or the rabbinic writings. In most communities there is a selection of such courses on various levels; or you can get some interested friends together and ask your rabbi, education director, or other knowledgeable teacher to start a weekly *shiur*, a Torah study class. Such study will not only be a *mitzvah* in and of itself but can eventually provide the basis to turn ordinary family conversations into Words of Torah by imbuing them with the depth of Judaic perspectives and values and with a range of Torah references.

• If you are unable to attend a class, read some books on the Jewish classics, sharing them with your spouse if possible. See the Resource Guide, pp. 316–318, for suggestions.

• Find out how Torah is taught at your child's Jewish school. Many Jewish educators feel that textual study should form the centerpiece of the Judaica curriculum. The study should be developmentally appropriate (see the Torah Taxonomy described earlier). By upper elementary grades, Torah study should go beyond learning stories to a direct encounter with texts and an exploration of the meanings to be found therein. In a day-school setting, children will be able to study texts and even commentaries, such as Rashi, in the original Hebrew; in supplementary schools they will generally study in translation, although key phrases and words can be studied in Hebrew to impart even greater meaning.

If you want to taste the real thing, Hebrew is it. No Jew who has read the Torah in Hebrew will call it the Old Testament again.

If you want to fall in love with where you come from, Hebrew is it. This is the language your ancestors dreamed in and died for.

If you want your children to feel passionately about being Jews, give them the key. If they don't learn to use it when they're young, not only won't they know Hebrew, but they'll be translating Jewish values, too, and diluting them in the process. For a language and its values are not separable. A *brit* is more than a covenant; *tzedakah* is more than charity; a *brakha* is more than a blessing. And if you do send your kids to a Jewish day school, jump up and down not only for great SATs but for outstanding Hebrew grades as well. Don't subscribe to the hidden agenda of many schools—that Hebrew is all very well but English is what counts. SATs will get your children into college, but Hebrew will get them into life.

—Nessa Rapoport[9]

LEARNING HEBREW

Many a Jewish educator has heard some variation of the following: "Why should my child learn Hebrew? Learning Hebrew isn't that important. I don't know any Hebrew myself, but I'm a good Jew."

Saying that Hebrew literacy is unimportant to being a good Jew is like saying that English literacy has nothing to do with being a good American. On one level, of course it doesn't. Knowledge does not necessarily develop character or make one morally superior. But I think that all of us agree that the English-literate, educated American is equipped to function much better as an American and to be a better citizen than is an illiterate person with a grade-school education. Similarly, the Hebrew-literate Jew is not automatically morally superior, or any such nonsense. But a Hebrew-literate Jew, the Jew who has gone beyond the usual grade-school Jewish education, is much better equipped to lead a fuller Jewish life, to learn more from classical Jewish texts (an integral part of Jewish spirituality), and to participate more intensely in the life of the Jewish people. Hebrew is an important core of the Jewish religious civilization, and learning Hebrew enables us to immerse ourselves more fully in our Judaic heritage.

Knowledge of more than one language, immersion in more than one cultural core, undoubtedly broadens one's intellectual and cultural outlook, but it is even more meaningful when that language bears one's own cultural heritage, as Hebrew does for the Jew.

Most of the Jewish classics are in Hebrew: the Jewish Bible, the *Mishnah*, the *Midrash*, the *siddur* (prayer book). (The *Gemara*, or Talmud, is written in Aramaic, a closely related language.) "Reading the Bible in translation is like kissing your mother through a veil," is the famous expression of Israel's poet-laureate Chaim Nahman Bialik.[10] While it's true that there are many new translations of the Jewish classics appearing each year, there is still nothing quite like studying Torah or understanding a prayer in the original Hebrew. There are dimensions and nuances of meaning that are lost in translation. And even a minimal knowledge of Hebrew can add depth to Jewish study.

Jews in their long Diaspora have traditionally been multilingual, speaking a Jewish dialect (such as Yiddish, Ladino, or Judeo-Arabic), as well as the vernacular, as well as at least a minimal knowledge of the Hebrew, the "holy tongue," and, for the better educated, Aramaic (the latter two in the past more likely to be learned by males due to the gender inequality in traditional Jewish education). Whatever daily language Jews spoke would become infused with Hebrew words that constituted a unique "values vocabulary" of Jewish life (see chapter 15 for more on Jewish values vocabulary).

Hebrew can serve as a bond between Jews from different countries. A Jew who can pray in Hebrew can enter a traditional service anywhere in the world and feel at home. And with the rebirth of Israel, Hebrew has once again become a living language, a language with a growing and important modern literature, a language that should serve as a cultural link between Jews around the world. Speaking Hebrew is one of the key elements of the Israeli Jewish identity; to be able to converse with Israelis in their native tongue is an important way to build ties with Israeli culture and society.

But although Hebrew literacy is the hallmark of an educated Jew, relatively few American Jews are fluent or even have a basic knowledge of Hebrew.

A study by Queens College sociologist Steven Cohen determined that in this country, 41 percent of Orthodox Jews (who make up 9 percent of the American Jewish population), 9 percent of Conservative, and 5 percent of Reform Jews describe themselves as having a minimal competence in Hebrew.[11] The vast majority of American Jews know their religion only in translation.

Why Hebrew remains a low priority among most American Jews is a complicated issue. Part of it is certainly a factor of the general American antipathy to bilingualism. In part, it may be related to cooling enthusiam for Israel and Jewish nationalism. Many Jewish educators have noted the decline in recent years in attempts to teach Hebrew as a living language, both in Hebrew school, as well as in "Hebrew speaking" camps. Others see speaking Hebrew as yet another demarcation of the difference between an increasingly educated and active Jewish elite and the majority of Jews who want a much less demanding Jewish involvement.

THE GOOD NEWS ABOUT HEBREW

Hebrew is accessible. Unless you have some particular language-learning disability, you can learn some basic Hebrew with relative ease. An adult can learn to read the Hebrew alphabet in a few weeks of weekly lessons and home practice (there is even a program that specializes in teaching Hebrew reading in a day!), and to understand much of the Hebrew prayer book in a few months. By studying for a couple of hours a week in an adult Hebrew program for a year or two (or spending a few months at an Ulpan, an Israeli language school), one can become reasonably conversant. It takes a number of years of serious study for most people to become truly fluent. In other words, learning the holy tongue is amazingly like learning any language!

At first, Hebrew will seem more different from English than say, Spanish, because it comes from a different language family and has a different alphabet. Yet many Hebrew words will be familiar from the context of Jewish life, and many modern Hebrew words have been borrowed from English. At the same time, Hebrew is a marvelously logical language, a language built on three-letter roots that blossom into words with great consistency and few irregularities. Once you learn some of the basic building blocks of Hebrew, putting words, phrases, and sentences together has an almost mathematical precision.

Ideas for Learning Hebrew

For Parents

Parents give their children as well as themselves a distinct educational advantage if they learn Hebrew for themselves before, or concurrent with, enrolling their children in a Jewish school of any type. Children generally learn Hebrew more readily when they see that Hebrew is a priority for their parents and when parents have at least a basic Hebrew literacy so that they can help their child. Even a few months of Hebrew instruction can help adults to better appreciate Judaism and provide some background to participate more fully in their children's Jewish educations.

Parents can learn Hebrew by attending a Hebrew language class at a Jewish Community Center, adult education program, synagogue, or local college. If no class is available in your community, ask the religious school director at your synagogue school or the principal at your day school to start Hebrew classes for parents. Some people are able to learn on their own with tapes and books. However, it is preferable to meet with a Hebrew-fluent tutor from time to time to check progress and correct errors.

For Children

Provide your children with the best Hebrew education you can. With all that is available today in the field of language instruction in general, and Hebrew in particular, every child whose parents and school are so motivated should be able to get a decent Hebrew education.

All Jewish schools should make Hebrew a central and fundamental part of their curricula. The day school, of course, can provide the optimum setting and enough time for substantive Hebrew instruction. Ideally, it can be a truly bilingual environment in which Hebrew is spoken much of the day and in which Jewish and general subjects are integrated as much as possible.

One problem outside the day-school environment is the time available for Hebrew instruction. The afternoon/supplementary religious school can maximize Hebrew education by using simple spoken Hebrew often in the Hebrew language component of the program, and by integrating Hebrew words and phrases into the school and synagogue life. There are good materials now available to make supplementary Hebrew programs more substantive than they have been in the past. Several years of Hebrew school should definitely impart more than the phonetic decoding of prayers without comprehension!

Whatever the setting, start early. Young children are at an advantage in acquiring a second language. The earlier one begins with oral language, the better. Absorbing some of the basics of speech and comprehension should come prior to introducing reading and writing.

In Israel

Of course, the ideal place to learn Hebrew is in Israel. Adults and teens can study intensively at a location such as Ulpan Akiva, an acclaimed Hebrew language school located in a pleasant resort on the Mediterranean (see Israel Resource Guide, p. 344). Young children can often absorb a lot of Hebrew simply by attending an Israeli day camp or playing with Israeli children. A couple of months of daily study in Israel may be worth a year of study elsewhere. (But try to learn whatever you can before your trip; even a small amount of prior study, such as learning to read Hebrew phonetically, can really give you a head start.)

Hebrew in the Home

Hebrew enrichment can continue at home through the use of conversation tapes, easy Hebrew stories, videos, Hebrew songs, everyday Hebrew phrases, and conversation (to the extent of the family's ability). In Texas, I taught a family of six in one of my Hebrew classes at the Jewish Community Center. The parents and children learned and studied together and tried to speak Hebrew at home as much as possible. They said that learning Hebrew was a result of their interest in and love of Israel. This family wasn't Jewish. Wouldn't it be great to see more Jewish families have this kind of active interest in Hebrew?

The Bilingual Family

For parents who are fairly fluent in Hebrew, language education experts will concur that the best way to make a child bilingual is by one or both parents *speaking Hebrew to the child from birth*. Eventually, she or he will probably answer in English, but you should persist. Introduce Israeli children's books, tapes, and videos into the home. Trips to Israel will bring out the child's passive language knowledge.

Confession: This is a case of "do as I say, not as I do." My husband and I gave up trying to speak

Hebrew consistently to our older children when they persisted in answering in English. We've been scrambling to make up for it ever since and invite you to learn from our mistake.

Family Projects with Hebrew Names

The use of Hebrew names can be another way to learn about Hebrew and our Jewish heritage. A Hebrew name—a literal Jewish identity—should not just be some secret code name trotted out for the rare ceremonial occasion. Ideally, one should use children's Hebrew names as their only names, or at least use them very often at home and in religious school. Here are some fun ideas and projects with Hebrew names:

● If in your family you don't use your Hebrew names all the time, at least choose a special time to use them among the family, such as Shabbat, or at least during Friday night dinner (or on any other occasion you select). This gives the children the opportunity to experience their Jewish identity as the primary one.

● Tell the children (from time to time), who they were named for and why. Tell stories about that person so that the child can identify with her or him.

● Using the *Encyclopaedia Judaica*, one-volume Jewish encyclopedias, and Jewish history books (you should be able to find these at your synagogue library), look up your Hebrew name and discover famous Jews who had the same name (if the name is a fairly traditional one), associations linked to your name if your name is a new one (such as a nature name), or both. If nothing turns up, ask a knowledgeable aquaintance (such as a Jewish education director, rabbi, or friend) for help.

● Celebrate your Hebrew name(s) by making personalized T-shirts, caps, bags, bibs, door plates, Lucite desk items. Parents are often advised not to let young children wear personalized items because of the slight chance that a potential abductor would learn the child's name that way (God forbid). Hebrew lettering pretty much takes care of that! Stencils (see Resource Guide, p. 320) can be used for the lettering, or lettering can be done freehand following the directions in such books as *The Handbook of Hebrew Calligraphy*, by Cara Goldberg Marks.[12] Supplies such as fabric paints and all-surface paint pens are available at crafts stores.

● Make a button with your Hebrew name. Button making supplies are available from crafts stores. Use your imagination to create other jewelry with your Hebrew name or those of your friends, using materials from the jewelry section of your crafts store.

● A personalized, ceramic, Hebrew door plate or wall decoration, or gold or silver Hebrew-name jewelry can be a meaningful gift for a birthday or holiday, as can a *kippah* with a Hebrew name crocheted on it, or painted (along with cute pictures) on suede. (These are available from many Jewish gift shops or by mail order. See the Resource Guide to Judaica for the Home, pp. 307–309. For doing it yourself, see the Resource Guide to Arts and Crafts, p. 316.)

YIDDISH AND OTHER JEWISH LANGUAGES AND CULTURES

Hebraist though I am, I would not want to exclude the importance of Yiddish for many Jewish families. Yiddish was the mother tongue (*mamaloschen*) of European Jewry for eight centuries before American Jews mostly gave it up and most of its European speakers were murdered by the Nazis. Many contemporary American Jewish families find a sense of meaning and continuity with the past by making Yiddish language, literature, songs, and proverbs a part of their home life.

While Ashkenazic Jews have strong emotional ties to Yiddish, Sephardic Jews treasure their own special languages. Those with a Spanish heritage have preserved songs, poems, and prayers in Judeo-Spanish and Ladino, while others speak and sing in various dialects of Judeo-Arabic. Along with their ancestral languages, many Sephardic Jews are careful to preserve their particular traditions of melody, prayer, song, dress, cuisine, and customs.

Even if one does not become fluent in the vernacular of one's ancestors, exposure to these languages can be particularly fulfilling, as it helps to forge a stronger link with one's personal history and heritage. See the Learning Resource Guide, pp. 320–321, for information on educational programs, music, and other materials on Yiddish and on Sephardic languages and culture.

In the following "family snapshot," Rukhl Schaechter-Ejdelman of New York tells why she and her husband, Leon, have decided to speak Yiddish in their home and to educate their children in this language.

FAMILY SNAPSHOTS

GROWING UP WITH YIDDISH

Historically, the Yiddishist movement was a secular, and sometimes antireligious, movement—led by young Jews at the turn of the century who were rebelling against their strictly observant parents of the "Old World." Many of these rebellious young Jews became nonreligious Zionists; many others became nonreligious socialists who wanted to express their Jewish identity through ethnic solidarity rather than religion. So they spoke Yiddish, created Yiddish schools, read Yiddish literature together, celebrated the historical Jewish holidays with Yiddish songs, and after the Holocaust, organized commemorations in Yiddish of the Warsaw Ghetto Uprising and integrated the themes of Holocaust and Israel into the poems, songs, novels, short stories, and memoirs that they continued to publish in Yiddish.

When my Rumanian-born father, a budding professor of Yiddish linguistics, married my American-born, Yiddish-speaking mother in 1955, they decided to raise their children in Yiddish. They sent us to the Sholem Aleichem Yiddish School in the neighborhood every afternoon, after we returned from the public school. No Sunday school today could compare to the education we received in the *shul*—Yiddish reading and writing, Jewish history, Bible, prayer, Hebrew, holidays, and reading Yiddish literature in the original!

However, my parents differed from the Yiddishists of the previous generation in that they kept kosher and fairly traditional *Shabbos* and holiday celebrations. Although our observance could objectively be considered Conservative rather than Orthodox, we did it all in Yiddish, so that, ironically, we felt more comfortable in an Orthodox synagogue where the rabbi could still make his *droshe* (sermon) in Yiddish.

My husband, Leon Ejdelman, was born and raised in Poland after the war. Living in a communist country, he has never had any (and to this day has no) interest in religion. Yet, ethnically, he feels a very strong bond to the Jews. Leon knows Yiddish from home and also studied it (reluctantly) in the government-controlled Jewish school in Poland. Until we met, however, he never thought he would raise his children in Yiddish. Now we have three sons—Menachem, Naftali, and Gedaliah. All three are fluent in Yiddish and English. We send them every Sunday morning to *Pripetshik*, a Yiddish immersion program for children.

Most of the Yiddishists I know in my generation are, like us, more traditional than the Yiddishists of previous generations. Other Yiddish-speaking families are modern Orthodox, traditional (that is, kosher, but not *shomer Shabbos*), and secular—in other words, Yiddishists today run the full gamut of Jewish life-styles!

I've enrolled Menachem and Naftali in a Jewish day school, *Kinneret*, which teaches Hebrew, prayer, *and* Yiddish.

I find that my children's fluency in Yiddish creates an automatic connection to senior citizens, Whether we're standing in an elevator, or on a shopping line, elderly Jews are delighted to hear these little kids asking Mommy questions in Yiddish! They seem to be getting *naches* from seeing young children who are not assimilated and are actually speaking a language that they themselves were raised in!

When we celebrate Shabbos and holidays, we supplement the celebration with Yiddish and *klezmer* music. And when we make the blessings, it's always in Ashkenazic Hebrew, which is the pronunciation that our forefathers used in Eastern Europe. Sephardic Hebrew is fine for speaking modern Israeli Hebrew, but when I'm reciting something traditional like prayers, it makes more sense to use the pronunciation that was traditional for my ancestors.

Speaking Yiddish also creates a natural connection to hasidic Jews. My husband is a salesman for a wholesale electronics company run by *hasidim*, and he finds it more comfortable making his transactions in Yiddish, even though many of them also can speak English. Several years ago, one of his colleagues invited us to his home in Williamsburg (a hasidic neighborhood) for Purim. It was fascinating to enter a world much like the *shtetl* in Eastern Europe, where everyone—including children—spoke Yiddish constantly. The store signs and advertisements were in Yiddish. At their home, his colleague's wife was equally fascinated with me—an apparently modern secular woman who spoke Yiddish as well as she did. She called in her neighbor and said to her in Yiddish, "Why, she's one of us!" Of course I'm not one of them, in many ways; but still, I appreciated the fact that we did feel this connection through Yiddish.

I've been to Israel three times; my husband, almost twenty times! My one gripe about Israel is their attitude toward Yiddish. It was bad enough that the Holocaust killed off the majority of Yiddish speakers; it hurts even more when our own Israel does so little to keep Yiddish alive. Ben Gurion was actually a virulent anti-Yiddishist and did whatever he could to prevent Yiddish from being used in Israel. It caused a lot of hostility and discrimination against Yiddish that is apparent to this day, even among the younger generation of Israelis. Occasionally, I run into an Israeli who feels a genuine warmth toward Yiddish; but for too many, Yiddish smacks of the "*galut*" (Diaspora) and is therefore something to be shunned or laughed at. Because Yiddish is such an integral part of my family's Jewish identity, I would find it very difficult to raise my children in Israel. It may sound funny, but I prefer my Yiddish-speaking children to grow up with American kids who have *no* opinion about Yiddish than to grow up with Israelis who have a *low* opinion of it.

—Rukhl Schaechter-Ejdelman

LEARNING ABOUT JEWISH HISTORY

Educators are scandalized by how poor a grasp of history many of today's young people have. Were they to look at Jewish children's understanding of Jewish history, my guess is that they would really be alarmed! Many Jewish youngsters do not even grasp the barest outlines of the Jewish experience.

For Jews, our history is inseparable from our religion and our culture. Part of being a "Judaist," a participating and believing Jew, is to maintain "a sense of the meaningfulness of Jewish history."[13] Our important days wed memories and visions. Without our communal memories and a sense of their meaning, our heritage would lose much of its significance.

History can be enjoyable to learn. Although the home need not be turned into a history lecture hall, there are many easy ways to integrate Jewish history into our family lives:

● For starters, investigate your own family history (see chapter 6).

● When on a trip, anywhere in the United States or worldwide, seek out Jewish historical sites and visit Jewish museums (of which there are several in the United States, and more than 120 in Israel!).

● Most Jewish holidays commemorate historical events. Use the holidays as opportunities to teach, learn, and remember Jewish history.

● The Jewish history book shelf: Parents can read adult books on Jewish history, while for children there are not only new and attractive history books, but books of historical fiction and "make-your-own (historical) adventure."

● There are even games that teach Jewish history. Try some at home.

● Current events are Jewish history in the making. Subscribe to Jewish periodicals for adults and for children. Read articles in the general press and watch television programs that deal with Jewish subjects. As a family, discuss the issues that arise.

● Use hobbies and hands-on activities to enhance your historical knowledge. Start an educational Israeli coin or stamp collection (see "Hanukkah gifts," p. 212). When you read about a historical period, you can bring it to life with crafts, dress up, paper-doll costumes, recipes, and art activities.

LEARNING ABOUT THE HOLOCAUST AND ANTI-SEMITISM

Although learning about Jewish history can be enjoyable, inevitably our children begin to ask those questions we are afraid of hearing: "But why did so many people hate the Jews?" and especially, "Why did the Nazis kill the Jews?" "Why didn't anyone stop them?" "Could that happen again?"

Learning about anti-Semitism, and particularly about the Holocaust, is difficult. It is painful and frightening enough for us to discover these dark chapters of history and lingering pockets of hate, but it is even more gut-wrenching when our children begin to become aware of them.

Becoming a parent makes the *Shoah*, the Holocaust, so much more devastating, if such a thing is possible. Looking at one's own precious children and realizing that a million Jewish children were wrenched from their parents' arms and cold-bloodedly murdered is too much to bear.

And when one's children begin to learn about the *Shoah* . . . I remember when my daughter Liora saw a television special narrated by a childhood friend of Anne Frank who was with her at the end of her short life. The woman, now middle-aged, described how they had been taken to a concentration camp and stripped of all their clothes. Liora looked at me in shocked disbelief and asked, "Mommy, did they really make them take off their clothes?" Believe me, that was one of the most painful moments I have ever experienced as a mother, to have to answer yes. And we weren't yet even talking about gas-chamber horrors, but simply about the humiliation and shame that Jews were made to endure.

Still, Jewish parents today know that the Holocaust must not be a taboo subject. "Never again" means that we must teach, remember, and fight anti-Semitism and racism in all forms. On the other hand, we don't want to instill a crippling fear in our children, or have them associate Judaism with persecution and victimization alone. We want them primarily to feel positive about being Jewish. Here are a few issues to consider:

● Many of us have lingering traumas of our own as a result of being the children of survivors, or simply as a result of the way the Holocaust was handled in our own educations. My youngest sister and I, as adults, discovered that both of us had severe childhood fears related to the Holocaust, despite our secure upbringing as third- and fourth-generation Americans growing up in a "wonder years" setting in south Texas. At any rate, all parents have to confront their own feelings about the *Shoah*.

● My own childhood fears have led me to be open, and yet I've very carefully exposed my children to the facts of the Holocaust. Fortunately, there are now many excellent books available that introduce these events gradually and sensitively to young children beginning with perhaps second grade. Such stories will generally focus on Holocaust survivors or escapees from the Nazi regime. Reading and discussing these stories with your children can convey the facts of the Holocaust to them without horrifying them with facts that they are too young to handle.

● Television programming about the Nazi era has become fairly frequent. Some programs can be very helpful in teaching about the events of this time while others are too frightening or too sensational for young children. Choose carefully; consider recording and previewing a program for later family viewing.

● Yom HaShoah, Holocaust Remembrance Day, is an important focus for learning and memory.

● Visit Holocaust memorials: Yad VaShem in Israel, as well as the Holocaust memorials in the United States, particularly the new Holocaust Memorial Museum on the National Mall in Washington, DC. An exhibit on "Children of the Holocaust" has been shown at Washington, DC,'s Capitol Children's Museum. Again, though, the caution is to avoid using the *Shoah* as the central focus of Jewish identity. Such powerful exhibits need to be balanced with positive, life-affirming Jewish experiences.

● This is the last generation that will be able to meet Holocaust survivors in person. Nothing else we can say or present has the same impact on young people, whether Jewish or Gentile, as meeting and listening to someone who lived through the Holocaust. My mother, as community relations director of our local Jewish Federation, several years ago developed an education program on the Holocaust that has had a tremendous impact on high school students in our area. The most effective part of the program continues to be the visits by survivors. Survivors should be invited to meet with children in Jewish schools, perhaps from grades three or four on (although the subject matter should of course be approached with sensitivity). Many places have begun to videotape the testimony of survivors, certainly a sacred task.

● Children should be taught about the actions of righteous Christians who, during the Nazi period, saved Jewish lives at the risk of their lives and the lives of their families. Even as the Holocaust demonstrates the depths of the evil to which humans are capable of sinking, the stories of these saintly individuals show the heights of altruism that the human spirit may attain.

● *Anti-Semitism today*: The past generation has seen a growth in Jewish pride, and in Jewish comfort and assurance of acceptance in American society. I would not want to exaggerate anti-

Semitism in this country, or use it as a source of paranoia or the eternal motivation for Jewish affiliation. Yet, in all honesty, some forms of anti-Semitism appear to be on the rise in the United States today, accompanied by other manifestations of racism and prejudice in our society. Today young people in public high schools, and especially on college campuses, report anti-Semitic remarks and attitudes. Parents of various religions have to band together to combat these trends in their own schools and neighborhoods. There are many educational programs that parents should push to introduce into their local schools, notably, "Facing History and Ourselves," which teaches teenagers about the Holocaust and racism in a context of self-examination.

Jewish young people should learn about the B'nai B'rith Anti-Defamation League (ADL) and other groups that fight anti-Semitism and prejudice. Consider inviting someone from the ADL or perhaps a Federation Community Relations director to speak at your Jewish school and at Jewish high school programs in your area. As Jewish young people grow up, they need to learn why we can never take democracy and tolerance for granted but should take an active part in the political and social processes that continue to shape our country's character.

12

LEARNING ABOUT GOD AND PRAYER

It seems hard for many contemporary Jews to speak about God. What's more, many find it difficult even to link their idea of their Jewishness with any sort of spirituality. They may compartmentalize their identities thus: Judaism is their ethnic and communal heritage, yet they themselves are secular and agnostic. Or, if they consider themselves spiritually oriented, perhaps their spirituality is universalist, or nondenominational.

What is the source of this dichotomy? Is it the legacy of a cultural reluctance to try to describe the ineffable . . . or perhaps of a cultural emphasis on deed above creed? Or is it that in modern America our Judaism has focused on the civil religion of organizational activity over and above the inner life? . . . Or could it be the painful legacy of the Holocaust that makes it hard for many Jews to express their Judaism in spiritual terms?

All of these and many other factors may be involved. To analyze the situation would require another book. Yet many Jews today are spiritually hungry, and institutional and organizational, ethnic, and national Judaism are no longer enough to satisfy their deepest inner needs. Whereas some Jews have turned away from Judaism to "wander in foreign fields," many others have begun to discover again or for the first time the unique beauty and preciousness of Jewish spirituality.

The very word *spirituality* is problematic because it implies a denial of either the material world or the body, and such denial is contrary to even the mystical strains in Judaism. And yet it remains the most adequate English word most of us can find to describe a sensitivity to the dimension of the holy or the numinous in everyday life.

Judaism has been described as a "God-intoxicated" way of life. Virtually every action of everyday life focused on holiness, on the service of the Creator. The mystics and *hasidim* constantly sought to cling to and be united with God. The late Dr. Perry London, who was a leading authority on Jewish identity formation, described one of the central challenges for contemporary Jewish parents and educators as raising children to a life that is "God intoxicated," and yet nonfundamentalist; spiritual, and yet actively involved in the larger world. A "God-intoxicated" life is one in which holiness and activism are balanced, in which our spirituality motivates us to a life of idealism and service.[1]

HOW WE RESTORE OUR SPIRITUALITY

How can we bring God back into our consciousness and into our Jewish homes? There is no single formula for restoring the spiritual life, but there are various approaches that many Jews find help to sensitize them to the spiritual dimension of life. They are organized here under three central themes of the Jewish tradition: creation, revelation, and redemption.

Twentieth-century Jewish philosopher Franz Rosenzweig[2] described these three themes as pillars of the Jewish tradition. Depictions of God as Creator of the World, Revealer of the Torah, and Redeemer of Israel and humanity continually recur in Jewish texts and liturgy. In every human being, there is likewise a potential for creativity, discovery, and activism, for human beings are created in God's image. Each of these central themes can also be an opportunity to nurture the spiritual dimension of family life.

In Creation

Time spent in natural surroundings and outdoors, learning about and experiencing the beauty of God's creation, has the potential to enhance the spiritual life of the family. I know this from my own experience, for a large part of my adolescence was spent at our family ranch in the Texas hill country, and many of our family vacations were spent at awe-inspiring natural locations such as the Rocky Mountains.

In such surroundings, I was able to develop an inner life and a capacity for contemplation not possible for many of my peers who spent every weekend in suburbia. What I didn't realize then was how Judaism, which was formed in an agrarian society, encompasses many observances and texts that emphasize themes of nature and the natural world. Likewise, the prophets, mystics, and later the *hasidim* were all known to seek communion with God in nature.

Reading the Psalms and reciting the *birchot hanehenin*, blessings over enjoyment of nature, are two traditional Jewish ways for heightening consciousness and appreciation of the wonders of God's creation. The *kavanah* (meditative intent) of saying a *berachah* may be heightened when one is able to grow or pick food, or to bake bread, experiences that can increase a sense of wonder at the work of creation and the human role as God's "partner" in it.

Appreciating "creation" doesn't take place only outdoors, of course. Learning about the many discoveries of the sciences with our families can also expand our awareness of the miraculousness of God's works.

We human beings also create, and being creative in our work and home can help us to experience the godly in ourselves. In particular, engaging in artistic pursuits can be an expression of spirituality. And enjoying the inspirational creations of artists, writers, and musicians can be a catalyst for our own inner growth.

In Revelation

The study of Torah is a primary spiritual pathway in the Jewish religion. Immersing ourselves in the "sea of Torah" can heighten our sense of the holy. Words of Torah can be studied and shared often in the Jewish home.

Revelation can also refer to relationships, for the Jewish concept of revelation is closely connected to that of love and relationship. In our moments of true relation to other people, and in our moments of teaching and learning with others, we may encounter the divine.

In Jewish tradition, teachers are important as models for, and conduits of, spiritual experience. I once asked Rabbi Harold Kushner, How can Jews relate to a transcendent, awesome, and abstract God? He said that one way is in our personal relationship with a teacher, *rebbe* (in the broad sense of a spiritual guide and teacher), or *tzaddik tzaddeket* (righteous one). The godly person is a living personification of God's teaching, the Torah, and our relationship to such a person nurtures our spiritual growth.

God is not only the endless *Ein Sof* (utter beyondness) who completely transcends our powers of understanding, but also *Shechinah*, the immanent, indwelling Presence. Meditation, prayer, and other spiritual disciplines can help us to turn inward and discover the spark of divinity within ourselves. Taking time to be alone and listen to the "still small voice" is important for our spiritual development, but Jewish tradition also stresses that the *Shechinah* rests upon human beings in the holiness of relationships and community—the congregation gathered for prayer, the friends exchanging words of Torah, the husband and wife uniting in holiness, respect, and love.

There are other ways in which the divine is revealed in our lives. Synchronicity, Swiss psychoanalyst C.G. Jung's term for meaningful coincidence, is a concept akin to the traditional Jewish idea of *beshert*. The meaningful coincidences we experience may become windows on the spiritual dimension of our lives that has always been there beyond our conscious awareness.

Dr. Kathy Chesto,[3] a family religious educator, has explained that the spiritual dimension of life is like the background music that most people don't notice in the hustle and bustle of daily existence. However, just as people are more likely to notice a familiar tune playing in the background, so does a familiarity with religious concepts and texts help to sensitize us to an awareness of the spiritual element in everyday life.

Often, the meaningful coincidences will be found in the texts themselves. Very often I find that Shabbat prayers, a verse in the Torah portion, or the *haftarah* selection seems to be speaking to me, addressing a pressing concern in my life. Attending services, engaging in a Judaic class or a congregational discussion, exchanging words of Torah with friends and family, reading the Bible, and studying other Jewish texts are all ways to reveal the spiritual meanings in our lives.

Likewise, Jewish rituals and traditions can be performed with a sense of meaning and spiritual awareness, of *kavanah*. We can focus on the meanings of specific prayers and rituals, as they are performed, or even articulate these formally before or after the action. In past centuries, verbal expressions of *kavanah* were formulated to be recited before and after the performance of ritual *mitzvot*. These generally begin: *Hineni muchan umezuman . . .* (Behold, I am ready to perform the *mitzvah* of . . .). After the *mitzvah*, one might recite a *Yehi Ratzon . . .* (May it be Your will, that just as I performed this *mitzvah*, so, too . . .) that would tie the performance of the *mitzvah* to a mythic worldview. Contemporary Jews can compose their own *kavanot* designed to focus their thoughts on the spiritual meanings of the rituals.

Ritual actions are not the only actions that can be done with spiritual awareness. Ideally, the "mundane" actions of life can also be done with a sense of *kavanah*, an awareness of the holiness and wonder of living.

In Redemption

For the family to learn together about Jewish history—to appreciate the miracle of our survival, our contributions to world civilization, and our return to our ancient homeland after two millennia—can be a way to heighten the family's religious consciousness.

Redemption is also linked to the moral imperative to become God's partners in "repairing the world" (*tikkun olam*). Social activism is an integral part of the Jewish concept of the spiritual life. It is when we engage in acts of redemption that we assume

our full stature as beings in "the image of God." Research confirms that good deeds can be as beneficial for us as meditation.

Living with a mission and a sense of purpose, with a desire to serve God and humanity however we are able—what could be more spiritual than this?

TALKING WITH CHILDREN ABOUT GOD

In the course of my work as a Jewish educator, parents occasionally ask me for advice on talking to children about God. Talking about God with children is like talking about any difficult subject. The parental task is first to clarify what they believe as adults, then to convey that to the child at an age-appropriate level that the child can understand. It's important to be honest and to avoid teaching our children things that we don't believe ourselves and that they will have to unlearn later on.

We can also explain that there is a whole spectrum of legitimate Jewish ideas about God. Judaism has traditionally valued "deed over creed" and has allowed a surprisingly wide range of theological flexibility. We, our children, and other Jews may have very different beliefs and still be good Jews.

Rabbi Harold Kushner, noted for his popular books on theology, suggests that we change the typical child's question of "where is God," to "*when* is God?" Kushner explains to children that the Ten Commandments forbid making a picture of God, because any human conception of God is inherently limiting. Children can be asked to suggest things they know are real but that cannot be seen or pictured. They can understand that feelings and ideas are real yet intangible forces. Just as we cannot draw a picture of love, we cannot draw a picture of God. But we can illustrate feelings and ideas by showing what people *do* as a result of their feelings and ideas. Similarly, children can discuss or even draw pictures of "God becoming real in people's lives"—when people are motivated to worship, to appreciate, to learn, to do good deeds, to act with righteousness, and to follow their consciences.[4]

Talking about God never happens in isolation. Our values and actions convey to our children much about the place of faith in our lives. When we pursue good deeds, tell Jewish stories, and make Jewish learning and practice a part of our everyday lives, our children are indirectly learning about God. But given the spiritual hunger of many Jewish young people, perhaps the time has come to do more formal talking about God within the family.

Talking about God, like talking about the "facts of life," seldom happens in one formal discussion. It can naturally occur as part of our daily interactions with our children. Natural times to talk about God with children can be grouped under the areas of creation, revelation, and redemption (as described on pp. 84–85). The theme of creation could include God-talk inspired by sharing our wonder at the beauty and complexity of creation, or the way we felt close to God at our child's birth. The theme of revelation could include talk about God that comes up when parents and children read traditional Jewish stories or study the Torah portion together. The theme of redemption could include talk about God's moral demands and the experience of God in Jewish history, including such issues as human free will and the choice of good or evil.

For parents who find it awkward to speak about God, there are excellent resources available to make the task less daunting. For example, "Hide and Seek," a game about God created by the Melton Resource Center as part of its *Together* program for parents and elementary-age children, encourages intergenerational sharing about beliefs through relating traditional Jewish stories and biblical episodes to personal experiences. *The Book of Miracles* by Rabbi Lawrence Kushner is suggested as a young person's guide to Jewish spiritual awareness "for parents to read to their children; for children to read to their parents." It makes an excellent Shabbat discussion starter for preteens and their families. These and other materials can be found in the Resource Guide, p. 322.

Before finding the correct language to communicate our beliefs to our children, though, we have to clarify those beliefs for ourselves. One helpful way to begin to articulate a personal theology is what Professor Neil Gillman of the Jewish Theological Seminary describes as the use of metaphors for God.[5] He is careful to stress that this does not mean that God *is* a metaphor or that we "pray to a metaphor," but rather that we need metaphors to be able to discuss ideas and concepts that would otherwise be beyond the range of human articulation. Nothing we can say about God and no metaphor for God can be *literally* true. Each is *more or less adequate* only in various ways. We can ask how it is more or less helpful in a given context to depict God as a warrior, shepherd, *mivkveh*, mother, king, or an endless light (all images from the Jewish tradition).

Jewish tradition, teaches Gillman, embraces a kaleidoscope of metaphors for God. The Bible (which is, we must recall, a library of books bound together in one cover) and later Jewish texts show a range of metaphors for God: the punishing God of Job, the forgiving and caring God of Jonah, or the loving "husband" of many of the prophetic works. Throughout the Jewish year, there is a similar range of metaphors. God is conceived of metaphorically as judge and sovereign on the Days of Awe, as provider and harvester on Sukkot, as general leading armies into battle on Hanukkah, and as one who sits in the dust and weeps for Jerusalem on Tisha B'Av.

Jews who come to services only twice a year are exposed to only one set of metaphors and may emerge with a one-sided concept of Jewish theology. Likewise, when Jews are well educated in secular fields, but when God metaphors have remained at a childish level ("An old man in the sky"), then it's no wonder they believe that they've outgrown religion. Before parents can begin to talk about God with their children, they need to question the adequacy of their own personal metaphors for God.

Despite the vast range of possibilities, Gillman finds four common elements that make a "core metaphor" which holds all of the Jewish God-metaphors together. The classic Jewish conceptions of God virtually always include the conceptions that:

- God is *Ehad*, meaning, not just that God is One (monotheism, unity), but that God is unique, alone. (Although God's immanence versus God's transcendence remains a Jewish theological issue, Jewish theology has historically been able to encompass both ideas.)

- God is personal. The biblical and midrashic God is not an abstract metaphysical principle, but a caring, involved, very personal God. However, some modern Jewish thinkers (notably Mordechai Kaplan) have conceived of God as a process rather than a being.

- God is sovereign. God's greatness, majesty, and power are paramount.

- God is vulnerable, as it were. Paradoxically, God is conceived of as "vulnerable." God has given us free will and thus is vulnerable to "suffering" because we disappoint Him/Her repeatedly; human beings can choose to sanctify or desecrate God's name. Another way of expressing this is that God permits evil, so God suffers with us.

Around this "core metaphor" have grown up a vast repertoire of Jewish metaphors for God. The Bible, the *siddur*, and other Jewish texts offer many metaphorical names and descriptions for God: Lord, Shepherd, Ultimate Being, Eternal, Holy One of Blessing, Indwelling Divine Presence, Refuge, Compassionate One, Utter Beyondness, Peace, Source of Life, Redeemer, and dozens of others. Understanding such names and descriptions in the original Hebrew reveals even deeper layers of meaning. The Yiddish language often expressed a certain intimacy with God, describing the divine in such terms as *Gottenyu, Zisser* (God Dear, Sweet One).

An important issue for contemporary Jews is the gender issue in our metaphors for God. To address or speak of God in exclusively masculine terms is clearly distorted. There is ample precedent in Jewish tradition, particularly in the mystical and kabbalistic strains, for feminine God-metaphors as well as for masculine ones. A number of contemporary *siddurim* have modified their gender language to reflect this sensitivity.

Children, even as early as upper elementary school, can discuss their own God-metaphors, or their name for God or what they think God is like. The object is not to decide if their metaphors for God are true, but to talk about how they feel that God is like a given metaphor. Such conversations should be repeated at different ages, so that children can begin to understand that our conceptions of God grow and develop as we mature. They can also begin to understand that Jewish ideas about God have developed over the ages and that different people may hold different yet valid beliefs. My daughter Liora, at age nine, joined an adult study session on the topic of metaphors for God and volunteered her own sophisticated and mystical metaphor: "A Rainbow without Colors."

PRAYER

I belong to a small congregation in a relatively small Jewish community. The members of this *minyan* do not, as a whole, come from very inten-

sive Jewish backgrounds or possess a remarkable amount of Judaic knowledge. But somehow, over several years, we have developed a prayer atmosphere that people find unusually inspiring, warm, and full of *ruah*, enthusiastic spirit. I think that what makes our congregation's services work may offer some good general guidelines for approaching Jewish prayer.

A core of our congregation members are committed to regular communal prayer. I'm sure that some of these faithful members come to services out of commitment and loyalty, especially on Shabbat mornings when they don't necessarily feel inspired to do so and would probably prefer sleeping in.

The service follows what is basically a traditional format (in an unusually nonsexist *siddur*), and involves a good amount of Hebrew, although translations and transliteration pages are available. This is striking, considering that many if not most of the members do not have a strong background in Hebrew or Judaic studies. Yet the atmosphere is so warm and informal that people feel supported and comfortable about learning the service. Congregants are willing and happy to do all kinds of things to improve their Hebrew skills: learning phonetic reading from tapes, getting a tutor, forming their own study groups to learn to understand the Hebrew of the *siddur*, organizing a class on the prayerbook as part of a community adult education series.

The service is highly participatory. We sit in a Sephardic-style, semicircular formation where we can see each other's faces. Congregational members lead most of the services themselves. Again, however, the atmosphere is supportive and caring, so people will go far beyond their comfort level to lead parts of the service and even to learn trope so they can read the *haftarah* and Torah. The congregation itself has sought out a variety of teachers, among them a number of rabbis, and also congregants who can teach. Informal commentary on the prayers is interspersed throughout the service.

Perhaps most important, our services are alive. There is a strong sense of fellowship, of being in a worshiping and learning community rather than in an audience. Participants sing (or hum if they don't know the words), sway, discuss the Torah portion together, and ask questions if they don't understand something. Children are welcome. We don't do stiff responsive readings; rather, we *daven* in the old-fashioned way expressed by that Yiddish word.

Finally, the congregation has major involvements other than prayer, including adult, child, and family education, as well as a strong commitment to social action. The values expressed in prayer are also expressed in the congregation's communal and individual deeds.

PRAYER IDEAS FOR THE FAMILY

Make prayer a regular part of life. For many traditional Jews, that means praying daily (three times a day is the Orthodox norm). For many others, that may mean faithfully going as a family to Shabbat services every week. Those who pray with the congregation only on the High Holidays should not reasonably expect to suddenly have a spiritual experience. It's like playing with a full orchestra once a year after having neglected to practice for 50 weeks (even having forgotten, perhaps, to tune the instrument).

Traditional Jewish prayer takes place in the context of a supportive community, the synagogue, and in the context of a supportive family, the home. Berachot (blessings) over food can be recited with young children from a tender age. Take children to an orchard to pick fruit, then say the *berachah* together and taste it in wonder. *Sheheheyanu* can be said when a happy occasion or milestone in life is reached. Special blessings can be learned for new clothing, seeing a rainbow, seeing beautiful sights in nature, and God's creation. *Modeh Ani*, the wake up prayer, can be sung by the family in the morning (I find that it fits very well to the opening stanzas of the second movement of Vivaldi's Concerto in D Major for Two Violins, Lute and Basso Continuo.) *Shema Yisrael* and other bedtime prayers can be said with children at night. Children can envision the four angels around their beds (there is a lovely visualization on this at the end of the *First Jewish Catalog*),[6] and a sheltering *sukkah* of peace over their heads. Songs from the liturgy have been set to beautiful new tunes that can be sung around the table at Shabbat meals (see Music Resource Guide, p. 313).

Singing helps children and adults to learn and eventually memorize the prayers, even as it infuses the service with spirit. Swaying and "shuckling" to the rhythm of the Hebrew songs (and other nonverbal features) are an important part of many traditional prayers; in the spirit of the Psalms, one prays with the whole body, with all one's limbs. Children can grow up with these sounds and movements of prayer in the home and synagogue. In many Jewish homes, the baby's first lullabies are Hebrew songs from the prayer service or the Psalms, accompanied by the swaying of a parent's body holding her or him close. Families can seek out relaxed, *heimish* (Yiddish "homey"), congregational settings where children feel welcome and can grow up with the sights, sounds, and feelings of authentic Jewish prayer.

When prayer is part of a supportive and loving context of family and community, children as well as adults will be more motivated to struggle with the challenges of learning Hebrew, understanding the prayer book, and the other details of learning the traditional service. Rather than dispensing with the difficulties by praying mostly in English or completely discarding the traditional service, it can be richly rewarding to make the effort to explore the layers of meaning and the many Judaic associations in the traditional prayers (the Hebrew prayer vocabulary itself is generally very simple, by the way). Of course, contemporary prayers and meditations in English or Hebrew can be a meaningful enhancement of worship services.

Traditional Jewish prayer needs to be studied to be fully appreciated. At home, parents can take time to discuss prayers with their children, or to study them as a family. One family we know has their own short *tefillah* (prayer service) at home each day. They've studied the major prayers by discussing them and illustrating them with beautiful drawings. In another family, the parents often sit and pray with the children on Shabbat, taking time to discuss the prayers with them. For parents without much background in Jewish liturgy, there are many books that can help them in their study of prayer (listed in the Resource Guide on pp. 321–324). Parents also need rabbis and teachers to whom they can turn with their own prayer questions. The more we understand about the Jewish prayers, the more meaningful they will be.

With prayer, as with so many other things, community is the key to Jewish life. The synagogue is called a *beit knesset* (house of gathering), and although the social and communal elements of synagogue life should not be trivialized, it is also a *beit tefillah* (house of prayer) and a *beit midrash* (house of study). It is really worth the effort to seek out a dynamic and supportive congregational or *havurah* fellowship with which to pray and build Jewish life together. (It is even worth the effort to create one, if necessary.)

At the same time, *prayer should be understood in its proper place*. Some American Jews think of religion as heavily focused on prayer, especially formal, fixed prayer. Prayer is only one part of Judaism, which is equally expressed in other ritual and interpersonal *mitzvot* (religiously mandated deeds), in Torah study, and in ethical behaviors and interpersonal relations.

Neither is Jewish prayer confined only to the recitation of set prayers at certain times. The Jewish practice of punctuating the entire day with blessings and acknowledgments of God's goodness expands our God consciousness in daily life. There is also a Jewish tradition of spontaneous conversations with God and meditation (see Jewish meditation, in the Resource Guide, p. 321). Meditation techniques can help to nurture the inner life in preparation for prayers with the congregation.

Blessings

The sages determined that one should say a blessing for each of life's pleasures, so as to focus one's consciousness in gratitude to God. Here are a few of the blessings we can say with our children (from an early age). More prayers of gratitude can be found throughout this volume and in most traditional prayer books. All of these blessings begin:

Baruch Atah Adonai, Eloheinu Melech HaOlam . . .

"Blessed Are You, Eternal Our God, Ruler of the Universe . . ." *or*
"Holy One of Blessing, Your Presence fills creation . . ."

For witnessing lightning, falling stars, great deserts, the sea, or other wonders of nature:

Oseh Maaseh Veresheet

"Who makes the wonders of creation."

On hearing thunder:

Shekoho ugevurato malei olam

"Whose might and power fill the world."

On seeing a rainbow:

Zocher habrit, vene'eman bevrito, vekayam et maamaro

"Who remembers the covenant (with Noah), and is faithful to the covenant and loyal to the promise."

On smelling fragrant scents such as woods or barks:

Borei minei besamim

"Who creates various kinds of scents."

On smelling fragrant fruits:

HaNoten re'ah tov baperot

"Who gives a good fragrance to fruits."

On wearing a new garment for the first time (unless it is made of leather):

Malbish Arumim

"Who clothes the naked."

For long-awaited experiences such as reaching a life-cycle event, meeting a long-lost friend, affixing a *mezuzah* to a new home, celebrating an annual Holy Day, or eating a fruit for the first time that year:

Sheheheyanu vekiyemanu vehigi'anu lazman hazeh

"Who has given us life, sustained us, and enabled us to reach this time."

FAMILY SNAPSHOTS

PRAYER

When our daughter Sadie was first born, the only way to get her to sleep at night was to walk with her and sing to her. I would take her out, wrapped in a blanket, often in the middle of the night (South Texas summer temperatures allow this), and walk under the stars singing to her all the prayers I could remember, *berachas* and songs from the service like *Ein K'Eloheinu*. My idea was to imprint her with the feeling of security, lying cuddled in her Daddy's arms and hearing the prayers. It seems to have worked, and she still calms down to those melodies now . . . but I must have been quite a sight walking down a dark, quiet tree-lined street in my bathrobe in the middle of the night, carrying a newborn baby and singing Hebrew blessings.

—Saul Rosenthal

13

JEWISH EDUCATION OUTSIDE THE HOME

SELECTING A JEWISH SCHOOL FOR YOUR CHILD

While a good Jewish school can form the centerpiece of an excellent Jewish education, it is only part of the total picture. Camps and youth groups, Israel programs, the synagogue, the general environment, peer groups, role models outside the home, and particularly the home itself may all play a critical role in a young person's Jewish education. In addition, more and more Jewish educators are convinced that Jewish education is something in which the entire family unit and community should participate (see Jewish Family Education, p. 95).

WHEN TO BEGIN?

With the increasing recognition of the early childhood years as important moments for a child's Jewish identity formation, combined with the increasing numbers of Jewish mothers in the work force who are in need of day care for their young children, the popularity of Jewish preschools is on the rise. You should consider carefully the educational quality and Jewish content of the program when you enroll your child. A quality Jewish preschool will reflect a philosophy of developmentally appropriate early-childhood education, as well as Jewish values, stories, symbols, holidays, and Hebrew conveyed through stories, songs, dramatic play, puppets, creative movement, art,

and everyday interactions in the classroom. Judaism will not be isolated as a separate subject but will be integrated into the life of the school in a holistic fashion—for example, by providing Judaic objects and costumes in the dramatic play area or by learning about the Jewish concept of *tzaar baalei hayyim* (concern for animals) and favorite animal stories from the Bible and *Midrash* when the theme of study is animals. For sources of materials for Jewish preschools, see the Resource Guide, p. 333.

WHEN TO GRADUATE?

You may have guessed—the traditional Jewish answer is "never." Jewish education, the study of Torah, is a lifelong pursuit. And yet research indicates that most Jewish youngsters do not continue their Jewish educations past age *thirteen*.[1]

As elaborated in the "teen" section of this book (pp. 280–283), the adolescent years are crucial to Jewish education. Every Jewish community that is large enough to do *anything* should do whatever it takes to provide quality Jewish high school programming, and every Jewish family should require their teens to attend.

DAY SCHOOL OR SUPPLEMENTARY?

The difficult question for many committed and involved Jewish parents may be the choice of day school or supplementary school.

Of all segments of Jewish education, in recent

years all-day schools have experienced the largest proportional growth, both in numbers and in variety. All major Jewish communities and 9 out of 10 intermediate-sized Jewish communities in this country have day schools.[2] It is estimated that the number of day schools in the United States now exceeds 520 Orthodox, 70 Conservative, 12 Reform, and 30 pluralistic community schools. The percentage of Jewish students enrolled in day schools has tripled or quadrupled between the early 1960s and the late 1980s. This growth can be attributed to a number of factors, pressures from both within and without the Jewish community. Jewish particularism has become more acceptable within the Jewish community at the same time that public schooling has declined in popularity among Jews in many areas.

The growing popularity of day schools can also be attributed to the excellent Jewish education they are able to provide. Day schools have many distinct advantages when it comes to Jewish education:

● The day school is looked at by parents and children as "real school"; Jewish studies are generally taken much more seriously.

● The day school has many more hours available to devote to Judaic and Hebrew studies. Pupils can gain much more depth and breadth of knowledge and understanding.

● The day school teaches pupils who are fresh and focused, rather than tired at the end of a long school day. The day-school choice means that afternoons and Sunday mornings will be free from supplementary school, so that the child can obtain a more extensive Jewish education while still having more leisure for extracurricular pursuits.

● Ideally, the day school can integrate Judaic and general studies in a holistic way that is educationally and emotionally beneficial to the child.

● The day school can provide a supportive environment and peer group to reinforce the classroom materials.

● The school functions by the Jewish calendar, reinforcing the family's religious values and eliminating the need for absences on Jewish holidays.

Having been involved as a parent and an educator in both day and supplementary Jewish schools, I am increasingly convinced of the advantages of a day-school education. My children had previously attended the best supplementary school I could find (I directed it!) and were pri-

vately tutored as well. But when two were enrolled in a Jewish day school, their progress in Hebrew and Judaic studies within only a year's time was impressive; simultaneously, I could sense an additional emotional security on their part from going to school in a Jewish environment. They were also receiving a quality private-school education. Studies now show the lasting positive effects of a day-school education on subsequent Jewish identification and behavior as an adult.[3]

Still, for a variety of reasons, a day school is not the answer for every family. A major reason may be that day schools are private, and private education is expensive. Affluent parents who want a private school education anyway will generally find a Jewish day school to be less expensive than many other private schools, and there are usually scholarships available for the needy. However, for middle-class Jewish families, this can be a definite case of the "middle-class squeeze"—tuition represents a genuine financial sacrifice, although the family has too much income to qualify for a substantial scholarship.

Some Jewish families have an ideological bias against "parochial" schooling. This viewpoint has lost popularity in recent years, as pluralism has replaced "melting-pot homogeneity as an American ideal."[4] I would venture to say that most of us today are pragmatists and not ideologues when it comes to our children's Jewish education. Of course, parents who choose to put their children in day schools would do well to encourage friendship with children of other religions and races in non-school settings, such as extracurricular classes, summer programs, scouts, and so on.

There are other circumstances that may weigh against the choice of a day-school education. Outside large metropolitan areas, Jewish schools may not be large enough to offer programs for children with special needs such as those with learning disabilities or physical handicaps. Some small Jewish communities do not have day schools, although they are increasingly available and many parents are willing to go to the considerable effort of helping to establish such a school.

In other cases, parents may feel that the local Jewish day school available to them does not have the facilities or staff to compete with the quality of their local public or private school. Or they may dislike the local day school's educational philosophy or methods. The parents may carefully weigh the trade-offs and decide that, for them, the benefits of the day school do not outweigh the disadvantages in their particular situation.

If your choice is a Jewish supplementary school,

select a program carefully. It should allow several hours of weekly instruction, preferably more than once a week, and include a curriculum designed to make the most of the limited time frame. Round out your children's Jewish education with family learning and with informal programs such as camps and youth groups.

Choosing the Particular School

Once the type of school (day or supplementary) is chosen, the parents must go about choosing the specific school for their child. With a supplementary school, the choice of school may affect the family's choice of congregational affiliation.

Many books are available that offer suggestions for choosing a school. Obviously, parents should visit the potential school for a reasonable period of time during routine school activities and ask themselves the basic questions about school philosophy (with a Jewish school this will clearly include the religious and ideological orientation of the institution): curriculum; nonacademic studies such as arts and physical education (especially in an all-day school); facilities and general atmosphere (would you want to spend hours there?); positive and effective classroom management; safety relationships among staff, pupils, and parents; as well as financial and logistical considerations. Try to meet pupils and graduates of the school and their families to evaluate the school's appropriateness for your child.

There is a relatively new body of research known as "effective schools research," developed in such places as the University of Texas Research and Development Center for Teacher Education. Effective schools research seeks to identify those qualities most associated with the most effective educational settings. (Of course, effectiveness alone is not the only consideration. A school may be very effective in carrying out its mission and goals, but its mission and goals may consist of shaping Jews and citizens who are very different from your own personal vision for your children! Clearly, the ideological content of the school's philosophy, curriculum, and educational setting must be taken into account.) Whether our children are in a supplementary school or day-school setting, these are some of the characteristics we can look for:

● *Strong instructional focus.* This includes such characteristics as maximum engaged time, favorable teacher-pupil ratio, and frequent direct one-on-one instruction.

● *Strong instructional leadership.* Principal offers vision and sense of mission for the school as well as strong programmatic leadership; teachers are experienced and responsive to individual student needs.

● *Monitoring of performance.* Clear educational objectives are set, including concrete curricular objectives by grade level; continual monitoring of performance is built into the school routine.

● *High expectations.* There is an assumption that everyone can learn and achieve to the maximum of his or her potential.

● *Parent and community involvement.* There is a high degree of support and involvement from the parents and the lay community, and there are strong lines of communication between school and home.

● *Positive campus climate.* The total school environment is a positive and supportive one, encouraging the fulfillment of the preceding characteristics.

In addition to evaluating their Jewish school on the basis of these criteria for effective education, parents can observe the kinds of learning experiences it offers. Many educational experts are of the opinion that effective learning, especially in the younger grades, should involve plenty of active, hands-on, nonlinear experiences. Children should spend more time "moving, touching, exploring," and learning with a variety of modalities and media, rather than being immobilized at their desks, listening to lectures. Thus they will be motivated to put the necessary effort into academic achievement.[5]

Parents observing Jewish schools for young children, whether of the day or supplementary variety, should expect to see children who are eager, engaged, and enjoying active, developmentally appropriate learning experiences. This does not mean that the school curriculum should be reduced to a series of random affective encounters or that the intellectual component should not be woven into the active experience. In a good school program, it is definitely possible to achieve a skillful integration of the experiential and cognitive elements of education.

If the school you've chosen meets the description of an effective educational environment, *mazal tov*! Support the school, principal, and staff in every way you can. If, however, your current Jewish school lacks some of the ingredients for effective education, you have three basic choices:

work seriously for change in your own institution, find someplace better, or do it yourself (with a community). There are many success stories in all varieties of Jewish schooling, largely as a result of grass-roots activism by educators and parents. A host of Jewish schools and educational organizations on this continent and in Israel as well were begun by concerned educators and parents looking for *something better.* Jewish parents, so committed to excellence in general education, can work with teachers and principals to create excellence in Jewish education as well. (See "An Invitation to Consider Yourself a Jewish Educator," p. 96.)

JEWISH SPECIAL EDUCATION

Jewish education for the physically challenged and those with special developmental needs is an area that has only recently begun to receive the attention it deserves. Here again, much of this has been due to parent advocacy. Resources and referrals in Jewish special education (day school, supplementary, and informal programs) are available from a number of national Jewish educational organizations, such as CAJE, the Coalition for the Advancement of Jewish Education (which has a Special Needs network); JESNA, the Jewish Educational Service of North America; and each of the denominational movements. (See the Resource Guide, pp. 333–334, for additional information.)

Equally important is the attitudinal change required. In a success- and achievement-oriented ethnic group such as our own, having a child who is "slow" or "different" is too often seen as a source of shame or failure. Acceptance and love for all members of our community is an important Jewish *mitzvah.* It is one in which increasing numbers of Jewish educational and communal agencies are taking a part, through the establishment of programs such as support groups for parents of special needs children.

JEWISH CAMPING AND YOUTH GROUPS: THE POWER OF INFORMAL EDUCATION

My own life experiences have served to convince me of the importance of informal Jewish education. When I look back at the transformative events in my Jewish life, I particularly note the powerful effect of my experiences at Jewish summer camps and in youth groups at the local, regional, and national level.

Indeed, many Jewishly involved adults credit their summers at Jewish camps for motivating future Jewish commitments. Camps can provide supportive peer frameworks, adult mentorship, and holistic environments in which to experience Jewish living. Shabbat, Jewish study, and Hebrew songs are interwoven with enjoyable experiences in nature, appreciating the beauties of creation.

There are also several Jewish youth movements that promote a variety of religious and ideological outlooks. They can provide preteens and teens with a framework for socializing with other Jewish young people, actualizing their idealism through volunteerism, and sharing religious experiences such as services and study programs. Many emphasize Zionism and include Israel programs for teens that involve touring, study, and service.

Even day camps can provide meaningful educational experiences. One of the most gratifying experiences I've had in Jewish education has been serving as a Judaica specialist at a Jewish Community Center day camp. The children responded warmly and enthusiastically to a holistic and integrated learning program, which included stories, songs, dances, a variety of large- and small-scale art projects, and other hands-on activities on themes of Israel and Jewish tradition.

In addition to youth groups and camps, Jewish Community Centers and YM-YWHAs around the country provide a variety of programming for youngsters, including sports, arts classes, drama groups, day care, and summer programs. These vary in their degree of Jewish content, but they do have the advantage of taking place in a supportive Jewish environment.

In choosing informal educational programs such as camps and youth groups, common-sense guidelines should be used. In the case of a camp, it's best if parents and children can visit the facility in advance. Beyond camp brochures and advertisements, try to learn about the specific details of daily programming, counselor qualifications, safety, and supervision. References are important in selecting either a camp or a youth group. Find out what other youngsters' experiences have been. In the case of a youth group, keep in mind that teen peers can have significant influence on your child, so try to find out whether the group is appropriately supervised and whether the members engage in behaviors that you want your child to adopt.

94

Despite the many benefits of youth groups and camps and despite the strong anecdotal evidence for their effectiveness, studies are conflicting as to their long-term effect on Jewish identity.[6] It is likely that the significance of the camp experience is dependent on the follow-up at home and in the local synagogue and Jewish community. The intense Jewish community experienced at camp should be integrated into a year-round experience of Jewish celebrations at home, Torah study, youth group programs, and so on. Also remember that merely bunking or socializing with members of their ethnic group is not the sole object of Jewish youngsters' camping and youth groups. Meaningful programming, study, and volunteer activities, and in the case of camp, a holistic Jewish environment (for observing Shabbat, and so forth) is what makes informal education truly worthwhile.

JEWISH FAMILY EDUCATION

Judaism is a very home-oriented religion, and effective Jewish education clearly requires the active and interested involvement of the family, both in the home and in community settings. Until recently, however, Jewish education in this country has focused overwhelmingly on children. Jewish Family Education seeks to bridge the gap between the Jewish school and the home.

Jewish Family Education is a new and rapidly growing educational field. Its goals seek to:

● empower parents once again as the primary Jewish educators of their own children,

● give children a model of Judaic learning as a lifelong pursuit,

● provide Jewish experiences for families to share,

● strengthen families, and

● create stronger and more vibrant Jewish communities.

Jewish Family Education has taken a variety of forms around the country. Programs include:

● publications (from small flyers to books such as this) that are devoted to the Jewish life of the family or to teaching about Jewish home observances;

● publications designed for parents and children to share;

● retreats, family camps, and similar settings for entire families to experience *Shabbatot* and Torah study together;

● workshops, large-scale events, celebrations;

● family prayer services;

● joint or parallel classes for parents and children; and

● family reading programs.

The ideal would be for each family to "plug into" family education classes, programs, materials, and retreats—not as a substitute for home observance, but as a vehicle for learning more in order to enrich and enhance the Jewish life of their own home.

I would encourage Jewish families to work with their own schools or congregations to develop family education programs in their locale. There is a growing body of resource materials available that can help. There are also programs available for learning about family education. The annual CAJE Conference generally has a variety of classes on the subject, and CAJE also has a Family Education Network involving many talented educators. The summer intensive program on Jewish Family Education at the Whizin Institute of the University of Judaism in Los Angeles is a week-long training program for educators, rabbis, and lay leaders who want to involve their synagogue or community in family education. See the Resource Guide, pp. 331–334, for addresses.

Resource Centers and Jewish Parenting Centers

Another important venture in Jewish education is the growing number of resource centers of various types throughout North America. If these exist in your community, take advantage of them. A resource center will generally offer materials for perusal or duplication, as well as classes and seminars on Jewish educational topics for teachers and often for parents. A parenting center will, of course, focus on family concerns, addressing them from a Jewish point of view.

To find out if there is a resource center in your

area, contact your synagogue, Jewish school, or central agency for Jewish education. Jewish parenting centers may be run by Jewish community centers, Jewish family service agencies, or congregations.

AN INVITATION TO CONSIDER YOURSELF A JEWISH EDUCATOR

According to the Torah, the parent is the primary Jewish educator. As a parent, you have the greatest stake in the Jewish future—your children. The Jewish life that you create at home, the Jewish communities that you involve your family in, and the words of Torah that are woven into the fabric of your life—these are probably the most significant influences on your child's "Jewish identity." Therefore, whatever your profession, it is proper to think of yourself as *also* being a Jewish educator.

Outside your home life, there are many other ways to get involved in Jewish education. You might:

● Serve on the education committee at your synagogue.

● Participate in, and help to develop, adult Jewish education programs in your community.

● Volunteer to work in your Jewish school; there are many areas in which to serve.

● Join (or start) a parent-teacher organization at your Jewish school.

● Get involved in your local Bureau of Jewish Education, central agency for Jewish education, or the education committee of your Jewish Federation.

● You might even want to consider Jewish teaching as a vocation or avocation. Teachers for Jewish schools are in short supply almost everywhere in the United States. Consider starting as a teachers' aide at your religious school. Read books on Jewish education and attend in-service programs and/or teacher certification programs if they are available in your area. (After several years of working in Jewish education, I realized that I had primarily begun in order to teach my own children! (For further information, see the Resource Guide, pp. 331–332.)

III

JEWISH INTERPERSONAL VALUES: TRANSMITTING A GOODLY HERITAGE

14

JUDAISM: MORE THAN HOLIDAYS

Holidays, customs, and rituals are part of the story of making a Jewish home. Equally important are the nonritual areas, the Jewish interpersonal values we practice and pass on to our children. So much of Jewish life today seems concerned with *how* and *who* ("How will Judaism survive?" "Who is a Jew?" "Who is a good Jew?"). Jewish values, by contrast, are about the essential question of *why* we are Jewish.

Why we want our children and grandchildren to stay Jewish after 4,000 years of history cannot be reduced to a simple desire for ethnic continuity or "tribal" preservation. Whether or not they conceive of themselves as religious, many (if not most) Jews believe at some level that our presence as a people—despite our small numbers—has had a profound impact on civilization and that it will continue to do so in the future. Our moral and ethical stance as well as our intellectual contributions have mattered to the world and should continue to do so.

The Jewish religious perspective is even more forceful: Jews are partners in a covenant with God, commanded to live as "a nation of priests and a holy people" (Exodus 19:5), a "light unto the nations" (Isaiah 42:6). Jews, our religion explicitly teaches (and experience clearly illustrates), are certainly not the only righteous people in the world! Neither is every Jew an exemplary human being. Yet, traditional Jewish faith ascribes to us a unique mission in history as a people covenanted with God, "chosen" for—or choosing—our task not as an indication of collective superiority but from a deeply perceived moral obligation to better the world in God's service.

No parent today can be apathetic toward the many social, environmental, and health issues affecting our nation and, indeed, the entire planet our children and grandchildren will inherit. The actions we take today will determine the quality of life for all our descendents. And what is true for any parent must be all the more so for Jewish parents, whose culture and religious heritage are predicated on a deep sense of moral obligation.

But strikingly, Jewish values and ethics are based more on the prophetic vision of global human redemption than on our reaction to possibilities of doom. At the end of the most apocalyptic *haftarah* (prophetic reading), the rabbis always added a verse or two of positive vision and comfort. Suspended as we are between the all-too-real nightmares of human disaster and our seemingly irrational visions of messianic fulfillment, we always tip the psychological scales in favor of the latter. We are to look at the possibilities of death and destruction, but we are always to turn and choose life.

On a day-to-day level, Jews who give of their time, resources, and energy to heal the world do these *mitzvot* with a sense of *simhah*, of joy and gladness. These actions stem not from guilt or fear, but because it is a wonderful privilege to serve God, to act as "partners" in perfecting creation. A *mitzvah* is so marvelous to do, said the sages, that the reward for one is simply the opportunity to do another! Committed Jews, then, are hardly surprised when science and psychology "discover" that doing for others is emotionally and even physically healthy, or when educators point out that service to others can have great impact on the emotional stability of adolescents and of families.

Children today suffer from feelings of powerlessness and fear about the world's problems. Jewish values help to counter these pervasive feelings by their emphasis on the importance and potential for good of each individual and the significance of seemingly small but regular actions. Judaism teaches that every individual matters, that every action counts, and that, with God's help, human beings can truly make a difference.

SOCIAL CONCERN IS A SPIRITUAL ISSUE

What message have you for young people?" asked Carl Stern of NBC in concluding a television interview with Rabbi Abraham Joshua Heschel shortly before Heschel's death.

Rabbi Heschel replied: ". . . Let them remember that there is a meaning beyond absurdity. Let them be sure that every deed counts, that every word has power, and that we all can do our share to redeem the world in spite of all absurdities and frustrations and disappointments.

"And, above all, [let them] remember . . . to build a life as if it were a work of art."

—Abraham Joshua Heschel[1]

Jewish values include both our relationship with God and our relationships with other people. In classic Jewish thought, the two are inseparable. In his book *To Raise a Jewish Child*,[2] Rabbi Hayim HaLevy Donin offers a summary of major Jewish values that includes both *spiritual* values—love and reverence for God, striving for holiness, study of Torah, and cherishing the land of Israel—and *social and moral* values—loving one's "neighbor," respecting human dignity, treating all people equally, regarding life as sacred, loving justice and compassion, and showing civic responsibility and creativity. He does not distinguish between the two or categorize them separately. Both are essential to Jewish education. Both are manifestations of the Jewish ethos.

Indeed, many of the ritual practices of Judaism serve to educate us toward sensitivity and ethical behavior. One small example: it is customary to cover the *hallah* during *kiddush*, as if to "protect its feelings," because it is not blessed first. A story tells how a husband once chided his wife for neglecting to cover the *hallah*. A noted rabbi who was their Shabbat dinner guest gently rebuked the husband: If we should be considerate of the "feelings" of a loaf of bread, how much the more so should we value the feelings of a person created in God's image.

The social and moral values of Judaism are traditionally known as the *mitzvot shebein adam lehavero* (interpersonal precepts), in contrast to the *mitzvot shebein adam laMakom* (commandments between a person and God). The section that follows focuses primarily on the interpersonal values, since issues such as learning, Shabbat and holiday observance, and Torah study are explored in depth in other sections. But it should always be kept in mind that the interpersonal values of Judaism flow from the spiritual values. It is *because* we love and revere God and *because* we learn and practice the Torah that we view life as sacred, for the Torah stresses that every human being is created "in God's image" and that human beings are God's "partners" in completing the work of creation. Because we believe in God as the supreme moral arbiter, we must never "follow a multitude to do evil" toward another person or group (Exodus 23:2).

For the Jewish believer, then, ethics are more than enlightened self-interest or social contract; they are a sacred obligation. Doing a *mitzvah* for another person is a spiritual expression just as much as is prayer. (Interestingly, some recent scientific studies indicate that the physiological effects of altruistic behavior are similar to those derived from meditation.)[3]

PARTICULARISM OR UNIVERSALISM?

Traditionally, Jews often lived in isolated, insular communities, and it was within our own communities that the interpersonal *mitzvot* were generously practiced. Even today, the most traditional Jewish communities give, loan, lend to, and help their own such as few other groups do. But what of a broader commitment to humanity? Is that a concern only for the assimilated, "universalist" Jew who has little interest in the traditional sources? I believe that the opposite should be the case.

A "particular universalism" means acting for the greater good of society, but out of our particular Jewish ethos, our unique moral heritage. Many Jewish activists today are working to bridge the perceived dichotomy between Jewish social values and conscious Jewish identity. This approach knows no political boundaries: One can find it in conservatively oriented publications such as Dennis Prager's *Ultimate Issues* (and his books and lectures), in liberal ones such as *Tikkun* (with its conferences and discussion groups) (listings in the Resource Guide to Periodicals, p. 326), as well as in the apolitical, humanistic orientation of Jewish writer-educators such as Danny Siegel. It is found in the growth of organizations such as Mazon, The Shalom Center, The Jewish Fund for Justice, the American Jewish World Service, and Shomrei Adamah, Jewish groups that approach "universalist" social concerns (hunger, world peace, poverty, social inequality, the environment) out of a distinctly Jewish consciousness.

The particular needs of the Jewish community are certainly no less worthy or legitimate than are those of other groups, and hard experience has taught us that we can't expect others to make them a priority if we don't. Yet we can hardly afford to emphasize *only* our internal communal needs to the exclusion of a world in which we are a tiny minority and to which the fate of every human being is linked. Serving as "a light unto the nations" means more than setting an example of pious communal behavior. It means that the world's Jewish community, small as it is, will continue to communicate a distinctive value framework, exemplify the moral life, and act as a catalyst for redeeming social change. (In an era when Jews have regained some political and military power, our ethical standards are put to their truest test. All of us are bound together in responsibility for the outcome.)

The tension between particularism and universalism is an old one in Judaism. As with many other issues, these ideas are debated in rabbinic sources. Part of the richness of Judaism is that, over the course of our long history, many seemingly opposing points of view have been woven together into a synergistic whole. For example, we have the *Alenu* prayer at the end of our service, which begins by thanking God for our particular identity as Jews but continues into a vision of *tikkun olam* and a universal kingdom of God. We can do the most for "universal" causes not by obscuring our unique heritage and identity, but rather through knowing who we are and by striving to be worthy of what the *Alenu* prayer calls our distinctive "destiny."

As Abba Eban has written, "A robust sense of identity has not prevented this people from sending the repercussions of its influence far and wide into the oceans of universal history. It is when historic Israel is most persistently distinctive that its universal vocation is enlarged. The lesson of history is plain. There is no salvation or significance for the Jew except when he aims high and stands straight within his own authentic frame of values."[4]

Or, as Hillel said it nearly two millennia ago: "If I am not for myself, who will be for me? And if I am only for myself, what (good) am I? And if not now, when?" (*Pirke Avot* 1:14).

SOME WAYS TO TEACH JEWISH VALUES

NAME THEM

Using Hebrew value-words and expressions often in daily conversation can place values education and discipline in the deeper context of our Jewish heritage. (See chapter 15, "Jewish Values Vocabulary.")

MITZVAH TALK

What do parents talk to their children about everyday? We've all heard about those studies that show that many parents spend but a few minutes a day communicating with their offspring, mainly discussing practical concerns ("Is your homework done?").

"Torah Talk," regular discussions of Jewish topics as a natural aspect of family life, are one way of enriching the discourse with our children (see pp. 73–74). Those Torah Talks, which revolve mainly around values and *tzedakah*, could be dubbed "*Mitzvah* Talk." (Of course, we want to do more than preach, but talking and teaching are important parts of the process.) Educators agree that parents shouldn't reserve values discussions for those times when a child has done something wrong, but should regularly talk about values in a positive way at the child's level. Here are some ideas:

● Discuss examples of values dilemmas from the Torah portion, holiday readings, or from other Jewish texts, stories, Jewish and general history, your own childhood or your child's world, and—as children grow—especially from current events.

● Clip articles, editorials, and political cartoons from newspapers and news magazines; discuss them at dinner. As children grow into adolescence, they need to begin to understand the complex causes of social and environmental problems.

● Some calendars cite daily historical events of social, ethical, or environmental significance, and these can provide materials for values talks.

● When learning about current events, encourage your children to ask themselves: What would I have done in this situation? What Jewish values apply to this situation? Is this a person I would like to emulate? How could I be like him or her?

MODEL, MODEL, MODEL

According to nationally noted child psychologist Eda LeShan, modeling the values we believe in is the number one, yet least acknowledged, way we teach our children how to act.[5] The moral character and behavior our children see in us have primary impact on their own moral development. As Heschel said, the parent must be "worthy of reverence." Our actions, both at home and in the larger community, will always speak louder than words. (The one time not to be an "anonymous donor" is with our children; part of their values education is knowing what our involvements are in *tzedakah*, *hesed*, volunteering, and so forth.) One writer says that in values education, in general, showing seems to be more effective than telling.

FAMILY TORAH STUDY

A simple family discussion of issues in the weekly Torah portion or other Jewish text can form a basis for teaching children about Jewish values and their meaning for our lives. For specific suggestions on family Torah study, see pp. 73–74.

JEWISH STORIES

Jewish stories can convey Jewish values in a context of love and warmth. Especially important are real-life stories of *tzaddikim*, righteous persons, or "*mitzvah* heroes," both from history and from contemporary life, who are worthy role models for children and adults. Make it a family custom to read and/or tell Jewish stories at least on each Shabbat and holiday.

CREATIVE EXPRESSION

For extra enrichment, consider creative projects: make a picture, poster, or bulletin board display to illustrate a Jewish values concept, saying, or quotation from the *Pirke Avot* or other text. Make and wear a button or T-shirt with a value-word or Torah saying. Rabbi Howard Bogot, formerly curriculum director for the Union of American Hebrew Congregations, suggests making a collage to illustrate a word of value-vocabulary, or writing various value-words (*mensch*, *hesed*) on peel-and-stick labels to be awarded to young children when they act out the behavior it describes.

EMPHASIZE THE ETHICAL ASPECT OF JEWISH HOLIDAYS AND LIFE-CYCLE EVENTS

Jewish holidays provide regular instruction about many ethical concepts, as I highlight in sections on Shabbat and the Jewish holidays. (See pp. 118–122 for a table of ideas on *tzedakah* projects for various holiday and life-cycle events.)

EVERYDAY *MITZVAH* PROJECTS

All the preceding strategies culminate in specific family activities: *mitzvah* projects, *tzedakah* projects, or whatever you'd like to call them. (*Mitzvah* is used here in the more colloquial sense of referring to the interpersonal values and precepts.) Just as the family regularly observes holidays, celebrations, and cultural or educational activities together and incorporates these into their regular routine, they should also choose *mitzvah* activities to do together on a regular basis.

Projects work best if generated from the children's real interests. For example, a child interested in animals might want to become involved with the animal shelter or the Delta Society (which brings pets to visit nursing homes and other facilities), while a youngster interested in physical construction might be "turned on" by volunteering for a group that builds inexpensive homes for low-income families. As children grow, a family discussion or meeting could be a good forum for deciding which projects to do. Optimally, these activities will include both monetary or material giving and actual hands-on action. Children learn by doing.

Children who experience *mitzvah* projects as a regular part of life often begin to surprise their parents by initiating projects on their own. So be prepared for the "price of success" when your children insist on recycling, caring for the poor or homeless, and generally getting involved despite the inconvenience.

Of course, the number, frequency, and sophistication of *mitzvah* projects depend on variables including family size, resources, time available, and so on; but every family can do *something*. In the Jewish view, modest but regular actions are valued, for "one *mitzvah* draws another." Even if we begin small, we have put our feet on the right path; there is a traditional Jewish belief that God will lead us further on whichever life path we choose.

The following section on *mitzvah* projects (chapter 16) offers suggested family activities organized into several key areas of the Jewish values scheme. The Resource Guide (pp. 336–339) lists organizations that work in each area, for those who want to give *tzedakah* and/or become more actively involved in specific causes.

Why *Mitzvah* Projects?

Rabbi Elazar asked: What was the blessing Moses recited before reading the Torah? "Blessed are You . . . Who has chosen this Torah, has made it holy, and has taken delight in those who fulfill it." He did not say, "those who work hard at studying it" nor "those who think deeply about it and expound upon it," but rather—"those who fulfill it," those who live out their lives according to the words of Torah.
—*Midrash* on Deuteronomy

If we want our children to appreciate music or reading, we don't just *talk about* music or books; we encourage our children to practice their instruments, we take them to the library and to concerts, and we make sure they see us reading. Similarly, with values, words alone do not suffice. Values education must include backing speech with action.

Some will say that this is mere tokenism: Our family collecting for the food bank will not stop world hunger; even a nation of food banks may be an evasion of the root causes of hunger and inequality. I would say, however, that the Jewish approach operates on all levels. There is *pikuah nefesh*, doing whatever immediate action is needed to preserve life. There is also the broader consideration of *tikkun olam*, setting the world aright. We have to consider immediate needs as well as work for long-term solutions.

The Jewish approach also affirms the importance of many small actions, many tiny steps that together produce the greater results: "Whosoever saves *one* life, saves an entire world"—neither "save the world" nor nihilism.

Families will find that *mitzvot* are habit forming. Once you get started, you want to experience that "*mitzvah* high" (*simhah shel mitzvah*) again. Some psychologists have noted that doing for others is a "positive addiction" just as much as meditation, yoga, or aerobic exercise can be, if not more so. Still other studies have indicated that service to others as a family is a trait that fosters family health. Those involved with adolescents particularly stress that volunteering and giving to others help teens transcend their self-absorption and put their personal problems into perspective. *Mitzvah* action also gives children the important, but all too rare, sense of their own personal power to effect constructive change. Obviously, it's best to get kids in the habit as early as possible, so that *mitzvot* are already a natural part of their life going into the vulnerable adolescent years. Although a Jew doesn't need a reason to do a *mitzvah*, she or he can readily appreciate the personal benefits that flow from it. Social and medical science are simply rediscovering what Torah knew all along: Doing good is good for us.

Most crucially, though, we do *mitzvah* activities because Jewish family life is directed outward as well as inward. The family should not be a lonely satellite, but a vital part of an interconnected web of community. We are dedicating/educating (it's virtually the same word in Hebrew) our children for a sense of purpose in life, for a sense of responsibility to the world, and for a feeling that our lives can and should make a difference. *Mitzvah* projects are "hands-on" education for *tikkun olam*. They are not only meaningful and often enjoyable activities in themselves, but are an integral part of the Jewish ethos.

15

JEWISH VALUES VOCABULARY

While the Eskimo language has many words for snow, Hebrew (and other Jewish languages such as Yiddish and Ladino) are ripe with "values vocabulary." For starters, we have dozens of names and expressions for describing God. We also have myriad rich, meaningful words that describe interpersonal values and ethics with refinement and power.

These "Jewish words" are much more than ethnic expressions. These are not simple translation of English words, but carry distinctively Jewish connotations. They reverberate with centuries of meaning in Jewish text and philosophy. The use of specific Hebrew values-words teaches our children that there is a specific framework of Jewish values, sometimes overlapping with, or inspiring or learning from, but always maintaining an essential distinctiveness from other religious or humanistic value systems. Being a Jew is much more than "being a nice person" who happens to observe different holidays a couple of times a year. Being a Jew encompasses a distinctive ethos, a particular life-orientation.

These words should be incorporated into everyday speech in the Jewish home. When children do something kind or considerate, rather than saying "You're a good boy," or "What a nice girl!" we can tell them instead: "That was really a *mitzvah*," or "You really did a *hesed*," or "You're behaving like a *mensch*." Or instead of, "You're being naughty," we can say, "How might you show your little brother *hesed*?" The difference is significant. We are no longer continually evaluating our children in a personal way (an approach that, when over-

done, tends to become hollow or even damaging): We are representing the Jewish heritage to them and educating them to take their place in it. Moreover, many common social behaviors, such as hospitality, pleasant speech, visiting the sick, which modern secular society views as mere etiquette, can become deep religious expressions when we see them in a Jewish perspective.

A PARTIAL LEXICON OF "JEWISH VALUES VOCABULARY"

All words are Hebrew unless noted as Yiddish.

THE CENTRAL CONCEPT

● *Tikkun olam*, "repairing the world," could be the overarching concept of Jewish values vocabulary. It is a term with origins in Kabballah (Jewish mysticism), which saw every *mitzvah* as an act of cosmic significance, repairing a shattering that dated back to Creation. Today *tikkun olam* has popularly come to mean the ultimate goals of Jewish activism: partnership with God and one another in transforming, healing, and improving life on this earth.

Classically, the end result of this *tikkun* is believed to be an anticipated messianic age, whether perceived in supernatural terms by traditionalists or in more humanistic terms by liberals. It signifies a faith in humanity's future on this earth. In recent years, some people have suggested that having children in this day and age is merely an act of selfishness in a deteriorating world. The concept of *tikkun olam*, by contrast, means that we see ourselves as positive instruments for change in the world and see our children as the inheritors of our sacred mission.

THE VOCABULARY OF RIGHTEOUS AND LOVING BEHAVIOR

● *Mitzvah* (plural: *mitzvot*): The colloquial translation is "a good or meritorious deed." However, *mitzvah* literally means a religious "commandment," "imperative," or "duty." Shabbat observance is a *mitzvah*, fasting on Yom Kippur is a *mitzvah*; so are giving *tzedakah* and seeking justice and pursuing peace and visiting the sick *mitzvot*. Taken together, *mitzvot* make up a lifepath (*halachah*) of actions through which we emulate and draw closer to the Divine. *Mitzvot* originally come from the Torah, together with the Oral Tradition expressed in the Talmud and other rabbinic writings.

Science is now demonstrating what Torah knew all along: Good deeds can be pleasurable, even healthful. Even when the particular situation at hand is not ostensibly a happy one, there is a deep ongoing satisfaction of living with a *mitzvah* orientation, *Simhah shel Mitzvah*, "The joy of (doing) *mitzvot*." The Talmud teaches that the Divine Presence (*Shechinah*) rests upon a person through the *joyful* fulfillment of *mitzvot* (*Shabbat* 30b).

● *Tzedakah*: This is the word usually translated as "charity." However, where charity implies something done out of the goodness of our hearts, *tzedakah* comes from the Hebrew word *tzedek*, meaning "justice," or "righteousness," thus implying that our action of giving or helping is the only just, right, necessary, divinely mandated thing to do. Since biblical times, *tzedakah* has been integral to Jewish life. It takes the form of concern for the weak, the poor, the stranger, the oppressed. According to the great medieval commentator Maimonides (the Rambam), the better the dignity of the recipient is preserved, the higher the level of *tzedakah*, and the highest form of all is enabling a person to become self-sufficient.

Tzedakah can be an entire life-orientation. "Personalized *tzedakah*," the term coined by *tzedakah*-activist Danny Siegel, means an acute sense of personal responsibility and the power of the individual, as well as a deep commitment to the dignity and humanity in every other person. It means weaving deeds of sharing, caring, and giving into the everyday lives of our families and communities.

● *Tzaddik*: Another variant of the same root, a *tzaddik* (feminine: *tzaddeket*) is a truly righteous, altruistic person, one who consistently goes beyond what the letter of the law demands (*lifnim meshurat hadin*) out of a passion for justice and mercy. This is the Jewish role model, the ideal that generations of Jewish parents held up to their children.

● *Mensch*: (Yiddish) A person, a human being—that is, what a human being is meant to be like. Maybe not everyone can merit to be a *tzaddik*, but everyone can try to be a *mensch*, a caring, mature, decent person. A *mensch* is what Jewish parents want their children to become, so this is an ideal word for household use. You can even make *mensch* stickers to recognize *menschlich* behavior.

● *Hesed*: *Hesed* means kindness, or more precisely, "compassionate love," "lovingkindness," or "giving love." *Hesed* is considered essential for a good marriage and family life. Hesed, however, is more than an attitude; it always implies action. As the inseparable partner of *tzedakah*, it is generally taken to mean the nonmonetary aspect of giving to others. It encompasses a range of caring actions known as *gemilut hasadim*, deeds of kindness. Such deeds include welcoming strangers, visiting the sick, dowering poor brides, and comforting the mourner, as well as simple everyday demonstration of care and concern for other people.

The rabbis called *hesed* even greater than *tzedakah*, because it applies to more potential recipients. And while *tzedakah* has limits (20 percent of one's income, said the Rambam), *hesed* does not. It is *tzedakah*'s more fluid partner.

THE VOCABULARY FOR PEACE AND THE SANCTITY OF LIFE

● *Shalom*: Peace. The word is also used as a Hebrew greeting and parting, "hello," and "goodbye"; on the Sabbath (and just prior to the Sabbath) it becomes "*Shabbat Shalom*." *Shalom* comes from a root word indicating "wholeness" or "completion"; thus its meaning is far deeper than a mere absence of hostilities. An important example is *shelom bayit*, peace in the home, domestic harmony, which is considered a primary Jewish value.

● *Pikuah nefesh*: Saving a life; the Talmud says that saving one life is like saving an entire world. In classic Jewish thought, any other commandment must be broken in order to save a life (including one's own), except for three capital offenses: murder, idolatry, and incest. *Pikuah nefesh* isn't always a dramatic act of rescue; helping to educate and support a child so she or he can have a better life may be a *pikuah nefesh* in the long run.

● Closely related is the *mitzvah* to ransom captives. Today *pidyon shevuyim* (redeeming captives) may be used to refer to action on behalf of Jews and others living under oppressive regimes or to obtain help for political prisoners in danger of torture or death.

THE VOCABULARY FOR PROPER BEHAVIOR AND ETHICAL DEVELOPMENT

● *Derech eretz*: The acceptable way, generally taken to mean good manners. This implies not merely etiquette, but high standards of honorable, dignified behavior, self-sufficiency, respectable appearance, and genuine concern for others' feelings. *Derech eretz* was viewed by the Sages as going hand in hand with observing the Torah. *Derech eretz* is the phrase that reminds children of the standards we hold for proper behavior.

● *Lashon tov*: "Good speech." The great emphasis on proper speech is one of the unique aspects of Jewish values. Jewish law considers the *kashrut* of what comes out of our mouths (words) at least as important as the *kashrut* of what goes into them. Especially to be avoided is *lashon hara*, "evil speech," which means any slanderous gossip about others, even if true. Children can make "Don't speak *lashon hara*" signs to place on the phone, as home reminders about the importance of watching one's words.

● *Musar*: Ethics: the *Musar* Movement in nineteenth-century Europe, founded by Rabbi Israel Salanter, strove to refocus Jewish sensibilities from pride in learning to building one's character and engaging in scrupulously ethical behavior. The ethicist movement also coined the Hebrew-Yiddish term *musar shmooze*, meaning a talk about values and behavior, a "heart-to-heart." In a certain form this was one of the *Musar* movement's key techniques for behavior modification. For the contemporary parent, I think it can also indicate the need to make values and ethics regular conversation topics.

● *Middah* (plural *middot* or *middot tovot*): (Desirable) qualities or character traits. The Jewish sages saw the emulation of Godly *middot* or qualities (compassion, patience, truth, lovingkindness) as a way to draw closer to the Divine. The thirteen *middot* particularly advocated by Reb Yisroel Salanter's *Musar* movement were truth, alertness, diligence, respect, peace of mind, gentleness, cleanliness, patience, orderliness, humility, righteousness, thrift, and silence.

Parents need to be consciously aware of what kind of *middot* we want our children to develop and if the way the children are being raised truly encourages these *middot*.

● *Emet*: Truth, honesty, fairness, the highest ethical standards in all areas of life. The attitudes our children absorb at home—everything from the issue of "white lies" to casual comments about our professional and business philosophies—teach them more than a thousand lectures on the subject. The Torah has a complete values vocabulary and set of laws for business ethics. Jews indicted for dishonest business dealings, even outbreaks of cheating in some Jewish schools, have rightly been viewed as serious symptoms of communal spiritual distress.

THE VOCABULARY OF DIGNITY AND HONOR

● *Kavcd*: Respect, honor, dignity. Jewish ethics are based on an attitude of respect for the dignity of every person, fear to cause another *bushah* (shame). "Let your friend's honor be as dear to you as your own (*Pirke Avot* 2:15). Every person on earth is seen as created in God's image. Each person is a priceless, irreplaceable *neshamah*, or soul. Jewish family relationships are also predicated on this attitude of respect and honor.

In particular, respect for parents and teachers is seen as the basis for respect for God. *Kibud Av Ve'Em*, honoring father and mother (the fifth commandment of the Ten Commandments), is a basic tenet of Jewish family relations. Jewish parenting is a balance between encouraging independence and cooperation while maintaining our authority as parents.

We also teach by the way we talk about and

relate to our own parents and older relatives. Honoring elders is a classical Jewish value that contrasts strongly with contemporary attitudes. Judaism mandates an attitude of respect and appreciation for the wisdom, experience, and talents that can come with years. Our children can learn from and make friends with older adults in a variety of private and community settings.

THE VOCABULARY OF CONCERN FOR ALL OF CREATION

● *Tzaar Baalei Hayyim*: (Concern for the) suffering of all living creatures. Jewish law is concerned with the welfare of animals as fellow living creatures of God. Many of the Torah's agriculture laws were concerned with the suffering of animals. The laws of *kashrut* are held by some to be a compromise with the ideal of vegetarianism, and hunting for "sport" has always been antithetical to Judaism. As animal rights become a greater concern for people, the Jewish perspective is worth examining.

● *Shemirat HaAdamah*: Guardianship of the earth, contemporary Hebrew term employed by Jewish conservationists to describe the proper human attitude toward nature: stewardship rather than exploitation. *Bal tashhit*, "do not destroy," is an expression for the Torah law against wantonly destroying fruit trees during a seige. By extension this became a prohibition of any type of needless destruction, either of food, property, or any of the earth's resources. In Jewish thought, the earth is our trust, not our property to exploit as we will.

16

FAMILY *MITZVAH* PROJECTS

Rabbi Simla'i sermonized: "The Torah begins and ends with acts of lovingkindness—it begins with an act of lovingkindness as it says, 'The Lord made clothing of skins for Adam and his wife, and He clothed them' (Genesis 3:20). It ends with an act of lovingkindness, as it says, 'And he buried Moses there in the valley' (Deuteronomy 34:6)."
—Talmud, *Sotah* 14a

It is good to give *tzedakah* before praying.
—*Shulhan Aruch, Orah Hayyim* 92:10

TZEDAKAH AND *HESED*: DEEDS OF CHARITY, JUSTICE, AND KINDNESS

As noted in the preceding values vocabulary section, *tzedakah*, although usually translated as "charity," properly means a righteous action, doing the right and necessary thing. *Tzedakah* may involve direct monetary contributions, material assistance, or, at its highest, providing the support and assistance that helps others become able to realize their fullest potential on their own.

Hesed, loving-kindness, or *gemilut hasadim* (doing deeds of loving-kindness), is a closely related concept. Here the emphasis is less on material assistance and more on personal interaction. In practice *tzedakah*, *hesed*, and the many variations

thereof are closely intertwined, so they are combined here.

FAMILY ACTIVITIES

● Make or purchase *tzedakah* boxes (*pushkes*) to place around the house; contribute frequently and involve the children. Tie the practice to Jewish celebrations by putting money in before candle lighting, or in honor of anything, from current events to *yartzeits*. The *yartzeit* notes for notable Jews in Michael Strassfeld's annual "The Jewish Calendar" [Universe] are a good source for such commemorations.

How to make your own *tzedakah* boxes: Various clean, dry containers can be recycled as *tzedakah* boxes, as long as you arrange a way for the money to get in and out. Cocoa boxes (metal or plastic) have a perfect shape and a removable lid. We've made very nice *pushkes* from white cardboard containers of various shapes, used for gift-wrapping cookies and ice cream, that we purchased from a store that sells wrapping and organizing supplies. The boxes were decorated simply with paint pens or more elaborately with glued-on collages of pictures and appropriate sayings, culled from magazines and old Judaica catalogs. Colored tissue scraps were glued on along with the pictures. The resulting collage was covered with a wash of *thinned* white glue. (Use brushes to attach the pictures and spread the glue wash.) The results can be beautiful, and adults as well as children may enjoy the artwork involved. The word *tzeda-*

kah, and perhaps some circles representing coins, can be written on with gold or silver paint pens.

If the box is for just a certain fund, add the name of the fund. The pictures can be thematic, too: nature pictures for an environmental fund, food photos for feeding the hungry.

● Have a family *tzedakah* council, perhaps as part of regular weekly or monthly family meetings. Keep a letter holder or file in which you save mail from charitable organizations to discuss at the "council" or at mealtimes. Decide which organizations to donate to as a family. Donations could come from your *pushke* savings and family fund-raising projects (a garage sale for *tzedakah*), as well as from a regular percentage of the family budget. You could also use this time for reading or studying Jewish texts or stories about *tzedakah*.

There are a variety of ways to organize a family *tzedakah* council. Issues to decide upon include consensus versus majority decisions, a set amount of money for each request versus judging each on its own merits, supporting one or two major institutions versus making some response to all. Parents may wish to decide in advance how much of the family budget will be devoted to *tzedakah* and how much of that amount the children can be involved in deciding its destination. Some families gradually involve older children in this level of decision making. (The classic Jewish standard was to tithe from 10 to 20 percent of one's income; even recipients of *tzedakah* were expected to donate a small amount. As with other *mitzvot*, where we fall short of the ideal, we can adopt an approach of gradual increases.)

● Open a special checking account set aside only for *tzedakah*. Make regular deposits and then decide at your meetings where to donate the money.

● With other families from your synagogue or *havurah*, organize a *tzedakah* collective. Members can pool money, learn together about various organizations, decide by consensus or vote where to donate money and/or other goods and services, spend some time at each meeting studying about the *mitzvah* of *tzedakah*. Make it fun by breaking afterward for music and refreshments. Here, too, there are a number of issues to be addressed; for example, does each family donate the same amount? If not, does each get the same voting power?

The Third Jewish Catalog, edited by Mary Gendler and Sharon and Michael Strassfeld,[1] has useful guidelines for both *tzedakah* collectives and family *tzedakah* projects.

● Get into what *tzedakah* activist Danny Siegel calls the "*tzedakah* habit." Purchase an extra non-perishable food (or personal toiletry) item each time you shop. Set aside a box or shelf for these *tzedakah* items, or decorate a plastic tub with paint pens and label it "tzedakah." When it gets full, bring it directly to a food bank or a collection point set up at your synagogue, Jewish Community Center, or school. If they don't have collection points yet, help to get them set up, with someone designated to take the full containers to a local food bank (the food bank will often pick them up).

● During *Elul*, decide on a family *mitzvah* project for the year ahead. Learn about the needs in your own community and consider what you have to offer. Examples: regularly visiting an elderly person who lives alone or in a nursing home (contact your Jewish Family Service, Jewish nursing home, or special outreach organization, if one exists in your area), packing food at a local food bank, working one evening a week at a shelter, clearing land for low-cost housing, helping with recreational activities for the mentally disabled, or delivering needed supplies or respite care for a handicapped child. If the project is something you must do reliably for an extended period of time, think the logistics through carefully and start small, but faithfully. If you can't take on a weekly or monthly responsibility at present, start with short-term efforts, such as packing Passover supplies for needy Jews, volunteering at a local Special Olympics, or waiting tables at a holiday dinner for the needy, as often as your schedule allows.

● *Hachnasat orchim*: The Jewish concept of hospitality is really looking at your home in a new way. You see your home not as a showplace, a "cocoon," or a castle, but as a central hub of love and caring into which you welcome others and make them part of your extended family. You start to be "on the lookout" for opportunities to invite those far from home and family, those who want to experience Jewish life, or simply people in need of companionship. Jewish Shabbat and holiday meals are the natural opportunities to begin this *mitzvah*.

Consider the needs of single people of different ages or single parents who may find it difficult to create the kind of celebrations they would like on their own. If you are a single parent or a parent with limited income who may feel isolated but can't afford to host others, consider "pot luck" Shabbat suppers with friends or a *havurah*. It's helpful, too, if synagogues set up a committee to make *shidduchim* between guests and hosts for Shabbat and festival meals.

● *Bikur Holim*: Visiting the sick may be a *mitzvah* in which it is problematic for young children to participate because they are not allowed to visit hospitals and very sick people. But often they are welcome to visit nursing and convalescent homes and indeed may bring much joy. You can look into respite care for handicapped youngsters, which can also teach your children to value people who are different.

Children can also make "get well" cards and calls, and can otherwise be introduced to this important *mitzvah*. It's so easy to forget those who are out of sight because of extended illness—and the needs and stresses of their families—yet Jewish tradition views this as a crucial *mitzvah*. It is one of the times that friends need us most, and modern science is corroborating the importance of a person's emotional well-being in promoting health and healing.

● Choose a "special *mitzvah*" of your own, and encourage your children to do likewise. *Hasidim* in days of old sometimes chose one special *mitzvah* (either ritual or interpersonal), which they would make special efforts to fulfill in the most exemplary way possible. These days, perhaps all of us ought to choose one "ritual-sphere" *mitzvah* to promote (Shabbat, Jewish education), and at least one interpersonal *mitzvah* to consider our special favorite that we'll almost always go out of our way to do. The latter needn't be something grandiose; indeed, it might be something as simple as giving rides to elderly people whenever the opportunity arises, or helping out new mothers, or inviting anyone who needs an invitation to your *seders*. (Ask older members of your family. I'll bet they had a "special" *mitzvah* or two, like my grandmother who always visited the sick and made them laugh and forget their troubles. These are the stories that children need to hear!)

"From the time our kids were toddlers we spent regular time visiting and playing with profoundly handicapped children as an extension of the *mitzvah* of *bikur holim*. This is easier to arrange and exposes the children to peers they might never meet," say Wendy and Stan Drezek.

● Does your synagogue have these two *active* committees: a Community Action or Social Action committee to foster members' (of all ages) participation in *tikkun olam* (bettering the world) in the local sphere and beyond—and a *Mitzvah* (or some such name) committee to look out for the group's own members who are in need of extra help, comfort, hospitality, and emotional or material assistance?

● Become a one-family *mitzvah* and community action committee, too. The busyness of contemporary life seems to militate against the traditional Jewish values of simply looking out for the unspoken needs, both material and emotional, of other human beings. Jewish tradition is replete with tales of exemplary men and women, admired not for their good looks, cleverness, or power, but for their lifelong concern for others. And that concern was generally a family affair in which each child was trained to be a *mensch* (decent, caring person) and even aspired to be a *tzaddik* or *tzaddeket* (truly righteous, altruistic person).

● Turn an ordinary bulletin board into a *mitzvah* message center. Decorate it and dedicate it to displaying things such as brochures about *tzedakah* organizations, articles about social issues in which you want to become involved, and notes to yourself about people who need a phone call or a visit. Keep it in your kitchen or family room as a visual reminder to do *mitzvot*.

● Make gatherings large or small into *tzedakah* opportunities, and always let your kids know about what you are doing and contribute ideas and participate as much as their ages allow. Ask participants to bring warm clothing, canned goods, or other donations. Share your joy with those less fortunate: Mazon, a Jewish organization that fights hunger, asks Jews to donate 3 percent of the cost of every *simhah* to feeding the hungry. (Many synagogues throughout the United States have voted to institute this practice.) Decide where you could cut costs on your event by making it less lavish and donating the savings to *tzedakah*. Don't throw out the leftover food and flowers. Food can be taken to a community soup kitchen. Flowers and decorations can brighten an old-age home. (But please don't forget employees or even attendees at the *simhah* who could benefit from tactfully offered gifts.)

See the table on pp. 118–122 for more suggestions on how to tie specific holidays and life-cycle events in with appropriate *tzedakah* projects. Judaism does not espouse asceticism, but Jewish communities throughout the ages have also instituted sumptuary laws that curbed conspicuous consumption. Lavishness is not only wasteful, but places painful pressures on less wealthy families to outspend their means in order to keep up with their neighbors.

● Hold a *"tzedakah* fair" at your Jewish organization. Set up tables with literature and promotional materials for various groups; visitors can learn, give, sign up, write letters. Selling buttons, bumper stickers, and money-raising items (such as crafts made by Jerusalem's Lifeline for the Old) tends to work well. Invite *"mitzvah* heroes" to address and inspire your group. Make sure that there are activities for adults as well as for youngsters.

● Use your professional abilities, business, or hobby for *tzedakah* by donating your time, talents, or goods on a *pro bono* basis. Again, don't be an anonymous donor with your own children; let them know about what you do, even accompany you at times if appropriate. Consider it part of their education.

● Recycle your possessions. "Recycling" isn't only about trash. Most of us own many things that we barely use. The Jewish view of property is basically stewardship of God's world. *Bal tashhit*—don't wantonly destroy—is a Torah commandment. (And giving things away is a *mitzvah* that children love to do, often as much as they love getting things.)

In traditionally religious neighborhoods in Israel one finds "GeMaH" (*Gemilut Hasadim*) funds, which loan out everything from tools to clothing to baby equipment. How about starting one in your synagogue or school? Or how about a match-up service or trading party for "hand-me-downs"? Given the high cost of living and the growing need to conserve resources today, we all need to share more.

Two caveats about giving things away: First, some thrift shops have been exposed as highly profit-making operations that give only a small percentage of their proceeds to the charities they are supposed to be serving. So check them out. You're on the safe side with organizations that give to direct recipients, such as battered-women's, children's, or homeless people's shelters, and to the nonprofit thrift shops and rummage sales run by many Jewish organizations. Second, sensitivity is required. Jewish *tzedakah* is very mindful of the personal dignity of the individual. In Maimonides' *tzedakah* "ladder," the greater the anonymity, the

higher the "rung." A direct handout that looks too much like a handout can sometimes undermine the value of giving. There are many creative ways to give while preserving the honor of the recipient.

● Many consumers are becoming more aware of the great financial power of everyday buying and investing. Consumer choice frequently has more dramatic impact than does legislation on industrial practices.

● One of the most significant ways American Jews can support Israel is not by handouts, but by the higher *tzedakah* level of investing in and supporting Israel's self-sufficiency. See the Israel Resource Guide, p. 343, for ideas.

FAMILY SNAPSHOTS

TZEDAKAH

Since our kids started talking, we have had a weekly family *tzedakah* council. There was a long time that it was perfunctory—a way of dealing with the barrage of requests we received. Over time, however, the import has changed; it has become the most "consciousness-raising" activity we do. Each week, all requests for *tzedakah* (received in the mail) go in the hopper. We scan the papers for additional items. Each request is assigned to a different family member to peruse and prepare. We set a semiformal annual goal in terms of percentage of gross and check our cumulative total as we make decisions. Our "presenter" suggests how the request should be handled and the suggestion is discussed, or more likely debated. Majority rules. Over time, the children have become more involved—championing specific groups, developing rationale for decision making. Our reactions to people have been humanized in the process.

To work, the family *tzedakah* council has to be regular and involve nontrivial amounts—unless you want to model making it trivial! We assign individual children to prepare the case for agencies they're promoting a week in advance so they have time to read or research. We've always been a "one *mensch*, one vote," family, so children feel the weight of decision making. Sometimes Stan and I lose the vote, but that's what makes it meaningful.

When we started a local *tzedakah* co-op, one of the reactions we got was that it wasn't right to deny our children everything they want in order to give to others. A mother of two suggested our children would grow up ungenerous, feeling they were denied, and that we should give our children a choice each week to give *tzedakah* or buy something for themselves. (This is an example of giving children age-inappropriate choice, in my opinion.) At any rate, at the next meeting, I asked the children what they thought of this idea. They just laughed and said, "How would you expect us to learn to give, if it wasn't something we *had* to do when we were little? Sure, we'd like more clothes and spending money, but that choice just isn't right."

Later, when we proposed cutting the percentage we dedicated to *tzedakah*, the kids were appalled that we would consider using *tzedakah* money for college funds or a fitness club!
— *Wendy and Stan Drezek*

SHALOM—PEACE

In a world becoming smaller every day, the Jewish imperative to be *rodef shalom*, a pursuer of peace, is more important than ever.

Shelom Bayit: Domestic Peace

Seeking peace begins with domestic harmony and radiates outward in ever-widening circles. *Shelom bayit* is the traditional Jewish ideal of creating a peaceful, loving atmosphere in our own homes. Rabbi Simon Glustrom, author of *The Language of Judaism*,[2] has pointed out that *shelom bayit* does not necessarily mean a hushed, quiet atmosphere. A home may seem peaceful on the surface, but be seething with anger beneath. Conversely, a noisy, vibrant, communicative family may experience a

great measure of confidence, inner peace, and mutual respect.

Of course, *shelom bayit* cannot be reduced to a formula or an activity, but constitutes an entire approach to family life, which means, among other things:

● A commitment to home and family as priorities, in deed as well as word,

● Quantity and quality time with our own families,

● Learning effective ways of resolving family conflict and creating intimacy,

● Nurturing Jewish values in the home, such as respect and kindness.

A Few Ideas

● Make your home into a warm, safe, loving place of peace by frequent positive interactions that involve touch, eye contact, and focused attention. Bedtimes, wake-up times, homecomings, and other transitions of the day are key opportunities for loving interaction. Jewish holidays and especially Shabbat provide regular, reliable times for being together. A family hug, holding hands and singing around the Shabbat table, and other loving traditions let family members know they matter.

● Small children will also respond to the occasional use of positive reinforcements; for example, cut out a heart or a house from construction paper and attach it to the refrigerator or bulletin board. (You can even write *shelom bayit* on it.) Then, whenever you catch each other being considerate or interacting peacefully, attach a heart-shaped sticker to the large shape—until you fill it up (children should be allowed to do this, too), then reward yourselves with an activity together.

● Encourage cooperation rather than competition among family members: avoid comparisons between siblings; strive to let each one know that she or he is valued as an individual. Good-natured, playful competition may be appropriate in some situations, but in general cooperation should be stressed and cooperative activities fostered. The Torah has many stories that illustrate the destructive potential of sibling rivalry and discrimination.

● Regular family meetings can create a framework in which communication lines stay open, problems are tended to early on, and family harmony is encouraged. Openly discuss the needs of the individuals involved in normal (nonemergency) family conflicts and brainstorm creative win-win solutions wherever possible. Shabbat meals also provide plenty of opportunities for more informal family discussion sessions.

● The parents' marital relationship, their mutual respect and love, set the tone for *shelom bayit* for the entire family. It's easy to make one's marriage a secondary priority when there are children; however, nurturing the marital relationship is one of the most important things that parents can do for their children. As the experts are always reminding us, parents need time alone as a couple, and they need shared activities and interests.

● One ingredient for *shelom bayit* is nurturing the spiritual needs of the marriage. Many couples learn some Torah (or any Jewish text) together for a few minutes each evening or half an hour every Shabbat. Reading and discussing books on marriage and family life together can also be a meaningful Shabbat afternoon activity. Praying together for strength and wisdom to deal with family concerns is also valuable; it's unfortunate that many of us see this form of prayer as foreign to Judaism. Many contemporary Jewish couples have discovered the observance of the traditional Jewish sexual disciplines revolving around the *mikveh* (see pp. 262–263) and feel that these add a greater measure of spirituality and commitment to their relationship.

● *Shelom bayit* is a concept that applies to all types of families, not only the two-parent, first-marriage type of family. Single-parent and blended families will often have many challenges to face in this area and will need to make *shelom bayit* a high, conscious priority. In the essay "Facing Divorce" in *The Hadassah Magazine Jewish Parenting Book*[3] Marilyn Shlachter Berger points out the importance of *shelom bayit* after a divorce as the atmosphere of tranquillity and wholeness (*shalem* means whole) that should be cultivated for the children in each parent's home. She explains that after a divorce parents should not view the family as incomplete or "broken", but should perceive the single-parent–children unit as a whole, complete family, observing Jewish traditions together at home and with other families, and remaining involved in a larger Jewish community. (See chapter 7 for more detailed discussion of these issues.)

● Be aware of the issue of family violence in the Jewish community. The positive stereotype is that spouse and child abuse don't exist in our communities; would that it were so! Victims and perpetrators of battering and abuse require special counseling approaches that differ fundamentally from regular marital counseling. Not all violence is physical, either. Emotional, verbal, social, and economic abusiveness are simply more insidious forms of battering. An atmosphere where a spouse or other family members are not respected and honored destroys *shelom bayit*. Although some rabbis and Jewish counselors are not yet equipped to deal adequately with this issue, awareness of the problem is growing. Jewish Family Service agencies around the country are introducing counseling, support groups, shelters, and other programs to deal with this problem.

PEACE EDUCATION

● Listen to Jewish songs and learn the many Jewish prayers in the *siddur* (prayer book) about *shalom*, such as *Oseh Shalom*, *Sim Shalom*, and *Shalom Rav*. At home, illustrate and dramatize them through art, dance, and creative writing. Engage in Torah talk about the deeper meaning of *shalom*, that is, not merely a cessation of hostilities, but real wholeness and understanding.

● Discourage war play and don't buy toys that glorify violence. One family I know forbade toy guns because of the pervasiveness of guns as weapons of violence in modern society; however, they allowed toy bows and arrows and toy swords because of their more removed, historical connotation. This allowed their children an alternative way to act out their anxieties and aggressions through play. As to the occasional toy weapon received as a gift, they admitted to ambivalence: They didn't want to refuse these gifts outright. In the end, they made sure that the war toys their children received as gifts had a way of "disappearing" faster than other toys.

A friend of mine who lives in Israel said that she finally decided it was too hypocritical to forbid her son a toy gun when his father carried one to reserve duty and in his job as security officer for their Galilee *moshav*. But she still feels uncomfortable about it. (Her internal conflict is an interesting extension of the contemporary dilemma of Jewish military power.)

Although the subject is complex, parents should be aware of the way their children play and should be ready to discuss play issues with them. Be alert to a preponderance of war themes in children's play, which may be an expression of underlying feelings of anger or fear.

● Parents should consider limiting their children's viewing of violent television and movies (including some cartoons, which can be surprisingly violent). Whether violence in the media reflects or encourages the violence in society is still up for debate, but it's hard to believe that watching thousands of murders on television doesn't harden children's sensibilities.

There are many strategies for keeping television viewing within bounds. Our silent television on Shabbat has had many unexpected benefits. Our Saturday mornings never include several hours of violent or overstimulating cartoons interspersed with seductive advertisements for questionable toys and sugary cereals. Throughout the day, learning, reading, interaction, and imaginative play take the place of isolated, passive television watching. (And it does seem to spill over into the weekdays, too.)

● Encourage peaceful, cooperative, life-affirming activities for children, such as caring for plants and animals, gently caring for younger siblings, parent-play with dolls for both sexes, creative art and music, and sports and active games that release energy in positive ways.

● Encourage nonviolent, educational television shows that broaden children's understanding of other people and of nature. Ask your librarian for suggestions from the many contemporary books that describe the lives of children from different cultural backgrounds. Learn about different cultures through music, art, and film.

● Seek diversity in your family's social interactions and in your children's experiences as well. Tolerance cannot be learned from books alone. In many locations, the Jewish community is more apparently homogeneous than the surrounding community in terms of socioeconomic status, race, and functioning, particularly for the child attending almost exclusively Jewish schools and extracurricular activities. (This should *not* be taken as a statement against Jewish day schools. Indeed, a child can be socially ghettoized without going to a day school, and a child who attends a school can have many extracurricular activities and neighborhood friendships with a diverse group of friends. The main purpose of sending a child to a day school ought to be Jewish education, not segregation.)

Often we assume a tolerance that is never

tested. A Jewish friend of mine with two adopted children of color tells me that her family's experiences with racism have been worse in the Jewish community than in the community at large. Others, sadly, find that their Jewish communities are not accepting of their children with mental or severe physical handicaps. Parents need to provide settings where children can interact naturally with people of other races, cultures, and generations, as well as people with physical and mental limitations.

● Discuss prejudice and intolerance in age-appropriate ways. There are plenty of examples in the media and in books. Obviously, pejorative labels for other religious and ethnic groups and racist "humor" do not belong in a Jewish home.

● Teach children how to acknowledge and express their feelings properly, rather than to repress or act out their aggressive feelings. Teach them by example and explanation how to express angry feelings without hurting others (for example, using "I language": "I feel angry when . . . What I want instead is . . ."). Provide healthy outlets for aggression, such as safe "roughhousing," a punching bag, fencing with "Nerf swords," tearing old papers or rags, drawing "mad" pictures, writing down angry feelings, punching clay or dough, and running.

● It may sound paradoxical, but self defense classes that foster self-confidence and self-control rather than violence (such as Kung Fu or Aikido) can be very positive. A good teacher will be skilled at helping students channel anger and aggression. Weakness does not equal peace; indeed, powerlessness can also foster rage. All teenagers can benefit from learning self defense.

● Support peace education in your children's school and your local school system. Peace education encompasses everything from teaching conflict resolution on the playground to learning about other countries, cultures, and different types of people, to artistic expression about peace.

● Jewish schools in particular need to deal with the many divergent *shalom* issues: *shelom bayit*, *ahavat Yisrael* (love for one's fellow Jews, harmony with other Jewish groups—a growing issue), *darkei shalom* (respect and good relations with non-Jews). The Coalition for the Advancement of Jewish Education (CAJE) and the UAHC's *Keeping Posted* magazine are among those that have produced classroom materials on such important subjects as the nuclear threat and Israeli-Palestinian relations. Find out how your children's school deals with these topics.

Seek Peace

There are many levels on which we can support Jewish groups and other groups that promote peace and understanding: in our homes, in our Jewish communities, among Americans of various races and religions, in Israel—between Jews and Palestinian Arabs, and in other troubled areas of the world such as Central America and Africa. We can support groups that are dedicated to international understanding, human rights, *pikuah nefesh* (saving lives), worldwide peace, and nuclear disarmament.

Support can take many forms, such as monetary donations, letter writing, teaching, public relations, and volunteer work. Young children should know about their parents' work for *shalom*; older children can be actively involved. (See the Resource Guide on p. 338 for some specific organizations.)

Evaluate where your family's money is spent and invested by peace, justice, and human rights criteria.

SHEMIRAT HAADAMAH: CONSERVATION

Shemirat HaAdamah—conservation, or "proper caretaking" of the earth summarizes a variety of *mitzvot* and Jewish values about the relationship between human beings and the rest of creation. Judaism views our proper relationship to the earth as one of reverent stewardship. Our holidays are strongly nature-oriented, our Shabbat is a weekly cessation of interference with nature.

Bal tashhit, which is the commandment in the Torah against cutting down fruit trees during a siege, is by extension a prohibition against wastefulness and wanton destruction of any resources. *Pikuah nefesh*, saving lives, is the essence of protecting human beings from toxins and a ravaged environment. *Tzaar Ba'alei Hayyim* means "the suffering of animals" and indicates the Jewish concern for the welfare of other species.

In the Garden of Eden story, the first people are given the tasks of caretakers of "the garden," the natural environment of the planet. A *midrash* tells that when the first human was created—from the earth—s/he was presented with a panorama of all of God's creation and bidden to preserve and not to destroy it.

According to the prophetic writings, the Jews were expelled from the land of Israel partly because of their failure to observe the sabbatical year in which the land lay fallow and was rejuvenated. The Torah is concerned even with the subject of proper sewage disposal. Having children should heighten our awareness of what we are doing to future generations who have to live on the same earth, breathe the same air, and drink the same water as we do. *Shemirat HaAdamah* is the Jewish (and universal) imperative to care for and preserve the earth, our home.

BAL TASHHIT: WASTE NOT

It's said that we have only a few short decades to halt and reverse the destructiveness of modern industrial society on the planetary environment. The time has come for all of us to adopt and to teach our children a more frugal, *bal tashhit* (waste not) life-style:

● At each "family meeting," or every Rosh Hodesh, we can choose together another step to take and make into habit. The following suggestions are only a few beginning steps. There are many new books available on simple steps that people can take to help restore the environment. (See the Resource Guide on pp. 335 and 338–339 for more extensive educational materials and pertinent addresses on this important subject.)

● Recycle newspapers and other mixed, low-grade paper, cardboard, aluminum, glass, plastic, and Styrofoam. Start with one kind of trash and you'll be stunned by the amount you've been throwing away. Jewish schools and institutions—which seem to generate mountains of paper waste—should recycle paper and buy and use recycled paper products. Children can quickly become involved in home recycling and will find such dull tasks as sorting items "fun." If you have a garden, they will also enjoy making a compost pile.

● Buy and use products wisely. Purchase recycled products and environmentally friendly product packaging. Switch back to old-fashioned reusable or recyclable items (such as canvas shopping bags, cloth rags and napkins, cloth diapers) rather than use throwaways. Buy natural or less-toxic cleansers and pest control products and learn ways of making your home environment healthier and safer.

● Conserve water: Use water-conserving devices in the sink, shower, commode, and hot water tank and teach your children saving ways: to shut off the faucet while scrubbing dishes or brushing teeth, to take short showers, and to minimize use of dishwashers. Water and chemical use can also be reduced with a drought-tolerant lawn and by watering in the evening. Israeli-style drip irrigation is another way to save water.

● Energy can be saved in many ways: Turn off lights and television when not in use (Shabbat-observant people can use a light timer rather than leaving many lights on all night.) Where possible, consolidate trips, carpool, use public transportation, walk, or ride a bike. Buy energy efficient appliances, cars, and home insulation. If you build your own home, look into making it an ecologically designed one based on principles of "permaculture." Moderate your thermostat. Explore solar power for your home's water heater.

● We can eat less wastefully: One important step is to eat less meat: Aside from humanitarian and health considerations, meat eating is wasteful. It takes sixteen pounds of grain and soy to produce one pound of beef; beef grazing erodes pastureland; and tropical rain forests are destroyed to make grazing room. Eat less highly processed, chemically preserved and overpackaged foods; where possible, purchase locally grown and organically grown produce. If possible, grow some of your own food, join a food co-op that buys in bulk, or join a CSA (Community Supported Agriculture cooperative), where a yearly membership fee in support of an organic farm gets you fresh chemical-free produce and a tie to the land, which children will love.

These principles can be extended to our Jewish observances: more moderate entertaining and celebrating are certainly in line with conservationism, social conscience—and the popular desire to eat less. Ultimately, these are just first steps toward transforming modern society into a more sharing, sustainable, gentle way of living on the earth. However, the Jewish approach to big problems is that every little step counts and the compound effects of many small actions can add up to great changes. We can transform our life-style, probably

not in one dramatic moment, but one modest step at a time. As Hillel said, "If not now, when?"

TZAAR BAALEI HAYYIM: CONCERN FOR ANIMAL SUFFERING

● Train your child to care gently for pets. The Torah mandates that animals be fed before we eat and that beasts of burden rest on the Sabbath. And of course, don't keep exotic animals as pets.

● Become an aware shopper. Choose "cruelty free" cosmetics and household products (not tested on animals).

● Keep your fur faux (sad to say, some of my little girls' friends already have real fur jackets). I like to tell my daughters and their pals that many glamorous women, including Britain's Princess Diana, refuse to wear real fur.

● Support local and national organizations that are concerned with animal welfare and species survival.

● Many contemporary Jews have chosen vegetarianism or near-vegetarianism as an extension of the humanitarian ideals of *kashrut* (see pp. 28–29).

TORAH AND GUARDIANSHIP OF NATURE

● Read together from the Bible, with particular attention to the emphasis on ecology and the beauty and grandeur of nature in such books as Psalms and Song of Songs and the prophets.

You might want to illustrate your impressions of your study artistically in the medium of your choice. Although Jews today are among the most highly urbanized peoples (including in Israel), our ancient heritage is closely intertwined with nature and the land. *Ecology in the Bible*[4] by Nogah Hareuveni and Helen Frenkly is a delightful introduction to the subject.

● Highlight the environment in Jewish holidays and celebrations. Tu BiShvat stresses the importance of trees; Shabbat teaches that there are limits to human manipulation of nature; the three pilgrimage festivals (Sukkot, Pesah, Shavuot) are tied to natural cycles and seasons. Shomrei Adamah—Guardians of the Earth (see the Resource Guide on p. 338) is a wonderful source for materials that emphasize the environment in Jewish rituals and celebrations.

● Parents and children can read, learn from, discuss, and act on publications from environmental groups. Subscribe to nature magazines for your children; read books and watch programs about nature together. Anxiety about pollution is one of the most widespread fears among today's youth. Explain that conservation is a *mitzvah* and help your children understand what the individual can do.

● Attend Sierra Club meetings and similar family programs in your area (and Society for the Protection of Nature in Israel programs when in Israel) to acquaint your family with the beauty of nature and the importance of environmental activism. Organize synagogue or *havurah* retreats in natural settings, and use these as further opportunities to learn about Judaism, nature, and conservation. As a family, vacation close to nature, treating your surroundings with respect. Take Shabbat walks in natural areas whenever possible, cultivating quiet and reverence for the environment.

● Get your synagogue or Jewish service group involved in local efforts to clean trash, recycle, and restore and beautify the environment.

● Plant trees, near and far. We're all well versed in the importance of tree-planting in Israel; it's time to promote Israel's success story as an example for worldwide reforestation. Trees are essential to preserving the land and atmosphere of the entire planet. The endangered tropical rain forests are of particular concern. How about "tree-twinning"? For Tu BiShvat, plant one tree in your local area or an endangered forest for each tree you sponsor in Israel. Rabbinic lore tells us planting trees is such a *mitzvah* that, should the Messiah

come while we're busy planting a tree, we should first finish planting the tree and only then run forward in greeting!

● Make financial and volunteer support to environmental groups a high *tzedakah* priority for yourself and your *tzedakah* co-op or *havurah*. Support their efforts to boycott environmentally destructive products and companies and to support legislative initiatives that reduce hazardous wastes, toxic chemicals, and environmental destruction. See the Resource Guide for some specific groups; a comprehensive directory of National Environmental Organizations can be purchased from U.S. Environmental Directories, Box 65156, St. Paul, MN 44165. (How about a copy for your synagogue library?)

Suggestions for Incorporating *Tzedakah* and *Hesed* into Holidays and Life-cycle Events

Judaism has institutionalized *tzedakah* practices in many of the existing holiday and life-cycle traditions. Here are some traditional and more innovative ways to make every celebration and remembrance an opportunity for interpersonal *mitzvot*. These activities are intended to involve as much of the family as possible.

Note: *Halachah* (Jewish law) prohibits handling money on the Shabbat and *Yom Tov* (see note, p. 177). When donations are referred to in conjunction with such days, the intention is that they would be given just before the holiday, rather than actually on it.

Addresses are listed separately in the Resource Guide on pp. 336–339.

Holiday or Event	Possible Family Project/Activity
Shabbat	Put coins in *tzedakah* box just before lighting the Shabbat candles (it can also be a reminder time to send in a larger donation). Expand your Shabbat and holiday guest list to those who are alone, experiencing difficult times of life, or hungry for friendship. Shabbat is a "foretaste of the World to Come"—consider *tzedakah* groups that help bring about a better world where all can enjoy the leisure, dignity, and peace inherent in Shabbat.
Elul	Honor the memory of a deceased relative with *tzedakah* donations to local Jewish organizations or to causes the person supported. Choose a family *tzedakah* project and/or a *mitzvah*-volunteer project for the upcoming year.

Budget a fixed percentage of income for *tzedakah* in the upcoming year.
Make this a time for healing and nurturing personal relationships; do those
thoughtful things that have repeatedly been put off.

Days of Awe

Elul and the Ten Days of Repentance are a classic time to give extra *tzedakah* as
well as to "mend fences" and pay extra attention to relationships with others.
For the "Birthday of the World," a day with universalistic themes, consider international *tzedakah* groups.
Send Rosh HaShanah greeting cards to Ethiopian Jewish youngsters in Israel
and support organizations that help them.
Yom Kippur: donate the money you would have spent on food to Mazon (see
Resource Guide, p. 336) or another organization that feeds people.
Synagogues and Jewish schools need donations and volunteers now. Also con-
sider a High Holiday "*mitzvah*-pledge" card: appeal for volunteers for community service projects and synagogue activities.

Sukkot

Dedicate your family or communal *sukkah* as a *Sukkah* of Peace through the
Shalom Center. Share the harvest with donations to the local food bank or soup
kitchen.
Emphasize the issue of shelter through volunteering or donations to local agencies for the homeless and political activism on housing.
Invite people who can't build their own *sukkah* to yours. Invite a Jewish special-
education or preschool class to your home *sukkah*.

Simhat Torah

Give *tzedakah* to Jewish educational organizations such as your local schools, Bureau of Jewish Education, or CAJE. Consider Jewish special-education organizations, such as the Jewish Braille institute and education for the Jewish handicapped. Volunteer to help at your Jewish school or to purchase special items the
school needs.
Start a year of family Torah study, concentrating especially on the interpersonal
values in traditional Jewish texts. Decide how your family can better *live* the
values of the Torah in the coming year.
Simhat Torah was a day when Russian Jews demonstrated their identity. Support organizations that aid in resettling Jews from the former Soviet Union.

Thanksgiving

Host a college student or service person far from home for Thanksgiving dinner.
If possible, invite the person to phone home at your expense. (Check with your
local JCC or synagogue whether they have a "match up" program.)
Volunteer as a family to work at a Thanksgiving dinner for the elderly or needy
or to deliver meals to shut-ins.
In advance of the holiday, donate meal-fixings to kitchens that feed the
homeless.
Emphasize world hunger organizations.

Hanukkah

Visit a Jewish nursing home and sing holiday songs with your children.
Decide how your family will "increase light" in the world this year.
Give away old and new toys or clothes to a *tzedakah* organization before giving
gifts. Make a new toy or gift to donate the admission to your Hanukkah party.
Have a coat drive through your synagogue or other Jewish group.
Decide on a *tzedakah* organization with which to share the family "gelt."
Between friends, agree to substitute donations to worthwhile organizations for
ritualized gift exchanges.
This is another traditional time to support Jewish educational organizations and
schools.

JEWISH INTERPERSONAL VALUES

Martin Luther King's Birthday	Support the NAACP. Support B'nai B'rith's Anti-Defamation League educational programs against prejudice.
January-February	Volunteer to help at your local Jewish Federation's "Super Sunday" fund-raiser, which raises money for local Jewish institutions and social welfare programs in Israel.
Tu BiShvat	Plant trees in Israel through the JNF. Plant trees anywhere with "Tree People" and similar groups. Support environmental organizations. Commit to ways to substitute reusable items for disposable ones, to recycle, to conserve.
Purim	Visit a nursing home in your Purim costumes. *Matanot Leevyonim* (monetary gifts to the poor) are the traditional *tzedakah* of the day. Make extra *mishloah manot* (the holiday goody baskets), not only for friends but for those in need of visitors and extra food, or donate food to a food bank to share your Purim feast. Emphasize other efforts for the poor, including political initiatives for better housing, educational opportunities, medical care. For this day of "costuming," donate extra clothing to a shelter.
Passover	"Let those who are hungry come and eat"—donate the cost of one or more *seder* guests to Mazon or another organization that feeds the hungry. Give your left-over *hametz* to a non-Jew who can use it or to a food bank. Donate to your local *Maot Hittin* fund, which provides Passover supplies to needy Jews (check with your local Jewish Family Service or synagogue). Volunteer to help pack supplies. Make the festival of freedom a time to write letters for, and otherwise support, organizations that work for human freedom and liberation. Invite people who are far from home or would find it difficult to hold their own *seder*. Consider various *Haggadot* and special prayers composed for inclusion in the standard *seder* that emphasize contemporary issues of freedom, liberation, and peace. Look into special Passover education/*tzedakah* projects from such organizations as the American Jewish World Service, CLAL, Mazon, and others (see Resource Guide, pp. 336–339), for inclusion in your *seder*.
Yom HaShoah	Honor the memory of those who perished in the Nazi genocide or risked their lives to save others by taking one action for *pikuah nefesh* (saving a life) of a person of any religion or race through an organization dedicated to human rights or care for the destitute. Donate *tzedakah* to organizations that commemorate the Holocaust for future generations, especially those that educate young people for tolerance and understanding. Donate to the Foundation to Sustain Righteous Christians, which supports righteous Gentiles who risked their lives to save Jews during the Holocaust, but who now live in poverty. Donate to organizations that educate Jews, since assimilation and ignorance are probably the greatest threats to Jewish survival today.

Yom HaZikaron   Support the Friends of the Israel Defense Forces (the Israeli "U.S.O.")
Support Israeli peace movements.

Memorial Day (also Veterans' Day)   Support the Jewish War Veterans of the U.S.A. (see Resource Guide, p. 337). Remember the cost of wars in human terms on all sides and support organizations that promote international understanding and peace.

Yom HaAtzma'ut   Donate to *tzedakah* organizations that work to make Israel a more peaceful, tolerant, democratic country (such as the New Israel Fund). Support Israeli environmental organizations such as the Society for the Protection of Nature in Israel (SPNI).
Invest in Israel: bonds, securities, and business endeavors in Israel.
Purchase and promote Israeli products.
Save for a trip to Israel in which your family will not only be tourists, but actively learn about, even contribute to, Israeli life.
Support educational programs and institutions in Israel and local scholarship funds that make it possible for young people to experience life and learning in Israel.

Yom Yerushalayim   Give to organizations that promote peace and understanding between Jews and Arabs and between religious and secular Israelis.
Support educational institutions in Jerusalem.

Shavuot   The holiday of Revelation is another good time to support Jewish education and commit more time to your own. Don't forget scholarship funds and informal education such as camps and youth groups; they have a great impact.

American Independence Day   Support organizations that promote democracy, pluralism, and tolerance in the United States.

Tisha B'Av   Support peace organizations that work to prevent a potential nuclear *hurban* (destruction).
Support the ingathering of the Jewish exiles by contributing to the UJA's Project Renewal and special funds to resettle former Soviet and Ethiopian Jews.

Every Rosh Hodesh   Have a family meeting to choose a *tzedakah* project for the month. Discuss the *tzedakah* mailings you receive, and think of ways to raise money and/or volunteer for the organization you choose.
At your family meeting, choose one more action your family can begin doing this month to live a more environmentally sound life-style.
Make this the day for your *tzedakah* co-op to meet (reschedule if it's Shabbat or Rosh HaShanah).

Any Day   Get in the *tzedakah* habit; purchase extra foods on your regular grocery shopping trip and keep a special shelf or box to save the food to donate to the local food bank (every synagogue, school, and JCC should have a collection area; personal items and clothing can also be collected).
Volunteer—the opportunities are limitless. Give *tzedakah*; open a checking account just for *tzedakah*.
Do someone a *hesed* (kindness); it might be just listening and caring. It could be a family member. Recycle. Share.

JEWISH INTERPERSONAL VALUES

Life-cycle Events	Possible Family Project/Activity
Birth	Sponsor a Save-the-Children child or donate to an organization such as the Children's Defense Fund, which helps underprivileged children in your area or anywhere.
Birthdays	Donate a multiple of the person's age to *tzedakah*. Let each person in the family choose a special "birthday *mitzvah*" for the family to do each year in honor of her or his birthday.
Benai Mitzvah	Donate a portion of the monetary gifts to *tzedakah*, or if the youngster is willing, indicate organization(s) and address(es) to encourage specific donations instead of gifts. Tie the *bar* or *bat mitzvah* or confirmation process to volunteer work within the framework of a special personal project.
Wedding	Donate the wedding dress to the Rabbanit B'rachah Kapach in Jerusalem (see Resource Guide, p. 337); she loans them to poor brides. Include a donation to help needy couples get a good start in life. Give the couple Jewish books and items for their home, subscriptions to Jewish periodicals, membership in a Jewish organization.
Memorials	Honor the deceased through a donation to an organization that represents his/her highest ideals in life. Do a *mitzvah*, teach Torah in his/her memory. Affirm life and human dignity through donations to medical research, services to the seriously ill, Jewish hospice.
Any Life-cycle Event	Donate 3 percent of the cost of the reception to Mazon—a voluntary program that many synagogues are now committing to urge their members to do. (In the past, and in some areas today, Jewish celebrations included tables for the needy to attend freely.) Look for at least one way to trim the conspicuous consumption or luxury of any "affair" (or organizational festivity or event); make it more modest and donate the money saved to *tzedakah*. Make a thanksgiving donation to your congregation or Jewish school. Ask guests to bring donations of money, food, clothing, coats, toys, toilet articles, blankets, or other goods to donate to shelters, food banks, and similar organizations. (Explain when and where to bring the items if the ceremony—such as *bar mitzvah*—is on Shabbat and you do not want them to carry the items to the *shul* on the Sabbath.) Buy a *tzedakah*-linked gift for the congregation. Donate the leftover flowers to a nursing home. Donate the leftover good food to a soup kitchen (people who have worked at the event might also appreciate the offer). Give a *tzedakah* donation in honor of the event or do a *mitzvah* in honor of the event and send the honoree(s) a card describing what you did. Purchase gifts of Jewish books, magazine subscriptions, musical or ritual items to enhance the Jewish education and life of the recipient.

IV

ISRAEL: THE JEWISH HOME AND THE JEWISH HOMELAND

17

THE IMPORTANCE OF ISRAEL IN THE LIFE OF THE DIASPORA JEWISH FAMILY

When the Lord brought back those that returned to Zion, we were like dreamers. Then our mouth was filled with laughter and our tongue with joyous song.
— Psalm 126:1–2

For nearly 2,000 years, the Jewish nation—the People of Israel—was exiled from the land of Israel, yet one has only to pick up a traditional Jewish prayer book to realize that our ancestral homeland always remained a central focus of Jewish prayer and aspiration, a central fixture of the Jewish consciousness. What a blessing, what a privilege is ours to witness the reestablishment of a Jewish nation in the land of our ancestors. The State of Israel, always a focus of our spiritual longings, is once again a living hub of Jewish life, learning, and culture.

As mentioned earlier, building and dwelling in the *sukkah* is one of the "holistic" *mitzvot*, a Jewish behavior that involves the "whole person" in a very literal way. If the *sukkah*, in which we spend at most a few hours of our time each day for a week once a year, can affect our family life so profoundly, how much more so can being in the land of Israel for a week, a summer, a year, or a lifetime! Indeed, researchers into Jewish identity find that the "Israel experience" can be critical to strengthening, even transforming, the Jewish identity of our young people—and ourselves.

Those who live in Israel today commit body, soul, and destiny to the Jewish nation, whether or not they label themselves "religious." To grow up in Israel is to speak Hebrew, to live in a society based on the Hebrew calendar and in a land of biblical landmarks. The sages of old compared residence in Israel to the observance of all the *mitzvot* of the Torah (*Sifre* 80).

For those who live in the Diaspora, entering Israel even temporarily usually has the powerful effect of a "core" or "immersion" experience (see pp. 7–9). Adults who go on study tours and "missions," and teenagers or young adults who go on educational programs, are often profoundly affected by even a short visit to the Jewish homeland.

The individual home needs to be connected to a heritage and a mission that go beyond the immediate family. Certainly Israel, the ancestral homeland of 4,000 years and the central focus of global Jewish life today, is an integral part of the heritage of every Jewish home, just as the rebuilding of Israel—aspiring, despite its difficulties, to become an exemplary society—is a central part of the Jewish "mission" for this generation and the future.

The partnership between Israel, the Jewish homeland, and the United States, the largest Jewish national community in the world, is a crucial one. Although the two communities in many ways appear to be drifting apart, they have been, and must continue to be, vital to each other's fulfillment.

Jewish families outside of Israel can make Israel a major part of their Jewish lives in a number of ways. Israel can be brought into the home by learning, both cognitive and affective. The family can travel to Israel for visits and longer stays; then they can contribute to goals they believe in. And—the most significant step—they can explore the possibilities of life in Israel for themselves. This chapter looks at all these opportunities in greater detail.

BEING IN ISRAEL: LIKE BEING IN LOVE

Several times, out of the blue, I've felt an irrational wave of compassion for, say, the checkout woman at my Texas supermarket: "Why, she'll probably never be in Israel!" I think to myself. It's as if anyone, of any religion or background, who never encounters Israel is like someone who has never been in love.

It's another case of naaseh venishma ("We will do, then we'll understand"; see p. 10). Without going there, one can't completely understand the pull, the beauty, the fascination of the country, the sheer love a Jew (and so many of other faiths) can feel for Israel. Can one understand Shabbat without doing it? Or understand being in love without experiencing it?

No one said that being in love was free of problems, either. Love can cause much suffering and emotional pain, yet most of us go ahead and love anyway. Marriage, as the utmost expression of love between the sexes, is simultaneously the most difficult and problem-prone relationship one can enter into, while also the most valuable, beautiful, meaningful, and life-affirming. The covenant of marriage acknowledges that one has a commitment for a lifelong relationship through good and bad. That's why Judaism stresses the importance of marrying and of helping people marry. And no wonder that Jewish texts have often compared our people's relationship to God to a marriagelike covenant.

A deep relationship to Israel is like a marriage in that sense. Sure, the honeymoon is over. We—and by "we" I mean both Diaspora Jews and those who live in Israel (and those of us who have done both)—have long since realized that a whole range of things related to the State of Israel can indeed cause us unhappiness, disappointment, or frustration as individuals and groups.

But, just as in a troubled marriage, it is more rewarding to cope with the problems, to work to heal, rebuild, and renew the relationship. Hasty divorces may be declining because people are

beginning to realize that the love of a really committed partnership is so many times stronger than the romantic illusions of a mere infatuation. So it is with our relationship to Israel. It's time to mature beyond the "infatuation" stage and to think in terms of the ongoing, committed, realistic yet devoted relationship.

And, just as in a marriage, the abiding, spellbinding love of youth is always ready to resurface. For myself, I know it is so. The love always wells up again whenever I'm in Israel; the longing is always there whenever I'm away.

TEN IDEAS TO BRING ISRAEL CLOSER

Between uninvolvement with Israel and actually "making aliyah" there are many possible intermediate steps. Here are ten possible avenues to take for the family who wants to draw closer to Israel:

1. Learn more about Israel through books, articles, periodicals from Israel, broadcasts, audio and video recordings, seminars, speakers.

2. Bring the sights, sounds, tastes, textures, and scents of Israel into your home through some of the following informal learning suggestions in Israel Through the Senses.

3. Learn as much Hebrew as possible and give your children a strong Hebrew education. Ideally, practice speaking Hebrew together as a family.

4. Get to know local Israelis in your community; yes, that means emigrés (yordim). Likewise, meet visiting Israelis who are in your community on sabbatical or as shelihim (Israeli government or organizational emissaries) and also talk to American-born Jews in your community who have lived in Israel for extensive periods. In many Jewish communities, there are real social barriers between former—or visiting—Israelis and other local Jews, which is a shame. These gaps need bridging. Most Israeli-Americans I know miss Israel, visit fairly often, will give you a generous list of people to contact when you visit there, and usually assert that they either will, or would like to, go back home. (Although the serious intent of this assertion varies, many well-educated Israelis are in the United States largely because of the Israeli "brain drain," resulting from the dearth of high-level professional positions available in a small country.)

5. Support pro-Israel organizations that you truly believe in, through financial donations, volunteer

service, political action, and so on. Some activist groups are listed in this chapter section. Become a critical, involved supporter of Israel, not just a passive "fan."

6. Support Israel economically through purchasing Israeli goods; by investing in Israel through Israel bonds, stock funds, and Israel-linked business ventures; by supporting joint economic enterprises on the state level (on the lines of the Texas–Israel Agricultural Exchange Commission).

7. Visit Israel—and visit again. If you haven't been back for a few years, you can be sure there have been many changes. Try to take the whole family on a family-oriented program or make your own custom-designed tour. If possible, stay for a month or an entire summer next time. Afterwards, main-tain ties with people you meet in Israel and help your children to do likewise with Israeli peers.

8. Involve your children in Zionist-oriented summer camps and/or youth groups. Send them to high school and college programs in Israel, particularly programs with a strong educational and values-oriented component.

9. Arrange to spend a few months to a year living, learning, and working in Israel, while your children go to a school *ulpan* (Hebrew program) and to classes with Israeli youngsters. Possibilities might include academic or research sabbaticals, volunteer professional work through Project Renewal, stays arranged through groups such as NAAM (North American Aliyah Movement). Let Israel become your "second home."

10. *Aliyah*: Make the Jewish homeland your—and your children's and grandchildren's—real home.

18

A SENSE OF ISRAEL IN THE AMERICAN JEWISH HOME

Israel" is a distant, abstract concept to young children—even to older ones who have never been there. Our parents' generation experienced the founding of the state. We vividly remember the dramas of the Six Day War and the Yom Kippur War. Israel had a much more palpable impact on most of us in our youth than it will on most of our children today—unless we make a special effort to give it a concrete and sensory manifestation in our homes.

Yet that's really not as hard as it sounds, and it can be enjoyable, too. Even those who haven't yet made that first trip to Israel can and should try out some of the following ideas. Israel-related school or community programs and classes can be connected to the home activities.

Of course, the ideal is to spend time in Israel as a family. Then these suggestions can serve to bring a little bit of that country back with you until the family returns again.

ISRAEL THROUGH THE FIVE SENSES

SIGHT

● Include posters and pictures of Israel among your family's wall decorations. Israel is a hauntingly beautiful country; however, many American youngsters have the idea that it's all a big desert. Visual images of Israel can include fine artwork,

posters, calendars, and photographs. Obtain these from galleries, quality Judaica gift shops, and catalogs (pp. 307–309). Some posters are available free or next to free from Israeli organizations, such as Israel Government Tourist offices in major cities and from El Al Airlines.

● Look at and discuss books of photographs of Israel together. It's a nice Shabbat afternoon activity.

● Hang a *mizrah* on your living-room wall. For more information, see chapter 4, pp. 23–24.

● Make an inexpensive stick-page photo album into a homemade Israel picture book by inserting family photos of Israel (if you have any), cut-up brochures, magazines, postcards, and greeting cards of Israel. If you haven't been to Israel yet, cut out photos of yourselves from family snapshots and glue in place over pictures of Israeli sites from tourist brochures. Include these in the album to imagine your future trips to the Holy Land!

● Make a more artistic collage by covering a poster board with glued-on pictures and cut-out words and sayings that illustrate your impressions of Israel or some facet of Israel. Fill in blank spaces with torn tissue paper. Cover all with a wash of *thinned* white glue and allow to dry.

● Watch videos about Israel for kids and families, such as the beautifully produced "Shalom Sesame," which uses the Israeli version of "Sesame Street" characters in addition to American actors and personalities. There are also videos for adults and older youngsters, ranging from travelogues to sing-alongs to Israel movies. And don't overlook "home videos" from people's visits to Israel. For specific video resources, see the Resource Guide, pp. 313–314.

● Have your own "Israeli Film Festival" with the family and friends; make some popcorn and sit back to enjoy any of the above.

● View programs about Israel on television from time to time, especially on Public Broadcasting; most of these focus on the political situation or the Arab-Israeli conflict and are of more interest to adults and possibly older children. (*Note*: Some highly evangelical religious groups use "Israel" or "Jerusalem" in the title and audiovisual content of their cable TV programs in order to attract unwary Jewish viewers. Other cable shows are produced by American Jewish and Israeli groups and *are* recommended family viewing!)

Reading

● Reading books and periodicals about Israel is, of course, one of the most effective ways to learn about Israel. There are many books for adults and a few good books for young people, although we need many more stories about life in Israel for school-age and preschool children (does this lack signal an ambivalence about the Jewish State?). See the Resource Guide, pp. 339–341, for suggested books and photography books about Israel.

● For books and other materials for learning Hebrew, see pp. 318–320.

● As a Shabbat study, read together from the *siddur* (or Torah portion and *haftarah*) for references to Israel, Jerusalem, and the Jewish longing to return to the land of Israel. Locate Jerusalem on a map of modern Israel. Do the same when you read any biblical selection or Jewish story that refers to places in Israel. The Jewish National Fund (p. 342) has inexpensive study-guide booklets such as *Israel in the Siddur* and *Israel in the Torah*.

HEARING: BEYOND "ZUM-GALI, GALI"

● If there's one area of Israeli culture that American Jews ought to experience more of, it's the range and beauty of Israeli music and its extreme importance to Israeli culture. There are folk songs of the pioneer days (those good old "Jewish Agency tunes"), children's songs (from lyrical to whiny), pop songs, biblical verses, and modern Hebrew poetry set to haunting folk tunes or included in the lyrics of pop music, and the ever-popular protest songs (which frequently echo Jewish sources—for example, Chava Alberstein singing a version of *Had Gadya* transformed into a lament for the Israel–Palestinian conflict). From nursery school to youth groups to communal sing-alongs, concerts, and songfests for adults, Israeli music is an inseparable part of Israeli cultural and social life.

The Music Resource Guide (p. 313) gives some basic ideas for discovering Jewish music. New series such as "The Israel Bookassette" introduce English speakers to Israeli folk songs and pop hits with lyric books that give English translations. There are also videos of Israel with accompanying lyrics for multimedia sing-alongs. Other albums and songbooks of Israeli "classic" tunes are readily available from companies such as Tara Publications (p. 313), and with a little effort one can also find the more up-to-the-minute Israeli songs (but these generally don't have translations, so if you don't know Hebrew, it's useful to get a friend who does to paraphrase or translate for you).

● Use any of the ideas from the Music section (pp. 64–66) for incorporating Israeli music into the home. Here are a few more suggestions: Play lively Israeli tunes as background music while you clean for Shabbat or get ready for Pesah. Play quieter songs during rest times, at bedtime, or during a family evening at home. Learn Israeli religious songs (for example, from the "Chasidic Song Festival") to sing around your Shabbat table. Play recordings during a Hanukkah, Purim, or Yom HaAtzma'ut celebration. Young children will often enjoy dancing to music, even if they don't understand the words; simple props such as streamers or rhythm instruments can enhance the experience. Family musicians can learn Israeli songs for their repertoire. For a multimedia experience, play Israeli music in the background while looking at books of Israeli photos, painting your impressions of the music, or even while having a Hebrew lesson together.

● If you have a shortwave radio, you can get broadcasts of "The Voice of Israel" in English, Hebrew, and other languages. Broadcast details can be obtained by writing to the English Service, Kol Yisrael, P.O. Box 1082, Jerusalem 91010, Israel.

● Attend performances by Israeli artists who visit your area.

A Taste of Israel

• Make foods from an Israeli cookbook together with your children. Try the dishes of various Israeli immigrant groups as new treats for each Jewish holiday. See the Resource Guide to cookbooks, pp. 309–310, for ideas.

• Make an Israeli Middle-Eastern-style meal from time to time: It can include foods such as pita bread, *humus* (chick-pea dip), *tehinah* (sesame-paste dip), *felafel*, Israeli salad (finely chopped tomatoes, cucumbers, green pepper, green onion), grated carrot salad sweetened with citrus juices, eggplant dip, olives and picante pickles, cold drinks.

• Make *bourekas* (an Israeli Sephardic snack): Purchase frozen phyllo dough (leaf pastry) and use according to package directions. Fill pastry triangles (or any shape) with a blend of spinach and onions (white and yellow cheeses optional), mashed potatoes, or whatever appeals to you. Do not overfill. Brush with margarine, sprinkle with sesame seeds, and bake in a medium oven until golden. Moroccan Jews fill the phyllo dough with spicy ground meat, roll up tight, and deep-fry in oil to make their famous "cigars."

• On a Sunday morning, serve an "Israeli breakfast": fresh Israeli salad, olives, hard-boiled eggs, the best-available rye bread, dairy products such as hard cheese, low-fat cream cheese, plain yogurt (to approximate the Israeli *leben*), jam, hot drinks.

• Try Israeli candies, cookies, chocolate spread (*oy!*) and packaged foods from your Jewish food market. Make Israeli sweets your traditional birthday, Hanukkah, or Purim treat.

Scent

On *Havdalah*, perhaps around Yom HaAtzma'ut, use as your spices (*besamim*) scents reminiscent of Israel, such as pine branches (abundant and fragrant in the Judean and Galilean hills), rosemary sprigs (rosemary grows all over Jerusalem), oranges and other citrus fruits—including an *etrog* if available at the time; spices used in Middle-Eastern cooking, such as cardamom, cumin, oregano; even Israeli perfume, Turkish coffee, or a whiff of Sabra liquor—why not?

Touch, Movement, and "Hands on"

• Do you have any "hands on" objects from Israel at home? Collect items such as olive-wood ornaments, Israeli dolls, jewelry, embroidered *kippot* and clothing in various ethnic styles, Jewish ritual objects, even stones and seashells collected on a trip to Israel. Use the ritual objects for Shabbat and holidays, wear the wearables, and make the rest into a home display in a child's room. Any of the above can also be conversation pieces for "home show-and-tell" with young children. Sources for collectors: trips to Israel, your local Jewish gift shop, and Jewish gift catalogs.

• Israel-oriented educational hobbies can include coin or stamp collecting. Check if there are clubs in your area and see the Resource Guide, p. 342, for pertinent addresses.

• Israeli folk dancing is not only a taste of Israeli culture and good exercise, but is also often a place to meet Israelis and those who have been to Israel, who would be willing to tell your family about their experiences.

• Play games that teach about Israel, such as "Going Up—The Israel Game," by Joel Lurie Grishaver (from A.R.E. Publishing, 3945 South Oneida St., Denver, CO 80237), for two–six players or teams, grade 4–adult.

More Ways to Bring Israel Home

The Israel Connection

• Strengthen your family's personal ties to Israel with pen pals. Renew correspondence with friends or family in Israel. The Jewish National Fund, Dept. of Education, 114E. 32nd St., Suite 1501, New York, NY 10016, sponsors a "friendship project" that matches schools in Israel to Jewish schools in the United States for the purpose of exchanging letters, photographs, poems, tapes, and other projects. Other possibilities, suggested by Barbara Sofer in *Kids Love Israel—Israel Loves Kids*,[1] her guide to Israel for families, are: advertising in the *Jerusalem Post*, Romema, Jerusalem, Israel, or writing Etty Moskowitz, "Pen Pals in Israel," ICCY, P.O. Box 8009, Jerusalem, Israel. Or ask Israelis in your locale for names of young friends and relatives back home whom your children could correspond with (Israeli kids begin learning English in fourth grade). American Jewish day school students may be capable of corresponding in Hebrew.

19

TIME IN ISRAEL AS
A FAMILY

Who walks four cubits in the land of Israel is assured
of a place in the world to come.

—Talmud, *Ketubbot* 111a

A PILGRIMAGE WITH
TRANSFORMATIVE POWER

There are few things that a Jewish family or
individual can do that will be as inspiring, educational, and generally mind-expanding as a meaningful journey—a pilgrimage, if you will—to Israel.
Just as a Hebrew-school teacher can't possibly
teach what Shabbat is really like to a child whose
family doesn't observe it, so all the books, lectures,
and even videos in the Diaspora can't really tell
you what Israel is really like. Like so many other
aspects of Jewish life, this is a classic case of *Naaseh
VeNishma*—we'll do it and *then* we'll understand it.

Israel is truly a family- and child-oriented
country and a wonderful place to visit with children. Israel has beautiful scenery—a rare diversity
of views and recreational opportunities in a com-
pact area: from the pine-covered hills of the Galilee
to Mediterranean beaches to the stark Negev, from
the eerie Dead Sea to the golden hue of Jerusalem
stone at sunset. And every view is immeasurably
enriched by the knowledge of the history of this
place and the impact these sites have had upon the
Western world. There's also a great diversity of
population, from all races and ethnicities, and it's

mind boggling to consider that most of these
people are Jewish, with so many stories, so many
histories. And of course the learning opportunities, from the wonderful museums to historic sites
to everyday experiences, are simply incomparable.

Still, it's not necessarily the historic sites or
major attractions alone that make a trip to Israel so
memorable. The little moments unique to your
personal experience may be the ones you treasure
most. My first trip to the *Kotel* (Western Wall) was
not particularly emotional, but for some reason
tears came to my eyes when I saw a *mezuzah* on the
doorpost of a Ford garage in Tel Aviv. A friend of
my parents was most moved while listening to an
Israeli child easily rattle off the four questions in
his native language at the Passover seder. For
another person, it may be something as "small" as
seeing a street sign named for Queen Esther. Or
kosher food at the central bus station. Or the daily
Bible verse and *HaTikvah* on television before
broadcasting ends each night. It's seeing Jewish
culture once again a natural part of national life in
its native environment that is such a different
experience for the Diaspora Jew.

For a child, the attractions might be quite different. For our children, growing up as young Jewish
kids in South Texas, simply getting on the plane
with so many people wearing *kippot* was a striking
experience! Children may enjoy the special foods,
water activities (so many varieties for an arid
country!), and Hebrew cartoons on television.
Older youngsters may be excited by Tel Aviv's
Diaspora Museum (*Beit HaTefutzot*) with its sophisticated computer programs and interactive exhib-

its, by a camel ride, by the underwater observatory in Eilat, or by the sites of real-life heroism and adventure from our ancient and modern history. Hebrew books, Israeli games, tapes, posters, and souvenirs purchased on the trip—as well as your own photographs or home videos—will provide many educational materials for the future.

Another striking feature of visiting Israel is seeing Judaism's metaphors become concrete. *Ta Shma*, "come and hear (learn)," is a key introductory phrase in the Diaspora masterpiece, the Babylonian Talmud. But Ta Hazi, "come and see," is the phrasing of the Yerushalmi, the Talmud of the land of Israel. In Israel, the imagery, prayers, seasons, and references of the holidays, Bible, and *siddur* take on three-dimensional life. *Aliyah* is not only an "ascent" to bless the Torah or an ascent to live in Israel, but the actual physical ascent from the coastal plain to hilly Jerusalem. Zion is not only the poetic name for Jerusalem or Israel—and the root of "Zionism"—but also a real (very modestly sized) hill in the center of Jerusalem. "Gehenneh," also known as *Gei Ben Hinom*, is a valley within Jerusalem city limits, site of an ancient trash dump and even more ancient site of child-sacrificial worship of the Canaanite god Moloch. Today it is a municipal park. Armageddon, also known as *Har Megiddo*, is a hill in northern Israel.

Another example: I was sitting at a sing-along at a large Jewish gathering a few years ago, singing the well-known words of Rabbi Nachman of Bratzlav: *Kol ha'olam kulo gesher tzar me'od, veha'ikar lo lefahed klal*, "The whole world is a narrow bridge, and the main thing is not to fear at all." Suddenly, in my mind's eye, I was back in Israel (where I had been the month before) driving on the road up to Jerusalem, when suddenly I saw a sign ahead: *Gesher Tzar*—Narrow Bridge.

This concretization of Jewish metaphors makes Jewish concepts more available and more memorable to our children, and perhaps explains some of the differences in mentality between American and Israeli Jews.

Some contemporary writers have, with humor but a trace of bitterness, blamed American Jews for looking at Israel as an exotic Jewish fantasyland where we go periodically "to recharge our Jewish batteries," then fly away to the stability and affluence of our American lives, leaving the Israelis behind to defend the country and deal with the difficulties of daily life there.

Well, there is some truth to that. But here's another side of it: Israelis, too, are obsessed with the country. They, too, find it a fascinating place,

are proud of it, and love to show it off. Israelis constantly tour Israel in families and groups; they take *their* young people on educational trips all over the country, write columns about this or that little-known site in their newspapers, and sing songs about the beauties of their homeland. I went on the same type of professionally guided intensive tours with my husband's Israeli Air Force unit as I did with my college *ulpan* (Hebrew course) group—and many Israeli students came along for those, too. It's not a simple matter of having few nearby places to go: for Israelis *tiyulim*, small excursions in their country, are practically a national ritual.

Also, tourism is a primary industry in Israel. Decreased tourism in tense political periods is a great blow to the Israeli economy. Tourism alone, even the unenlightened bourgeois variety, is a major *mitzvah* for Israel.

But our stays in Israel can be much more than tourism. A stay in Israel can be a spiritual pilgrimage (*aliyah laregel*), an unparalleled educational adventure, and even more important, a chance to learn new ways to contribute something to Israel and to forge personal, meaningful links with the Jewish homeland. A trip to Israel shouldn't be a one-time thing, but can lead us to increase our ties and our children's ties to the country and to the Jewish people. The ideal is that, if we don't make Israel our actual home, we will *really* make it our second home.

"BUT IT'S SO EXPENSIVE!"

Yes, it is expensive, but it's also a matter of priorities. For the affluent, it may simply be a matter of placing Israel higher on the agenda of places worth visiting (and many Jews with the means to travel anywhere in the world have found that Israel is their favorite destination). For the less affluent, it really is worth scrimping and saving and finding ways to make the trip less expensive. Make it a priority, even a necessity. As Theodore Herzl said, "If you will it, it will not remain a dream." Start a separate savings account for your trip, then open another one as soon as you get back.

WAYS TO SAVE MONEY ON ISRAEL TRIPS

● Go on a subsidized program or a volunteer program (most are directed at youth and young singles, but there are some family opportunities; see the Resource Guide on pp. 343–344).

● Cut costs by staying with friends or relatives (if this is a realistic option for all concerned), camping part of the time, trading homes, renting a nonluxury apartment or a suite in an "apartment–hotel" for your stay (renting an apartment may be more comfortable for a family and will also facilitate a less touristy, more integrated stay).

● Go to Israel off season.

● Various family members go separately: for example, parents go alone first, then save money for the children to go on educational programs when they are teenagers.

● Some airlines are less expensive than EL Al, but I personally would rather spend the extra money and fly with greater comfort, the special atmosphere (you're "in Israel" as soon as you step on the plane, and the quality of service today is excellent), and a greater sense of security. I have also found EL Al more family-oriented than the other carriers when it came to traveling with small children.

GETTING READY

● If you are considering an organized tour or program, it is imperative to get the names and numbers of *several* people or families who have been on that program, to get an idea of what it is really like.

● Use any of the techniques under Israel in the Home (see pp. 129–131) to learn about Israel with the family.

● Read from the many insightful guidebooks, which tell a lot about the character of the country and give many useful hints and suggestions.

● As experienced parents know, travel with children is quite different from adult travel. The pace needs to be slower and more relaxed, the places visited more child-oriented and "hands-on," and the trip needs to include a greater amount of recreation and fun. *Kids Love Israel, Israel Loves Kids: A Travel Guide for Families* by Barbara Sofer (Kar-Ben), is a godsend for parents traveling to Israel with children. It contains all sorts of "insider hints" and descriptions of special child- and family-oriented places and programs that the average

tourist could easily miss. It also includes listings of Israeli summer day and overnight camps for children.

● Subscribe to Israeli periodicals (see p. 345); learn as much as possible about current events and trends in advance of your visit.

● Make as many personal connections as you can. Talk to Israeli friends or acquaintances in your community about recommendations of places to visit and numbers of people to call (they'll have plenty, don't worry). Write to anyone you know in Israel (see "Israeli pen pals," p. 131). Ask friends who've been to Israel recently for their impressions and suggestions. The Israel Government Tourist, which has offices in various Israeli cities (the addresses of which are listed in guide books) can arrange home hospitality with Israel families.

● Learn some Hebrew (see Learning section). You can generally get by very well in English, especially in major cities and areas frequented by tourists, but knowing some Hebrew can be a boon, and it's also a wonderful experience to be able to use your Hebrew in Israel.

● Keep a journal. Begin before your trip by recording your expectations: How realistic do they seem? Later, you can describe how Israel (or what you encounter of it) compares with your expectations. After your trip you might ask: What can you do to maintain and strengthen your ties to Israel, to teach your children, preserve memories, contribute? How will you keep the initial posttrip enthusiasm from fading? When will you go back? There are some special journals prepared just for a trip to Israel, but of course you can create your own.

HOW TO GIVE SOMETHING BACK

● The tourist looks at Israel as an "experience," whereas the committed Jew also feels ties of responsibility and caring. Learn about the major issues facing Israel today: establishing peace and a political solution to the Israeli-Palestinian conflict, strengthening democracy, building the economy, enhancing civil rights and pluralism, improving the quality of life, and preserving the natural environment. All these are areas in which both American immigrants and American-Jewish organizations can offer experience and knowledge.

● Go to Israel on family volunteer programs, on a sabbatical to volunteer your professional services, or, if otherwise staying there for an extended time, get involved in volunteer work or causes you believe in.

● Even on a short visit, some of your time can be spent visiting the headquarters of organizations and causes you support in Israel, or visiting and perhaps even working with some of Israel's unique *mitzvah* people." (Danny Siegel's *Munbaz II and Other Mitzvah Heroes*, described in the Values section, p. 334, is a good source for the locations of *"mitzvah*-doers.") Call to make an appointment; preferably, write in advance for details. The New Israel Fund schedules regular tours throughout the summer of a number of the organizations that they benefit. For other large organizations, call the American headquarters or "American Friends of . . ." that particular organization.

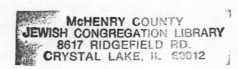

20

AMERICAN AND ISRAELI JEWRY: RIVALRY OR PARTNERSHIP?

The relationship of the two major world Jewish communities, Israel and the United States, is by no means a simple one. While for two millennia Jews perceived themselves in exile from their ancestral homeland, most contemporary American Jews feel at home right where they are. Meanwhile, their Israeli counterparts are raised with the notion that every Jew in the world should naturally feel a need, if not an obligation, to live in the Jewish homeland. Sometimes the rhetoric from opposite sides of the Atlantic has made the two great Jewish communities sound like rivals.

Yet it cannot be denied that American Jewish life has been profoundly influenced by the State of Israel. The very existence of a strong, independent Jewish state has given American Jews more confidence to develop and display our own particularistic Jewish identity. The renewal of Hebrew as a spoken language has facilitated Jewish learning and scholarship. A large percentage of rabbis, educators, and other professionals in the American Jewish community have studied in Israel as part of their training. Many Jewish American lay leaders have been deeply influenced and motivated by intense programs in Israel, and numerous young adults have rediscovered Judaism as the result of sojourns there. Israeli thinkers, writers, educators, artists, and public figures have helped to shape the contemporary Jewish world. In many ways, the Jewish world has seen a realization of Israeli philosopher Ahad HaAm's vision of "Cultural Zionism," not of Israel as a "negation" of the Diaspora, but of Israel as a cultural center for world Jewish revival.

The American-Israeli dynamic should come to be characterized by partnership rather than rivalry. In recent years, many American Jews have begun to work together more closely with Israelis to make the Jewish state better fulfill its ideals. The UJA's "Project Renewal" and the New Israel Fund are two examples of this personal brand of involvement. American Jews have much to give back to Israel, not only through financial contributions and political support, but also by sharing ideas, values, and experience.

AMERICAN *ALIYAH*

While about 99 percent of American Jewry is satisfied to enjoy a long-distance relationship with the Jewish homeland, there are thousands of American Jews who have chosen Israel as their actual home. *Aliyah* ("ascending," the word means literally; to live in Israel) perhaps provides the ultimate way to raise one's children as Jews, to ensure that one's descendants are likely to remain part of the Jewish people. Judging by current demographic trends, in the not-too-distant future Israel will overtake the United States as the world's largest Jewish community. While American Jewry continues to age and assimilate, Israelis have more children and a new wave of *aliyah* is arriving daily from the former Soviet Union.

It's natural to raise Jewish children in Israel. Hebrew is the spoken language, Bible and rabbinic texts are learned in public school, Jewish holidays are the national holidays, and the week revolves around Shabbat (as a day of religion for some, recreation for others).

Family life in Israel can be very satisfying. Israel is a country with strong family values where one can be more confident of living within easy visiting distance of grown children and grandchildren. Family values in Israel, unlike the contemporary United States, are supported by both social attitudes as well as by social welfare legislation. (On the other hand, it can be painful to live in such a family-oriented society when one's own family of origin still lives far away in North America.)

For many American Jews, especially the Modern Orthodox, Israel may be the place to experience a more fully integrated and holistic Jewish life. (About 20 percent of Israel's population is Orthodox.) On the other hand, religiously liberal Jews such as Reform, Conservative, or Reconstructionist will find that their approach to Judaism is in a small minority in Israel. Most Israelis who are not Orthodox have a secular, nationalistically based Jewish identity that is foreign to most American Jews.

American immigrants have much to contribute to Israel. So much of what many American Jews would like to see happen in Israel—more democracy, pluralism, tolerance, feminism, religious variety, even better efficiency and courtesy—would be facilitated by increased American *aliyah* and a wider spectrum of American Jews as *olim*. The relatively few Americans who have made *aliyah* have already accomplished a lot in many areas of Israeli life; how much more thousands more of us could contribute! In a small country like Israel, the social activism of each individual has the potential to make a profound impact.

While recognizing the obvious fact that most Diaspora Jews have not opted for *aliyah*, the American Jewish community could do much more to encourage and facilitate *aliyah*, through youth programming, substantive Hebrew instruction, Zionist educational emphasis, subsidized travel, and sabbatical programs in Israel for young adults and families. It's a "Catch-22" situation; the very problems that keep Americans away are the problems that we have the potential to be most instrumental in helping solve were we there in more significant numbers. We can still work for our goals from afar, but not at all with the same impact.

Aliyah is seldom easy; it's a difficult and life-changing move. Most *olim* must leave families and friends behind, forge new personal ties, learn a new language, deal with culture shock, carve out new identities, adapt to a more modest standard of living, and live in a society where the difficult security situation and extensive military service are pervasive facts of life.

Like many of my Jewishly committed friends, I am familiar with the *aliyah* dilemma. I lived in Israel for several years. My husband was raised in Israel and our family all holds dual American and Israeli citizenship. In recent years we've been back to Israel frequently and have continually explored the options for a more permanent return. Going back feels like going home in many ways, but it also means the difficulty of leaving my side of the family and a familiar, in many ways easier, way of life in the United States.

Although *aliyah* can be difficult, many *olim* feel that the rewards more than compensate for all the difficulties and sacrifices. Jews have waited centuries for the chance to build a nation in our ancestral homeland. Now that it is at last a reality, we can choose to support Israel from the sidelines—or we can move there and be a part of it ourselves. *Aliyah* means that you and your family have the opportunity to participate in a 2,000-year-old sacred dream, doing your part to help make it come true.

There are moments in history which are unique, moments which have tied the heart of our people to Jerusalem forever.

These moments and the city of Jerusalem were destined to radiate the light of the spirit throughout the world. For the light of the spirit is not a thing of space, imprisoned in a particular place. Yet for the spirit of Jerusalem to be everywhere, Jerusalem must first be somewhere.

—Abraham Joshua Heschel[1]

I asked some friends who have made *aliyah* (and love it!) to share some of their thoughts about living and raising kids in Israel. What follows are some of their "family snapshots."

FAMILY SNAPSHOTS

RAISING JEWISH KIDS IN ISRAEL

[The Reisses—Sue and Chayim, and their young children, Amit, Navah, and Karin—live on

Moshav Shorashim, near Carmiel, in the Lower Galilee. Sue grew up in Texas, Chayim in New York. Shorashim is a settlement affiliated with the Conservative movement, and Sue describes Shabbat there as "like back at summer camp!" Shorashim's economy includes high tech industry, a little agriculture, and a translating office where Sue works with some friends. They maintain ties with other regional communities, both Jewish and Arab. *Moshav* children experience a kind of freedom and security that most American city kids would envy.]

What is it like to raise kids in Israel? It's hearing your son explain to a friend, "Christmas is the Christian's Hanukkah." It's explaining to the kids that an eagerly awaited event is "three Shabbats away." It's taking an autumn walk to see the *sukkot* on people's lawns.

Still, religious education is not "automatic" for the non-Orthodox. One of the problems in raising non-Orthodox Jewish children in Israel is teaching them to look beyond the many negative models in the "religious" communities. The line between religious and political is blurred in Israel, and the ultra-Orthodox play some "dirty games" in the name of religion. The challenge then becomes teaching children that the ultra-Orthodox (and often the "crocheted *kippah*" ultranationalists) might be observant, but that doesn't necessarily make them good Jews.

One of the shocks for me in raising kids in Israel was that living in Israel didn't release me from the responsibility of giving my kids a *Jewish* education. In fact, for the non-Orthodox family, it might be harder in Israel, because you can't just send the kids off to Hebrew school a number of times a week.

Of course, in Israel kids are fluent in Hebrew, and in the secular Israeli schools they study the Bible as a literary, historical book. And the holidays are stressed in the schools. But the kids won't feel comfortable in a synagogue, won't know their way through a *siddur*, and so on, unless the individual family makes an effort to impart these things.

We chose a life-style in Israel based on a community committed to Conservative Judaism—Moshav Shorashim in the Galilee. The community synagogue is an important part of the social as well as the religious experience here. One of the Israeli-born parents here—from a secular *kibbutz* that actively rejected particularistic Jewish values—told us that one Friday afternoon his three-year-old daughter refused to take a bath. "No bath, no Shabbat services," he threatened her, and then shuddered to think that this actually *was* a threat for her!

The two most positive aspects of raising children in Israel are related to time and place. The fact that the Hebrew calendar is the dominant one in national and cultural life makes the Jewish holidays a part of every Israeli's life. Suddenly, prayers like the Sukkot prayer for rain make sense in the Israeli context. Hearing holiday-related songs on the radio, finding holiday foods available, and so on, all contribute to more meaningful celebrations of all the Jewish holidays.

Concerning place: A trip anywhere in Israel is linked to Jewish history, both ancient and modern. Israelis love to hike in their land, and it certainly adds a dimension to learning Jewish history to visit key places, such as the Old City of Jerusalem, Safed, and Mount Meron. My six-year-old son can tell you who Josephus was, name major crusader forts in "the Holy Land," describe the battle for Jerusalem in the Israeli War for Independence, and so on. The kids feel that they are a link in the long chain of Jewish history—especially today, with planeloads of Jews arriving almost every day from Russia, Argentina, or Ethiopia.

—*Sue Reiss*

FAMILY SNAPSHOTS

P.R.
FOR ALIYAH

[Charley Levine is founding president of CLC, a leading Jerusalem public relations consulting firm. His wife, Shelly, is owner-operator of Tivuch Shelly, a Jerusalem-area realty agency. This "modern Orthodox" couple and their children, Doni (Doniel), Dori (Dvora), and Zvi, live in Ma'ale-Adumim, a town just outside Jerusalem in the Judaean Desert. (Interestingly enough, in this case he is from Texas and she is from New York.) Charley has always stressed that *aliyah* for him doesn't mean throwing away his American past to "pick oranges on a *kibbutz*," but rather it's combining the best of American know-how with the spiritual benefits of living in the Jewish homeland.]

One standard motivation for coming to live in Israel is the anticipated fashion in which parents can raise their children—freer, more Jewish, more natural than in the Diaspora.

Indeed, our own theoretical plans for *aliyah* turned concrete at precisely the stage when our firstborn, Doni, made his appearance. His birth triggered a bout of introspection in which Shelly and I were confronted with a soul-searching examination of our *aliyah* plans: Were we serious about our long-held desire to move to Israel, or was it some idyllic dream?

Our answer came in December 1978, when we boarded the EL AL airliner to come home to Israel, ending a three-generation wholly positive experience by our respective families in the American Diaspora. Originally from Galicia and Lithuania, our families had fleetingly settled—in New York and Texas, respectively. We decided to join that trickle of American Jews who hear the different drummer, and our children, both present and hoped-for, figured significantly in the decision.

Without conjuring up the routine ideological truisms, suffice it to say that Israel enjoys one capability that absolutely no other place in the world can claim—the ability to imbue Jewish children with a sense of majority mentality and control of their national destiny.

In *Galut*, Jews pick and choose their identification. Do the kids miss any days for religious holidays, or all of them? Do they take their own sandwiches for the class party, clearly setting them apart, or do they eat the McDonald's hamburgers like everyone else, or perhaps order a fish-burger? Do they learn a little Hebrew, do they continue their religious education after *bar/bat mitzvah*, and so on. Make no mistake, this randomness applies equally to the most nominally affiliated Jews and to the insulated ultra-Orthodox alike, for both are defining their Jewish identity and practice within the much larger context of a thoroughly non-Jewish, or even Christian, if you will, society.

With all its oddities, Israel takes that method of self-definition and turns it on its head. No matter how religious you are in the Jewish state, you are an integral part of the majority culture.

The life cycle and annual rhythm is totally a Jewish one. Schools educate about, and close on, our holidays, even the nonceremonial ones like Tu BiShvat and Lag BaOmer. Hebrew is the *lingua franca*. The Bible is the national history book and archeological guide. Children may not be observant, but every child has a concept of what keeping kosher means, what motivates people to wear *kippot* and *tzitziot*, and so on. In comparison with the frighteningly low level of similar knowledge amongst the vast majority of Diaspora Jewish children—not those who attend day school full-time—the difference is tremendous in terms of both quantity and quality of knowledge and feeling.

An excellent case in point was our eldest son Doni's recent bar mitzvah. In addition to his intensive training for the big day itself—he read the entire Torah portion on Shabbat, the *haftarah*, and so on—I felt that we would be remiss not to add other dimensions—the dimensions of history and religious meaning—to his budding awareness of being Jewish and being responsible for his own acts. Israel provided a unique proscenium for this purpose, and this is something that people living outside Israel can adapt to their own needs.

For a six-month period, we used Israel as a showcase and testing ground for delving into Jewish history and religious meaning. We talked about politics, and we went to see the Good Fence and the Knesset in Jerusalem. We discussed the Holocaust, and the poignant displays of Yad Vashem. We explored the millennia of Jewish history, and visited Bet Hatfuzot (the Diaspora Museum). There were also the stories and lessons of Masada, Gamla, Latrun, and the Temple Mount.

The process culminated about a month before Doni's bar mitzvah. Being a big advocate of father-son getaways (a vestige of the ethical code I picked up from *Father Knows Best* and *Leave It to Beaver*), Doni and I left Jerusalem and checked into a modest mountaintop resort in the Judaean hills. For Doni, who is interested in sports, we spent the evening in Tel Aviv at a fast-paced Maccabi basketball game, but the next morning was all work.

We hiked to the proverbial global vantage post and sat and talked. We covered the full gamut. What is life all about? What are we doing in Israel? What kind of person is each member of our family, and what kind of person did Doni aspire to be as he grew up? What were his professional and academic ambitions? What does God expect of us—day by day and over the course of a lifetime?

I took some mental notes, and as frequently happens something emerged from our talks—we had the rudimentary outline of Doni's bar mitzvah speech prepared before we trekked back to the hotel.

I think back to what I remember as a child, and I get a real kick out of providing positive "memories"—even the kind that I manipulate into exist ence—that our children can carry with them until they are 120. I believe that the memories of Doni's bar mitzvah period will stay with him for a good while, and the meaning he drew from our various visits and talks will, I hope, provide him with a clearer understanding of his role, and even more important, of the fact that we have to address the big questions in life, not just the petty tasks and duties of everyday living.

—Charley Levine

V

THE JEWISH WEEK, MONTH, AND YEAR

In family life, we are accustomed to placing great emphasis on places: the neighborhood where we will live, the home we will buy, the schools to which we will send our children. But the decisions we make in regard to place are only part of the picture. The most important decisions we make as parents involve the way in which we will live our time. What we do with our time teaches our children what we value. When and how we mark special occasions teaches our children how to celebrate and commemorate. What we do with time really shapes our character as individuals and as a family.

Judaism, as Rabbi Abraham Joshua Heschel explained in *The Sabbath*,[1] was perhaps the first religion to sanctify time above place; to stress the holiness one can make of time. Finding eternity in the present life, to paraphrase Heschel, is one of our tradition's salient themes.

The section that follows deals with the recurring cycles of the Jewish calendar: week, month, and year. Shaping our home life around these ancient cycles also has the potential to strengthen and nurture our families.

As elaborated in the section on "Home and Heritage," p. 4, research into strong families demonstrates that the major traits they have in common often include spiritual values, rituals and traditions, time together (especially meals together), communication, and appreciation. The Jewish Shabbat and holiday cycle encourage these traits. Obviously, the holidays are important religious celebrations, which center on spiritual values. They involve rituals and traditions, spending time together as a family, communicating about important values, and appreciating one another, our community, and God. A commitment to observe these special days is a commitment to family life, to Jewish community, to Judaic and humanistic values and ideals. The yearly cycle presents numerous recurring opportunities in which to transform family life from secular to sacred.

Observing Shabbat and holidays together—not just by rote, but with insight and creativity—can be an important element in strengthening and enriching family life and in transmitting our deepest values to our children.

21

SHABBAT: THE HEART OF JEWISH LIFE

Saturday: Weekend. Movies. Cartoons. Cocktails. Entertaining. The Mall. Eating out. Spectator sports. Yardwork. Housework.

Shabbat: Sabbath. Torah. Stories. *Kiddush*. Hospitality. The Synagogue. Home-cooked meals. Family Time. Walks. *Home*.

Friday Night/Saturday or Shabbat: Each is a day-long period in time, but the former is merely time spent, while the latter is time made holy. Every Jewish family can decide whether Friday night brings just another weekend or "a sanctuary in time."

The choice is ours.

Choosing to make Shabbat with one's family is one of the primary steps—perhaps the one most important action—in creating a Jewish home and identity.

Your family's Shabbat orientation may be Orthodox, Reform, Conservative, Reconstructionist, or eclectic! For while they may disagree on the details of observance, *all* the major Jewish movements affirm that Shabbat is the high point of the Jewish week and the mainstay of the Jewish calendar. Every Jewish family, regardless of "denominational" identification, can make Shabbat a meaningful element of family living.

Shabbat has been a pillar of Jewish life throughout the centuries. Just as Jerusalem is our physical center, the Sabbath is our temporal center. Time and again, Jewishly active adults recall that their increased commitment to Jewish life began with the Shabbat experiences in their own or another home, or at camp, youth group, or in college—or maybe it was a trip to Israel—any one of these experiences might have touched the physical center or the temporal center, or both.

When I look back at what made me want to learn more about Judaism as an adolescent, I remember the Shabbat evenings at a Jewish sleepover camp that my parents sent me to when I was about twelve. Changing out of our grungy camp duds into white "Shabbat clothes" and then attending services in a lakeside chapel created a break from the week that I had never experienced before. In the next few years, there were more camp and youth-group Shabbats and later Shabbats in the homes of observant Jews. The total *gestalt* of a Shabbat, not easily translated into words, convinced me that I, too, wanted to create that beautiful experience with my own family. The experience of Shabbat taught me more than any book or course on Judaism could have. Shabbat was the catalyst of my Jewish life.

The power of Shabbat observance tends to spill over into other areas of Jewish life. As a family begins to create its personal Shabbat experience on a regular basis, its whole orientation tends to become more Jewish; as the sages would say, "one *mitzvah* draws another." Or in the words of writer and Zionist philosopher Ahad HaAm, "More than

Israel has kept the Sabbath, the Sabbath has kept Israel."[2]

Shabbat is not only critical for Jewish continuity, but it can be vital in fostering family closeness. Shabbat is the ideal framework for developing many of the qualities that researchers have found to characterize strong and healthy families (see p. 4). In particular Shabbat is an opportunity to nurture the important qualities of appreciation (in our prayers to God and our words to one another) and time together—including "table time" and meaningful conversation and communication. Of course, Shabbat is a time for rituals, traditions, and learning, which enhance "spiritual wellness" and religious identity. Shabbat can also be a time for service to others when we give *tzedakah* before candlelighting or invite someone to share our Sabbath joy. Commitment is another one of those important family qualities, and a commitment to Shabbat is de facto a commitment to family life and family values. "Coping," too, can be enhanced: In today's hectic world, Shabbat can be an island of peace and relaxation in otherwise stressful schedules.

Shabbat is a powerful means for transforming the Jewish home from a secular space into a holy place.

WHAT IS SHABBAT?

Shabbat (Israeli Hebrew/Sephardic pronunciation) or *Shabbos* (Yiddish/Ashkenazic pronunciation) is the Jewish day of rest that begins at sundown on Friday evening and lasts until dark on Saturday night. The Shabbat or Sabbath day is first mentioned in the Creation story in the book of Genesis: "For in six days the Eternal made heaven and earth, and on the seventh day God rested. . . . Therefore the Eternal blessed the seventh day and made it holy."

Shabbat is also the fourth of the Ten Commandments:

"Remember the Sabbath day to keep it holy. Six days you shall labor and do all your work, but the seventh day is a Sabbath to the Eternal your God: you shall not do any work: You, your son, your daughter, your manservant or maidservant, your cattle, nor the stranger that is within your gates. For in six days the Eternal made heaven and earth, the sea and all that is in them, and rested on the seventh day; therefore the Eternal blessed the Sabbath day, and made it holy." (There are two versions of this commandment, "Remember the Sabbath day" in Exodus 20—and "Observe the Sabbath Day" in Deuteronomy 5. The traditional explanation is that the different versions allude to the two aspects of keeping the Shabbat: the positive observances and the negative commands [the "thou shalt nots"], respectively.)

Three central features of Shabbat are *kedushah* (holiness), *oneg* (delight and pleasure), and *menuhah* (rest). The atmosphere of Shabbat is one of physical delight and enjoyment—the finest foods of the week are eaten, nice clothing is worn, songs sung, guests invited. At the same time there is a sense of tranquillity, spirituality, and peace.

MAKING SHABBAT

Shabbat doesn't start just on Friday evening. The mood and experience of Shabbat is greatly enhanced when preparation goes on all week.

Preparing for Shabbat, or "making Shabbat," is the necessary prelude to the actual Shabbat experience. This is often the case in Jewish observance. Passover is not just the *seder*, but is cleaning the house and removing the *hametz*. Rosh HaShanah and Yom Kippur ideally have a month of spiritual and interpersonal preparation preceding them. Likewise, part of the Shabbat experience is preparing for Shabbat during the week.

ONEG SHABBAT

● It's traditional to save anything new or special to be used first on Shabbat, in order to enhance the pleasure of the day (*Oneg Shabbat*). So if you buy new clothes for family members, they can be worn for the first time on Shabbat. New toys can be played with first on Shabbat, new books read on Shabbat. Especially delicious foods can be saved to be served on Shabbat or new or unusual produce over which to say a *sheheheyanu*. You can obtain fresh flowers, especially new ones for the season. Once children are old enough to postpone gratification a bit, it should be pointed out to them that the things are being saved for Shabbat. They will come to associate "Shabbat" with "special, best."

● You can also follow the talmudic saying that one should have special clothes for Shabbat. Even

Outline of a Traditional Shabbat

All week long — Shabbat is kept in mind:

Guests invited; special foods, books, toys, or clothing set aside.

Around Thursday: Shabbat grocery shopping, cleaning, baking, and cooking usually begin (purchase extra for a food bank).

Friday — Getting ready:

Hallah baked at home or purchased, along with foods and Shabbat supplies, flowers for the table.

Afternoon: cooking and cleaning accelerate as sunset draws near.

Family bathes and dresses in nice clothing.

Orthodox/traditional Shabbat: family may set a timer to turn off lights, a hot plate/electric urn to keep foods and water hot.

Table set: a white tablecloth, two *hallahs* and cover, salt (to dip the *hallah* in), *kiddush* wine cup, candlesticks, nice dishes.

Just before candlelighting: give *tzedakah*.

Friday — *Just before sunset* — Welcoming the Sabbath:

Candles are lit at home no later than 18 minutes prior to sunset.

Traditional synagogues: a brief afternoon service is held, followed at sunset by the *Kabbalat Shabbat* (Receiving the Sabbath) and fairly short evening services.

Friday Night — The Shabbat Evening Meal:

A festive dinner is held at home: *Shalom Aleichem* is sung, followed by blessing the children and *Eishet Hayil* ("A Woman/Wife of Valor," Proverbs 31). (To make this more egalitarian, some households add Psalm 112 or other verses of praise for the husband/father.) Kiddush, ceremonial hand-washing, and *HaMotzi* prayer over the *hallah*. Then the meal, which includes singing Hebrew songs (*zemirot*), conversation and happiness, stories, words of Torah, and finally *Birkat HaMazon* (grace after meals).

Guests are often present at any Shabbat meal (it's a *mitzvah* to invite those who otherwise wouldn't enjoy a nice Sabbath meal).

Later Friday evening:

Some congregations hold the Shabbat evening service at fixed, later hours (after dinner) year-round. In some Reform synagogues, this is the major service for the week. Some congregations hold an *Oneg Shabbat* ("Sabbath Delight," social gathering).

Shabbat morning — Prayer and Torah:

Traditional practice: the longest, most leisurely and well-attended synagogue service of the week. Includes reading from Torah and prophets (*haftarah*). There may be a junior congregation or other programs for children during services. After services, *kiddush* is often held at the synagogue.

Shabbat noon — The second Shabbat meal:

Another *kiddush*, hand-washing, HaMotzi over the two *hallahs*. Between courses or after eating, more songs — long, leisurely ones — words of Torah, conversations, and enjoyment of being together, concluding with *Birkat HaMazon*.

Shabbat afternoon — Leisurely "at home" time:

A more "personalized" part of the Shabbat. Relaxation, naps, conversation, reading, learning. Children may hear a story read aloud, play with siblings or friends, or go for a family walk with parents, perhaps to a playground, park, or other nearby natural setting. Visiting or hosting friends informally (it's always a *mitzvah* to visit the sick).

Shabbat late afternoon:

A light "third meal" (*se'udah shlishit*) is served. Traditional synagogues: a brief afternoon and evening service, sometimes combined with a short study session and/or the meal. Some synagogues and *havurot* have other Shabbat afternoon activities, such as youth group meetings, study or discussion groups, social gatherings.

Saturday night — *after dark:* Parting from the Shabbat:

At least 42 minutes past sunset (that is, an hour past candlelighting time): brief *Havdalah* service held at home, with blessings over wine, spices, and the flame of a braided candle. Concludes with songs like *Eliyahu HaNavi* (Elijah the Prophet) and *Shavua Tov* (A Good Week). *Melaveh Malkah,* or escorting the "Queen" Shabbat on "her" way, is an extra meal some serve after *Havdalah*. Sometimes synagogue or *havurah* groups will host a festive *Melaveh Malkah*, which might include Jewish music, songs, or folk dancing.

Shalom until next week . . .

Go back to the beginning of this section and repeat . . .

if a best dress is also used for other occasions, it can be labeled, "my Shabbat dress." My fantasy for Jewish life in America is that little Jewish kids will call their best shoes "my Shabbat shoes."

● Create things throughout the week in anticipation of Shabbat. Involve the children as you purchase food, invite guests, or plan menus or activities for the Sabbath. Make ritual objects for the Sabbath. A Sunday afternoon once a month might be set aside to bake and freeze *hallahs* and other Shabbat goodies.

CLEANING AND COOKING AS A FAMILY

The rhythm of the Jewish week includes an acceleration of activity as Shabbat draws near. By Thursday—Friday, certainly—there's an atmosphere of bustling anticipation as the house is being cleaned and favorite dishes cooked. (Some of us might never clean if it weren't for the Jewish calendar—it has been a bit embarrassing on that rare Tuesday when I get in a housewifely mood, only to have one of my children say, "But, Mommy, it's not Shabbat tonight"). "Making Shabbat" is a true creative handiwork.

Gone should be the days when the mama should be expected to clean and cook and bake for Shabbat on her own. The more people involved, the merrier, for several reasons.

For busy, two-career families today, we may have to be creative and flexible in our approach to preparing for Shabbat. It might be logistically impossible to devote much of Friday to the traditional cooking and cleaning. Different strategies could be used: cook and freeze in advance, use more ready-made food, hire help if appropriate. And of course, involve the spouse and children. The main thing is not that we bake our own *hallahs* or roll our own strudel dough the way great-grandma did, but that our weekly rhythms build toward the Shabbat in a way that is authentic for our own lives. We may need that Shabbat respite from the world of materialism and competition even more than our ancestors did!

But even if we have household help and don't do all our own cleaning and cooking, some hands-on involvement in the Shabbat preparations is a *mitzvah*, both for us and for our children's education in becoming independent and capable and making significant contributions to family life. Anticipating and creating Shabbat at home is a

drama in which the entire family can share. The Talmud records that even noted sages did quite menial chores in honor of Shabbat.

Another reason to involve children in Shabbat and holiday preparations is that it provides one of today's rare opportunities to give youngsters meaningful household work. Teaching children about work is the important counterpart to teaching them about rest (Shabbat). In the rhythm of Jewish living, the two go hand in hand. Noted child psychologist and author Eda LeShan points out in *When Your Child Drives You Crazy*[3] that modern parents have a particular problem teaching children about work, since children's work is no longer a necessity for survival as it was in the past. Likewise David Elkind[4] emphasizes that children today have many external trappings of premature "adulthood," but few areas of real responsibility. The few chores we require, such as straightening one's toys, seem dull and inconsequential to children. As a result, we often have trouble gaining their cooperation in what seems like only a few reasonable requests for help. Not only in the past, but in rural societies today (including the *kibbutz* in Israel), children and adolescents have a much greater opportunity to see that the work they do is of real value to the family or community they live in.

Making Shabbat together gives children an opportunity to be involved in a cooperative venture, working to create something of real importance to the family. Children can have the chance to choose projects that have meaning to them, such as baking or cooking special dishes, making a centerpiece and decorating the table. Moreover, when it comes to Shabbat, even the mundane chores are leading to a special result that has value to the adults in the family as well as to the children.

There are a number of ways to change the mood from chore time to family Shabbat-making. Playing some Jewish music/Hebrew songs with a lively beat really helps to set the *erev* Shabbat mood (Friday afternoon is when Israeli radio stations play Hebrew songs rather than American pop imports).

Work together with children, especially with young ones. They are nearly always more interested in "grown-up" jobs they see parents doing or can do together with parents. Frankly, I also find it much easier to clean when it's a family project and not my particular burden. It's helpful to set a regular "family clean-up time" that children will expect so that they don't feel we're "springing it on them" in the midst of other activities. Gradually they can begin to work more independently. Some families like to cap the clean-up sessions with a treat such as a video, story-session, or special snack.

Young children are thrilled to do "grown-up" jobs. At first it will seem that their "help" is really more work for us. But if they are ever to learn, we have to be patient and take the time to show them what to do, step by step. The extra work of letting them help while they're young is setting the stage for real contributions later on. By age seven or eight children can make really significant contributions to the work of the house, and often they will actually enjoy themselves and feel proud of their abilities. By that time, I don't even call it "helping"; that seems too patronizing. I call it, "doing their part."

(*Note*: I've focused on indoor jobs in these lists because I'm concentrating on Shabbat preparation, but of course children can do outdoor work such as gardening or raking.)

● Tots: bring unbreakable things to help set table (enjoy the "fetching phase" while it lasts!)
> sprinkle seeds on the *hallah*
> place cookies on sheet
> grease pans (an all-time favorite)
> pour ingredients in bowl
> scrub vegetables with a brush
> play with a bit of dough or mix a bit of anything

● Preschoolers can also:
> partially set table (nonbreakable items)
> mix things
> chop soft things with a butter knife
> start to shape things: meatballs, *matzah* balls, cookies, rolls
> dust
> clean part of glass doors and appliances with a squirt bottle and a wet rag (lay down a bathmat to avoid slipping)
> entertain an infant
> clear their places
> dress themselves
> pick things off floor and put in a hamper or other central container
> put own possessions away

● Younger school-age children can also:
> crack eggs (with supervision)
> peel vegetables
> make a fruit or vegetable salad (with some help with knives)
> mix, shape, spread, portion, decorate foods— can really help here

help cook and plan menus
polish *kiddush* cups, candlesticks, furniture (avoid toxic polishes)
vacuum or use carpet sweeper; use hand-held mini-vacuum
dust mop
wet mop with a sponge mop
hold dustpan; sweep with broom or whisk broom
set and clear table, including making a centerpiece
scrub a sink or tub
wash dishes or fill dishwasher with supervision
put dishes away/sort silverware (good opportunities to learn about *kashrut* for those who keep kosher)
bathe and dress themselves
entertain younger children, help dress them
put dirty clothes in hamper and possessions in place/keep own room in order with minimal help (plentiful containers and organizers encourage order)
empty small trash containers
fold clothes and put away (some children can start at four or five)

● Older elementary-school–age children and pre-teens can also:
> clean bathrooms—avoid toxic cleaning products
> completely cook or bake simple dishes/use microwave oven
> sweep and mop
> clean windows and mirrors with a squeegee
> do hand laundry and run washing machine (need to teach carefully)
> fold laundry
> simple mending—teach boys, too!
> plan and help with hospitality—set up, serving, and clean-up
> learn to shop, carry groceries and packages, plan menus
> greater help with younger children and infants
> outdoor work, cut flowers for centerpiece
> collect and take out trash/sort trash for recycling

CREATIVE SHABBAT PREPARATIONS

Getting ready for Shabbat can include more than housework and cooking. There are lots of creative projects that children can do by themselves or together with parents. These range from decorating food and making centerpieces and place-markers/decorations, to preparing an entertainment for the family or researching a discussion topic for Friday night or Shabbat afternoon. In the Shabbat tradition of hospitality (*hachnasat orchim*), they can invite guests and perhaps plan special foods or activities for them. Depending on their ages and interests they could teach a song, plan a puppet show based on the Torah portion or holiday, select a story to tell or be told, or—for older children—prepare a simple *devar Torah* (Torah talk). It's traditional to review the Torah portion in advance of the Shabbat, which is what you'll be doing if you plan some Torah talk.

SHARING OUR SHABBAT JOY

Each week there is a Shabbat lesson that the Jewish way is to share one's joy. Traditionally, before one lights the candles and welcomes Shabbat into the home, one first puts a few coins into the family *tzedakah* box(es); children are to be encouraged to participate in this *mitzvah*. Rabbi Yitz Greenberg encourages us to expand this *mitzvah* by actually stopping before Shabbat to write a check to some worthy project that we've perhaps been meaning to support, but have put off during the week.[5]

Another, simple way to share our Shabbat joy is to get into the *tzedakah* habit of buying some extra item each time we shop for Sabbath or holidays. Collect these on a special shelf or in a decorated box and donate regularly to a local food bank. Similarly, as children outgrow those special Shabbat clothes, consider donating to a shelter or thrift shop. Always involve children in these actions.

Not all who are needy are financially needy. There are people who need companionship or those who hunger for spiritual things. We may be privileged to help them by welcoming them into our home on Shabbat, and sharing not money, but friendship and Shabbat joy. The Jewish view of hospitality is not an exchange of social obligations, but a sharing of whatever bounty we have with our fellow travelers (*orchim*) in life. In the process it is often the giver who is enriched.

AS SHABBAT APPROACHES . . .

When my older children were tots and I ran out of things for them to "help" with while I rushed around with last-minute preparations, they would often keep happily occupied by playing *Erev Shabbat* (Sabbath evening) with some small candlesticks, cup, head coverings, and a cloth for their play table.

● *Dress for Shabbat*: Dressing for dinner sounds like something out of Miss Manners in our fast-food world—which gives it all the more impact. After an afternoon of cleaning for Shabbat (or cleaning after work on Thursday evening, with last-minute jobs on Friday afternoon), the mood begins to change. We're probably still in a hurry, but now it's (we hope!) an exciting hurry, like dressing up for a party. Shortly before Shabbat begins everyone can bathe and dress nicely. Washing away the weekday dirt and changing our clothing is a physical process of transformation that our children can feel and appreciate.

● Imagine the Shabbat "Queen": The traditional image of Shabbat is a beautiful bride/queen who graces us with her presence each Friday evening. You can ask the children if the house is beautiful enough for the Shabbat Queen, if everyone is dressed nicely to welcome the bride. Tell them to close their eyes and picture her coming in the door. What does she look like? Imagination is an important part of every cultural heritage; in Judaism it's known as the aggadic tradition (*Aggadah* means story, oral tradition, myth, lore, legend).

We're honoring not only the shabbat, but also our family. After all, we dress up and spruce up the house when important visitors are coming, but how often do we do this for our own family? The Jewish tradition provides a weekly opportunity.

We're ready for Shabbat!

Aviva's Famous
Hallah

2 packages instant dry yeast
1 cup sugar
5 lbs. (1 bag) all-purpose flour
 (Part whole-wheat flour may be substituted.)
1-1/2 sticks margarine, softened
1 tablespoon salt
4 cups warm water
5 eggs (plus one egg for egg-wash)

(All ingredients should be at room temperature.)

Sprinkle the yeast over 1 cup warm water, adding 1 tablespoon sugar. Let sit for about 2–3 minutes or so, until bubbly. Add to the remaining ingredients (adjust amount of flour as necessary to make a smooth dough) and mix well.

Knead on a floured surface about 10 minutes, until smooth. Place in an oiled bowl, cover with a towel, and allow to rise in a warm place until double in bulk (approximately 1-1/2 hours). Punch down dough.

Cover and allow dough to rise a second time. Punch down and knead for a couple of minutes. (Separate a piece of dough, about the size of a very large olive, for "hallah.")* Let rest for about 5 minutes. Divide the dough into 7 parts. Roll each portion of dough into 3 or 4 strips. Braid together into 7 loaves; place in greased pans. Allow to rise in a warm spot for about an hour, or until doubled.

Brush tops with beaten egg. Sesame or poppy seeds may be sprinkled on the loaves (this is said to symbolize the mannah that fell in the Sinai desert). Bake in a 350° F oven for 30–35 minutes, or until golden brown. When done, the loaves of bread will sound hollow when tapped. (Loaves of various sizes and shapes may be made; adjust baking times accordingly.)

This makes a very sweet hallah. For a less sweet bread, decrease the sugar by 1/4 to 1/2 cup, and use an extra teaspoon or two of salt.

RITUAL ITEMS TO MAKE FOR SHABBAT USE

Hallah Covers

Possible motifs for decoration include the word "Shabbat" or "HaMotzi Lehem Min HaAretz" in Hebrew letters, Shabbat designs such as hallahs, candlesticks, kiddush cup/decanter with grape clusters, or flowers, fruits, wheat, crown, Magen-David, abstract designs.

For any of the simple covers, you can use any piece of white cotton cloth in a size large enough to cover two hallahs. Sheeting or even large handkerchiefs are possibilities. Cut with pinking shears or tear and fringe edges.

● Crayon cover: For a simple hallah cover with no sewing involved, decorate the cotton cloth with crayon drawing, pushing hard to leave a lot of crayon on the cloth. Pencil in first if desired. Older children could use a permanent marker or laundry pen to outline the design. Cover with a piece of paper bag and iron lightly to make design permanent. (Or use special crayoning kits available from crafts stores, in which case the design is made in reverse onto a piece of paper and ironed on.)

● Paint cover: Crafts stores and dime stores have a variety of fabric paints, gold leaf kits, and decorative sew-on items that are used to decorate clothing. Experiment on a hallah cloth, following package directions to set the design. Use Jewish-symbol stencils if desired. A backing may be needed.

● Felt cover: Cut Shabbat symbols from felt or other cloth scraps and glue to a large piece of white felt or other cloth. Glue or sew on sequins or beads if desired. A spool or other object can be dipped in fabric paint and used to print designs. For fabric-tape design, use iron-on fabric tape. Cut out designs and arrange on cloth. Adult irons designs in place.

● Tie-dye cover: For an abstract design, knot a cloth with rubber bands and dye the color of your choice with commercial fabric dye (instructions on box).

● Needlework cover: Those with needlework ability might enjoy helping a child make a hallah cover design in simple cross-stitch, more elaborate embroidery, needlepoint, applique, or patchwork. Choose any cloth you like, from velvet to denim. Edges should be hemmed and the entire cover could be backed with a satiny or velvet cloth, with corner tassels if desired. Or crochet a lacy border. There are commercial kits available (see p. 308) or design your own picture.

● Batik cover: A craft for older children, this needs thorough adult supervision. To make a batik

---

*This hallah symbolizes the offering that was given to the Cohanim in the time of the Temple. (The popular name of the bread comes from the hallah offering.) Since the destruction of the Temple, Jews have separated a piece of dough and burned it in the oven. When the hallah is taken, the following blessing is said:

Baruch Atah Adonai, Eloheinu Melech HaOlam, asher kidshanu bemitzvotav, vetzivanu lehafrish hallah.

Holy One of Blessing, Your Presence fills Creation, You make us holy with Your mitzvot, and have bidden us to separate hallah.

hallah cover, paint a design (drawn in lightly with chalk first) on a cotton cloth with hot paraffin wax. Heat the wax in a coffee can placed in a pot of hot water and reheat as needed to keep it fluid. Wax must soak through cloth. Then dip in commercial fabric dye according to package directions. For a multicolor design, use multiple dyeings. Whatever part of the design is not covered with wax at each stage will absorb the newest color of dye, which will also mix with previous colors. For example, you paint on the white cloth first: all that is covered will remain white. Then dip in red (protect hands with rubber gloves). Now cover with wax all parts of the design you want to stay red. Dip in blue: all exposed parts of the cloth (previously red) will now be purple. Cover what you want to stay purple with more wax and dip in black, which in addition to making black whatever you've left exposed will also add a "veined" effect. Between dippings, rinse the cloth in clear water (do not wring) and hang to dry. When finished, iron on hot between several brown paper bags to melt out and absorb the wax.

Candlesticks

For *candles*, see techniques under "Havdalah candles," p. 153.

● Clay candlesticks: Unless you have access to a kiln, use clay that is meant to air dry only or that can be baked at home; self-glazing clays are available in crafts stores. Candlesticks can be shaped as desired from a coil of clay, a ball, braid, or other shape of clay. Make a candle-sized hole by pressing a candle in the clay. You may wish to use inexpensive metal candle holders (the kind that are used to cover and protect silver candlesticks) or foil to protect your candle holders from heat and wax each time they are used.

● "Collage" candlesticks: Using extra-strength adhesive, glue metal soda-bottle caps onto just about anything you would like to use as candleholders: wooden spools (paint gold or silver) or other wooden constructions, large open seashells, or other natural objects.

● Mosaic candlesticks: Support candles inside cleaned baby-food jars with layers of colored sand (craft or aquarium store) or layers of dried peas and beans. Do not use thin glass for candleholders; it may shatter from heat.

Tzedakah box

See pp. 109–110. *Tzedakah* is customarily given before lighting the Sabbath or holiday candles.

Kiddush Cups

Decorate small plain glasses with paint pens or special paints (from crafts store) for mock "stained-glass." Or decorate plastic wine goblets with permanent markers and even stickers, if desired. They're less durable but unbreakable and you can make enough for a crowd. Avoid the rim of the glass when decorating.

Bentschers

● *Bentschers* (Yiddish) or *Birkonim* (Hebrew) are the small booklets that include the Grace after Meals (*Birkat HaMazon*) and often contain other prayers and the traditional Shabbat songs (*zemirot*). They are often available in inexpensive soft-cover versions from Jewish gift shops. You can make *bentscher* covers out of construction paper or felt or other cloth. For paper, decorate with construction paper cut-outs, drawings, or a collage of pictures and if desired cover with Contac® paper, which can be extended slightly over the ends of the book-cover to hold it in place. For cloth, use any of the techniques described for the *hallah* covers. The words *"Berachot U'Zemirot"* can be written on the cover in Hebrew, or "Blessings and Songs" in English. You can also make covers for your *siddur* (prayer book) or make place markers from paper or felt.

● One family we know made their own Shabbat song books by photocopying songs and readings they liked and binding these into copies (you can use a folder with brads) for weekly use. They decorated the covers, too.

Light-Switch Covers

● Those who are traditionally *shomer Shabbat* (Shabbat observant) may like to make light-switch covers to remind the children not to turn the lights off and on on the Sabbath. Make from felt or even posterboard pieces decorated with Shabbat symbols and use small strips of magnetic tape or Velcro (both available at dime stores and crafts stores) on the cover and on the switch plate, to attach and detach before and after each Shabbat.

Table Decorations

Making centerpieces is one area where children really enjoy expressing their creativity. There are myriad possibilities: arrange store-bought or wild flowers and greenery, make tissue-paper flowers, make a doll-sized Shabbat table with ritual objects from play clay or paper and tiny birthday candles, display something children made in school that week or items connected with some important event in their week, objects connected with a seasonal holiday, or just natural objects of the season (fruit, fall foliage, summer seashells), even souvenirs from a family excursion.

Children or adults can make placecards with special "I love you," "I appreciate . . ." or "You are a blessing because . . ." messages inside them. Young children can make placemats from paper or posterboard decorated with crayons or markers. Glue on paper or magazine cut-outs or pressed flowers and then cover with clear Contac® paper or laminate if you have access to a machine. Use some of the cloth techniques for cloth placemats.

Havdalah Items

There are a number of crafts items you can make for the *Havdalah* ceremony that separates the Sabbath from the week to come.

● Wine cup: Use methods as for *kiddush* cup, p. 152.

● Spice box: Use any container you can fill with fragrant spices to smell. An empty spice-bottle that has a top with small holes in it is ideal. Open the top and refill with whole spices; because it is clear, children can see the spices inside. A friend added tiny artificial flowers for visual interest. Or decorate the outside with gold or silver paint pens. (Caution: Use plastic rather than breakable glass spice jar with very small children; supervise them at all times with small objects such as whole spices.)

Or cover a small container of choice, such as an empty Band-Aid® box or match box with Contac® paper or regular paper and decorate with markers, sequins, and the like. Fill with whole spices and open for smelling.

● Tray: The *Havdalah* items are often stored together on a tray. Decorate a plain purchased tray with paint pens or use the previous placemat instructions to make a plastic-covered mat to protect the table during *Havdalah*.

● Candles: The ambitious can make their own *Havdalah* (or Shabbat) candles by repeatedly dipping wicks in a pot of melted wax (heat in a coffee can inside a pot of hot water). Children from about age eight and up can do this with *constant* adult supervision. The wax on the taper must cool slightly in the air between each dip. Hold a piece of cardboard underneath to catch drips. It takes patience! You can tie three wicks to a stick of pencil so that they dip at the same rate. Leave some wick at the top for lighting. When desired thickness is reached and candles are still warm (or redipped to resoften), braid into a single candle and trim wicks to desired length. If you want different colors, make another pot of wax and melt colored crayons or commercial wax color in it. Dip an entire taper in this or use for a few final dips to coat with the color. Candle-making supplies are available from crafts stores.

For "cool" candle making without hot wax, purchase sheets of honeycomb beeswax at a crafts store. Keep in a warm place as it tends to crack if cold. Simply lay a wick along one end (let the wick extend out about an inch for later lighting) and roll into a taper. To make into a *Havdalah* candle, pinch ends of two tapers to stick together, then twist together, or try braiding three thin rolls. Roll only a few inches of wax sheet so it won't be too thick to twist.

FRIDAY NIGHT IS FAMILY NIGHT

There is a non-Jewish religious group that urges its member families to set one night a week aside as "family night," when the members of a household will make the commitment simply to spend enjoyable time together in one another's company. This practice is said to work wonders for increasing family closeness and solidarity. Of course, Judaism has had such a "family night" practice for centuries; for traditional Jews, Friday night, or *Erev Shabbat* (Sabbath eve), has always been "family night."

One of the disturbing trends in contemporary family life is the trend away from the family dinner table. "Family table time" with its conversations and "togetherness" has been found to be one of the building blocks of family health. But with pressured two-career couples and children involved in more extracurricular activities than ever, more and more families tend to eat on the run and rarely find the time for a shared meal.

When we make the commitment to "Friday night is family night," we give our children the security that at least one dinner a week will be a time for all of us to be together—eating, singing, learning, or just talking in a relaxed, pleasant manner. (It's to be hoped that commitment will be expressed as, or grow into, a realization of the entire Shabbat—Friday evening until Saturday night—as a special family and community day.) Friday night is time for:

our best clothing, prettiest table, and special treats to eat

candlelighting	prayers
songs	blessings
words of Torah	conversation
laughter	touch
family, relatives, and guests	*hallah*, wine, and favorite foods

Here are some of the highlights for making it your own:

You would not think of time as having texture, yet in a traditional Jewish household it becomes almost palpable. On Shabbat, I can almost feel the difference in the air I breathe, in the way the incandescent lamps give off light in my living room, in the way the children's skins glow, or the way the trees sway. Immediately after I light my candles, it is as if I flicked a switch that turned Shabbat on in the world, even though I know very well the world is not turned on to Shabbat. Remarkable as this experience is, even more remarkable is that it happens every seventh day of my life.

—Blu Greenberg[6]

CANDLELIGHTING TIME

The Shabbat is welcomed into the home with candlelighting and blessings. The lights (traditionally kindled no later than 18 minutes before sunset) glow with the Shabbat spirituality, peace, and joy.

Local candlelighting times can be found in Jewish community newspapers, synagogue bulletins, and some Jewish calendars. Some communities welcome the Shabbat early during daylight savings time so that dinner isn't at 10 P.M. In traditional Judaism, one can welcome Shabbat early or bid it good-bye late, but one cannot shorten it.

Lighting the Shabbat and Yom Tov candles has traditionally been a woman's special *mitzvah*; however, the main thing is that someone light them (the reverse goes for reciting the *kiddush*, traditionally the province of the husband/father). To a lot of people—whether temporarily apart from spouse, single parents, intermarried, or just experimenting with new roles—it's important just to know that it's all right, even in a traditional perspective, to have someone other than the "customary" person perform these rituals. Indeed, it's a *mitzvah* to make *kiddush* and light candles in the home for Shabbat, no matter the gender of the people doing the actions.

Generally two candles are lit, although there are other customs, such as adding an additional candle for each child born to the family. Sometimes each daughter, beginning at age three (or some other age you choose, such as at *bat mitzvah*) lights her own candle. In other households, the children may simply gather around the mother (or other adult) as she (or he) lights the candles. They might say the blessing together or just answer, "Amen." Again, there's no reason boys should not participate if they wish. (When a boy leaves home to be on his own, say to go to college, he is responsible for lighting candles on his own, so there is ample reason to train him as well.) In some households, candlelighting is a family experience in which everyone participates. Guests for Shabbat can be invited to join in the candlelighting if they desire.

It's traditional to cover the head at candlelighting (of course, many traditional Jews cover the head at all times). When I was growing up, we used to cover our heads with paper tissues when we lit the candles each Friday night, which I must have imagined was an ancient custom instituted by the Kleenexite sect. I've now reluctantly abandoned this familial practice, opting for more poetic headcoverings. I like to indulge my dramatic (Sephardic?) side with romantic lacy mantillas.

There is a gentle choreography to the candlelighting. The candles are first lit, then the person lighting them encircles them three times (or more) with outstretched fingertips, as if drawing the light inward. She covers her eyes, says the blessing (and perhaps additional prayers), and then uncovers her eyes to behold the Shabbat lights. The reason that the eyes are covered is that the Torah forbids lighting a fire on the Shabbat itself. But once the blessing has been recited, the Shabbat has been welcomed into the house. To overcome this halachic dilemma, the candles are lit, but then one covers the eyes so as not to see the lights until the blessing has been said. (On Yom Tov, when it is permissible to light from a preexisting flame, most people say the blessing before lighting.)

After lighting the candles, some add the traditional *Yehi Ratzon:* "*Yehi Ratzon*—May it be Your Will, Adonai our God and God of our ancestors, that the Holy Temple (*Beit HaMikdash*) be rebuilt speedily in our days; and grant our portion in your Torah."

(I myself say this, although my concept of building the next *Beit HaMikdash* is decidedly on the metaphorical side.) Others might wish to compose their own *Yehi Ratzon*.

This is also one of the traditional Jewish times for spontaneous personal prayers. Many women quietly whisper their own prayers for their family. I especially like to mention all my friends or others I know who are in need of physical or emotional healing, or sometimes individuals on whose behalf we are working to emigrate from lands of distress. The beautiful thing is that my older daughters have begun to imitate my example and will stand there with eyes covered saying their private prayers even longer than I do! It's one of the best frameworks I have found for encouraging them to pray, without even any nudging on my part.

I also like to bless the children after candlelighting, although the more traditional time is at the evening meal (see the following section).

Kabbalat Shabbat takes place in the synagogue with a beautiful service of poems and psalms originating with the sixteenth-century mystics in Safed, in the upper Galilee. They used to go out into the mountainside fields each Friday evening to welcome the "Sabbath Bride." It is appropriate to sing or say the service at home if family members are unable to attend the synagogue service. Maybe in nice weather you could pray outdoors, too.

To the philosopher the idea of the good is the most exalted idea. But to the Bible the idea of the good is penultimate; it cannot exist without the holy. The good is the base, the holy is the summit. Things created in six days He considered *good*, the seventh day He made *holy*. . . . The law of the Sabbath tries to direct the body and the mind to the dimension of the holy.

— Rabbi Abraham Joshua Heschel[7]

THE SHABBAT MEALS: THE TABLE IS AN ALTAR

In contemporary society, food is much more than a means for survival. Today, food and eating have become multimillion-dollar industries with massive advertising campaigns at the same time that food and eating may be the subjects of behavioral problems (compulsive eating and dieting, anorexia, and so forth). Sometimes it seems that food must be gourmet, trendy, healthful, effortless to prepare, take no time to eat, satisfy various emotional deficiencies of life—and of course, be "lite"!

Judaism proposes a different dimension to the eating experience. Eating, which sustains holy life, can be a holy act. The talmudic rabbi Yohanan likened a person's table to the altar of the Holy Temple (*Berachot* 55a). In Jewish life, the most mundane everyday actions become holy when we realize and acknowledge that all of life's necessities are gifts from God.

If this can be so with every little snack on any Wednesday afternoon, how much the more so on the holy Sabbath, when we have the time and the focused energy to truly make our meal into a holy gathering. The customs and rituals of the Shabbat meals might be termed, "a choreography of holiness."

The Friday night meal traditionally begins with the song, "*Shalom Aleichem*" ("Peace Unto You"). Some families hold hands around the table or in a circle, a lovely custom that reinforces family closeness. A talmudic legend (*Shabbat* 119b) has it that two angels accompany each Jew home from prayer on Friday evening, and this song is to greet them. One is a "good angel" and the other a "bad angel." If the home is ready for Shabbat and a peaceful, loving mood prevails, the "good angel" blesses the home, "May the next Shabbat and always, also be so," and the "bad angel" must respond "Amen." However, if conditions are quite the opposite, then the "bad angel" gets to say, "May it always be so," and the "good angel" is compelled to respond, "Amen." This legend makes a lovely Shabbat story for children, and a nonjudgmental way of encouraging them to help get ready and act nicely to one another: "so the *good* angel can bless us."

Families who cannot attend evening *Kabbalat Shabbat* services might add songs such as *Lechah Dodi* ("Come my beloved," with its traditional imagery of the Shabbat Bride) or other selections from that service prior to being seated for the meal.

This is the traditional time to bless the children,

another priceless opportunity to reinforce family closeness and the holiness of the parent-child relationship (see details following).

Other songs may be sung before *kiddush*. The traditional selection is *"Eishet Hayil"* (A Woman/ Wife of Valor), Proverbs 31. In order to make this more egalitarian, some households now add Psalm 112 or other verses of praise for the husband and father. (Although in some mystical traditions, *"Eishet Hayil"* is viewed as an allusion to the *Shechinah* or Divine Presence, and is sung together by all assembled). At any rate, the Friday night meal is certainly an appropriate time to express our appreciation and gratitude toward other members of the family as well as to God.

Next the *kiddush* is recited over a cup of wine. *"Kiddush"* means "sanctification," or "making holy," and the full text of this prayer testifies that God created the world and brought us out of Egypt to observe the Shabbat in holiness. The prayer actually sanctifies the *day*; the wine itself is a symbol of our Shabbat joy. Most families stand for the *kiddush* (sitting to drink the wine), although there are other customs. Although most of us associate *kiddush* with "the papa," like candle-lighting this is a ritual that should be done in and for the home, whether or not the customary person does it. A Sephardic custom is for the father to lead the prayer, but everyone to join in as it is sung. In some families each person holds his or her own *kiddush* cup and says the blessing together. Sometimes older children are encouraged to recite the *kiddush* in order to learn it. Everyone takes a sip of the *kiddush* wine.

The ritual handwashing or *netilat yadayim* ("lifting up of hands") that follows, reminiscent of the ritual washing of the Temple priests, again emphasizes that "the table is an altar." It is not for hygiene, but to focus our thoughts on the holiness of eating. Water is poured from a cup two or three times onto each hand (there are special cups available for purchase, but a regular cup may be used). Parents may wish to pour the water on their children's hands, spouses for one another, as another gesture of love. The blessing recited afterwards (while drying one's hands) is:

Baruch Atah Adonai, Eloheinu Melech HaOlam, asher kidshanu bemitzvotav vetzivanu al netilat yadayim.

Holy One of Blessing, Your Presence fills Creation, You make us holy with your commandments and bid us concerning the washing of hands.

After handwashing, it is customary to refrain from speaking, in order to maintain the level of *kavanah* or focus, until the *hallah* blessing is recited and the bread eaten. Children are often amused by this practice and take delight in "shushing" one another.

Finally, the two *hallahs* (two are used at each meal in memory of the double portions of *mannah* that the Israelites received in the desert prior to each Shabbat; small rolls or whole pieces of *matzah* may be used instead of large loaves) are uncovered and blessed with the *HaMotzi*. Pieces are cut or torn for everyone present and dipped in salt, another ritual associated with the ancient sacrifices, another reminder that eating in our "small sanctuary," the home, is likened to a holy offering in the Holy Temple.

The meal that follows involves not only *gefilte* fish and soup (or whatever your family favorites happen to be), but singing (*zemirot*), conversation, and it is hoped some words of Torah (*divrei Torah*). But don't feel that you need to become a Judaic scholar or a cantor to "make the table an altar": It can also be quite meaningful simply to share recent experiences and family stories, or take turns telling everyone something you've appreciated about them that week. (If you want to learn more songs, try some of the tapes or song books in the Resource Guide, pp. 347–348; or best of all, find some friends who can teach you. For suggestions on planning an informal Torah discussion, see pp. 73–74.) Conversations, storytelling, laughter, talking about the week's events with the family and guests can all be part of the joy of the Shabbat meals. If the time is truly freed from workday commitments, the television is off, the phone allowed to go unanswered, the Shabbat meal can be a time for intimacy and joy. It much more than fills the "family health" prescription for shared table time. Even infants learn to anticipate and love the weekly lights, singing, clapping, and family "togetherness." Finally, *Birkat Ha-Mazon* (grace after meals) ends the meal with thanks to God who is the ultimate source of all physical and spiritual nourishment.

A traditional Shabbat evening menu might include, besides the *hallah* and wine, fish (*gefilte* fish for Ashkenazim, stewed fish for Sephardim) and salads, soup, chicken or vegetarian main course, and side dishes such as *kugel*. Fruit or dessert and tea might complete the meal.

The Saturday noon meal is similar to the Friday night meal, except that it begins directly with *kiddush* (there is a different introductory text, which can be found in most prayer books and

Shabbat guides). One traditional main course for this meal (at least in cold weather) is *chulent* or *hamin*—a hot stew of meat (optional), beans, grains, and such—that is prepared prior to Shabbat and cooked overnight on a *blech* (hot plate) in a low oven or in a slow-cooker. *Chulent* is actually a "polemical" food, a kind of culinary theological statement against the Karaites, an early medieval sect who rejected the talmudic/rabbinic laws and followed the Torah literally, prohibiting any fire in the home during the Sabbath, even if lit beforehand. Another option is to heat precooked foods on a hot plate, *blech*, or low oven; the halachically observant should consult their rabbi for guidelines.

SHABBAT BLESSINGS: CANDLELIGHTING

Baruch Atah Adonai, Eloheinu Melech HaOlam, asher kidshanu bemitzvotav vetzivanu lehadlik ner shel Shabbat (Kodesh).

Holy One of Blessing, Your Presence fills creation, making us holy with Your commandments and calling on us to kindle the (Holy) Shabbat lights.

Blessing over the wine—the blessing over the wine itself is:

Baruch Atah Adonai, Eloheinu Melech HaOlam, borei pri hagafen.

Holy One of Blessing, Your Presence fills creation, forming the fruit of the vine.

The full *kiddush* includes paragraphs that can be found in most prayer books. The texts are different for Friday night and Saturday.

HaMotzi over the bread—recited over any meal with bread:

Baruch Atah Adonai, Eloheinu Melech HaOlam, hamotzi lehem min haaretz.

Holy One of Blessing, Your Presence fills creation, bringing forth bread from the earth.

Birkat HaMazon—blessing for nourishment:

This traditional Jewish grace after meals is a longer prayer said or sung after any full meal, that is, a meal with bread (there are shorter traditional blessings after other foods). The images are of God as the merciful source of life and nourishment. It can be found in most traditional prayer books and in many of the Shabbat books listed in the resource guides (some offer abridged versions). Children might begin by singing the first paragraph with their parents or by reciting parts of the *Birkat HaMazon* in English.

BLESSING THE CHILDREN

One of the most beautiful and meaningful Shabbat ceremonies is the weekly custom of blessing one's children. It's truly indicative of the holiness and importance of family ties in Jewish life. Traditionally done by the father at the Friday night dinner table after "*Shalom Aleichem*," it is now often given by either or both parents. Blessing the children indicates to them in a concrete way that the parent–child relationship is something sacred.

How to: The parent places both hands on the child's head and says the blessing. The traditional formula, used every Friday night for centuries, is:

For a daughter:

Yesimech Elohim KeSarah, Rivkah, Rahel veLeah.

May God make you as Sarah, Rebecca, Rachel, and Leah.

For a son:

Yesimcha Elohim KeEfraim vecheMenashe.

May God make you as Ephraim and as Menasseh.

(Ephraim and Menasseh were Joseph's sons; this refers to the blessing their grandfather Jacob gave them in Genesis 48.)

Many add the priestly (Cohanic) blessing for all the children:

Yevarechecha Adonai veyishmerecha,
Ya'er Adonai panav elecha viyehuneka,
Yisa Adonai panav elecha veyasem lecha shalom

May the Eternal bless you and keep you;
May the Eternal enlighten you and be gracious to you;
May the Eternal bestow favor upon you and grant you peace.
(Numbers 6:24–27)

There are so many personal variations on the traditional blessing that it can become a very intimate, special experience. In some families this is a fairly formal ritual, each child waiting in turn for the blessing. In our house, as in others, it's a kind of informal but loving custom each week as I go to each child after candlelighting and bless her or him, then say the "priestly" blessing for all of them. Even if the blessing is brief, I try to really focus, to feel a sense of spiritual and emotional energy flowing between us.

Some parents change the traditional formula or keep it but also add their own references to Jewish history, upcoming holidays, or the weekly Torah portion (such as, "May God make you like Judah Macabee who was brave enough to struggle for his beliefs." "May God make you like Miriam, a leader and a poet.").

Like other parents, after the traditional blessing is said I often whisper personal messages about important experiences each child has had that week or is looking forward to in the week to come. Especially around the New Year and birthdays I try to convey especially meaningful thoughts for the year ahead. I spend a few moments alone with each child, and of course, hugs and kisses are an important part of the routine. In some families, the children bless the parents as well (ours used to do this when they were little).

If grandparents are present—a double *berachah*!—it could be meaningful and memorable if the grandparents bless you—their own children—as well as the grandchildren. (You can never have too many blessings, right?) They probably don't need any suggestions about what to say, either!

The blessing ritual is another one of those "little" things that really grows in value as the years go by. Parents of preteens and teens often say that over the years, the reliability of this simple weekly custom has helped add an extra measure of respect and harmony to their relationships.

We want to give our children so much: material things, a good education, happiness. A parent's blessing—a spiritual outpouring of love from our hearts to theirs—is a gift that costs us no money, yet whose value is priceless.

FAMILY CUSTOMS

Many families develop personal Shabbat customs that enhance their sense of closeness and love. Ours include holding hands around the table (guests welcome to join in) as we sing "*Shalom Aleichem*," the traditional song that welcomes the Shabbat angels said to accompany each Jew home from prayer on Friday nights. We'll also often do a little informal folk dancing with the kids at *Havdalah*.

Once, when our children's Friday night enthusiasm seemed on the wane, my husband sug-

gested that the three girls take turns dressing up as the "Shabbat Queen" and we would dance around her singing "*Lechah Dodi*" and other Shabbat songs. It didn't become a permanent custom, mainly because the role of Shabbat Queen was too popular and they had trouble waiting their turns and arguing over who got more time in the spotlight!

A custom in my parental home—like so many others—was to say "*Shabbat Shalom*" or "*Gut Shabbos*" and kiss everyone right after candlelighting. Of course I do it with my own family now. It's a simple expression of love, week after week, that many Jewish families find meaningful.

Family life today can be hurried and stressful; how good to take that time out once a week when children know we will touch, kiss, sing together, spend a few moments telling them we love them.

SHABBAT TABLE TALK

Shabbat meals are meant to provide food for the spirit as well as the body. Singing and conversation are certainly part of that "soul food."

1. Shabbat table talk can be on any subject that draws family and friends closer in meaningful dialogue. Here are a few ideas:

● Share a pleasant experience each person in the family has had that week.

● Go around the table and have each person tell something she or he appreciates about every other person present; or for each person present, let the others finish this statement: "You are a blessing; you . . ."

● Share something beautiful (or holy or "a *mitzvah*") you saw, heard about, or experienced that week. Or tell something that you are thankful for this week.

● Discuss a current event or issue, particularly emphasizing what your Jewish values could suggest as appropriate responses.

● Discuss everyone's Hebrew name: after whom each was named, what the name means, and if possible, point out its significance in Jewish heritage and historical role models (look up in *Encyclopaedia Judaica* or a one-volume Jewish encyclopedia, or if you need to, ask a knowledgeable person for assistance).

● Discuss your family history, what countries each branch was originally from, how they came to this country, challenges they had to face.

● Recount family stories from older generations, your childhood, your children's early years.

● Recount your experiences in connection with significant events in contemporary Jewish history, for example, parents share memories about how the Six Day War affected their lives and identities, grandparents about the period of the founding of the State of Israel.

2. Stories: Shabbat meals, evening or afternoon, are also ideal times for reading or telling Jewish stories. See pp. 59–63 for ideas and a resource guide on Jewish storytelling.

3. Discussion about Jewish texts such as the week's Torah portion (*Parashat HaShavuah*) can be especially meaningful and educational:

Divrei Torah (singular *devar Torah*: words of Torah, or "Torah talks") can greatly enhance Shabbat meals. The sages of the *Mishnah* taught that when Jews sit together and discuss Torah, the divine presence is between them. Since "Torah" in its broadest sense means all of Jewish learning, the possibilities for such Torah talk are nearly endless. Pages 73–74 give ideas for home Torah study.

FAMILY SNAPSHOTS

SHABBAT

Every Friday evening, before the *kiddush*, we hold up our *kiddush* cup and say: "We praise God with this symbol of joy and thank God for the blessings of the past week and for life and health, for home, love, and friends, for the discipline of our trials and the happiness which has come from our labors—and this week we give special thanks for . . ." (at this point we think back over the past week and every member of the family adds things that he or she or the family have to be thankful for, especially our love for one another). It's a wonderful review and a way of putting our week in perspective.

—*Saul and Cindy Rosenthal*

ATTENDING SERVICES WITH CHILDREN

Although the home is the primary focus of Shabbat, it is a day for community as well. At the least, attending synagogue shows children that Judaism is part of the life of an entire community, not something done only by our particular family. At the synagogue, children may develop a peer group of Jewish friends with common religious experiences, especially important if they are in a public or non-Jewish private school. And of course, Shabbat is more than a day of vacation or nice meals. It is a holy day for prayer, contemplation, Torah readings, and *kiddush*. A *bar* or *bat mitzvah* is usually celebrated on Shabbat, as are other rituals such as a baby naming or individual blessings at the Torah. Fairly regular synagogue attendance as a family brings our children into contact with the vibrant life of the Jewish congregation. In the words of Rabbi Harold Kushner, "Religion is . . . the community . . . through which we learn what it means to be human."[8]

Although we may pray at home (and children should certainly see us doing so and ideally be involved in the prayers), there are some prayers (*Kaddish*, *Kedushah*) that are only said in the holiness of community.

Of course, various synagogues differ in their approach to children's involvement in services. Some congregations (often of the traditional or *Havurah* bent) are completely tolerant of children running up and down the aisles or wandering in and out of the sanctuary. Others are much more formal, and such behavior would be nigh unto scandalous. Still other synagogues provide a full range of youth activities from baby-sitting for the youngest to preschool, child, and youth congregations. Again, the quality of such programs varies greatly, so it's important to observe the actual programs to get a sense of what they are really like. Some synagogues have initiated special family services or programs geared for parents and young children.

In choosing a congregation, it's important to discover how comfortable you will feel bringing your children there, and whether some of your spiritual, emotional, and intellectual needs as a Jewish family can be met in the settings it makes available. Or, unite with friends who are willing to organize (or upgrade) family programs or other participatory services.

For those times when you don't pray with the

congregation, a short prayer service at home can enhance the holiness of the day. If you already *daven* (pray) on your own, you could still take a short time to say some prayers with the children and learn together from the Torah portion. Your children's ages, attention spans, Jewish knowledge and interest can set the guidelines for this experience, which might range from saying the *Shema* and singing some *Shabbos* songs to the basic elements of a Shabbat morning or afternoon service.

SHABBAT AFTERNOON: THE JOYS OF DOWNTIME

Some houseguests who have spent Shabbat with us have found our traditional Sabbath afternoons—reading, naps, lolling around, and maybe going for a walk—to be too dull for their tastes. They can understand the Sabbath meals and even spending the morning at services. But a whole afternoon just to . . . rest! It's more than some people can take, and we don't hold them prisoner if they believe their afternoon is better spent shopping or at a gallery.

But other friends of ours, who were already beginning to have a regular Shabbat meal on Friday night and to attend services and *kiddush* on Shabbat morning, confessed to jealousy over our lazy Sabbath afternoons. They were still using that time to squeeze in shopping trips and to take the children to various activities, and our nap looked better all the time. Our children played pretty independently, yet knew that we were nearby when they wanted us. Why, we didn't even answer the phone! (Although, slaves to the era as we are, we do leave on the answering machine.)

A Sacred Day Off

Shabbat—although philosophers rhapsodize over its layers of historical, mystical, psychological, and sociological meaning—is, still, also a day of REST. The root, in modern Hebrew, comes to mean "to go on strike." In addition to being a spiritual experience, Shabbat is also a day off.

Sociologist Arlie Hochschild[9] found—as if we needed a study to tell us!—that today's employed mothers tend to be chronically rushed and over-tired, nearly obsessed with the subject of plain old sleep. It carries over to their children, whom the mothers are perennially hurrying along.

The hard truth is that we live in a rushed, overoccupied, overworked society. "Baby boomer" men tend to work longer hours than did their fathers, and more and more women work another entire job in addition to carrying most of the traditional housewife's burden. Heavens, we need a day of rest! (Not to carry the nap business too far, but Robert Ornstein, Ph.D., and David Sobel, M.D., devote several pages of their book *Healthy Pleasures*[10] to the myriad physiological and emotional benefits of same. But of course, any mother of tots could have told them—there's nothing like a nap!)

So, after Shabbat lunch, we flaunt convention by reading or resting, while our nonnapping offspring have been reasonably trained to spend the time playing by themselves or with guests. (When they were younger we usually took turns supervising the wakeful dears.)

But when do we get all that housework and shopping done? It's amazing that once one makes Shabbat sacred for rest, other times can be found for mundane pursuits ("Parkinson's Law": work expands to fill the time allotted it). And usually much more energy results from taking that time off regularly. The truth is that people rearrange their schedules to fit their priorities, and Shabbat rest can become a priority. Thousands of observant Jews do it. And the rhythm of preparing for Shabbat has in many ways led to our family sharing those home jobs more equitably.

Suggested Shabbat Afternoon Activities in the "Slow Lane"

● Study Hebrew, the Torah portion or other biblical selections, *Pirke Avot* (the traditional summertime study).

● Read a Jewish or other periodical. Read a library book.

● Sit outside and read the paper. Drink lemonade.

● Take the kids on a walk to a park or playground or just around the neighborhood. Stop to look at things or talk to people. Enjoy the changing seasons.

● Read Jewish stories aloud to the children. Let them sit on your lap. Look together at those beautiful "coffee table" books you never have time for. Look at family albums while you tell family stories.

● Read a book aloud with your spouse and discuss it. Read each other poetry.

● Play chess or checkers. Play Frisbee in the backyard. Play "hug tag" (you're "safe on base" only when hugging someone). Just hug.

● Children can make up plays or puppet shows to do for parents.

● Parents can do a puppet show for young children or tell a story with a homemade felt board, about the Torah portion, holiday, or other topic.

● Talk without being rushed.

● Ask questions that take some time to ask or to answer.

● Sing Hebrew songs or anything you like.

● Play. (You really have to use your imagination. No TV.)

● Think. Daydream.

TIPS FOR SHABBAT AFTERNOON WITH TOTS

● If your child naps or has a quiet afternoon time, make that yours, too.

● If your young children are the restless type, it tends to work best if the parents trade off rest and "on-duty" times.

● If possible, find a third party to help out so parents can have some private time together. Even an older sibling who baby-sits can be a major help.

● Set aside certain very desirable toys for Shabbat afternoon, perhaps in a Shabbat box for play on the Sabbath and holidays only. It could include puzzles and other toys with especially Jewish themes.

● Check out Jewish children's books from the synagogue library to read aloud.

● For children who like to do artwork, if you observe the Shabbat prohibitions, you can substitute a felt board, magnets, or Colorforms® kind of game for coloring.

● Spend some time outside, weather permitting. During inclement weather, my kids would enjoy gentle sorts of "horseplay" such as piggyback rides or "flying tummy rides" (their tummies on our feet, while we lay back on the carpet, bouncing them up and down). A minitrampoline on the rug also helped let off pent-up energy.

WAKE-UP TIME

In religious neighborhoods in Israel and in traditional Diaspora Jewish communities, where Shabbat is observed more or less organically, the Shabbat afternoon follows a typical pattern: long noon meal, then nap or rest time, and later in the afternoon a more active time. It is at that time (perhaps four-ish; it varies with the changing seasons and hours of Shabbat) that families walk together or friends drop by for a short visit, children flock to the playgrounds, youth groups meet in the park, synagogue study groups meet in homes or in the *shul*. In some areas in Israel, museums and zoos are open at no charge or with prepaid admission.

Late in the afternoon there is a lighter "third meal" at home or in the synagogue, often between the afternoon and evening services. The *seudah shlishit* (*shalosh seudos* is the Ashkenazic term) dates back to the rabbinic period when it was customary for most people to eat only two meals a day. To make Shabbat special, a third meal was added (the first two meals are on Friday evening and Saturday noon; remember that the Jewish day begins at sunset). There is not a separate *kiddush*, but one does say *HaMotzi* over two breads again. It's a nice time for low-key entertaining, partly because the traditional fare is simple: *hallah*, cake, salads, maybe a *kugel* or two.

At many traditional *shuls*, the *third* meal is not much more than a snack—herring-and-piece-of-*matzah* type—eaten in the synagogue by congregants (usually mainly men) who come to pray in the afternoon. But at one such synagogue we went to, the third meal evolved from that into a truly festive weekly gathering of many families, complete with lots of singing and some words of Torah. It was especially nice for the children to be involved in that feeling of a warm "extended family" that most of them had little opportunity to experience.

Another community I have been involved with gathered about once a month in different congregants' homes for late Shabbat afternoon socializing and an informal learning and discussion session, along with a buffet afternoon meal. Children were welcome and had many friends to play with. The evening concluded with the *Havdalah* service.

You can organize a similar Shabbat afternoon communal gathering simply by inviting friends on your own, or organize a more formal rotation with a synagogue or *havurah* group. Ask some people to prepare a few words of Torah and lead in song.

Young people can be in on the planning. It's ideal to have a multigenerational group. The food should be simple, leaving the emphasis on the warm community feeling.

GIVE SHABBAT AFTERNOON A TRY

When a family begins to observe Shabbat, they usually start with the most obvious acts—candle-lighting, family meals, attending services, Havdalah. The unstructured Shabbat afternoon often gets a low priority and is quickly filled up with errands and ordinary activities.

But do give it a try, if you haven't. Shabbat afternoon—unproductive, unstructured, daringly unexciting—allows something that can be very positive for the family. It's an opportunity for the family to discover that elusive experience of "quantity time."

Our weekdays are just as hectic as those of many other over-busy modern families. But on the Sabbath afternoon, although we may do some socializing, we usually spend a good solid chunk of time together as a family. In large part because of those "laid-back" Shabbat afternoons, we are together a lot as a family. At least once a week, we are just there for one another. Our children can count on that time when Mom and Dad will be accessible. Even if they don't need a heart-to-heart talk or a big dose of hugging every week, a reliable framework is built in for those weeks when they do need it. And that, the "family health" experts tell us, is no small matter for families today.

HAVDALAH: BIDDING SHABBAT GOOD-BYE

The Havdalah ("separation") ceremony is a short but beautiful home ritual during which the family bids the Sabbath goodbye with blessings over wine, spices, and the light of a braided candle. Havdalah is especially compelling to children because it involves all the senses: smelling the spices, seeing the flames and the play of light and shadow, hearing the songs, tasting the wine, touching the spice box or holding the candle (use foil or a holder to protect fingers from dripping wax), and perhaps holding hands for a brief dance.

Distinctions are important to children as they grow and try to make sense of an often confusing world. Havdalah, which literally means "distinction," sets a boundary in time between the Sab-

bath—a holy time—and ordinary days. In teaching in various Jewish schools, I've found that trying to explain Shabbat as the time period from "Friday sunset until Saturday after sundown," is a rather amorphous concept for young children to try to grasp. But "from candlelighting on Friday evening until Havdalah on Saturday night" is vivid and concrete to children—if they experience it, week after week. One parent-child textbook explains it as "framing" the beautiful Shabbat just as we would frame a lovely picture.[11] And of course, that experience can be created with any regularity only at home.

Havdalah is one of those ceremonies that is making a comeback among contemporary American Jewish families. I personally never saw a Havdalah ceremony until my teens; now I observe one each week with my family, as do many of my friends with similar backgrounds.

Havdalah marks the distinction from the Jewish emphasis on holiness to the Jewish emphasis on activism. For it is during the weekdays that we are most able to affect the world, to change and heal society or our small corner of it. Holiness and activism continually infuse each other in Jewish life. Hopefully we will carry the Shabbat awareness of the holiness of time into the coming week. During the week, we will continue to remember that time is precious and that what we do with our time—during the "six days of action" as much as during the day of rest—is the weightiest question in the world.

SUGGESTED ACTIVITIES FOR HAVDALAH TIME

● Make your own ritual items for Havdalah time (p. 153) or purchase an attractive set. However, don't let a lack of ritual items stop you. In a pinch, use a plain candle, small glass for the wine, and any spice jar on your shelf.

● Hold hands in a circle as you sing "Eliyahu HaNavi," "Shavua Tov," and other Hebrew songs at Havdalah time. A few simple "invent your own steps" circle dances can add to the atmosphere.

● Try the Sephardic version of besamim: fresh herbs such as mint, often presented on a silver tray. My father-in-law blesses these fresh herbs with a slight variation: "borei isbei besamim," "who creates the various fragrant herbs." Grow your own or sample various kinds from a greengrocer.

● Prior to Shabbat, grind whole spices with a mortar and pestle. The scent of the spices is meant to cheer us in the bittersweet moments of bidding

Shabbat goodbye, to hearten us as we take leave of the "additional soul" (*neshamah yeterah*) that Jewish tradition says we gain each Shabbat.

● Make seasonal *besamim*, such as an apple with cloves stuck in it around Rosh HaShanah; the same with an *etrog* after Sukkot.

● In addition to the traditional spices, ask each family member to bring a favorite fragrance to *Havdalah*: fresh flowers, potpourri, lemon, even a baking essence such as vanilla (you can soak cotton balls in various essences; store in airtight containers). Very young children can be helped by a parent to find a favorite scent. (I used to read to a blind friend at Tel Aviv University; she kept bottles of scent essences to smell on her desk as sighted persons might place attractive knickknacks on theirs.)

● Wish everyone a Good Week with the words, "*Shavua Tov*" (Hebrew) or "*a Gut Voch*" (Yiddish) before you turn to other activities.

● Invent your own Saturday night household tradition, such as playing Jewish music on the stereo (or with your own instruments—even better!), eating a certain favorite family food for a *Melaveh Malkah* ("escorting the Shabbat Queen"; Sephardim call this "King David's meal"), going out for a brief family "date" (or have one at home—popcorn and video), reading a Jewish story as a bedtime story.

● A musical *Havdalah* service is perhaps the loveliest of all. Learn *Havdalah* melodies from a tape or from friends.

Havdalah Blessings

The candle (usually a braided *Havdalah* candle) is lit, after which a brief introductory prayer may be recited (found in most prayerbooks). Then the *Borei Pri HaGafen* blessing is recited over the wine, which is not drunk until the end of the ceremony. *Besamim*—Prayer for smelling fragrant spices:

Baruch Atah Adonai, Eloheinu Melech HaOlam, borei minei besamim.

Holy One of Blessing, Your Presence fills creation, forming various spices.

Prayer over the *Havdalah* candle:

Baruch Atah Adonai, Eloheinu Melech HaOlam, borei me'orei ha'esh.

Holy One of Blessing, Your Presence fills creation, creating the lights of fire.

(It is customary to look at the shadows made by one's fingers on one's palms in order to see the distinction of light and dark and in order actually to make use of the fire's light.)
HaMavdil—Separation/distinction Prayer:

Baruch Atah Adonai, Eloheinu Melech HaOlam, hamavdil bein kodesh lehol, bein orlehoshech, bein Yisrael laamim, bein yom hashiviyi lesheshet yemei hamaaseh. Baruch Atah Adonai, haMavdil bein kodesh lehol.

Holy One of Blessing, Your Presence fills creation, distinguishing between holy and profane (mundane), between light and darkness, between Israel and the nations, between the seventh day and the six days of creation. Holy One of Blessing, You distinguish between holy and profane (mundane).

The wine is drunk and the candle extinguished in a few drops of wine. It is customary also to sing "*Eliyahu HaNavi*" (Elijah the Prophet, who tradition says will herald the coming of the Messiah) and perhaps "*Shavua Tov*" (A Good Week).

The reason why the Shabbat has so central a place within Jewish law lies in the fact that the Shabbat is the expression of the central idea of Judaism: the idea of freedom. . . . When I speak of the principle of the Jewish Sabbath, I am not referring to all the details of the Jewish Shabbat law. . . . Although I believe that even these details are important to create the full atmosphere of rest, I do not think that—except perhaps for a small minority—one could expect people to follow such cumbersome practices. . . . But I do believe that the principle of the Shabbat rest might be adopted by a much larger number of people—Christians, Jews, and people outside of any religion. The Sabbath day, for them would be a day of contemplation, reading, meaningful conversation, a day of rest and joy, completely free from all practical and mundane concerns.

—Erich Fromm[12]

THOU SHALT NOTS: SHABBAT PROHIBITIONS

If I could be so bold as to venture a sweeping generalization, the main difference between a traditional and a liberal Shabbat lies not mainly in the "Thou Shalts" of Shabbat, but in the "Thou Shalt Nots." At least in principle all Jewish movements have a vision of Shabbat that includes a day of rest, services and Torah reading, festive meals, a special atmosphere, candles, *kiddush* and *hallah*, family time, and finally *Havdalah*.

The more traditional Jews, however, also observe many Shabbat prohibitions (not to imply that liberal Jews observe no prohibitions!; see the following, "A Liberal Shabbat"). As noted, the two versions of the Fourth Commandment, "observe" and "remember" the Sabbath day, were interpreted by the rabbis to mean that Shabbat has two facets, the prescribed and the proscribed. In other words: "Thou shalt" remember the Sabbath by praying, making *kiddush*, eating three meals, and so forth. "Observing" means that "thou shalt not," in the words of the Fourth Commandment (Exodus 20:10 and Deuteronomy 5:14), do any sort of *melachah*, or creative work.

Melachah is explained in the Talmud to mean 39 broad categories of creative work connected with building the sanctuary during the Israelites' trek through the Sinai wilderness—a building process recessed every Sabbath. These categories include activities related to agriculture and food preparation, making clothing, leatherwork, writing, making shelter, making fire, completing work, and transportation of goods. They don't necessarily mean work in terms of "exertion." One could walk five miles to *shul* and not violate the prohibition against *melachah* (as long as in doing so one remained within the same city and didn't violate the prohibition against travel on the Sabbath). In addition to the commandment against "work," there are also specific Torah prohibitions against traveling from one's place (Exodus 16:29) and kindling fire (Exodus 35:3).

The rabbis added extra prohibitions to preserve the spirit of the day. *Muktzeh* means that things prohibited for use on the Shabbat (such as a pen for writing or a sewing needle) should not be handled on the Shabbat. *Shevut* expands some of the prohibited activities in order to preserve the Shabbat spirit. *Uvdin vehol* means that "everyday" or "secular" kinds of activities and even discussion should be eschewed on the Sabbath. For example, reading the stock-market reports involves no prohibited labor but is a "weekday" activity. Technically, a timer could be used to enable one to watch television on the Sabbath, but that would make Shabbat too much like an ordinary weekday.

In practice, all these prohibitions mean that (among other things) Orthodox Jews won't do the following on the Shabbat: drive a car or travel by other vehicle, cook (though food may be kept warm on a hot plate), turn lights on and off (although timers may be used to do so), use a telephone, light a fire, write, sew, draw or paint, cut or tear paper, go to work or shop or handle money at all, do most housework or any yardwork. The halachically observant Jew won't carry items on Shabbat in a "public domain," that is, outside a home or building; however, an *eruv* or special wire may be strung up on telephone poles around an entire neighborhood—around entire cities in Israel— to make it all one "private domain" in the view of Jewish law. In such areas carrying, pushing a child's stroller, and such things, becomes halachically permissible.

Children growing up with this observance learn to put away their crayons, scissors, and battery-operated cars before Shabbat. Amazingly, they manage to grow up without Saturday morning cartoons or phone calls (two excellent arguments in favor of traditional observance!).

While all these prohibitions may sound oppressive to those who don't observe them, those who do insist that they set the Shabbat day apart as a "sanctuary in time." Shabbat is no "blue Sunday," but a day of joy and delight. Precisely by refraining from asserting our power over the natural world, we liberate ourselves to appreciate, contemplate, relate. The peaceful, holy atmosphere of Sabbat is fully experienced when all weekday concerns are put aside for 25 hours.

In Jewish law the concept of *pikuah nefesh*, saving a life, always overides the Shabbat (contrary to anti-Semitic myths throughout the centuries). An observant Jew would be *commanded* to break the Shabbat the minute that there was a life-threatening situation.

A LIBERAL SHABBAT

Obviously, in the contemporary pluralistic Jewish community, not everyone's Shabbat will conform to these traditional patterns.

Some families choose to combine some of the traditional Shabbat activities such as learning, prayer, and special meals with other recreational pursuits they personally feel are in the spirit of Shabbat, such as a visit to a museum, recreational sports, time spent in natural settings, listening to music.

While the more liberal approach to Shabbat might not include a strict observance of the various prohibitions, it would strive to maintain a Shabbat *gestalt* of rest, enjoyment, meaningful interaction, and spiritual versus material pursuits. In the words of Rabbi Irving Greenberg, a liberal approach to the Shabbat would still involve "more than a day of leisure; *it is a shift in the mode of being*. The foundation of Shabbat is a negative commandment: to cease being manipulative on this day . . . on this day, one shifts from tampering, control, and aggression to harmonizing behavior. Being, friendship and relationships become the central mode of existence."[13]

There are value judgments to be made by those who want to observe a family Shabbat outside the clear guidelines of traditional *Halachah*. For the more one clears away weekday activities that conflict with the Shabbat spirit, the more psychic space is created in which to realize that precious sense of Shabbat peace and respite. A liberal Shabbat might include a commitment to keep the Sabbath as free as possible of professional work, house and yard work, shopping, and perhaps even electronic interruptions (using an answering machine instead of letting the phone interrupt your family meal can really be liberating, and experiencing all or part of a day without television can be nigh unto revolutionary!). One Reform Shabbat guide explains that liberal Jews should keep the Shabbat qualities of *oneg*, *menuchah*, and *kedushah*—joy, rest, and holiness—in mind as they choose what activities they consider appropriate to their Shabbat observance.

One problem for those making a commitment to observe a "liberal Shabbat" is that outside the Orthodox and very traditional Conservative fold, there may be a lack of communal structure to reinforce the family's choice for Shabbat observance. It may actually take more personal tenacity to maintain some kind of Shabbat standards "on one's own," as it were. A family might take a gradual approach to rediscovering more and more of the Shabbat day, beginning perhaps with Friday night dinner and gradually appropriating the entire Shabbat as a holy time, with a special spirit. Involvement in a *havurah* or synagogue group where other families participate in regular Shabbat services or activities can help reinforce one's own commitment to observing a "liberal" Shabbat.

Of course, there is a whole spectrum of Shabbat observance. Some families drive only to services or Shabbat-related events (while Orthodox Jews would stay home all Shabbat rather than drive to the synagogue). Some observe a portion of the traditional restrictions but not all.

We may choose to observe Shabbat in different ways, but like all of the Jewish heritage, Shabbat belongs to every Jew. The choice is ours: to ignore Shabbat and live like "everyone else" or to voluntarily create this unique Jewish experience for ourselves and our children.

SHABBAT: NOT ALWAYS ECSTATIC

Although Shabbat is a central element of Jewish family living, I would be too propagandistic if I gave the impression that it's *always* an ecstatic, joyful, or spiritual experience. One book termed this the "Jewish Good Housekeeping Family" myth. We all probably have some picture tucked away in our minds of a happy, well-dressed family gathered around a beautifully appointed table, singing Hebrew tunes in perfect harmony.

In reality, Shabbat—while a "taste of the world-to-come"—still transpires for the time being in this imperfect world of today. Dinner might not be a gourmet delight. If you are traditionally observant, you might sometimes forget to turn on the hot plate or the light-timer. A long Shabbat afternoon with tots may turn out to be far from restful. School-age children may tease each other at the table. Older children might grumble about conflicts with outside activities.

My family has observed a fairly traditional Shabbat in less than ideal circumstances and sometimes in relative isolation, and I would be lying to say that it has always been the wonderful family experience of my dreams. Sometimes I have made compromises in my desired level of observance in order to preserve the spirit of the day. On the other hand, more often the Shabbat has dictated life decisions—for example, our Shabbat observance has become a key factor in choosing a community and neighborhood in which to live.

But of course, that's precisely the case with all important life commitments. We usually enter marriage full of rosy expectations, only to find out that a real marriage commitment involves real-life problems such as boredom and conflict. Having children also tends to defy our happy dreams of joyful nurturing. Real children mean messes and squabbles and whining. However, marriage and children also mean love, support, and continuity along with the "normal" problems.

It's the same with a commitment to Shabbat. Those whose first experience of Shabbat is at camp, at a youth program, or otherwise outside the realm of family life, may dream of "making Shabbat" in their own homes someday, not anticipating the normal stresses that can occur when Shabbat is observed at home with children. Furthermore, Shabbat observance often has less social reinforcement than do one's other life commitments. In fact, observing Shabbat today is very likely to bring criticism from some quarters because it goes against the popular life-style. So when Shabbat fails to bring instant or constant fulfillment, we may conclude that it's not worth it.

Yet when love is part of everyday life, one learns to live with the imperfections of another even as one tries to better the relationship. And when Shabbat is part of the fabric of family life, the imperfections are part of the package, even as we continually work on making it more dynamic, meaningful, or spiritual. Like any life commitment, the results of Shabbat merit accepting some imperfections while working for improvement.

It should be mentioned that the rewards do come. As children grow up with Shabbat as a natural part of life, they begin increasingly to participate in the preparations and observances of the day. It becomes less and less something we do for them, and more and more something we all do together.

Not only can Shabbat really be a key factor in imbuing our children with a Jewish identity, but Shabbat can truly be a focus for sanctity in family life. On Shabbat we can realize that family life is more than mundane; that home can be a holy place; that time can be holy. Shabbat teaches our children that relationships and heritage and holiness are more valuable to us than achievements and acquisition.

I and many others believe that Shabbat is worth the effort.

FAMILY SNAPSHOTS

Shabbos is a time to recharge and renew mentally. At first glance that can seem ridiculous: Some people always have a houseful of guests, which means a lot of tedious domestic tasks. I have to admit that when we first began to keep *Shabbos*, it seemed very confining, particularly with regard to children. But the key is to live among others who value the gift of *Shabbos*, so that you and your children can share it with a community. *Shabbos* provides a rhythm to life that otherwise wouldn't exist, like a 6/7 time signature in music.

—*Jody Crane*

[Hedy Rutman is a clinical psychologist, and Joel Rutman is a pediatric neurologist. They are the parents of young adults Jessica, Nathaniel, Jeremy, and Gabriel. The couple helped establish a Jewish day school in San Antonio.]

Our rule was Friday night, the kids stayed home and had dinner with the family. (We also had many family Shabbat activities on Saturday.) We enforced this through high school, and Jessica missed all the football games. Finally, when she was a senior and president of the student council, and it was the homecoming game, we gave her permission to go. She really appreciated "breaking the rule" one time. But it wasn't a constant struggle, because that was the way it was. The kids had to tell us in advance if there was some major thing they wanted to do on Shabbat.

It was nice at home on Friday night. It was very secure, with family, with company. We had a good meal and did all the traditional things and then adjourned to the living room to play games. No TV or radio. Maybe they resented it sometimes, but the truth is that they could go out any other night.

And even though there was some antagonism sometimes on her part, Jessi said many times to us how many of her friends admired our family life. Her friends recognized that our Shabbat observance helped our family to be a "real family." To some extent they were wistful, even envious, because many of their families didn't have a special time set aside to be together.

It's never ideal, especially when the kids are teens. Somebody's always "rebelling," somebody's not participating the way you'd like, but in general the family atmosphere is enhanced by these observances. We had always made it a point to have dinner at home together six nights a week, but when the children started high school that practice of having regular family meals began to disintegrate. We started to feel out of touch, especially with the more rebellious among our four children . . . but Friday night they knew that they had to be home, and that helped to strengthen family life.

— The Rutmans

This, then, is the answer to the problem of civilization: not to flee from the realm of space; to work with things of space but to be in love with eternity. Things are our tools; eternity, the Sabbath, is our mate. Israel is engaged to eternity. Even if they dedicate six days of the week to worldly pursuits, their soul is claimed by the seventh day.

— Rabbi Abraham Joshua Heschel[14]

PERSONAL REFLECTIONS ON SHABBAT

Shabbat has been described in many ways by Jewish thinkers and philosophers: a sanctification of time, an island of peace, a day-long experience of our fullest human potential, a taste of the messianic age to which we aspire.

Shabbat is also an antidote. It's an antidote to the materialistic values of modern society, which equate a person's earning power and possessions with his or her worth. It's an antidote to life-styles that center around how much one can achieve and acquire.

Shabbat is a day that glorifies *non*-earning and *non*-achievement. The basic principle of the Shabbat prohibitions is to forbid any creative craft, any manipulation of nature on this day. One writer pointed out that Shabbat is a day when carrying money becomes a desecration.

This despite the fact that Judaism is not an ascetic way of life. Indeed, Judaism stresses our active creativity as God's "partners" to better the world. Material wealth is not condemned, but rather seen as a wonderful resource for serving God through the *mitzvah* of *tzedakah*. Power is not inherently evil, but can be a necessary force for redemption.

Still, Shabbat comes to teach that there has to be a measure of humility along with our wealth, power, and manipulation of nature. On Shabbat, we are bidden to step back and realize that we ourselves are creatures of a higher power. We

reserve one day out of seven to things other than attainment and acquisition. One day a week is devoted to appreciation, introspection, learning, reflection, relating.

The *Havdalah* prayer, which separates the Sabbath from the weekdays, is usually translated "Who separates between the holy and the profane." However, the word *hol*, translated "profane," could also mean simply "secular," or "mundane." Our lives today take place mostly in that realm of the secular. And the typical American Friday night-Saturday is perhaps the most secular, the *least* holy time in the secular week—a day for the week's most trivial pursuit of entertainment or for the discharging of duties such as housework and errands. Although for some it is a family day, it's now more likely to be a day when everyone in the family goes his or her separate way. This secular life-style is "profane" because it's so superficial, so materially oriented that there isn't any time for contemplation, for nurturing an inner life, for relating to others on more than a superficial level.

Experiencing Shabbat as a young person showed me that there are alternatives to the completely secular life. Saturday, the adolescent's day to "kill time," became Shabbat, the day to realize the sanctity of time as the essence of life. By my late teens, I decided that it was more meaningful to spend Friday nights at *Kabbalat Shabbat* than at a football game. I opted for *kiddush* over keg-parties, services over shopping, the *mitzvah* of welcoming guests over the secular ritual of "socializing." I discovered that the mall and the stadium house only crowds, but the house of worship is home to a community; that Saturday errands and chores maintain housemates, but Shabbat meals, songs, and Torah-talk nurture a family.

Even now, I suspect that some family and friends are too polite to tell me that they can't believe I have chosen such a "dull" way of life. On the contrary, I feel that they don't know what they're missing. I love cultural events, trips, shopping, as much as anyone, yet if I did even the nicest of those things on Shabbat, I would feel that I had been deprived of something irreplaceable: my holy time, rest, delight, and rejuvenation.

What's more, setting aside one day a week of holy time has gradually shaped my perceptions until I find more and more holiness in the "secular, mundane" days as well. Just as loving one child can make us realize that all of life is precious, so keeping one day sacred can begin to infuse us with a knowledge that every day, every minute, is holy.

167

It's led me to want to put more quality, meaning, and beauty into the way I live every day, whether it's a day of work or a day of leisure.

The Genesis story that God created the world in six days need not be literal to contain truth. To me it says, if six days were enough for God to create a world, then six days a week must be enough for me to run a household and earn a living, even if that means a less elegant household and a more modest living. Six days a week will also have to be enough for my children to run to organized activities. Six days a week has to be enough to shop and run errands and go to the movies.

Because I want at least one day a week devoted to more enduring things, freed for finding meaning in life.

I want a limit on the time devoted to bettering our "standard of living," because otherwise we might never find the time to step back and appreciate what we have. I want a limit on the days we spend bettering our own and our children's potential "status," because otherwise we might never find the time to nourish our souls, to nurture our inner lives. I want at least one day a week when the phone is not our master or the television our household idol, a day with time for reading, talking, and introspection.

There can be much fulfillment found in work, and satisfying work is a psychological necessity. However, one of the banes of the present generation is "workaholism." Many young professional adults work far longer hours than did their parents, not only because today's economy is more brittle, but because their identities are so much more dependent on their professional life than on any other aspect of life. It is an externally oriented, one-dimensional life-style that leaves the individual vulnerable when the job is lost or a life crisis arises. For these workaholics, too, Shabbat can be an antidote, if they can allow themselves to make room for it in their lives. Shabbat is a day where one can find meaning and identity beyond the work place.

Over the years, I have also learned to appreciate and respect different ways that families "make Shabbat," and that for some of our friend-families a greater measure of freedom along with tradition is what makes this day enjoyable and restful for them. The important thing is that these families, too, have come to consider Shabbat a unique day of the week; they call it Shabbat, and not just "Saturday," and they really strive to make it meaningful. Their children, like ours, know that Shabbat is special.

Shabbat provides children with a security that is becoming increasingly rare and precious in contemporary family life: the security of a "family day" when they get real quantities of time with their parents. And in an age where more and more kids have schedules that look like a career diplomat's, Shabbat gives children the certainty of a simple, dependable rhythm to their week. For these reasons alone, it's worth it. However, Shabbat is definitely not something I "do" for the children's sake. Although my Shabbat observance isn't a static thing and continues to take new forms over the years, Shabbat is something I've grown to feel that I couldn't live a satisfying life without.

Club Med advertises itself as the "antidote to civilization," and that's what Shabbat is for me. It's a time for me to stop *doing* and concentrate on just *being*.
—Diana Bletter[15]

SHABBAT AND HOLIDAY OBSERVANCES FOR "BEGINNERS"

Readers who are just beginning to introduce Shabbat and other Jewish observances into their homes can look upon it as an intriguing adventure. With any new observance, it's best to take a gradual, incremental approach. This is certainly consonant with Jewish sensibilities: "one *mitzvah* leads to another." It might be best to try one new practice for a month before adding more.

The main pitfall is an all-or-nothing approach. If we are too tired to provide a four-course meal just like *Bubbie* used to do, that certainly doesn't mean that we can't make *kiddush* before our take-out dinner! One prominent Jewish family educator told me how liberated a single mother felt when told that it was "OK" for her to serve pizza for her Friday night *Shabbos* dinner. Since permission was given to make the table an altar with pizza, this mother and her son have enjoyed wonderful Friday evenings together. Sometimes we just need to give ourselves permission to be Jewish in our own way.

When we spend a meal or afternoon or day with our families, that can be holy time for us. It all depends on how we view it. Shabbat doesn't have to mean that we are singing cantorial music in four-part harmony or delivering talmudic discourses at the table. Reflecting on the week gone by, going for a walk, or playing games together is also part of a sacred enterprise—building and strengthening family life.

Begin by reading this chapter and some of the books in the resource guide about Shabbat, talking to people who observe it, and if at all possible attending Shabbat and holiday events such as congregational retreats and celebrations. Best of all is to get yourselves invited to the homes of other families who observe Shabbat in various ways, to experience first-hand how Shabbat is lived. If you don't know of anyone, perhaps a rabbi or Jewish school director could make you a *shiddach* (a match) with another family. Many families who are Jewishly observant are happy to share their knowledge with others; in fact, they feel it is a *mitzvah*. As with other Jewish observances, remember that there are various ways people keep Shabbat, so don't be put off if one experience seems too rigid or another not traditional or dynamic enough. The aim is to find the comfortable level and type of observance that enhances your own lives.

As your research progresses, decide on which Shabbat home practices would mean the most for you to start with. The Torah itself (Exodus 31:16) calls observing Shabbat, literally "making" Shabbat. We *make Shabbat happen* in our homes through our decisions and actions. Consider the three basic Shabbat elements: *kedushah* (holiness), *menuhah* (rest, recreation), and *oneg* (pleasure, delight). How could your family gradually develop each one of these elements in making your own Shabbat? *Kedushah* could mean observing rituals and customs such as candlelighting, *kiddush*, and attendance at services; *menuhah* could be found in a decision to abstain from housework, take the phone off the hook, or postpone errands; *oneg* could be discovered by making Shabbat meals the most special of the week, with the best dishes and flowers on the table.

For many families, Shabbat observance begins with the Friday night candlelighting, *kiddush*, and dinner. After that, many choose to attend Saturday morning services together, and the next step may be to hold a *Havdalah* service on Saturday night. Saturday afternoon may gradually become a special family time, as well. This chapter, the resource guide, and your personal contacts can help you decide where to start and continue.

Parents of babies and tots are pretty free to make these decisions on their own, and even with slightly older children, the Shabbat observances can be introduced with a positive attitude as fun new family traditions, without in any way making them optional.

When preteens are involved, however, the process may be much more pleasant and meaningful, and the results more successful, if the young people themselves are in on the new decisions, planning, and experimenting, perhaps in the context of ongoing family meetings in which they play a significant part.

As for parents of teens, the issue is trickier because the young people now have much more of a life of their own. If parents choose to begin Shabbat observances at this point, they may have to be satisfied in making these changes for their own benefit as adults. The parents can invite the teens to join in, but not create another issue for rebellion by *insisting* that teens who haven't grown up with Shabbat suddenly change their life-styles to accommodate their parents' new observances. If teens are interested, youth-group programs and Jewish camping experiences that involve exciting Shabbat experiences may be positive additions.

At any age, it's helpful, and generally more rewarding and pleasant, if the family is part of a community in which to share the learning and joy of Jewish observance with others. A *havurah* or congregational group can often provide the support network that reinforces and enhances the family Shabbat. Shabbat and other Jewish observances were never meant to be observed in a vacuum or in the splendid isolation of the nuclear family alone. At some point, it's virtually essential to connect with others.

How long can the Jews go on dreaming [of a world perfected]? . . . Living with a dream is a treacherous business. . . . Dreams can give life purpose or rob it of value and meaning. Dealing with this double edge has been a major challenge for the Jewish people on their great trek through history toward redemption. . . . The classic Jewish answer to our dilemma is to set up a rhythm of perfection. The first movement is to plunge into this world as a participant. Then, just when there may be a danger of complete absorption into this world, there is an alternate reality to enter into: the Shabbat. Stepping outside the here and now, the community creates a world of perfection. Through total immersion in the Shabbat experience, Jews live the dream *now*.

—Rabbi Irving Greenberg[16]

22

ROSH HODESH: A FESTIVAL OF RENEWAL IS RENEWED

Rosh Hodesh, the celebration of the new Hebrew month, is an ancient festival finding renewal among contemporary Jews. It presents many wonderful family opportunities. Rosh Hodesh means the first of the month, just as Rosh HaShanah means the first or "head" of the year. Rosh Hodesh begins on the evening in which the first silver of the new moon can be sighted in the sky.

In ancient times, Rosh Hodesh was a major festival, but its significance waned after the destruction of the Temple. Traditionally, the advent of the new month is still announced in the synagogue on the Shabbat preceding Rosh Hodesh (except for Rosh Hodesh *Tishrei*, when Rosh HaShanah takes precedence). On Rosh Hodesh itself, a special blessing (*"yaaleh veyavo"*) is added to the *Amidah* and the *Birkat HaMazon* (Grace after Meals), and the *Musaf* (additional service) and partial *Hallel* (Psalms of Praise) are recited in the synagogue. Rosh Hodesh also became a day traditionally associated with new beginnings, a day preferred for dedications and other happy events. Fasting and mourning were curtailed on this day.

A week to fifteen days after Rosh Hodesh, when the new moon is more visible (generally after *Havdalah* on a Saturday night), worshippers go outside to bless the moon. This brief, poetic ritual can be found in most traditional prayer books. Worshipers greet each other with, *"Shalom Aleichem"* (Peace unto you) and answer one another, *"Aleichem Shalom."* Mystical thoughts expressed in these prayers link the restoration of the Jewish kingdom to a mythical restoration of the moon from its secondary, fluctuating role to a primordial glory equal to that of the sun.

Rosh Hodesh is traditionally considered a "semi-holiday" for women as a reward, it is said, for the Israelite women's refusal to donate their jewelry to make the golden calf. Some Orthodox and *hasidic* women take this day off from heavy housework, leaving it to the men of the family. Dinner will often include an extra dish. Sephardic women may light a candle at home; I have observed my mother-in-law kindle floating oil lights on Rosh Hodesh, each in memory of a righteous person.

Because of these traditional associations, some contemporary Jewish feminists have reappropriated Rosh Hodesh as a special women's festival. They identify traditional Jewish mythology about the restoration of the moon's primordial glory with an expansion of women's roles. The day may be marked by lighting a floating candle in a round bowl, which combines the motifs of the moon "floating" in the sky, roundness and cycles, and the symbolism of water, the womb, and renewal. Prayers and poetry from traditional sources and more contemporary feminist writings may be read. A special meal is served, often containing new fruit (over which *sheheheyanu* is recited) and crescent-shaped or round breads and foods. *Tzedakah* may be given, another traditional Rosh Hodesh practice. Music, dancing, or discussion may be included.

171

ROSH HODESH WITH THE FAMILY

Rosh Hodesh can be an excellent family day as well. Most of us live primarily with a consciousness of the Gregorian calendar, more or less just "pasting" Jewish holidays onto a Christian year. Doing special things on Rosh Hodesh helps to emphasize the rhythms of the Hebrew calendar. It also sets aside another regular opportunity for family closeness and tradition building. Since there are few rigid requirements for the celebration, there is plenty of room for creativity in establishing a family observance of Rosh Hodesh.

Since Rosh Hodesh is sometimes two days, that gives you more options for family activities. If Rosh Hodesh falls on Shabbat, Shabbat becomes even more special, with extra prayers in the synagogue and perhaps extra treats on the Sabbath table. However, more "secular" Rosh Hodesh activities (such as a family meeting, see the following) might be held on the next day. As for Rosh HaShanah, the first of Tishrei when the New Year supersedes the New Moon, you might want to have a special activity about a week before, in preparation for the Days of Awe (see pp. 180–182).

ROSH HODESH IDEAS

● Have a nice family dinner on each Rosh Hodesh. (Like any "Jewish" day, Rosh Hodesh lasts from sunset to sunset. You might have your family dinner on the eve of Rosh Hodesh in winter months, on the day of Rosh Hodesh during the summer.) In biblical times, Rosh Hodesh was a day for especially festive meals. Decorate the table attractively with a seasonal centerpiece, or one that highlights an upcoming festival. Light candles with appropriate colors or scents for the season. Play music related to Jewish holidays that arrive that month or musical selections linked to the changing months and seasons. Include the blessings for the new month in the grace after meals.

● Read the partial Hallel (found in most prayer books) at home, even if you do not pray the daily service or attend a *minyan*. You might read or sing selections aloud as a family.

● If possible, serve a new fruit and say the *sheheheyanu* (p. 89). (Wearing new clothes on this day would be another reason to say the blessing.) You might also serve crescent- or round-shaped breads or other foods that resemble the phases of the moon.

● Give *tzedakah*. Rosh Hodesh is also a good time to allocate the previous month's *tzedakah* collection.

● Adapt some of the new/old Rosh Hodesh customs to your home. Light a candle or candles, perhaps a floating wax or oil one in a round bowl. Traditionally, no fixed blessing is said, but you might choose to read some meditations from Jewish sources or selections from the Blessing of the New Moon in traditional prayer books. Building on the Sephardic tradition, you might dedicate the lights in memory of righteous women or men from history.

● At dinner, discuss upcoming holidays and events in the new Hebrew month. Plan activities.

● Use Rosh Hodesh (after the meal, perhaps) as the day for a monthly family meeting. At first we tried having weekly family meetings, but it quickly became burdensome. Having one once a month on Rosh Hodesh is perfect for us. Our own style is a fairly laid-back forum for discussing issues, brainstorming solutions, and facilitating communication.

We generally begin our family meetings with a brief *devar Torah* (Judaic discussion) about something associated with that Hebrew month. In addition to the usual family issues, we try to include a discussion of family *tzedakah* allocation and topics related to Jewish holidays in the month ahead.

● Make Rosh Hodesh the day to distribute allowances—guaranteed to make it a memorable day! We do this right after the monthly family meeting.

● Choose Rosh Hodesh, where appropriate, as a day for special family events such as housewarmings or parties. We had one daughter's naming celebration on Rosh Hodesh *Elul*. That way it could be held in conjunction with services, but without the Shabbat restrictions on travel and activities. (It also happened to be Labor Day, which didn't hurt!)

● Say the *Kiddush HaLevanah* (Blessing the Moon) prayer outdoors with your family on a clear night seven to fifteen days after Rosh Hodesh (generally it is said after *Havdalah*). Experience the changing seasons, explain why the moon appears to wax and wane, look through a telescope, identify constellations. Bake cookies shaped like moons and stars. In pleasant weather, sit and tell stories or just enjoy being outdoors.

● Memorize the name of the Hebrew months (they are actually Babylonian in origin):

Fall: *Tishrei, Heshvan, Kislev*
Winter: *Tevet, Shevat, Adar*
Spring: *Nissan, Iyyar, Sivan*
Summer: *Tammuz, Av, Elul*

My friend Chaike Charles has taught me how children can memorize the Hebrew months easily by singing them to the tune of "Pop Goes the Weasel"! Start with *Tishrei* to learn the order from Rosh HaShanah, with *Nissan* if you want to begin with the first Hebrew month, the spring "new year."

23

AROUND THE JEWISH YEAR

The Jewish yearly cycle is no less than an amazing learning experience for our families. "The Jew's calendar is the Jew's catechism," wrote Rabbi Samson Raphael Hirsch over a century ago.[1] When studied and celebrated fully, our holidays and holy days teach Jewish history, texts, philosophy, values, and ethics. They offer psychological, spiritual, and moral insights. Yet all of it is presented in a hands-on, experiential—and quite often fun—way.

In the course of the yearly cycle we travel as a family and community through peaks and valleys of communal memory and 4,000 years of shared history. Rather than learning this volume of material in a linear, academic way, we are immersed in it holistically as we experience the rituals and traditions of each holiday. We learn with our senses, our emotions, and our intellect together. What's more, this learning experience can help foster family closeness and create treasured family memories.

The chapters that follow will take families on a journey through the Jewish year. Each holiday section includes several elements. There is a broad overview of the holiday or holiday period, with emphasis on insights at the adult level. A brief outline of the traditional holiday practices is given. "Family Activities" for the festival will offer suggestions on how to involve children in the traditional holiday practices as well as how to introduce creative new ideas (crafts, food, imagination and play, and so on) for expanding on the holiday themes. The ethical content of each holiday is stressed, with specific suggestions for family

projects. The Resource Guide on pp. 348–355 will suggest books, music, audiovisual materials, and other supplies that can enrich holiday experiences at home. These books and materials will hopefully help supply topics for family Torah talks, discussions about holiday themes and issues. Included also are "*Derashot* for Parents," Midrashic-style interpretations that (as the word literally means) "seek out" meaning for contemporary family life from traditional Jewish sources.

Like the rest of *The Jewish Parents' Almanac*, this holiday guide is meant to be used in the way most helpful to you. If you wish, you can use it as a general guide to the holidays. Or you can pick and choose activities and ideas that appeal to you and seem to hold potential for your family. The volume of possible extra activities for each holiday means that not even a superparent could crowd them into one year. Fortunately, the holidays return each year, bringing more opportunities.

THE JEWISH HOLIDAYS TODAY: A DOUBLE CHALLENGE

As modern Jewish parents, we have two challenges in bringing the Jewish holidays to life for our families. While some of us were fortunate to grow up in homes where Jewish traditions were observed, for many of us they played a minor role in our childhood experiences.

STEP ONE: THE REDISCOVERY

Foremost for many of us there is that process of gradually rediscovering the culture and traditions of our people, filling our homes with the sights and sounds, tastes and smells of Jewish living.

I grew up as did many other American Jews of our generation, defining my Jewishness more by what I didn't believe in or do (didn't have a Christmas tree or an Easter basket) than by what I did believe or observe. Although my family observed most of the Jewish holidays at home or at Sunday School or the temple, and I enjoyed them, they didn't loom very large in my consciousness as the non-Jewish holidays did. When it was Halloween or Christmas, the "whole world"—public school, stores, television—seemed to revolve around the celebration. By contrast, Jewish rituals were rather small, private affairs. Some of them were more entrenched, while others were somewhat optional. There were Jewish holidays and observances that I had barely heard of (like Shavuot) or never encountered before adolescence (Tisha B'Av).

I don't think that my experience was unusual among American Jewish youngsters. Repeatedly, I've been surprised during Jewish celebrations, when Jewish adults of my acquaintance who are fairly involved—even very prominent—in Jewish organizations and synagogues will point out to me that they are attending a Simhat Torah observance or eating in a *sukkah* for the first time in their lives, that year.

Step one, then, is to rediscover the holiday traditions, to make some of our times sacred times. For those just beginning, it usually needs to be a gradual process. But it's important to feel that all of the Jewish heritage belongs to us and that we can begin to reclaim it for ourselves and our families.

I think, though, that it's important to pay heed to the wholeness of the Jewish year. Each holiday is linked to the entire cycle, and none is meant to stand out of the total context. A family needs a Jewish calendar in order to plan ahead for each festival. It's hard to expect one's children to take Jewish observances very seriously if they can be "forgotten" or observed sporadically. Would we forget our children's birthdays? Thanksgiving? How seriously do we take our Jewish heritage? Our children quickly learn what we really value. A basic observance of the major festivals is a key building block in creating a Jewish home and instilling Jewish values.

STEP TWO: THE MEANING BEHIND THE RITUALS

But simple observance isn't enough—especially in today's world. Our second, no less important task, is to introduce the more abstract qualities of the holiday cycle—the psychological and philosophical insights, the Jewish values and ethical content. Some of us grew up observing the holidays, but rarely being exposed to the deeper meanings behind the rituals. We had little appreciation of the intellectual content of our heritage.

When we go beyond the experiential and emotional content of the holidays to the psychological, intellectual, and ethical dimensions, we transcend the simple cycle of the year. Each year, the holidays have the potential of serving as catalysts for new insights, discovery, and growth. The yearly cycle thus becomes an ascending helix, a striking image proposed by Professor Edward L. Greenstein in his accompanying commentary to Michael Strassfeld's *The Jewish Holidays—A Guide and Commentary*. He compares our journey through Jewish "sacred time" to ascending "a spiraling ramp, like the one in the Guggenheim Museum, able to look down at least a year and forward to next year at each curve on the journey."[2]

But we can grow and ascend as individuals and families only if we use each year as an opportunity to learn at a more profound level than we did last year. One problem many Jewish parents face today is that of transmitting Judaism at increasingly sophisticated levels as their children grow and develop. As children grow, the holiday experiences and learning must fit their development. A secularly well-educated and ambitious Jewish teenager who sees "apples and honey" as the main message of Rosh HaShanah would doubtless draw the conclusion that she or he had outgrown Judaism. By reading and learning about the deeper meanings of the holidays and then discussing the holiday themes with our families, we can introduce our children to Jewish ideas that are stimulating, challenging, thought and action provoking.

Observing the holidays with our children should be, in the main, pleasurable and enjoyable. Warm, loving family memories can be woven around these ancient and modern days of celebration. The Jewish holiday cycle combines learning and values with festivity and fun. In observing the holidays together, we not only transmit the messages of our heritage to the next generation, we convey values that have the potential to strengthen our families and communities and to strengthen our people in its ongoing dedication to helping to improve the world.

HINTS FOR "BEGINNERS" AT HOLIDAY OBSERVANCE

When it comes to Jewish resources, the holidays are the most plentifully supplied. You can find many books that explain the holidays at any level you are interested in from lofty philosophy to practical how-to.

Buy or check out holiday stories and read them for each holiday. Tapes and records will also help to set the mood. (See the Resource Guide, pp. 348–355, for specifics.) Introduce new observances gradually. You might want to try a couple of new practices for each holiday around the year. Remember, the holidays return each year, bringing new opportunities for learning and observance.

Possibly the best help is to find another family to learn with or from as your personal resource people. Join a *havurah* that celebrates the Jewish festivals together. Attend family education programs at your synagogue or Jewish community center, then use what you learn there to enhance your home observance. Ask your rabbi or education director for suggestions.

Finally, see the section for "Shabbat Beginners" (pp. 168–169) for a more elaborate explanation of how to introduce new Jewish observances into the home.

WHAT IS A *YOM TOV*?

Yom Tov, literally a "Good Day," is the Hebrew expression for the holier holidays of the Jewish year: Rosh HaShanah and Yom Kippur, as well as the biblical pilgrimages of Passover, Shavuot, and Sukkot. These holidays all have their origins in the Torah itself.

In traditional Jewish observance, a *Yom Tov* carries the same restrictions on *melachah* (creative work) as a Shabbat, except that cooking for the holiday, using fire from a preexisting flame, is permitted, as is carrying in a "public domain." Yom Kippur, the weightiest *Yom Tov*, is observed like a Shabbat in that all work is prohibited (indeed the fast of Yom Kippur supersedes the usual prohibition of fasting on the Sabbath). Passover includes days of *Hol HaMoed*, intermediate weekdaylike days of the festivals, when work is permitted, framed by the holier *Yom Tov* days at the beginning and end. Sukkot consists of *Yom Tov* followed by several *Hol HaMoed* days, capped off by the extra *Yom Tov* of Shemini Atzeret and Simhat Torah.

A *Yom Tov* is inaugurated by the lighting of candles, as for Shabbat, with the blessing parallel to Shabbat, except that it ends, *lehadlik ner shel Yom Tov* (to kindle the candle of *Yom Tov*; on Yom Kippur this is changed to *lehadlik ner shel Yom Hakippurim*, to kindle the candle of the Day of Atonement). A festival *kiddush* is recited on the holiday eve and the next day at noon; special meals are eaten as on Shabbat, with special additions to the Grace after Meals. Several special prayers are recited in the synagogue.

Before the Hebrew calendar was fixed, the advent of each new month was publicized by bonfire signals on hilltops, and later word was sent by messenger to outlying areas. Jews who lived far away from Jerusalem, in the Diaspora, were in danger of observing some of the festivals on the wrong days, so the rabbis added a *Yom Tov Sheni* or second *Yom Tov* day to each biblical one (except Yom Kippur), when observed in the Diaspora, in order to ensure that the correct day would be observed. Rosh HaShanah was the only *Yom Tov* extended to two days even within the land of Israel: as it was observed on the first day of a new month, it was dependent, even there, on the correct witnessing of the new moon.

After the calendar was fixed, these extra days of *Yom Tov* continued to be maintained by Jewish communities outside the land of Israel. Today, the additional day of *Yom Tov* is still observed in the Diaspora by Orthodox and many Conservative Jews. Rosh HaShanah is still traditionally observed for two days, including in Israel. Liberal Jewish congregations no longer observe the *Yom Tov Sheni* days, and many observe only one day of Rosh HaShanah.

24

THE FALL HOLIDAYS: SEASON OF RENEWAL

The year is turning. The long, hot days of muggy summer are fading away. Children have actually begun to tire of vacation and look forward with a mixture of excitement and trepidation to the new school year. Soon fresh autumn breezes will clear away the summer doldrums. In the crisp air, our thoughts are easier to focus. Change is in the air. It's the perfect setting for a new beginning.

The Jewish year is inaugurated now with a special season of fall holidays that focus on personal, interpersonal, and communal revitalization. This is a key time for Jewish families. The traditional holiday observances of this season can foster family closeness, love of heritage, transmission of values. They can set the tone for a year in which we strengthen our family circle as well as reach out to a broader community.

The season of *teshuvah*, of renewal and return, has come.

ELUL: PREPARATION FOR A SPIRITUAL JOURNEY

When a family plans a vacation, they usually begin weeks in advance to prepare by obtaining passports and other documents, sending for travel brochures, reading the guidebooks, and making plans. I've yet to meet the clan who would show up at the airport one morning, suitcases in hand, and hope that they'd eventually get somewhere.

Similarly, for the spiritual journey through the Days of Awe to be meaningful for us and to our children, a certain amount of advance preparation is called for. If we "wing it" by embarking on this most intense season "suddenly one Rosh HaShanah morning" in the synagogue, we're taking our chances. Without adequate preparation, we and our children are like travelers who take a spur of the moment trip to a place we haven't been for a long time—we may chance upon some exciting new experience, but we're really more likely to end up feeling like strangers, finding that we've forgotten some of the language and customs of the place.

The Hebrew month of *Elul* provides an opportunity for Jews to prepare physically, psychologically, and spiritually for the New Year. *Elul* is the month directly preceding Rosh HaShanah, so it usually falls around mid-August to mid-September. Rosh HaShanah, Yom Kippur, Sukkot, and Simchat Torah all occur in the next Hebrew month, *Tishrei*.

Beginning to set the holiday/Holy Day mood in *Elul* can enhance the meaning of the upcoming fall holiday season and the Jewish year to come.

TRADITIONAL *ELUL* PRACTICES

● *Shofar*: The *shofar*, an ancient instrument made from a ram's horn, is blown daily (except on Shabbat) in traditional synagogues after the morning services beginning with the first of *Elul*. According to the Rambam (Maimonides), the *sho-*

far's call is intended to wake us from our spiritual doldrums and move us to *teshuvah*.

● Services and Prayers: In the nights before the New Year, many Jews gather for *Selihot*, or penitential prayers. The first night's service is at midnight, and additional ones are said just prior to sunrise. This is another traditional practice that is making a "comeback" even among more liberal congregations, many of which hold at least the Saturday night service.

Psalm 27, which expresses trust in God, is added to each morning and afternoon service from the beginning of *Elul* through Hoshanah Rabbah (the seventh day of Sukkot). The psalm could be used as a seasonal meditation whether or not one attends daily services.

Elul is a good time to obtain a *mahzor*, the special holiday prayer book, and study the prayers with the commentaries and notes.

● Personal reflection and mending relationships: *Elul* is a time for introspection, for reviewing actions of the previous year, and for deciding how to improve oneself in the year to come. But introspection and prayer are not in themselves enough. According to Jewish beliefs, all one's prayers and good intentions cannot absolve a wrong toward another human being unless one first obtains that person's forgiveness and makes whatever restitution is necessary. *Elul* has traditionally been the time of year in which Jews make a special point to end quarrels, ask forgiveness for unkind remarks, and basically mend relations with family and friends. Considered equally important is the sometimes difficult matter of forgiving others.

● Greetings: Beginning in *Elul*, it's traditional to wish people, in person or in letters, *L'Shanah Tovah Tikateivu* ("May you be written [in the 'Book of Life'] for a good year"). A modern extension of this greeting custom, both in the United States and in Israel, is to send Rosh HaShanah greeting cards to family and friends.

● Visiting the cemetery: A widespread custom during the month of *Elul* is to visit the graves of loved ones who have died. Rosh HaShanah is a time for remembrance, and the holiday season resonates with themes of death and life. It's a good time to talk to children about loved ones whom you miss and their legacies that you hope to keep alive in your lives.

● Other practices: Although Rosh HaShanah is a Day of Awe, it is a festive day as well. Buying something new to wear, sprucing up the house for the New Year, and starting to cook, bake, and invite for the upcoming holidays all add to the general air of anticipation in the household.

FAMILY ACTIVITIES FOR THE MONTH OF *ELUL*

Shofar Experiences

See Rosh HaShanah Activities, pp. 184–185.

Selihot Services

The word *selihot* means pardon or forgiveness. *Selihot* usually begin the Saturday night preceding Rosh HaShanah with a midnight or close to midnight service. (It will begin the week earlier if Rosh HaShanah falls on a Monday or Tuesday.) Check with your congregation for details. There will often be a late study session and refreshments (and coffee!) preceding the services. Going to pray in the middle of the night can be a memorable experience for older children as well as for adults. There is a special atmosphere there that can really set the mood of awe that characterizes the Jewish New Year.

With younger children, you might adapt the idea of the *selihot* by taking a few moments of quiet at bedtime, shortly before Rosh HaShanah, for everyone to think about his or her actions and talk silently to God about what he or she wants to improve in the coming year.

Person to Person

This is the time to stress to children that making amends with others is just as essential a part of *teshuvah* as praying in the synagogue. Here parents set the example for youngsters, all year long, when they are able to admit that they've been wrong and to ask their children (or spouse's) pardon. As in all areas of parenting, modeling is essential. It can also help to tell some stories from your own childhood about making up and making amends.

A family might establish their own tradition each year in which they sit around the table after Friday night dinner, *Havdalah*, or a family meeting during a set date in *Elul* and exchange feelings about the events of the past year and hopes for enriching their relationships in the coming year. Include a chance for all the members to compliment one another for things they've appreciated in the past year.

For a lighter reminder that this is *teshuvah* time, you might make everyone in the family buttons to wear with the word "*teshuvah*" in Hebrew or English or a "*teshuvah*" magnet for the refrigerator door (write on a scrap of wood or cardboard; attach with magnet tape from the dime store), in order to make a rather abstract, difficult concept a bit more concrete for children.

It's a good time for family meetings that focus on plans, goals, and mutual behavioral changes for the coming year. Try to keep the goals positive, gradual, loving—and mutual. You might all decide by consensus on one family behavior for everyone, children and adults, to improve during the upcoming year, for example, better communication, more pleasant speech, greater community involvement. (State it positively, rather than "less yelling" or "less messing the house.") You can brainstorm some positive steps to take: family meetings every Sunday, a commitment to a certain number of meals together each week. Reinforcements might be used to encourage improved behavior. For example, anyone of any age who observes another family member doing the desired behavior can drop a marble in a jar; each time the jar is filled, the family celebrates with a treat. Or cut a posterboard in the shape of a house, then fill with heart-shaped stickers in the same way. If you have regular family meetings, you can all review your progress each month, but even a few weeks' effort could affect a change for the better.

Making New Year's Cards

Making and sending Rosh HaShanah cards to family and friends is an activity that can be adapted to any age level. And what grandparent isn't thrilled to receive a custom-made holiday card from a grandchild?

Hold your own Rosh Hashanah card workshop. One afternoon during *Elul*, set up a table with paper and art supplies; the older the children, the more varied and sophisticated the choices that can be offered. For preschoolers, it may help to cut out some holiday symbols in advance or make tagboard cut-outs for the children to trace before cutting out. For older children you might provide, or compile with them, a list of holiday motifs they might want to illustrate: *shofar*, apples and honey jars or honey bees, round *hallah* candles and *kiddush* cup, *mahzor* (holiday prayer book), *tzedakah* box, scales, "Book of Life," dove of peace, Jerusalem-

style skyline, friends together or hands clasped together, and so on. If needed, write out the Rosh HaShanah greeting for the children to copy:

LeShanah Tovah Tikateivu VaTehateimu.

May You Be Written and Sealed for a Good Year.

For an additional challenge, look for phrases of blessing in the Psalms, Proverbs, or prophetic books of the Bible to include in your cards.

Younger children can write:

Shanah Tovah

A Good Year

Gather a variety of supplies. Use paper of various kinds, such as plain and colored construction paper, white bond or drawing paper, tissue paper, colored cellophane, gold and silver foil, old wallpaper samples, origami papers, and the like. Provide various drawing implements, such as crayons, colored chalk, colored pencils, and markers, along with scissors, glue, crayons, squeeze-on glitter, and stickers. Children can cut up old Rosh HaShanah cards, Jewish magazines, catalogues, and old Israel travel brochures to paste on for a collage effect. Then have fun! Decorate the cards with some of the symbols as you provided or with collages and write your *Shanah Tovah* greetings and personal messages inside.

New Year's Card Ideas

● Cut out Rosh HaShanah symbols from contrasting paper or from felt or other scraps. Glue on cover of card.

● Make a mini-collage from cut-up pictures of Jewish scenes or symbols from old Rosh HaShanah cards, magazines, travel brochures of Israel, even spare family photos. If "mass-production" is desired, unfold the card and photocopy the results, then refold the copies. Children may want to color in the copied picture, perhaps with markers. A full-color picture can be reproduced by the laser-printing method.

● Cut the card itself in the shape of a *Yom Tov* symbol, carefully cutting on a fold so that the card will have two sides.

● The card can also be one-sided, three-sided, or accordion-pleated.

● For a stained-glass effect, cut out a holiday design (such as a *shofar*) from the front of a construction-paper card, then glue a piece of colored cellophane and tissue paper over the back of the cut-out. Or fold the paper in half horizontally, then vertically, so that you have doubled pages. Then unfold, cut a design from the front page only, starting from a hole in the center so just the design is removed. Place a contrasting paper over the next inside sheet, which will be exposed when you refold the page. Or cut the design from both front folds simultaneously and paste some tissue paper or colored cellophane inside, between the two folds.

● Cut the end of a potato or a sponge in the shape of a holiday symbol and print the card with poster paint or ink. You can also get linoleum block print supplies from an art-supply store for more sophisticated prints.

● Equally important is the message you write inside the cards (after the glue dries!). Older children and adults can write a few lines, while younger ones can dictate.

The Family Mailbox

Rosh HaShanah is a good time for a family mailbox. You can use a box covered with adhesive paper, a compartmentalized letter-holder, or even an old toy mailbox. Encourage each family member to leave personal messages for the others during the month of *Elul*.

Tzedakah

Tzedakah is considered especially important at this time of year. "*Teshuvah* (repentance), *tefillah* (prayer), and *tzedakah* (justice and charity) avert the evil decree," states the traditional Rosh HaShanah liturgy. Jews start the new year by helping others, thus shaping a better future for all. Make a point of deciding as a family where to give some New Year's donations. With young children, you might explain in simple terms where you are giving some money to ("to help feed hungry people who are poor"). They can also put some coins in the *tzedakah* box.

As the children grow up a bit, you could establish a family tradition of taking *Elul* as a time to make decisions not only regarding personal growth, but also to choose a personalized *tzedakah* project for the year. You might decide to "adopt" a shut-in or nursing-home resident to visit on a regular basis, to volunteer for work with the handicapped, to purchase extra food and donate it to a food bank, to write letters and raise money for an organization that you believe in.

General Preparations

As for Shabbat, children can be involved in the cooking, baking, and cleaning for the holidays ahead. If possible, it's fun for everyone to have at least one new item to wear for the New Year. At the same time, children can pass their outgrown clothes along to siblings and friends or donate some to *tzedakah* organizations. For the blessing over new clothes, see p. 89.

You can also shop fruit markets for a fruit that you haven't eaten yet this year on which to make a *sheheheyanu* prayer on the second day of Rosh HaShanah.

THE DAYS OF AWE

The fall holiday season reaches its peak during the ten days of Rosh HaShanah through Yom Kippur. These form a period known in the Jewish tradition as the *Aseret Yemei Teshuvah*, the Ten Days of Repentance, or *HaYamim HaNoraim*, the Days of Awe. This period is also often called the "High Holidays" or "High Holy Days." The *teshuvah* process of introspection, of reviewing the year and renewing ourselves, which began in the month of *Elul* (see previous section) culminates with these days. Traditionally, this is a time marked not only by extra prayer and observance but by extra acts of *tzedakah*, kindness, and attention to relationships.

The Days of Awe are among the most widely observed of Jewish holidays in the United States, yet there is often a difficulty in relaying them to children. Because the themes of these days are so adult, it may be difficult to convey the holiday concepts to children. For very young children, "apples and honey for a sweet year" and "the birthday of the world," are appropriate themes to emphasize. As children grow up, however, we have to offer increasingly sophisticated insights into these days. The Days of Awe offer the family an opportunity to teach important processes, which are rarely taught in school but are essential to human growth and happiness: things such as self-examination, personal growth, and working on relationships.

As an extension of this personal aspect, the liturgy and themes of the Days of Awe resound with an awareness of communal responsibility and global interdependence. These two traditional Jewish concepts have now become virtually essential to transmit to the next generation if we are to see human civilization and our planet survive and flourish.

A Derashah* for Parents: Wake-up Call

Maimonides wrote that the *shofar* is sounding a wake-up call to "sleepers," that is, to those who are going about their business unconscious of their creator's demands for righteous living (*Mishneh Torah*, Laws of Repentance 3:4).

Relationships in a family can use such a wake-up call from time to time. It is so easy to get into ruts, habitual responses, automatic conflicts. This is true in any relationship, but particularly in responding to children with their many demands. I know that there are many times when I've related to my children as if I were asleep, not really listening to or looking at them, just giving an automatic response while thinking of something else (an "I-it" interaction, to borrow from Buber). But then I remember that they are growing up so fast. I ask myself: If not now, then *when* will I relate to them with full attention and awareness?

The *shofar* can be a wake-up call for parents.

THE DAYS OF AWE: TURNING TOWARD ONE ANOTHER AND GOD

Traditional Observances for the Days of Awe

Rosh HaShanah

Rosh HaShanah, the New Year (literally "head of the year"), the first day of the Hebrew month of *Tishrei*, is solemn yet joyful. It is known by several names, including: *Yom Harat Olam*, the birthday of the world, *Yom HaZikaron*, the Day of Remembrance, *Yom Teruah*, the Day of Sounding the Shofar, and *Yom HaDin*, the Day of Judgment.

The Torah scrolls, the curtain covering the holy

ark, and the garments of those leading the service are white to symbolize the theme of purification. Services are longer than usual and feature the themes of God as sublime sovereign as well as loving parent, as epitomized in the traditional prayer *Avinu, Malkeinu* (Our Father, Our King). The theme of judgment of all mankind for the coming year is found in such classic Rosh HaShanah prayers as *Unetaneh Tokef* (Let Us Declare the Holiness of the Day).

The day begins, like all Jewish holidays, the previous evening with candlelighting, *kiddush*, and a festive meal. Special foods of the day are a sweet round *hallah* (symbolizing the cyclical year or the crown of kingship) and other sweet foods, particularly apples and honey, for a sweet year. Rosh HaShanah is observed as a *Yom Tov* (see p. 177) similar to a Sabbath as a day of abstaining from creative work.

Rosh HaShanah is traditionally observed for two days, both in Israel and in the Diaspora. This practice dates back to ancient times before the calendar was fixed and the sighting of the new moon in the sky was confirmed only by witnesses. Some liberal congregations observe one day of Rosh HaShanah. The talmudic rabbis called the two days *Yoma Arichta*, one long day. So in order to properly be able to recite the *sheheheyanu*, which celebrates newness and renewal, on the second day, it became customary to wear a new garment or to eat a new fruit.

The *shofar* is sounded many times—traditionally one hundred times in the course of the service. Its cry recalls many peak moments in Jewish history— the binding of Isaac, when a ram in the thicket was sacrificed in his stead; the revelation at Mount Sinai, when thunder and *shofar* calls were heard; and the beginning of the biblical jubilee year, the fiftieth year in which slaves were freed and property restored. In olden times the *shofar* was sounded for every new month, and it is traditionally believed that *shofar* calls will herald the arrival of the Messiah.

Tashlich is one of those seemingly quaint Jewish customs, dating back to the Middle Ages, that is making a comeback as more of us discover our roots. On the first day of Rosh HaShanah (second if the first day falls on Shabbat) many congregational and *havurah* groups stroll to a body of water such as a river, lake, or ocean, and empty a few crumbs from their pockets into the stream, thereby symbolically "throwing away" their sins into the purifying waters. Prayers, and often singing and folk dancing, accompany the ritual.

---

*Derashah A midrashic-style interpretation, lit."seeking out" meaning.

183

The Ten Days of Repentance

The Ten Days of Repentance, which include the high holidays and the intervening days, is the period of the year most intensely devoted to *teshuvah*. The day after Rosh HaShanah is the Fast of Gedaliah, a minor (dawn to dark) fast that commemorates the death of Gedaliah, the last Jewish governor of Judaea during the Babylonian exile. The Sabbath that falls during these days is called *Shabbat Shuvah*, the Sabbath of Return, and is considered one of the major Sabbaths of the year.

In Jewish lore the completely righteous are seen as "written and sealed" for a good year in a celestial Book of Life on Rosh HaShanah. But ordinary people are written in, penciled in as it were, on the New Year, then given the Ten Days of Repentance to complete their *teshuvah*, after which they can hope to be "sealed" in the Book on Yom Kippur. The greeting during this period therefore changes to "*Gemar Hatimah Tovah,*" "Finish with a Good Sealing-In." The good verdict is metaphorically weighing in the balance—scales to weigh the good and bad deeds are another Rosh HaShanah motif. In the broadest sense the *teshuvah* period is seen as extending all the way from the first of *Elul* through Hoshanah Rabbah, the seventh day of Sukkot.

Yom Kippur

Yom Kippur or *Yom HaKippurim*, the Day of Atonement, is the holiest day of the Jewish year. It is a 24-hour fast that involves abstention from food, drinking, bathing, anointing the body, wearing leather shoes, and having sexual relations. As with all Jewish fasts, the full fast is observed by adults (past *bat* and *bar mitzvah* age), unless health reasons proscribe fasting. Yom Kippur is also, like the Sabbath, a day of abstention from creative work.

A family meal is eaten prior to the fast and children are blessed by parents as on Shabbat. White, symbolizing purity, is customarily worn on Yom Kippur, and in Orthodox synagogues many men wear the *kittel*, a garment symbolic of purity. *Tallitat*, prayer shawls, are worn at night *and* during the day only on this holiest of days.

The evening service begins with the haunting tune of the *Kol Nidre*, a formula for the annulment of religious vows. The prayer is said to recall Inquisitionary days, when many Jews were forced to take vows of Christianity but practiced their religion in secret. The next day is devoted to worship, beginning with the morning service, then *Musaf* (the additional service), which on this day recalls the ancient Temple rituals of atonement. The afternoon service includes Torah readings on sexual morality and (unlike other holidays and Shabbat) a *haftarah* selection, the book of Jonah. The long day of prayer concludes with a special final service: *Ne'ilah*, the "closing of the gates."

A central prayer of the day is the "*Al Het,*" a communal confession of sins and plea for divine forgiveness. The long day of prayer concludes after dark with a single blast of the *shofar* and the words "Next Year in Jerusalem!"

In traditional synagogues, the short evening service and the *Havdalah* are recited immediately after the *shofar* is blown. Then, after a light "break the fast" meal at home, it is customary to begin building the family *sukkah* that very night. In a few days, Sukkot and Shemini Atzeret-Simhat Torah will complete the fall holiday cycle.

FAMILY ACTIVITIES FOR THE DAYS OF AWE

Prepare for Rosh HaShanah during *Elul*

See the previous section on activities for the month of *Elul* (pp. 180–182) for suggestions on how to make original New Year's greeting cards and family letters, and also on *Selihot* services, making amends with family members, the family mailbox, *tzedakah*, new clothes, and other High Holiday preparations.

Holiday Poster

To concretize the rather abstract Days of Awe, make a holiday poster. As a family, paste items such as New Year's cards and holiday photos on a large poster board. Using colored markers, write or draw holiday memories. Display the poster in your *sukkah* or family room.

Shofar Activities

See, feel, hear a real *shofar*. Borrow one or purchase your own from a Judaica gift shop or ask if you can handle a *shofar* at your synagogue or Jewish school. Besides examining the *Shofar*, try to blow it. Is it hard to blow? The trick is to keep your lips close together and create vibrations by blowing very hard. Even if you don't have a real *shofar*, you and your preschooler can pretend to blow one, imitating the *shofar* calls.

Toy *shofars* are (noisy) fun for very young children, although they don't sound much like a real *shofar*. You can make your own by cutting a *shofar* shape double from construction paper, inserting a dimestore kazoo, and stapling shut at the top. The kazoo can be used to mimic the sounds of the *tekiah* (one *shofar* call of moderate length), *shevarim* (three shorter sounds), *teruah* (nine quick blasts), and the High Holiday *tekiah gedolah* (one *very* long *shofar* call). What do the sounds remind you of? How do the sounds make you feel?

Preteens, with plenty of parental supervision, can even try their hands at making a real *shofar* from a ram's horn. Instructions, which could turn anyone into a vegetarian, can be found in *How to Run a Traditional Jewish Household* by Blu Greenberg, *The Jewish Holidays—A Guide and Commentary* by Michael Strassfeld, or in *The Rosh HaShanah Anthology*, Phillip Goodman, editor.[1] In some cities, the hasidic organization Chabad-Lubavitch sponsors *shofar*-making workshops.

Blessing Before Hearing the Shofar:

Baruch Atah Adonai, Eloheinu Melech HaOlam, asher kidshanu bemitzvotav vetzivanu lishmoah kol shofar.

Holy One of Blessing, Your Presence fills creation; You have made us holy with commandments and bid us to hear the sound of the shofar.

(This is the blessing said for liturgical purposes—not when simply blowing the *shofar* for fun.)

Sweet Foods for Rosh HaShanah

There are several special foods associated with the New Year. Honey is the naturally sweet ingredient eaten in several forms "for a sweet year." Recipes with honey and related crafts are child-pleasers, but honey should not be fed to infants under age two, as it may be associated with infant botulism. Kids will enjoy arranging a platter of different kinds of apples: green, gold, Delicious, Macintosh, and others, with some bowls of different flavors of honey. My children love the honey that comes in a container shaped like a teddy bear.

At Rosh HaShanah dinner, the apple is traditionally dipped in the honey with the blessing over fruit (*Borei Pri HaEtz*), followed by the words: "*Yehi Ratzon . . . shetehadesh alenyu shanah tovah umetukah.*" "May it be Your will to renew for us a good and sweet year."

● *Make a Honey Jar*: Take a clean, small jar such as a baby-food jar and decorate as desired with stickers (use the kind with Judaic motifs, appropriate pictures such as apples, or make your own abstract designs with geometrical stickers) or paint pens. If you start collecting jars early enough, you could make individual honey jars, for everyone at the table. For an unbreakable version, decorate small disposable plastic cups rather than jars.

● Bake a Honey Cake with Your Children:

Try this recipe:

Mrs. Rosenberg's Honey Cake[2]

3 eggs
1 cup sugar
1 cup honey
1 cup oil
1 teaspoon baking powder
1 teaspoon baking soda (heaping)
1 cup cold black coffee
3 cups flour
1 cup chopped pecans (opt.)

(Hint: measure the oil before the honey so it won't stick to the cup.)

Beat eggs and sugar well, then add honey and oil. Sift dry ingredients and add alternately with the coffee. Add ½ cup pecans, if desired. Oil and flour an oblong pan and pour in the batter. Add rest of pecans on top, if desired. Bake at 300° F for one hour.

For mini honey cakes, bake in muffin papers in a muffin tin for 20 to 25 minutes.

New Fruit and Other Symbolic Foods

● New Fruit: As mentioned in the section on traditional observances, it's customary to eat a new fruit on the second day of Rosh HaShanah. Make it a family tradition to go shopping with the kids to discover a new fruit that no one has eaten all year.

Our family also observes the Sephardic custom

of eating pomegranate *(rimon)* seeds on Rosh HaShanah with the words: "May our merits multiply like pomegranate seeds."

● Other Symbolic Foods: There are other foods customary for Rosh HaShanah dinners. Most of these will appeal to children, except perhaps the venerable custom of eating fish heads with the saying: "May we be the head and not the tail." The Sephardic equivalent, eating brain and meat from a sheep's head, is not likely to excite American kids either.

Sephardic Jews also serve a whole variety of symbolic foods that, like the apples and honey, have special blessings, often involving a play on the Hebrew name of the food. For fish, for example, they say, "May it be your will, our God and God of our ancestors, that we will be fruitful and multiply like fish, and you will watch over us with 'open eyes.' " Or you might invent your own family food traditions for the holiday.

Tzimmes, a sweet vegetable dish made featuring carrots, is a traditional Ashkenazic New Year's dish that kids may like. The Yiddish word for carrots is *"meyrin,"* which also means to increase (one's wealth, privileges, and family). The round carrot slices also resemble gold coins, prosperity for the coming year. *Tzimmes* can include meat or be a *parve* dish.

● Round *Hallah*: The round *hallah* of the Days of Awe symbolizes the cycle of the year, or the crown of sovereignty, a seasonal theme. Even if you don't usually make *hallah* at home, you might enjoy taking an afternoon prior to the New Year to bake some loaves with the kids. You can freeze the bread for use over the many fall holidays. Simply braid the dough as usual and shape into a circle before it rises. Raisins are often added for additional sweetness. (See p. 150 for *hallah* recipe.)

Some other traditional *hallah* motifs that children might enjoy making with the dough are ladders, symbolic of ascending prayers. Doves of peace are also traditional motifs.

The *hallah* is traditionally dipped in honey rather than salt throughout the Days of Awe; some do this throughout the fall holidays. Friends of ours keep a jar of honey on their Shabbat table from the beginning of *Elul* through Simhat Torah, to dip *hallah* in and to reinforce the completeness of the season.

● Round *Hallah* Cover: Although you can certainly use your regular Shabbat *hallah* cover, your children might enjoy decorating a round cover.

Some plain white cloth can be cut into a circle with pinking shears (trace around the rim of a large bowl) and then decorated with fabric crayons or use one of the other suggestions for *hallah* covers in the Shabbat section (pp. 151–152). The youngest can simply decorate a large round coffee filter with crayons for an instant *hallah* cover.

MISSING SCHOOL FOR THE HOLIDAYS

One of the advantages of full-time Jewish schooling is that the school calendar is built around Jewish life. But if your children are not enrolled in a Jewish preschool or day school, you're bound to face some conflicts between Jewish observance and non-Jewish school schedules. (In some areas with a dense Jewish population, public schools close for Rosh HaShanah and Yom Kippur, but problems may arise with other holidays.) Sooner or later, two important values are going to conflict, and families will have to make value judgments.

Although American Jews are highly oriented toward academic achievement, our actions should make the statement to our children that school and work, while very important, are not our ultimate values. Our commitment to our faith and heritage is of such importance to us as adults that we are willing to miss work for Jewish holy days and to require that our children do not attend school on these days (with the understanding that some, such as physicians, are permitted to work on Shabbat on holidays, when preservation of life is involved).

It's helpful to write a letter that includes a schedule with dates of the year's Jewish holidays to the school office and your child's teacher at the beginning of the school year, plus reminder notes before each holiday. (You can also include a simple explanation of any related religious practices your family observes, such as *kashrut*.) It's also usually helpful to make an appointment before school begins, for a friendly talk with your child's teacher, and with the principal if it's a new school, to explain your family's observances.

By law, a child should be able to miss school for religious holidays without discrimination. The child should be given assignments in advance or given enough time to do make-up work. If problems arise, such as a major test when a teacher knows that it's a Jewish holiday, and if you can't work it out with the teacher or administration on your own, contact the Community Relations

Council of your local Jewish Federation for support.

My experience and many of my friends' is that most public-school teachers we've dealt with are supportive and understanding of our children's differences from the majority. I've even heard some non-Jewish public-school teachers express their dismay that they have Jewish pupils whose parents don't consider their religion's holidays an important enough reason to miss school.

Your Community Relations Council may also be able to provide you with a printed calendar of the holidays to give to your school. Through a church-state committee, the Community Relations Committee should be troubleshooting on a citywide level by mailing its own calendars of Jewish holidays with appropriate explanations to all local schools before the fall term begins, and this may even be a volunteer area you want to get involved in with your local Federation.

HIGH HOLIDAY SERVICES WITH CHILDREN

Many synagogues arrange special youth, junior congregation, or family services for the holidays, either parallel to or at a different time from the main services. Check with your congregation well in advance for details. Ask if the synagogue or school offers a family education series with holiday activities that parents and children can attend together.

The preschool nursery usually available during holiday services needn't be a mere parking lot for tots if the synagogue arranges for an early-childhood teacher or parent volunteers to organize some loosely structured activities such as songs, stories, simple dramatic play (for example, my puppet asks your puppet's forgiveness for Yom Kippur), and appropriate refreshments such as apples and honey while saying the correct blessings. Holiday books and puzzles can be available for free play.

Youth or family services that involve older children can include simplified versions of some of the major prayers, as well as appropriate stories, discussions, and songs to involve youngsters in the spirit of the day.

Even if there are youth services, children should begin to spend at least a short time at the regular adult services, to impress upon them precisely that services are an adult activity that they are going to be privileged to grow into. You can start by bringing tots to hear the *shofar* sounded, to see the Torahs brought out of the ark and the other more "dramatic" parts of the service. As children learn more at school and home, they should be expected to remain in the adult services for increasingly longer periods. At first, this might mean being there for the *Avinu Malkeinu* and other familiar prayers. I may hold a child close and translate a few prayers for her (read the translation and explain in simple language if you don't know Hebrew). As they grow and learn, they should stay for the *Amidah*, *Al Heit*, and more introspective parts of the service.

Of course, a lot depends on the atmosphere at your synagogue and whether it's considered acceptable for people to enter and leave the sanctuary during services. Generally, the traditional synagogues and the *havurah*-type settings are more relaxed about this. It's all part of the larger issue of finding a congregation that accepts families and helps children grow into their adult roles as Jews.

Tashlich

After a morning spent more or less quietly in *shul*, what child wouldn't appreciate the opportunity to walk, frolic, and play by a stream? On the afternoon of the first day of Rosh HaShanah (second if the first day is Shabbat), it's an old Jewish custom to walk to a natural body of water and symbolically "cast away one's sins" as the participants empty some crumbs in their pockets into the water, symbol of purification. There's usually some singing and folk dancing as well. This rather quaint custom, dating back to the Middle Ages, is making a comeback as more Jews discover their "roots." Now not only Orthodox congregational groups, but members of *havurot* and liberal synagogues are also observing this custom, which is especially fun for kids. You might ask everyone in the family to think of which attitudes and behaviors each would like to "cast off." It's also the sort of concrete activity that helps youngsters to anchor the somewhat abstract ideas of Rosh HaShanah. Besides, no one tells them to sit still during *tashlich*!

THE TEN DAYS OF *TESHUVAH* AND *SHABBAT SHUVAH*

The days between Rosh HaShanah and Yom Kippur, and especially *Shabbat Shuvah*, the intervening Sabbath, are traditionally a time for extra synagogue attendance, Jewish study, *tzedakah*, deeds of kindness, and more intense observance in general. The themes of introspection and reconciliation with other people continue at an even greater intensity as Yom Kippur approaches. Each family can develop its own customs for this special time of year:

● At home, this can be a time to discuss the High Holiday themes and to continue to work on person-to-person reconciliation. With young children one doesn't always have time to get around to everything, so these days can be a time to bring up any holiday themes or activities you may have missed.

● It's especially appropriate to focus on kind deeds and *mitzvah* projects that involve the entire family. You might choose "a *mitzvah* a day" from Rosh HaShanah to Yom Kippur. It can be something very simple each day: holiday cards to Ethiopian Jews, a visit to a shut-in, dropping off a donation of clothes to Goodwill or a local Jewish organization's thrift shop, a *tzedakah* donation.

● As during *Elul*, this is another good time for the family to decide together on a *tzedakah* project for the year, be it hands-on work for a local organization or long-distance support of a national or international cause you believe in.

YOM KIPPUR EXPERIENCES

If you've been using the past month and ten days, or at least the past ten days as preparation time, by working on interpersonal relations in the family and outside it, sending greetings, giving *tzedakah*, attending services, and discussing the concept of *teshuvah* at the appropriate levels, then the mood has been set for the most solemn day of the Jewish year. Here are a few suggestions for making Yom Kippur eve (*erev* Yom Kippur) a special family time and for managing with young children on the holy day itself.

Erev Yom Kippur

This should be a serenely spiritual day, with an air of anticipation and awe. However, with all the preparations for the pre- and post-fast meals, and just the pre-Yom Kippur tension many feel, it can become a stressful time. Especially when you have children, if at all feasible, it's best to eliminate outside obligations for most or all of the day. However, for employed parents who've struggled

just to get Yom Kippur itself off from work, this isn't always possible. If you have to work all or part of *erev* Yom Kippur at an outside job, be sure to cook as much as possible of the pre- and post-fast meals in advance, by using the evenings in advance of the holiday to prepare as many details as possible. It will help to ease the last-minute rush.

● *Mikveh*: In traditional circles, *erev* Yom Kippur is one of the few times when men customarily immerse in the *mikveh*, or ritual bath. This recalls the ritual immersion prior to entering the Holy Temple in ancient times. (See pp. 262–263 for more on the *mikveh*.)

● *Kapparot* (atonements) is the name for a rather exotic custom still observed among some very traditional Jews. On *erev* Yom Kippur a live chicken (for females) or a rooster (for males) is twirled three times around each family member's head, with the following formula recited: "This is in exchange for you. This is in place of you. This is your atonement. This chicken (rooster) will go to its death, but you will go on to a good and long life and peace." The birds are later slaughtered in the kosher manner and given to the poor.

My guess is that your children and mine would not enjoy this ritual (even medieval rabbis found it too superstitious), but many families have modernized this old custom by substituting money tied in a handkerchief in place of the ill-fated fowl. "This money will go to *tzedakah*," is then substituted for the line about the chicken. The family can decide together where to give the money, or each person can give it to the charity of choice.

● Sneakers to *Shul*: Young children get a kick out of the fact that on Yom Kippur they get to wear their sneakers to synagogue. In addition to the sneakers, dressing in white, which symbolizes purity, is exciting for many young children, who enjoy the drama of any type of "costume." (In fact, *Sneakers to Shul* is the title of a Yom Kippur book by Floreva G. Cohen beloved by preschoolers.)[3]

The reason for wearing sneakers or other non-leather shoes is that part of the fast, for children (from age six) as well as for adults, involves abstention from wearing leather shoes on Yom Kippur. Leather shoes were considered the most comfortable, and on a fast day we relinquish the comforts and pleasures of the flesh. Wearing sneakers or nonleather shoes also serves the purpose of making one feel more humble. (One year we stayed at a motel on Yom Kippur, in order to attend services nearby. In the flurry of holiday preparations and packing five sets of clothes, I forgot my own sneakers and resorted to wearing plastic "flip-flops" the entire day. I felt humble indeed!)

● The Prefast Meal: Once everyone is dressed, you're ready for a sit-down prefast family meal. Other than the traditional round *hallot* and honey, there aren't specific prefast foods. It used to be thought that a very heavy prefast meal was helpful, but it's now realized that more moderate fare—such as light protein and complex carbohydrate foods, vegetables, and fruits or juice and other liquids—better facilitates the fast. Very spicy or salty foods should be avoided, as they produce thirst.

The candles are lit after the meal, because lighting them ushers in the fast day. Before the candle lighting is an appropriate time to donate *tzedakah* money. The candle blessings are:

Baruch Atah Adonai, Eloheinu Melech HaOlam, asher kideshanu bemitzvotav vetzivanu lehadlick ner shel Yom HaKippurim.

Holy One of Blessing, Your Presence fills creation; You have made us holy with Your commandments and bid us to kindle the Yom Kippur lights.

Baruch Atah Adonai, Eloheinu Melech HaOlam, sheheheyanu vekiyemanu vehigianu lazeman hazeh.

Holy One of Blessing, Your Presence fills creation; You have kept us alive, sustained us and enabled us to reach this moment.

Yahrzeit candles are also lit if the family is remembering a loved one who has died. This can be the time to take a few moments to share some precious memories of these departed relatives with the children.

● Blessing the Children: After the meal is a special time for family members to ask each other's forgiveness for any wrongs during the year and for the parents to bless the children. The blessing is usually the same as the Shabbat evening blessing (p. 157), but extra messages of love and care for the year ahead may certainly be added. It's a special time for parents and children to step outside the daily routine and recall how important they are to one another.

Tips on Fasting with Kids

Fasting can be difficult, especially with young children who demand one's attention. To make it easier, it's helpful to completely prepare the children's food in advance (in traditional practice, one doesn't cook on Yom Kippur). Traditional halachic sources encourage giving young children a nice meal in honor of the day.

Extra snacks, changes of clothing and diapers, and some favorite quiet toys can be left at the synagogue nursery before the holiday, especially if you're planning to spend most of the day in at the synagogue. Although older children should be expected to spend part of the day in youth and regular services, books (preferably with Judaic themes) and other quiet amusements can also be prepared in advance. Once children are old enough to understand, you can talk to them in advance about why you are fasting and how they can help by behaving especially well.

Although children are not supposed to fast a full day, it is traditional to encourage them, in a relaxed, nonpressuring way, to gradually get used to fasting a few hours more each year from age nine or so. Some preteens seem to feel it is a mark of honor to fast all or most of the day. They can start by skipping snacks at an even younger age.

One other piece of advice for coffee- or tea-addicted parents: Gradually phase out the caffeine in your life by the week prior to Yom Kippur, to avoid a big caffeine-withdrawal headache.

Children and Holiday Services

See under Rosh HaShanah activities, p. 187.

Break-the-Fast

This light, usually dairy meal, is one that children can help prepare before Yom Kippur begins. They can help make cream-cheese spreads, salads, and desserts in advance. A buffet format is nice and can be a pleasant occasion for several families to share together. You can all go outside after the meal and spend a short time beginning to assemble your family *sukkah*.

THE HIGH HOLIDAYS: RATED PG-13?

The Days of Awe, with their serious themes of moral responsibility and personal introspection, often seem difficult to convey to children. We can, of course, focus on the concrete rituals and customs, from the *shofar* and *tashlich* ceremony to the apples and honey. These concrete experiences should not be disregarded, for children develop their identities early by linking strong emotions to tangible symbols. But the primary qualities of these days are in large part serious and abstract: awe, repentance, atonement, renewal, responsibility. How to teach them to our children—and should we even try? Should the Days of Awe be rated "PG-13"—post *bar mitzvah*, parental guidance recommended?

It may be a challenge, but in order to do the best for our children as well as to do justice to the Jewish tradition, it is important to begin teaching our children the moral and ethical dimensions of the Days of Awe while they are young.

By translating abstract, "adult" ideas into concrete actions, it is possible to teach even very young children about the more lofty themes of the Days of Awe. Of course, one wouldn't give preschoolers a graduate-level lecture on the Aramaic liturgical poetry of Yom Kippur. But one can find age-appropriate ways to convey the less-concrete aspects of these Days.

There are three central imperatives of the Days of Awe: *teshuvah* (repentance), *tefillah* (prayer), and *tzedakah* (justice, charity). Here are some suggestions for beginning to convey these three adult concepts to children.

Teshuvah

Even very young children can begin to learn about *teshuvah*. For preschoolers, dramatic play and stories are appropriate ways to learn and broaden experiences. For example, when my older girls were preschoolers, we would act out asking forgiveness with puppets. Most children's holiday anthologies (see Resource Guide, pp. 349–350) have at least one High Holiday chapter with a *teshuvah* theme, and we read many of these.

The *Elul* activities, such as the *Elul* family meeting, family mailbox, and other ideas (pp. 180–182) can be useful in teaching about *teshuvah* as children grow older.

But according to many psychologists and educators, the best way to teach moral concepts is by modeling them ourselves. If we, as parents, embody qualities such as tolerance, patience, ethical concern, and forgiveness, our children will be much more likely to develop them, too.

Indeed, the Jewish concepts of *teshuvah* and ethical responsibility are important to begin teaching young children all year long. The idea of seeking forgiveness and "making *shalom*" should begin even in preschool. The actual steps of *teshuvah* can be taught from early elementary school: (1) recognition and regret for wrongdoing (along with asking forgiveness and making all possible amends to those wronged), (2) rejection of the behavior by ceasing to do it, and (3) resolving to behave better and taking steps to act differently in the future. Rabbi Irving Greenberg calls these the "three R's of repentance": regret, rejection, and resolution[4] (see pp. 105–108 for more on the use of Hebrew value words in child guidance).

In other words, if a child says, "I'm sorry," after hurting a sibling or cheating on a test, encourage her or him to go further and "do *teshuvah*" as she or he is able. Help the child through the steps in a nonblaming way. Brainstorm ideas for change. Help the child discover ways to channel innate qualities (a need for attention, a drive for achievement) toward more positive use. The *teshuvah* process is more than behavior modification. It includes discovering what one's underlying needs and drives are and then redirecting them toward more positive ends. According to Rabbi Greenberg, that rechanneling is the real meaning of the Jewish concept of *kapparah*, or atonement.

We should strive to create an atmosphere where a child is able to talk about any problem. Maimonides stressed the importance of verbal confession. A child should learn from a young age that it is safe to talk to parents and be helped to do *teshuvah* when behaviors need changing. The child should feel that she or he is loved unconditionally, but that some kinds of behaviors have to change. As the sage Beruriah said to her husband, Rabbi Meir, "Pray that sins, not sinners, will cease" (*Talmud, Berachot* 10a).

Teshuvah is freeing because a child can feel that mistakes can be overcome. The Jewish view is that the one who does *teshuvah* is renewed, is a new person. The slate can be wiped clean and guilt alleviated, not just by tossing out an automatic "I'm sorry," but by sincere efforts to make amends and to change. A child can always be sure of our unconditional love, a crucial element in self-esteem and family strength.

There are other High Holiday messages that children can learn that are related to *teshuvah* and renewal. One is about personal stock taking. Secular New Year's resolutions are usually not taken seriously. But the idea of self-examination and sincere goal setting for the year ahead are appropriate components of the Jewish New Year.

Goal setting is an effective tool for life that families can instill in their children. Setting goals need not be limited to strictly material areas, such as finances or physical fitness. Material goals are important; however, spiritual, intellectual, and other less tangible aims can also be formulated as goals.

The family can set yearly or monthly goals that deal with family life, as well as with *mitzvahs* and *tzsedakah*. Young children, from age five or six, should be told about the parents' goals for the family. And as they grow, they can be more and more involved in the goal setting and progress evaluation processes. It helps when parents set the example by formulating their own goals and visions, both individually and as a couple.

As they grow up, young people can be encouraged also to formulate personal yearly goals, not only in academics and personal improvement and achievement, but also in such areas as service to others, spiritual growth, Torah study, ethical improvement (*musar*), character development (*middot*), and so forth. Judaic tradition, from the Talmud to the nineteenth-century *Musar* (ethicist) movement, has stressed personal ethical growth as a way of emulating godliness and drawing closer to God.

A *Rosh Hodesh* family meeting (see Rosh Hodesh section) could allow several minutes for each person to review her or his goals and ideally could show that help can be asked for where needed. Inability to fulfill a goal should not be taken as a sign of failure but as an indication of the need to look at it more closely, perhaps reformulating it. Examine why the goal is not being met and how it can be reframed into easily achievable components.

Tefillah

See "Kids and Synagogue Services" (p. 187) for general suggestions on easing children into increasing participation in the holiday services. Special holiday prayerbooks (*mahzorim*) for children can be used to learn or review key prayers.

You can play recordings of the High Holiday music during the month of *Elul* prior to Rosh HaShanah. If desired, go a step further and sing some of the major prayers with your children. Read some of them aloud from the *mahzor* or from one of the children's prayer books and discuss at the child's level of understanding.

You can set the mood of spirituality with some of the *Elul* practices, such as attending the mid-night *Selihot* services or a daily reading of Psalm 27. You could read aloud a short selection from a High Holiday anthology or from the *mahzor*, in the month prior to the High Holidays. After learning some of the traditional High Holiday motifs, write your own personal prayers for the new year and read aloud if desired. Or write new verses for some of the traditional prayers, such as the *Avinu, Malkeinu* (Our Father, Our King) or the *Al Heit* (communal confession of sins). Doing this makes one take a closer look at these prayers. You can also illustrate some of the feelings you have from the prayers or from the holy days in general.

Tzedakah

Another important message of the Days of Awe is moral responsibility. As we read on Yom Kippur, the prophets condemned those who fasted and prayed, but continued to ignore the poor and oppressed. *Tzedakah* (justice, righteous actions, charity) is mentioned in the holiday liturgy as the essential complement to prayer and *teshuvah*. We can teach our children from their early years that the High Holy Days are meant to spur us toward greater sensitivity and humanitarianism throughout the year.

The Days of Awe are a traditional time for special *tzedakah*, so it's an ideal time for the family, or several families, to get together and decide where to give some donations for the New Year. It's become a growing custom in the American Jewish community for people to take the money that would have been spent on food on Yom Kippur and to donate it to Mazon or another organization that feeds the hungry, in order to alleviate the suffering of those who fast nearly every day because they have no food. (See Resources on Jewish Interpersonal Values, pp. 336–337.)

This can be the time of year to raise our goals and standards of *tzedakah* and *mitzvah* actions for the year to come. What concrete action can our family take each week or month this year to work for *Tikkun Olam*, perfecting and healing God's world? Brainstorm with your kids about possible actions on different levels, from family relationships to global concerns. (For specific *mitzvah* ideas, see the section on Jewish Interpersonal Values, pp. 109–112.) The family can start off the new year with *mitzvot* such as inviting Russian immigrants for a holiday meal, giving *tzedakah*, giving our outgrown clothes away when we buy new holiday clothes, buying extra food for the food bank when we purchase food for the holidays, or paying a holiday visit to an elderly Jew living alone or in a nursing home.

Never Too Young

Children aren't too young to learn about the deeper meanings of the holidays. I think of the years that my parents played classical music in my home when I was a child. They didn't do it to "give me culture," but because it was something that truly meant something to them, and *besides* that it was good for me to hear. Although much of the music was over my head and little appreciated when I was young, by early adulthood I began to love fine music. What's more, that continued exposure as a child had given me a more discriminating ear than some of my college friends who had never heard classical music played at home.

In the same way, children will absorb the more adult messages of the Days of Awe (and Jewish values in general), even if the honey cake and the new clothes are more exciting to them at the present time. On some level, the ideas we teach are making an impression, becoming a part of the fabric of their lives. When they grow more mature and are ready, those years of exposure to the classical ideas and values of our heritage that we exposed them to during childhood will be fully appreciated.

Just as my parents didn't keep me listening to nursery music as I grew up, we can soon go beyond the "apples and honey" to introduce our children to the great ideas and values of our people while they are young. It's an investment in their future.

A Derashah for Parents: On Parenting and Teshuvah

The Days of Awe focus on a central theme of Judaism: *teshuvah*. Usually translated as "repentance," *teshuvah* literally means "return" (to righteous ways, to behaving as our true selves in the image of God, to Jewish tradition). The word carries a connotation of renewal and revitalization. In addition to its other meanings, *teshuvah* also means "a response." *Teshuvah* is the Jewish way to respond to human failings.

Teshuvah is often thought of today as a return to ultratraditional Judaism. The phenomenon of the *baal teshuvah* as a "born-again Jew" has captured the contemporary Jewish imagination. Several books and any number of impassioned articles have been written on the subject. The more traditional definition of *teshuvah* is a change of behavior. There is a whole process defined by Maimonides as examining one's conscience, renouncing sin, and finally withstanding temptation in the future. This is *baal teshuvah* in the sense of penitent.

There is also a broader meaning to the word *teshuvah*. Rather than strictly a return from sin, *teshuvah* can represent the human ability for renewal, for making a new beginning. When I used to picture *teshuvah*, I envisioned it as a "return" in the literal sense, as if we had gone astray and were now going back to where we belonged. But I've begun to see that action of return as an upward movement, an ascent toward our higher, truer selves, and thus closer to our Source. *Teshuvah* is an act of transcendence.

The Days of Awe are a period set aside for self-examination and renewal by the entire Jewish community. Yet *teshuvah* can, and should, also take place at any time. Whenever we miss the mark in life there exists a possibility for a new beginning.

Teshuvah is seldom an effortless act. It is a gradual process of mastery. The term *baal teshuvah*, one who has "done *teshuvah*," literally means a "master of *teshuvah*." Having accomplished *teshuvah*, one is not merely "back on track," but better and stronger from the process. As the rabbis said, "In the place where one who has done *teshuvah* stands, even a totally righteous person cannot stand."

In parenting, there are so many moments for *teshuvah*. So often one feels inadequate, even like a failure. Yet the paradox of *teshuvah* is that in failure lies the seed of success. I've yet to meet an expert, an educator or psychologist, who says that his or her own parenting has been smooth and easy. One of the parents I admire most, who holds a doctorate in education and is extremely devoted and idealistic, has told me that sometimes she just drives away from the house because she thinks she might "blow up" at her adolescent children. On the other hand, she knows many parents who over the years acted as if parenting gave them nothing but gratification, while all the while serious problems were breeding underneath the surface. Her many uncomfortable moments of regret over the years have saved her from greater regrets as her children grow up.

The renowned pediatrician and author Dr. T. Berry Brazelton said in a television interview that he loves to hear parents expressing their self-doubts and uncertainties. He said that their insecurity and occasional feelings of failure were an indication of how concerned, caring, and dedicated they really are.

So how, then, do we go about doing *teshuvah* as parents? We can model our *teshuvah* on Maimonides' description of the process. First there is the recognition and regret that we're doing something insensitive, thoughtless, or inconsiderate of our children's needs or feelings. Unconscious, automatic living is a danger to every relationship. We have to live with more *kavanah*, more awareness of our actions and their present and future effects on our children.

Parenting has its sins of omission and of commission. We give in for the sake of quiet when we know we'll regret it later on, we refuse to engage with our children when they truly need our attention, we use hurtful speech or other subtle degradations of a child's self-worth. Or we may push them to do something that's really for our gratification, not for their good. There are so many ways, large and small, that we may miss the mark in parenting. The Hebrew word for "sin," *heit*, literally means "missing the mark."

So phase one is "regret." But regret shouldn't be something to wallow in; it should be turned into a force for change, for *teshuvah*. In the Jewish mystical tradition, the energy of our regrets can be used to propel us higher, and whatever personal qualities have led us astray can be rechanneled into constructive purposes.

We need to ask forgiveness of our children when we wrong them. In Jewish tradition, Yom Kippur is seen only as a day for forgiveness and atonement from God. For our sins against human beings, we must first go to the person we've wronged and ask for forgiveness, making whatever restitution is possible. This certainly applies to members of our own family. We are the models from which our children learn to forgive and to ask forgiveness. Children are usually very tolerant of our lapses, but we also have to put up with our discomfort at those times when they do feel so hurt that their forgiveness is a while in coming.

Maimonides' next step in *teshuvah* is rejection. The penitent is supposed to reject his or her present way of life and change for the better. As parents, that means we can't just regret that we're yelling at our kids so often, but we actually have to take the steps to change our behavior. We must learn new responses, whether on our own by increased thoughtfulness, experience, and aware-ness, with the help of parenting books and courses, or with counseling and support groups if the problem is severe. As Rabbi Irving Greenberg has described this phase: "In the Jewish tradition, actions speak louder than words." Certainly to children, our actions toward them speak louder than our many words.

Finally, there is resolution. The person doing *teshuvah* must resolve to change course in the future. I've heard success described as a process of "ready, fire, aim." Even if we didn't hit the target this time, if we "missed the mark" yet again, we will come closer to our goals in the future if we've made the effort to learn from our mistake. To use a Jewish mystical expression, we'll have "descended in order to ascend." Having mastered *teshuvah*, we can turn to the future even stronger and more sensitive than before.

Teshuvah is an ongoing process, a lifelong journey. One descends and ascends many times. Mastering an attitude of *teshuvah* means learning to live in the everyday with a heightened sensitivity and empathy for others. It means constantly struggling to grow, to transcend selfishness, to be, in short, a *mensch*.

SUKKOT AND SHEMINI ATZERET-SIMHAT TORAH

THE FALL FESTIVALS

Sukkot and Shemini Atzeret-Simhat Torah have always been my favorites. Maybe it's the result of growing up in Texas's hot climate. There's a tangible relief when the muggy weight of summer lifts, replaced by crisp blue skies, cool and sparkling air. Autumn can mean the pageantry of leaves changing colors, the cornucopia of harvest fruits and vegetables.

The Jewish holidays of this season are a pageant as well. The majestic white of the Days of Awe kaleidoscopes into a burst of joyful colors: a *sukkah* festooned with colorful decorations and fruits, a Simhat Torah parade bright with flags and scrolls in their beautiful mantels. The fall holidays are full of impressive experiences: parading with the *lulav* and *etrog*, beating the willow branches, dancing for hours with the Torah scrolls.

Sukkot in particular has long been one of my favorite holidays. I remember the *sukkah* at our temple, enormous to my child eyes, fragrant with palm leaves, fruits, and gourds. I remember being given an apple and a piece of raisin *hallah* each Sukkot, a bag of candy and a flag every Simhat Torah. As a teen, I remember that my parents built our first family *sukkah* in our backyard, methodically following the directions in *The First Jewish Catalog* and hanging the sides with bright red and blue cloths. And I enjoyed Sukkot in the Texas hill country: we transformed the grape arbor at our ranch into a *sukkah*, and at my Confirmation-class retreat we built a *sukkah* out of branches and boughs in a hilltop wood.

In Israel, we bought our own prefabricated *sukkah* long before we bought an apartment. I also visited even more unusual *sukkot*: my brother-in-law's "penthouse *sukkah*" on a rooftop overlooking the Mediterranian coast in Ashdod, jumbo communal *sukkot* built by the families of American immigrants in Petach-Tikvah. My in-laws have to set up a double-sized *sukkah* to accommodate whichever of their 11 children and more than 30 grandchildren decide to show up for holiday meals.

Our current hexagonal *sukkah* is decorated each year with palm branches and arches of bamboo to remind my husband of the *sukkot* back in Morocco. Almost every year, another family among our friends decides to have their own *sukkah*; some friends improvised a three-sided one on the deck of their home at the outskirts of the city. How enchanting it was to sit there in the candlelight, feeling the hill-country breeze and breathing in scents of cedar boughs and fruits and gourds they had hung from the roof.

The fall holidays celebrate the family and home, symbolized by the *sukkah*, as well as the community, represented by the synagogue festivities such as on Simhat Torah. These are days to thank God for our blessings and to savor the joys of being together with the ones we love.

TRADITIONAL OBSERVANCES FOR SUKKOT AND SHEMINI ATZERET-SIMHAT TORAH

Four days after Yom Kippur marks the beginning of Sukkot, "The Feast of Tabernacles," one of the three pilgrimage festivals mentioned in the Torah. For a week, Jews dwell, or at least take meals and spend time, in huts or booths known in Hebrew as *sukkot* (singular: *sukkah*). These *sukkot* recall the huts our ancestors lived in, in the wilderness on their way from Egypt to Israel. They were later used as temporary housing during the ancient pilgrimages to Jerusalem.

Sukkot is also known as *Hag HaAsif*, the harvest festival. *Sukkah* booths were used by Israelite farmers during harvest time. The American festival of Thanksgiving is said to have been modeled by the pilgrims on the biblical harvest festival of Sukkot.

Yet another name for Sukkot is *Zeman Simhateinu*, the season of our joy. Sukkot and Simhat Torah are times of rejoicing after the solemn mood of the Days of Awe. They embody the faith that God has judged us positively.

Another biblical observance during Sukkot is to take and shake the *arbaat haminim* or four species of plants, consisting of a palm branch tied together with willow and myrtle branches (the *lulav*) and the fragrant citron fruit, the *etrog*. In traditional synagogues, there is a daily procession around the sanctuary with the four species in hand, while special prayers called *hashanot* (from their central phrase *hosha-na* or "please save") are recited. The *lulav* and *etrog* are also shaken ritually as *Hallel*, a special selection of psalms of praise, is recited during the daily synagogue services.

The first two days of Sukkot (first day only in liberal practice and in Israel) are holy days or *Yom Tov*, similar in observance to a Sabbath. Festival meals are eaten in the *sukkah*, *kiddush* is recited, and holiday candles are lit.

The next five days are known as *Hol HaMoed*, the weekdaylike days of the festival. During this time the positive observances such as eating in the *sukkah* and waving the *lulav* are maintained, along with the festive atmosphere (nice meals, nice clothes) but most of the holiday prohibitions against creative work are lifted. Special prayers and Torah readings are given in the synagogue. The Shabbat that falls during these days is known as *Shabbat Hol HaMoed*.

The seventh day of Sukkot is called Hoshana Rabbah, or the Day of Great Praise, when extra *hashanot*, those prayers imploring God's mercy for the coming year, are recited. In traditional synagogues there is a parade of seven circuits around the sanctuary by congregants bearing the *arba minim*. In a ceremony that harkens back to the ancient Temple in Jerusalem, the congregants beat bunches of willow branches on the floor so that the leaves fall off, symbolic of casting off sins, a continuation of the High Holiday themes. *Hoshana Rabbah* is traditionally considered the final day for the High Holiday period, the last chance for a good verdict in the divine judgment. The night of *Hoshana Rabbah* acquired mystical connotations in the Kabbalah, so that even today some Jews devote this night to study and prayer.

The eighth day from the beginning of Sukkot is actually an additional holiday known as Shemini Atzeret, meaning the "eighth day of assembly." Some people continue to eat in the *sukkah*, but the blessing for dwelling in the *sukkah* is not recited, nor is the *lulav* waved. This is a *Yom Tov*, with the special meals, candles, and *kiddush*, services and observances. A special prayer for rain in the land of Israel is recited in traditional synagogues, as well as *Yizkor*, the memorial service.

The ninth and final day of this holiday cycle is Simhat Torah, the day of rejoicing with the Torah. This day is combined into one with Shemini Atzeret in Israel and in liberal Jewish practice.

On Simhat Torah, the annual cycle of Torah readings is completed and immediately begun anew. Both at night and the following morning, the Torah scrolls are paraded around the sanctuary in circuits known as *hakafot*, and the holiday is joyously celebrated with songs, dancing, and waving decorative flags.

Blessings for Sukkot:

Prior to eating or drinking in the sukkah, after the usual blessing for the food, say:

Baruch Atah Adonai, Eloheinu Melech HaOlam, asher kidshanu bemitzvotav vetzivanu leishev ba-sukkah.

Holy One of Blessing, Your presence fills creation; you made us holy with Your commandments and bid us to dwell in the *sukkah*.

On taking and shaking the *lulav* and *etrog*, say:

Baruch Atah Adonai, Eloheinu Melech HaOlam, asher kidshanu bemitzvotav vetzivanu al netilat lulav.

Holy One of Blessing, Your presence fills creation; you made us holy with Your commandments and bid us to take up the *lulav*.

FAMILY ACTIVITIES FOR SUKKOT—SIMHAT TORAH

A Family *Sukkah*: Why and How to

Having your own *sukkah* is not only the main *mitzvah* for Sukkot, it's probably one of the most significant Jewish observances you can do with your children. My admittedly irrational, subjective observation is that families who make the effort to build their own *sukkah* seem to be far ahead when it comes to making Jewish memories and building Jewish identities. In this secular, non-Jewish society, how many chances do most of us get to literally surround our children with something Jewish? Building a *sukkah* is one of those rare opportunities.

The main requirements for any *sukkah* are that it be a temporary structure with at least three walls and a roof of natural materials. The frame is generally made of wooden boards. The covering of *s'chach*, natural materials, covers most of the *sukkah*'s top while allowing enough gaps to see some stars through the roof at night. The *s'chach* materials must be cut off from growing things. *S'chach* often consists of palm branches, evergreen, or bamboo (the latter can be reused each year). Ordinary deciduous greenery tends to dry out and turn brown by the end of the holiday, but it is acceptable.

Walls are made of material such as cloth, canvas, wooden trellises, or split bamboo shades with a makeshift door-opening. Existing outside walls can be used, as long as the roof is of *s'chach*. Some people even have a porch or patio with detachable roof that is used for a *sukkah*. Inside, you'll need a table and chairs or benches, optional floor covering (such as an old carpet), and plenty of decorations (see the following). For night lighting, an electric bulb can be attached to a long heavy-duty extension cord, or a camp lantern (or candlelight, with great care) could be used. Mosquitos are often a bother in southern climates. Spray the area well in advance of dinner or use citronella candles, which repel insects.

There are basically three methods to choose from in building a *sukkah*: the lean-to method, the serious method, and the "yuppie" method. Choose the method that best suits your taste, skills, and pocketbook.

The lean-to method consists simply of improvising a *sukkah* booth from whatever materials you happen to find handy. A *sukkah* is supposed to be an impermanent, somewhat flimsy structure, and this one probably will be! But even if this year's *sukkah* is patched together from the backyard clothesline, an old folding screen, and some crates, that might be enough to get you hooked on *sukkah* building for years to come.

For a more solid *sukkah*, go the serious route. If you're the handy type, you can design your own booth with a frame of wooden boards, even making use of preexisting walls. The roof should be of natural materials, as explained earlier.

If you have friends who build a *sukkah* each year, they can give you some suggestions. Or ask your synagogue to connect you with some congregants who are experienced *sukkah* builders. The synagogue may even have a teen *sukkah*-building committee or a youth group that could help out.

Children can be involved in the *sukkah* construction at their level of ability. At seven, six, and three ours came along to help carry palm leaves and bamboo stalks that Aba cut (with permission, we explained) from neighborhood trees, then helped to sweep the *sukkah* floor and put up the decorations. As they get older, supervised children can do more of the actual construction, such as hammering nails.

For those who are willing to build but not design, full *sukkah* plans can be found in *The First Jewish Catalog*. These plans are repeated in *The Jewish Holidays, A Guide and Commentary*.[5]

Finally—the "yuppie" method: Simply buy a prefab *sukkah*. (Just have the butler set it up every year in the parking lot next to your BMW.) These ready-to-assemble *sukkot* consist of poles that fit together and may include their own sized-to-fit canvas walls and bamboo poles for use as *s'chach*. In major metropolitan areas, purchase directly from a large Jewish gift shop or a *sukkah* market. If you live in a smaller Jewish community, your synagogue or Jewish gift shop may be able to order you one. *Sukkot* and the four species can be mail-ordered from "America's Jewish Bookstore" (see Resource Guide, p. 307). Be prepared: These upscale *sukkot* aren't cheap. But they do save a lot of time and trouble for harried professionals. And since it's going to be used year after year, a prefab *sukkah* could be seen—yuppies take notice—as an investment. (In truth, the instant *sukkah* is an old standby, but can be expensive if ordered from afar and shipped long distances.)

Sukkah Decorations

One of the most fun things about making a *sukkah* is decorating it. Although the concept of *hidur mitzvah*, beautifying the *mitzvah*, has been associated more with the selection of a beautiful *etrog* and *lulav*, the *sukkah* decorations themselves are also part of the esthetic emphasis of this holiday. But I have to be honest. Although in recent years our family *sukkot* have been quite tasteful, we have been known to overdo. We once dubbed our *sukkah* the "disco *sukkah*" because of the effect of strings of tiny flashing colored lights.

A good approach with *sukkah* decorations, as with Rosh HaShanah cards, is to hold an informal holiday workshop. Set up the kitchen or rec-room table with an assortment of art supplies, such as various types of paper, magazines, and travel brochures, glue, scissors, colored pens, and so on. As the children get older they can help prepare these items; for young ones the parent does the preparation. You can work right alongside your children, stopping when needed to offer some suggestions and guidance, but letting the kids make their own creative designs rather than trying to achieve a preset result.

Note: For any type of paper decorations in the *sukkah*, it's ideal to laminate the items, or at least cover on both sides with clear Contac® paper so that they won't be damaged so much if it rains. Many schools, resource centers, and print shops have laminating machines that can be used for a fee. Likewise, be advised that crepe paper isn't good for a *sukkah* because it tends to bleed dye when rained on. Mylar® wrapping paper holds up well and reflects light.

Here are some ideas for *sukkah* decorations:

● Paper chains: try using different types of paper, such as metallic (may have to be stapled rather than glued). Elementary-school–aged children often know how to make quite complicated chains, such as gum-wrapper chains, which they have perfected in dull moments at school!

● Rosh HaShanah greeting cards hung from a long piece of yarn or string.

● Laminated posters depicting holiday scenes or sites in Israel.

● Strings of beads, popcorn, cranberries, or paper cutouts strung at intervals.

● Artificial fruit that is saved from year to year.

● Real fruit: minimize waste by using items with tough peels that can be used later or by displaying a harvest centerpiece that will be used for food or given away later. Traditional produce would include the "seven varieties" for which the land of Israel is praised in the Bible: grapes, figs, dates, olives, pomegranates, wheat, barley. Pictures of these can also be hung.

● Ornamental gourds, squashes, and Indian corn.

● Cutouts or three-dimensional constructions depicting fruit, doves of peace, holiday symbols, and the like, can be suspended from the roof.

● Mobiles are a *sukkah* favorite: Simple ones can be made by hanging cutouts from a dowel or a clothes hanger, or a strip of poster board can be made into a circle from which objects are hung at various lengths. Four holes are made at even intervals around the circle and strings threaded through two opposite holes, so that they crisscross and then are tied above for hanging.

● Paper "lanterns": Fold colored construction paper in half lengthwise. Cut evenly spaced slits over the fold, then open the fold and attach the ends of the paper so that the cuts run vertically.

● A miniature *sukkah* made of ice cream sticks (you can buy packages of them in crafts stores and dime stores) and decorated with paper scraps can be used as a centerpiece or suspended from the beams.

● An *Ushpizin* chart (see the following).

● A *Beruchim HaBa'im*—Welcome sign for the *sukkah* entrance. Hospitality is an important theme of the festival.

Ushpizin: *Sukkah* Visitors from Jewish History

Aside from pictures of the "seven species" of Israeli produce mentioned in the Bible and perhaps a picture of an Israeli shrine such as Rachel's tomb or the *Kotel* (Western Wall), the truly classic *sukkah* decoration is an *Ushpizin* chart. A mystical custom begun by the sixteenth-century kabbalists of Safed, Israel, is to invite *Ushpizin*, Aramaic for "guests," to "visit" one's *sukkah* each night. The purpose of the chart is to list the names of the guests and which evening each will be invited.

The guests, one each evening, are Abraham, Isaac, Jacob, Joseph, Moses, Aaron, David (the order may vary, depending on local traditions). Some traditional holiday prayer books include a formula to recite when welcoming each guest. In recent years many people have added parallel female guests, such as Sarah, Rebecca, Leah, Rachel, Miriam, Deborah, and Esther.

Although the original meaning of this ceremony was kabbalistic, with each guest representing a different emination of divine influence, the custom of the *Ushpizin* can also have educational meaning for the modern family. Like Elijah the Prophet at the *seder* or the Shabbat Queen on Friday night, the *Ushpizin* become part of our children's Jewish imaginations. Besides reciting the traditional prayer from the prayer book, children can be encouraged to imagine the guests as they visit the *sukkah*. In the dark autumn evening, with stars glittering overhead, it's not hard to do. Here are

several suggestions for some informal educational expansions on the *Ushpizin* ritual:

● Using your Bible or *Humash*, make a family tree of the Patriarchs and Matriarchs to familiarize the family with them.

● Give out parts to different members of the family to portray the "guests." You could do this informally, or quite elaborately, with costumes and props.

● Ask the "guests" questions about both their own lives and how they might react to current events and issues today.

● In addition to the traditional *Ushpizin*, decide as a family on other guests from Jewish history (or even contemporary life) whom you would like to invite to your *sukkah*. They could range from a recently freed Soviet refusenik, to a biblical figure, or even your great-grandma who came to the United States from Poland. You could also include "*mitzvah* heroes" (Jewish or not), such as those from one of Danny Siegel's books such as *Munbaz II and Other Mitzvah Heroes*.[6] Friends of ours symbolically invite *tzedakah* and peace heroes to their *sukkah*. You could do this daily during the holiday or make an annual tradition of one night on which you do it. Then research the person or people you have chosen in appropriate books or the *Encyclopaedia Judaica* at your synagogue library, and either discuss them or actually have someone in the family portray them and answer questions.

Ushpizin in Reverse: The *Sukkah* as Jewish Time Machine

Torah Aura Productions' *Building Jewish Life*[7] series refers to the *sukkah* as a "Jewish time machine," an image I find particularly engaging. They suggest taking some time in the *sukkah* for guided imagery in which the children imagine that they are living in a temporary hut in the Sinai wilderness, wandering with the Israelites on their way to the promised land. Later, they take an imaginary journey to the ancient land of Israel at harvest time, where they learn the Torah laws about sharing with the poor. Finally, the children are told to envision a pilgrimage to the Holy Temple in ancient Jerusalem. A *sukkah* is their "hotel" for the duration of the festival, a time of ecstatic joy and celebration.

You could adopt this concept at home by taking your "time-machine" *sukkah* on a short imaginary trip to a different place or period in Jewish history. Describe it to the children as they close their eyes. Focus on details and the use of the five senses. Afterward instruct them to "wake up" slowly and tell everyone something they remember from the "journey."

A DERASHAH FOR PARENTS: SUKKOT IS A TIME FOR WELCOMING

Ushpizin is more than a ceremony. It reflects a central Sukkot theme of hospitality and sharing. Sukkot is the ideal time for sharing our bounty, whether that means food for the body or for the spirit.

In today's mobile society, many Jews feel alienated from the Jewish community because they aren't part of a traditional family unit. For example, the Passover seder, with its heavy emphasis on home and family, makes them feel excluded. We may say, "all who are hungry, come and eat," but many still feel left out.

By contrast, the sukkah seems an appropriate gathering place for a new type of "family." The sukkah is no one's permanent home. We can build one as a group of friends or havurah fellowship, each contributing what she or he is able. Such a communal sukkah can be erected at a synagogue, community center, or in rotation in people's backyards. As the group gathers for holiday meals, they feel themselves become, for the moment, a family.

A charming children's story for Sukkot, The Big Sukkah by Peninnah Schram, tells of Berl and Rivke and their large family who are always a bit abashed because they don't have a large home to host their relatives for the holidays. Then one year they build a gigantic sukkah and so are able to perform the mitzvah of hospitality, as they have always dreamed. Sukkot is the ideal model for taking us outside the usual walls of social categorization by offering a more flexible structure for hospitality and community.

Many contemporary Jewish thinkers have emphasized the sukkah as a symbol of the joyful yet fragile nature of human existence. Often today's fellowship seems fragile compared to the apparently sturdy communal structures of the past. But they can be all the more precious to us for their tenuous and sometimes temporary nature. Michael Strassfeld has pointed out[8] that the traditional Ushpizin figures were all exiles or wanderers at some point. Drawing from the Ushpizin theme,

we can learn to gather in the temporary "home" we create together, to welcome everyone as holy, everyone with an open heart.

If You Can't Make Your Own Sukkah

If you can't make your own sukkah at home, Sukkot should certainly not be passed by. Here are some suggestions for celebrating the holiday if you don't have a sukkah of your own. (Some of these are good ideas even if you do have your own sukkah.)

● Do as many other Sukkot activities as possible: attend services during the various phases of the festival (there will probably be a kiddush in the synagogue sukkah after the prayers), wave the lulav and etrog, learn about the festival, read holiday stories.

● Prior to the holiday, make decorations as a family for the sukkah of a friend, the local Jewish nursing home, the Jewish Community Center, or your synagogue and go with your children to hang them up. If possible, actually help build a communal sukkah, such as one at a synagogue, or help friends build a sukkah.

● Visit and eat in the sukkah at your synagogue, Jewish Community Center, or Jewish school and say the appropriate blessings. If possible, don't just visit when the synagogue sukkah is crowded with people after services, but take the children to visit it at a quiet time when they can sit inside and really appreciate it. If the local Jewish nursing home has a sukkah, you can do a double mitzvah by visiting the residents with your family.

● Get yourself invited to other people's sukkot. (You'll be helping your host fulfill the mitzvah of hospitality.) This may be easy if you live in a dense Jewish neighborhood, or it may be a challenge if you live in a city with few sukkah builders. If you're new in town, politely ask your new synagogue if they can make you a shiddach with a sukkah-building family. Ask your hosts if you can make and bring some decorations or some s'chach for the roof. With a havurah group, you might make an arrangement to build a sukkah for several families at a different residence each year and share it.

And may you merit to build your own sukkah next year.

Play *Sukkot*

Although the focus of the Sukkot festival is on the real *sukkah*—preferably at home or at the synagogue or community center—toy *sukkot* can be fun and can serve as a reinforcement. If Sukkot consists solely of making an ice-cream-stick model *sukkah* at religious school, we may be giving the message that Jewish holidays aren't serious. But in conjunction with more serious observance, imaginative play can be a constructive force in developing our children's identities. Any type of house makes a popular toy, and a play *sukkah* is a uniquely Jewish one. Here are some suggestions:

• Make a toy *sukkah* large enough for children to actually play in by using a discarded appliance carton or large pieces of packing cardboard held together with strong masking tape. If only three sides are made from cardboard, it can be opened wide but will tend to be unstable; a card table in back can help give balance. Some cardboard strips can be taped across the top and decorated with real or artificial greenery, plastic or paper mâché fruit, or other decorations.

• Make a doll-sized *sukkah* from wood scraps or popsicle sticks, or from a small box. Real, small vines can form the *s'chach*, and fruit can be shaped of play clay. Especially nice is an annual *sukkah* for the family dollhouse.

Challenge school-age children to construct an edible *sukkah* as a centerpiece. Comestible art is a perennial childhood favorite. It could consist of raw vegetables held together by toothpicks or graham-cracker pieces cemented with icing. (Full directions for an elegant gingerbread *sukkah* can be found in *The Jewish Holiday Cookbook* by Gloria Kauffer Greene.)[9]

The Four Species (*Lulav* and *Etrog*)

Other than the *sukkah* itself, the four species are the major symbol of the Sukkot festival. The book of Leviticus (23:40) commands Jews to gather together a palm branch with willow and myrtle sprigs (the *lulav*) and the fragrant citron, or *etrog*, a lemony fruit with a distinctive tip.

Into our children's suburban, automated world the *lulav* and *etrog* bring a verdant reminder of the Land of Israel. Like the *sukkah*, they surprise the senses, involve more of the person than the mere sights that make up so much of contemporary experience. Waving them, one ushers visions of ancient rituals, of a long chain of history leading back to an agrarian past.

While living in Israel we enjoyed the experience of selecting our *lulav* and *etrog* in the open-air market. In the United States, in some areas with large traditional Jewish populations, one can also select the four species from street vendors. In selecting the four species, emphasis is placed on *hidur mitzvah*, finding the most perfect and unblemished specimens of the plants, especially the *etrog*. Once children are old enough, a visit to such a market makes an interesting family outing.

But have no fear, even in hinterlands the four species can be ordered through Jewish gift shops or bookstores, and where you don't have even those, your synagogue office can probably order you a set. You won't be able to select your own, though, and the price with shipping will generally be much higher than on New York's Lower East Side. Part of the excitement of the season is waiting for the *lulav* and *etrog* (inevitably) arrive at the last minute. But it always seems to be worth the effort once you receive them.

Our local botanical gardens has also been generous in allowing us to cut myrtle and willow branches to freshen up a *lulav* and *etrog* that has dried out in its long journey. Perhaps you have such a resource in your community. It's also interesting to see these plants and trees.

• How to wave a *lulav*: The *lulav* ritual can be performed at home or outside in the *sukkah*. To do it, hold the *lulav* in the right hand and the *etrog* in the left while the blessing (see p. 195) is recited. The *lulav* should at least be shaken gently, allowing the leaves to rustle, or it can be shaken in the ritual way: One faces to the east, extends the *lulav* a bit and shakes three times, drawing the *lulav* in with each shake, and then, going clockwise, continues to shake it three times in each direction of the compass, followed by three times upward and three times slightly downward. This symbolizes God's blessing over the "four corners" of the earth.

• *An Etrog Box*: Most Jewish gift shops sell decorated etrog boxes for storing the etrog. As a crafts project, children and parents can decorate a cardboard or plastic container or perhaps a pantyhose container, if the *etrog* will fit inside, with stickers or glue-on items. Be sure to cushion the container with cotton or the flax in which the *etrog* came packed. (The *pitam*, or tip, must remain intact for the *etrog* to be considered "kosher" for use. However, if the tip breaks off after the holiday begins—such as when a marauding toddler breaks it off!—it is still allowed to be used.)

Activities with the *Lulav* and *Etrog*

● Compare the *etrog* to other citrus fruits, such as an orange, grapefruit, or lemon. What are the similarities and differences? You can save the *etrog* after the holiday. If you keep it from moisture, it can stay quite a long time (some people keep them for years). Cloves can be pressed into the sides in rows and then it can be used for *besamim* at *Havdalah* time.

● If there are myrtle bushes, willow trees, or palm trees in your area, you can point them out to children as the type of trees on which parts of your *lulav* grew. If not, try to find pictures of them in a book. *Ecology in the Bible,* by Nogah Hareuveni in association with Helen Frenkly,[10] has photographs of the four species growing in their natural habitats in Israel.

● After the holiday, the *lulav* is not thoughtlessly tossed away, but is allowed to "biodegrade" outdoors (a possible starting point for a discussion on ecology). To link the holiday cycle together, some people save part of the *lulav* (the palm branch) and use it to sweep up the *hametz* crumbs before the *seder*.

● Shaking the *lulav* in all directions shows that God is everywhere and that we pray for God's blessings to be felt everywhere in the world. This may be an opportunity to talk about the Jewish belief in God's omnipresence.

● Here are two traditional interpretations of the symbolism of the *lulav* and *etrog*. Actually touching and experiencing the four species as you talk about them will help bring these interpretations to life for children.

1. Hold the *hadas*, myrtle (the three short branches with small roundish leaves), by your eye: What does it look like? (an eye). Place one of the *aravah*, willow, leaves over your lips: What does it look like? (lips). Similarly, hold the *lulav* carefully by someone's back; it's like a spine. And the *etrog* can be held by the chest; it's like a heart. From this the rabbis of old learned that we should serve God with all our body. How can we do that? How can different parts of our body serve God? (Think of examples both from religious ritual and in service to other people.)

2. Pass the *lulav* and *etrog* around and carefully feel, see, and smell the different parts. Examine the *etrog*: It has both taste and fragrance. You can taste it after the holiday. The small *etrogim* we purchase in the United States are generally quite sour, but some people collect and make them into jam. In Israel the Yemenite Jews prefer very large *etrogim* that can be cut and eaten as is. They taste much like a grapefruit. The rabbis compared the *etrog* to a person who possesses both Torah learning and good deeds. The palm tree has no fragrance, but it produces dates that taste good and can be eaten, so it is compared to Jews who possess learning but not good deeds. The pretty myrtle has a fragrance but no taste. It is compared to Jews who possess good deeds but not learning. The willow has no taste or smell, and thus is compared to Jews who lack Torah learning *and* good deeds. Yet the rabbis pointed out that all four plants are bound together to create the four species. None can be lacking, even the willow. Just so, every kind of Jew is needed to make the Jewish community complete. Each person has a special role to fill.

This simple *midrash* has become more and more meaningful to me as I've traveled in the Jewish world and met Jews who embody varying combinations of impressive Jewish scholarship or noble values and ethical actions. Each one, even the seemingly ignorant and assimilated Jew, has a role to play.

One could point out that everyone in the family, large or small, is important, too, and is needed to make the group complete.

Simhat Beit HaSho'evah

In ancient times Sukkot was the time for the annual water-drawing ceremony for a libation at the Holy Temple in Jerusalem. *Simhat Beit HaSho'evah*, the rejoicing at the place of the water-drawing, became synonymous with total joy. According to the Talmud, the entire city was alive with light, and the great sages showed their happiness by dancing, singing, and even juggling. "One who has not seen the rejoicing at the place of the water-drawing has never seen joy in his life," said the sages.

Indeed, the Bible emphasizes that, among the festivals, Sukkot is a special time of *rejoicing* (Deuteronomy 16:14). Although the original *Simhat Beit HaSho'evah* is no longer performed, some synagogues, *yeshivot*, and hasidic groups today hold celebrations during Sukkot that are called *Simhat Beit HaSho'evah* and may involve dancing and singing, Torah lectures, and reciting Psalms. Sometimes it's just a small gathering in the synagogue's *sukkah* late at night, with a mystical feeling in the air.

You could have your own version of *Simhat Beit HaSho'evah* at home by inviting guests for an evening in the *sukkah* that includes refreshments, Jewish music, folk dancing, stories, and discussion. An appropriate discussion topic might be water motifs in Jewish sources (check out a biblical concordance in the synagogue library) or conservation of earth's seas and rivers.

Hoshana Rabbah

Speaking of mystical feelings, there's a night at the end of Sukkot that could capture any child's imagination. *Hoshana Rabbah*, the seventh and final day of Sukkot, is the occasion for synagogue ceremonies and is traditionally considered the final day for the High Holiday season. Perhaps because it was considered a last chance for a good verdict for the coming year, a mystical tradition grew up that at midnight on *Hoshana Rabbah*, the gates of Heaven open and one's wishes or prayers are granted. Some spend the night in study and prayer, and writers like Isaac Bashevis Singer have spun wonderful stories about this night.[11]

Since children like any reason to stay up late, you might let them stay up a bit on this night—but not to watch the late show, rather to read Jewish stories or play games with Jewish themes and to make a special wish at (or near!) midnight.

The daytime pageantry of *Hoshana Rabbah* is another potential memory maker. In traditional synagogues there is a procession around the sanctuary with Torah scrolls, *lulavim* and *etrogim*, as the *hoshana* prayers imploring God's mercy and help are sung. Again, the preciousness of rain and water is a theme, for in Israel, the crucial rainy season is about to begin. Willow branches are beaten on the floor so that the leaves fall off, symbolic of casting off sins. Except for Orthodox men, most Jews miss out on this service, which is a pity. Especially when *Hoshana Rabbah* falls on a Sunday, some traditional synagogues are now encouraging families to attend and for children to participate in the rituals. Some liberal synagogues are creating innovative rituals for the day. Even if it means a visit to a different kind of *shul*, attending this service with kids can be quite an experience. Discuss some of the *hoshana* ("Please Save") prayers found in the traditional holiday prayer book, the *mahzor*. Can your family write some of your own *hoshana* prayers with modern themes? What do we need God to help us do in our times, in order to save and redeem our world?

Foods for Sukkot

There is no classic Ashkenazic Jewish food associated with Sukkot in the way that, say, *matzah* balls are associated with Passover or *hamentashen* with Purim. However, anything reminiscent of the fall harvest would be appropriate and fun to make as a family, from apple cider to fruit breads or strudels to vegetable soups and stews. Round *hallot* with raisins and honey are often served as symbols of the new year and of joy.

A Sephardic dish that we associate with the holiday is my mother-in-law's pumpkin soup. It's one of the rare recipes I know that makes my children enjoy eating vegetables.

Moroccan Sukkot Soup (American Adaptation)

1 small onion, finely chopped
2 cloves garlic, minced
2 tablespoons oil
4 cups acorn squash or pumpkin meat, cut in chunks
(may bake first to soften; save the seeds for roasting)
1 large sweet potato and 4 large carrots, peeled and chopped
2 kosher-parve, beef-flavored bouillon cubes
1/2 cup cooked chick-peas (may use canned, drained chick-peas)

Seasonings:
1/3 cup brown sugar
1/2 teaspoon paprika
2 dashes of pumpkin-pie spice (or one pinch each ground ginger, nutmeg, allspice, and cinnamon)
1/2 teaspoon additional cinnamon
1–2 teaspoons soy sauce
1 tablespoon lemon juice
salt or additional bouillon to taste, if desired

In a 4–6 quart pot, saute the onion and the garlic in the oil until golden. Cover with water and add the squash or pumpkin meat. Add water to cover all, plus about two inches. Bring to a boil, add bouillon, and lower heat. Mash the vegetables gently from time to time as they soften, until the soup has a thick, pureed texture. Add the cooked chick-peas. Cover and continue cooking on low heat until everything is tender (the chick-peas should remain intact). Before serving, add the seasonings to taste.

A Sukkot *Derashah* for Parents: Surrounding Our Children with Judaism

For the purpose of various studies, sociologists of the Jewish community have come up with a variety of criteria for determining the level of Jewish commitment in a household. These criteria include such actions as lighting Shabbat candles, affiliating with a synagogue, giving to Jewish charities. To my knowledge, whether or not a family builds a *sukkah* has never been selected as one of the criteria for evaluating Jewish observance. Yet my subjective impression is that building a *sukkah* is of special significance in the building of Jewish identity.

Perhaps it's because the *sukkah* builders are just getting started when the "twice-a-year" Jews have recessed until Hanukkah. Or perhaps it is related to the fact that our Diaspora Jewish children are surrounded by a non-Jewish culture. The media, stores, and advertisements, perhaps the children's schools, all emphasize the Christian holidays. Compared to this sort of media blitz, Jewish holidays can easily seem like peripheral experiences to many Jewish youngsters.

By contrast, a *sukkah* is one of the few opportunities we have to surround our children (and ourselves) with something Jewish. In the *mitzvah* of *sukkah*, our children participate in building a miniature Jewish environment in which to dwell, if only for a short while. They participate with all their senses, with physical effort, with imagination and spirit. The *mitzvah* of *sukkah* is a special experience of immersion in Jewish culture.

In traditional Jewish thought, no *mitzvah* is labeled with having greater absolute importance than another (although some may have precedence over others; for example, saving a life supersedes almost any other *mitzvah*). Yet Jewish sources from the Talmud to the hasidic teachings have noted that such *mitzvot* as living in the land of Israel, observing the Shabbat, and dwelling in the *sukkah* are special *mitzvot* that involve the whole person, body and soul. These are *mitzvot* that surround and encompass those who observe them. They could be called holistic *mitzvot*.

A Jew who lives in Israel, for example, whether or not labeled "religious," speaks Hebrew, lives in a society governed by the Jewish calendar, and walks among biblical landmarks. Body, soul, destiny—every aspect of life is committed to Israel. Those who live in the Diaspora are almost invariably amazed by the intense emotional and spiritual effect of a pilgrimage to the Jewish homeland.

On a much more limited scale, building and dwelling in a *sukkah* also demands a complete personal involvement. It's not as overwhelming as a pilgrimage to Israel, of course, but it is an opportunity to become fully immersed in a Jewish experience.

The *sukkah* becomes a metaphor for trying out a more complete Jewish life-style. Even though our fancy, modern, western-style house is still where we live almost all the time, for one week a year our flimsy little Jewish house has more importance. We step outside the walls of assumption and convention that have protected us until now and enter a place where the walls and roof have openings to see beyond.

Like the other holistic *mitzvot*, *sukkah* involves a person's whole complex, physical, earthy, sublime self. It involves effort, beauty, humor, and community.

As the Baal Shem Tov, the founder of hasidism, said, "I love the *mitzvah* of *sukkah* because a person can enter the *sukkah* with his entire body, including the mud on his shoes."

Shemini Atzeret

Shemini Atzeret, "The Eighth Day of Assembly," is an additional holiday with all the observances of a *Yom Tov*, such as special meals, services, candles, and *kiddush*. The *Yizkor*, memorial service, is held on this day, and *Tefillat HaGeshem*, a special prayer for rain in the land of Israel, is recited in traditional synagogues. Although it is no longer a *mitzvah* to eat in the *sukkah*, some people continue to eat in it without the blessing. In Israel, and in liberal Jewish practice, the two days of Shemini Atzeret and Simhat Torah are combined into one day of *Yom Tov*.

If you are observing *Yizkor* for a deceased relative, you might spend a while talking to the children about the person. Perhaps when you light a *yartzeit* memorial candle on the holiday eve would be a good time. Talking about those who have gone is one way to keep their memories alive for the next generation.

Regarding the prayer for rain: In Israel rain falls only in the fall and winter, approximately between Shemini Atzeret and Passover, and in Israel's arid climate, this rainy season is crucial to the entire year. Of course, our prayers and liturgical cycle are in sync with the seasons of Israel, not of North America. If you move to Israel or spend a year there, you are struck by the links between the Jewish religion and the natural world.

Simhat Torah

Simhat Torah, the annual celebration in which we conclude the yearly cycle of Torah readings—and immediately begin again—is the last *Yom Tov* of the fall holiday season. Like Shemini Atzeret, it's a *Yom Tov* day of rest, candles and *kiddush*, and special meals. But the essence of this holiday really can't be fully appreciated at home; it needs to be experienced in the synagogue: dancing, singing, parading, and celebrating with the community.

On the eve of the holiday, and again the next morning, the Torah scrolls are removed from the ark and paraded around the sanctuary, sometimes outside into the street, in seven circuits known as *hakafot*. All this is accompanied by singing, dancing, refreshments, and candies (tossed or given in bags to the children), as well as carrying flags or sometimes banners, so it's an exciting and memorable experience for the young and the young at heart.

Another high point for youngsters is *Kol HaNe'arim*, the traditional practice of calling up all the children once in the year to recite the Torah blessings under an outstretched *tallit* held by adults. Following the children's second *berachah*, the congregation blesses them with Jacob's blessing from the book of Genesis: "May the angel who redeems me from all evil bless the youths, and let them be called by my name and the name of my fathers, Abraham and Isaac, and may they multiply in the midst of the land."

Simhat Torah Crafts

Although synagogues usually distribute paper flags for the children to carry during the *hakafot*, you can also make your own beautiful ones before the holiday and bring them. You can take the "holiday workshop" approach and provide an assortment of crafts supplies along with some suggestions, leaving plenty of room for imagination and creativity. You can make flags, banners, model *Sifrei Torah*, Torah scrolls.

● To make flags: The stick can be a thin wooden dowel from a crafts store or lumber store, or a paper-towel roll, or even a strip of cardboard or a wooden ruler. Depending on the materials used, attach the flag to the stick with glue, tape, staples, or hot glue (the latter two done by adult only). The flag itself can be construction paper, other paper, felt, or other cloth. Decorate with a variety of materials: paints, crayons, markers, fabric paints, stickers, sequins, beads, collage, or cutouts. Decorate with pictures of Torah, Jewish symbols, Simhat-Torah celebrations, and the like. Or make a special personalized flag with motifs that represent you or even a family flag with items special to your family. For special effects you can create a three-dimensional picture: Draw a picture of an ark with Torah scrolls and cut out two rectangular pieces of construction paper for the door. Glue in place as "doors" along the outer one-quarter inch of each rectangle and fold the rest open to form the open doors. Or cut a Torah from construction paper and make it "pop" out by gluing onto a small strip of paper folded back and forth several times (as one folds a paper fan).

● Banners: You can make your own from felt or other cloth stapled or sewn in place to hang from a long dowel or even a yardstick. Two people carry it from the ends. Again, you can depict Jewish holidays or motifs with special meaning to your family.

● Model Torahs: Use ice-cream sticks, empty paper-towel rolls, or dowels for the rollers. Glue or staple these to a long roll of paper or cloth, which you can leave plain or decorate with scenes from the Torah. Then roll it up and make a mantel from decorated construction paper or felt.

● Toy Torah mantel: To cover your model Torah, or to recover a purchased model Torah, you can easily make a beautiful felt cover with no sewing. Cut with a piece of felt to fit around the model Torah, allowing about an inch overlap. Decorate the front with paint pens, fabric paint, glue-on sequins, or beads. (You can use safety pins to delineate where the front, sides, and back of the cover will fall, so the decorations will end up in the right place when the cover is put on.) To close, simply attach stick-on Velcro® strips, which can be purchased in a dime store and need no sewing.

● Sephardic-style Torah: The Sephardic Jews put their Torah scrolls into decorated round metal or wooden cases rather than cover them with soft materials. To make something approximating a Sephardic-style Torah, instead of cloth wrap heavy-duty foil into a cylinder around your homemade scroll. It should be long enough to leave several inches at the top, which are pinched into a dome form. (With real Sephardic Torahs, the case is hinged to open on one side, and the wooden rollers of the scroll protrude through the top of the case). Or decorate an inexpensive cardboard cylinder from a crafts or container store to look like a Torah case.

● Toy and model Torahs: Even stuffed versions are available for tots, at Judaic gift shops. Children often enjoy carrying one during the *hakafot*. You might want to make an "ark" from a cardboard box covered with wood-grained Contac® paper.

25

THE WINTER HOLIDAYS

HANUKKAH: KEEPING THE LIGHT OF OUR HERITAGE AGLOW

Ask nearly any American Jewish child what her or his favorite Jewish holiday is, and the answer will come back, "Hanukkah." Hanukkah means lights and songs, *dreidl* games, and special treats to eat. The profusion of presents, parties, and decorations that now accompany this once-simple holiday have made it irresistible to kids. However, there are deeper and more meaningful dimensions to this most commercialized of our festivals. Hanukkah, which literally means "dedication," is a time to rededicate ourselves to the sacred task of keeping the lights of our heritage aglow.

THE STORY OF HANUKKAH: RATED G AND RATED PG-13

The first Hanukkah was celebrated in Jerusalem on the 25th of *Kislev*, 165 B.C.E. Jews in the land of Israel, led by the group known as the Maccabees, rebelled against their Syrian-Greek oppressors and the dictator Antiochus. They recaptured Jerusalem (eventually achieving a brief Jewish independence) and rededicated the Holy Temple. According to a story in the Talmud, the victors found only enough pure oil to light the Temple *menorah* for one day, but the oil miraculously lasted eight days—which is why we light our Hanukkah lamps at home for eight nights.

So goes the story of Hanukkah as we learned it back in Sunday school. But there's also the "PG-13" (post-*bar-mitzvah*) uncut version, a more sophisticated look at the Hanukkah story. According to historians, the Maccabean revolt began as virtually a civil war between those Jews who went along with the Hellenistic (Greek) way of life and those who clung to traditional Jewish ways. The Greeks had conquered the Persian Empire, including Judaea, two centuries before. At first the Greeks were fairly tolerant, and many Jews adopted Greek names, dress, and life-styles. In fact, the meeting of Greek and Jewish ideas throughout the centuries led to some of the greatest creative developments in Jewish life.

When Judaea came under the rule of the Syrian-Greek Seleucids and the notorious ruler Antiochus, Jewish observance became increasingly less tolerated. Hellenists embraced the more corrupting aspects of Greek culture and saw the "old" Jewish ways as backward and unaesthetic. The split between Hellenist and traditionalist deepened. At times, the Hellenists even urged on the Syrian regime in their sanctions against Jewish traditionalists. The *Cohen Gadol* (High Priest) was replaced with a Greek puppet. As the rift among the Jews themselves deteriorated into civil war, the Greek rulers cracked down, banning major Jewish practices like Shabbat and circumcision. Cruelty and atrocities multiplied. A famous story about this period is that of Hannah and her seven sons, who one by one chose death over disloyalty to the Jewish faith.

Families fled to the countryside hoping to live in peace, but Antiochus' mercenary soldiers pursued them there, as well. In one town, Modi'in, which lies halfway between Jerusalem and Jaffa (not far from Ben Gurion airport today), an elderly Cohen named Mattathias rose up and killed a Jew who was about to sacrifice a pig in obedience to Antiochus' laws. Mattathias tore down the pagan altar and called on the faithful to join him as he and his five sons fled to the hills and soon began a guerilla rebellion against the Greeks. These farmers-turned-fighters came to be called the Maccabees for Judah Maccabee, the famous middle son.

Against the odds, the Jewish rebels fought for three years and finally liberated Jerusalem and recaptured the Temple mount. The victorious Jews cleansed the Holy Temple and rebuilt the altar. The gold *menorah* was relit. In the thick of the fighting the Jewish rebels had been unable to observe the Sukkot festival. Now, on the 25th of *Kislev*, they celebrated an eight-day festival of rededication, modeled perhaps on the eight days of Sukkot–Shemini-Atzeret. Only in later generations did the story of the miraculous cruse of oil become a central element in the festival.

This original partial victory was a precursor to a fuller independence achieved after a quarter century of struggle. But the independence won by the Hasmonean dynasty, Mattathias's descendents, was a fragile one. The Hasmoneans fought among themselves, and in ironic reversal they themselves became Hellenized and even welcomed foreign intervention into their internal struggles. The end result of their internacine struggle was that Rome conquered Judaea three quarters of a century later. (There may be a message here for our own day: zealousness, which may be needed to win a desperate cause, can also lead to tragedy down the road if it goes untempered.) Still, the original hard-won victory of a few dedicated believers outshines the corruption of later generations, and it is this dedication that we continue to celebrate each year at Hanukkah.[1]

TRADITIONAL HANUKKAH OBSERVANCES

Hanukkah is a home-centered holiday. Although lights are kindled in the synagogue and special prayers like the *Hallel* and the *Al HaNissim* ("for the miracles") are added to the prayers there, the central practice of the holiday is the lighting of the Hanukkah lamp for eight nights at home.

The lamp is popularly called a *"menorah,"* meaning candelabra in Hebrew, although the more specific Israeli name that is catching on in the United States as well is *"hanukkiyah."*

Although only one *hanukkiyah* per household is required to fulfill the *mitzvah* of candlelighting, it is increasingly popular to light several, even one for each family member. And although most modern Hanukkah lamps burn candles, burning real oil (olive oil, or any vegetable oil) is the more authentic method.

The main requirement for a "kosher" *hanukkiyah* is that all the lights be separate, yet on the same level, except for the *shamash,* or service candle, which is used to light the others. Thus one sees at a glance which night of the festival it is. However, an artistic *hanukkiyah* that doesn't conform to these standards may be lit in addition to a kosher one. The lights should be big enough, or enough oil should be used, to burn for at least half an hour.

How to Hold the Candle Lighting Ceremony

The *hanukkiyah* is lit as soon after dark as possible, although the ceremony may be delayed to enable the entire family to participate. On Friday night the *hanukkiyah* is lit before the Sabbath candles, and on Saturday night it is lit after *Havdalah,* in order not to violate the prohibition of kindling a fire on the Sabbath.

The candles are placed in the *hanukkiyah* beginning at the right as you face it. Each night a new candle is added toward the left. The lights are kindled, however, from left to right.

Blessing the Lights:

While holding the lighted *shamash,* or service candle, the following two blessings are said or sung:

Baruch Atah Adonai, Eloheinu Melech HaOlam, asher kidshanu bemitzvotav vetzivanu lehadlik ner shel Hanukkah.

Holy One of Blessing, Your Presence fills creation; You made us holy with commandments and bid us kindle the *Hanukkah* light.

Baruch Atah Adonai, Eloheinu Melech HaOlam, she'asah nissim laavoteinu bayamim hahem bazman hazeh.

Holy One of Blessing, Your Presence fills creation; You performed miracles for our ancestors in days of old, at this season.

On the first night only, the *sheheheyanu* blessing is added (see p. 89). The lights are then kindled, after which it is preferable to place the *hanukkiyah* in a window so that passersby can see the lights. This is known in Hebrew as *pirsum ha'nes*—publicizing the miracle. I believe that the rabbis were referring to the miracles of the oil, but perhaps they meant the victory of the few against the mighty. Perhaps the miracle to be proclaimed is the survival of Judaism against the odds. One writer has suggested that nowadays it may be even more appropriate to display the Hanukkah *menorah* inside the house, to publicize the light of Jewish living to our own families.

The Hanukkah lights are supposed to be dedicated only to *pirsum ha'nes*, and not used for reading, lighting other candles, or other mundane purposes (hence the *shamash*). It is customary, in fact, to abstain from work while the flames are burning—some sources say that women particularly abstain from work at this time in thanks to the active role of women in the Hanukkah story.

After lighting the candles with the appropriate blessings, there are several prayers that can be added, beginning with *HaNerot HaLallu*, which can be found in the prayer book. Sephardic Jews recite Psalm 30, and the medieval hymn *"Ma'oz Tzur"* or "Rock of Ages" is usually sung. It is customary and fun to add other holiday songs.

During Hanukkah, the *Hallel*, psalms of praise and thanksgiving, as well as passages thanking God for the victories and miracles, *Al HaNissim*, are added to the traditional prayer services and to the *Birkat HaMazon*, grace after meals.

It is customary to eat foods fried in oil during Hanukkah, in remembrance of the miracle of the oil. Gifts of money (*gelt* in Yiddish, *demei Hanukkah* in Hebrew) are traditional, as is the game of *dreidl*, played with a four-sided top.

Hanukkah Today

The popularity of Hanukkah has ebbed and waned through the centuries. In our own day, it has become a very popular festival, but the reasons are different in different Jewish communities throughout the world.

Israeli Jews tend to identify with the Hanukkah story in a nationalistic way. The story of a small group of Jews struggling for independence against many enemies reminds them of Israel's own struggle to be born. The emphasis in Israel is on public celebration, such as *menorahs* on rooftops and music festivals for children. There are torch relays from Modi'in and radio programs for adults that retrace the footsteps of the Maccabean forces.

Jews in the former Soviet Union often drew inspiration from the holiday story of the Jewish loyalists, who resisted assimilation and government terror to preserve their heritage.

We American Jews generally place a great deal of emphasis on Hanukkah, sometimes more than on such major Jewish holidays as Sukkot and Shavuot. A partial explanation is that most other Americans are celebrating their major religious holiday, Christmas, at the same time.

Suggested Activities to Enrich the Home Celebration of Hanukkah

Hanukkah is a fun holiday, with eight days to hold plenty of activities and celebrations. And since it's not a *Yom Tov* like Passover or Shavuot, tradition places few special restrictions on one's behavior. There's a lot of leeway for inventing creative celebrations or new family customs. Home activities for Hanukkah include enriching the candlelighting ceremony, making *hanukkiyahs*, home decorations, food, games, gifts, parties, and special *mitzvahs*.

Enriching the Candlelighting Ceremony

With a little extra planning the candlelighting ceremony can become a meaningful gathering for the family. Begin with attention to the *menorah*. A simple foil *menorah* can be every bit as kosher as an expensive artist's version, and some of our grandparents used a *menorah* made from a potato when that was all they could afford. But if you can manage, it's preferable to get a nice one. What we value enough to spend money on makes a statement to our children. You'll also be practicing *noy mitzvah* (beautifying the *mitzvah*).

You can use more than one *hanukkiyah* so that more people can take turns participating in the actual lighting. If possible, everyone can have his or her own. If the *hanukkiyot* have stories behind them ("We got this one on our trip to Israel," "Rachel made this one in first grade," "This one belonged to Grandpa"), so much the better. We find it fun to have one or more of the miniature children's *hanukkiyot* in addition to full-size *hanukkiyot*. A real oil-burning *hanukkiyah* is particularly authentic and beautiful to behold. Of course, you can collect *hanukkiyot* without feeling obligated to light all of them. Light a couple and use the rest for a special Hanukkah display on the mantlepiece or buffet.

Before or after the lighting, family members can take turns doing some readings or saying some words of Torah that pertain to the holiday or to other current concerns. See the Resource Guide for books that contain holiday readings.

After the candlelighting is the time for singing Hanukkah songs, playing recordings of Hanukkah and other Jewish music, maybe a little folk dancing, telling stories, eating *latkes*, playing *dreidl* and other games. There is a custom not to do any work while the lights are burning. The atmosphere is warm and cozy as the colorful candles or golden oil burn brightly in the dark winter's night. You might want to adopt a family tradition of reading one story or section nightly from books that are divided in sections for the holiday. (See Resource Guide, pp. 351–352, for suggestions.)

Making *Hannukkiyot*

Although there are now an impressive variety of beautiful Hanukkah lamps on the market, it can be fun to make your own *hanukkiyah* (Hebrew plural: *hanukkiyot*) at home. For a candle-burning *hanukkiyah*, just remember the guidelines: eight lights on a level for the eight nights, plus a *shamash* set apart by height or location. On a wooden base, glue any eight nonflammable objects in a row (plus one to the side for the *shamash*)—try bolts, bottlecaps, spools with bottlecaps glued on top, or sea-shells. The *hanukkiyah* can be painted gold or silver, if desired. Attach the candles to their holders with a bit of modeling clay or melt the bottoms to stand them in place. (For more ideas see the Resource Guide to Arts and Crafts Books, p. 316.)

An Oil-Burning Hanukkiyah

An oil-burning *hanukkiyah* is beautiful and can also give children an idea of how oil can be used as fuel in lamps, as in the Hanukkah story. They can be expensive to buy, but you can make your own easily with a few purchased pieces. Start with a rectangular wooden board for a base. This should be covered with heavy duty foil, long enough to accommodate 10 small votive candle glasses. Place eight of the glasses in a straight row on the base, and in the middle of the row, place one glass upside down, with another right-side-up on top of it for the *shamash* (or the *shamash* can be placed on a small square piece of foil-covered wood). To light the oil, you need wicks that float, and the simplest way to do it is to purchase a kit of little plastic floaters that come with disposable wicks. Be sure you've bought enough floaters for all the containers; you may need two boxes. It helps to buy the floaters first, then select votive glasses that will hold them with just enough room to float, although the floaters can be trimmed a bit to fit if needed.

To use the oil-burning *hanukkiyah*: Fill each glass about two-thirds of the way with water. Then gently pour in about one-quarter inch of oil (with experience, you'll see how much is needed—a little goes a long way). Insert the wicks into the floaters according to instructions on the box and gently place on the oil to float. At candlelighting time, light the flames from the *shamash*, using a candle to transfer the flame. The effect is enchanting.

Decorations

Decorating the home for Hanukkah is a relatively new American practice. Traditionally, decorations were for Shavuot (flowers in the synagogue, paper cuts) or for the *sukkah*. Recently, the Christmas influence has led to a boom in the Hanukkah-decoration business. A profusion of commercially made Hanukkah decorations are available in Jewish gift shops or by mail order. Hanukkah decorations for the home are virtually unknown in Israel. Some very traditional Jews reject this kind of "foreign" influence. I think that the more realistic view has been that Judaism has always adopted some ideas and practices from other cultures (even the Shavuot greenery is thought by some to have been borrowed from church festivals).[2] Meetings with other cultures have often resulted in creative developments. More importantly, Jews have adapted outside influences to reflect Jewish themes and values. So, rather than refuse to decorate the house or give gifts on Hanukkah because that makes it too much like Christmas, I prefer to retain these already ingrained practices but ensure that they reflect Jewish priorities and values.

The main "decoration" of Hanukkah is the glowing *hanukkiah*, so it's proper not to overwhelm it with quantities of tinsely decorations. Likewise, the main message of Hanukkah is a spiritual one, which is often in danger of being overshadowed by materialism. Despite the overwhelming commercialism of the season, we as parents can still do a lot to set the tone; and the younger we start with our kids, the easier it will be.

It's fun to use a holiday workshop approach to

making decorations. Set up a table with all the arts and crafts fixings (older kids can help select them) and then sit down with your children and make things together. The parent is there to offer help and suggestions rather than to make sure that everyone's *Magen-David* comes out the same.

Hanukkah Decoration Ideas

You can start with a few simple paper chains, or paper cut-outs of Jewish and holiday symbols. Try to expand beyond the usual Star of David to *menorahs*, *hanukkiyahs*, oil jugs, candles, *dreidls*, shields, Lions of Judah, or elephants (which the Greek soldiers rode). Mae Shafter Rockland in *The Chanukah Book* (Schocken Books, 1975) mentions among other possible Hanukkah symbols the eight-pointed star used on coins by the Hasmoneans (in the form of a circle surrounded by eight points), a crown motif, or a bell to symbolize the liberty that the Maccabees "proclaimed throughout the land." Elaborate by hanging some of the cut-out symbols from a long ribbon or paper chain, or by taping the paper chains on the wall in the shape of a symbol. You can make some of these into mobiles by cutting them from sturdier materials and suspending them with string or thread from hangers, dowel sticks, or a circle made from a band of tagboard.

Hanukkah decorations that are made of materials like colored foil, tissue, or cellophane and hung in a window to catch the light are especially attractive and can reinforce the traditional holiday themes of light and "publicizing the miracle." You can even cut the decorations from thin translucent plastic, an idea we've adapted from a general crafts book, *Crafts for Fun* by Virginia S. Rich.[3] Plastic theme-book covers from the dime store or school-supply store are perfect. Simply spray the windows lightly with water and the shapes will stick, even after the water dries. They can be peeled off later.

Crayon "stained glass" is another type of light-catching decoration to hang in a window. These ideas require complete parental supervision, however. One method is to place crayon shavings in a design between two sheets of waxed paper (shiny side out). Parent presses the pieces together with a medium iron, melting the crayons. An alternate method comes from a crayon company. Place a piece of construction paper over a hot plate, which is then set to the *lowest* possible setting. Coloring on top of the warm (not too hot!) paper causes the crayon to melt slightly into the paper, which creates a translucent effect when the drawing (or design can be cut out later) is hung in the light.

An alternative Hanukkah decoration is a center-piece that the family can make from a jug reminiscent of the pitcher of oil, Israeli coins, a *dreidl* collection, and the like. Or make a display of a doll's Hanukkah celebration with a miniature *menorah* (from a gift shop or make from plastecine) with birthday candles, the tiniest *dreidl* you can find, *gelt* cut from foil, and miniature presents.

A friend whose two boys were attracted to the Maccabean-soldier aspect of Hanukkah found that they enjoyed making small Maccabee figures from a variety of disposable foil baking pieces. They also made shields from foil pizza pans or oven liners. Heavy-duty foil stretched over a piece of paper towel over cardboard was "embossed" with a pencil to create a metallic decoration.

For a fabric wall hanging, cut out a *hanukkiyah* from felt and glue it to a felt background. Attach Velcro® tabs where each flame (or entire candle) goes. Make the flames or candles from felt that is attached to the complementary piece of Velcro®; then you can stick on a flame (or candle) each night! This could even be done on a T-shirt; draw on the *menorah* with fabric paints.

Food for the Holiday

Hanukkah began in the days long before Pritikin, which is why no one thought twice about foods fried in oil, the official holiday treats. The cooking oil symbolizes the miracle of the eight-burning oil. The traditional Ashkenazic treat is *latkes*, or potato pancakes, usually served with applesauce and sour cream (or plain yogurt, for the nutrition-conscious heretic. I know some people who have even made *latkes* without oil or salt, which I think qualifies them for excommunication. Some liberal opinions allow the substitution of no-stick cooking spray, however).

The Sephardic Hanukkah goody popular in Israel is *sufganiyot*, fried doughnuts. Cafes all over Israel do a hefty business with these heavy-duty treats, which are sometimes filled with caramel or jam. These aren't exactly like American dough-nuts, which are baked as well as fried, but bakery jelly doughnuts have become the American equiv-alent at a lot of Hanukkah parties. French dough-nuts made from a mix come close to the Israeli item.

Dairy foods are also a Hanukkah tradition in some communities because of the story of Judith in the Apocrypha, which came to be associated with the Maccabean period. While the Jews in one city were under seige, Judith wooed the Syrian general with plenty of thirst-producing food, especially cheese. She then quenched his thirst with lots of wine, which made him sleepy. While he was asleep, she beheaded him, thus turning the tide of the battle.

Sugar cookies cut with Hanukkah-symbol-shaped cookie cutters (available from Judaica gift shops) are also fun, even if the tradition doesn't date back to the Second Temple.

Another idea for kids is to make an edible "*hanukkiyah*": spread a rectangular strip of bread or fruit-bread with cream cheese, then insert thin carrot pretzel sticks upright for "candles." Attach "flames" (raisins) to the tops with a dab of cream cheese. Or challenge the kids to make their own "edible *hanukkiyah*" sculpture from fruits, vegetables, and such (on condition that they eat it!). Friends of ours make a working *hanukkiyah* from *mandelbrodt* (almond cookie) each year. Use a standard *mandelbrodt* recipe from any Jewish cookbook and shape into a long piece for the base, with small circles attached for each candleholder. The candle holes spread a bit as they bake, so either make them in the dough with a smaller candle than the ones you will light or fill them a bit with foil. After using for lighting, you can remove the waxy parts and eat the rest. *The Children's Jewish Holiday Kitchen* by Joan Nathan[4] suggests an "edible *dreidl*" for dessert made from a chocolate kiss and marshmallow stuck together on a toothpick.

Potato
Latkes

Grate together:
8 medium potatoes
1 small onion
Add 2 eggs (lightly beaten), 2 tablespoons flour, 1 1/2 teaspoon salt, 1/4 teaspoon each baking powder and pepper. (The baking powder helps keep the potato from darkening.)
Mix all together and allow to set a couple of minutes. Drop by tablespoons into hot oil (1/2 inch deep) and fry until brown. Serve with applesauce and sour cream.

Easy Applesauce

Making your own applesauce seems amazing to most kids who are used to getting it out of jars or little lunch-box containers. Use as many ripe apples as you have people to serve. Quarter and pare the apples, remove core and seeds, then simmer until soft with a little water or apple juice (about 1/2 cup for eight medium apples). Stir occasionally and add liquid if needed. Carefully add brown sugar or honey to taste while hot, then simmer a bit more until blended. Season with cinnamon and other sweet spices as desired, plus a squirt of lemon juice. Or you can toss in a few red cinnamon candies while it cooks and watch them melt and turn the sauce redder.

Aviva's Israeli-Style
Sufganiyot

Make dough as for Aviva's *hallah*, p. 150. (Recipe can be halved; use 2 eggs.) Shape dough into walnut-sized balls and allow to rise about 1/2 hour. Fry dough balls until golden brown in 2 inches hot oil. (Balls should rise to surface immediately.) Turn once during frying. Drain on paper towels. Sprinkle with powdered sugar. Serve with mint tea and spread the insides with a dab of jelly or chocolate cream.

Goldie's
Mandelbrodt[5]

4 eggs
1 cup sugar

1 cup oil
4 cups flour
3 teaspoons baking powder
1 teaspoon baking soda
3 teaspoons vanilla
1 teaspoon almond or lemon extract
1/2 cup chopped almonds, pecans, or walnuts
1 teaspoon cinnamon mixed with 1/2 cup sugar

Beat eggs and sugar, add oil, and stir until blended. Add sifted dry ingredients, vanilla and almond extract, and then add nuts. Knead pieces of dough on floured board. Form into long rolls on greased cookie sheet. Bake at 350 degrees for 30 minutes. Cut into 3/4-inch slices while warm. Turn on sides and sprinkle with sugar and cinnamon mixture. Return to oven and toast for 10 minutes. (Or shape as desired and adjust baking time appropriately.)

Games

The long winter evenings of Hanukkah were traditionally considered one of the few times in the Jewish year when game playing was a respected pastime. One explanation is that game playing was used as a cover-up for the studying of Torah when the Greeks forbade it in the days of the Hanukkah story. The most widely played Hanukkah game is spinning a top, known in Yiddish as a *driedl*, in Hebrew as a *sevivon*.

The familiar *driedl* with four sides displaying the Hebrew letters *nun*, *gimmel*, *hey*, and *shin* is an Ashkenazic version dating from the Middle Ages. The letters are the initials for *Nes Gadol Hayah Sham*—A Great Miracle Happened There. In Israel the final letter is a *pey* for the word *"poh,"* making the meaning "A Great Miracle Happened *Here*." My husband remembers as a boy growing up in Morocco that on Hanukkah the children played with a regular top that was spun with a string, rather than the type with the letters. A *driedl* collection can be fun for kids, too, especially now when there are so many novelty kinds available of all sizes and materials. You can get them at any Jewish gift shop. And don't forget the hollow ones that can be filled with Hanukkah goodies such as holiday balloons, stickers, chocolate coins, and tiny toys.

● *To play the game:* All players put an agreed-upon amount of goodies (see the following) into the pot. They then take turns spinning the *driedl*. If it lands with *nun* on top, you do *nothing*; if *gimmel*, you get everything in the pot (and everyone puts another piece back in); for *hey* you get *half*, and *shin* means you put one item (or whatever amount was agreed upon) back *in*. (Actually, the original directions used Yiddish words that began with the four Hebrew letters–with the same meanings as noted: *nun* for *nicht*, "nothing"; *gimmel* for *ganz*, "all"; *hey* for *halb*, "half"; and *shin* for *shtel*, "put.") The game continues until one player takes all or until everyone has had enough. Nintendo it's not, but for some inexplicable reason the game continues to have appeal for every generation of children. Really cool nine-year-olds can spin the *dreidl* upside down (the *dreidl*, not the kid).

● *Dreidl games for tots:* For preschoolers who still can't spin the *dreidl* well, there are other games you can improvise: hide and find the *dreidl* (everyone sing louder if they're "getting warm," softer if they're far off); put a few colored *dreidls* in a row—while child covers eyes, you remove one and child then looks and must try to tell which one is missing; put the *dreidl* in a paper bag with several other objects and the child must try to find it by touch alone.

● *The goodies:* Once upon a time, back in the *shtetl*, children thought it was a treat to play *dreidl* for ordinary nuts. Nowadays, the possibilities are myriad: you can play for gold foil-covered chocolate coins or for carob-covered raisins, for pennies or *shekels*, for pop-beads, crayons, or stickers.

● *Other games:* Making up other Hanukkah games can be fun and can be an enjoyable challenge for school-age kids. For example, you might make a Lotto game. For playing boards, divide cardboard squares into nine pieces, like a tic-tac-toe board. Draw in Hanukkah symbols in each square. Make each board slightly different. Also cut out cards or pieces of paper that fit over the squares. Draw a different symbol on each board. To play, take turns picking cards out of the pile and try to match all of your squares. You can also make pairs of cards with matching Hanukkah (or other Jewish and holiday) symbols and use them to play "memory": lay out face down, then turn over two at a time and try to make a pair; you keep the pairs you make and try to collect the most cards.

Hanukkah Parties

With eight days, and much of it often occurring over winter break from school, Hanukkah is the perfect time for a party. Children's parties are great, but how about a multigenerational Hanukkah celebration to show that Hanukkah belongs to adults as well? It might even become your yearly tradition. Children can help make invitations. Try to invite some people of ages and generations beyond your usual crowd, perhaps to include someone lonely or far from home. Tell or read stories, sing songs, play live or recorded music, and play games. Serve *latkes* or other Hanukkah specialties.

You can ask each person or family who comes to bring a *hanukkiyah* with candles to light or display. Each child could also bring a small grab-bag gift if desired. They could also bring a small gift (if wrapped, attach a note saying what is inside) to be given to a less fortunate child through a Jewish or general charitable organization.

Gifts

Giving Hanukkah money, *gelt* in Yiddish or *demei Hanukkah* in Hebrew, is a fairly old custom that represents the minting of coins, symbolic of the national sovereignty that is central to the Hanukkah story. Some families give Hanukkah *gelt* on the fifth night of the holiday because that is the day that more lights are lit than are unlit; others give it every night. The giving of elaborate gifts for Hanukkah is a fairly new custom in North America and other Western countries. In Israel the custom is little known. Like decorations, it's no secret that the emphasis on gifts probably started in response to the massive Christmas gift giving that takes place at the same time of year. The problem is that for many children, gifts may become the major focus of the holiday.

It's easiest, of course, to establish a climate of moderation while the children are young, for soon competition with peers who are getting expensive Hanukkah or Christmas gifts comes into play. We've decided to give the bigger gifts on the last night of the holiday. The last night, with all eight candles aglow, is traditionally called *Zot Hanukkah*, "This is Hanukkah," and is the climax of the festival. On the other nights we might give each child a tiny gift such as chocolate coins or a holiday pencil. Or gifts from relatives are distributed after candlelighting.

One family we know agrees on a reasonable limit to spend per person, which can either go toward one large gift or several small ones. They also visit book fairs during Jewish book month (the month prior to Hanukkah) and let the children draw up a "wish list" of books. The children then get one book for each night of Hanukkah.

Before the holiday we take time to sort through the children's outgrown clothes and old toys and let the children select things to give away. Shelters for the battered and homeless, and other charities, need toys and other children's items in good condition. It's wonderful if you can also take your children shopping for new items to donate.

Giving *gelt* can also be imbued with new meaning when the family agrees to give some of their holiday *gelt* (including Mom and Dad's holiday check from Uncle Meyer) to *tzedakah*. You can pool your donations or make them separately.

You can enhance the *gelt* giving with other creative ideas, as well. Some families give a certain amount each night, which can be a very shiny newly minted coin from the bank. Or start an educational "Jewish hobby" with a starter set of Israeli coins. (Write to: Israel Government—Coins and Medals, 350 Fifth Avenue, New York, NY 10118.) If you have a local Israeli stamp club, you might make it a stamp collection.

But the *gelt* needn't be monetary alone. Family members can make each other pretend coins or bills on which they write or draw an I.O.U. promising special favors, help, or a special shared activity. Examples: "This coin good for one afternoon at the park," "Trade in for a morning of watching the kids," or "Good anytime for a hug—reusable."

Another variation is to have the family draw names for Hanukkah secret pals and secretly do a favor or give a small surprise each day to the family member whose name each drew. For prereaders, draw envelopes that contain photos of family members. Guess who your pal was on the last day of Hanukkah.

Give to others by doing an extra good deed each day of the festival. Visit a shut-in, give *tzedakah*, feed the hungry birds, send a holiday card to someone far from home, and so on. Or make a Hanukkah "care package" together. Include an inexpensive or homemade *hanukkiyah*, candles, a *dreidl*, potato pancake mix, homemade decorations, and chocolate coins. Then mail it to someone far from home.

The word Hanukkah is related to the Hebrew word *hinuch*, education. This is an appropriate time to give donations to Jewish schools and educational organizations and to give presents of Jewish books, or subscriptions to Jewish periodicals.

In recognition of all the Jewish practices that the Greeks and other oppressors throughout the ages outlawed, such as Shabbat observance, Shabbat items or other Jewish ritual items would make particularly appropriate gifts.

P.S. What about Christmas?

When Jewish parents consider the "December Dilemma," chances are they don't mean how to celebrate Hanukkah or what kind of gifts to give. Rather, the term has become the catch phrase for the range of uncomfortable feelings that many Jews, in particular Jewish parents, experience while most of the rest of the country is celebrating Christmas. It's as if the year's biggest party is going on, and we've decided not to be invited.

I don't think we should run away from our discomfort with Christmas, because it serves to remind us that, for all of our comfort and acceptance in this best of Diasporas, we still have chosen not to live in our national homeland, Israel. All year long we may feel totally at home, but once a year we're reminded that at some level it's still *galut*, exile. Ironically, Christmas may do a better job of that than Yom HaAtzma'ut.

The December Dilemma is just the most obvious manifestation of the larger dilemmas we have to deal with as American Jews. The more involved we are in the general society, the more we are going to feel the tension at this time of year. Not only Jews in Israel, but those who live in densely Jewish enclaves, work within the Jewish community, or send their children to Jewish day schools or preschools will be more insulated from the dilemma than those who are more immersed in the general society. It's all a part of the bigger issue of how we balance our lives between particular and universal, between our identities as Jews and our identities as Americans.

I think that the people who experience the most problems with children and Christmas are those for whom December is practically the only time of year in which their children feel distinctively Jewish. If the main experience of Judaism is that you can't have fun on Christmas, then it becomes negative. The time to bolster our kids' Jewish egos is back at Purim and at Simhat Torah, or every week on Shabbat. When family observances revolve around the Jewish calendar, we know who we are, not just who we aren't.

There is a less palatable factor at play here, too. The Judaism most families observe places few restrictions on children's life-styles—until December. If you can eat exactly what your non-Jewish friends do and spend your Saturday mornings the same way they do, then aren't you more likely to

resent it once or twice a year when suddenly you can't have or do something fun just because you're Jewish? Children in homes with more intense Jewish observance, including the discipline of some of those unpopular "thou shalt nots," *all year 'round*, are far less likely to rebel at not having a Christmas tree. Some amount of restrictions (related to *kashrut*, Shabbat, and so forth) can have a very positive effect on children's Jewish identities, provided that Judaism overall is perceived in an affirmative and meaningful way.

Children should be taught that, despite its contemporary secularization, Christmas is a sacred religious holiday for our Christian neighbors. To appropriate their observances in our homes is a trivialization of both of our faiths. On the other hand, going to the extreme of acting as if Christmas didn't exist is unrealistic and even counterproductive. It's to be hoped that we are secure enough in our identity as Jews that we can feel comfortable in visiting Christian friends' celebrations or admiring their decorations and lights. Likewise, we should feel comfortable inviting our Christian friends to see what Hanukkah and other Jewish celebrations around the year are about.

At the same time, children in public schools should not be required to take part in any Christmas celebrations. This is a violation of the constitutional separation of Church and State. Including a token Hanukkah element merely puts Hanukkah in competition with Christmas, but in reality, it's often what happens. Any December celebrations, such as "winter carnival," in public schools should have a secular orientation. Or a unit such as "holidays around the world" could introduce children to the many ways that people of different cultures celebrate their special times. Despite the vast differences between groups, certain central motifs, such as faith and light, are found in winter celebrations of many cultures. And yet each group interprets these symbols to fit a particular set of values and beliefs.

The reality is that most public schools *do* incorporate so-called "secular" Christmas symbols such as trees (actually a religious symbol of eternal life), reindeer, and Santa Claus. Most Jewish children and their families take a certain amount of this in stride, with a note to a teacher or a brief conference usually proving sufficient to alert the faculty to one's sensitivities. And many parents, no matter what their organizational leaders prefer, are willing to accept a few Hanukkah decorations for "balance." But if situations arise where a teacher reads from the New Testament, displays a crèche scene, chides a Jewish child for not singing "Silent Night," or otherwise seriously infringes on the separation of Church and State, then it is time for parents to take action. If the school administration is not cooperative, the Community Relations Council of the local Jewish Federation is usually the best place to turn for help.

Christmas is a time that may make us question things, such as the educational setting we've selected for our children. These problems don't arise in a Jewish day school. But do we want to urge the Jewish community to leave the public schools in droves and give up its efforts at achieving pluralistic education? Like the Israel/Diaspora problem, there are no easy answers.

For Jews in mixed marriages or for those in which one parent or both have converted to Judaism, and for whom other branches of their family celebrate Christmas, the issues at this time of year can get really tricky. The kids may be confused and anxious, or they may take contradictions in stride. I don't presume to offer any instant solutions. It's ideal for both the parents and the in-laws involved to agree on what the holiday policies will be, but even this doesn't always happen. Talking to others who have brought up families with similar circumstances, perhaps in a support group for intermarried couples (many Jewish Family Services and some liberal synagogues sponsor such groups), or looking into some of the books on mixed marriages (pp. 306–307) may offer some helpful strategies.

When I was a child, in public school, with two Jewish parents and few Jewish friends, I begged for a Christmas tree, but the answer was always no (except that I had a tiny toy one in my dollhouse). My desire peaked around sixth grade, when even my teacher seemed surprised that my parents stubbornly refused to let me have "even a little tree in my room." Every Christmas Eve we did hang up stockings, though, and we visited a Christian family for Christmas afternoon (they came to us for Thanksgiving). Of course, we celebrated Hanukkah with candles and blessings as well as presents and decorations. I'm happy today that my parents never gave in. But it's interesting to note that my own children, who are being raised in the same general environment but with many more Jewish observances than I was, have virtually never exhibited any jealousy of Christmas. I don't think that Christmas per se is always the great dilemma we make it out to be; rather it stands for our greater dilemmas as American Jews.

In Israel, Hanukkah is still the minor festival it was for centuries. Here in North America it is assumed by many people to be "the" Jewish holiday because it takes place alongside "the" Christian holiday. The notion has always frustrated me, and I've tried repeatedly to explain that Hanukkah has nothing to do with Christmas.

Yet what could be more appropriate at this time than the message of Hanukkah—the rededication to Judaism in the face of overwhelming pressure to conform to the majority culture?

One of the ongoing miracles of Hanukkah is that, generation after generation, we continue to do so.

A DERASHAH FOR PARENTS: HANUKKAH FAITH

Oil gives both light and nourishment, just as a parent should give his or her children both spiritual inspiration and emotional nurturance. The most repeated Hanukkah miracle is the story of the small cruse of oil that contained enough fuel for only one day, yet burned for eight days. That Hanukkah miracle (whether understood literally or metaphorically) says, in the fashion of David Ben-Gurion: Sometimes the dreamer is the only realist. Hanukkah faith means going ahead and starting small, with belief that whatever has been in short supply can grow. Hanukkah faith means lighting that one candle rather than cursing the darkness.

So many times, especially with small children, I've felt, to make the metaphor apt, "burned-out." The sages taught that one is not to rely on miracles. Parents shouldn't expect to give constantly, without any self-nurturing or help to ease their task. The biblical concept that a parent should be "honored" (and not just respected) indicates an understanding for the needs of the parent as a person. Of course, we need to take care of our own needs—spiritual, emotional, physical, and intellectual—in order to be able to give abundantly to our children.

However, few of us know how much we are capable of giving until we become parents. Often our inner resources continue to flow long after logic would indicate that the capacity to give should have been spent. We discover a greater source of love and nurturance that replenishes us when we feel that, logically, we should have run out of energy long ago.

Parenting can be a faith-building experience.

TU BISHVAT: PLANTING FOR THE FUTURE

Tu BiShvat, the Jewish Arbor Day, has gone from being merely a marker on the calendar to being a minor festival that once focused on Jewish longings for the land of Israel and has now become an important national celebration encompassing Jewish mysticism, ecology, and reclamation of Israel's natural resources. In this age of growing concern for the planetary environment, Tu BiShvat may be a holiday whose time has come.

It's not a major festival with many prescribed rituals and observances, but it can be a great opportunity to experience unusual customs, invent creative family traditions, and explore important aspects of our Jewish heritage.

The name "Tu BiShvat" is simply a Hebrew abbreviation made by combining two Hebrew letters, *tet* and *vav*, whose numerical equivalents add up to fifteen. So Tu BiShvat literally means "the fifteenth of the Hebrew month of *Shevat*." (A longer name, *Hamishah-Aser BiShvat*, means the same thing.)

Tu BiShvat is first mentioned in the *Mishnah*, where the rabbis explained that it is the New Year for trees, just as Rosh HaShanah is the New Year for people. It is also known as "the birthday of the trees." It was held to be the preliminary day of spring, the day on which the winter rains begin to wane and the sap once again begins to rise in the trees. And as every Israeli schoolchild knows, it's the time when the almond tree, the *shekediyah*, whose name means "industrious," first displays its delicate white or pink blossoms.

In the Talmud (tractate *Rosh HaShanah*) the fifteenth of *Shevat* was described as the day after which all fruit harvested would be included in the coming year's calculations for the tithe, the 10 percent of the harvest that Jewish farmers had brought to the Temple in Jerusalem.

For centuries after the exile from Israel, Jews used Tu BiShvat as a day to recall their ties with their homeland by eating the fruit of its trees. While snow lay on the ground, the fragrance and tastes of raisins, dried figs, dates, almonds, and especially the hardy carob, known in Yiddish as *bokser*, brought to life the national memories of springtime in the land of Israel. This custom was not confined to Ashkenazic Jews, but was kept among North African Jews as well. Our children's Sephardic grandmother, Savta Mazal, still prepares a Tu BiShvat "party" of dried fruits and nuts for the extended family in Israel just as she always did in her native Morocco.

Since the rise of modern Zionism in the last century and the subsequent establishment of the State of Israel, tree planting has become the more well-known practice of the day. In Israel it is the occasion for a major annual outing by all the schoolchildren. Outside of Israel, many Jews give money to the Jewish National Fund (JNF) to plant trees in Israel. In warmer climates, such as in Texas where I grew up, Jewish schools may plant a tree every year on the holiday, as well as sponsoring trees in Israel.

Families can easily elaborate on these old and new traditions to create their own meaningful Tu BiShvat home celebration.

FAMILY ACTIVITIES FOR TU BISHVAT

Fruit Feasts

The simplest kind of Tu BiShvat celebration is a little party with refreshments of fruits reminiscent of Israel. You can plan a meal around it or have an elaborate afternoon snack. Traditional foods would include representatives of the "seven varieties" of produce for which the land of Israel is famed: "wheat and barley. . . (grape) vines, figs, and pomegranates . . . olive trees and (date) honey" (Deuteronomy 8:8). Children who are old enough can look up or at least read the biblical reference with you. Other traditional foods include the almond, the first tree to bloom in Israel in the spring, and the carob, which was traditional since it traveled well from Israel to faraway lands. Oranges, avocados, bananas, and even kiwis are more modern Israeli fruits. If you can get real Israeli produce, such as Jaffa oranges, so much the better.

These fruits can be served in their natural form or in a recipe, such as tabouli from cracked wheat or a carob-powder milk shake. Should you want to innovate a little upon the fruit-feasting tradition, here are some other fun treats to try:

● Roast chestnuts: Roasting chestnuts over an open brazier is a Sephardic Tu BiShvat custom that my husband, Avraham, remembers from his Moroccan boyhood. It sounds like a very cozy custom to try if you have a fireplace or even a hibachi on the porch or patio. To prevent their bursting, one must split the chestnut shells by cutting a small cross all the way through the hard shell on the flat side of the nut. Place the nuts in a popcorn popping basket and hold just over the flame. Shake occasionally and avoid direct contact with the flame, which could char the outside before the inside is cooked. Roast until the shell is blackened (about one quarter of an hour). Let cool enough to touch, then peel and eat while still warm.

You can also bake the slit nuts in a 350° F oven for about half an hour. When cooked, they will be rather firm on the surface but soft inside, and the shell and inner skin will peel easily.

● Fruit Art: Young children, and older ones too, enjoy making an edible picture from small pieces of fruit on a backdrop of lettuce leaves on a plate or tray. As they get older they might enjoy making three-dimensional edible fruit sculptures with the aid of toothpicks.

● Trees' Birthday Cake: Since Tu BiShvat is the trees' "birthday," young children may ask, "Where's the cake?" Here are two recipes for trees' birthday cakes; the first uses one of Israel's favorite fruits and dates, with the optional addition of carob powder, also in honor of Tu BiShvat. It is a variation of a cake that a friend made for me after my first daughter was born in Israel.

Israeli Date Cake

(An adult must do this first step.)
In a large mixing bowl, pour:
  1/2 cup boiling water
over 1 lb. (1/2 kilogram) chopped dates
Add:
  2 cups chopped pecans or walnuts
  1 cup sugar
  2 tablespoons butter
Beat slightly:
  2 eggs

Add to other ingredients.
Mix together in another bowl:
  3 1/2 cups flour
  2 teaspoons baking soda
  1/4 cup carob powder or cocoa (optional)
Add to wet ingredients.
Add:
  2 teaspoons vanilla
  dash cinnamon

Bake in a lightly greased 9" × 13" pan at 350° F for about one hour; do not overcook. Allow to cool before serving. To make a snowflake decoration on the top, place a large paper doily over the cake. Dust with powdered sugar, then very carefully remove the doily. This reminds me of the snow that fell on the ground in cold climates while Jews ate the sweet dates of Israel on Tu BiShvat.

Another very easy fruit-filled cake for the trees' birthday is this Southern recipe:

Hummingbird Cake[6]

Mix together:
  3 cups flour
  1 teaspoon each baking soda, salt, cinnamon
  1 cup sugar
  1 1/4 cups oil
  3 eggs
  1 8-ounce (1 cup) can of crushed pineapple in its own juice
Add these and mix again:
  2 medium or 3 small chopped bananas
  1 cup chopped pecans or walnuts
  1/3 cup shredded coconut
  1/2 cup chocolate chips (optional)

Pour mixture into a greased tube pan. Bake at 350° F for one hour, or in a 9" × 13" pan for 45 minutes. Allow to cool one hour in pan before turning out.

———————

● You could even invent a special Tu BiShvat dinner. Start with appetizers that grow on trees, such as cold fruit soup, assorted olives, or avocado slices sprinkled with lemon juice. A salad of "biblical" and Israeli-favorite fruits could be served as a side dish. Perhaps bake a *hallah* with a tree design on top. The main course could be a *tzimmes* with dried fruit in it or maybe a vegetarian nut loaf. Or maybe an Enchanted Broccoli Forest.

The following recipe, which looks like a miniature forest when prepared, seems like the perfect Tu BiShvat entree. (You might want to modify the spicy seasonings if you have picky eaters or very young children.)

The Enchanted Broccoli Forest[7]

Preheat oven to 325° F. Butter a 10" × 6" pan or its equivalent.
Prepare the following:

1 1-lb. bunch of broccoli (Cut off bottom several inches of stalk. Shave off the tough outer skin, and cut the broccoli into spears. These will be the "trees.")

2 cups (raw) brown rice. Combine in a saucepan with 3 cups water. Bring to a boil, lower heat, and cover. Cook until *just* done: 20–30 minutes. Fluff with a fork.

Saute all the following ingredients together over medium heat, stirring, until the onions are soft and translucent (8–10 minutes). Add to the cooked rice and mix well:

1 tablespoon butter
1 cup chopped onion
1 large clove garlic, crushed
1/2 teaspoon salt
1/2 teaspoon dill weed
lots of black pepper
1/4 teaspoon dried mint
cayenne pepper, to taste

Beat the following together well, then beat into the rice mixture. Spread evenly into your buttered 10" × 6" pan:

3 large eggs
1/4 cup freshly minced parsley
1 1/2 packed cups grated cheddar or Swiss cheese

Steam the broccoli "trees" until bright green and *just* tender. Rinse immediately in cold water;

drain. Arrange these broccoli trees upright in the bed-of-rice mixture and drizzle the trees with lemon butter (juice of one lemon combined with 2 tablespoons melted butter). Cover gently, but as firmly as possible, with foil. Bake 30 minutes. Makes four servings.

For dessert, have dried fruits and nuts or a "Tree's Birthday Cake."

A *Seder* for Tu BiShvat

In some communities, particularly Sephardic ones, the Tu BiShvat fruit-eating ritual became highly symbolic. The number, order, and types of fruits eaten were imbued with mystical significance. The most elaborate Tu BiShvat celebration was the *seder* (ordered ritual meal) instituted by the kabbalistic mystics of sixteenth-century Safed, a town in the Northern Galilee region of Israel. Their ritual, described in the text *Pri Etz Hadar* (Fruit of the Goodly Tree) has enjoyed something of a renaissance in modern America and Israel. Once an exotic celebration, the Tu BiShvat *seder* is now enjoying such a comeback that it is a common celebration even at Jewish nursery schools.

You can hold a Tu BiShvat *seder* with your own family, with guests, with a *havurah* or synagogue group, or in a school setting. The basic format of the *seder* consists of the following:

● Eat three groupings of up to ten kinds of fruits and nuts:

1. Those that have a hard outside shell that cannot be eaten. This includes all hard nuts with an outer shell, pomegranates, and coconuts.

2. Those that have a soft outside but an inedible pit, such as olives, dates, cherries, apricots, plums, and peaches.

3. Those fruits that are wholly edible, such as grapes, figs, apples, pears, raspberries, blueberries, and carobs.

Each of these groupings represents an increasingly higher, holier, and more spiritual level in relation to God, as seen by the kabbalists.

Modern adaptations of the Tu BiShvat *seder* may change the categories, for example, to plates of fresh fruits, nuts, dried fruits, and canned fruits, respectively.

● In between eating the fruits and nuts, drink four cups of wine. Beginning with white wine, symbolizing the dormancy of winter, each cup is made redder by the addition of red wine until the fourth cup, representing the full bloom of spring, is all red. For children, grape juice and white grape juice or apple juice can be substituted. The cup is filled before the fruit course is served and then is drunk after eating the fruit.

● Read selections from Jewish sources about trees. Consult a biblical concordance or see the Resource Guide, p. 352, for some complete *Haggadahs* for Tu BiShvat.

Blessings for Tu BiShvat

Before eating fruit:

Baruch Atah Adonai, Eloheinu Melech HaOlam, borei pri ha'eitz.

Holy One of Blessing, Your Presence fills creation; creating the fruit of the tree.

Before drinking wine:

Baruch Atah Adonai, Eloheinu Melech HaOlam, borei pri hagafen.

Holy One of Blessing, Your Presence fills creation; creating the fruit of the vine.

For the first time one sees a tree in bloom each spring:

Baruch Atah Adonai, Eloheinu Melech HaOlam, shelo hisar meolamo davar, uvarah vo briyot tovot veilanot tovim, lehanot bahem benai adam.

Holy One of Blessing, Your Presence fills Creation; You left nothing lacking in Your world, and created in it goodly creatures and beautiful trees to delight people's hearts.

PLANTING

Besides fruit eating in its many variations, the other major custom of Tu BiShvat is tree planting. Most children enrolled in a Jewish school will experience this in some way, but it is doubly special to enjoy this *mitzvah* as a family. Actually, it is always a *mitzvah* to plant trees in Israel. Should the holiday occur on Shabbat, the tree planting is postponed until Sunday.

Planting Trees in Israel

Unless you live in Israel or are visiting on Tu BiShvat, your Israeli tree-planting experience will have to be vicarious. Although it has become the stuff of greeting cards ("In honor of your birthday a tree has been planted in Israel—Your day to water it is Thursday!") in reality the tree planting and other work of the Jewish National Fund (JNF) has become quite sophisticated and remains pivotal in turning Israel's wastelands into fertile greenery. JNF also provides books, posters, and other educational materials on Israel, Judaism, and ecology.

At dinner or a family meeting you can decide who or what to plant your trees in honor of. The JNF will mail your honoree a certificate. Or you and your children might decide to plant the tree in honor of an important family, community, or world event, or in honor of a famous person or date in Jewish history.

The JNF can provide you with details about choosing either the type of tree planted or a special forest in which to plant, such as the forest in honor of Soviet Jews, or one in memory of children who perished in the Holocaust. Family members can decide together which tree to plant or which forest to plant in (the JNF normally allows only one of the two choices per tree).

Planting Where You Live

Contributing to Israel's reforestation is important, but it can also be enjoyable and beneficial on Tu BiShvat, to plant a tree where you live, if you live in a temperate climate. There's a plum tree on my mother's front lawn that I planted one Tu BiShvat while I was in high school. If you don't have a yard or just want to do a *mitzvah*, ask a local Jewish agency, school, or nursing home if your family can plant a tree on their grounds for Tu BiShvat. Trees for planting can be found at local plant nurseries, which will also provide you with information on how to plant and care for the sapling.

Be sure that there is someone who will water and care for the seedling if it is not being planted at your own home, unless you are willing and able to take on that responsibility.

In these days of environmental crisis, it is certainly a great *mitzvah* to sponsor tree planting anywhere on the planet. (There are several worthy organizations in the tree-planting business. A notable one is "Tree People," 12601 Mullholland Dr., Los Angeles, CA 90210, (818) 769-2663.)

Indoor Gardening

If you live in a cold climate where tree planting on Tu BiShvat is out of the question, or if you simply find it too ambitious, you can still carry out the planting theme in other ways with your children.

You can save the seeds from your Tu BiShvat fruit party or *seder* and plant them in moist potting soil in paper cups, small pots, or even an egg carton. Orange and lemon seeds can produce lovely plants with fragrant foliage. It would be even more meaningful to bring some of your plantings to shut-ins or nursing-home residents.

On Tu BiShvat, hasidic Jews pray that a beautiful *etrog* will grow for their Sukkot use. In *The Jewish Holidays—A Guide and Commentary* by Michael Strassfeld, Zalman Schachter-Shalomi suggests keeping *etrog* pits in the freezer until a week before Tu BiShvat, then sprouting them in moist cotton for planting.[8]

Another way to link the holiday cycle is to plant parsley seeds on Tu BiShvat and grow your own parsley in time for the Passover *seder*.

Other Tree-Planting Traditions

In ancient Israel, a cypress was planted when a girl baby was born, a cedar for a boy. Later, when the youngsters grew up and married, branches from their trees were used to construct the *huppah* (marriage canopy).

You can create your own family traditions involving tree planting, whether in Israel, at your own home, or both. These needn't be confined to Tu BiShvat. You might decide to plant a tree for each child at birth, at age three, upon beginning or completing a school, at *bat* or *bar mitzvah*, or at other times. If you plant one at home and sponsor one in Israel, the family can imagine how their home tree's counterpart is growing and flourishing in Israeli soil.

Other Activities for Tu BiShvat

Feed the birds: Feeding the hungry birds in winter is an example of concern for *tzaar baalei hayyim*, the suffering of animals. But take care to feed them only infrequently or absolutely consistently, for they will learn to depend on the feedings once you begin them. Some Jews have the custom of feeding the birds the week of *Shabbat Shirah*, the Sabbath of Song, which occurs around Tu BiShvat, because the song of the birds is a praise to God.

THE ORIGINAL EARTH DAY?

Although Tu BiShvat is a minor holiday, one that is sometimes relegated to the appendix of Jewish holiday books, I believe that it conveys important messages for our time. Massive deforestation of the Amazon rain forests and elsewhere (including North America) has focused world attention on the importance of trees. Forests and ecosystems must be saved, new trees must be planted, and paper must be recycled.

Shomrei Adamah is a Jewish organization dedicated to protecting the environment and exploring the importance of the natural world in our Jewish heritage. They would like to make Tu BiShvat a focus, not only for Jews, but for all people who are concerned about the future of the environment. Synagogues and *havurot* can join their coalition; individuals and families can support them and use their materials on highlighting the environment in Jewish holiday and Shabbat celebrations. (See Resource Guide, pp. 338–339.)

Tu BiShvat can hold new meanings for a changing world.

A *DERASHAH* FOR PARENTS: THE IMPORTANCE OF ROOTS

He (Rabbi Elazar ben Azariah) used to teach:

"When a person's wisdom exceeds his good deeds, to what may he be compared? To a tree with many branches but few roots. A wind blows, uproots it and topples it over, as it is written, 'He shall be like a desert scrub that never thrives but dwells unwatered in the wilderness, in a salty, solitary land' (Jeremiah 17:6).

"However, when a person's good deeds exceed his wisdom, to what may he be compared? To a tree with few branches but with many roots. All the winds of the world may blow against it, yet they cannot move it from its place, as it is written, 'He shall be like a tree planted by the waters that spreads its roots by the stream. Untouched by the scorching heat, its foliage remains luxurious. It will have no concern in a year of drought and will not cease from bearing fruit' (Jeremiah 17:8)."

—*Pirkei Avot* 3:22

We live in an age that values externals, the foliage. While in the talmudic age and for centuries in traditional Jewish society, wisdom and Torah scholarship were the most esteemed attributes; today it is professional and financial success, as well as physical beauty and style, that are society's valued qualities.

Even when it comes to child rearing, more and more emphasis is being placed on outward appearances. Parental success is usually measured by how attractive and "achieving" our offspring are. There are magazines that tell us how to dress our children in the latest fashions. There are programs to ensure that babies learn academic subjects and begin nursery school smarter than the baby next door.

Children's schools, from early childhood through college, have frequently become status symbols. The children must be accepted into the right schools and make near-perfect grades. After school, they are often involved in competitive activities or in lessons and classes designed to make them more talented, more achieving, "winners."

In our status-oriented culture, children are sometimes in danger of becoming yet another status symbol.

Certainly, we would not be able to, or even want to, discard all externals. We should do our best to help our children feel comfortable with their physical appearance, succeed in school, and develop their individual talents and abilities. To a certain degree, externals are important to our children's self-esteem and enable them to be happier and more valuable members of society. A tree that never has leaves or fruit would be a pitiful sight to most.

But if we place all or most of our concern as parents on external qualities, on pruning the foliage, we give our children a very shaky base for life. Foliage, after all, is something that comes and goes with the changing seasons. Too much of it may make the tree topple in a strong wind. Our modern society, for all its external success, is in many ways weak at the roots, unstable on the personal level. Upward mobility and material success have often been acquired at the expense of personal security, family cohesion, and traditional values.

As parents, we can't protect our children from every storm, and some storms uproot even great trees. But constant nurturing of the roots, the nonexternals, is one of our crucial tasks. The roots are the firm foundation that support all the outward attraction and achievements we hope our children will have.

What are these roots? Just as Rabbi Elazar ben Azariah taught, good deeds are significant. Doing for others and engaging in *mitzvot* and *tikkun olam* (transforming the world for the better) need to be as essential to our children's education as are music lessons, sports, and even academics. Writes American *tzedakah* activist Danny Siegel, "someone has to believe that a Good Life of *Mitzvahs* can ease those years of growing up without so much craziness. . . . I've said it in my lectures again and again: the more *mitzvahs*, the less teen-age suicides. And certainly the more *mitzvahs*, the less depression and confusion and downright, bald unhappiness."

Think about the unseen sources of strength in a person's life and you will think of more "roots"— faith and belief in something beyond the self, heritage, values, family closeness, self-respect, strength of character. These may not be the items that are most valued in today's competitive society, yet these are the kind of firm roots a child needs to sustain him or herself in life, to "be like a tree planted by the waters that spreads its roots by the stream . . . (which) will have no concern in a year of drought and will not cease from bearing fruit."

PLANTING FOR THE FUTURE

The Talmud tells of a legendary figure named Honi HaMe'agel. One day Honi happened upon an old man planting a carob tree. Honi asked him how long it would take for the tree to bear fruit.

Replied the man, "Seventy years."

Honi then asked if the elderly man ever expected to eat the fruit of the tree he was planting. The man answered, "I enjoyed the fruits of trees which my parents and grandparents grew. Even as they planted for me, so I plant for my children."

Planting for the future is a lot of what parenting is about. Much of what we do day after day has no immediate or obvious effect, and yet the influence of our small, everyday interactions with our children may have great bearing on their futures and even upon the futures of generations yet unborn. "Just as the twig is bent, so the tree is inclined," says the Book of Proverbs.

By making the effort to create a "small sanctuary" in our homes, we plant the seed of our people's continuity in the ways of Torah that is called "a tree of life to them that hold fast to it."

PURIM

Purim is a time for rejoicing. Purim has the gaity and spirit of a fiesta, carnival, April Fool's day and New Year's eve—yet all with a Jewish flavor and meaning. It's a day for costumes, dramas and satires, eating, drinking, and making merry.

Purim is celebrated as much by adults as by children both among the more traditional sectors of the American Jewish community and in Israel among the "religious" and "secular" alike. However, when I was growing up, my Purim memories were primarily of a carnival for children in the Sunday school basement. Purim has probably suffered even more than Hanukkah from the problem of "pediatric Judaism." Fortunately, in recent years, Purim has seen somewhat of a revival in the broader American Jewish community.

Purim, held on the 14th of *Adar* (usually in March on the secular calendar), celebrates the deliverance of the Jewish people from destruction by a Persian tyrant during the period of the Babylonian exile in the fifth century B.C.E. The story, related in the biblical book of Esther, tells how King Ahasuerus's evil vizier Haman hatches a plot to kill all the Jews in the kingdom because one, Mordechai, has refused to bow down before him. Haman casts lots (*purim*) to determine the day of the Jews' destruction. But the intervention of the brave and beautiful young Jewish queen, Esther, guided by her cousin and guardian, none other than Mordechai, saves the day for the Jews.

The wicked Haman is executed, and Mordechai becomes the king's new prime minister. The Jews, who are enabled to defend themselves from their enemies, rejoice. To commemorate their celebration, Purim has continued to be observed.

In modern times some scholars have called into question the historicity of the book of Esther. Whether historically exact or not, the Purim story resounds with recurrent themes of Jewish history in its long Diaspora. Time and again, Jews have been objects of anti-Semitism and baseless hatred. Many a Jewish community throughout the ages celebrated its own special "Purim," commemorating a local deliverance from destruction. Some Jews, like Queen Esther, have assimilated into the highest echelons of non-Jewish society, only to be confronted with the need to face their identity as Jews: "Imagine not that you shall escape in the king's house more than all the Jews" (Esther 4:12).

Purim has gained a new interpretation among contemporary American Jews. The earlier commentators tended to view Esther as a traditional Jew who was faithful to her heritage even in the king's palace. Modern commentaries often picture her rather as an assimilated Jew (by virtue of her own and Mordechai's non-Jewish names and the fact that she married the non-Jewish king) who discovers her identity at a critical moment. The idea of an assimilated, intermarried queen rediscovering her identity and finding that it is possible to be prominent in the non-Jewish world while open about her Jewishness fits in more with the American Jewish self-image than with that of the more traditional, pious Esther.

The Book of Esther and the festival of Purim may even be taking on the status of a new myth for American Jews. Journalist and scholar Charles Silberman even chose a phrase from the Book of Esther as the title of *A Certain People—American Jews and Their Lives Today*, his popular book on American Jewry, explaining that the words "a certain people" were used by Haman to single out the Jews as different, dangerous and proper targets of persecution. Silberman contends that this negative perception of Jews, prevalent for two millennia, no longer exists in modern American society. He writes: "There is a striking parallel, therefore, between the Book of Esther's legend of salvation— the capital city of Shushan (Susa) rejoices when Haman is hanged and Mordechai succeeds him as prime minister—and the post World War II experience of American Jews, who have moved from the periphery of American society into its mainstream."[9] Just as Israeli Jews identify with the Hanukkah story of national liberation, perhaps American Jews are beginning to reinterpret Purim to fit in with our image of success in the Diaspora.

BE HAPPY, IT'S *ADAR*

"Mi shenichnas Adar, marbim besimhah" ("When *Adar* arrives, rejoicing increases") goes the rabbinical saying and popular Hebrew folk song. *Adar*, the month in which Purim falls, is traditionally considered a lucky and joyful month. (I agree; it's my birthday month—actually I was born in the Jewish leap month of *Adar* II—the additional month added in to the calendar seven years out of every nineteen to reconcile the lunar and solar years. When there's a leap year, Purim occurs in that second *Adar*.)

To set the mood, get in the spirit with a festive family dinner on Rosh Hodesh *Adar* (see p. 172). You could even put up "Be Happy—It's *Adar*" signs and banners (an ancient custom dating back perhaps to the *First Jewish Catalog*); make *Adar* T-shirts to wear that feature smiley faces, fish (the zodiac sign of *Adar*), and happy slogans; tell jokes from Jewish humor books; or read a story about the "wise men" of the mythical Chelm.[10]

TRADITIONAL PURIM OBSERVANCES

There are four major Purim observances: listening to the *megillah* reading, sending gifts of food to friends, giving to the needy, and eating a festive meal. Each of these activities lends itself to family involvement.

You and your children can pick and choose the activities you want to especially elaborate on this year. School-age youngsters might enjoy holding a Purim workshop for the family or friends shortly before the holiday, when you can help them set up tables with materials for making *graggers* (noise makers), food baskets, costumes, and so on. (In fact, there are so many possibilities for a one-day holiday that it can be difficult to avoid the "super-parent" routine. Before I resolve that this year I'll bake every whole-wheat *hamantash* from scratch and make the ultimate *mishloah manot* baskets with full family participation, I need to ask myself if it's realistic. After all, nothing seems less in the Purim spirit than doing anything with a sense of grim determination!)

FAMILY ACTIVITIES AROUND THE FOUR TRADITIONAL OBSERVANCES

Listening to the *Megillah*

Hearing the *megillah*, the parchment scroll containing the Book of Esther, read is the central Purim observance. In traditional synagogues, the reading is held on the evening of Purim and repeated the following morning. Although the reading may take place at home or another gathering place, the usual location is the synagogue. The reading *can* be long with small children in tow (they don't call it "the whole *megillah*" for nothing), but the kids are usually having so much fun with their *graggers* and costumes that they enjoy themselves anyway. Many synagogues provide a party, Purim play, or Jewish music concert after the reading.

Costumes

Costumes are *de rigueur* for Purim festivities, particularly for the *megillah* reading. In many places adults wear them as well as children. Planning costumes together can be a fun family activity. The costumes may represent characters in the Purim story or any kind of gorgeous or silly fantasy you and your kids can dream up.

Some Suggestions

● Save old clothes and accessories in a "dress-up" drawer that can also be used for Purim costumes. Crowns and scepters can be quickly shaped from aluminum foil.

● Buy packaged costumes sold for Halloween on sale right after that holiday and save them for Purim. Birthday crowns are also a favorite among young royalty.

● For serious costume-couture: visit a thrift shop, rummage sale, costume rental store, theater shop, or party-goods store.

● Old make-up or face paints can create Queen Esthers or monsters from outer space. Those too "grown-up" for costumes may still want to color pictures on their faces.

● Half- or full-face masks can be made by decorating paper plates or construction paper. Cut eye and mouth and nose openings; punch holes and thread or staple on string, ribbon, or elastic to keep the mask on.

● Older children can make paper-mâché masks. Inflate a balloon. Dip one-half-inch-wide strips of newspaper in liquid starch or flour-and-water paste, squeezing off the extra paste. Cover half the balloon. Add one layer at a time, allowing to dry somewhat between layers. Let dry hard for a couple of days before popping the balloon. Cut holes for eyes and mouth and on sides to thread strings for tying mask on. Decorate with poster paints.

● For a minicostume—instead of conventional head coverings, wear a totally out-of-place hat (Stetson, sombrero, fez) for the *megillah* reading. Although in Texas, where I come from, there's no assuming that the cowboy hat is a costume. Wore 'em to *shul* all the time—Purim word of honor.

Noisemakers

Every time during the *megillah* reading that the name of the villainous Haman (who in a sense represents all anti-Semitic enemies of the Jewish people throughout history) is mentioned, the congregation drowns it out with boos, shouts, and noisemakers. In Jewish tradition, the obliteration of a name, of a memory, is considered the ultimate destruction. Yet the jeering is part of the celebration, at once serious and farcical.

This is definitely a high point for children, the

one time of the year when they are encouraged to make lots of ruckus! Getting them to quiet down again is another matter; many synagogues use signals involving flags or signs of some kind to indicate when the noise has to stop. (Since the *mitzvah* is to hear every word of the *megillah*, considerate parents will do their best to keep their kids relatively quiet between "Haman"s.)

Most synagogues give out small metal noisemakers, which have sharp edges underneath and are not for tots. You can also make your own, the only major caution being to avoid the use of small swallowable objects with very young children who still put things in their mouths.

In Yiddish the noisemakers are called *graggers*, in Hebrew they are *raashanim*. (*Raash* means noise.)

Great Graggers

● A closed empty plastic soda bottle (individual or large size) with one marble to rattle around inside it. Optional additions: sequins, beads, beans, decorating the outside with stickers and ribbons.

● An empty juice can or empty metal Band-Aid box filled with anything noisy (nuts and bolts, pebbles, buttons, beans, jingle-bells), securely covered and sealed with adhesive-backed paper and decorated with stickers or rick-rack.

● Any unbreakable container with anything noisy secured inside. Even a paper plate can be folded in half with a few noisy small objects inside, stapled closely shut and an ice-cream stick handle stapled on the outside.

● "Found" *graggers* might include a tom-tom, maracas, spoons beaten on an upside-down pot, toy rhythm instruments, or cymbals.

● A pie plate tambourine can be made by punching a few holes around the edge of a disposable pie pan and attaching jingle-bells through the holes with twist-ties.

Learning the Story

To familiarize kids with the Purim story, read aloud or let them read to themselves some of the Purim books in the Resource Guide, pp. 352–353. Even if they are going to hear the *megillah* reading, they may find it difficult to follow the entire reading and will enjoy it more if they review the story in advance. There are a couple of books listed that contain pictures to cut out and reassemble into a toy *megillah*. Children can also make their own model *megillah* by illustrating the story on a long strip of paper such as computer paper that is then attached to a dowel stick or a paper-towel roll. Acting the story out for parents or younger children with puppets is also fun and in line with the Purim tradition of drama and masquerade. As children get older, the show may become more of a satire, or Purim *shpil*.

Puppet Ideas

● Very easy puppets can be made from paper lunch bags. Color or glue on features from construction paper or collage materials.

● Older children can make sock puppets by sewing on features from felt, buttons, yarn, pom-poms, fake fur, and fabric. "Googly eyes" from the dime store add a special touch. Features can also be attached with a parent-held glue gun.

● Make collage faces on paper plates and glue or tape on large ice-cream sticks available in craft stores and dime stores. Puppet bodies can be cut from construction paper and ice-cream sticks attached.

● Finger puppets can be made by cutting the fingers from cloth or rubber gloves and drawing faces on with permanent markers. Glue on hats from colored felt or yarn hair. Or decorate each finger of a garden glove as a different character from the Purim story.

● You can make a puppet stage from a cardboard carton or box with performing area cut out. Or perform from behind a table or chair back.

Mishloah Manot: Gifts of Food to Friends

This is another example of a traditional Jewish practice that was becoming forgotten outside all but Orthodox enclaves and is now making something of a comeback in the broader Jewish community. *Mishloah manot* (*Shalach Manos* in the Ashkenazic form) are gifts of food that, like the other practices of the day, recall the celebrations of the Jews of ancient Shushan, Persia, where the Purim story took place.

At least two kinds of ready-to-eat foods (that is, foods on which two different blessings would be said) are sent to at least one friend, although most families send *mishloah manot* to a number of friends. Usual foods consist of *hamantaschen*, cook ies, fruit, candy, nuts, juice, wine, and the like. The gift is usually sent in a decorated box, plate, or basket. Since the word *"mishloah"* implies something sent by messenger, it is customary to have the gifts "delivered" to the friends, usually by a child. This gives children a special role in the *mitzvah*.

Children can also participate in making and filling the *mishloah manot* containers. They will enjoy giving some of their own food gifts to friends and teachers as well as participating in the family giving. We've found it particularly rewarding to give *mishloah manot* to those who've never received them before.

Rather than just giving the *mishloah manot* to friends, add one recipient each year who may be somewhat isolated or lonely, such as an elderly person living alone or someone far from home. Taking your children, perhaps with some friends, dressed up in their Purim costumes and some *mishloah manot* to a nursing home can be a wonderful Purim *mitzvah*.

Mishloah Manot *Containers*

● The simplest can be made from sturdy paper plates. Decorate the rims with stickers, or glue on rick-rack or collage materials such as sequins or paper decorations. Or line with colored tissue paper or decorative napkins. Place the foods on the plate, then cover with colored or clear plastic wrap if desired, or wrap the whole thing in colored cellophane and tie on top with a bright ribbon.

● Alternately, inexpensive woven baskets can be purchased from a dime or crafts store. Again, line with napkins or tissue. You can weave a ribbon through the basket and tie in a bow. Or make your own baskets by attaching pipe-cleaner handles to berry baskets or through holes punched on either side of the rims of sturdy plastic disposable bowls (not Styrofoam; the handle will break through).

● Use any kind of clean, safe container, including coffee tins covered with adhesive paper, empty boxes from the craft shelf, colored paper bags that are used for gifts. In the interests of conservation, the best idea could be to save a variety of empty containers in advance and "recycle" them as *mishloah manot* dishes. Kids can help do the decorating and filling or adorn napkins with stickers to cover the goodies.

● Some Jewish gift shops carry ready-to-use *mishloah manot* boxes or bags.

Maot Purim

Moroccan Sephardim distributed gifts of money to the children on Purim. This was known as *Maot Purim*. I think it's a great way to give Hanukkah some competition.

The Content: Suggestions for Goodies

● *Hamantaschen*, cookies, slices of cake, *halvah*, or other sweets

● Fruits—fresh or dried (including miniboxes of raisins)

● Granola or dried fruit bars

● Small containers of juice, miniature kosher wine bottles

● Small bags of chips or pretzels, crackers, popcorn, nuts, trail mix made of dry cereal, dried fruit, nuts or seeds, carob or chocolate chips. Children can also make edible necklaces (cereal with holes strung on yarn for younger ones; add popcorn, dried fruits, mini-pretzels, and older kids can string on thick thread with a blunt darning needle). The recipients can then wear the necklaces as part of their Purim costumes.

● For the ambitious: miniature roll-size *hallahs*, mini-*kugel* portions baked in muffin tins.

Here is a *hamantaschen* recipe that children will enjoy making. It's particularly easy, since it uses a cake mix as a base; yet it won first place in our congregational *hamantaschen* bake-off!

Hutzpah Hamantaschen[11]

1 pkg. deluxe yellow cake mix (1 lb. 2.25 oz. package)
1 cup all-purpose flour
2 eggs
2 tablespoons water

hamantaschen filling (below)

With electric mixer, combine dry cake mix, flour, eggs, and water until well blended. Dough will be soft. Chill for 1 hour or more. On a lightly floured surface, roll out a quarter of the dough 1/8 inch thick. Cut into 2 1/2- to 3-inch circles.

In the center of each circle, place 1 teaspoon filling. Bring edges together to form a triangle, pinching seams together from top down to corners, leaving a small opening in center. Repeat with remaining dough, working with a quarter of the dough at a time.

Place on a lightly greased cookie sheet. Bake at 375°F for 6 minutes or until lightly browned. Remove and cool on rack. Makes about four dozen.

Selected *Hamantaschen* Fillings

Apricot-Pecan
1/2 cup dried apricots
1/2 cup firmly packed dark-brown sugar
1/2 cup water
1/2 cup chopped pecans
1 tablespoon lemon juice

In a pan, combine apricots with firmly packed dark-brown sugar, water, chopped pecans, and lemon juice. Bring to a boil over medium heat, stirring constantly. Continue cooking, stirring occasionally, until mixture is thick, about 8 minutes. Cool. Makes filling for approximately four dozen *hamantaschen*.

Prune Filling
1 cup mashed, cooked pitted prunes
3 tablespoons honey
2 teaspoons lemon juice

Mix together mashed fruit, honey, and lemon juice. Place a rounded teaspoonful of filling on center of each *hamantaschen* circle. Makes enough for two dozen *hamantaschen*.

Honey-nut Filling
2 pounds walnuts, finely chopped
1 pint honey
1/2 teaspoon cinnamon
grated rind of 1 lemon
1/2 teaspoon vanilla extract

Heat honey in saucepan over medium flame. Add nuts, cinnamon, vanilla extract, and lemon rind. Bring to a boil. Lower flame and cook slowly for about 5 minutes. Cool. Makes filling for approximately four dozen *hamantaschen*.

Children will also enjoy concocting their own original fillings from fruit preserves, a bit of lemon juice and rind, and some crushed dry cereal flakes. Nuts, chocolate chips, or dried fruits can also be added.

Gifts to the Needy: *Matanot La'Evyonim*

Gifts to the needy, *Matanot La'Evyonim*, also recall the Purim celebrations of the Jews of Shushan. At least a small amount of money is given to at least two individuals, or alternately to two charitable funds. This can also be accomplished by putting money in two *pushkes* or sending two *tzedakah* contributions. Even young children are encouraged to join in this *mitzvah* by putting some coins in the *tzedakah* box.

A rather elaborate *mishloah manot* including extra-nourishing foods that keep well could itself be a useful gift for someone on a limited income. The Rambam (Maimonides) wrote that "gifts to the needy" can include food as well as money. In either case, children can and usually should be involved in the giving.

Another Purim *tzedakah* custom is *mahatzit hashekel*, meaning half a *shekel* coin. The practice of each Israelite donating half a *shekel* to maintain the Temple in Jerusalem is mentioned three times in the book of Exodus. Today it is recalled in many synagogues by donating *tzedakah* money in the synagogue prior to the evening *megillah* reading.

In all the excitement and fun of Purim, taking a few moments to emphasize the practice of *Matanot La'Evyonim* teaches children that sharing one's joy is a Jewish value. We can't celebrate wholeheartedly without helping others as well. The nonsupernatural tone of the *megillah*, as well as the Purim, focuses on human interactions more than on rituals, highlighting the humanistic side of Judaism. They teach our children the importance of sharing food and friendship with other people.

The Festive Meal

The fourth Purim *mitzvah* is to enjoy a festive holiday meal, a *seudah* in Hebrew. Feasting, like the other *mitzvot* of the day, is prescribed in the Book of Esther.

The meal is held late in the afternoon. No special *kiddush* is recited, but a special prayer, *Al HaNissim*, thanking God for the Purim miracles, is added to *Birkat HaMazon*, the grace after meals (as well as to the daily synagogue services). The Purim *seudah* menu could be any festive dinner the family enjoys. *Hamantaschen* are often the dessert. For fun you could serve other triangular foods: soup with *kreplach* or maybe Sephardic-style *bourekas* (purchase frozen phyllo dough and fill as desired). We usually serve Moroccan *couscous* (the instant, packaged variety). It would also be in the Purim spirit to serve foods that look like something they aren't (scoop out melons and refill with sherbet of the melon's color) or with unusual ingredients of the sort featured in a magazine for April Fool's Day.

Although no formal *kiddush* is recited (some people do a kind of spoof *kiddush*) liquor or liqueur is often served at this meal. Indeed, beginning in talmudic days, Purim became one of the rare times when respectable Jews drank enough alcoholic beverages to become slightly tipsy. According to the Talmud, one drinks *Ad Delo Yada*—until one cannot distinguish clearly between "cursed be Haman" and "blessed be Mordechai." The rabbis said you should still exert moderation: Drink enough just to take a snooze! *Adloyada* has also become the name for the festive Purim parades held in modern Israel.

The prescribed use of alcohol in certain set situations—Purim, Passover, Simhat Torah—coupled with prescribed moderation most of the year (a modest amount at Shabbat *kiddush*) is believed by some to be among the reasons that in the past, Jews have been thought to have had a lower rate of alcoholism than the surrounding society. Alcohol was permitted—nothing to rebel against by drinking it—but not glorified. Jewish celebrations in the home and synagogue taught young people how to celebrate and enjoy life's pleasures, but in a climate of structured moderation, in a context of sanctification. Today, when Jews are more integrated into the general social mores (and perhaps a bit more open about acknowledging the limitations of positive stereotypes), we are coming to know that unfortunately we, too, are not immune to substance abuse. We have to be more sensitive to the dangers of alcohol as a drug and not to assume that "Jews don't drink."

Although Jewish law permits working on Purim, it is ideal to take at least part of the day off for the celebrations, including the leisurely meal. If that's not possible, at least try to have a festive family dinner. In most sectors of the American Jewish community, Purim is yet another celebration to be transplanted from the home (the festive meal) to the synagogue (carnivals). Especially if most of the Purim celebrations your children take part in are happening at the synagogue or school, the *seudah* will bring the holiday back home for them.

Children can be involved in the *seudah* by:

● Cooking or helping parents to cook.

● Making centerpieces or napkin rings. (Try crazy flowers: outline a child's hand on construction paper; cut out and decorate with glittery sequins; then staple onto pipe-cleaner "stems" that you insert into a modeling clay or florist's foam base cut to fit inside a small flower pot.)

● Decorating the room—perhaps with Purim pictures, balloons, streamers, masks, clown hats, or fish (the symbol of the Hebrew month of *Adar*).

● Inviting friends.

● Leading some of the singing or choosing background music.

● Performing a puppet show or other Purim *shpil* (see the following) after dinner.

● Helping to clean up!

The Purim *Shpil*

The tradition of the Purim *shpil*, or Purim play, dates back perhaps to the Middle Ages. It's traditional to present a parody or a somewhat farcical version of the Purim story. Even the *megillah* reading becomes an opportunity for dramatic interpretation. Puppets are also common at Purim time.

Nahafoch Hu (things were turned topsy-turvy), says the *megillah*, which well summarizes the spirit of Purim. On Purim even staid *yeshivah* students have free reign to parody their respected rabbis and teachers, while Israeli and American Jewish periodicals print satires and spoof important issues of the day. I recall while living in Israel that one year, just prior to Purim, I heard what I assumed was a tongue-in-cheek radio newscast reporting that Israel was about to change its currency to the *shekel*, a coin of biblical origin. Imagine my surprise when the report turned out to be true! But then again, there's a little bit of the Purim spirit every day, in Israel.

A home Purim shpil

For a home version, children and/or parents can do a "straight" or satirical Purim play or puppet show at the *seudah*. You might get to act out some fantasies! A family with older kids could produce a spoof family newsletter or mock announcements on the family bulletin board. Or compose some Purim *midrashim*—mock discourses on silly subjects by imaginary rabbis (for example, "Rabbi Simon Ben Noodnick's classical ruling on weeknight bedtimes"). For families (parents especially) with a very good sense of humor: Let family members role-play one another for a time. It could be enlightening.

A DERASHAH FOR PARENTS: COSTUMES AND ROLES

Often the Torah portion directly preceding Purim, unless Purim occurs in the Jewish leap-month of *Adar Sheni* (Second *Adar*), is *Tetsavah* (Exodus 27:20–30:10), a portion that is largely devoted to an elaborate description of the garments worn by Aaron, the *Cohen Gadol* (High Priest) and the other priests.

More than forty verses are given to a detailed explanation of the priestly clothing, including the robes, headpieces, and the High Priest's breastplate. The late Rabbi Pinchas Peli wrote in his book *Torah Today—A Renewed Encounter with Scripture*,[12] ". . . almost all commentators agree that the garments—and especially the detailed instructions for their production which were immortalized in the Torah—are not there merely as a manual for their makers, but are laden with mystical and symbolic meaning." Peli elaborates on the *ephod* and the breastplate, which he explains teach us that Aaron's wearing of these articles symbolized that even in his high position, his duty as a leader was to carry the burden of the Israelites' needs on his shoulders, as well as always feeling compassion for the people in his heart.

Peli also explains that clothing has played an important role in the Jewish tradition. Since Adam and Eve, clothing in the Bible and talmudic literature has signified dignity and civilization.

In today's multifaceted Jewish society, clothing is often used to make a symbolic statement about group affiliation or ideology. In the streets of Jerusalem, for example, insiders can often tell which religious, ethnic, or even political group a passerby adheres to merely by the shape of a hat or the style of clothing. Often, the only way to be accepted by a certain group is to adopt its style of dress.

On the one hand, it would seem that costume, and the roles it symbolizes and supports, is everything. And yet, but a few days later on Purim there is a *nahafoch hu*, a total reversal of things. On Purim we celebrate the absurdity and utter relativity of all costuming, of all roles. Everyone can wear a mask or costume, try on any new role. One can be a clown or a queen for the day. Children dress as wise rabbis, and the rabbi may be dressed as a science-fiction hero. In the Purim shpils of the day, nothing seems sacred, and everything is subject to mockery and jest. A Jew can become an Arab. A secularist can play a hasid. The Hebrew motto of the celebration is *Ad Delo Yada*, to celebrate until the usual sharp distinctions begin to blur. To take the idea to the extreme, one can note that in the *megillah*, even God goes into "hiding," behind a mask, as it were. God's name is never explicitly mentioned in the *megillah* of Esther.

All this has a direct bearing on parenting. On the one hand, our role as parent is everything. The Torah states and the Talmud and later commentators expound that a child must be taught to honor and respect his or her parents. For example, a child should never sit in a parent's chair or call a parent by her or his first name. Even as an adult, a child is not supposed to directly contradict a parent. This extreme respect is seen as the foundation of a strong Jewish society, the basis on which rests the continuity of our heritage from generation to generation.

This aspect of parenting can be summed up with the word *hinuch*, education of children, which carries connotations of providing discipline and also of dedicating the next generation to a sacred role.

"But on the other hand," as Tevye the dairyman was wont to say, things can never be quite so straightforward in Jewish thought. Yes, our role, our costume, our position as parents is everything. We are not our children's pals. But at the same time, roles are relative. Someday we may parent our parents; someday the little ones we parent may be caring for us like parents. A child may be more mature in some ways than a parent.

Even more, in the absolute sense of Purim, roles really have no meaning. Purim is sometimes referred to as *Yom KePurim*, a day like Yom Kippur! In the absolute sense of Yom Kippur, we are all as nothing before God. In the absolute sense of Purim, all of our precious roles and costumes are nothing at all. Who are we really, to call ourselves parents? Do we really know anything in comparison to the vast unknowns of the universe?

Sometimes a child comes to me in the night to be comforted, thinking that I am bigger and stronger, that I have no fears. Sometimes I wonder who is holding whom.

In the absolute sense of *Kippurim* and *Purim*, there is no hierarchy but that of God above all else. Yes, there are High Priests and there are queens, but their only real function is to represent the people as a whole. All else is artificial. In this sense, we do our duties as parents, fill our roles in the household, all the while knowing that we are but souls like our children. Jewish parenting forces us to confront the truths of our being, its total limitation and its boundless meaning. Then we face our children as soul to soul, as "I and Thou," in the philosophy of Martin Buber. We meet each other in pure relation, as two beings, two creatures of the same Creator.

For in Judaism every human relationship is ultimately another window to our relationship with the divine. Each moment of real relation to our children has the potential to bring us closer to the infinite.

That is why Purim is a sacred holiday, why the *midrash* has the *hutzpah* to say that when the Messiah comes at last and all the other festivals will be abolished, only Purim will remain forever.

This *derashah* is dedicated in remembrance of Rabbi Pinchas HaCohen Peli, may the memory of the righteous be a blessing.

26

THE SPRING HOLIDAYS

Warmth returns, the air fills with the scent of flowers. Children begin to shed coats and sweaters in favor of lighter, freer clothing and to run and play outdoors.

Nissan is the Hebrew month of spring, the first month of the year. It is a time for rebirth, for new freedom, a new outlook. Passover focuses our attention on the many meanings of freedom, even as it focuses our energies on our homes and families.

Passover is the beginning of a spiritual journey from the Exodus to Mount Sinai, where we will celebrate the giving of the Torah on Shavuot, which comes fifty days after Passover. In between the two, the seven weeks of counting the *Omer* will bring several special days that remind us of key turning points in Jewish history—particularly the dramatic events of our own century.

"Behold, the winter is past . . . the flowers appear on the earth . . ." (Song of Songs 2:11).

PASSOVER

Passover, or *Pesah* in Hebrew, is a major Jewish festival commemorating the Exodus of the Israelites from Egyptian bondage. Although it took place three thousand years ago, every Jew is enjoined by the tradition to see him or herself as one who actually came out of Egypt. And each is required to pass the lesson of freedom on to his or her children. Indeed, Passover might be called the didactic holiday. It's almost impossible to separate

"activities" from the holiday observances themselves, for the observances are largely designed to engage the entire family and to teach children in the home setting. The extensive preparations—cleaning the house, buying and preparing special holiday foods—all focus on the centrality of the home in Jewish life.

TRADITIONAL PASSOVER OBSERVANCES

Passover begins on the fifteenth day of the Hebrew month of *Nissan*. For eight days (seven days only in Israel and in liberal Jewish practice), Jews eat *matzah* rather than leavened foods, to remind us of the unrisen bread eaten by the Israelites during the Exodus. The holiday begins with the festive *seder* meal, which re-creates the drama of the Exodus and its lessons for the Jewish people. The first and last two days (first and last day only in Israel and in liberal practice) are *Yamim Tovim*, Holy Days (plural of *Yom Tov*), when one refrains from work in a way similar to a Sabbath. The intermediate days are known as *Hol HaMoed*, the weekdaylike days of the festival.

Hametz and *Matzah*

Hametz (leavened food) is prohibited for use during Passover (see Exodus 12:19). *Hametz* includes foods, drinks, and other products made from wheat, rye, barley, oats, millet, and derivatives of the same. Ashkenazic Jews and some Sephardic groups also customarily refrain from eating rice, peas, corn, and beans (*kitniyot*) and products made from them during Passover, because of their similarity to *hametz*.

Matzah is unleavened bread made from flour and water that is mixed and baked at very high temperatures in under eighteen minutes. This quick baking does not give the dough any time to rise. It is eaten during Passover instead of bread, in recollection of the unleavened bread eaten by the Jews as they fled Egypt in haste (Exodus 12:15). Some very traditional Jews customarily use *shemurah matzah*, *matzah* made from wheat that has been specially guarded from mixture with water prior to baking, especially at the *seder* itself. The earlier the "guarding" starts, the more select (and expensive) the resultant *matzah*. *Shemurah matzah* is often round and shaped by hand the old-fashioned way. If you live within field-trip distance of a traditional *matzah* bakery, call and ask if you can come observe. Chabad Lubavitch (a hasidic group) organizations in many communities hold a "model *matzah* bakery" where children can actually participate in making *matzah* the traditional way.

Today, a variety of special baked goods (made with *matzah* ground into a fine meal in place of flour) and other kosher-for-Pesah products are readily available from kosher stores and some supermarkets. Rabbinical certification of *Kasher lePesah*—"kosher for Passover" products—is indicated by special seals on the labels.

Preparations for Passover*

Cleaning the Home

"Behold, the winter is past, the rain is over and done. The flowers appear on the earth, the time of the singing has come, and the voice of the vacuum-cleaner is heard throughout the land. . . ."

In order to remove all traces of *hametz*, the home is thoroughly cleaned in preparation for Passover. Often a complete "spring cleaning" is done to the house (as well as the office, and the car) to remove lurking *hametz* crumbs. The biggest cleaning storm hits the areas most likely to harbor *hametz*, especially the kitchen, where all surfaces are cleaned and usually covered. Areas where actual cooking is done are *kashered* (made kosher) with boiling water or heat. Foods containing *hametz* and dishes used during the year are stored away, and different dishes are taken out for Passover use. Some-

---

*This is not intended as a halachic guide, but as a general overview of the traditional preparations for Passover. For more detailed information, see the Resource Guide, pp. 305, 348, and 353, for this section or consult a rabbi.

times the dishes can be *kashered* for Passover with boiling water, soaking, or by other methods.

Care for Others

In the midst of preparations that center on our homes and our personal lives, Judaism mandates that we consider others as well. As with the Purim gifts to the poor and the pre-Shabbat *tzedakah* donations, Passover has institutionalized kindness and care for others through two main concepts:

● *Maot hittin*: "Wheat money" is the special *tzedakah* contribution made prior to Pesah, to help needy Jews afford the necessary supplies for the festival. Many synagogues and Jewish Family Service organizations establish a fund for this purpose.

● *Kol Dichfin*: "All who are in need" are invited to the *seder* to share the meal with us. It is a beautiful *mitzvah* to invite extra guests to the *seder*, beyond family and friends. Again, synagogues and Jewish Family Service usually know of many people—service people, students, single parents, newcomers, elderly—who find it difficult or impossible to hold their own *seder* and would truly appreciate an invitation.

The line at the beginning of the *seder*, "all who are hungry, let them come and eat," has been expanded to become a rallying cry for organizations like Mazon and the American Jewish World Service, who use this opportunity to call upon Jews to share their bounty with others. Families can donate the cost of one (or more) guest at the *seder* to an organization that helps feed the hungry all over the world.

Mechirat Hametz (sale of *hametz*)

Since *Halachah* (traditional Jewish law) forbids the use of *hametz* that had been kept by a Jew over Pesah, those who have large amounts for personal or business use would suffer a serious financial loss each year. Besides that, even the minute amount adhering to dishes or forgotten in cupboards presents a problem, since even the slightest trace of *hametz* is forbidden.

Talmudic rabbis devised a way to rid oneself of "excess" *hametz* for the duration of the holiday, without incurring severe loss. Traditional Jews go to a rabbi and sign a paper giving him authority to act as their agent for "selling" their *hametz* to a non-Jew. They then seal the *hametz* away in closed cupboards for the entire holiday. The non-Jewish buyer enters into a contract with the rabbi on behalf of the community. The buyer puts down a token deposit, leaving a balance payable at the end of the holiday—but each year at holiday's end, he doesn't pay the balance and consequently forfeits the purchase. So, the *hametz* is legally in the non-Jew's possession for the entire holiday, but always ends up being restored to its original owners at holiday's end. In Israel, the *hametz* of the entire country is sold by the chief rabbinate to a certain Druze gentleman for the week! (Luckily, he's never decided to keep it after the holiday.)

Bedikat Hametz (the search for *hametz*)

A dramatic moment, especially appreciated by youngsters, is the search for *hametz* the evening before the *seder*. Traditionally, it is done by the light of a candle, while a wooden spoon and feather are used to sweep found crumbs into a paper bag. (You can sometimes even find little kits with candle, spoon, and feather; call an Orthodox synagogue and ask.) It is customary to hide ten (wrapped) pieces of bread so that *hametz* will definitely be found during the search. The blessing before searching for *hametz*:

Baruch Atah Adonai, Eloheinu Melech HaOlam, asher kidshanu bemitzvotav vitzivanu al bi'ur hametz.

Holy One of Blessing, Your presence fills creation; You have made us holy with commandments and bid us regarding the removal of *hametz*.

Biyur Hametz (burning the *hametz*)

Early in the morning the day of the *seder*, the *hametz* that was found during the search or left over from breakfast is disposed of by burning. Unless you live in an apartment building with an incinerator, a small fire can be made outside in a metal container such as a coffee can. (Obviously children should never be left alone with the fire.) *Bitul hametz*, a declaration of nullification of any overlooked *hametz* (found in the traditional *Haggadah*) is recited.

Fast of the Firstborn

The eve of Pesah is a traditional fast day for firstborn sons, in memory of the sparing of Israelite firstborn sons when the Egyptian firstborn were slain in the tenth plague. However, firstborn sons are allowed to break the fast for a religious meal, which many traditional synagogues hold on the day in honor of completing a unit of talmudic study.

Obsessive or Ingenious?

To Orthodox or other traditionally minded Jews, the preceding practices are unquestioned. The Passover preparations may be difficult, but their value is never doubted. But to Jews who don't identify with these traditional forms, the pre-Pesah orgy of cleaning, the seemingly obsessive process of "selling" the *hametz*, the searching for and burning the crumbs and then—as a last "just to be on the safe side" measure—reciting the *bitul hametz*, all may seem a bit excessive, if not downright compulsive.

However, as with other Jewish rituals, there are many layers of symbolism and meaning involved: educational, psychological, spiritual; so much so that I'd say it's worth doing *some* kind of Passover preparations, whether one is in the traditional camp or not. Many of Judaism's superficially "archaic" and "outdated" elements can turn out to be meaningful and educational processes where families draw closer to one another and to the Jewish heritage. I know a family who doesn't keep kosher all year, yet cleans the house for Pesah and produces a special set of kosher dishes and foods for the holiday. I don't think they're hypocritical. I think that they've made a decision that this is an important Jewish experience worth preserving and re-creating annually.

The educational value is paramount. This is "hands on" at its utmost. The Passover preparations, especially the somewhat theatrical moments like the candlelight search or burning the crumbs, create a living drama that can involve children more than a hundred Sunday school lessons on the subject can. Studies show that the Passover *seder* is one of the most widely observed Jewish rituals in the United States. House cleaning, changing the dishes, shopping for the special foods, participating in the holiday-eve rituals—each activity chosen can increase the impact of the upcoming *seder*. The key is to involve the children and the entire family, rather than to let it all fall solely on the wife and mother's shoulders.

The very drudgery itself can be part of the experience. My husband and I often satirically sing the song, *"Avadim Hayinu,"* "We Were Slaves," as the family cleans the house in the days before Passover. But educationally, that's the point. We identify more with the Hebrews when we've experienced a bit of "forced labor." Call it affective learning!

Psychologically, cleaning the house in the spring offers a chance to act out a sense of renewal in our lives. The physical cleaning concretizes the psychological process of ridding ourselves of slavery to old behaviors and attitudes in a necessary prelude to personal change and liberation.

The two great changes of season (in Israel) are the harbingers of personal, familial, and communal renewal. The Hebrew calender has two major new years—one at Rosh HaShanah, the other at Passover. In the preautumn month of *Elul* (through the Days of Awe) we do spiritual "housecleaning," wiping the slate of our behavior clean. In early spring, the physical preparations for Pesah signal a second season of renewal. But now the focus is especially on our homes and the family unit.

Spiritually, the *hametz* has been explained as symbolic of puffy human pride and ego, while the flat, simple *matzah* represents humble faith in God. The liberation of Pesah is really the freedom to serve God rather than a false taskmaster: "Let my people go, that they may serve me." We become free not for selfish purposes, but to live the life of a "holy nation."

As hands clean together and the house is transformed, spirits can awaken with the spring to new learning, new growth, new directions, and new opportunities to serve. Can we do this without the demanding physical *mitzvot*, the concrete rituals? Of course . . . sometimes, when we're inspired, when circumstances are right. The genius of Judaism is to institutionalize this chance for liberation into an annual process. Moreover, the traditional Passover preparations, followed by the *seder* and the holiday week, create a vehicle, a *kli*, for passing on important teachings to the next generation.

A Derashah for Parents: Hametz: A Lot of Hot Air

Before we can observe Passover, we must rid our house of *hametz*, all the fluffy leavened foods. Although a certain amount of drudgery is involved in the task, it is also often exhilarating to give the house a thorough cleaning, to throw out lots of old junk we don't really need.

The puffy *hametz* could symbolize all the "hot air" in our lives, all the overinflated business that takes up so much of our time and energy. Just as the crumbs of bread may often be found in every nook and cranny of the house, "crumbs" of overblown nonessentials may have invaded every facet of our lives.

Cleaning out *hametz* and subsisting on *matzah*—

the most basic food—gives us a chance to reflect on the essentials versus the extraneous parts of our lives. Are important things like the family crowded out by "hot air" tasks?

Sometimes we must clean out a lot of fluff, even to live on "the bread of bare basics," in order to be really liberated.

Finally, the *Seder*

The first two nights of Passover (first night only in Israel and in liberal Jewish practice) bring the *seder*, a ritual meal that reenacts the Exodus from Egypt through readings, songs, and symbolic foods. The word *seder* means an "order," or "program." The *seder* ritual is contained in the *Haggadah* (literally, "telling"), a classic of Jewish literature that has taken varied artistic and literary forms over the ages. Although many synagogues now feature communal *seders*, the *seder* is essentially a home ritual. The central element of the *seder* is "tell your child in that day." It's a didactic meal, and many aspects of it are especially designed to hold the interest of children.

Setting the **Seder Table**

In addition to the *Haggadot* and *matzahs*, the table contains a *seder* plate with the following symbolic foods: roasted lamb shankbone (commemorates the paschal sacrifice), roasted egg (commemorates the festival offering and the destruction of the Temple; the egg is associated with mourning and the life cycle), *karpas* (greenery such as parsley—green for spring, to be dipped in salt water for slaves' tears), *maror* (bitter herbs, usually horseradish—the bitterness of slavery), *haroset* (a sweet mixture of chopped fruit such as apples, nuts, and wine, resembling the mortar that the slaves used for building). There is also salt water for dipping, enough wine for four cups per person during the course of the *seder* (grape juice may be substituted), and pillows for reclining to dramatize our free status. Three ceremonial *matzot*, representing the Jewish groups of Cohen, Levi, and Israel, are in a special partitioned container or under a cover. A glass of wine for Elijah the Prophet, symbolic *seder* guest, is on the table.

The Order of the **Seder**

The order of the *seder* is traditionally recited in fifteen steps:

Kadesh—Sanctify	Recite the *Yom Tov kiddush*
U'rhatz—Wash	Hand washing without blessing
Karpas—Greens	Parsley or other greens dipped in salt water and eaten
Yahatz—Divide	Leader breaks middle *matzah* in pile of three; wraps larger piece in napkin and hides for *afikoman*
Magid—Recite	The centerpiece of the ceremony is the recitation of the Passover story
Rahatzah—Wash	Ritual hand washing with blessing
Motzi	Blessing for meal
Matzah	Blessing for the *mitzvah* of eating *matzah*
Maror—Bitter herbs	Bitter herbs are dipped in *haroset* and eaten
Korech—Combine	Bitter herbs and *matzah* are eaten together in Hillel the sage's "*matzah* sandwich"
Shulhan Orech—The meal	The meal is traditionally begun with an egg and salt water, symbol of mourning for the Temple/rebirth of spring
Tzafun—Hidden	Children search for the hidden *afikoman* and may demand a reward to turn it over to the *seder* leader before it is eaten as "dessert"
Barech—Bless	Blessing after meals and other prayers are recited
Hallel—Praise	*Hallel*, psalms of praise, are recited
Nirtzah—Accepted	The *seder* conclusion—the final words are "Next Year in Jerusalem!"

As pointed out by Ron Wolfson in *The Art of Jewish Living: The Passover Seder*,[1] the *seder* can also be seen as organized into "a talk feast in four acts": The Beginning, which includes *kiddush* and the early actions of the meal; The Tellings, four rabbinic accounts of the Exodus, which together comprise the *Maggid* section of the *seder*; The Feast, including blessings before and after eating; and Redemption, the final, climactic psalms and prayers of the *seder*.

HOME ACTIVITIES FOR PASSOVER

It's hardly necessary to create activities for Passover, since the traditional observances are already oriented toward family and children. The key is to involve the children as much as possible in the preparations and observance. Arts and crafts and cooking projects are also a natural for this holiday.

In addition, expanding on the *seder* is already a traditional notion for Passover. Each family can personalize the ceremonial meal in ways that are meaningful to them.

Crafts Ideas

A pillow to recline on: It's traditional to recline on pillows at the Passover *seder*, to demonstrate that we are no longer slaves but are free people. Children can decorate their own pillows, or even one for every guest, with holiday motifs (cups of wine, *seder* symbols, *matzah*) in advance of the holiday. Here are some suggestions:

● A paper pillow (good for young children): Make a pillow from a large white paper bag. Child decorates with crayons or washable markers. Child stuffs this "paper pillowcase" with scrunched-up newspaper (scrunching is fun) and then parent closes the bag, folding over, stapling, and covering the stapled edge with sturdy masking tape. The pillow can also be made from butcher paper folded over and stapled.

● Decorate a plain white pillowcase with paint crayons or fabric paints available in crafts stores. (Use over a pillow or stuff with folded towel.) Some crafts stores even sell plain white pillows to decorate.

● Tie-dye a pillowcase by knotting pieces of the case with rubber bands and dyeing according to instructions on packaged fabric dye.

● Draw in a simple line design of Passover symbols or scenes. Cover with cross-stitches. Older kids and teens who know embroidery can put their skills to use for more elaborate pillowcases. They can also sew their own pillows from fabric odds and ends by sewing three sides of two fabric squares together, reversing, stuffing, and then sewing the fourth side shut.

A Seder *Plate* (Kaarah)

Making a *seder* plate can be educational. Children can make a small *seder* plate for themselves, for the "children's table" at a family *seder*, at a very large *seder* for extra so that there is enough for all, or for a model or play *seder*. Some suggestions:

● Draw, or cut from construction paper and paste, the *seder* plate symbols (roast egg, shankbone, *haroset*—chopped nuts and fruits, *maror*—bitter herbs, green vegetables—some plates include both *karpas* [usually parsley] and *hazeret* [usually lettuce], some just the *karpas*) on a sturdy paper dinner plate. Cover carefully with a large piece of clear Contac® paper.

● Instead of drawing the items, glue muffin cups onto the paper plate. Write the Hebrew and/or English name of each item with markers next to the muffin cup.

● A more elaborate plate can be made by first attaching the center of the paper plate with a brad to an upside-down paper soup bowl.

● For a more permanent plate, purchase a kit to make a plastic plate. They are available at toy and crafts stores. You color a paper pattern as a *seder* plate with markers (no smudges or erasures allowed), mail it in to the company with a small fee, and your completed plate is returned to you in six to eight weeks. (If you can't get the supplies locally, write: "Small Fry" Plastic Manufacturing Co., P.O. Box 769045, Dallas, TX 75376-0945.)

● Older children and families with more advanced artistic skills, such as pottery, ceramic painting, or glass painting, can put them to use to make a more sophisticated product. Get an artist to teach an applicable workshop for your congregation or Jewish Community Center.

A Matzah *Cover*

Use some of the techniques for making a *hallah* cover (pp. 151–152) to make a *matzah* cover for Shabbat and *Yom Tov* meals. It can be decorated with holiday motifs and verses from the *Haggadah* in Hebrew or English. For an actual *matzah* case for the *seder* service you will have to sew three layers together, leaving openings for the three *matzahs* used.

A Matzah *Box*

Cover an 8"-square, 3"-deep box with Contac® paper. Glue Passover symbols around the box or decorate as desired. Use to hold *matzahs* on the table during Passover.

A *Bookmark for the* Haggadah

Children can make bookmarks for everyone at the *seder*:

● Cut strips of construction paper and draw on Passover motifs with crayons or washable markers, or cut out designs from old Passover cards or from magazines. For added sturdiness, cover with clear Contac® paper.

● Make from felt, decorated with glued-on felt cut-outs or sequins.

● Cut 1" × 6" strips from a manilla file folder. Mark a line with a brown marker 1" from the top, then decorate the resultant top square front and back with lines of brown dashes, to look like pieces of *matzah*.

Haggadah *Cover*

Cover your old paperback *Haggadahs* with construction paper or butcher paper that the children have decorated with Passover motifs and the words "Passover *Haggadah*" or "*Haggadah Shel Pesah*," in Hebrew. Tape in place or, for added strength, cover with clear Contac® paper, which can be extended a bit over the edges of the cover so that it actually holds the cover in place.

Make a Haggadah

For a more elaborate, educational project, help youngsters make a child's *Haggadah* for themselves or for a younger sibling with each page representing a stage in the *seder* (see the preceding). The parent could label each page in advance to simplify the process. For *Maggid*, the actual telling of the story, the child can illustrate scenes from the Passover story. Textured items can be glued on for added effect, such as purple cellophane for the wine, a piece of real *matzah* for the *afikoman*, and so forth. Staple the pages together and use construction paper for the covers. This project might take several sessions to complete.

Wine Cups

Decorate plain glasses with stained-glass paint and plastic "leading" (available from crafts shops), or decorate small disposable plastic cups or plastic wine glasses with stickers and/or paint pens. Avoid decorating near the rim. Kids can make one for every *seder* guest or just very small ones for the children. You could even decorate paper plates to place under the wine glasses, especially for the ritual of spilling the drops of wine for the Ten Plagues.

Decorated Bag for Hametz Search or for Afikoman

Children can decorate a paper bag, gift bag, or even a large envelope with holiday motifs. Use stickers, markers, crayons, and glue-on pictures. Label one to be used for the *hametz* crumbs during the search, another to hold the *afikoman*.

Decorations for the Seder Table

An arrangement of springtime flowers and greenery is just right for this "festival of spring." A collection of *Haggadahs* displayed on a side table would be nice for early arrivals to peruse.

Place Markers

Make place markers for the *seder* table. Decorate with Passover symbols. If possible, write the person's English and Hebrew name.

Involving Children in the Passover Preparations

It's hard to overemphasize that Passover should be a holiday with lots of build up. In some very traditional Jewish neighborhoods in North America, and especially in Israel among all, Passover is really felt as a holiday season. It's in the stores, the media, the atmosphere, in conversations with friends. In the weeks before the holiday, Israelis talk about how the cleaning is going (if observant), or what kind of *tiyul* (outing or short trip) they'll be taking for the holiday. People buy gifts for relatives and friends: food, new clothes, household items.

For those of us who don't live in that kind of atmosphere, it's possible to create a sense of excitement and anticipation at home by involving the whole family as much as possible in the holiday preparations. Parenting involves a certain amount of drama and artistry. Whatever your personal brand of Passover observance, your children can be involved. Here are some suggestions:

Clean the House Together

Clean to whatever degree is meaningful to you, and involve your children. (See Shabbat section, p. 149, for ideas on what children can do.) Even if you don't do it out of traditional motivations, you still have three thousand years of tradition behind you when you clean your house for Pesah! It creates a feeling that the home is really undergoing a transformation, that something of significance is coming up. And when the home receives attention, it's also a form of recognition that home is an important place.

But make it fun. Create an atmosphere by playing Passover music in the background, wearing T-shirts or aprons labeled, "Let My People Go!" with fabric paint, or having the kids make signs reading "Kosher for Pesah—*Hametz* Keep Out" for rooms that have been cleaned. Some kids find the kashering process of the various dishes fascinating, although one must be careful around children with some of the kashering processes that require heat. For added motivation, cap off the major cleaning sessions with a truly *hametz* treat.

Buy New Things for the Home and Family

Like Rosh HaShanah, Passover signifies a new beginning. Rosh HaShanah is the first of the year, but *Nissan*, the month in which Passover occurs, is also a new year, the first month of the year when we number the months. It's a good time for buying dishes and such, since they can be used first for Passover and then saved for each Passover or used during the year instead. Pesah is a good time for buying new spring clothes or at least token items so that everyone will feel she or he has something new for the holiday. Any house or garden items you might be purchasing anyway can gain more meaning if they are pronounced "bought in honor of Passover." When any of my in-laws' eleven children come home for the *seder*, they always bring a gift like household goods, Passover sweets, liqueur, or flowers. If you're a guest at a *seder*, your children could help pick out a gift for the hosts, and you could donate to *tzedakah* in their honor.

As with Hanukkah gifts, it's more meaningful if you first clean out the old and donate to *tzedakah*. This fits right in with Passover cleaning. And speaking of Hanukkah, associating gifts and new things with Rosh HaShanah, Purim, Pesah—*any other Jewish holiday*—will give that often overdone holiday some deserved competition!

New Foods

Take the children shopping for Passover foods. Let them help to put the *hametz* foods away for the holiday or to give to a food bank or to a needy non-Jew before the holiday.

Get the children involved in some cooking over the holidays. Cooking on Passover with those unusual, once-a-year ingredients seems more intriguing to children.

Search for Hametz

Whether or not you follow all the traditional practices surrounding the disposal of *hametz* (see the preceding) is obviously up to your own Jewish beliefs. I do think that trying out some of them can be fun and especially meaningful to children. In particular the search for *hametz* by candlelight can be a dramatic and memorable experience for children.

Seder Preparations

Let the children help cook for the *seder* (*matzah* balls and *haroset* are the big "messy" favorites), set the table, arrange the *seder* plate, make crafts items for the event.

Educational preparation is equally important. Take time before the holiday to learn about the festival. Read Passover stories (see Resource Guide, p. 353) at bedtime before and during the holiday. On *Shabbat HaGadol* ("The Great Shabbat," the one before Passover) afternoon, take some time with the kids to go over the *seder*, or at least ask questions (remember the *haroset* on the table? What does it mean?) to renew their memories from last year.

Learn to say the four questions, in Hebrew if possible. Older children can help prepare special additions to the *seder* (see the following).

Tzedakah

Apply the traditional Passover principles of *Ma'ot Hittin* and *Kol Dichfin* (see p. 230) to your family holiday preparations. Whenever Jews celebrate, it's incomplete unless we share our joy and further the process of redemption.

Model Seders and Play Seders

Model *seders* are often held by Jewish schools to familiarize the children with the *seder* program, songs, and prayers. If you're involved in planning one, you might consider it an opportunity to introduce more child-oriented material than you would ordinarily want to have at a family *seder*. Puppets, dramatics, children's holiday songs, decorations, even holiday videos are all possibilities (see Resource Guide for ideas). Although the model *seder* often amounts to a "rehearsal" for the real thing (and is often a showcase for the school), it would probably be more engaging to the children to introduce some variety.

A less formal variation of the preceding is a play *seder*. When my husband was a boy growing up in Morocco, Passover was one of the few times a year when the children were given toys—play dishes that they took to the olive grove for picnics and for playing house (perhaps to keep them out from underfoot during the holiday preparations). Passover was the picnic season for them. When my older girls were preschoolers they enjoyed making their own play *seder* on a small table with a small plastic *seder* plate, toy dishes, and *matzah*. Imaginative play is an age-appropriate way for preschoolers to learn and besides, it's fun!

Personalizing the Seder

The Passover *seder* is already one of the most widely observed rituals among American Jews. The other side of the coin is that very often the *seder* is little more than a nice family meal with a brief bit of ritual thrown in. That in itself has some value, but the *seder* has much more to offer. The *seder* is more than just a festive meal; at its best, it's an event that binds families, friends, generations together, an important vehicle for transmitting the Jewish heritage and values.

One problem that's been brought up in some Jewish publications is when one person wants to make the family *seder* more meaningful and substantial, but other members of the extended family resist. ("Since when did you become a rabbi?") That's when having two *seders* can come in handy!—one can keep harmony with the relatives one night, enjoying the family gathering on its own merits, then have a more "meaningful experience" with congenial friends the next. Or compromise by introducing new experiences to the family gradually. Ask them to prepare a part or write additions to the *seder*; you may be surprised how involved they get.

Recognize and Build on Ways in Which the Seder Involves Children

The *seder* is actually designed to hold children's interest. Imagine walking into a classroom to find that the room had been rearranged in a very unusual way. Odd objects are on the teacher's desk. In addition, you are promised a game at the end of the class if you pay attention to the lesson very closely. Wouldn't you pay attention and probably learn something?

That's exactly what's supposed to happen at the Passover *seder*, but it takes place at the dinner table rather than in the classroom. We don't just sit and tell the story of the Exodus, but rather arrange things artfully to provoke an affective educational experience. Things have been changed from a traditional meal (of the time the *Haggadah* was composed, of course) in order to provoke questions that became standardized in the text. The *seder* plate contains symbolic objects that are intented to provoke more questions. The search for the *afikoman* keeps children's interest, though the hour is late. And their fantasies and imaginations are engaged as they check to see if Elijah really did take a sip from the cup we put out for him.

If we just read through the *Haggadah* like an ordinary book, we may miss a lot of the educational potential. The *Haggadah* is meant to be a starting point for learning. The *Haggadah* teaches that we learn best by asking questions, including questions of our tradition.[2] "All who expand (on the core text) are to be praised," is the traditionally innovative approach stated in the *Haggadah* itself.

Take time to discuss the questions and symbol, a little beyond the text in the *Haggadah*. Add to the four questions. Let children and adults alike ask spontaneous questions. Try to have a well-annotated *Haggadah* or two, plus some Jewish reference books handy to help answer the more concrete, informational questions that arise. But remember that there are some philosophical questions that may be asked, even by children, that we each have to answer for ourselves.

Another way to enhance the children's experience is to provide them with children's *Haggadot* (see Resource Guide or make your own), if they aren't old enough to follow in the regular *Haggadah*. Help them follow the course of the service in their own books, which will parallel the adult version.

The story of the four children in the *Haggadah* points out another important educational principle, that we should teach each person at his or her level of understanding and moral development.

The Passover story has to be conveyed to children and adults in a way dependent on their backgrounds, personalities, and values. It's important to maintain the children's interest and introduce elements that engage them, without making the *seder* into another manifestation of "pediatric Judaism." Parents have to find a balance between maintaining children's interest and reducing the *seder* to a child's level. One solution for those who hold two *seders* might be to have one *seder* geared more toward the children's interest, the other at a more adult level. If the discussion gets too abstract, that might be a good time for the kids to go look for the *afikoman*. As they get older, though, they need to be required to participate more and more each year. An unspoken lesson is being taught at the *seder*—whether or not our religion is an important, interesting, adult concern that children can strive to *grow into*. (On the other hand, "out of the mouths of babes" adults may be challenged to grow, too. We should be open to learning from our children and the questions they ask, just as the great rabbis of old said they learned from their students.)

Take Time to Read the Haggadah in Advance

There are now many versions of the *Haggadah* with introductions and footnotes to enhance the reader's understanding. Assign parts in advance or simply take turns reading around the table, so that everyone can participate. (At one particularly memorable *seder*, we had guests from different countries who each informally translated the *Haggadah* selection into their native tongues as we went around the table!) At a smallish gathering, it can be nice to have several versions of the *Haggadah* for participants to refer to. If that would be unmanageable, look through several different versions in advance and choose selections to add to your standard *seder*. Photocopy the extra parts or simply compile a list of *Haggadah* names and page numbers and where each reading will be inserted. Some may wish to go further, compiling their own *Hagaddah* that is precisely tailored to their family's needs. People who do so are usually enthusiastic about the process and the results.

"Expand" on the *seder* by taking time to discuss it rather than just rushing through it.

Whoever Expands Is to Be Praised

"Whoever expands on the Passover telling is to be praised," said the Jewish sages. The Passover *seder* is a product of the rabbinic period, in the early centuries of the Common Era. Throughout the centuries, additions have been made, and especially in modern times the *seder* has been a forum for the expression of timely issues in Jewish life. For example, some of the secularly oriented *kibbutz* movements hold a *seder* that emphasizes human struggles and national concerns rather than a religious viewpoint. Literally hundreds of editions of the *Haggadah* have been published over the ages, many modern ones highlighting whatever variation of the Passover liberation theme that the authors felt most relevant. Some contemporary American *Haggadot* have been written to focus on not only particularistic Jewish concerns like the birth of Israel, Soviet Jewry, and the Holocaust, but on such diverse (and sometimes controversial) topics as civil rights, vegetarianism, feminism, humanism, concern for Central American peoples, concern for Palestinian rights alongside Israel's rights, and many others. Ecumenical groups have written *seders* combining Jewish and Christian concerns. Additional readings for the *seder* have proliferated on topics ranging from Soviet and Ethiopian Jewry to nuclear disarmament.

The family can research and photocopy special readings for insertion in the *seder*. It could be a selection from Natan Sharansky's autobiography or an account of the Warsaw Ghetto uprising, which took place around Passover, or any contemporary theme of freedom that has meaning for you. Various Jewish organizations distribute readings and prayers on current issues that you can include, or try composing your own. Your family can meet before the *seder* to plan one or more topics of concern that they wish to add to the *seder*. If you hold two *seders*, you might want to make one more traditional, one more innovative, or focusing on two different themes. (Consider the possibility that participants will disagree with the ideas you are presenting. That's actually quite positive— *if* the atmosphere is one where everyone agrees to disagree, to make it a "dispute for the sake of Heaven." But don't forget that *shelom bayit*, family peace, is also an important Jewish value.)

Be sure not to overlook the traditional content of the *seder* in the search for "relevance." Often, the most meaningful additions are those that draw on traditional forms for their power. Make any additions you create reinforce the classic *seder* elements; for example:

● Write new verses—on modern concerns—for the traditional songs (like *Dayenu* or *Had Gadya*, or even a new "psalm" of praise for the *Hallel*).

● Ask a fifth question. Ask four more questions.

● Add a fifth child to the "four children."

● Add a new cup of wine like Elijah's for—whom?

● An empty chair for—whom?

● Add a modern interpretation to an ancient *seder* symbol. What else could the *matzah*, *maror*, *karpas*, and the other symbols mean to you?

● Ask each individual or family who comes to the *seder* to "produce" one part of the service by explaining the historical background, teaching a tune, or writing a modern addition. You might especially try to invite at least one guest who can contribute a special perspective on freedom from his or her own life experiences. Additions to the *seder* could take the form of new tunes, illustrations of scenes from the *Haggadah*, dance, poetry, or other artistic expressions.

Creative Customs

Adapt Jewish customs from other countries and communities to enrich your *seder* experience. Various Sephardic communities have introduced a sense of extra drama to the *seder* by acting out parts of the story. Some groups carry a pack and dress for the flight from Egypt. Sometimes one person dresses as a pilgrim from Jerusalem, heralding the ultimate Redemption.

This type of drama can be introduced to your own home *seder* by a small gesture, such as walking around the house with staffs and bundles of *matzah* to symbolize the journey, or in a more dramatic way be having someone dress up as a character from the Passover story. One year a communal *seder* that we attended adapted this sort of drama by having someone make a "guest appearance" as Elijah the Prophet, complete with fake flowing white beard and long robe.

If your family is the adventuresome type, research some exotic Passover customs from far-off lands and see if they could be adapted for your *seder*. My Moroccan in-laws hold a vase of flowers over each person's head and circle it around as a sign of blessing while singing holiday songs at the beginning of the *seder*. Iranian Jews have an interesting custom of playfully swatting each other with leeks while reciting *Dayenu*. They tell me it's a real psychological release!

● *Don't Overlook Your Own Family Customs:* Even something as simple as the children's furtive peeks at Elijah's cup to see if he's had a sip of the wine becomes a custom. Treasures may be hiding under our own floorboards, as the hasidic tale at the beginning of this book has it. Interview older family members for Passover memories that may have become forgotten and that could be reintroduced to your family. Value and preserve the special memories and customs your family has imparted to the *seder*.

Passover as a Metaphor for Liberation

One tactic for appreciating the *seder*, described by Israeli Rabbi Adin Steinsaltz[3] and others, is to make the *seder* an inward experience by relating the themes of the exile and redemption to one's personal experiences. Rather than focusing exclusively on the outward aspects of redemption, we can experience the traditional themes as archetypes for human growth. Obviously, this is a rather sophisticated approach that can't be appreciated by young children, but it could be meaningful to adults as well as to adolescents who are much concerned with growing up and getting "free." Mature young people may be amenable to more abstract discussions on the meaning of freedom and enslavement. You could start by discussing (at the *seder* or at another time during the holiday) different forms of personal "enslavement": bondage to chemicals and addictions, different kinds of compulsions, slavery to possessions and materialism, unhealthy relationships, blind following of social pressures, and the like. Each kind of "enslavement" is a personal "Egypt," a *mitzrayyim*, the Hebrew word connoting a narrow, confining, limiting way of life.

On an even more sophisticated level, one can explore personal redemption using the national liberation of Passover as a model. The Passover liberation did not take place in one step, and neither does our personal liberation. As explained by Rabbi Pinchas HaCohen Peli (in *Torah Today*), there are four phases of redemption in the book of Exodus, traditionally symbolized by the four cups at the *seder*.[4] I believe that these four steps or phases can be adapted to personal redemption as well. Step one: "I will bring you out from their burden." Peli points out that the word for burden in Hebrew, *sivlut*, is related to the word for patience or tolerance. Just as the Hebrews lost their tolerance for slavery, a person must first lose patience with the particular enslaved situation she or he has accepted in the past. Step two: "I will deliver you from their bondage": a person must

take the concrete steps to free herself or himself from the dependency. This may involve learning, prayer and meditation, therapy, support groups, or whatever methods are best suited to the individual.

Step three: "I will redeem you with an outstretched arm." Peli links this step to the realization of national independence. On the personal level it could represent the growing realization of personal integrity and the glorious reclaiming of the long-neglected inner self. Finally, the fourth step: "I will take you as my own people." Personal redemption is complete only when we find our place in the context of community, of relationships to people, and to God.

But there is always an extra cup on the *seder* table. So too, there is another verse in Exodus that points to a fifth step down the road: "And I will bring you to the land which I promised. . . ." Even when the "problem" on which we have been so focused is solved, there is a long process of growth ahead, a wandering in an uncharted land, a receiving of new teachings and gifts along with challenges and temptations. And somewhere at the end of many years of learning is—not perfection—but rather our personal "promised land," a state of maturity that can be attained only after years of the inner journey.

A land of thorny hillsides and rocky soil may yet abound with milk and honey.

Additional Passover Ideas

Please Don't Eat the Hametz:

Although I grew up not observing *kashrut* at all, we still didn't eat *hametz* on Passover. I remember how shocked I was to realize as a teenager that some of my Jewish friends' families actually ate bread on Passover! I recall my late father telling us, while on a visit "back East" during the holiday one year, how he had forgone eating delicious New York breads—something he really missed in south Texas—even though some relatives actually chided him about this observance. If he were alive today, I would thank him for having the courage of his convictions, because I really think that this mild discipline once a year influenced our Jewish identities for life. The Torah describes the penalty for eating *hametz* on Passover (and other major lapses like not fasting on Yom Kippur) as *karet*, being "cut off," a vague expression that has attracted a lot of interpretation. Let me venture that a modern way to understand this might be that if we relinquish the most basic expressions of the Jewish religion (such as not eating *hametz* on Passover) we take the first step to cutting ourselves and our descendents off from our heritage and our people. But if we do uphold some basic standards of observance, we show our children that maintaining our heritage is worth a certain amount of effort and dedication.

Recipes for Passover

Haroset (for the *seder*):

Chop up apples, pecans or walnuts, and raisins as much as needed to make a mixture reminiscent of bricks or mortar. For younger kids, a parent can cut apple slices that the child then chops with a butter knife. Moisten with wine. Make extra for snacking.

Haroset around the World:

Each country has its own *haroset*, with such diverse ingredients as pomegranates and chestnut paste. For an enjoyable dimension to the *seder*, make several types of *haroset* from various countries from Jewish holiday cookbooks (see Resource Guide, pp. 309–310; *The Jewish Holiday Kitchen*, by Joan Nathan, features several international varieties).

Matzah Pizza:

This was my children's favorite preschool Passover lunch. Spread *matzah* thinly with seasoned tomato sauce or ketchup. Top with shredded cheese and heat briefly in oven until cheese is bubbly. To make mini-pizzas, use the small crackers as the bases.

Matzah Brie:

Beat the number of eggs you wish to serve with a bit of milk, salt, and pepper to taste. For each egg used, use one half of a *matzah*. Moisten the *matzah* briefly and then break into small pieces and add to the egg mixture, beating lightly. Scramble in a small amount of butter or margarine. Serve with cottage cheese and jelly, if desired.

Frozen Treats:

As a substitute for commercial frozen desserts during Passover, freeze any fruit, especially single grapes or bananas (the latter should be peeled and wrapped in freezer wrap first). Or mix one part pure juice concentrate with one part water and freeze in paper cups or Popsicle molds.

Judy's Matzah-Meal "Rolls":

These have a taste that appeals mainly to children; to me they taste like fried *matzah* balls. But they come in handy when the kids are craving bread, and they are messy fun to make, too.

Matzah-Meal "Rolls"

2 cups *matzah* meal
1 teaspoon salt
1 tablespoon sugar
1 cup water
1/2 cup oil
4 eggs

Boil the water with the oil. Combine 2 cups *matzah* meal with 1 teaspoon salt and 1 tablespoon sugar. Boil one cup of water with 1/2 cup of oil. Add to the *matzah* meal mixture and mix well. Beat in 4 eggs very well, one at a time. Let mix stand 15 minutes. With oiled hands, shape into rolls. Bake on a greased cookie sheet at 375°F for 50 minutes or until golden brown. When cool, split and fill with jelly, butter, or any sandwich filling. For whole wheat "rolls," grind whole-wheat *matzahs* into meal in a blender; use instead of plain *matzah* meal.

After Passover

Maimouna: Various Jewish communities around the world have held some sort of *hametz* party to celebrate the return to regular eating after the holiday. There are often traditional dishes served at these times. One such celebration with special meaning for our family is the Moroccan Jewish festival of Maimouna.

This North African Jewish festival, the evening and day after Passover, is held to be the *yartzeit* of the father of Maimonides. The word "Maimouna" also sounds like the Hebrew words for fortune (*mamon*) and faith (*emunah*). Yet another explanation is that it's related to the faith that the Messiah may come on the day after Passover. In my husband's boyhood home of Marrakesh, the holiday was observed when the final *Yom Tov* at the end of Passover ended at night. The Passover dishes were put away, and Arab neighbors brought dairy products and other dishes that the Jews customarily refrained from eating on the holiday. Special confections of dates, coconut, ground nuts, and such were prepared during Passover itself but not eaten until Maimouna. Sugar was not eaten on Passover, among the Jews of Marrakesh, apparently because they couldn't count on it being free of *hametz*. Only dates were used for sweetening until Maimouna. The table was covered with these elaborate sweets and the dairy products (milk and *leben*, soured milk), and a bowl of sugar. Families went from house to house, visiting and hosting one another. The festivities continued the next day with an outdoor picnic and cookout.

In Israel today, Maimouna has enjoyed a resurgence as a day of ethnic pride for the country's large Moroccan Jewish community. Of late, Israelis of many national backgrounds participate, and the holiday is said to represent "unity of the people." Ashkenazic and Sephardic Jews alike join in the day's many festivities, which include large picnics in public parks, with entertainment by costumed dancers and musicians from the Israel's diverse population.

Maimouna has a special meaning for our family because it's the day on which our eldest daughter was born. We gave her the middle name Emuna ("faith"—her entire name, Liora Emuna, thus means "faith is my light") in honor of the day.

After we put away our Passover things on the evening after the holiday, we set the table for a family Maimouna with flowers, candles, beverages (often all the wine and liqueur bottles in the house are displayed virtually as decorations and not drunk from—a good reflection on the traditional Jewish moderation with alcohol), sweets, snacks, and even a pitcher of milk and a bowl of sugar as in Morocco. We make a *Yom Tov Havdalah*, perhaps using spring flowers for the *besamim*. We wear Moroccan ethnic clothing and play and dance to recordings of Moroccan and Israeli music.

We have also sometimes held a special Maimouna celebration in our backyard on the holiday or the next Sunday afternoon, including a cookout, Moroccan-style salads, and other Middle Eastern foods. We dress in our Moroccan kaftans and encourage our guests to come in folk dress. We play Moroccan music, Israeli music, and especially albums like Shlomo Barr's "Natural Gathering" (known in Hebrew as *HaBreirah HaTivit*, which means "the natural choice"), which specialize in a unique brand of music that blends East and West. Jackie Elkayam is another contemporary Moroccan-Israeli singer whose music is available through larger Judaica shops in North America. To explain the holiday, we may photocopy some information to distribute. Over the doorway we

put a banner with the special Judeo-Arabic greeting of the day, *Tirbechu U'Tsa'adu*, which means "Triumph and Succeed."

A Maimouna celebration like ours could be adapted by other families. For an evening celebration, simply decorate the table with flowers, fruits, nuts, dried fruits, and sweets. The traditional Moroccan beverage, *Nana*, sweet mint tea made with regular tea, fresh mint leaves, and sugar, is considered essential. Play some appropriate Middle Eastern music. Unfortunately, really authentic Moroccan-Jewish music is hard to obtain in most places in North America. But your local Jewish gift shop and music companies listed on p. 313 probably have several recordings of Sephardic tunes. The uninhibited can try some free-form, Middle-Eastern-style dancing. For added effect, any kind of embroidered ethnic clothing or jewelry will do, if you don't have your own Moroccan kaftan and fez in the closet.

The major elements of a daytime Maimouna party are an outdoor environment, outdoor cooking, Middle-Eastern-style foods, and the same music and clothing mentioned.

Even if you don't have a Maimouna party, the family can adapt the idea by holding a post-Passover *hametz* party in the kitchen. After everyone helps put the Passover utensils away, enjoy your favorite *hametz* foods.

A *DERASHAH* FOR PARENTS: PARENTING AND FREEDOM

The Lord God of the Hebrews has sent me to you, saying, "Let my people go, that they may serve me in the wilderness."

—Exodus 7:16

As soon as there is some kind of ordering leading to a final goal—be it material, spiritual in a broad sense (knowledge, truth, love), or specifically religious (divine enlightenment, etc.)—one must judge each situation and each action, not according to its "comfortableness" but according to whether or not it is likely to bring one nearer to that goal. . . without inward strife there can be not life. . . what a man endures is not mere "punishment" being exacted of him as an individual but the way of all men. . . . Indeed, man's question should not be how to escape the perpetual struggle but rather what form to give it, at what level to wage it.

—Adin Steinsaltz[5]

God, I do not ask why I never suffer, but only whether my suffering be for your sake.
— Rabbi Levi Yitzhak of Berditchev[6]

"Let my people go," which began as Moses' call to Pharaoh, has become a classic rallying cry not only for Jews in different ages but for many oppressed peoples throughout history.

But there is a second, often overlooked, phrase to the verse: "that they may serve me." Freedom, in the Jewish ethos, is not a value unto itself, but is valued because it liberates people to serve God. The words for servitude, *avdut*, and service, *avodah*, have the same root in Hebrew and in English. The difference hinges on whom we are serving. True freedom, in the Jewish sense, is not mere license; it is the freedom to serve God and humanity with the best and highest in our collective and personal lives.

Being a parent can feel like slavery. Whether you're up all night with a sick baby, listening to the hundredth sibling conflict of the week, or helping an adolescent deal with peer pressures, it certainly doesn't feel like freedom. No sooner do the physical burdens of infancy lighten a bit, then the emotional load begins to increase. Jewish tradition has long recognized that parenting is full of struggle and sacrifice. "In sorrow you shall bear children" (Genesis 3:16) was interpreted by the rabbis to mean that raising children will inevitably entail *tzaar*, suffering.

It's a Sephardic family joke to refer to sleepless babies as *Paro*, Pharaoh, after the midrashic tradition that the Egyptian Pharaoh never slept. Indeed, caring for a fussy baby can feel like slavery to Pharaoh in Egypt!

One gives up a lot to be a parent. From the first day of morning sickness to the children's teen years and beyond, we sacrifice our comfort, time, money, energy, and most of all our freedom, in order to be a parent.

The Western worldview holds forth a promise, found in most child-rearing books today, that we can conquer the suffering. If only we learn the right techniques, our struggle will be overcome. But we soon find that each answer is but a step on our journey. We learn; things improve, but soon new challenges arrive.

The Eastern worldview is that it is our inner outlook that must change so that we achieve inner peace, inner wholeness. According to this view, once we realize that we and our children are part of the same universal whole, strife will cease. But

while Judaism values peace and inner growth; peace alone is never enough. "Peace is a vessel that can contain blessing, but it can also contain nothing at all, it can be an *empty* vessel," explains Israeli philosopher Rabbi Adin Steinsaltz.[7]

The Jewish view bridges East and West. Like the Western outlook, we want to eliminate needless suffering. We believe in redemption on the concrete, human level. But when we eliminate basic needs, we free energies to struggle with higher concerns. Human beings, by virtue of being alive, will always struggle in some way.

Like the Eastern outlook, our orientation is also inward. But we seek redemption, not Nirvana—the Promised Land, not the Garden of Eden. The Jewish goal is not so much wholeness as holiness.

The Jewish question is not how to avoid the struggles of life and of parenting, an impossible task, but at what level we choose to struggle. In the words of Steinsaltz, it is whether our struggles will be carried out "in the ash-heap" or "in the heavens."[8] "The guardian of Israel neither slumbers nor sleeps," says our liturgy—and neither does the false taskmaster, Pharaoh. The choice is not whether to serve, but whom to serve.

The crucial variable is a vision of what we are struggling for. By "vision," I don't mean a graven image of what our children should become to fulfill our own ego needs, but rather the goal of creating a family in which the highest in each individual, the *Tzelem Elohim*, or divinity in all of us, is free to develop and be expressed.

Sometimes parenting seems like drudgery, week after week. But we can transcend the drudgery when we come to perceive of parenting not as a burden but as a holy task. We have the power to decide that we are not slave laborers at all, but rather builders of the *Mikdash*, creators of dwelling places for holiness in this world. Indeed, the traditional Jewish ideal of a home is a *Mikdash Me'at*, a small Holy Temple.

The task is ongoing; we may forget the larger picture, get lost in the day-to-day toil again and again. (Like the yearly *seder*, where we taste liberation for a moment, but conclude by admitting, "Now we are slaves. Next year may we be free . . . next year in Jerusalem!" And even if we do make it to Jerusalem next year, we pray, "Next year in rebuilt Jerusalem.")

The rhythm of Jewish life is to constantly rediscover holiness in the everyday. We choose between *avdut*, servitude, or *avodah*, service, not just once, but over and over. Every action carries within it the seeds of its own redemption.

(If thinking in such spiritual terms as "serving God" is awkward, we can begin by asking, "Is my way of living and relating right now worthy of my highest self?" For that highest in us is the *Tzelem Elohim*, the "image of God." And we can ask if we are honoring that divine image in other human beings.)

Avodah means sacred service, but it also means *work* in Hebrew. The Jewish view is that meaning, holiness, redemption are achieved through work, struggle, action. Oftentimes, it is through mundane and repetitive action that we serve God. Especially in parenting, the great goals may be far away. The daily service may take place, as the verse in Exodus states, "in the wilderness," years before the "promised land" comes into view.

Home can be a *mitzrayim*, a limiting place, an Egypt where we serve in slavery—or a *merchavYah*—a great free, open space with God.

JOURNEY TO SINAI: THE *OMER* PERIOD

Pesah is over. The special dishes are put away. The *Haggadahs* lie forgotten in a drawer, and you're wondering what to do with all of that leftover *matzah*.

But Pesah was meant to be not an end, but a beginning.

The Exodus was only the first step in preparing the Jewish people for the receiving of the Torah, an experience that is commemorated by the next major Jewish holiday, Shavuot, which occurs seven weeks from the second day of Pesah.

When the ancient Temple stood in Jerusalem, Jews celebrated the start of the grain harvest by bringing an *omer* (measure or sheaf) of barley on the second day of Passover as an offering of thanksgiving (Leviticus 25:15–21). From that day, seven weeks were counted until Shavuot. Although the Temple no longer stands, the seven weeks are still literally counted day by day by many Jews, using a brief formula found in traditional prayer books. This is known as *Sefirat HaOmer*, counting the *Omer*. The seven-week period counted between Passover and Shavuot is therefore often referred to as the *Sefirah* period or just the *Omer*, for short.

TRADITIONAL *OMER* CUSTOMS

Among Orthodox and other traditional Jews, the *Sefirah*, or counting period, is a time of semi-mourning. Although the exact origins of this mourning period are somewhat obscure, it serves to recall the memory of persecutions against the Jews in the land of Israel during Roman times, and of later persecutions. On the agricultural level (and most Jewish holidays hearken back to our ties to the land), this is a tense season of waiting and anxiety for the coming wheat harvest. As during times of mourning, men do not shave, and people don't get haircuts. No weddings, parties with music, or other joyful events are held except during the miniholiday of Lag BaOmer, and among many also on Israel Independence Day and on Jerusalem Day. (In some traditions, the mourning is lifted after Lag BaOmer.)

The thirty-third day of the *Omer* is Lag BaOmer, a minor festival. Tradition holds that, during the days of Roman domination in second-century Israel, a plague during the *Omer* period killed many of Rabbi Akiva's followers: scholar-soldiers and potential leaders in the revolt against Rome. The plague may be an allusion to the Roman persecutions themselves. On the thirty-third day of the *Omer* (the Hebrew letter *lamed* [=30] + the letter *gimmel* [=3], or LaG in Hebrew numerology) the plague suddenly ceased. In addition, there is a tradition that the messianic Jewish general Bar Kochba's ill-fated revolt against the Roman occupation of Israel met with a temporary victory on this day.

All *Omer* mourning practices are lifted for Lag BaOmer. Because of the connection with Rabbi Akiva, this day became a scholars' and school children's holiday. Outdoor picnics and play with bows and arrows are customary on this day to commemorate that, during the Roman period, pupils of the legendary Rabbi Shimon Bar Yochai would take bows and arrows as if going hunting but really would travel to a cave in the hills to learn with their rabbi. More simply, the bows and arrows also recall the Jewish revolt, which Rabbi Akiva supported until his martyrdom at the hands of the Romans.

The most dramatic celebration in Israel is the Lag BaOmer pilgrimage to the mountainside grave of Rabbi Shimon Bar Yochai in Meron, near Safed in the upper Galilee. Lag BaOmer is observed as the anniversary of his death, a day he requested be celebrated with much rejoicing. Large crowds of people, especially Sephardic and hasidic Jews, spend the night singing and dancing around bonfires near the rabbi's tomb, and three-year-old boys traditionally receive their first haircut during the celebration.

It is striking that, while the traditional holidays of the *Omer* period relive the last day of an independent Jewish commonwealth in the land of Israel, there are also several modern observances in this period that commemorate the events surrounding the resurgence of Jewish sovereignty in our own day. The primary modern observances are Holocaust Remembrance Day (Yom HaShoah, which takes place on 27 *Nissan*) and Israel Independence Day (Yom HaAtzma'ut, 5 *Iyyar*). Yom HaAtzma'ut is preceded by one day by Yom Ha-Zikaron, Israel's memorial day for all fallen soldiers of pre- and post-independence. Jerusalem Day (Yom Yerushalayim), the anniversary of the reunification of Jerusalem during the Six-Day War in 1967, occurs on the twenty-eighth of the Hebrew month of *Iyyar*.

The final three days prior to Shavuot are known from the Torah as *shloshet yemei hagbalah*, "the three days of restrictions," in preparation for receiving the Torah. *Sefirah* prohibitions such as those against shaving and haircuts are lifted at this time.

HOME ACTIVITIES FOR THE PERIOD OF *SEFIRAT HAOMER*

By observing the daily *Omer* count, we link the two holidays of Passover and Shavuot with a sense of mounting anticipation. Just as we prepared physically for Pesah, we prepare spiritually for receiving the Torah on Shavuot and increase the holiday's meaning for our families. Even as we go about our daily business, on another level we are progressing to Sinai. It's a way of reinforcing the Jewish calendar and year in our lives, reminding ourselves that we have another rhythm besides the secular, that we also live in holy time.

In addition, by marking the special observances of the season, the *Omer* period can be an important opportunity for learning about Jewish history. Two pivotal periods in Jewish history are superimposed on each other during this time, so that as we relive the distant past we increase our awareness of the recent past—and of today's Jewish history in the making.

An *Omer* Calendar

The complete *Omer* ritual can be found in most traditional prayer books. It numbers the days (and weeks, after the first one) from Pesah to Shavuot. The count is generally recited each evening as the new Hebrew day begins at sunset, but anytime during the following day is allowable. However,

Halachah permits that one recite the *berachah* for the count only if one is really counting steadily, in other words, if not a day along the way has been forgotten. (Otherwise, it's recited without a blessing, or after answering *amen* to the blessing of a less forgetful worshiper!)

To Make an *Omer* Chart

On a piece of paper or poster board, draw seven hortizonal columns for the seven weeks of Pesah. Each column should display seven squares for the days of the week. Label the columns "one" to "seven" or with the Hebrew letters *"alef"* through *"zayin,"* beginning from the top (or the bottom, which would make it an ascent). Divide each column into seven squares. Starting with column one, number the squares one to forty-nine, increasing from right to left (the Hebrew way), in each column. If desired, also write in the Hebrew and English date in each square. The chart can be decorated any way, with any sort of appropriate seasonal motifs (*matzot*, sheaves, bows and arrows, Ten Commandments, Torah, harvest fruits of Israel). Or, if you make the chart go from top to bottom, you could outline the chart with a mountain outline representing Sinai. The columns can also be vertical, numbered as in Hebrew reading from right to left, with the squares numbered from top to bottom. You can highlight the special days, such as Lag BaOmer, with a highlighter pen or with a sticker. Check off each day as you count it (Shabbat can be checked off on Saturday night).

Alternatively, cut forty-nine small pieces of adhesive-bucked Velcro,® one for each day of the *Omer*. Stick on a poster board in one of the suggested calendar designs mentioned. Cut out a small felt design such as a Torah Tablets of the Covenant and attach the complementary side of the Velcro® to it as a backing. Stick it on the current day. Small children love the fun of moving the Velcro® piece, so you might want to make them a separate design that they are allowed to move around the chart as much as desired. The calendar is reusable (if you don't write in the English dates), although you may need to make a new marker piece if it gets worn out.

In chronological order on the Hebrew calendar, here are some suggestions for home activities and observances for the special days of the *Omer*.

Yom HaShoah

(Holocaust Remembrance Day, 27 *Nissan*, twelfth day of the *Omer* count): On or close to Yom HaShoah, Jewish synagogues and communities will have some kind of public observance, which often includes prayers, readings, testimony by survivors, and rituals such as lighting memorial candles. *Kaddish* is recited for the millions who have no one to say *kaddish* for them, whose day of death went unrecorded. It will probably take many years for this observance to evolve into a formal ritual to commemorate the bleakest chapter in Jewish—and human—history. It's important that children who are mature enough to understand the significance of the day attend community memorials with their parents. However, more people are calling for ways in which families can observe Yom HaShoah at home, since home observance is a key element in preserving a majority of Jewish memories and traditions.

At home some families light a *yartzeit* candle; some light six. Simply sitting quietly for a few moments after the lighting can give a time for contemplation and for the family to talk about their feelings if they wish. In Israel, sirens go off on Yom HaShoah morning, and everyone in the country gets up and stands in silent attention for a couple of minutes. Even cars stop on the highway and the drivers get out and stand beside their cars. You might also select together appropriate Holocaust-related books for family members to read around this time of year, and these could be discussed now, or short selections could be read aloud. There are now many age-appropriate materials available for children (See "Learning about the Holocaust," pp. 79–81 for more on the subject.)

Even if you do not observe the *Omer* restrictions, it is appropriate to preserve the spirit of this solemn day by refraining from playing music, attending or giving parties, buying new clothes, and other expressions of joy.

An Israeli friend told me that on each Yom HaShoah when he was in school, every child was given a small pin to wear that said simply, *Zachor* ("Remember"). He thought it would be an appropriate gesture for American Jews to adopt this practice. When anyone asked what it meant, we could tell them that this was a day for remembering those who perished in the Holocaust, for remembering what evils humanity is capable of, in order that they might never happen again.

You can make your own pins at home, as designed by my friend Gayle Fish. Glue a strip of black ribbon to a small strip of wood and glue a pin piece (from a crafts store) to the back of the wood. Write "*Zachor—Remember*," on the ribbon with a gold paint pen. You can trim with tiny bows of fine yellow ribbon.

Noted educator Rabbi Noah Golinkin proposed in an article in *Moment* magazine[9] that families have a home observance modeled on other Jewish holiday observances. But rather than holding it around a festive dining table, we should gather around a table bare of food. Children would learn about the Holocaust in their Jewish schools and the family would gather memorabilia and photographs of family members who perished in the Holocaust. (Arthur Kurzweil, in his book on Jewish genealogy, *From Generation to Generation*, points out that most Jewish families of European origin lost family members in the Holocaust. With a little research into our family trees we will find whole branches that stayed behind in Europe and were destroyed.)[10]

Golinkin goes on to suggest that the family light six candles and the parents offer personal meditations on the day, followed by a moment of silence. They could sing "*Ani Maamin*" ("I Believe") and songs of the Resistance movement, read selections from Holocaust literature, and discuss the Shoah and the Righteous Gentiles who risked their lives to save Jews. He also suggests discussing anti-Semitism and oppressed Jewry today. Golinkin encourages families to pledge $18 (= *Hai* = Life) to organizations that commemorate the Holocaust. (I would also encourage donations to Jewish educational organizations, for I believe that ignorance and apathy are Diaspora Jewry's greatest enemies today.)

Rabbi Golinkin suggests that Jews adopt the yellow tulip as a symbolic flower for Yom HaShoah. He wrote: "Tulips are the flower of Holland, and Holland, Denmark, Sweden and Bulgaria were the only countries that saved Jews during the Holocaust. Tulips flower in April, at the time of Yom HaShoah. They are a symbol of renewal and rebirth. Yellow gives pride to the yellow star that the Nazis forced Jews to wear." He suggests planting early- and late-blooming tulips in the fall with the children, since the twenty-seventh of *Nissan* may fall between April 7 and May 6 in different years. Six of the flowers would be placed beside the six lit candles on the table (by the youngest child in the family, Golinkin suggests).

As the years go by and there are fewer and fewer actual survivors of the Holocaust to bear witness, ritual and symbol will have to be developed to memorialize the period for future generations. Considering the importance of concrete symbols in Jewish continuity, Rabbi Golinkin's proposal deserves serious consideration. He hopes that the yellow tulips would symbolize that "there is goodness in every one of you. Let it flower. Let it be an eternal blessing."

We cannot undo the horrors of the Nazi era, but we can respond. One of the lessons of the Holocaust should be that we do not remain silent or passive in the face of injustice anywhere in the world. An especially appropriate *mitzvah* for Yom HaShoah day could be to take at least one positive action for human rights and *Pikuah Nefesh*, saving lives. For example, the family could learn as much as possible about a child who persished, and to honor that child's memory could redeem a living child from hunger, ignorance, and probable early death through an organization such as "Save the Children."

The family could honor the memory of an adult tortured and killed in the death camps by writing letters for Amnesty International on behalf of a political prisoner. A family who was denied sanctuary from Hitler's Germany in the 1930s could be remembered and honored by actions on behalf of Syrian Jews or of Central American refugees. The memory of a Righteous Gentile who saved Jewish lives could be honored by joining the Shalom Center and pledging to do one positive action a month for world peace.

Positive action can help youngsters psychologically as they deal with the feelings of powerlessness and fear often brought on by learning about the Holocaust. Moreover, positive ethical action is a classically Jewish way of responding to suffering. The Torah tells us: "Remember the heart of the stranger because you were strangers in the land of Egypt." Today the world is smaller, human life on this planet more endangered than ever. The Holocaust is not only our private wound, teaching us to never again be powerless victims, but, like Hiroshima, it is an eerie last *shofar* call warning all humanity of its potential for destruction. In today's world, we can't afford to let our terrible national suffering be turned wholly inward. Rather it must sensitize us to injustice and oppression, push us as Jews into the forefront of those who work to heal the world. We, more than any, must know the heart of the persecuted and oppressed everywhere, because we were victims in Nazi Europe.

Yom HaAtzma'ut: Israel Independence Day

(*Iyyar* 5, twentieth day of the *Omer* count): It's important to take children to attend communal celebrations of Israel's independence, to let them experience how we share our joy as a people over Israel's birth. In the Diaspora, local communities often sponsor parades, entertainment, Israeli folkdancing, parties, film festivals, walkathons, and the like. These may be on the fifth of *Iyyar*, the Hebrew date on which Israel was founded, or on the English date of May 14. There's plenty of opportunity for home celebration as well.

It's important to teach children about the birth of Israel through books, audio or video recordings, and discussion. Children today grow up with Israel as an accepted fact, and many American Jewish children lack the most basic understanding of the Jewish national history of exile and return.

In Israel, Memorial Day (Yom HaZikaron) comes the day before Yom HaAtzma'ut. Oddly, this day isn't usually observed by many American Jewish communities (although Yom HaAtzma'ut is), and in fact is often omitted from Jewish calendars made in the United States. Yet if it weren't for the sacrifices made by those who fought and those who died defending Israel—and their families—there wouldn't be an Israel to celebrate on Yom HaAtzma'ut. The nation wasn't delivered "on a silver tray," as Natan Alterman's famous poem by that title (often read on this day) says. At the least, Jewish families in the Diaspora as well as in Israel could take a few moments during the day to contemplate the many sacrifices made so that the State of Israel could exist. Our local Jewish community recently began holding a community-wide Yom HaZikaron service, followed by a joyful Yom HaAtzma'ut celebration. It was indeed a stirring experience.

In Israel, as on Yom HaShoah, a siren is sounded and a period of silence observed, but in this case it is immediately before the country changes to the party mood of Yom HaAtzma'ut—a rather jarring contrast. At home, your family might observe a similar moment of silence before dinner or before leaving to participate in a Yom HaAtzma'ut celebration. There are many Israeli poems and songs which deal with themes of war and loss that can be found in collections of Hebrew poetry, and a couple of these might be read. A memorial candle might be lit as well.

Many Jews are uncomfortable with the secular character of the usual Yom HaAtzma'ut celebrations. If returning to Jewish nationhood after two millennia is a turning point of sacred dimensions, then the Jewish religion should recognize it through religious observance. More and more, this is happening. Various groups and movements on all ranges of the religious spectrum have compiled services, guidelines, and suggested rituals for the day. These include a recitation of the *Hallel* and appropriate psalms, or Torah readings from the book of Deuteronomy, which deal with settling the Land of Israel. Prophetic selections such as Isaiah 10–12 and Ezekiel 37 may be read, and psalms such as Psalm 107 and Psalm 126 may be read or sung.

While each synagogue and religious movement has a responsibility to adopt appropriate observances for the day, the family at home should also be an active participant in Yom HaAtzma'ut observance. A *seudat mitzvah* (religiously mandated festive meal) could be served as it is on Purim and other festivals. Hebrew songs from Israel could be sung after the meal, and the *Birkat HaMazon* recited with "*Shir HaMaalot*" (Psalm 126), as for a festival.

Informal Ideas for Celebrating Yom HaAtzma'ut at home:

● Learn about the history of the return to Israel in modern times. Some have suggested the development of a Yom HaAtzma'ut *seder* with a *Haggadah* being formulated to teach the story of this modern-day redemption. Meanwhile, try some of the books and educational materials in the resource section, perhaps during an after-dinner program for the family, friends, or a *havurah*.

● Decorate with blue and white streamers and balloons. Cover a poster or bulletin board with pictures of Israel from magazines or travel brochures.

● Have a "birthday party" for Israel, serving foods such as *felafel*, *hummous*, and *tehina* on pita bread, orange juice, and a birthday cake with white-and-blue icing. Play Israeli music in the background.

● If your idea of Israeli music is limited to "*Hava Nagilah*," this is a good day to expand your horizons by playing recordings of contemporary Israeli music at home. Or rent videotapes of Israeli movies. (See the Resource Guide, pp. 313, 341.)

● Start or contribute to a savings account for family members to visit, study, or volunteer in Israel. Have a family meeting to look at books and/or travel videos about Israel and plan your first (second, third) trip—even if it seems as if it would take years to achieve. If you have preteen children, look over some brochures of high-school-age programs that they might be able to attend in Israel in a few years.

● Serve the day's meals Israeli style: an early, hearty breakfast including hard-boiled eggs, cheeses, good bread, tomato and cucumber salad, and olives, a full dinner (with soup please) at noon (you'll need a nap after lunch, the way Israelis do), and a light dairy snack (plain yogurt, a roll and jelly, more tomato and cucumber salad) around seven for supper. Don't forget tea and cake at ten and four. This should provide you with the energy to work several hours in the citrus orchards at a *kibbutz* or maybe just chase buses and *shlep* shopping bags up flights of stairs in Tel Aviv!

● Invite an Israeli family in your community or a friend who has spent time in Israel to tell your family about life in Israel (photos encouraged). Ask how they celebrated Yom HaAtzma'ut in Israel. Parades, fairs, and picnics in the Israel countryside are popular celebrations in Israel itself.

● Donate to a *tzedakah* organization in Israel that supports projects you believe in. Rabbi Irving Greenberg suggests investment in Israeli through Israel bonds or stocks in Israeli companies as the best *tzedakah* for the day because helping someone become self-supporting is the highest form of *tzedakah*. He adds that on a communal level, Yom HaAtzma'ut is an especially appropriate time for fairs that publicize Israeli goods and services.[11]

Lag BaOmer

Although some Jewish schools plan outdoor events for this "scholar's holiday," it's an ideal time to celebrate with an outing to a park or the country and a family picnic. If the holiday falls on a Sunday, you've got it made. Otherwise, if a half or whole day off can't be arranged, perhaps plan a picnic dinner. Children are often given (not too sharp) toy bows and arrows to play with in recollection of the Jewish soldier-scholars of Roman times. Jewish folk music and natural decorations at home would also be appropriate for the day's celebrations.

You can also adopt the favored Israeli custom for the eve of Lag BaOmer: a campfire with plenty of songs and refreshments. In Israel on the holiday eve, campsites, vacant fields, and even parking lots alongside apartment complexes are all dotted with the red glow of fires. The fire departments are on alert just as they are in the United States for Fourth of July fireworks! Toasted marshmallows are unknown, but roast potatoes and coffee brewed over the coals are fuel for hours of singing nostalgic Hebrew folksongs. Like the bows and arrows, the bonfires recall the precarious outdoor lives of those who strove to preserve the Torah and maintain a measure of Jewish independence at the nadir of the second Jewish commonwealth.

Rainbows

The rainbow is also a motif associated with Lag BaOmer, thanks to the great second-century rabbi, Shimon Bar Yohai, to whom authorship of the mystical *Zohar* is attributed. A *hilula*, or memorial festivity, is held at Bar Yohai's tomb at Meron in the Galilee on every Lag BaOmer. The rainbow, according to the story of the Flood in Genesis, is a sign that God will not destroy the world with flood again. A rainbow was thought to be God's way of saying, as it were, "I'm angry enough to send a flood again, but I'm keeping my covenant with humanity and not doing it." Bar Yohai was so consumately righteous, goes the legend, that not one rainbow appeared in the sky during his lifetime.

Possible ways to carry out the "rainbow" theme: art activities with rainbows, learning the colors of the spectrum, making "rainbows" with prisms, and learning the blessing upon seeing a rainbow (see p. 89).

Yom Yerushalayim: Jerusalem Day

Jerusalem Day (*Iyyar* 28, forty-third day of the *Omer* count) marks the reunification of Jerusalem during the Six-Day War in 1967. For the first time in roughly 1,900 years, a united Jerusalem was under Israeli sovereignty. Judaea and Samaria (the West Bank), the Golan Heights, Gaza Strip, and Sinai were gained as well. The latter was returned to Egypt as part of the peace treaty made a decade later with Egypt.

Yom Yerushalayim is the newest and latest of the important dates marked during the *Omer* period. From the War of Independence in 1948 until 1967, Jerusalem was a divided city, with Jordanian rule over the eastern half, and Israeli rule over the western side. Jews were not allowed to visit the Western Wall or any Jewish sites in the Arab-controlled portion of the city, nor for that matter anywhere in the Jordanian-controlled West Bank of the Jordan river. Only as a result of Israel's stunning victory in a war imposed by the surrounding Arab countries did Jews finally return to these holy sites and allow free access to members of other religions to their holy places.

In Jerusalem itself there are special public events marking the day. Hallel, psalms of praise, are recited in many synagogues worldwide. Other readings, such as Psalm 107, may be added to the service.

Yet the joy of Jerusalem Day is marred. The large Palestinian Arab population in the territories gained in the '67 war are unwilling subjects of Israeli military governance. The situation in these territories has grown increasingly tense and violent over the past few years. While recent peace talks bring hope, in the absence of a political solution to the Israeli-Palestinian conflict, some have found Jerusalem Day celebrations too ironic, presumptuous, or even immoral.

Nonetheless, while unmitigated celebration would be arrogant at the least, the Six-Day War and aftermath, in all its miraculous, glorious, triumphant yet difficult, dangerous, morally problematic, and sometimes tragic facets, is one of the key turning points in Jewish history. Ignoring it or seeing it as wholly negative seems an equally gross distortion. Jerusalem Day remains an important day for remembering and learning, for giving thanks for a great redemption, yet also for struggling with the incompleteness of that redemption and our responsibility in bringing it to full fruition.

At home, Jerusalem Day provides an opportunity to share your memories of the Six-Day War with your children. Many American Jewish young people know next to nothing about this key event in the recent Jewish past. How about your children? My most eye-opening experience as a Hebrew-school teacher came when I found out that my pupils had no idea that Jerusalem had ever been divided, that from 1948 to 1967 Jews had been expelled from the Jewish quarter of the Holy City, synagogues there were destroyed, cemeteries were desecrated, and holy places were unattainable. These sixth graders said they had never heard the song, "Jerusalem of Gold." (When *I* was in elementary school, the sixth-grade music class at my south Texas public school had performed the English version of that song at an assembly.) Suddenly I had aged a generation. I'd lived through a significant turning point in Jewish history that my pupils hadn't, and I was now the one to transmit a Jewish memory.

So, depending on your children's ages and ability to understand, make your memories of 1967 a dinnertime topic on this day. How did you feel then? How old were you? Prior to the victory, were you worried that Israel might literally be destroyed? Did you sense Israel's growing isolation or feel the potential for a second Holocaust? Were you old enough to understand what was happening? How did your parents feel and what did they do? (Ask them to share memories if possible. Ask an Israeli friend to share memories if at all possible.) How did you feel to see pictures of Israeli soldiers praying at the Western Wall? How do you feel today about the problems and moral dilemmas brought on in the wake of victory and the military rule subsequently established over an unwilling Arab population? What can we do to bring a more peaceful future? (Discuss the hopeful potential of the recent peace accord.)

Adapt an ancient Jewish custom by hanging a *mizrah* on an eastern wall of your home. The *mizrah*, meaning east, indicates the direction of Jerusalem, where Jews face when for prayer. (See pp. 23–24 for ideas on making a *mizrah*.)

Other ideas: Read a book about Jerusalem or the Six-Day War. Give *tzedakah* as a family to a charitable organization in Jerusalem. It would be appropriate to use this opportunity to support organizations that seek to bridge the widening gaps in Jerusalem between religious and secular Jews, between Arabs and Jews.

Shavuot—A Taste of Milk and Honey

Shavuot—a holiday of myriad dimensions. It's the lightning, thunder, and awesome solemnity of the Revelation at Sinai, the single most significant event in Jewish history. It's the quiet intensity of a group of Torah scholars learning deep into the night to reveal yet another layer of God's teaching.

Shavuot is also the full bloom of early summer, the radiance of harvest time in Israel—harvest of wheat and the first fruits of the season. It's the glorious pilgrimage to ancient Jerusalem and the joyful contemporary harvest celebrations in Israel's *kibbutzim* and *moshavim*.

It's an extraordinary story of love and devotion: "Whither thou goest, I will go . . . thy people will be my people, thy God my God" (Ruth 1:16). Ruth: eternal symbol of loyalty.

Shavuot is a synagogue alive with greenery. It's a mystical taste of milk and honey that has even been described as a "marriage" between God and the people Israel.

It also happens to be one of the most neglected Jewish holidays.

Studies have shown that the average American Jew is much more likely to light candles for Hanukkah than to participate in any kind of Shavuot observance. This despite the fact that Shavuot is a far more major holiday—one of the three pilgrimage festivals from the Torah (the other two are Passover and Sukkot).

Sociologist Marshall Sklare theorized that American Jews are most likely to observe occasional holidays and rituals which can be reinterpreted to reinforce our identities as modern Americans and do not isolate us socially.[12] The rituals most observed are child-centered and provide a Jewish alternative to a popular Christian celebration. The most popular observances that fulfill these criteria (or can be molded to do so) are Hanukkah and the Passover *seder*.

Shavuot doesn't really do any of these. It doesn't take place around Christmas or Easter, and proper observance means missing school and work (isolating and separating oneself from the general society). Shavuot's fairly abstract nature makes it hard to transform into a child-centered holiday, as has often, not necessarily for the best, been done with Hanukkah, Purim, and Simhat Torah. The Shavuot theme of receiving the Torah reinforces Jewish particularism rather than a universal ideal such as freedom or religious liberty.

In addition, Shavuot lacks distinctive symbols such as the *sukkah* or the *matzah*, which mark the other festivals. That makes it harder to anchor memories with it. Shavuot also usually occurs in early summer, when Jewish schools may have recessed for the summer vacation, so it might not be taught as intensively as the other major holidays. It tends to be a low priority for Jewish publishing. Plenty of not-terribly-assimilated American Jews have a hard time remembering what Shavuot commemorates.

So Shavuot tends to be downplayed. Yet without Shavuot observance, one misses out on a lot of important themes and lessons of the Jewish year. Moreover, without it the holiday cycle is drastically incomplete. It's significant that Shavuot is linked to Pesah by the counting of the *Omer*, for without Shavuot and the receiving of the Torah, the Pesah loses its essential conclusion. Without Shavuot, Sinai, and Torah, the dramatic liberation of Passover would merely have let us out into the desert.

Traditional Observances for Shavuot

Shavuot is a major Jewish festival commemorating the giving of the Torah at Mount Sinai. The word *shavuot* means "weeks," and the holiday falls on the fiftieth day following the seven-week *Sefirah* count begun on the second night of Passover (see previous section). The Hebrew date of Shavuot is the sixth and seventh of *Sivan*. Only one day is observed in liberal Jewish practice and in Israel. Shavuot is a *Yom Tov*, a day of refraining from work, similar to a Sabbath.

Shavuot is known by several other names, which reveal different facets of its character. *Hag Hakatzir*, "Festival of the (wheat) Harvest," and *Yom HaBikurim*, "Day of the First Fruits," highlight the ancient, agricultural side of the holiday, which has been revitalized in modern Israel. *Zeman Matan Torateinu*, "the season of the giving of our Torah," emphasizes the spiritual aspect, which became the dominant theme of the holiday as Judaism shifted from an agricultural society situated in Israel to a widespread and mobile Diaspora.

Because Shavuot is associated with the receiving of the Torah, it is a traditional day for studying Torah and for more recent ceremonies, such as Confirmation, which are connected to Torah study. Like the other biblical pilgrimage festivals, it has an agricultural aspect, the offerings of the wheat loaves and first fruits. This is usually marked by decorating the synagogue and home with flowers and greenery.

In the synagogue: the account of the revelation of the Ten Commandments is read from the Torah. In many synagogues, the congregation stands to mark the significance of the reading. On the second day of the Festival (or the first day when one day is observed), the biblical Book of Ruth is read. Since Ruth deals with the story of a righteous convert, the holiday has become an occasion when the Jewish press, particularly in Israel, carries interviews of Jews-by-choice.

Confirmation is a special service led by young people who are publicly confirming their commitment to Judaism as they complete the tenth grade of religious school in Reform and many Conservative synagogues. Often the class selects a theme and writes its own service. At one time this fairly modern ceremony was intended by the Reform movement to replace the *bar mitzvah* rite, partly because the latter was thought to be too premature a ceremony for entering "adulthood." Nowadays, many youngsters participate in both, and the Confirmation class is made into an intensive year involving Shabbat retreats and study of topics relevant to adolescents.

Other ceremonies connected with Torah learning are often held by Jewish schools at Shavuot time. Youngsters may be presented with their first *Humash* (Five Books of Torah) or *siddur* (prayer book). In previous generations, Shavuot was the time that a youngster's formal Jewish schooling began. It was the custom in many communities, both Ashkenazic and Sephardic, to spread honey over the letters of the Hebrew alphabet on a slate, which the child licked off as he learned them. (For suggestions on modern equivalents, see p. 278.)

Yizkor, a memorial service, is held (on the second day by those who observe both days). An appeal for the giving of *tzedakah* is customarily made at this time. The *Akdamut*, a medieval liturgical poem in the Aramaic language, is traditionally chanted prior to the Torah reading on the first day. The synagogue is customarily decorated with flowers and greenery.

Sephardic Jews recite a different liturgical poem "*Azharot*," which lists the 613 commandments found in the Torah. In addition, they read a symbolic *ketubah*, or marriage contract, describing the eternal covenant established this day between God and the people Israel.

In Israel, children wear garlands of flowers, and the agricultural aspect of the holiday is stressed with harvest pageants in the *kibbutz* and *moshav* settlements. Baskets of produce are decorated with flowers.

At home, Shavuot has no obvious external symbols to compare with the Passover *matzah* or the Sukkot booth. Basically, it is observed as a *Yom Tov*, with special meals, candles, and *kiddush*, and by refraining from work. Some people decorate the house with greenery and flowers to recall the spring harvest in Israel as well as the tradition that Mount Sinai bloomed with greenery as the Torah was given.

Traditional foods for Shavuot are dairy delights such as blintzes and cheesecake, which allude, among other things, to Israel, the "land flowing with milk and honey," as well as to the words of Torah that are likened, in the biblical words, to "milk and honey . . .under your tongue" (Song of Songs 4:11).

An exotic custom that is making a comeback in modern adaptation is the *Tikkun Leil Shavuot*, an all-night Torah study session the first night of Shavuot. The tradition of studying a wide selection of Jewish texts all Shavuot night was begun by medieval Jewish mystics. The traditional list of texts studied—eight to ten solid hours of them!—can be found in *How to Run a Traditional Jewish Household* by Blu Greenberg.[13] The more common adaptation is for synagogues to sponsor abridged sessions or late-night study groups on themes associated with the holiday.

Home Activities for Shavuot

Since Shavuot is a relatively short festival without complicated observances comparable to the Passover *seder* or the Sukkot booth, there is a fairly wide margin for creativity within the traditional practices. The family can expand on the traditional customs of decorations, study, and special foods.

Floral Decorations:

Please decorate for Shavuot! Hanukkah needs all the competition it can get. Seriously, shiny Hanukkah decorations are merely a decades-old response to Christmas, while Shavuot decorations go back at least several hundred years. The decorations of greenery, flowers, branches, and even small trees represent both the harvest element (the first fruit baskets were decorated with greenery) and the belief that the area around Mount Sinai was once a green pasture. In addition, there is a talmudic tradition that Shavuot is the day of judgment for fruit trees. Yet another tradition is that Moses was rescued in his basket of reeds on Shavuot. Fragrant spices and grasses have sometimes been scattered about synagogues to enhance the effect.

Roses were a traditional favorite because of a playful interpretation of the biblical verse, "And the decree (*dat*) was proclaimed in Shushan" (Esther 8:14), to mean that the Law was given with a rose (*shashan*). The mystical *Zohar* compares the nation of Israel to a rose as well: "As the rose among the thorns, so is my love among the maidens" (Song of Songs 2:2). This seems in line with the marriage motif of Shavuot. *Shavouslech*, papercut Shavuot decorations that depict roses, flowers, or Shavuot motifs, are another old European tradition that is being rediscovered. They were hung in windows facing the street.

Prior to the holiday, the family can collect or make decorations for the house. Bring in some house plants, purchase flowers and ferns—maybe even an ornamental fruit tree or two. If possible, gather garden or wildflowers and grasses (the latter for non-hay-fever sufferers!). Put vases around the house or adorn the mantlepiece. You could put some fresh potpourri in dishes around the house. Quality artificial flowers are a good supplement. Well-made silk flowers look fairly realistic and can be used year after year. You can also make your own as a family. Attractive paper flowers can be made from colorful tissue paper folded, rolled and "scrunched," and snipped into the shape of various types of flowers. Attach with florist's tape from a craft shop to purchased stems or green pipe cleaners.

Baskets:

For *bikurim* (first fruits) baskets, decorate wicker baskets with artificial or real flowers. A large one could serve as a centerpiece or buffet decoration. Small ones could be made from berry baskets or miniature wicker baskets and used at the table to hold fresh fruit for dessert. To add the other Shavuot theme of Torah, a miniature Torah or ark could be included in the display. A *siddur* or *Humash*, particularly one with an ornate cover, could be added. Or how about clay "Tablets of the Law"? (The ones I made in nursery school broke into bits, but Daddy consoled me by explaining that Moses broke his first set, too!)

To concretize Shavuot services for children, some synagogues provide small decorated *bikkurim* baskets of fruit and miniature Torah scrolls for the youngsters to carry when the Torah is taken from the ark for reading. We introduced this at our small congregation and found it a successful way to involve the children. They were also called up for a communal *aliyah* under an outstretched *tallit*, as at Simhat Torah.

Wreaths:

Children can make floral wreaths to wear, as the young children do in Israel. Use long-stemmed flowers such as daisies. Hold one flower horizontally and keep adding flowers one by one vertically behind the first blossom. Bend the stem of the latest flower added up around the horizontal stems to make a chain. When the chain is long enough to wear, tuck in the stem ends firmly. For more professional results, secure flower stems to florist's wire with florist's tape before making the wreath. A wreath of a flowering vine such as honeysuckle could also work. We have made easy floral wreaths out of cloth flowers with long flexible stems, which we simply twisted together into the right size and shape for a wreath. The children selected the flowers and I did most of the twisting, which took only a few minutes. A few strategically placed twist-ties are helpful for keeping it together.

Paper Cuts, Shavuoslech:

Paper cuts can be made from all kinds of colored paper: construction, tissue, origami paper, or wrapping paper. The cut paper could be plain black or white that is glued onto a piece of tissue paper. Younger children can stick to snowflake-type designs: Fold a thin sheet of paper several times and then snip a few triangles around the edges and unfold. Older children and adults can fold a sheet of paper in half and draw a design, realizing that it will come out exactly double when cut. Shade the areas to be cut out, then cut out using a pair of small, sharp scissors. Possible motifs include: tablets of the Ten Commandments, Torah crown, roses and flowers, sheaves of wheat, stars of David, pomegranates, or vines. Hang in a window to catch the light.

Ketubah:

Since the *ketubah*, or marriage contract, is connected with the Shavuot theme of marriage, you might make a point of showing yours to the children or displaying it during the holiday.

Dairy Foods

Besides the references to "milk and honey" mentioned here, dairy foods are also said to commemorate the giving of the *kashrut* laws in the Written and Oral Torah; when the Israelites first received the Torah they ate uncooked dairy meals until they could *kasher* their cooking utensils. Or could it be because the Hebrew word for milk, *halav*, equals forty in *gematria* (Hebrew numerology), the exact number of days that Moses spent on Mount Sinai?

You can make your *Yom Tov hallot* (see Shabbat section for recipe, p. 150) a bit sweeter than usual to commemorate the "honey" of the land of Israel. The loaves can be made a bit longer than usual to symbolize the Wave Offerings brought by the Jews to the Temple on this holiday.

Cheesecake, blintzes, *kugels*, cream cheese, *bourekas* (Sephardic filled leaf-dough pastry), and cheese-filled *kreplach* are all popular. How about ice-cream sundaes, lasagna, or cheese enchiladas?

1/2 pint sour cream
1 cup milk
1/2 stick margarine or butter
1/2 lb. cottage cheese
1/2 cup raisins
1 teaspoon vanilla
1/2 lb. broad noodles (cooked and drained)

Soften cream cheese. Cream all ingredients (except noodles) together in order. Add noodles. Place in a well-greased 9″ × 14″ pan. Bake for about 1 hour at 350°F. When cool, cut in squares.

Celia's Fruit Noodle
Kugel (Parve)[15]

1 large package broad noodles, boiled and drained
2 eggs, beaten well
1 small can crushed pineapple
1 can unsweetened sliced apples
1/2 cup maple-flavored syrup
1/2 cup white raisins
1 small can sliced peaches
1/2 cup brown sugar
1 stick margarine, melted
1 teaspoon grated lemon rind
crushed cornflakes, for topping

Add all of the ingredients except the cornflakes to the beaten eggs. Fruit may be diced, or left sliced. Place mixture in greased baking dish and top with crushed cornflakes. Bake for 1 1/2 hours in 325°F oven. Stir twice while baking.

Barbara's Dairy
Noodle *Kugel*[14]

1/4 lb. cream cheese
3 eggs
1/2 cup sugar

Mount Sinai
Cake

Seven-layer cakes representing the "Seven Heavens" (*Siete Cielos*) were customary in some Sephardic communities. An adaptation popular with children is the "Mount Sinai" cake. Buy or make a loaf-shaped pound cake. Cut in three pieces: small, medium, and large. Pile like blocks in a tower. Cover the "tower" with a generous amount of whipped cream. Garnish with strawberries and a few mint sprigs for "greenery" and decorate the top with a paper cut-out of the tablets of the Ten Commandments.

Torah Study

As already explained, the first night of Shavuot is the traditional time for *Tikkun Leil Shavuot*, a late-night, or all-night, study of Jewish texts and topics. Your congregation or *havurah* may wish to sponsor an appropriate study group for the holiday. Usually, it will be a few hours long rather than all night. The topic may be the Ten Commandments, the concept of covenant, or another theme of the holiday.

Children are thrilled at the chance to stay up late. Synagogue youth groups may (with a little encouragement from parents, perhaps) sponsor special nighttime study sessions for preteens and teens. If well planned and supervised, these can be quite successful.

Finding child care can be a big obstacle for parents who want to participate in study groups (you could volunteer to have a group meet in your living room, thus eliminating the need for a baby-sitter). My night-owl children have participated nicely in adult sessions. You might participate in a synagogue-sponsored event the first night of the holiday, then have a small family event the second night.

Younger children could simply be allowed up an hour or two past their regular bedtime in order to take part in the family Torah study. They might get ready for bed first, to avoid extra arguments if they get overtired. Keep any program simple: Perhaps tell the story of the giving of the Ten Commandments (adapt from Exodus 18–20; 24:1–18; 34:27–35; also Deuteronomy 5:1–6:9). A puppet show to depict the story of Ruth with puppets (which could be made by the children from paper bags before the holiday) is another possibility. We would first tell the story to familiarize the children, then prompt the action by whispering to them what comes next as we acted out the story together.

Older kids might enjoy a game of biblical charades, in which teams act out biblical stories that the others try to guess. There are a number of "read-aloud" stories about the giving of the Torah that can be found in books like *The Classic Tales* by

Ellen Frankel.[16] This could warm them up for a more serious discussion of the Ten Commandments.

Naturally, the event wouldn't be complete without some Shavuot dairy refreshments, such as make-your-own-sundaes, honey cookies in the shape of Hebrew letters, cheese and crackers, miniature cheesecakes, or minibagels and cream cheese. For a real "slumber party," let the kids sleep in the living room in sleeping bags.

Water Works

When spending Shavuot with my in-laws in Ashdod, Israel, I was introduced to a North African Jewish custom that is sure to appeal to any child: water-splashing. The holy Torah is compared to life-giving water, and anyone who steps outside in Ashdod on Shavuot is fair game for children who are eagerly waiting with pails and bucketsful of the Torah's metaphorical equivalent. (To be fair, I remember that they gave synagogue-goers time to get home before beginning to splash people.) My husband, Avraham, recalls that in Morocco the water games made their way even into the house. He remembers that being doused with water was very refreshing in the arid Saharan climate of Marrakech. But then, he was only twelve years old at the time!

This custom demonstrates the playful, joyful element in Sephardic observance. So if you're game and the weather is hot, how about a little water play in your backyard on Shavuot?

A SHAVUOT DERASHAH FOR PARENTS: GOD'S TORAH—THE MEANING IN THE SPACES

Of what is Torah composed? 'Black fire on white fire.' In this world we read the letters, which are black, and ignore the background, which is white. In reality we are living in a negative of the true print, and the letters in the 'Heavenly Torah' are formed of white light, while the spaces are black, as in a negative. What we see as letters—the darkness—are only vessels, while the shining white spaces contain the real meaning.

—Dr. Freema Gottlieb[17]

We are familiar with the *Sefer Torah* (Torah scroll) in the synagogue ark, written with ink on parchment. Its black letters are said to contain more wisdom than a person could hope to discover in a lifetime. But the Midrash tells us that the original Torah, God's Torah, the blueprint of the universe, was written with black fire on white fire (*Midrash Tehillim* 90:3). Moreover, as contemporary philospher and Jewish mystic Freema Gottlieb explains, God's Heavenly Torah shines forth in the white spaces between the black letters.

Together with our families, all of us are busy writing the stories of our lives. We want to make them full of meaning and significance, like the letters in a *Sefer Torah*. Yet every word we work so hard to inscribe in our book of life is only half of life's story. The *spaces* of life—the opportunities for being, for relating, for wondering and appreciating—often contain the real meaning. When we pause from life's busy enterprise and allow space for family, for love and for being together, we may find God's heavenly Torah shining through.

The *Midrash* (*Midrash Shir HaShirim* 1:4) tells that before God would give the Torah to Israel, he told Moses that the Jews would have to provide a guarantor who would prove that they would continue to observe the Torah. First the Israelites offered their holy ancestors, the Patriarchs and Matriarchs, as guarantors, but God would not accept it. Then they suggested the prophets, people of passion and vision. But still the Holy One was not satisfied with their suggestion.

Finally, the Israelites said that their children would be the guarantors that they would observe the Torah. And God accepted.

Often, having children makes us face the need to teach, to articulate our values, to stand for something. Striving to make Judaism come alive for our children may be the act that moves us to rediscover it for ourselves. As we transmit the Torah to another generation, we may confront it for the first time on an adult level. Thus, as we pass the Torah on to the next generation we may become even more receptive of it ourselves, motivated to learn more, to claim more of the riches of our heritage, the words of Torah that are richer than milk, sweeter than honey.

27

SUMMER: A SOMBER PERIOD IN THE JEWISH CALENDAR

Summer is a favorite time of year for most families. Therefore it may seem incongruous that between vacations, picnics, and trips to the swimming pool the Jewish tradition asks us to devote part of these seemingly carefree days to remembering some of the darkest events in Jewish history—but to remember them with faith and hope.

The days referred to are those surrounding Tisha B'Av, meaning simply the ninth day of the Hebrew month of *Av*. Tisha B'Av marks the day when both the Holy Temples in Jerusalem were destroyed, the first by the Babylonians in 586 B.C.E., and the second by the Romans in the year 70 of the Common Era. Later, numerous other destructions and persecutions of the Jewish people occurred on or near the ninth of *Av*, including the exile of the Jews from Spain in 1492 and the beginning of the deportation from the Warsaw ghetto to the Treblinka death camp in 1942.

THE TISHA B'AV PERIOD

Tisha B'Av is a complete (24-hour) fast day, like Yom Kippur. Adults (*bat* and *bar mitzvah* age and up) abstain from food, drink, bathing, use of cosmetics, wearing leather shoes, and having sexual relations.

Yet the mood of Tisha B'Av is different from that of Yom Kippur. The mood and ambience of Yom Kippur is one of purity, cleansing; everything in the synagogue is white. On Tisha B'Av the synagogue is dark and sad. In many places worshipers sit on the floor while the biblical book of Lamentations, which describes the horrors and desolation surrounding the destruction of the Temple, is read along with *kinot*, dirges and prayers of mourning. Even happy greetings are traditionally omitted on this day of sorrow, and Torah is not studied since its study brings joy.

Tisha B'Av, like many other significant Jewish days, does not stand alone. It is the climax of three weeks of semimourning and restriction on festivities to recall the period between the Babylonian breaching of the walls (the seventeenth of *Tammuz*, a minor, dawn-to-dusk fast) and the actual destruction of the First Temple.

The mood intensifies beginning with Rosh Hodesh *Av*. During these nine days, traditionally observant Jews abstain from eating meat and drinking wine (except on the Sabbath) and from other sources of comfort or recreation such as swimming and bathing for pleasure, home improvements, even laundering clothes (beyond absolute essentials).

On each Shabbat of the three weeks preceding Tisha B'Av, the *haftarah* portions deal with themes of retribution and destruction, particularly the week preceding Tisha B'Av, *Shabbat Hazon* (Sabbath of Prophecy), when the first chapter of Isaiah is read.

On the eve of Tisha B'Av, a large meal is eaten in the afternoon, but just prior to the fast there is the *seudah mafseket*, concluding meal, which consists of the mourner's foods of a hard-boiled egg and a piece of bread. Some actually dip the bread in ashes as an act of mourning for the Temple. Other Tisha B'Av customs center around enacting the mourning and exile through physical discomfort, such as sitting on the floor and sleeping without a pillow. These concrete rituals create a sort of psychodrama or affective education on Jewish history. They conjure up our difficult national memories of sieges, exiles, and deportations.

Yet the mood is not one of abject despair. There is mourning for the past, for the terrible *hurban* (destruction) that ended Jewish sovereignty for nearly nineteen centuries and scattered the Jewish people as wanderers without a homeland.

At the same time, Tisha B'Av signals an indestructible hope for the future of Judaism and humanity. One tradition holds that the Messiah will be born or make his appearance on this day, ushering in a new era of peace and wholeness for the world. (In a more abstract sense, this means that even amidst the worst destruction, the Jewish spirit finds seeds of redemption and rebirth.) The prayers of the afternoon service are more hopeful, the prayer shawl and *tefillin*, not worn in the morning, are donned again, and some communities, especially among the Sephardic Jews, have a custom of cleaning their homes on the afternoon of Tisha B'Av; for after all, the Messiah may arrive that day. . . .

On the night Tisha B'Av ends, the new moon is blessed, another symbol of renewal and emerging wholeness. (Mourning practices such as not eating meat are extended onto the tenth of *Av*, because much of the destruction of the Second Temple continued that day.)

In the weeks following Tisha B'Av, the mood changes. Life is renewed. Even the month itself is now called *Menahem Av—Av* the comforter. For the next seven weeks biblical prophecies of consolation are read as the *haftarah* selections, beginning with the hauntingly beautiful *Nahamu nahumu ami* ("Comfort ye, comfort ye My People"—Isaiah 40) read on *Shabbat Nahamu*, the next Sabbath after the ninth of *Av*. The *haftarah* readings foretell that the exiles will someday return to Israel, the wastelands will be rebuilt, the deserts will bloom again.

REDISCOVERING TISHA B'AV

Tisha B'Av seems foreign to many North American Jews. In fact, many outside the Orthodox world have scarcely heard of it, since it takes place in the summer and receives scant attention in many Hebrew schools. I never knew it existed until high school, when I went to a Jewish summer camp sponsored by the Reform movement. Fasting was "optional but encouraged," and as I recall we teens spent most of the day talking about food. Rather than the destruction of the ancient Temples, the programmatic emphasis of the day was on the Holocaust, the *hurban* of our own era.

The first time I went to the Western Wall in Jerusalem, the only remnant of the ancient Temple retaining wall, was on a Tisha B'Av. I fasted but found it hard to join in with those overcome by genuine weeping and mourning over an ancient cataclysm, as if denying that Jerusalem was being rebuilt, under Jewish sovereignty, right before our eyes.

Like many other Jews, I oppose a Jewish education that focuses exclusively on anti-Semitism and the negatives of Jewish history. However, the painful memories are also part of our experience and in many ways have enabled us to endure and rebuild.

As the years have passed, Tisha B'Av has come to mean more to me. Those who observe such a day seem to be those who feel a deeper, more profound tie to Jewish history. By this observance, they are linking themselves and their families and communities to the great chain of our past experience—and thus to our future as well.

Blu Greenberg and Rabbi Irving Greenberg, a married couple and each a leader and pathfinder in the American Jewish community, have each articulated the continued relevance of Tisha B'Av. In *How to Run a Traditional Jewish Household*,[1] Blu Greenberg uses moving personal memories to make the point that it is through the merit of all the generations before us who kept the memory of the national destruction alive that we are privileged to see the national rebirth in our lifetime. Our continued observance is a way of keeping the faith with our fathers and mothers.

Rabbi Greenberg, in *The Jewish Way—Living the Holidays*,[2] places Tisha B'Av in the context of an entire year cycle that, throughout the long years of Jewish exile, became ever more clouded with mourning. In our own day, with the rebirth of Israel and the reunification of Jerusalem under Jewish sovereignty, the cycle of the Jewish year shifts more and more to joyful rebirth. Yet again, it has been those rituals and seasons of national remembrance that kept the hope and will for redemption alive until our day.

Today, according to Rabbi Greenberg, we are not yet ready to give up Tisha B'Av, for the complete redemption of our people has not come. Yet it would show ingratitude to God for the miracles of the return to Israel and Jerusalem if we continued to mark Tisha B'Av with the same sort of pathos of generations past, when Jews could not even visit the Holy Land. The chief rabbinate of the Israeli Army and the Religious Kibbutz Movement have taken first steps in a new understanding of the day, by composing new prayers for the afternoon service of Tisha B'Av that reflect the 1967 reunification of Jerusalem.

Tisha B'Av has global implications as well. It occurs very close to Hiroshima day, an awful synchronicity that points toward the human potential for a *hurban* of all civilization. In addition, the accounts of death by starvation (during the Babylonian siege of Jerusalem) in the Book of Lamentations, particularly the deaths of children, would move any sensitive parent to action against hunger, poverty, and military victimization of the innocent.

Throughout our history, we Jews, with our national memories of devastating destructions—from Tisha B'Av to the Nazi genocide of this century—have used memory to turn pain toward healing and rebirth. If we can begin to teach the world to remember what destruction mankind is capable of, we can also begin to extend a lesson of hope and peace. Perhaps today we need the message of Tisha B'Av more than ever.

Suggestions for Tisha B'Av

● If you have not observed this period on the Jewish calendar in the past, consider gradually easing into it, perhaps by reading the special prophetic readings for the three Sabbaths before Tisha B'Av and reading the biblical Book of Lamentations on Tisha B'Av itself. It's important to follow up with the *haftarahs* of consolation in the seven weeks *after* the fast. Listings of the readings can be found in many Jewish calendars. Reading about Jewish history would seem an appropriate accompaniment. With older children, some of these selections could be read aloud. With younger children, you could orally summarize the story of the *hurban* (explaining also about the return to Israel in our day).

● Take children to your own or another synagogue where the day's rituals of sitting on the floor and reading the special prayers are observed. Explain in advance the significance of the readings and rituals and how people are expected to behave (serious, quiet, no cheerful greetings).

● The fast and accompanying rituals of mourning have an emotional, educational impact. Like Yom Kippur, children under *bat* or *bar mitzvah* age are not required to fast, although beginning a few years before, they may gradually be encouraged to give up snacks or fast for part of the day. Unlike Yom Kippur, even children would appropriately forgo desserts and other treats on Tisha B'Av.

● We observe the Sephardic custom of cleaning our home well on Tisha B'Av afternoon, a symbolic gesture of reorientation from destruction to redemption.

● Write special prayers for Tisha B'Av that reflect the return to Zion in our day. Write prayers for Jews and others who are not free and still suffer exilic oppression.

● As suggested, use the Tisha B'Av experience as a starting point for redemptive social-action activities focusing on peace, feeding the hungry, child welfare, or aiding Jews in Ethiopia or other lands of distress. Perhaps donate the money you would have spent on food on Tisha B'Av to help feed the hungry, through organizations such as Mazon or the American Jewish World Service.

Tu B'Av

A few days after Tisha B'Av is Tu B'Av, the fifteenth day of *Av*, a day associated in Jewish tradition with divine mercy and forgiveness. It became a day of dancing and courting in ancient Israel, and even today is considered a special day for weddings. Some Jews are now rediscovering it as a kind of Jewish sweethearts' day.

Ideas

● Tell family members some of the things that you love and appreciate about each person. Married couples can take some time to express love to their spouse, for that love is a wellspring of family life.

● Have a special family dinner, with flowers, candlelight, soft music, and a heart-shaped cake for dessert.

● Tu B'Av can also serve, in the words of Michael Strassfeld,[3] "as a transition from the mourning of Tisha B'Av to the renewal of *Elul* and the New Year." Some people begin from this day to end their letters with the blessing, "May you be inscribed for a good year."

Return us, Eternal, to You, and we will Return. Renew our days as of old.

—Lamentations 5:21

A *Derashah* for Parents: Broken but Holy

Tisha B'Av is only one of the ways in which Jews commemorate the destruction of the Temple. The sages decreed that there be many small brokennesses and incompletions in our lives to recall the loss: a glass broken at every Jewish wedding, a portion of every home left unfinished and undecorated.

These gestures also speak of the brokenness in every life. What marriage or home is forever whole and unblemished?

Jewish mysticism is replete with images of shattered vessels of holiness whose fragments we must gather up, of cords to the divine cut asunder but then retied. Our tradition tells us that the tablets that Moses broke were also sacred and were also preserved in the holy ark (Talmud, *Baba Batra* 14b).

Judaism affirms that our lives, homes, and relationships need not be perfect. Our very struggles toward *shelom bayit*, the wholeness and peace of our homes, are holy. We sanctify and celebrate the incomplete, broken, patched-up, and retied reality of our humanity.

The popular American notion that only a "perfect" marriage or relationship was worth saving is being replaced by the realization that perfection is an illusion, that commitment and relationship is worthy of continual efforts toward renewal and repair. In that sense the popular culture is catching on to an ancient Jewish notion.

That which is imperfect may also be holy.

VI

SPECIAL TIMES IN THE LIFE OF A YOUNG JEWISH FAMILY

The more high-tech and secularized our daily lives become, the more we seek "high touch" and spiritual meaning at our vulnerable moments of life passage and transition. This is one probable reason why the popularity of Jewish life-cycle ceremonies seems to be gaining, despite decreased observance in many other areas. At moments of crisis and change Jews still seek meaning and support in traditional (or "innovatively traditional") forms. Birth, puberty, marriage, death and mourning, and other significant life passages are times when many of us want to link our profoundly personal experience to a greater destiny or communal myth through the "artistic" media of ritual and symbolic action.

The present volume focuses not on these dramatic occasions, but on ordinary daily living and the recurrent experiences of the Jewish week and year. Although the natural tendency is to concentrate on major occasions such as a wedding or a birth, what counts in the long run is the quality and content of everyday life. It's of little use to have a grand baby naming or *bar mitzvah* if there is no continuity of Judaism afterward. Likewise, the most magnificent wedding counts for little if the marriage can't thrive amid ordinary day-to-day experiences.

Still, life-cycle events—whether once-in-a-lifetime or annual occurrences like birthdays—can be potent nexus points when we are open to new expressions of our Jewish heritage and new developments in our life orientation. For our children, life-cycle events can add to their "storehouse of Jewish memories" as treasured moments of Jewish living to be shared with generations yet to come. For the older child, a life-cycle event like a *bat* or *bar mitzvah*, when perceived as truly meaningful, has the potential for propelling the young person toward intensified Jewish identification and involvement.

28

IN THE BEGINNING

Beginnings are always difficult.

— Hebrew saying

Few things change our lives as does becoming parents. We are no longer a couple, but a family, with our personal stake in the future (of our family, community, the Jewish people, the nation, humanity) staring us solemnly back in the face. Our network of relationships, our feelings about our own parents, our past assumptions about goals and priorities—all are subject to change in ways both confusing and exciting.

A story goes that a couple went to a *rebbe* asking when a child's Jewish education should begin. He answers that if education does not mean mere formal instruction, but the entire orientation with which a person grows and perceives of the world, then education begins at birth. Indeed, the educational environment begins to be created long before birth with the attitudes and life orientation of the parents.

In that spirit, this look at the life-cycle events for a young family begins even before the birth itself, with the considerations and issues that are likely to arise prebirth.

FERTILITY ISSUES

A BIG FAMILY?

"Be fruitful and multiply" is the first *mitzvah* in the Torah, and raising a family has been a central Jewish value since Genesis. Our sources, liturgy, and even our mysticism are replete with familial metaphors. Judaism has no monastic orders or clerical vows of celibacy, for marrying and having children are viewed among life's greatest obligations and blessings. In traditional Jewish communities both in Eastern Europe and the Middle East, large families were admired and a family with only one or two children was viewed as abnormally small. Childlessness has been viewed as a tragedy since the first book of the Torah (see the following).

Yet today's American Jewish couples are marrying later and having smaller families, averaging less than two children per family. The effect is compounded by those who don't marry at all and those who intermarry without the spouse's conversion or an active commitment to a Jewish family. The most recent surveys indicate that American Jewry is in serious demographic decline, having fallen in population by more than 8 percent from the 1950s to 1990, a period during which the general United States population rose 65 percent.[1]

Raising Jewish children can have a special poignancy for Jews in this generation, since only a few decades ago over one million Jewish children were among the six million Jews—one third of the world Jewish population—brutally murdered by the Nazis. Each Jewish baby today represents our reaffirmation of the sanctity and preciousness of life, our faith in God and the future, and our commitment to rebuild the Jewish people in the wake of our greatest tragedy.

Despite the general trend toward smaller Jewish

families, there are many Jewish couples today who do choose to have that third or fourth child, because of traditional religious values as well as a desire to perpetuate the Jewish people in the wake of the Holocaust.

In Israel, where demographic considerations are felt more acutely and social norms are also more traditional and family-oriented, couples still tend to have an average of three children, and it's said to be fashionable today to have a fourth child when the others are nearly grown.[2] And most everywhere in the contemporary Jewish world, Orthodox and other traditionally minded families tend to have more children than the general Jewish population.

While social and economic issues appear to be the major factors in family-planning decisions, world population control is increasingly given as a reason to limit family size. It is undeniable that the human population boom is a worldwide crisis, particularly in developing nations. Yet Americans, who as a nation have a negative birthrate, each squander many times the natural resources of those in less-developed nations. As Jews, we must balance a strong commitment to conservation with a desire to perpetuate our people.

In general, a family's mind-set, and often their social set as well, has to become much less secular and a lot more traditionally "Jewish" before the perceived burdens (the virtual stigma, in some circles) of raising a large family are offset by the value and joy to be found in doing so. Having another child will require some trade-offs, even some sacrifices. But for many Jews it is still, more than ever, a very important way to "choose life."

FERTILITY PROBLEMS AND ADOPTION

Ironically, many Jews who want very much to have children, or to have more children, encounter fertility difficulties. The figure is perhaps as high as 20 percent.[3] Infertility is almost always a painful situation, so much the more so for couples with a strong Jewish orientation who dream of a house full of offspring.

Those who have never been through that emotional mill need to put forth a special effort to empathize. For my part, I recall the disappointment, worry, yearning, and secret jealousy of pregnant or new-mother friends (and strangers) that I experienced after having a miscarriage before my first child was born. Yet my situation was

easily resolved when I conceived again a few months later. It was nothing compared to the emotional, financial, and often physical stress and suffering endured by those who go through years of waiting, tests, and expensive and uncomfortable procedures, only to be disappointed again and again. If they are Jewish, this is frequently compounded by a residual stigma that is attached to "barrenness," and by the thoughtlessness of those who assume that childlessness is always a conscious choice. Thus, infertility is not an issue for the infertile alone, but should concern everyone in the Jewish community, if only to make us more sensitive in our interactions with others.

Adoption may be the answer for many couples with fertility problems. Jewish adoption goes back to Moses, whose "adoption" by Pharaoh's daughter made possible the eventual redemption of the Israelite nation. The Talmud recognizes that raising a child is like bearing a child (Sanhedrin 19b). Yet the Jewish idea of adoption is not entirely parallel to the American legal definition. A full discussion of the Jewish aspects of infertility, pregnancy loss, neonatal death, fertility treatments, and choosing, seeking, and living with adoption is beyond the scope of this book. See the Resource Guide, pp. 355–356, for some excellent publications on these vital topics.

Bearing children is easier than raising them.
—Yiddish folk saying

CONCEPTION: THE *MIKVEH*

The desire to conceive a child may prompt us to view our sexuality with a new reverence, as the miraculous capability to create new life. Planning the birth of a child has prompted some Jewish couples to use the *mikveh*, or ritual pool of "living waters," for the first time, or the first time since their wedding, as a uniquely Jewish sanctification of their sexual relationship. Although *mikveh* immersion is traditionally a woman's *mitzvah*, there's no reason why the husband shouldn't immerse as well. (In some Jewish communities, the groom as well as the bride immerses in preparation for the wedding, and some Jewish men immerse in the *mikveh* prior to Shabbat or Yom Kippur. Some communities have separate *mikveh* facilities for men and women, others have special hours for men.)

The *mikveh* is a ritual pool used for immersion at various transformational moments of Jewish life, including conversion. Among the many laws of constructing a *mikveh*, the water must come directly from a natural source, or be mingled with water from a natural source. The most common use of the *mikveh* is within the marital relationship. The Torah forbids sexual relations for a week following the onset of menstruation, and talmudic law extended the separation to a minimum of five days for menstruation plus a week of "white" days thereafter. Following the wife's immersion in the *mikveh*, the couple is sexually reunited.

This sexual discipline (known generally as *taharat hamishpahah*, "family purity") was historically among the major *mitzvot* observed by Jews. In many sectors of the Jewish community, *mikveh* practices fell out of favor in modern times, when they began to be viewed as a primitive and outmoded taboo superseded by modern hygiene. But ironically, at the same time that some women were pointing to the menstrual separation as another indication of oppressive patriarchy, other women were reclaiming the practice on equally "feminist" grounds, as a Jewish affirmation of feminine spirituality and sexuality.

Observance of *mikveh*, with the separation at menstruation and reunion around ovulation, creates a more feminine-centric sexuality for the couple. Their intimate life revolves around the wife's body rhythms. It may also heighten a couple's fertility awareness and the religious and Jewish dimensions of their family-planning decisions. The *mikveh* may be seen as symbolic of the womb and rebirth. In Jeremiah 17:13, God is metaphorically described as the "*Mikveh*" (which also means "Hope") of Israel, the "Source of living waters."

Overrationalization of the *mikveh* is traditionally discouraged, for like *kashrut*, it is a *hok*, an "ordinance" to be observed simply out of service to God. But the benefits of *mikveh* observance are widely appreciated by observant couples. *Mikveh* observance helps to extend the spiritual dimension into that most elemental aspect of life: one's sexuality. Many couples have found that the discipline of *mikveh* observance can help to stabilize a marriage by linking a most private relationship to something both ancient and transcendent. Also, as the talmudic sage Rabbi Meir noted, the periodic sexual abstinence helps to refresh a couple's sexual interest, transforming a wife of many years into a

"bride" each month (*Niddah* 31b). While dozens of books and articles offer "secrets" to revive a marriage-gone-dull, especially after the birth of children, *mikveh*-observant couples have a built-in monthly mechanism for renewing desire.

European Jewish women of centuries past composed special penitential prayers called *tehines* for important moments of life, including *mikveh* immersion. The modern woman who immerses in the *mikveh* in preparation for conception may wish to add a personal prayer or meditation (*kavanah*) after the traditional blessing (men do not say a blessing—except for conversion—but could certainly add personal meditations).

After birth, the Torah (Leviticus 12) specifies a minimum wait of seven days for postpartum bleeding plus an additional week if a male is born, an additional two weeks for a female, before immersion in a *mikveh*. Some scholars suggest that producing another potential life-bearer may explain the longer waiting period after a daughter's birth.[4] (Much longer waiting periods described in the same biblical chapter apply only when the Temple is standing.) At any rate, the postpartum flow generally lasts longer, and few obstetricians approve of sexual relations within the first three weeks after birth.

The drama of giving birth creates physical and emotional changes that still call out for religious recognition. Perhaps the first postpartum visit to the *mikveh* could become the time for a new ceremony or ritual in which women together would celebrate childbirth as a female life passage.

See the Resource Guide, p. 355, for books that provide more information on *mikveh* observance.

In addition to prayers at the *mikveh*, there are Jewish meditative techniques that can be used when hoping to conceive a child. Rabbi Aryeh Kaplan explains some of these talmudic and kabbalistic sexual practices and meditations in "Between Man and Woman," in *Jewish Meditation—A Practical Guide*.[5]

PREGNANCY AND CHILDBIRTH PREPARATION

There are a number of ways in which the pregnant couple can prepare to become a Jewish family, or to grow as a family. Childbirth classes can instill confidence and dispel anxiety. Likewise, attendance at LaLeche League meetings prior to delivery often proves very helpful for those wishing to breast-feed. A number of Jewish community centers and Jewish Family Service agencies have introduced the "Jewish childbirth class," which includes not only physical preparation for childbirth but an introduction to Jewish traditions regarding parenthood, birth, and the related ceremonies.

The issue of Jewish genetic diseases should be reviewed with one's physician, preferably prior to conception. As for any ethnic group, there are a number of such disorders prevalent in various Jewish gene pools. For example, genetic testing and counseling is recommended to prevent giving birth to a child with Tay-Sachs, an incurable neurological disorder for which one in thirty Ashkenazic Jews is a carrier.

Prenatal care and childbirth classes are only the beginning of preparing for the real changes that having a child will make in your life. Reading books that deal with the postpartum period can be helpful. For new parents, spending time with other people's babies and children is generally a good idea. Cook ahead, arrange for household help if you can, and get as many details of the new-baby festivities planned ahead as possible, so that after the birth, you will be able to devote your limited energies to baby and the rest of the family.

The growth of the child within often prompts a new introspection. Pregnancy can bring spiritual as well as physical growth! It is said that Jewish education begins before birth, with the spiritual values of the parents. This can be a time to meditate and pray more, to learn more about the Jewish heritage that you will soon be "teaching unto your children." If you're not already involved in a congregation or *havurah*, now is the time to find such a support system for creating your Jewish life as a family.

Among Turkish Sephardim, a special women's party is held in honor of a woman in her fifth or sixth month of pregnancy. A cloth is cut from which the baby's first swaddling clothes will be made, onto which sugar-coated almonds are placed as a sign of blessing. Some American Jewish women are creating new customs and rituals to celebrate pregnancy as a female life-cycle event. In *The Jewish Baby Book*, Anita Diamant describes several innovative celebrations in which blessings, songs, and gifts appropriate to birth and Jewish observance are shared with the mother-to-be.[6]

JEWISH ISSUES IN THE MATERNITY WARD

If you keep kosher, be sure to check about the availability of kosher food well in advance of a hospital or birthing-center stay.

The traditional or Orthodox mother-to-be will find that her rabbi should be able to answer any halachic questions (about *kashrut*, Shabbat observance) related to the hospital stay. Blu Greenberg, in *How To Run a Traditional Jewish Household*,[7] discusses "Shabbat contingency plans" and other concerns.

Remember that you need to say "no" to the often routine hospital circumcision of boys in order to have the proper ritual circumcision. I found it ironic that our son had a large note attached to his bassinet, reading, "No Circ." I penciled in underneath, "He's having a *brit*!"

PLAN AHEAD FOR NEWBORN CEREMONIES

Despite the thoroughness with which many couples plan for a baby, planning and preparing for the *brit* or naming ceremony is often neglected until after the birth, which adds stress to an already stressful period. Unless you're sure of the baby's sex, it helps to be prepared for either possibility: have the names and numbers of a couple of *mohalim* should you need to have a *brit milah*, and choose a girl's ceremony as well. Bake ahead and recruit friends and relatives to do so (or choose a kosher caterer); draw up a guest list with phone numbers. Those who want to send formal birth announcements can line up the calligrapher or printer in advance, too. Few first-time parents realize the sheer exhaustion that accompanies a birth and care of a newborn. The more done ahead, the more pleasant, rather than stressful, the baby ceremonies can be.

JEWISH STATUS

If you are an intermarried couple, pregnancy might be the time to examine your future children's Jewish status. "Who is a Jew?" has become a strained debate within the Jewish community. If the mother is Jewish, all Jewish groups will consider her children to be Jews. The Reform and Reconstructionist movements also recognize patrilineal descent (accepting the child of a Jewish father as Jewish if the child is raised in the Jewish faith); Conservative and Orthodox do not. The attitudes of lay people (and sometimes of individual rabbis and congregations) do not always match the official stances of the movement to which they subscribe; they may be either more flexible or less so.

If the mother converts before conceiving or while pregnant, the child is considered a Jew from birth. If not, or if the child is adopted, traditional Jewish groups will insist on conversion if the child is to be considered Jewish. Yet the more traditional groups do not always recognize the conversions performed by those denominations to their left, and that creates the potential for problems should the family or the child later decide to become more traditional or to live in Israel, where the Orthodox rabbinate holds sway over matters of personal status such as conversion, marriage, and divorce. More immediate problems might include situations in which an Orthodox *mohel* would not be willing to perform a *brit milah* for the baby, or a child might be expected to convert prior to becoming *bat* or *bar mitzvah* at a Conservative or Orthodox synagogue.

My purpose in touching on these potential problems is not to pressure or offend intermarried couples, but to suggest that they might consider any future difficulties their children may encounter if they are considered Jewish by some and not by others. I hope for the day when the Jewish community will find the solution to the "Who is a Jew" question by placing Jewish unity over denominational struggles. Until then, the answers remain highly individualized. Discussing the issue with others in similar situations, and with rabbis of differing outlooks, may help you to resolve how you will choose to deal with this issue.

Interestingly, there is no special ritual or blessing for women that marks the act of giving birth. (Could it be that if men had been giving birth all these centuries, some fantastic ritual would have developed by now?) Whatever, it has become a time to savor the miracle in a very personal, individual and intimate way.
— Blu Greenberg[8]

BIRTH RITUALS

Despite the traditional dearth of formal Jewish ceremonies related to birth, every culture has rituals of some sort that accompany labor and delivery. Our great-grandmothers had amulets and folk rituals that haven't totally disappeared in some traditional Jewish communities. Today, for most Jewish couples, the cultural rituals connected to childbirth are called "Lamaze methods" or "hospital procedures." In other words, they come from the general, secular culture and lack a religious dimension.

The miraculous and emotional moments of life's beginning can be more than secular. They can be accompanied with prayers, meditations, and perhaps even new rituals. Here are just a few such approaches that I have read about and tried for myself. [The NCJW Women's Resource Center in New York (see Resource Guide) has a variety of innovative rituals composed by women to celebrate female rites of passage such as birth.]

Kavanah, or meditative awareness, is helpful in understanding the physical and spiritual aspects of childbirth. The paradox is that giving birth, the most purposeful of goals, can often best be accomplished by left-brained meditative awareness: staying fully engrossed in the present moment and cooperating with one's body by the use of relaxation and breathing techniques (and massage or hand-squeezing, if helpful), enhanced by the spiritual dimension of meditation and prayer.

While I like to focus on my husband's eyes during active contractions, other laboring women have found it helpful to focus on a Hebrew calligraphic design. One mother wrote in a Jewish publication a few years back of the mandala-like Hebrew design she created while pregnant, focused on during delivery, and later hung in her daughter's room.

Auditory focuses are helpful as well. Some laboring Jewish couples have used soothing Jewish folk music as background music for labor. It's a good idea to keep the tapes in your hospital room after delivery; they can provide a welcome alternative to cable television during nursing. A woman whom I met at a conference of Jewish educators told me how she meditated while in labor on the Hebrew biblical verses: "Open for me the gates of righteousness, I will come through them and praise the Eternal/This is the gate of the Eternal, the righteous shall enter through it" (Psalm 118:19–20). I found this meditation very helpful myself, focusing on it during contractions and visualizing how every contraction was opening the "gate" of the cervix in preparation for birth.

Saying prayers and reading psalms are two venerable Jewish approaches to facing the drama of labor and deliver. As I was waiting to be admitted to the maternity ward of Hadassah Hospital on Mount Scopus, Jerusalem, to give birth to my second child, I was pleased to find that the lobby held several copies of the Book of Psalms, a touch of Jewish spirituality so integral to this place of healing in the Holy City. Eagerly, I picked up a copy; opening it at random, my eyes spontaneously alighted on these timeless words of comfort: "Trembling took hold of them there, pangs as of a woman in travail!" (Psalm 48:7). I had to laugh; so much for the solace of spirituality!

By contrast, when I was in labor with my fourth child, I opened up my husband's little book of *Tehillim* (Psalms) and discovered the following: "Bless the Eternal, O my soul; and all that is within me, bless God's holy name!" (Psalm 103:1). That proved a very meaningful verse for childbirth meditation and praying the rest of that Psalm was comforting and inspiring.

European Jewish women of centuries past composed *tehines*, or penitential prayers, to ask for God's grace and protection at times such as their own labor, or for a friend or relative in labor. They would use the name of the laboring woman as "daughter of" her mother's name, calling upon God in the names of the memories of righteous women and female prophets of the Bible to help the one giving birth, to make the newborn child a righteous person who would merit to see the true Redemption. However, to modern ears, these prayers have an antiquated and often, Matriarchs aside, a decidedly antifeminist tone.[9] Contemporary couples might wish to compose their own personal prayers for themselves or for expectant friends—or you might just find you want to pray spontaneously!

That Books of Psalms in the lobby of Hadassah's labor ward are evidence that Jews have always turned to God at difficult and wonderful times such as childbirth. The metaphors we employ for God in contemporary *tehines* might be "Deliverer," "Healer," "Opener of Gates," "Freer of captives," "The Merciful One" (*HaRahaman*—the word is related to *rehem*, "womb"). "She Who Dwells Within" (*Shechinah*), which represents the feminine aspect of God in kabbalistic tradition, is linked to Mother, and to Inner Understanding or *Binah*, which is associated with "pregnancy" in the kabbalistic schema. (The word "metaphor" signals our merely human attempts to imagine and express the ineffable [see "Talking about God with Our Children," pp. 86–87].)

It is traditional to recite the following prayer after a safe delivery or upon receiving the good tidings of a birth:

Baruch Atah Adonai, Eloheinu Melech HaOlam, HaTov veHaMeitiv.

Holy One of Blessing, Your Presence fills Creation, You are good and do good.

The Reconstructionist movement has introduced a new blessing, based on traditional verses, to be recited upon holding one's newborn child for the first time. My husband and I read it at the birth of our fifth child. It can be found in *Kol Haneshamah Shirim U'vrachot: Songs, Blessings and Rituals for the Home.*[10]

Birkat HaGomel, the prayer of thanksgiving for deliverance from danger, is to be recited after birth in the presence of a *minyan*. It may be said at the *brit* or naming ceremony or at services (depending on your synagogue) by the mother herself, or by her husband on her behalf at any regular service after the delivery:

Baruch Atah Adonai, Eloheinu Melech HaOlam, HaGomel lehayevim tovot, asher gemalani kol tov.

Holy One of Blessing, Your Presence fills Creation, bestowing goodness on the undeserving, granting me kindness.

Those present respond: "May the One who granted you kindness deal kindly with you always."

WHAT ONLY BECOMING A MOTHER COULD TEACH ME ABOUT GOD

Among God's many names is *HaRahaman*, The Merciful One. The name comes from the root word, meaning "womb." Becoming a mother, carrying children in my womb, has taught me another way to apprehend God.

To the baby in the mother's womb, mother is All. The baby lives and exists because of mother, surrounded by mother, nourished by mother. No two beings could be closer.

And yet the baby, while in the womb, is not aware of who the mother is at all.

To the mother, no one could be closer than the

baby inside her. She carries the child within her, feels its every move, knows that child more intimately than she could know anyone.

And yet, she doesn't yet know the child at all, not even the most basic information about it: its gender, the color of its hair or eyes.

So it is with my relationship to God. I feel surrounded by God, my entire life deriving from and nourished by God. In a way that transcends logic, God is "in" me (the Immanent), and I am "in" God (the Transcendent). And yet, the God who is my life and gives me life and guides my life is still, in so many ways, a complete and utter mystery to me.

. . . At least in this womb, this stage of becoming.

NAMING THE BABY: PHILOSOPHY AND FASHION IN JEWISH NAMES

In life, you discover that people are called by three names: One is the name the person is called by his father and mother, one is the name people call him, and one is the name he acquires for himself. The best one is the one he acquires for himself.
—*Midrash Tanhuma, Vayakchel*

Every person has a name/that God gave him/ and that his parents gave him/ and that his stature and way of smiling gave him . . .
—from "Every Person Has A Name,"[11] Zelda

The act of naming does not imply power over the thing named. According to the rabbis, Adam named not only the animals but also God [*Bereshit Rabbah* 17:4].

—José Faur[12]

Speech is the human faculty in which we are most reflective of the Creator's divinity. The Torah describes God's creation of the world as an act of speech and naming. In God's image, people use language and naming to make meaning of the world. Thus Adam, the first human, is privileged to name the other creatures in Eden. According to Jewish tradition, the biblical foremothers named their children with a measure of prophecy. Biblical figures' names are frequently linked to their characters or destinies, and God changed certain peo-

ple's names as a sign of profound changes in their lives or personalities. Hebrew names have obvious meanings to the Hebrew-speaker, unlike English names for which the nonlinquist must look up the derivation to know the meaning.

When we name our children, we make one of the most significant marks on their destiny. This name we give will be for them the most important word in their lives, their very identity. A Jewish tradition suggests that the parent is endowed with *ruah hakodesh*, the holy spirit, at the important moment of naming a child.

In Jewish tradition, naming a child after a relative (deceased relatives for Ashkenazic Jews, sometimes living relatives for Sephardic Jews) imparts a sort of immortality. Family names are meant to live on in subsequent generations. But a Jewish child is virtually never named for a parent, for each person is supposed to bear his or her own identity, not a parent's.

Anyway, why would we want to name our children after what our parents chose for our identities? We prefer to give our children the name we wish we had been given, the identity we would choose for ourselves. This is especially true of Jewish life in recent generations. My own family can serve as an example. My grandparents Anglicized their own Yiddish names (Feigel to Fanny), then gave their children "apple-pie" American names, Betty and Charles. Our "All American" generation got appellations suitable to our future careers in Hollywood: Julie, Missy, and Ali, tenuously referring to our Yiddish-named antecedents Gitel, Michle, and Elke.

When the time came to name my children, the pendulum had long since swung back. Now Great-Grandma Rose's (née Ruchel) namesake is known as Shira Rachel. While some Jewish parents are still transforming "Shlomo" into "Stuart," many more are blithely (and with equal disregard for the name's meaning) changing Grandpa George's name to Joshua (more Jewish, but not too un-English), Gil (obviously Hebraic, Israeli-sounding; they're toying with the idea of *aliyah*), or back into the original Chayim (they've become *baalei teshuvah*). Like Phillip Roth's Portnoy thought that "spatula" was a Yiddish word, my kids think that Avi, Ari, Shira, and Liora are English names. In fact, my Shira has known about as many other Shiras (even in Texas) as I grew up with Lauras and Anns.

Anglo-biblical names, with their Jewish yet American-Colonial sound, have enjoyed a renais-

267

sance: plenty of Benjamins, Rebeccas, Sarahs, Joshuas, and Hannahs in Hebrew school these days. And the Bubbe and Zeide (Gram and Gramps) names are trendy now, too: whoever expected that American Jewish children would once again be named Sadie and Rosie and Max?

Meanwhile, those of the baby-boomer generation who have rediscovered Judaism and become neotraditionalists, Modern-Orthodox, or have made *aliyah* are particularly given to poetic, meaningful, or religious Hebrew names, which a friend of mine dubs "Hebrew flower child" names. So Nancy and Stu may be the parents of Tiferet ("splendor"), Amikam ("my people arose"), or Ayelet-Hashachar ("Dawn-star"). The more traditional Orthodox world tends to the faithful maintainance of Ashkenazic pronunciation and Yiddish names like Moishe, Sheina, and Mendel.

Since every Hebrew name has a meaning understood by all Hebrew speakers, Israeli parents can be quite poetic in naming their offspring. Typical Israeli names may come from nature, places in Israel, or from lesser-known biblical characters. Rapidly changing fashions in Israeli names can be found in my husband's family. His brothers and sisters have traditional biblical names: David, Avraham, Daniel. Some of his older nieces and nephews had lesser-known biblical names that had become popular in Israel: Michal, Merav. A few years later, poetic names were in fashion: Yaniv ("He will be fruitful"), Yariv ("He will be great"), Ortal ("Light-dew"). The latest trend is to one-syllable names, traditionally rare in Hebrew: Li, Mor, Bar, and Rom are among the youngest family members.

Nicknames have always been popular in Israel's informal society: Rami, Tami, Uzi, and Gidi. One writer, an American immigrant to Israel, remarked that he found an Israeli class roster sounded to him like a list of the seven dwarfs! Cutesy nicknames (Dubi, Kobi, Bibi) are almost mandatory for those possessed of too-long names, especially if they are generals, politicians, and entertainers. Orthodox Israeli parents still tend to select the biblical, traditional, or religiously meaningful names.

IDEAS FOR PARENTS SELECTING A HEBREW NAME

Naming a child is a deeply personal matter (at least until you begin to consider all of your relatives' preferences!). Each couple must make this impor-tant decision for themselves, but here are a few things you might consider:

● According to a *midrash*, the Jews kept their identities alive while in Egypt in large respect because they persisted in using their Hebrew names. Hebrew names almost always resonate with Jewish tradition and meaning. They say that we are truly proud and confident in our Jewish identities. I strongly advise joining the many contemporary parents who are calling their child by a Hebrew (or sometimes Yiddish or Ladino) Jewish name that will be used all the time, rather than on a few ceremonial occasions or just in Hebrew school. The Hebrew name is the "real" name, then, the real identity.

There are also many English names derived from Hebrew, so that the Hebrew and English names are essentially one and the same (although pronounced a bit differently), such as Rachel/Rahel, Nathan/Natan, Hannah/Chana, Abigail/Avigayil, Benjamin/Benyamin, Daniel/Danniel. Lesser known are the Hebrew-English cognates, such as Keren, Sheli, Sharon, Tom, and Tami, which all sound like common English names but have Hebrew meanings.

While there is no religious requirement that one's Hebrew name and English name bear any relation, I can verify from my personal experience that having a clear connection helps to create a more unified identity. When I lived in Israel, my different sounding Hebrew and English names created such a real identity crisis for me that I eventually legally changed to my Hebrew name on my Israeli documents.

● As noted, Ashkenazim frequently name after deceased relatives; Sephardim may also name after living relatives (other than the parents themselves). It's important for the child to know whom she or he was named after and something about the person.

If you want to name a child after a relative, it's considered most meaningful to use the relative's actual Hebrew name, rather than randomly choosing something with a similar sound. If you want a different first name, the relative's name could be used as a middle name. If you want to translate a Yiddish name to Hebrew, or a masculine name to feminine (or vice versa), do take the time to research the optimum translation, rather than asking your rabbi to come up with a hastily selected "equivalent" at the last minute.

One obvious but often overlooked source for

finding out ancestors' Hebrew names is gravestones. Everyone told me emphatically that Aunt Janet "didn't have a Hebrew name"; then I saw her headstone, and it said "Yocheved," a beautiful Hebrew name indeed. Family records, such as a *ketubah* (marriage contract) or family tree can be useful sources, if you can obtain them. Everyone thought that my Grandpa Sam's Hebrew name "must be" Shmuel, until I read his and Grandma's *ketubah*, where I discovered that it was Yishayahu (Isaiah). Non-Hebrew readers can find someone to help with translating.

● "Name your child for a righteous person," said the sages. Name for a role-model, relative, or nonrelative. Many names appear over and over throughout Jewish history. Jewish children have often been named for biblical figures. Or choose a role model from the Talmud or from later Jewish history until our own day. Look through the Bible, history books, Jewish encyclopedias. There are books today on Jewish women's history that might inspire a new generation of Jewish names for girls. But for the naming to be meaningful, you must explain its significance to the child periodically as she or he grows up.

● Derive the name from a character or word in the Torah portion or *haftarah* of the week the child is born, or a name connected with a holiday or season (Esther for Purim, Nissim ("miracles") for Hanukkah). Our oldest daughter, Liora, was given the middle name Emuna ("faith"), in honor of the Moroccan-Jewish folk holiday of Maimouna, on which she was born.

● Choose a name that represents a quality: Noam/Naomi (pleasantness), Shalom/Shlomit (peace), Adin/Adina (sensitive), Orit, Lior (light, my light), and so forth. Or a name from nature: Vered (rose), Yona/Yonit (dove), Aryeh/Ariella (lion [of God]). These latter three names, like many others, also have connotations in Jewish tradition or mystical thought. Hebrew names have also been given for places in Israel and to honor historical events.

● Those with some Hebrew background will find it easiest to consider, or even "compose," Hebrew names, but others can be helped by name books and by knowledgeable friends. Common Hebrew name-components are "el," which means "God," and "i" or "li," which means "mine." Many Hebrew names can be transferred from masculine to feminine by adding "ah" or the feminine diminu-

tive, "it," or vice versa by removing these endings (Shlomo—Shlomit, for example). A few names are gender-neutral, and some others have changed their gender-association over the years.

● Despite a common belief to the contrary, Jewish law does not forbid one to change his or her Hebrew name. A Hebrew name may either be given by the parent or adopted by common use. The former Hebrew name could be maintained as a middle or third name, to preserve one's namesake heritage.

AFTER THE BABY ARRIVES

CARING FOR THE NEW MOTHER

Jewish cultures of the past emphasized the special attention and pampering due a paraparturent woman. In Eastern Europe, the new mother was called a *kimpetor*, a Yiddish word that became synonymous with someone particularly in need of coddling and solicitous care. A maid or relative came in to do the housework and to feed the mother nourishing foods. Yemenite tradition included the ceremonies of *Yoledet* ("one who gives birth"), in which the new mother was attended to by her women friends.

With all the excitement of the pregnancy, birth, and baby "ceremonies," few first-time parents are prepared for the impact the new baby will have on their lives. It would be welcome to see more Jewish communities revitalize some of the old practices of helping mothers and fathers when a new baby arrives. A synagogue "*mitzvah* committee," a *havurah*, a Jewish women's group, or relatives and friends can get together to help the new parents with things like housework, cooking, and errands.

Don't be afraid to ask for help assertively. People may be afraid of "bothering" you, or they may simply be busy. Ideally, father should have a paternity leave or take vacation time when the baby is born. If you're fortunate enough to have extended family living nearby, take advantage of their offers of help. Plan before the birth to get household help, to streamline meals (freeze ahead, take-out), and to take off enough time from outside responsibilities so that you can relax, recuperate, and really devote yourself to baby and to self-care.

Local Jewish Family Services or Jewish Parenting Centers can provide the location and staffing for seminars and support groups for new parents, especially new mothers. Today's parents may be well educated and sophisticated achievers who find themselves unprepared to adjust to the vastly different role of caring devotedly for a demanding infant. Such agencies can be a great resource to the couple or the new mom in particular.

CARING FOR BABY

Traditional Jewish infant care was oriented toward lots of touch and closeness. Popular "natural" baby-care methods today, such as sleeping with or near the baby, infant massage, rocking, and breast-feeding, go far back into our history. The Talmud viewed the first two years as the period of infant nursing (*Ketubot* 60a). The idea of banishing the baby to splendid isolation in the nursery is quite foreign to traditional Jewish culture, as we can find in this classic description of the infant's life in the Eastern European *shtetl*:

"The first months of the baby's life are a constant bath of warmth, attention and affection. At first it sleeps with the mother, then it is placed in its own cradle or swinging crib, near her bed. She may hold a string attached to the baby's cradle, which she rocks incessantly, even in her sleep. . . . Several times a day the [infant's] swaddling is removed and the baby is massaged and allowed to move freely, always with an obligato of loving coos and murmers. . . . Wrapped and pillowed, the baby is carried around a great deal by grownups and by older brothers and sisters. . . . It is sung to, petted, addressed with endearments that usually end in the diminutive "leh.". . . . The father sings to it, visitors coo over it, speaking in baby talk and in a special singsong voice. . . . The warmth and affection of this outer womb in which the baby lives comes to be associated also with food, for he is offered the breast whenever he seems to want it. . . . To suckle one's own child, her 'own flesh and blood,' is regarded as a rewarding and desirable experience, pleasurable for the mother as well as for the child."[13]

When Rabbi Hanina was eighty years old, he was still able to stand on one foot and remove from the other. He said: "My strength in old age comes from the frequent warm baths and anointing in oil given my body during infancy."

—Talmud *Hullin* 24[14]

BRIT CEREMONIES: WELCOMING A JEWISH CHILD INTO THE COVENANT

Having a baby is a personal and intimate wonder, but Judaism is a religion that emphasizes the importance of community. The baby is not only our own child, but the continuation of our people, and this is recognized in the joyful ceremonies and celebrations we hold after the birth to name our children and welcome them into our community and into the covenant between God and the people of Israel.

SHALOM ZACHAR/SHALOM BAT

A traditional custom in advance of the more formal *brit* ceremonies is the old practice of *shalom zachar*, welcoming the baby son (*zachar* means "male") on the Friday night that precedes the circumcision. Nowadays, many parents have extended this custom to welcome a daughter, *shalom bat*. Light refreshments, including the traditional seasoned chick-peas for good luck, are served, and guests may enjoy singing or listening to *divrei* Torah (words of Torah). The *shalom* party is usually held at home.

WELCOMING A DAUGHTER

Back in less-enlightened days (like when we were babies), welcoming a baby daughter was a pretty quiet affair, in Ashkenazic communities, at least. This was in stark contrast to all the fanfare that traditionally accompanied the birth of a son. The father, or perhaps the grandfather, made an *aliyah* to the Torah, after which the girl was named with a brief Hebrew blessing. In centuries past, in Europe, this might be paralleled by a women's party at the new mother's bedside. (There is fragmentary evidence of other Ashkenazic ceremonies for the birth of a baby girl, of which most of the details have been lost to history.)

Yet in only the past couple of decades, beautiful ceremonies to welcome and name a daughter have become *de rigueur* in nearly all sectors of the Jewish community, spreading rapidly from the more liberal denominations into the Modern Orthodox world (even in the most traditionally Orthodox families, one at least holds a nice *kiddush* in honor of the baby girl's naming these days). In Israel, friends tell me that it's become fashionable to have a large party known as a *britah* (feminine of *brit*) to celebrate the birth of a girl. Some hold the ceremonies for a baby daughter on the eighth day, like the boy's *brit milah*, while other families wait two weeks (the biblical purification period after a daughter's birth) or a month (the traditional period of viability in Judaic sources), or to the nearest Shabbat or Rosh Hodesh. These ceremonies are so new that there is no uniform name; they may be called *simhat bat*, "rejoicing in a daughter," or *brit banot* (covenant of daughters), among other titles. While many parents put together their own ceremony, or get one from their rabbi or friends, the Reform prayer book has formalized an official ceremony, "The Covenant of Life," which can be found in *Gates of the Home*, the UAHC home prayer book.

Many Ashkenazic Jews remain unaware that a Sephardic ceremony for welcoming a daughter has long been a formalized part of the Orthodox Sephardic prayer book and ritual. The *zeved habat*, or "gift of a daughter" ceremony (the Hebrew echoes the words of Leah before she conceived her daughter [Genesis 30:20]), was traditionally held at home, although in Israel today it may be held in a rented hall and the style may be as lavish as a wedding, including live music, a multicourse meal (*seudah*), and fancy decorations. The baby is usually dressed in a long white gown. While her grandmother holds the infant, a *piyetan* (cantor) sings the traditional "naming" blessing for the newborn child, with the classic Middle Eastern cantillation. These naming prayers quote from the Song of Songs and ask that the baby be blessed in the name of quite a number of the biblical Matriarchs and heroines. (Although, after heaping blessings upon the infant and her parents, the traditional prayer sneaks in the aside: "[and may they also have] male sons"! I'm happy to note that today, the phrase "sons and daughters" or "children and grandchildren" is usually substituted.) Special verses are inserted if the daughter is a firstborn, which loosely parallels the *pidyon haben* for a firstborn male.

Among Jews of Moroccan origin there are several *piyutim*, poetic liturgical songs composed especially for the birth of a daughter, which draw on feminine imagery from the Psalms and the biblical Song of Songs.[15]

Today's naming and *brit* ceremonies for a daughter can be held at home, at the synagogue, or elsewhere. Possibilities for a creative ceremony include Hebrew songs, readings, words of Torah, or ritual actions such as candlelighting or ritual hand and foot washing. The accompanying *seudah* (festive meal) might be a full meal, a Shabbat or holiday *kiddush*, or an informal brunch or buffet. Various honors may be given out to different members of the extended family or to friends: carrying the baby in, holding her during the ceremony, saying various prayers, or leading readings. As with a *brit milah*, honorees may be designated "godmother" and "godfather" (*kvatterin* and *kvatter*, in Yiddish), and *sondak* or *sondeket*, the person who holds the baby during the naming. Another Sephardic custom is to gently pass the baby from person to person, while each extends blessings and wishes to her. Be sure that older siblings have a featured part in the ceremony, if they so desire. (The Resource Guide, p. 355, lists sources for a variety of creative naming and covenant ceremonies for a baby daughter.)

BRIT MILAH

Since the days of Abraham and Isaac (Genesis 17:10–12), a baby boy on the eight day of life has been brought into the covenant—*brit*—through circumcision—*milah*, hence the name *brit milah* (often called a *bris*, with the Ashkenazic pronunciation). The boy is given his Hebrew name at his *brit milah*. Despite persecution over the centuries, Jews steadfastly persisted in circumcising their sons, not infrequently at risk of their own lives. Circumcision is regarded by the Torah as one of the most primal of Jewish commandments, without which, as it says in Genesis 17:14, one is "cut off" from the Jewish people. (No, no pun intended, wiseguy.)

While for Jews, circumcision is a religious rite, a physical sign of the covenant, it has been practiced by many other peoples for various reasons. Circumcision was almost universally adopted for hygienic purposes in the United States in the past couple of generations. More recently, some health professionals and parents no longer feel that circumcision is necessary for hygiene, although many still hold that it is preferable. For Jews, the traditional motivations are religious; it is a *mitzvah*.

At the same time, parents should not berate themselves for feeling uncomfortable or anxious before the operation; almost all parents are bound to have some feelings of anxiety, ambivalence, or tension, a mixture of emotions well recognized in Jewish sources. For example, among Ashkenazic Jews the joyful *sheheheyanu* blessing is not said at the *brit milah*, partly in consideration of the baby's pain. However, with an expert *mohel* in attendance, the baby's pain should be brief, and he will quickly be comforted with a bit of wine and his parents' attentions. (A local anesthetic is sometimes used, although its effects are generally short-lived. Consult the *mohel* in advance if this is important to you.)

Medical circumcision in the hospital is by no means less painful because it is out of earshot (many who have witnessed hospital circumcisions and the traditional *brit milah* affirm that the latter tends to be quicker and less traumatic), and it does not have the same religious significance as welcoming one's son into the covenant by *brit milah*. In traditional Jewish law, a child who undergoes surgical circumcision is still in need of a *hatafat dam brit*, the symbolic drawing of at least one drop of blood from the skin of the glans. Writes Jacob Neusner: "The contemporary practice of having a surgical operation in no way carries out the rite of circumcision. For what changes the matter is not only circumstance. It is the formula, the words of blessing . . . the medium of enchantment that transforms the birth of a child to an individual couple into an event heavy with meaning: a metaphor for something more, for something that transcends."[16]

Brit milah takes place on the eighth day after birth, whether that day is Shabbat, Yom Kippur, or any other day. Generally, it may be postponed only for medical reasons, in which case it will not be held on the Sabbath or Yom Tov, but will await the nearest weekday.[17] Remember that the Jewish day begins at sunset, so this must be taken into account when scheduling the *brit milah*. Traditionally, one does not extend an "invitation" to a *brit milah*, since attendance at one is a *mitzvah*, and no one should have to refuse a *mitzvah*. Rather, one "informs" at least a *minyan's* worth of participants about the event, and these understand that they are invited. (Although not obligatory, a *minyan* is preferable. Remember that your *mohel*, if of the traditional variety, will count only men in the *minyan*.)

The father is actually the one obligated by the Torah to carry out the circumcision. Officially speaking, the *mohel* (ritual circumcisor) acts in his stead, as his *shaliah*. The *mohel* is a pious Jew who is carefully trained in his craft. Some *mohalim* (plural) are also physicians by profession. The Reform movement has begun to train physicians to become *mohalim*—or *mohalot*—female *mohels*. Besides the *mohel's* fee, you will also have to pay travel expenses if you live in a small Jewish community without a resident *mohel*. If your rabbi

leads the service, it is customary to pay an honorarium or to make a donation to the rabbi's discretionary fund at the synagogue. (Contact your synagogue office for suggestions.) To find a *mohel*, consult your rabbi and if possible get some recommendations from friends who have engaged the services of the same *mohel*. It's ideal if you can see local *mohalim* "in action" at other circumcisions prior to the time you actually need to choose one for your son.

The Ceremony of *Brit Milah*

The ceremony itself can be found in most traditional *siddurs* and a number of books (see Resource Guide, pp. 323, 355). It may be held at home, at the synagogue, or in the social hall. Some hospitals in major Jewish population centers provide rooms for *brit milah*.

The child is brought into the room by the *kvaterin* (godmother), who hands him to the *kvater* (godfather). All present rise (they remain standing throughout the ceremony) and welcome him with "*Baruch HaBa*." Songs may be sung, particularly in Sephardic practice. This may be the time for some of the more innovative practices, such as a prayer by the mother for the miracle of birth.

In Ashkenazic tradition, the child is then placed on a chair designated the *kiseh shel eliyahu* (chair of Elijah the Prophet, who is the symbolic guest at every *brit milah*), where someone holds him briefly while the *mohel* recites the first prayers. Then he is given to the *sondak*, the one who actually holds him during the ceremony, often on a table, but sometimes in his lap. In Sephardic tradition, the *sandak* is actually seated on the chair of Elijah, which is elaborately decorated. (Diplomacy and *shelom bayit*, domestic harmony, should take precedence in distributing these honors. Our *mohel* quickly read the family situation and suggested that both grandmothers take the part of the *kvaterin* rather than having a man and woman act as godparents.)

The *mohel* recites a blessing and performs the circumcision, which he may do with either a clamp or a surgical knife. (A special clamp called a Mogen clamp is often used, and I have found physicians as well as *mohalim* to be enthusiastic about this method.) This is followed by another blessing by the father, and sometimes the mother as well if the ceremony is from a more liberal perspective. Those present respond: "*Keshem shenichnas lebrit, ken tikanes leTorah, ulehuppah, ulema'asim tovim*"—"Just as he has entered into the covenant, so may he enter into the world of Torah, the marriage canopy, and the fulfillment of good deeds."

Meanwhile, the *mohel* is busy tending to the baby, blessing the wine and drinking some (although in some traditions, another person recites the *kiddush*). The baby is given a drop of the sweet wine, which usually quickly pacifies him. Other traditional prayers follow, including the giving of the name. In Sephardic tradition, fresh mint is distributed, and the blessing is recited for smelling sweet herbs. The baby is soon given to his mother to be nursed and comforted.

Some parents introduce some extra readings or short words of Torah at this point. It can be a good time for older siblings to participate. Our nine- and ten-year-old daughters held the baby and read an explanation of the baby's name and namesakes. Other brief additions might include personal prayers, blessings, readings, songs and music, or the reading of Bible verses or acrostic poems containing the baby's Hebrew name.

There is increased participation of the mother and other women in the *brit milah*; the mother may recite the *Birkat HaGomel* or join the father in some of the traditional prayers; or she may offer another reading or words of Torah. Likewise, today the baby's name may be announced as "son of"—*Ben*—the mother's name as well as the father's. If you desire a more innovative ceremony, select a *mohel* who will go along with your plans.

The feast that follows, whether an elaborate meal or a light brunch, is considered a *seudat mitzvah*, a *mitzvah*-feast. Special liturgical songs may be sung, and special verses are added to the Grace after Meals. (As usual, a kosher meal is thoughtful whether or not you are personally kosher observant.)

Some parents prefer to change the traditional format to hold the circumcision itself in a private area, then to bring the baby out for the celebrations. This is reminiscent of traditional Sephardic practices described to me by my Moroccan-born in-laws, that the circumcision itself was a fairly quiet religious occasion, followed by a big dinner the next day.

The *mohel* generally offers complete directions about care of the newly circumcised infant. Your pediatrician should follow up.

When I first wrote the chapter about a *brit milah*, I had three daughters and so had no first-hand experience of being the parent of a newborn son. Looking over what I'd written after the *brit milah* of our son, I realized that I had gotten most of the details right but by no means had anticipated the drama of the event. With my third daughter's naming, I took a month to get the ceremony ready and to pick the perfect date and location. With a *brit*, there is much more time pressure, since the ceremony is held so soon after birth (and since our son was the only one of our children born by Caesarian section, everything was even more exhausting). Family tensions seem destined to surface during that eight-day period. But thanks to a wonderful rabbi, excellent *mohel*, and in-laws who cooked for four days straight, we had a memorable Thanksgiving day *brit*, full of love and community, from the Sephardic songs to the hasidic dances.

MORE IDEAS FOR CELEBRATING AND WELCOMING YOUR NEW BABY

● An old custom, being revived by some, is to make a Torah binder, or wimpel, *vimpel* in Yiddish, from fabric used to wrap the baby at the *brit*. A recent variation, described in the book *Jewish and Female*,[18] is a textile-work Torah breastplate, made from fabric by artist Ita Aberland, used to wrap a baby girl at her naming.

● Plant a tree or trees in Israel in honor of your baby or a friend's. In ancient days, a cedar was planted for every boy, a cypress for every girl; when they married, branches from the trees were used to hold up their wedding canopy. When Liora was born in Petach-Tikvah, Israel, we received an artistic certificate from the city council, stating that a tree had been planted in honor of her birth, as for each child born there. You could also plant a tree in your own yard or elsewhere in your hometown. As you watch the local tree grow, you can imagine how your tree in Israel is growing, too.

● Give to *tzedakah*, perhaps in multiples of 18 (the numerical equivalent of *hai*, life) or of 120, the number symbolic of long life. Consider donating 3 percent of the cost of your *simhah* to Mazon, a Jewish organization that feeds the hungry (see p. 336). Another possibility would be to sponsor a child from an organization such as "Save the Children" to help a child in impoverished circumstances as you raise your own (God willing) in relative plenty and ease. A donation to your congregation and local Jewish organizations is also appropriate.

● Provide a guest book in which attendees have space to write personal messages, blessings, and wishes to be treasured for years to come.

- Record your baby's ceremony with photographs or videotape.

- Many Jewish parents today choose to send out birth announcements that include the baby's Hebrew name and Hebrew birth date, and perhaps also calligraphic designs with the Hebrew letters, Jewish motifs, and appropriate verses from Jewish sources. Some include an explanation of the baby's Hebrew name and namesake(s). Local Judaica gift shops or those listed in the Resource Guide on p. 308 can probably direct you to a Hebrew-English calligrapher, or ask your rabbi or friends whose Jewish birth announcement or wedding invitation you've admired. Some parents make their own birth announcements that include Hebrew press-on letters or Hebrew computer graphics.

- Similarly, naming and *brit* certificates, special blessings to hang in the nursery, and even Jewishly oriented "baby books" are available from synagogues, calligraphers, and gift shops.

PIDYON HABEN: REDEMPTION OF THE FIRSTBORN SON

The Torah tells that firstborn males were to be dedicated to God's service (Exodus 13:1–2). Later, only the Levites, and in particular the Kohanim, were consecrated instead (Numbers 8:18). Still, the firstborn was required by the Torah to be ritually redeemed from his service by his father's payment of "five *shekels* of silver" to a *Cohen* (Numbers 18:15–16). And so until our day, traditionally observant Jews will celebrate the *pidyon haben*, redemption of the (firstborn) son, on the thirty-first day after the birth (unless that falls on a Shabbat or *Yom Tov*, when it will be postponed until the next day).

Pidyon haben is held only if the boy is the firstborn son of his mother by natural "opening of the womb"; thus it is traditionally not held if the firstborn of the family is a daughter, if a miscarriage past three months' pregnancy preceded the live birth, or if the child was born by a Caesarean section. Likewise, if the child is a Cohen or Levi, he is considered "dedicated to God's service," anyway, and no *pidyon* is done.

The ceremony is brief and can be found in many traditional prayer books. The father presents his son to the *Cohen* and says that this is the firstborn and he is commanded by God to redeem him for five *shekels*. The *Cohen* then asks if the father chooses to give him the child or redeem him. The father answers: "To redeem him." The father recites the blessing for redeeming his son and gives the Kohen five silver dollars. Turkish Sephardic Jews use five silver spoons. There are even specially minted solid silver coin sets available from the Israeli mint.

Sheheheyanu is recited and the *Cohen* waves the money over the child's head and says a blessing for him, followed by the traditional priestly blessing. Then he blesses the wine, and this is followed by a *seudat mitzvah* (*mitzvah* meal), and singing or words of Torah as the family desires. The *Cohen* is entitled to keep the money, although in general he will return it to the parents as a gift for the baby, especially if it's an expensive commemorative set. The money may also be given to *tzedakah*.

While each child in a family is equally precious, the arrival of the firstborn is usually the most life-and-perspective changing experience for a couple. Some liberal Jewish groups have written new *pidyon* ceremonies to celebrate the birth of a firstborn, whether boy or girl, or however born. For those who are interested, such new ceremonies may be found in Diamant's *The Jewish Baby Book*. (See Resource Guide.)

WEANING

The Torah relates that Abraham and Sarah made a feast when Isaac was weaned at the age of three. (All of us who have nursed a child until that age can readily understand!) Today, weaning ceremonies and celebrations have made a reappearance as part of the process of creating new rituals for the female life cycle. Although weaning is best a gradual process, once it is more or less complete, it could be celebrated with a festive *kiddush* and a gift to *tzedakah*. A *sheheheyanu* could be recited (over a new fruit or new garment for traditionalists). A silver *kiddush* cup, engraved with baby's name and the Hebrew date, could become a future heirloom. (See the Resource Guide, p. 355, for the sources of more complete rituals and ceremonies.)

Behold, how good and pleasant it is for siblings to dwell together in harmony.

—Psalm 133:1

SIBLING RIVALRY

The story of Cain and Abel comes to tell us, among other things, that sibling rivalry is virtually as old as mankind. With Isaac and Ishmael, Jacob and Esau, Joseph and his brothers, sibling rivalry continues as a motif of our sources. Some commentators have suggested that biblical stories such as the tale of Joseph and the coat of many colors should teach parents the dangers of favoring one child over others.

The rivalry that occurs when a new baby arrives is usually quite mild compared to the heights kids can bring it to in years to come. Older children should not be ignored during a new sibling's *brit* or naming ceremony, or when lots of guests and relatives are making much of the baby. Special treats and roles at this time can help to smooth things over, but most of all the older child needs to be reassured that she or he is still actively loved in a unique way.

Sibling rivalry is normal and virtually universal, but it often intensifies when children feel in need of emotional nourishment or have anxieties over tensions in the home. Whenever I think to myself, they're just doing it to get attention, I quickly realize that, yes, they really are in need of more focused, personal attention. With several children, I've found that special notes, bedtime trysts, individual learning or story-reading, and even occasional "dates" with each one help them each to feel unique and special.

Siblings Without Rivalry, by Adele Faber and Elaine Mazlish,[19] is a useful resource for helping parents understand and deal with the normal jealousies and conflicts between siblings. Part of the wisdom of their approach is to encourage parents to think in terms of giving children what each uniquely needs, rather than trying futilely to give "equally" to everyone at all times.

Listening to the classic rivalry stories from the Bible can actually help children resolve their inner feelings of aggressiveness toward siblings. A certain someone in our family *really* liked hearing that story "about how Joseph's brothers threw him down that hole!"

And Jewish tradition, from biblical tales to modern *tzadikim* (righteous people), also has many stories of sibling love and cooperation for our children to hear. The *Midrash* tells that Rachel willingly helped Leah to be married to Jacob first, in her stead, in order to spare her sister humiliation. Another famous Jewish story (from the *Midrash*, *Vayikra Rabbah*) tells of two brothers, one of whom had a family and one of whom did not. During one lean year, each brother thought his sibling worse off than he, and they simultaneously smuggled grain into each other's barns during the night. Finally one night, the two met during their secret task and discovered that each had had the same idea. On that spot in their field, they stopped and embraced. Because of their brotherly love, the place of their embrace merited to become the future site of the Holy Temple. (This story is retold as *Brothers—A Hebrew Legend*, in a beautiful children's picture edition by Florence B. Freedman, illustrated by Robert Andrew Parker.)[20]

After all, there *is* the other side of having sisters and brothers: the intense love, companionship, and sharing that is possible. We are apt to notice the rivalry and conflicts and to take the friendship and love of siblings for granted. Most grown-up "only children" I know wish very much that they had a brother or sister. My own sisters are my best friends. Likewise, everytime we see our children playing together for hours, or walking and talking together intensely, my husband and I know that it's all worth it: How good it is for siblings to live together in harmony!

29

BIRTHDAYS

Here are some ideas to make birthday celebrations extra special and to enrich them with Jewish meaning:

● Sponsor a *kiddush* or *oneg* Shabbat at your synagogue in honor of the birthday. If desired, a parent can give a short birthday *devar* Torah.

● Donate to *tzedakah* in honor of the birthday, especially to a fund of special interest to the birthday child. Perhaps give a multiple of 18 = *hai* (life).

● Choose a "birthday *mitzvah*" for each family member. Do an extra act of *tzedakah* or kindness in honor of the person's day.

● Say the *sheheheyanu* prayer (p. 89) to thank God for another year of life. (Some Orthodox authorities stipulate that the blessing should be said while wearing new clothing or eating a new fruit on the birthday, because there is not a clear mandate to say the blessing on a birthday prior to the seventieth![1]

● Bless the child, on the birthday or the nearest Shabbat, with a special and personal blessing.

● Sponsor a tree planting in Israel, and another in North America or elsewhere, to honor the child's birthday.

● Sing *"Yom Huledet Sameah"* to the tune of "Happy Birthday to You."

● Make sweets from Israel your special birthday treat.

● Make a birthday a special time to give a gift of Jewish significance: perhaps a *kippah*, personal prayer book, Judaic books, audio or videotapes, games, jewelry or room decorations, or a subscription to a Jewish periodical. How about a "Hebrew kit" containing items such as Hebrew stampers, magnets, and stencils?

SPECIAL BIRTHDAYS

FIRST BIRTHDAY

The first birthday has no particular ancient Jewish traditions that I know of (my husband did tell me that it was often the time for the first haircut in Morocco). Indeed, with each baby we say that we are going to keep it a small family gathering, but every time we find that that first birthday party is a major celebration. Any of the preceding suggestions (where age appropriate) could be employed to add a Jewish dimension.

THIRD BIRTHDAY

The third birthday does have certain traditions associated with it, ostensibly derived from the biblical requirement of waiting three years before eating the fruit of a new tree. Age three represents the transition from infancy to early childhood. In very Orthodox and hasidic circles, a baby boy's hair is trimmed for the first time at age three, leaving it very short except for the side-locks (*pe'ot*), which are left long according to biblical mandate. The boy will also begin wearing a *kippah* and small fringed garment (*tzitziot*) at all times. The Lubavitcher hasidim (Chabad) in particular promote the custom for girls to begin lighting one Shabbat candle by their mother's side, beginning at age three. More liberal Jews would extend this to boys' participation as well.

FIFTH BIRTHDAY

The fifth birthday has been considered the traditional time to begin study of Torah. A lovely custom of generations past in both Ashkenazic and Sephardic communities was for the child (back then, this meant a boy) to be brought to the *heder* school for the first time, wrapped in his father's *tallit*. As the child learned each Hebrew letter on a slate, it was covered in honey for him to lick off, so that Torah would be associated with sweetness, with "honey under the tongue." (Among some groups, this was done at age three. There are also other related customs, such as giving the child a special honey cake.)

Some contemporary schools have revitalized this custom. (In many Reform congregations, it's known as "consecration.") At one Talmud Torah (religious school) our children attended, my kindergartener was in a group of children who came on the first day of school wearing white. The director had ordered a wreath of daisies for every little one's head. With much ceremony, each child was given a letter *alef*, written with honey on a paper plate, to lick off. At our current synagogue, we observe a variation of this custom on Simhat Torah. Each child beginning his or her formal Jewish education that year receives a model Torah scroll from his or her parents, as well as a sweet chocolate lollypop in the shape of a Torah. Many day schools hold a ceremony to present young children with their first *siddur* or *Humash* (Pentateuch).

These ceremonies symbolize the way in which Jewish parents have classically introduced their young children to the way of life embodied in Torah—by making Jewish traditions tangible, sweet, and desirable.

BAT MITZVAH AND *BAR MITZVAH*

The most significant childhood birthday in the Jewish tradition is the attainment of age twelve (*bat mitzvah*, for a girl) or age thirteen (*bar mitzvah*, for a boy). Most liberal synagogues observe a girl's *bat mitzvah* at age thirteen as well. The plural is *benai mitzvah*. These names, meaning literally "daughter, son, or children of the Commandments," respectively indicate a legal status attained at puberty, when a young person becomes liable for her or his own deeds under Jewish law. They do not indicate *full* adulthood in the Jewish tradition, which occurs at age twenty.[2]

Assumption of the "adult" responsibilities for Jewish observance has been marked with a similar sort of celebration for several centuries, although traditionally this was only for boys. The *bar mitzvah* assumes responsibility for daily prayer and putting on *tefillin* each weekday. Among Sephardim, the full-sized tallit is worn beginning at *bar mitzvah*. The traditional ceremony includes participation in the prayer service according to the youngster's ability and local custom. Minimally, this meant reciting blessings over the Torah reading; maximally it could include chanting the *maftir* section of the Torah portion (or even the whole portion, in some communities), chanting the *Haftarah*, and leading the *musaf* service. The honoree offers a *derashah* (*devar* Torah). In past generations, this would often be at the meal; today it is usually given during the service itself. A festive *kiddush* or meal (*seudah*) follows.

While the *bar mitzvah* ceremony has remained similar for generations, the celebratory aspect has grown by leaps and bounds in this century. Recent decades have also seen the popularization of the parallel *bat mitzvah* ceremony for girls. The first contemporary *bat mitzvah* ceremony was held early in this century for Judith Kaplan, the daughter of Mordechai Kaplan, founder of Reconstructionism. Today, in Judaism's more liberal denominations, girls generally participate in *bat mitzvah* services in the same way that boys have always done for *bar mitzvah*. In Modern Orthodox settings the *bat mitzvah* may be celebrated with a *kiddush* or *seudah* (often the Shabbat afternoon Third Meal), where the young woman gives a *devar* Torah or even chants the *Haftarah*, a nonsynagogue service such as a much-augmented *Havdalah*, or even to a female-led synagogue service at which the girl reads from the Torah and does everything a boy would do (the male guests may then be the ones to sit behind the *mehitzah*, the partition separating the sexes during prayer in Orthodox synagogues). The adoption of various new *bat mitzvah* customs among the Modern Orthodox represents a striking change from the mores of even a couple of decades past. Among the more traditional Orthodox, *bat mitzvah* is still not marked with a religious ceremony but may be celebrated with a party or a school program.

BENAI MITZVAH CELEBRATIONS

A true *bar mitzvah* story:

A young boy was born to a poor but pious Jewish family in Poland. He left home at a tender age to engage in the study of Torah and Talmud. Once, on a visit to a relative, where he knew he could receive a good meal, his kinsman said to him: "Do you know . . . I believe you are *bar mitzvah*. By my reckoning you have passed your thirteenth birthday." The lad calmly borrowed a pair of *tefillin* and thus said the morning prayers. After a long time he was able to scrape together enough money to buy a pair of his own.

Thus was the "*bar mitzvah*" of one of the most legendary *tzaddikim* (righteous ones) of our century: Rabbi Aryeh Levin, "the *tzadik* of Jerusalem."[3]

I tell this story not to argue that a wonderful *bar* or *bat mitzvah* celebration can't be a memorable and meaningful experience to a young person, but to put the whole thing in perspective a bit. It is important for a young person to see the passage into adolescence in the religious and cultural framework of Judaism. On the other hand, the social and performance aspects of the occasion have often been inflated. The *bat* or *bar mitzvah* has often become the major focus of Jewish education, especially the supplementary variety (around the country, enrollment in Jewish schools peaks at age thirteen, then sharply declines).

The following are some ideas being instituted around the country in order to make *benai mitzvah* a more meaningful experience. Ideally, such suggestions would be implemented as congregational or school policies; minimally, the individual family can consider adopting some on its own.

● Be sure that *benai mitzvah* represents the beginning and not the end of intensive and sophisticated Jewish education. Research on Jewish education suggests that teens should attend Jewish high school programs through twelfth grade. (More on this in the section, "Looking Ahead to the Teen Years.")

● The celebrant should donate a portion of the monetary gifts received to *tzedakah* funds of his or her own choice. A tithe, or 10 percent, is a traditional Jewish standard of giving. Some particularly sensitive youngsters ask for *tzedakah* donations instead of gifts, although such a decision should not be pressured by the parents. Alternately, the celebrant could ask for *tzedakah* donations to a certain fund without stating that these are in place of gifts. This could be tied to a special-focus "*tzedakah* project" of several months to a year prior to the ceremony.

● The family could ask guests to donate goods to a *tzedakah* group: for example, food for the local food bank, even warm coats or other clothing for a local shelter. If you do not want guests to bring items on Shabbat, be sure to include that information in the invitation.

● Decide on a way to make the celebration less lavish and donate the proceeds to *tzedakah*. *Tzedakah* activist Danny Siegel tells of young people who make a centerpiece of books or canned goods that will be donated, or just a card on each table stating that in place of a centerpiece, the money has gone to certain *tzedakah* fund.[4]

● Make a synagogue *benai mitzvah* policy that sets limits on the lavishness of celebrations. Such "sumptuary laws" are an honored Jewish tradition that both prevents wastefulness and protects the less affluent from pressures and embarrassment when they cannot compete.

● Donate 3 percent of the costs of your *simhah* to Mazon, a Jewish organization dedicated to feeding the hungry and addressing the problem of world hunger (address on p. 336).

● A donation to your congregation and Jewish school is particularly appropriate.

● Given that the *benai mitzvah* period is already such a focus of Jewish education, many schools and synagogues have begun to institute special programs for this age group that focus on the meaning of growing up, adolescence, Jewish life, and future goals. Such programs often involve intensive projects, whether in learning, the arts, or service to the community. Ideally, parents should also be involved as active participants in some of the programs.

● Some synagogues and study programs offer personalized possibilities for the *bat* or *bar mitzvah* ritual that enable the young person to have a ceremony or celebration uniquely tailored to her or his abilities, interests, personality, and desires.

The best way to make yours personally meaningful is to plan far enough ahead to ensure that differences between your family's concepts of the event and those of your institution mesh, or that you can work out other possibilities either in your current institutional framework or elsewhere.

● Make up your own personalized program of spending extra time with your *bat* or *bat mitzvah* youngster, learning together, doing *mitzvot* together, talking about the teen years ahead and priorities and goals.

● Some people who were never able to have a *bat* or *bar mitzvah* ceremony as a child choose to have one as an adult. Traditionally, of course, the age of *mitzvot* and not the ceremony itself is the important thing. However, many people (most often it is women) find that such an adult *bat* or *bar mitzvah* is a meaningful and emotional event, and many synagogues have instituted programs to enable adults to have them. Sometimes the parent and child even celebrate their *benai mitzvah* ceremony together!

● Design a special invitation in both Hebrew and English, possibly with calligraphic design, which could include biblical versions from the *parashah* or related to the celebrant's name. The same goes for a commemorative certificate.

● At my *bat mitzvah* ceremony, a small Torah scroll was literally passed from generation to generation, from my great-grandmother to my grandmother to my mother to me. The same was done at my eldest daughter's *bat mitzvah* service. Such intergenerational participation can create treasured memories.

FAMILY SNAPSHOTS

BENAI
MITZVAH

We have tried in our children's *benai mitzvah* experiences to stress process and participation rather than pomp and circumstance. For Rebekah's, we initiated a series of study sessions, beginning the year before. Different friends hosted groups to study the service, her *parashah*, Reconstructionism, *tefillin*, and so forth. We had a special session for non-Jewish friends. Rebekah studied and prepared an annotated teaching service that she led. Photocopied portions had been sent to each participating family in advance.

All three children had lay-led services, photocopied invitations, and parties at our house. While some invitees didn't take the occasions seriously, since they were used to foil-lined envelopes, service rehearsals, and hotel receptions, the people who mattered to us didn't mind.

For Joseph's *bar mitzvah*, we did a variety of activities relating to *tzedakah*, including making *tzedakah* coloring books, studying Danny Siegel's materials, starting a *tzedakah* collective, and collecting food for the local food bank. His *devar Torah* also carried through this theme.

—Wendy and Stan Drezek

For Jessica's *bat mitzvah*, we could not have it with her reading from the Torah, and so on, at our Orthodox synagogue, so we did it at home. We borrowed a Torah from the Reform Temple. It was on Sukkot, so we planned around that. We set up "the world's biggest *sukkah*"; it covered practically the whole backyard. A box lunch was arranged to eat in the *sukkah*. Our *havurah* helped us to build the *sukkah* and decorate it, which made it a special experience for them, too.

The day before the *bat mitzvah*, it was raining and raining and raining. We covered the *s'chach* with plastic, which kept the ground dry, but the *sukkah* started to cave in! The *bat mitzvah* was held on Sunday of *Hol HaMo'ed Sukkot* (the intermediate days of the festival), which turned out to be a nice day, after all.

Jessica still remembers that she did *Hallel* for Sukkot, and she still knows it and leads sometimes. Joel, who regularly fills the role of congregational *hazzan* (cantor), taught her (and later her three brothers) the trope. She read the special reading for Sukkot and gave a talk.

The three boys' *bar mitzvahs* were more traditional, at the synagogue with a ceremony and sit-down luncheon. What we did not do was have big parties; the kids weren't much interested in that, anyway. We simply entertained the visiting relatives in the evening after the *bar mitzvah*. For Nathaniel's, we took our out-of-town guests "country and western" dancing, for Gabe's, we took them to the symphony, and for Jeremy's, we went to a recreational site in the area.

—Joel and Hedy Rutman

We enjoyed many Sephardic customs at Liora's *bat mitzvah*. Her father and grandfather sang a *piyyut* (liturgical song) when she went up to the Torah, as her paternal grandmother and aunt tossed candies for children to collect. She sang her *haftarah* with the Sephardic tune, learned from her father. For Liora's party, at our home, we wore Sephardic caftans, served Moroccan food, and played Middle Eastern music. We also observed the Moroccan custom of placing henna (a vegetable dye) on participants' palms for good luck. It was truly a "first" for San Antonio, Texas!

— The Author

LOOKING AHEAD TO THE TEEN YEARS

The teen years may be the most important years in forming your child's lifelong commitment to Judaism. But the time to start thinking about them is while your child is still quite young.

When I moderated a discussion on Jewish parenting at a recent national Jewish educational conference, I expected to get parents of preschoolers, wanting to discuss ideas about holiday arts and crafts, or perhaps parents of elementary-school–age children, looking for ways to teach the Torah portion at home. To my surprise, I was confronted almost exclusively with anxious parents of teens. They were wondering why there weren't more teen activities in their local Jewish communities, how to get their teens involved in Jewish life, what to do about interdating (which they all seemed to permit, but worried about), and if their future grandchildren would be Jewish. Yet they all seemed to be good Jewish parents, the kind who had always been involved in Jewish life. What had happened?

One major problem is that the teen years may be too late to worry about the teen years. The time to start thinking about the teen years is when children are still young. Parents of elementary-school–age children should look at programs for teens in their own communities: Is there a Jewish high school program? What is the quality; is it popular and well attended? What kinds of Jewish youth-group programs are there? Are they just for partying (in ways you may find negative), or do they have religious, ideological, and service content? How well attended are they? Do the youngsters go

to regional and national Shabbat events and summer camps? Is there a local trip to Israel program (considered one of the most potentially powerful experiences) for teens? Does it include educational preparation? Does it continue with any follow-up programming?

If you live in a major Jewish population center, or a particularly active smaller community, the opportunities may be many or at least high quality. But in many areas, teen programming is thin. The teen years are currently possibly the weakest link in Jewish education in this country. Jewish education around the United States peaks at age thirteen (*bar mitzvah*, of course), then drops precipitously. By eleventh grade, it's estimated that a mere 6 percent of American Jewish teens are enrolled in Jewish schools! Camps and youth groups are still important, but in many cases have changed from the more ideological nature they had in the sixties and seventies.

While some parents are prepared to actually move to a larger Jewish community or one with more intensive educational settings, the alternative is to get involved in lobbying for and building better Jewish programs for teens in your local community, preferably while your children are still young. It's important to bring these issues to the attention of as many parents of your children's Jewish peers as you can, because peer influence is a crucial factor for teen involvement.

Why go to all the trouble? The answers are significant: "Continuation of Jewish studies through high school is considered by some researchers to be one of the *critical* predictors of adult Jewish identification, communal participation and observance. . . . Alumni of intensive Jewish high school programs (day or supplementary) have been found to belong to and be more active in Jewish organizations and synagogues, be more observant, read and study more about Jewish issues, visit Israel more frequently and to intermarry less." Some researchers have even argued that supplementary Jewish education has almost no long-range positive effect on Jewish religious involvement *unless* it is continued through high school graduation![5]

Expect your child to participate in the best Jewish high school program you can find, through twelfth grade. If a private Jewish high school is possible, your teen is among a Jewish educational elite. An excellent supplementary program is also worthwhile. The ideal supplementary high school Jewish education program for teens, whether synagogue or community run, might involve weekend

Shabbaton and fellowship programs, integrated youth and camping programs, a social service *mitzvah* component, and a well-developed Israel experience.[6]

In one synagogue (which, by the way, feeds its teens pizza every week when they come to study), youngsters who continue in the program through high school receive a *shofar*, which they are invited to blow together at the next High Holiday *tekiah gedolah*, the long *shofar* blast at end of Yom Kippur. The education director overheard two kids discussing whether or not they should continue their Jewish studies after *bar mitzvah*. Said one to the other, "Hey, man, I'm going for the horn!"

In addition to formal education, here are some other areas in which to encourage teen Jewish involvement:

● Jewish youth groups can be important to strengthening Jewish identity. Some are primarily social, some strongly Zionist, some more religiously oriented, whether Reform, Conservative, or Orthodox. Major groups include NFTY (Reform), USY (Conservative), NCSY (Orthodox), B'nai Akiva (Orthodox Zionist), BBYO (B'nai B'rith Youth), and Young Judaea (Zionist). Try to steer your teen to a local chapter or to regional and national events with a significant amount of Judaic, spiritual, and social-action content. Many Jewish teens are sorely in need of spiritual nourishment, community, and a passion for ideals.[7]

● Jewish camping can be a powerful factor in the teen years. It certainly was so for me and many of my friends. Just bunking with Jewish kids isn't really enough. At camps such as the major youth movements' regional and national camps, teens meet peers from all over the country and the world while spending the summer in a holistic Jewish environment, generally with a meaningful Jewish studies component. Find ways to carry over the camp experiences into home and community life.

● Israel programs can have a powerful transformative effect on young people, particularly if they involve preparation, educational content, and meaningful follow-up activities. A year in Israel after high school (such as Young Judaea's "year course") seems to have an especially significant impact on Jewish involvement in college.

● *Tzedakah* and volunteer activities can have a positive effect on teen self-esteem and alleviate the self-centeredness of these years. They are particularly positive within a peer-group framework. *Tze-dakah* activist Danny Siegel suggests making use of the family car contingent on spending a minimum number of hours driving it for *tzedakah* work.

● Provide Jewish role models other than parents. A certain amount of charisma is an important factor to look for in Jewish youth workers and teachers of teens. Time spent with other Jewish families whose values you share can be positive, since teens will often find the same values much more attractive when presented by anyone other than parents! (Some parents swear by "trading" their teens with those of friends or relatives for a vacation. Especially great if the relatives live in Israel!)

● Be aware that interdating, even in the teen years, is related to an increased likelihood of intermarriage later on.[8]

● Home observances, such as Shabbat, and family customs and traditions are just as important, if not more so, with teens. Your kids may grumble, but many of their peers are starved for just such family closeness and tradition.

● Get involved with a Jewish community such as a very participatory congregation or *havurah* while your kids are still young. This will not only provide them with "extended family" who do Jewish things together, but can also help parents confront and work together on the changing phases in their families' Jewish lives. After the kids leave home, the adults should be able to confront together how they can continue to live and learn in a Jewishly meaningful way. (One of the saddest things I've heard from a Jewish youngster is, "It seems like my family doesn't 'do Shabbat' any more since my older sister left for college.")

● Make Jewish life on campus an important criterion in choosing a college for your child. You can't force your young adult to be involved, but you can increase or decrease the odds, depending on where you send her or him. The atmosphere on most campuses today encourages many young adults, even those from seemingly strong Jewish backgrounds, to drift away from Jewish affiliation and involvement. Is this a campus in an area far removed from centers of Jewish life, or is it known as a place with many Jewish activities and a large Jewish population? Is there an active Hillel House? What kind of Jewish studies programs are available on campus? What kinds of opportunities are there for community service in a Jewish context?

Tzedakah activist Danny Siegel writes: "Parents—ask yourselves exactly what you would hope your child would be like as a human being and as a Jew when he or she graduates [from college] 4 years down the road. Don't be afraid to discuss it with your child, this Jewish thing. Don't be afraid to say, 'Now is the time when you can integrate your *Tzedakah* work with your other training and education more fully.' It is *their* choice to listen or not, but it is *your* obligation to raise the issue. Discuss the relationship of wisdom and knowledge with them and how both subjects will be presented at college. Discuss the relationship of thinking to action, philosophy to life-style, and all of those other issues you *really* think are critical. Begin intensive discussions from the moment College Board exams become a necessity. That would be a good time to ask your kid exactly 'what he or she wants to be when he or she grows up.' Compare Profession to Life; discuss Success, Happiness and Security in depth.'"[9]

PROPOSAL: A *HAI* (*CHAI*) RITE OF PASSAGE AT AGE EIGHTEEN

Given the data that over 80 percent of Jewish youth "drop out" of formal Jewish education after the *bat* or *bar mitzvah* ceremony (those same Jewish young people who are overwhelmingly likely to receive a college degree in a secular field), and given the evidence for the crucial importance of those high school years in the development of future Jewish commitment, it seems wise for the Jewish community to explore new ways to keep more youth involved in Jewish education during the teen years. Although many liberal synagogues have a Confirmation Class in tenth grade, one wonders about the message given when the Jewish "graduation" ceremony takes place in tenth grade. (What if those same youngsters left their *secular* high schools after their sophomore year?)

I propose that the Jewish community undertake to make age eighteen (*Hai*) the age for a new rite-of-passage appropriate to contemporary society and its developmental stages. Eighteen is the age when most Jewish young people leave home to attend college. At this age, they will venture forth into an ideologically open (and sometimes anti-Semitic, anti-Israel) environment. Should we send them off having had their last formal Jewish educational experiences as children of thirteen or even as high school sophomores?

The *Hai* ceremony would not replace *benai mitzvah* (as confirmation was once intended to do),

but would be an incentive for keeping young people involved in Jewish education at least through high school. (It's to be hoped that they would be even more likely to continue their studies at the college level.) I am not proposing the specific content for the ceremony itself; I think that the main thing is to have it! (However, I would like to see it have a more *yiddishe tam*—Jewish flavor—than some of the "white-choir-robes-and-corsage" confirmation ceremonies I've seen.) The *Hai* program might be structured by local synagogues and communities to involve participation in a Judaic high school that would include study of Jewish source materials as well as informal camp or retreat experiences and a well planned Israel component. Young people might undertake a yearlong *tzedakah* service project together during their eighteenth year. They might learn about prayer and synagogue skills in a serious way, beyond memorization. They might study Hebrew intensively and qualify for advanced placement in college.

Many Jewish life-cycle customs have evolved out of grass-roots community practices, including *bar* and *bat mitzvah* themselves. The *bat mitzvah*, girls' *brit* ceremonies, and confirmation are all fairly recent innovations. There is no reason why the Jewish community could not put forth the effort to establish another life-cycle rite-of-passage that could provide so many benefits to the community and to our children. I believe that it's a concept that deserves the serious consideration of those who care about the future of the Jewish community.

FAMILY SNAPSHOTS

JEWISH LIFE WITH TEENS

The biggest area of neglect in the Jewish community is the teen years. Parents still have a lot of control during elementary school (we helped to found a Jewish day school in our community). Later on, in college, many of the finest colleges have excellent programs in Jewish studies and a wide range of Hillel activities. But the high school years can be a kind of vacuum, especially in the smaller communities. (When our older children were teens there was no ongoing organized Jewish high school study program as there is now in our community, although we did organize various tutorial arrangements for them, and Joel studied with them on Shabbat.)

We keep a traditional, but not strictly Orthodox, home; our main congregational involvement is with an Orthodox synagogue. Where possible, we sent the children to various camps and Israel programs and trips (we have family in Israel and have considered *aliyah* for ourselves). Sometimes these experiences were very positive, but some actually turned out to have a negative influence. The caliber of the peer group was often a significant factor. One of our sons was completely "turned off" to Orthodoxy by an intolerant group of kids at an Orthodox summer camp. But another son was heavily involved in the Young Judaea youth group and synagogue activities and has now chosen to go on a yearlong program in Israel before starting college.

Peer relationships and role models had an important effect. Friendships with more observant teens—or conversely with teens from assimilated Jewish households who admired our family's more active Jewish life-style—influenced some of our children. Personal role models of observant young adults turned out to be a very positive Jewish influence for our daughter when she was at Harvard and when she was on a college program in Israel.

Peer influence is so significant at this stage, but finding a Jewish peer group for teens is a terrific problem in smaller Jewish communities. We would like to see more of the Jewish community's resources allocated to providing professional staff to work with high school kids, more than what the youth groups alone can currently provide. There should be weekly teen activities and much greater use of Jewish camps.

We wonder about the extent of parental influence. Although we have raised our children in a Jewishly observant household and have given them the best Jewish education we could, we find that right now two are very involved Jewishly, while the other two seem relatively uninterested at this point. (Of course they are still young adults and one doesn't know how they will grow and change in the future.) This seems to be true not only for us, in our small Jewish community, but for friends and relatives in larger Jewish communities and more traditional Jewish settings.

Since there are no guarantees, what is an appropriate and realistic goal for Jewish parents?

Joel: "I want them to 'be just like us.' How can you really have any other goal, if you believe in the way you are living?"

Hedy: "You can only raise them to be knowledgeable Jews. We gave them the best education we could give them Judaically in our city. Once they become adults, we can't choose how they will live. You can only raise them with hopes, not with expectations."

Joel: "The expectations guide them in a direction, though."

—Hedy and Joel Rutman

30
TALKING TO CHILDREN ABOUT DIFFICULT LIFE-CYCLE ISSUES

SEX EDUCATION

When it comes to sex education, parents have two major obligations: to convey factual information and to convey values. We are all aware that many young adults harbor a lot of misinformation about contraception, sexually transmitted diseases, and AIDS. Yet providing the factual information is really the easier task. There are many books in almost every bookstore and library to read and discuss, to honestly yet gradually explain sex to children at their level of understanding.

The more complicated task is to convey our values. This goes far beyond the proverbial heart-to-heart talk about the birds and the bees. Sex education is conveyed in our own attitudes about ourselves as men and women, by the example of how mother and father relate to each other. It is also conveyed in the love, acceptance, and appropriate attention that both parents continue to devote to their children of both sexes as they begin to develop into young men and women.

The Jewish attitude toward sexuality is the multifaceted product of thousands of years of development and contact with many surrounding cultures. Yet a general ethos emerges, one that is decidedly at odds with the usual American secular approach to sexuality.

The American approach with which the media bombards us presents a double standard. It continuously tantalizes, yet the lingering effects of puritanism militate against honesty and education. (So much sex on television, yet few condom ads.)

Sexuality is also prostituted to commercial ends: to sell toothpaste, for example.

The Jewish approach is different. Judaism does not emerge from a puritanical approach that finds sex "dirty," nor from a libertarian approach that worships sex, but rather from a belief that sex and sexuality are God-given pleasures and drives that are wonderful blessings—in the right context, the context of holiness and moderation—traditionally, of marriage. Judaism (outside a few pockets of extreme prudishness that were almost inevitable in such a long and varied history) has had what could be called an accepting and wholesome attitude, positive yet conservative, toward the sexual needs of both men and—so different from most societies—of women. Even back in talmudic days, Judaism encouraged sex education (including instruction in sexual techniques to young marrieds). Judaism, particularly the mystical trends, is replete with imagery of love and even sex to symbolize the religious love for God. The great Rabbi Akiva said that the Song of Songs, the biblical love poem, is the "holy of holies."

By exploring Jewish sources as well as honestly facing and articulating their own attitudes toward sexuality, Jewish parents can help to give their children a meaningful sex education. The pressures of society and the media don't bode well, but we can all do our best within our own homes and the social groupings in which we choose to raise our families.

While on the subject of love and sex, I must include a brief note about children and Jewish weddings. Certainly the ideal of a Jewish marriage should primarily be modeled in the home, but attending plenty of joyful Jewish weddings can't hurt our efforts to present Jewish couplehood as a desired state. Yet I've received so many invitations to Jewish weddings stating that they are for "adults only." I find this very sad. In Israel, a wedding is an occasion for *everyone* to celebrate, from babies to great-grandparents. The emphasis is on *Yiddishe simhah*, Jewish joy, rather than on formality and etiquette. Israeli children may go to several weddings each year. While I was growing up, I didn't get to go to one Jewish wedding! Of course, one can't insist on bringing one's offspring to "crash" Jewish weddings where they aren't welcome. But the exclusion of children from life-cycle events seems to be just one more manifestation of Jewish assimilation into majority cultural modes. It's something for all of us to consider when it's our turn to do the inviting.

TEACHING ABOUT DEATH

The Jewish tradition can be of great help to parents in teaching their children about death, whether it is in facing an actual death in the family or simply learning about death as a normal issue of growing up.

Too many Jewish parents think that Judaism is an exclusively this-world religion that has no belief in an afterlife and little comfort to give in the face of death. On the contrary, Judaism, while certainly emphasizing this life and lacking rigid dogma about the next, has also developed a wide range of beliefs in the life to come, including concepts of spiritual survival, spiritual reward and punishment (although never in the classical Christian sense of "eternal damnation"), resurrection (perceived in various ways), and even reincarnation. Many of the near-death, out-of-body experiences currently being studied by scientists have striking parallels in Judaism's kabbalistic literature. The vision of a loving light at death conforms to its descriptions of the revelation of the *Shechinah* to one who has just died.

At the same time, Judaism offers a sound psychological process of gradually adjusting to a death in the family: the intense week-long *shivah* period of mourning, followed by less-intense thirty-day and up to a yearlong periods, depending on the closeness of the relationship. Reciting the mourner's *kaddish* helps the mourner achieve the difficult task of reaffirming faith and life within the context of a supportive community.

Children's understanding of death goes through a natural evolution over the years, but parents can generally influence whether death becomes a source of terror and fear or is seen as a natural part of the life cycle. I believe that Sephardic Jews have much to teach westernized Ashkenazic Jews about facing death. They are much more natural in their approach to mourning, much less likely to put up a cheerful facade in the face of tragedy. Sephardic Jews also emphasize the commemoration of a death and visits to the graves of departed relatives and holy people, often bringing children and grandchildren along. A memorial meal and service is held in the deceased's home on the anniversary of his or her death. Sephardic Jews don't treat death as a taboo subject, as Americans are wont to do. Following the Sephardic approach I learned from my in-laws, I have not hesitated to take my children on visits to my father's grave, their great-grandparents' graves in Israel, and to the graves of holy people in Israel.

Another thing I have found helpful is to become involved in a *Hevrah Kaddisha*, the group of Jewish volunteers who take on the sacred duty of *taharah*, washing and preparing the dead for burial in accordance with traditional Jewish law. I served on such a group for a year or so. The dead person is not made up like a doll for display, but is "purified" with washing and prayers, then dressed in simple shrouds and placed in a closed wooden coffin so that the body can gradually return to the earth.

Certainly, not everyone will want to be involved in this *mitzvah* (which is considered the greatest act of *hesed*), but there are ways to become involved in many *Hevrah Kaddisha* groups without doing the actual *taharah* ritual. Some *Hevrah Kaddisha* groups will take only older adults to do this work, some will accept only Orthodox-observant Jews. However, smaller communities are much more likely to be flexible about who participates. Frequently, the group also needs volunteers to sit with the body, which is never left unattended prior to burial, to visit mourners, to explain the *Hevrah*'s work, to speak to schools and other groups, to write articles for local Jewish publications, and to make phone calls to notify volunteers when their services are needed. However, I would not rule out the possibility of becoming involved in the actual *taharah*. The American terror of death robs us of what may be a very profound spiritual experience, an experience that also graphically brings home that the body we are so identified with is really just a shell, like the chrysalis of a butterfly. Telling my children about my involvement in the *Hevrah Kaddisha* has also given them a more natural view of death.

Like teaching about God, sex, or any other emotionally charged subject, teaching about death involves clarifying our own beliefs and their place in the Jewish tradition, rather than looking for the "Jewish party line" to be able to tell our children. As on so many other subjects in our people's lengthy history, there is not just one official dogma. Parents will find it helpful to study Jewish sources as well as to honestly deal with their own fears, hopes, and beliefs.

EPILOGUE

SEARCHERS FOR A WAY

Every generation is the last but for the next, the one that it creates; and the generations that face the twenty-first century—the fourth and fifth and the sixth beyond the mass murder and migration—have sound reason to wonder, "What will you give me, for I continue childless?" (Genesis 15:2) In that setting, the power to believe does stand for righteousness, or so I think.

—Jacob Neusner[1]

My first year at college was spent at the University of Texas at Austin, my second year at Bar-Ilan University in Israel. By odd coincidence, I had the same Hebrew literature professor at Bar-Ilan who the previous year had been my teacher while he was on a sabbatical at the University of Texas. In Texas, he was notorious for dwelling on the superiority of Israeli students, while back in Israel he frequently remarked on the excellence of American students. (I scored my first points in social acceptance by pointing this out in class one day, simultaneously extracting his first public laugh at himself.)

What remains in my mind about this professor, aside from what I retain of his teachings on modern Israeli literature, was that he lived in Jerusalem and attended a synagogue called *Mevak-shei Derech*, meaning "Searchers for a Path/Way," which I later found out was an Israeli Reconstructionist-style synagogue.

What a marvelous, honest name—Searchers for a Path/Way! I believe it would be appropriate for every synagogue and Jewish institution to consider adopting this name as a kind of subtitle. For we, committed Jews at the end of the twentieth century of the common era, are all Jews groping in search of a way—a way back "home" to the intellectual and spiritual wellsprings of classical Judaism, which is simultaneously a way forward into a global future where Judaism will have something to say to a world in ecological, political, moral, and spiritual crises, as well as to those who choose our particular path.

So why this Jewish book for parents in particular? Because as parents we are in the remarkable position of seeking to effectively transmit Judaic ethos and culture, even as we are groping for it ourselves. We care deeply that our children will be Jewish, even as we are just beginning to discover what Judaism means to us (I refer not only to the assimilated or ignorant Jew; even after years of study we are—I hope!—grappling with the full meaning of living as Jews today).

We are all caught in what the late scholar Simon Rawidowicz—echoed recently by Jacob Neusner and Leonard Fein—called the syndrome of "the ever-dying people."[2] What Jewish parent today isn't concerned with the Jewish identity of the next generation? Yet Rawidowicz pointed out that the Jewish people have been "dying out" from the days of Abraham, who somehow believed God's word that his descendents would number like the stars, although he and his wife were still childless at a ripe old age (Genesis 15)—to the Talmud, where the death of each great sage was counted as an end of some essential quality of the world (*Sotah* 49b)—to the great Hebrew poets of the last century who wondered—how ironic it seems now—for whom they were even writing! And as I write this, I have just read an article by a Hillel director from UCLA, which concludes, "rapid assimilation is already underway and the Jewish future is withering before our eyes."[3] And parents I hear from in the United States (and even in Israel, but in different ways) agonize out loud over whether their grandchildren will be Jewish, what it means to be Jewish, what kind of Jew it matters to be, and what kind of Judaism it matters to preserve.

This book has been concerned more with Judaism in practice than with just being Jewish. While I am aware that there are many Jews who consider themselves Jewish without being Judaists (that is, observers of some form of Judaism as "a complex of faith and social ethics").[4] I don't know how effectively to transmit the idea of being Jewish apart from some sense of Judaism. Judaism is different and more than a "religion" in the Western sense (as dogma and ritual); it is a distinctive ethos and life path (or a religion–philosophy *cum* culture). Even so, Judaism is not fixed, but is legitimately expressed in various ways and continually interacts with other philosophies and cultures—sometimes in ways that detract from it and sometimes in ways that enrich it.

I hope that this book has encouraged the reader to learn more from Jewish sources and to seek more about Jewish spirituality. What's more, I hope that it has made a small contribution in accompanying some Jewish families on the journey that goes so far to find what is so near.

The first Jews, Abraham and Sarah, were commanded by God to go on a long journey (Genesis 12:1). The Hebrew words of that command echo to us across the ages: "*Lech-Lecha*," "Go for/to yourself." The ambiguity of the Hebrew words suggests that the journey was to be a journey outward, as well as a journey inward. Spiritual growth in Judaism is linked to the demand for ethical behavior and social justice. In Judaism, the authentic spiritual journey, the journey toward our truest selves, is also a journey outward, a journey toward a new social order, toward a blessing "for all the families of the earth"(Genesis 12:3).

THE WINDOWS OF THE HOUSE SHINE OUTWARD

And for the House he made windows wide without, and narrow within.

—1 Kings 6:4

The Temple windows were narrow within and widening outward, in order to send forth light into the world.

—from the *Midrash*

I have set you for a light of the nations: to open the blind eyes, to bring out prisoners from the prison, and they that sit in darkness out of the prison house.

—Isaiah 42:6

The world we live in, the world our children will inherit, is beset by social, environmental, and moral problems. Our homes cannot be our cocoons or our castles; they should not (indeed, they cannot really) function as walled fortresses in which we hide from the stresses and troubles of society. Yet neither must we allow them to simply receive all outside influences, to be a small mirror of the pathologies of society.

Judaism proposes an alternative: home may be—in the traditional Jewish sentiment— *mikdash me'at*, a small holy temple, a sanctuary. The home is not a perfect place; indeed, there is a Jewish tradition to leave a small part of the home decor empty and unfinished, a symbol of the destruction of the great Temple and of all the brokenness in our lives. Yet the home may be a dwelling place for holiness.

Tradition has it that the Holy Temple did not need to receive the light of the sun or the moon. The Holy Temple, the *Beit HaMikdash*, gave forth a light of holiness that was said to illumine the world.

Our homes, if we merit it, may give forth their light to the world. True, our homes are only small holy places; our candles are tiny, and the darkness is great. But joined together as community, as nation, we may hear the command to shine. We may open blind eyes and break open the doors of the darkened prison-house, letting in a great light.

Light is associated in Jewish tradition with the divine, with God. To increase the light, to make our homes a beacon of light, we must rediscover the sense of divinity and holiness within our lives as human beings and as Jews. With a renewed spiritual dimension, a sense of sanctity, and a command to activism, each of our homes may merit a part, however modest, in making our children's world what it may become.

The windows of the home may yet shine outward.

NOTES

PART I: HOME AND HERITAGE

CHAPTER 1: JUDAISM AND STRONG FAMILIES

1. This is adapted from a classic hasidic tale with many variants. I have highlighted only one dimension of its possible meanings. One version of the story "Reb Eisik's Treasure" can be found in Ellen Frankel's *The Classic Tales* (Northvale, NJ: Jason Aronson, 1989), pp. 545–546. For an illustrated version that is suitable for reading aloud to children, see Uri Shulevitz, *The Treasure* (New York: Farrar, Straus & Giroux, 1978). Since choosing this story as the opening for this book, I have found variations of it in two or three other contemporary Jewish guidebooks. It seems to speak to American Jews in a special way.

2. See Sylvia Barack Fishman, "The Changing American Jewish Family in the 80's," *Contemporary Jewry* 9:2 (1988): 1–31; and Chaim I. Waxman, *America's Jews in Transition* (Philadelphia: Temple University Press, 1983), pp. 159–183. This book is primarily geared to families in North America. Israeli Jews exhibit more traditional family patterns, but they, too, have their own set of problems to deal with in formulating a Jewish identity in the modern world.

3. See *Secrets of Strong Families* by Nick Stinnett and John Defrain (New York: Little Brown/Berkley, 1985/1986); and *Traits of a Healthy Family* by Dolores Curran (New York: Winston Press/Ballantine, 1983/1984), for two separate studies involving families, and professionals who work with families, respectively.

4. Leonard Fine, *Where Are We? The Inner Life of America's Jews* (New York: Harper & Row, 1988), p. 171.

5. Ibid., pp. 143–144.

6. A term coined by Bernard Reisman. See Bernard Reisman, "Jewish Family Education," *Pedagogic Reporter* 28 (Spring 1977):5, as cited in Janice Alper, "Introduction to Jewish Family Education," *Learning Together—A Sourcebook on Jewish Family Education* (Denver, CO: Alternatives in Religious Education, 1987), pp. 1–15.

CHAPTER 2: MAKING LIFE MORE MEANINGFUL

1. Adin Steinsaltz, *The Thirteen Petalled Rose* (Northvale, NJ: Jason Aronson, 1992), p. 127.

2. Franz Rozenzweig, draft of address at the opening of the Freies Jüdisches Lehrhaus in Frankfurt, 1920, from *Franz Rosenzweig: His Life and Thought*, presented by Nahum N. Glatzer (New York: Schocken, 1976), p. 231.

3. Chaim Potok, *The Chosen* (New York: Simon & Schuster, 1967).

4. More on drawing closer to the Jewish cultural core through study and observance will be found in the sections on learning and on the Shabbat and holidays. For a guide to using the Jewish holidays and Shabbat as a way to get closer to the core of Judaism, see Rabbi Anson Laytner's *The Wheels of Observance: A Growth Guide to the Jewish Holidays* (New York: CLAL, 1988). A full description can be found in the Resource Guide to the Holidays, p. 348.

5. See Victor E. Frankl's *Man's Search for Meaning* (New York: Touchstone Simon & Schuster, 1984).

6. *The Insecurity of Freedom* (New York: Farrar, Straus & Giroux, 1966), p. 84. As quoted in *I Asked for Wonder: A Spiritual Anthology of Abraham Joshua Heschel*, ed. by Samuel H. Dresner (New York: Crossroad, 1986), p. 65.

7. This analogy is found in another form in Joan Borysenko's *Minding the Body, Mending the Mind* (Reading, MA: Addison-Wesley, 1987), p. 27. Borysenko quotes a teacher as saying that all of life's experiences are like zeros in a long number and that peace of mind is the missing digit.

8. Jacob Neusner, *The Enchantments of Judaism* (New York: Basic Books, 1987), p. 95.

9. David Weiss, *The Wings of the Dove—Jewish Values, Science, and Halachah* (Washington, DC: B'nai B'rith, 1987), p. 21.

10. Abraham Joshua Heschel, *The Insecurity of Freedom* (New York: Schocken, 1966), pp. 231–232.

11. Arthur Hertzberg, *The Jews in America: Four Centuries of an Uneasy Encounter* (New York: Simon & Schuster, 1989), pp. 387–388.

12. Acknowledgments to Professor Perry London for enlarging my understanding of Jewish identity formation in young children (lecture, Whizin Institute for Jewish Family Life seminar, University of Judaism, Los Angeles, June 1990), and to Rabbi David Nelson for the exercise on early Jewish memories.

13. Herbert Weiner, *The Wild Goats of Ein Gedi* (New York: Atheneum, 1970), p. 213.

14. Quoted by Dov Peretz Elkins, "Tzedakah—The Jewish Way of Giving," *The Hadassah Magazine Jewish Parenting Book*, ed. Roselyn Bell (New York: Free Press, 1989), p. 201.

15. Adin Steinsaltz, *The Strife of the Spirit* (Northvale, NJ: Jason Aronson, 1988), pp. 241-242.

16. Arlene Rossen Cardozo, *Jewish Family Celebrations* (New York: St. Martin's, 1982). Among Ms. Cardozo's other books is *Sequencing* (New York: Collier/Macmillan, 1989).

CHAPTER 3: PARENTING AS A SPIRITUAL PATH

1. Abraham Joshua Heschel, *The Insecurity of Freedom* (New York: Schocken, 1966), pp. 39-40.

2. "Actions in God's Image," based on a lecture by Dr. Kathy Chesto, Whizin Institute for Jewish Family Life seminar, University of Judaism, Los Angeles, June 1990. I am grateful to Dr. Chesto, a noted Roman Catholic family educator, for an experience of what interfaith dialogue can really mean.

3. This section was greatly facilitated by source materials and study guides from the Shalom Hartman Institute for Advanced Jewish Studies in Jerusalem (provided by the American Friends of Shalom Hartman Institute), particularly two study units on the Jewish family: "Authority and Independence in Jewish Family Relationships" and "Education for Inter-Dependence in the Jewish Family."

4. "You are children of Adonai your God" (Deuteronomy 14:1). Admittedly, in the traditional *siddur*, much of this is in masculine gender language (e.g., "Our Father, Our King"), but there are also biblical metaphorical descriptions of a motherly God (e.g., Isaiah 66:13), as well as the traditional name for God, *HaRahaman*, The Merciful One, while, although masculine in gender, stems from the same root as the Hebrew word for "womb." Jewish mysticism (Kabbalah) vividly describes both "fatherly" and "motherly" aspects of the Godhead. Also, note that *both* parents, not only the father, are to be honored and revered and that these attitudes toward both allude to the human–God relationship.

5. Franz Rosenzweig, *The Star of Redemption*, tr. William W. Hallo (Boston: Beacon, 1972).

6. Seymour Rossell, *Managing the Jewish Classroom* (Los Angeles: Torah Aura Productions, 1988), pp. 157-161. Rossell expounds on Eugene Borowitz's 1974 article, "*Tzimtzum*: A Mystic Model for Contemporary Leadership," which has been reprinted in *What We Know About Jewish Education*, ed. Stuart Kelman (Los Angeles: Torah Aura Productions, 1992), pp, 331-341.

7. Ibid., p. 28.

CHAPTER 4: THE ART OF JEWISH PARENTING

1. *The Enchantments of Judaism* (New York: Basic Books, 1987), p. 12.

2. The definition of *art* in this chapter is derived from a lecture, "Art and Jewish Continuity: Towards a General Theory of Art in Jewish Education," given by Dr. Yehudah Wurtzel, director of the Jerusalem Media Workshop, at the Conference on Alternatives in Jewish Education, Jerusalem, August 1988.

3. Ibid.

4. Neusner, *Enchantments*, pp. 205-216.

5. Ibid., pp. 3-12.

6. Joan Borysenko, *Minding the Body, Mending the Mind* (Reading, MA: Addison-Wesley, 1987), p. 52.

7. Lawrence Kushner, *Honey from the Rock—Vision of Jewish Mystical Renewal* (San Francisco: Harper & Row, 1977), p. 53.

8. *The Jewish Communities of the World—A Contemporary Guide*, 4th ed., ed. Antony Lerman (New York: Facts on File, 1989), p. 178.

9. Menachem Lubinsky, "The Show That Helped to Shape an Industry," *Kosher Gourmet* (March 1990), p. 16.

10. Marshall Sklare, *Jewish Identity on the Suburban Frontier, 2nd ed.* (Chicago: University of Chicago Press, 1979, ch. 3), as elucidated in *A Certain People—American Jews and Their Lives Today* by Charles E. Silberman (New York: Summit Books, 1985), pp. 233-234.

11. Interview with Gershom Scholem in *Shdemot* (Spring 1975), quoted in *On Jews and Judaism in Crisis—Selected Essays of Gershom Scholem*, ed. Werner J. Dannhauser (New York: Schocken, 1976), p. 10.

12. Richard H. Schwartz, *Judaism and Vegetarianism* (Pompano Beach, FL: Exposition Press, 1982), p. 122.

CHAPTER 5: CHILD DEVELOPMENT AND JEWISH PARENTING

1. David Kraemer, "Images of Childhood and Adolescence in Talmudic Literature," in *The Jewish Family—Metaphor and Memory*, ed. David Kraemer (New York: Oxford University Press, 1989), p. 70. See also Shoshana Matzner-Bekerman's *The Jewish Child—Halachic Perspectives*, Part III, "The Dimensions of Development" and Part IV, "Child Development in the Social Context" (Hoboken, NJ: Ktav, 1984).

2. See *Studies in Cognitive Development: Essays in Honor of Jean Piaget*, ed. David Elkind and J. H. Flavell (New York: Oxford University Press, 1969); Jean Piaget and B.

Inhelder, *The Psychology of the Child* (New York: Basic Books, 1969); Erik H. Erikson, *Childhood and Society*, 2nd ed. (New York: W. W. Norton & Co., 1963); and Lawrence Kohlberg, *The Philosophy of Moral Development: Moral Stages and the Idea of Justice* (New York: Harper & Row, 1981). For a popular exposition of developmentally appropriate practices, see *The Hurried Child* by David Elkind (Reading, MA: Addison-Wesley, 1988).

CHAPTER 6: FAMILY HERITAGE: JEWISH HISTORY BEGINS WITH GRANDMA AND GRANDPA

1. As quoted in *From Generation to Generation* by Arthur Kurzweil (New York: Schocken, 1982), p. 79.

2. Lecture by Arthur Kurzweil, San Antonio, TX, January 20, 1988. See also his book *From Generation to Generation*.

3. Ibid.

CHAPTER 7: THE CHANGING JEWISH FAMILY

1. Sylvia Barack Fishman, "The Changing American Jewish Family in the 80's," *Contemporary Jewry* 9:2 (1988): 27.

2. As quoted in *Divorce and the Jewish Child* by Thomas J. Cottle, Ph. D. (New York: The National Jewish Family Center of the American Jewish Committee, 1981), p. 17.

3. Lecture, "The Jewish Family in Israel and the United States: A Comparison," Dr. Jonathan Woocher with Dr. Rivka Bar-Yosef, mod. Sherman Rosenfeld, Conference on Alternatives in Jewish Education, Hebrew University, Jerusalem, August 1988. See also Fishman, "Changing American Jewish Family," p. 27. *Jewish Marital Status*, ed. Carol Diament (Northvale, NJ: Jason Aronson, 1989); and the *National Jewish Population Study, 1990* (New York: Council of Jewish Federations).

4. Woocher lecture. See also Arthur Hertzberg, *The Jews in America—Four Centuries of an Uneasy Encounter* (New York: Simon & Schuster, 1989), pp. 377–388.

5. Egon Mayer, "Intermarriage and Modern Jewish Family Life in the United States: A Research Perspective," in *Jewish Marital Status*, ed. Carol Diament (Northvale, NJ: Jason Aronson, 1989), pp. 246–252.

6. Chaim Waxman, "Toward a Strategy for Integrating Single-Parent Families within the Organized Jewish Community," in *Jewish Marital Status*, ed. Carol Diament (Northvale, NJ: Jason Aronson, 1989), p. 205.

7. Barbara Kalin Bundt, "The Divorced-Parent Family and the Synagogue Community," in *Jewish Marital Status*, ed. Carol Diament (Northvale, NJ: Jason Aronson, 1989), p. 197.

8. Nemzer Brodbar, as cited by Fishman in "Changing American Jewish Family," p. 27.

9. Mayer, "Intermarriage and Modern Jewish Family Life," p. 247.

10. Nathalie Friedman with Theresa F. Rogers, *The Divorced Parent and the Jewish Community* (New York: National Jewish Family Center of The American Jewish Committee, 1985).

11. Marilyn Shlachter Berger, "Facing Divorce—Shielding the Children," in *The Hadassah Magazine Jewish Parenting Book*, ed. Roselyn Bell (New York: Free Press, 1989), p. 293.

12. Bundt, "Divorced-Parent Family," p. 199.

13. Linda Gordon Kuzmack and George Salomon, *Working and Mothering* (New York: The National Jewish Family Center of The American Jewish Committee, 1980), pp. 18–19.

14. Cottle, *Divorce and the Jewish Child*, pp. 22–27.

CHAPTER 8: THE IMPORTANCE OF COMMUNITY

1. See Susan Handelman, "Family, a Religiously Mandated Ideal," and Martha A. Ackelsberg, "Family or Community?" in *Jewish Marital Status*, ed. Carol Diament (Northvale, NJ: Jason Aronson, 1989), pp. 319–325 and pp. 326–330.

2. Jacob Neusner, ed., *Contemporary Judaic Fellowship in Theory and Practice* (New York: Ktav, 1972). For more on the development of the American *havurah* movement, see Bernard Reisman, *The Havurah: A Contemporary Jewish Experience* (New York: UAHC, 1977).

PART II: LEARNING, LEARNING, LEARNING

CHAPTER 9: JEWISH EDUCATION BEGINS AT HOME: THE IMPORTANCE OF INFORMAL LEARNING

1. *The Insecurity of Freedom* (New York: Farrar, Straus & Giroux, 1966), p. 42.

2. From a letter to J. L. Magnes, September 18, 1910, as cited in Joseph L. Baron, ed., *A Treasury of Jewish Quotations* (South Brunswick, NJ: A. S. Barnes and Company, 1965), p. 271.

3. Jacob Neusner, "Talmudic Thinking and Us," in *Invitation to the Talmud* (New York: Harper & Row, 1984), p. 275.

4. Chaim I. Waxman, "The Contemporary American

Jewish Family," in *America's Jews in Transition* (Philadelphia: Temple University Press, 1983), p. 160.

5. Sylvia Barack Fishman, *Learning About Learning: Insights on Contemporary Jewish Education from Jewish Population Studies* (Waltham, MA: Cohen Center for Modern Jewish Studies, Brandeis University, 1987), p. 16.

6. Jacob Neusner, "Study of Torah and Modern Scholarship: Yeshiva, Seminary and University," in *The Way of Torah—An Introduction to Judaism*, 4th ed. (Belmont, CA: Wadsworth, 1988), pp. 141–144; quotation here from p. 142. See also Arthur Hertzberg, "The End of Immigrant Memory—What Can Replace It?" in *The Jews in America—Four Centuries of an Uneasy Encounter* (New York: Simon & Schuster, 1989), pp. 377–388; and Rabbi Hayim HaLevy Donin, "Jewish Respect for Scholarship: An American Myth," in *To Raise a Jewish Child* (New York: Basic Books, 1977), pp. 13–15.

7. Isa Aron, "The Malaise of Jewish Education," *Tikkun* 4:3 (1989): 32–34.

8. Conversation with Vickey Kelman, Whizin Institute for Jewish Family Life seminar, University of Judaism, Los Angeles, June 1990.

9. Aron, "Malaise of Jewish Education," 32–34.

10. David Elkind, *The Hurried Child—Growing Up Too Fast Too Soon* (Reading, MA: Addison-Wesley, 1988), pp. 65–66.

CHAPTER 10: JEWISH STORIES, MUSIC, PLAY, AND IMAGINATION

1. Peninnah Schram, "Storytelling, Five Steps to Teaching Others," *Ten Da'at* (Heshvan 5748 [1987]).

2. See David Elkind, *The Hurried Child* (Reading, MA: Addison-Wesley, 1988), p. 35; and Jim Trealease, *The Read-Aloud Handbook* (New York: Penguin, 1985).

3. Schram, "Storytelling."

4. Ibid.

5. From the translation by Sir Leon Simon (Zionist Federation of Great Britain and Ireland, 1944), p. 28.

6. Lawrence Kaplan, "Education and Ideology in Religious Zionism Today," in *Religious Zionism: Challenges and Choices* (Jerusalem: Oz veShalom), p. 37.

7. Louis Ginzberg, *Legends of the Bible* (Philadelphia: Jewish Publication Society, 1956).

8. Peninnah Schram, interview with the author, Conference on Alternatives in Jewish Education, University of Washington, Seattle, August 1989.

9. Preface to Judith Kaplan Eisenstein's *Heritage of Music* (New York: UAHC Press, 1972).

10. "On Science," cited in Lewis C. Henry, *Best Quotations for All Occasions* (Greenwich, CT: Fawcett, 1969), p. 112.

11. Howard Bogot, "Art Is Not Extracurricular," in *The Jewish Principal's Handbook*, ed. Audrey Friedman Marcus and Raymond A. Zwerin (Denver: Alternatives in Religious Education, 1983), pp. 311–314.

12. See Zalman Schachter, "A First Step: A Devotional Guide," in *The First Jewish Catalog*, ed. Richard Siegel, Michael Strassfeld, Sharon Strassfeld (Philadelphia: Jewish Publication Society, 1973), p. 302.

CHAPTER 11: JEWISH CULTURAL LITERACY

1. Norman Linzer, *The Jewish Family: Authority and Tradition in Modern Perspective* (New York: Human Sciences Press, 1984), p. 112.

2. Barry Holtz, lecture, Conference on Alternatives in Jewish Education, Hebrew University, Jerusalem, August 1988.

3. Jacob Neusner, "Jewish Law and Learning," in *The Enchantments of Judaism* (New York: Basic Books, 1987), p. 136.

4. José Faur, *Golden Doves With Silver Dots—Semiotics and Textuality in Rabbinic Tradition* (Bloomington, IN: University Press, 1986), p. xv.

5. Abraham Joshua Heschel, *The Insecurity of Freedom* (New York: Farrar, Straus & Giroux, 1966), p. 182.

6. David Epstein and Suzanne Singer Stutman, *Torah With Love—A Guide for Strengthening Jewish Values Within the Family* (New York: Prentice Hall Press, 1986).

7. Joel Lurie Grishaver, "The Technology of Making Meaning—A Systematic Inquiry Into the Task of Enabling the Teaching of Jewish Texts," a report on the research and design efforts of Torah Aura Productions (Los Angeles: Torah Aura Productions, 1988), in-house article.

8. Acknowledgments for this idea to Kathy Chesto, lecture, Whizin Institute for Jewish Family Life seminar, University of Judaism, Los Angeles, 1990.

9. "In Living Hebrew," *Hadassah Magazine* (October 1990).

10. See Leo Rosten, *Leo Rosten's Treasury of Jewish Quotations* (Northvale, NJ: Jason Aronson, 1988), p. 519.

11. *The Jewish Observer* (July 19, 1990).

12. Cara Goldberg Marks, *The Handbook of Hebrew Calligraphy* (Northvale, NJ: Jason Aronson, 1990).

13. Definition of a Judaist from Raphael Lowe, as explained by Jacob Neusner, *The Way of Torah: An Introduction to Judaism*, 4th ed. (Belmont, CA: Wadsworth, 1988), p. 27.

CHAPTER 12: LEARNING ABOUT GOD AND PRAYER

1. Perry London, lecture, Whizin Institute for Jewish Family Life seminar, University of Judaism, Los Angeles, June 1990.

2. See Nahum N. Glatzer, *Franz Rosenzweig: His Life and Thought*, presented by Nahum N. Glatzer (New York: Schocken, 1961).

3. Kathy Chesto, lecture, Whizin Institute for Jewish Family Life seminar, University of Judaism, Los Angeles, June 1990.

4. Harold Kushner, "The Idea of God in the Jewish Classroom," in *Creative Jewish Education*, ed. Jeffrey L. Schein and Jacob J. Staub (Chappaqua, NY: Reconstructionist Rabbinical College Press and Rossel Books, 1985), pp. 193–197.

5. Neil Gillman, workshop, "Writing a Theology," Conference on Alternatives in Jewish Education, Ohio State University, Columbus, August 1990. See also Neil Gillman, *Sacred Fragments—Recovering Theology for the Modern Jew* (Philadelphia: Jewish Publication Society, 1990).

6. Zalman Schachter, "A First Step: A Devotional Guide," in *The First Jewish Catalog*, ed. Richard Siegel, Michael Strassfeld, Sharon Strassfeld (Philadelphia: Jewish Publication Society, 1973), p. 302.

CHAPTER 13: JEWISH EDUCATION OUTSIDE THE HOME

1. Sylvia Barack Fishman, *Learning About Learning: Insights on Contemporary Jewish Education from Jewish Population Studies* (Waltham, MA: Cohen Center for Modern Jewish Studies, Brandeis University, 1987), p. 61.

2. Ibid., p. 36.

3. Alvin I. Schiff, "What We Know About . . . The Jewish Day School," in *What We Know About Jewish Education*, ed. Stuart Kelman (Los Angeles: Torah Aura Productions, 1992), p. 156.

4. Fishman, p. 37.

5. See "Education: A Consumer's Handbook," *Newsweek Special Edition* 116:28 (September 1990).

6. Perry London, lecture, Whizin Institute for Jewish Family Life seminar, University of Judaism, Los Angeles, June 1990.

PART III: JEWISH INTERPERSONAL VALUES: TRANSMITTING A GOODLY HERITAGE

CHAPTER 14: JUDAISM: MORE THAN HOLIDAYS

1. Samuel A. Dresner, ed., *I Asked for Wonder: A Spiritual Anthology of Abraham Joshua Heschel* (New York: Crossroad, 1983), p. 63.

2. Rabbi Hayim HaLevy Donin, *To Raise a Jewish Child* (New York: Basic Books, 1977), pp. 22–40.

3. See Robert Ornstein, Ph.D., and David Sobel, M.D., *Healthy Pleasures* (Reading, MA: Addison-Wesley, 1989), pp. 222–237.

4. Abba Eban, *My People* (New York: Behrman House and Random House, 1968), p. 522.

5. Eda LeShan, *When Your Child Drives You Crazy* (New York: St. Martin's, 1985).

CHAPTER 16: FAMILY MITZVAH PROJECTS

1. Mary Gendler, Sharon Strassfeld, and Michael Strassfeld, eds., *The Third Jewish Catalog* (Philadelphia: Jewish Publication Society, 1980), pp. 29–32.

2. Simon Glustrom, *The Language of Judaism* (Northvale, NJ: Jason Aronson, 1988).

3. Marilyn Shlachter Berger, "Facing Divorce, Shielding the Children," in *The Hadassah Magazine Jewish Parenting Book*, ed. Roselyn Bell (New York: Free Press, 1989), pp. 288–294.

4. Nogah Hareuveni with Helen Frenkly, *Ecology in the Bible* (Kiryat Ono: Neot Kedumim, 1974). Available from the Jewish National Fund Department of Education, 114 E. 32nd St., Suite 1501, New York, NY 10016.

PART IV: ISRAEL: THE JEWISH HOME AND THE JEWISH HOMELAND

CHAPTER 18: A SENSE OF ISRAEL IN THE AMERICAN JEWISH HOME

1. Barbara Sofer, *Kids Love Israel, Israel Loves Kids* (Rockville, MD: Kar-Ben Copies, 1988), p. 19.

CHAPTER 20: AMERICAN OR ISRAELI JEWRY: RIVALRY OR PARTNERSHIP?

1. Abraham Joshua Heschel, *Israel—An Echo of Eternity* (New York: Farrar, Straus & Giroux, 1974), p. 13.

PART V: THE JEWISH WEEK, MONTH, AND YEAR

1. Abraham Joshua Heschel, *The Sabbath* (New York: Farrar, Straus & Giroux, 1951).

CHAPTER 21: SHABBAT: THE HEART OF JEWISH LIFE

1. Found in M. M. Yosher, *Saint and Sage* (New York: Bloch, 1937), as quoted in *A Treasury of Jewish Quotations*, ed. Joseph L. Baron (South Brunswick, NJ: A. S. Barnes, 1965), p. 425.

2. Ahad HaAm, *HaShiloah* (1898), quoted in *A Treasury of Jewish Quotations*, Joseph L. Baron (South Brunswick, NJ: A. S. Barnes, 1965), p. 427.

3. Eda LeShan, *When Your Child Drives You Crazy* (New York: St. Martin's, 1985), pp. 293–301.

4. David Elkind, *The Hurried Child* (Reading, MA: Addison-Wesley, 1988).

5. Rabbi Irving Greenberg, *The Jewish Way—Living the Holidays* (New York: Summit Books, 1988), p. 164.

6. Blu Greenberg, *How to Run a Traditional Jewish Household* (Northvale, NJ: Jason Aronson, 1989), pp. 25–26.

7. Abraham Joshua Heschel, *The Sabbath* (New York: Farrar, Straus & Giroux, 1951).

8. Harold Kushner, *Who Needs God* (New York: Summit Books, 1989), p. 106.

9. Arlie Hochschild with Anne Machung, *The Second Shift: Working Parents and the Revolution at Home* (New York: Viking Penguin, 1989).

10. Robert Ornstein, Ph.D., and David Sobel, M.D., *Healthy Pleasures* (Reading, MA: Addison-Wesley, 1989).

11. Vicky Kelman with Joel Grishaver and Jane Golub, *Together: A Child-Parent Kit*, part 3 (New York: Melton Research Center, 1984), p. 48.

12. Erich Fromm, *You Shall Be As Gods* (New York: Henry Holt, 1991).

13. Rabbi Irving Greenberg, *The Jewish Way—Living the Holidays* (New York: Summit Books, 1988), p. 177; italics his.

14. Heschel, *Sabbath*.

15. Diana Bletter, *The Invisible Thread—A Portrait of Jewish American Women* (Philadelphia: Jewish Publication Society, 1989), p. 220.

16. Irving Greenberg, *The Jewish Way*.

CHAPTER 23: AROUND THE JEWISH YEAR

1. Quoted in *A Treasury of Jewish Quotations*, ed. Joseph L. Baron (South Brunswick, NJ: A. S. Barnes, 1965), p. 39.

2. Edward L. Greenstein in Michael Strassfeld, *The Jewish Holidays—A Guide and Commentary* (New York: Harper & Row, 1985), p. 106.

CHAPTER 24: THE FALL HOLIDAYS: SEASON OF RENEWAL

1. Blu Greenberg, *How to Run a Traditional Jewish Household* (Northvale, NJ: Jason Aronson, 1989), pp. 310–311. Michael Strassfeld, *The Jewish Holiday—A Guide and Commentary* (New York: Harper & Row, 1985), p. 99. Phillips Goodman, ed., *The Rosh Hashanah Anthology* (Philadelphia: Jewish Publication Society, 1973), pp. 345–346.

2. Agudas Achim Sisterhood, *Love and Best Dishes* (San Antonio, 1978).

3. Floreva G. Cohen, *Sneakers to Shul* (New York: Board of Jewish Education, 1978).

4. Rabbi Irving Greenberg, *The Jewish Way—Living the Holidays* (New York: Summit Books, 1988), pp. 203–205.

5. Richard Siegel, Michael Strassfeld, and Sharon Strassfeld, eds., *The First Jewish Catalog* (Philadelphia: Jewish Publication Society, 1973), pp. 129–130; and Michael Strassfeld, *The Jewish Holidays–A Guide and Commentary* (New York: Harper & Row, 1985), p. 138.

6. Danny Siegel, *Munbaz II and Other Mitzvah Heroes* (Spring Valley, NY: Town House Press, 1988).

7. Joel Lurie Grishaver, *Building Jewish Life: Sukkot & Simhat Torah* (Los Angeles: Torah Aura Productions, 1987), p. 47.

8. Strassfeld, *Jewish Holidays*, p. 129.

9. Gloria Kauffer Greene, *The Jewish Holiday Cookbook: An International Collection of Recipes and Customs* (New York: Times Books, 1985).

10. Nogah Hareuveni and Helen Frenkly, *Ecology in the Bible* (Kiryat Ono: Neot Kedumim, 1974). Available from the Jewish National Fund Department of Education, 114 E. 32nd St., Suite 1501, New York, NY 10016.

11. Isaac Bashevis Singer, "A Tale of Three Wishes," in Singer's *Stories for Children* (New York: Farrar, Straus & Giroux, 1985), pp. 8–14.

CHAPTER 25: THE WINTER HOLIDAYS

1. For a fuller explanation of the period, see Lee I. A. Levine, "The Age of Hellenism," in Hershel Shanks, ed., *Ancient Israel* (New York: Prentice Hall, 1988), pp. 177–204.

2. Michael Strassfeld, *The Jewish Holidays—A Guide and Commentary* (New York: Harper & Row, 1985), p. 72.

3. Virginia S. Rich, *Crafts for Fun* (Valley Forge, PA: Judson Press, 1986), pp. 24–27.

4. Joan Nathan, *The Children's Jewish Holiday Kitchen* (New York: Schocken, 1987), p. 59.

5. Agudas Achim Sisterhood, *Love and Best Dishes* (San Antonio, 1978), p. 179.

6. Ibid., p. 147, adopted.

7. Molli Katzen, *The Enchanted Broccoli Forest . . . and other timeless delicacies* (Berkley: Ten Speed Press, 1982), p. 229.

8. Strassfeld, *Jewish Holidays*, p. 183.

9. Charles Silberman, *A Certain People—American Jews and Their Lives Today* (New York: Summit Books, 1985), p. 9.

10. See Simon Solomon, *The Wise Men of Helm and Their Merry Tales* (1942) and *More Wise Men of Helm and Their Merry Tales* (1979), both from Behrman House, West Orange, NJ.

11. Mildred L. Covert and Sylvia P. Gerson, *The Kosher Cajun Cookbook* (Gretna, LA: Pelican Publishing, 1987), pp. 129–131.

12. Pinchas HaCohen Peli, *Torah Today—A Renewed Encounter with Scripture* (Washington, DC: B'nai B'rith, 1987), p. 86.

CHAPTER 26: THE SPRING HOLIDAYS

1. *The Art of Jewish Living: The Passover Seder* (New York: Federation of Jewish Men's Clubs and the University of Judaism, 1988), pp. 48–51.

2. See Arthur Waskow, *God Wrestling* (New York: Schocken, 1978), pp. 76–86, "The Question Is the Answer: Education and Passover."

3. Yossi Klein Halevi, "Travelling with Light: A Kabbalistic Passover," *Jewish World* (April 10–16, 1987): 20.

4. Pinchas HaCohen Peli, *Torah Today* (Washington, DC: B'nai B'rith, 1987), pp. 59–62.

5. Adin Steinsaltz, *The Strife of the Spirit* (Northvale, NJ: Jason Aronson, 1988), pp. 5, 7, 8.

6. Joseph L. Baron, ed., *A Treasury of Jewish Quotations* (South Brunswick, NJ: A. S. Barnes, 1965), p. 482; and in *Leo Rosten's Treasury of Jewish Quotations* (Northvale, NJ: Jason Aronson, 1988), p. 498.

7. Steinsaltz, *Strife*, p. 4.

8. Ibid., p. 8.

9. *Moment* magazine (June 1989).

10. Arthur Kurzweil, *From Generation to Generation* (New York: Schocken, 1980), pp. 136–139.

11. Rabbi Irving Greenberg, *The Jewish Way—Living the Holidays* (New York: Summit Books, 1988), pp. 401–402.

12. See Charles E. Silberman, *A Certain People—American Jews and Their Lives Today* (New York: Summit Books, 1985), pp. 233–234.

13. Blu Greenberg, *How to Run a Traditional Jewish Household* (Northvale, NJ: Jason Aronson, 1989), p. 463.

14. Adapted from Agudas Achim Sisterhood, *Love and Best Dishes* (San Antonio, 1978).

15. Ibid.

16. Ellen Frankel, *The Classic Tales—4,000 years of Jewish Lore* (Northvale, NJ: Jason Aronson, 1989).

17. Freema Gottlieb, *The Lamp of God—A Jewish Book of Light* (Northvale, NJ: Jason Aronson, 1989), p. 10.

CHAPTER 27: SUMMER: A SOMBER PERIOD IN THE JEWISH CALENDAR

1. Blu Greenberg, *How to Run a Traditional Jewish Household* (Northvale, NJ: Jason Aronson, 1989), pp. 468–478.

2. Rabbi Irving Greenberg, *The Jewish Way—Living the Holidays* (New York: Summit Books, 1988), pp. 283–303.

3. Michael Strassfeld, *The Jewish Holidays—A Guide and Commentary* (New York: Harper & Row, 1985), pp. 92–93.

PART VI: SPECIAL TIMES IN THE LIFE OF A YOUNG JEWISH FAMILY

CHAPTER 28: IN THE BEGINNING

1. Joshua O. Haberman, "The New Exodus Out of Judaism," *Moment* 17:4 (August 1992): 34–35. See also Sylvia Barack Fishman, "The Changing Jewish Family in the 80's," *Contemporary Jewry* 9:2 (1988): 1–31.

2. Rivka Bar-Yosef, lecture, Conference on Alternatives in Jewish Education, Hebrew University, Jerusalem, August 1988.

3. Michael Gold, *And Hannah Wept: Infertility, Adoption and the Jewish Couple* (Philadelphia: Jewish Publication Society, 1988).

4. Baruch A. Levine, ed., *The JPS Torah Commentary—Leviticus* (Philadelphia: Jewish Publication Society, 1989), p. 250.

5. Aryeh Kaplan, *Jewish Meditation: A Practical Guide* (New York: Schocken, 1985), pp. 154–160.

6. Anita Diamant, *The Jewish Baby Book* (New York: Summit Books, 1988), pp. 32–34.

7. Blu Greenberg, *How to Run a Traditional Jewish Household* (Northvale, NJ: Jason Aronson, 1989), pp. 235–236.

8. Ibid., p. 236.

9. Tracy G. Klirs, lecture, "*Tkhines*: Women's Yiddish Prayers," Conference on Alternatives in Jewish Education, University of Washington, Seattle, August 1989. See also Chava Weissler, "The Traditional Piety of Ashkenazic Women," in *Jewish Spirituality II—From the Sixteenth Century Revival to the Present*, ed. Arthur Green (New York: Crossroad, 1989), pp. 245–275.

10. *Kol Heneshamah: Shirim Uvrahot—Songs, Blessings, and Rituals for the Home* (Wyncote, PA: The Reconstructionist Press, 1991), pp. 114–115.

11. *The Penguin Book of Hebrew Verse*, ed. and trans. T. Carmi (New York: Viking and JPS, 1981), p. 558, lines cited were retranslated by the author.

12. *Golden Doves with Silver Dots—Semiotics and Textuality in Rabbinic Tradition* (Bloomington, IN: Indiana University Press, 1986), p. 38.

13. Mark Zborowski and Elizabeth Herzog, *Life Is With People—The Culture of the Shtetl* (New York: Schocken, 1962), pp. 308, 329. See also Menachem M. Brayer, *The Jewish Woman in Rabbinic Literature*, vol. 1, A *Psychosocial Perspective* (Hoboken, NJ: Ktav, 1986), pp. 108–110, on the importance of breast-feeding in Jewish culture.

14. Quoted in *The Talmudic Anthology* (West Orange, NJ: Behrman House, 1945), p. 71.

15. See Meir Elazar Etya, *Sefer Shirei Dodim* (Hebrew only), pp. 34–37; available from Rehov HaMa'philim 35, P. O. Box 1043, Givat Olga, Hadera, Israel. The only way I know of to learn the tunes to these songs is to hear them from a Sephardic *piyetan* (cantor).

16. Jacob Neusner, *The Enchantments of Judaism* (New York: Basic Books, 1987), pp. 44–45.

17. There are some contemporary rabbinic opinions that it is permissible to postpone the *brit milah* from a Sabbath if the celebration could lead to guests violating the Sabbath. Consult your rabbi if this is an issue of concern to you.

18. Susan Weidman Schneider, *Jewish and Female—A Guide and Sourcebook for Today's Jewish Woman* (New York: Simon & Schuster, 1985), p. 127.

19. Adele Faber and Elaine Mazlish, *Siblings Without Rivalry* (New York: W. W. Norton, 1987).

20. Florence B. Freedman, *Brothers—A Hebrew Legend*, ill. Robert Andrew Parker (New York: Harper & Row, 1985).

Chapter 29: Birthdays

1. Shoshana Matzner-Bekerman, *The Jewish Child—Halakhic Perspectives* (Hoboken, NJ: Ktav, 1984), p. 225.

2. David Kraemer, ed. *The Jewish Family—Metaphor and Memory* (New York: Oxford University Press, 1989), pp. 71–74.

3. Simcha Raz, *A Tzaddik in Our Time* (New York: Feldheim, 1976), p. 19.

4. Danny Siegel, *Gym Shoes and Irises (Personalized Tzedakah), Book Two* (Spring Valley, NY, 1987), pp. 156–178, "Bar and Bat Mitzvah."

5. "The Impact of Post Bar/Bat Mitzvah Education on Jewish Communal Involvement," *Trends* 13 (Fall 1987): 1.

6. Recommendations of a report by the Board of Jewish Education of Greater New York, June 1987.

7. See Gary D. Eisenberg, *Smashing the Idols—A Jewish Inquiry Into the Cult Phenomenon* (Northvale, NJ: Jason Aronson, 1988).

8. See Mark L. Winer, "Mom, We're Just Dating," in *Jewish Marital Status—A Hadassah Study*, ed. Carol Diament (Northvale, NJ: Jason Aronson, 1989), pp. 228–230.

9. From material shared with the author by Danny Siegel.

EPILOGUE

1. Jacob Neusner, *The Death and Birth of Judaism* (New York: Basic Books, 1987), p. 328.

2. Ibid.; and Leonard Fein, *Where Are We?—The Inner Life of America's Jews* (New York: Harper & Row, 1988), pp. 139–142.

3. Chaim Seidler-Feller, "Jewish Life on Campus Today, 3," *Shema* 20:393.

4. "Judaist," term coined by Raphael Lowe, elucidated in Jacob Neusner, *The Way of Torah—An Introduction to Judaism*, 4th ed. (Belmont, CA: Wadsworth, 1988), pp. 23–28; quotation from p. 28.

GLOSSARY

Afikoman   Small piece of *matzah* that is reserved for "dessert" at the *seder* meal. Children try to find it and exchange it for a prize.

Aggadah   Legends, lore, stories, and other non-legal material from rabbinic literature. Also used in modern Hebrew to mean a fairy tale.

Aliyah   An ascent: to Jerusalem, to the bima to bless the Torah. Also means immigrating to Israel.

Amidah   Standing prayer, also known as the *Shemoneh Esrei* or *Tefillah*. It is the central prayer of the Jewish worship service and consists of up to nineteen blessings of praise, petition, and thanksgiving. Middle section varies from weekdays to Shabbat and festivals.

Ark   Sacred storage area for the Torah scrolls, located in the front of a synagogue sanctuary.

Ashkenazic   Pertaining to Ashkenazic Jews, those whose ancestors came from Germany, Eastern Europe, or Russia.

Bentsher   (Yiddish) A small booklet containing the Grace after Meals and other prayers.

Berachah   A blessing. A *berachah* is a basic unit of Jewish worship. There are *berachot* (plural) that are recited for many different pleasures and occasions of life, as well as those recited before performing a *mitzvah* and those that are part of the prayer service.

Bikur holim   The *mitzvah* of visiting the sick.

Bimah   Raised platform at the front of a synagogue from which prayers are led and the Torah read. In the Sephardic synagogue, the *bimah* is customarily found in the center of the room.

Birkat HaMazon   Blessing for Nourishment, the Grace after Meals, recited after a meal that includes bread.

Brit   A covenant. The *brit milah* is the covenant of circumcision into which Jewish males are entered on the eighth day of life.

Cohen (pl. *Cohanim*)   Descendent of the priestly family of Aaron who served in the ancient Holy Temple in Jerusalem.

Daven   To pray in the traditional Jewish way.

Dayenu   Traditional song from the *seder* ritual that describes God's many beneficent acts toward the Children of Israel. The refrain *dayenu* means, "It would have been enough for us."

Derashah   Interpretation, homily, Torah discourse based on a Jewish text.

Devar Torah   "Word of Torah," a sermonette or Torah discussion.

Dreidl   (Yiddish) A four-sided top that is played with on Hanukkah.

Eliyahu HaNavi   Elijah the Prophet. Since the Bible describes his ascent to heaven in a fiery chariot, Jewish folklore holds that he never died but that he returns to perform acts of kindness, to visit the *seder* and *brit milah*, and will eventually announce the coming of the Messiah.

Elul   Month preceding Rosh HaShanah on the Hebrew calendar.

Erev Shabbat   Sabbath eve. Jewish holidays start at sundown the night before.

Etrog   The citron, a citrus fruit native to Israel that is one of the "four species" used in Sukkot rituals.

Gut Shabbos   (Yiddish) Good Sabbath.

Had Gadya   "One Only Kid": a traditional *seder* song that is held to be an allegory for Israel and its relationship to God and the nations.

Haftarah   Reading from the prophetic or historical books of the Bible that concludes each Sabbath or holiday Torah reading.

Haggadah   Book used at the *seder* meal to retell the story of Passover.

Halachah   Jewish law.

Hallah   Bread baked for the Sabbath and festivals.

Hallel   Psalms of praise that are recited or sung as part of the worship service on festivals and Rosh Hodesh.

Hametz   Leavened food, forbidden for Passover consumption.

GLOSSARY

HaMotzi Blessing recited before eating bread or a meal that includes bread.

Hanukkiyah Eight-branched candelabrum (plus a servant, or *shammash* candle, used to kindle the Hanukkah lights). Also known as a *menorah*.

Hasidism Pietistic movement begun in eighteenth-century Poland by the charismatic leader the Baal Shem Tov. Hasidic practices are characterized by the emphasis on mysticism and the joyful service of God.

Havdalah Short ceremony held on Saturday night to mark the separation between the Sabbath and the weekdays.

Havurah Jewish fellowship group.

Hazzan Cantor, prayer leader.

Hesed Kindness, love. *Gemilut Hasadim* means "deeds of kindness."

Hinuch Education.

Hol HaMoed Intermediate days during the festivals of Sukkot and Passover, which are not as holy as *Yom Tov*. The Sabbath that falls during these days is known as *Shabbat Hol HaMoed*.

Humash Pentateuch, Five Books of Moses. Often printed in a book, organized by Torah portions, together with the *haftarot*.

Kabbalat Shabbat Service to welcome the Sabbath on Friday evening.

Kasher To make kosher.

Kashrut The practice of observing the Jewish dietary laws.

Kavanah "Direction," intention, attentiveness, meditative awareness while performing a religious act. In this volume, also used to describe a spiritual awareness in everyday life.

Kedushah Holiness.

Keva Fixed, regular habit in religious observance.

Kibbutz Communal agricultural settlement in Israel. The *kibbutz* settlements were instrumental in building the state of Israel and providing many of its early leaders.

Kiddush Prayer sanctifying the Sabbath or festival, recited over a cup of wine. Also refers to a light meal or snack, sometimes served for a *Simhah*, eaten after the recitation of *kiddush* in the synagogue.

Kippah Skullcap traditionally worn by Jewish men, and more recently by some Jewish women, as a sign of respect for God. In Yiddish, *yarmulke*.

Kosher "Proper," in accordance with Jewish dietary laws.

Knesset Israel's parliament.

Kotel The Western Wall in Jerusalem, a retaining wall that is the only standing remnant of the ancient Holy Temple.

Lulav Palm branch, waved during Sukkot rituals as part of the four species. Also refers to the palm, myrtle, and willow branches that are waved together.

Maimonides Moses ben Maimon, also known as the Rambam, famous twelfth-century Jewish philosopher, commentator, and physician.

Mahzor Festival prayer book.

Melachah Craft, specific creative acts that are forbidden by *halachah* on the Sabbath.

Mensch (Yiddish) "A person," i.e., a decent, mature, caring person.

Messiah (Hebrew *Mashiah*) Literally, "Anointed One," whom Jewish tradition says will be appointed by God to lead the world into an age of peace and fulfillment. Liberal Judaism describes a nonsupernatural messianic era as humanity's goal.

Mezuzah Parchment scroll containing biblical verses that is attached to the doorposts of a Jewish home as a sign of dedication to God.

Midrash Rabbinic exposition of Scripture, and collections of such expositions, dating back to the Second Temple period. More recently, also used to refer to contemporary creative reinterpretation of Jewish sources.

Mikveh A gathering of waters from a natural source, used as a ritual pool.

Mikdash Me'at Small Holy Temple, traditional term for the Jewish home.

Mishnah Collection of rabbinic legal decisions, completed about 200 C.E. in the land of Israel, in the Hebrew language. It forms the core text of the Talmud.

Mitzvah (pl. *mitzvot*) Torah commandment, religious imperative.

Mizrah "East," a decoration placed on the eastern wall of a home to indicate the direction of Jerusalem, which is faced during prayer.

Moshav Agricultural settlement in Israel.

Omer period See *"Sefirat HaOmer."*

Parashat HaShavua Weekly Torah portion.

Pesah Hebrew name for Passover, spring holiday that celebrates the Exodus from Egypt.

Pidyon HaBen Redemption of the (Firstborn) Son, a brief ceremony traditionally held when a son who is his mother's firstborn is a month old.

Pirke Avot *Chapters of the Fathers*, a collection of sayings from the sages that forms a tractate of the *Mishnah* and is often studied at home and in the synagogue.

Rabbi Authoritative teacher of Jewish law and tradition. "The rabbis" refers to the ancient Jewish sages who argued and expounded on the Oral Tradition at the core of classical Judaism.

Rashi Rabbi Shelomoh Yitzhaki, eleventh-century French Jewish scholar who wrote definitive commentaries of the Bible and Talmud. Rashi script is a style of Hebrew print often used for traditional commentaries.

Rebbe Revered leader of a hasidic group or sect. In contemporary usage, may mean a charismatic leader of any Jewish group.

Rosh Hodesh "Head of the month," new moon on the Hebrew calendar.

Seder Literally "order," ritual meal held on Passover to recount the story of the Exodus.

Sefer Torah Scroll containing the Five Books of Moses, handwritten on parchment by a scribe.

Sefirat HaOmer Period of seven weeks, counted between the second day of Passover and the festival of Shavuot.

Selihot Penitential prayers recited prior to Rosh HaShanah.

Sephardic Pertaining to Jews whose ancestors came from Spain, the Mediterranean region, and Moslem countries.

Shabbat The Jewish Sabbath, which begins Friday evening at sundown and lasts until dark on Saturday night. Also known as *Shabbos*, in the Ashkenazic pronunciation.

Shabbosdik Appropriate to a Sabbath atmosphere.

Shalom "Peace," also used as a greeting. Just prior to and during Shabbat, the greeting is "Shabbat *Shalom*," a peaceful Sabbath.

Shavua Tov "A Good Week," greeting for the end of the Sabbath on Saturday night.

Shavuot Feast of Weeks, early summer festival that celebrates the giving of the Torah.

Shechinah Divine Presence, in Jewish mysticism the feminine, immanent aspect of God.

Shema "Hear O Israel," major prayer declaring God's unity.

Shiddach A match, as in marriage or other pairing.

Shoah The Holocaust, genocide against the Jews in Nazi Europe.

Shofar Ram's horn blown on the High Holidays.

Shtetl Small village in which many Jews lived, in Russia or Eastern Europe.

Shul (Yiddish) A synagogue.

Siddur Jewish prayer book.

Simhah Joy, happiness, a happy occasion.

Simhat Torah "Rejoicing with the Torah," festival on which the annual cycle of Torah readings is concluded and begun again.

Sukkah Hut or booth constructed for the biblical festival of Sukkot (Tabernacles). It is covered with natural materials or greenery known as *s'chach*.

Tallit Four-cornered prayer shawl with ritual fringes (*tzitzit*). Orthodox men and boys wear a small *tallit* (*tallit katan*) under their clothing all day.

Talmud Encyclopedic collection of Jewish Oral Law and lore, consisting of two parts, the *Mishnah* (in Hebrew, completed in the land of Israel about 200 C.E.) and the *Gemara* (in Aramaic, completed in Babylonia about 500 C.E.).

Tefillin Phylacteries, small leather boxes containing scriptural verses, bound on the forehead and arm during prayer in accordance with biblical commandment.

Tekiah Gedolah Long sound blown on the shofar at points during the Rosh HaShanah service and to signal the end of the Yom Kippur fast.

Teshuvah Repentance, return to righteous ways.

Tikkun Olam Repairing the world in "partnership" with God; a mystical concept. In contemporary Jewish thought it is often used to describe social activism.

Tisha B'Av Late-summer fast that commemorates the destruction of the First and Second Temples.

Torah The Five Books of Moses. Also used to mean all of Jewish teaching. The Written Torah refers to biblical Scripture, while the Oral Torah refers to the rabbinic works, which were originally oral in nature.

Tu BiShvat Jewish arbor day, held in early spring.

Tzedakah Righteousness, generally refers to charitable activity and giving.

Yamim Nora'im The High Holy Days: Rosh HaShanah, Yom Kippur, and the days in between.

Yartzeit (Yiddish) The anniversary of a death.

Yizkor Memorial service held on Yom Kippur and festivals.

Yom HaAtzma'ut Israel Independence Day.

Yom HaShoah Holocaust Memorial Day.

Yom HaZikaron Israel's Memorial Day.

Yom Kippur Day of Atonement, marked by fasting and prayer.

Yom Tov Holy day of a festival, marked by ritual observances and abstention from work, similar to a Sabbath.

RESOURCES

RESOURCE GUIDE FOR HOME AND HERITAGE

BASIC JUDAISM

Understanding Judaism—For Adults

Judaism: An Anthology of the Key Spiritual Writings of the Jewish Tradition, rev. ed., edited and interpreted by Arthur Hertzberg (New York: Simon & Schuster, 1991), is an updated edition of "The Classic Introduction to One of the Great Religions of the Modern World," presented through excerpts from the classical Jewish texts.

To Life! A Celebration of Jewish Being and Thinking, by Harold Kushner (Boston: Little, Brown & Company, 1993), is Rabbi Kushner's warm, humorous, sensitive, and welcoming presentation of basic Judaism.

Jewish Literacy, by Joseph Telushkin (New York: William Morrow, 1991), includes more than 600 pages of lucid essays on "the most important things to know about the Jewish religion, its people, and its history."

A Glossary of Jewish Life, by Kerry M. Olitzky and Ronald H. Isaacs (Northvale, NJ: Jason Aronson, 1992), is a comprehensive dictionary of Jewish words, concepts, values, and individuals that goes beyond definitions to convey the Jewish feeling associated with each term. Contains more than 2,400 entries.

The Rhythms of Jewish Living—A Sephardic Approach, by Marc D. Angel (New York: Sepher-Hermon Press, Inc., 1986), presents the Sephardic approach to Jewish living, written by a noted Sephardic rabbi and author.

Guides to Practice—For Adults

(For books that focus specifically on holidays or Shabbat, see the appropriate sections.)

How to Run a Traditional Jewish Household, by Blu Greenberg (Northvale, NJ: Jason Aronson, 1989), has quickly become a classic reference to all facets of modern Orthodox Jewish home life. Goes into great detail about observance while remaining warm and conversational in tone.

The Complete Book of Jewish Observance by Leo Trepp (New York: Behrman House/Summit Books, 1980), "a practical manual for the modern Jew," this book is an excellent basic reference guide. Includes more than 80 photographs.

The Jewish Home: A Guide for Jewish Living, by Daniel B. Syme (Northvale, NJ: Jason Aronson, 1989), is an informative introduction to Jewish life practices, based on a liberal Jewish and Reform perspective.

Living a Jewish Life, by Anita Diamant and Howard Cooper (New York: Harper Perennial, 1991), is a guide to "Jewish Traditions, Customs and Values for Today's Families," from a liberal Jewish perspective.

The First Jewish Catalog, compiled and edited by Richard Siegel, Michael Strassfeld, and Sharon Strassfeld (Philadelphia: Jewish Publication Society, 1973); **The Second Jewish Catalog**, compiled and edited by Michael Strassfeld and Sharon Strassfeld (Philadelphia: Jewish Publication Society, 1976); and **The Third Jewish Catalog—Creating Community**, compiled and edited by Michael Strassfeld and Sharon Strassfeld (Philadelphia: Jewish Publication Society, 1980): a best-selling series of creative and entertaining guides to just about every aspect of Jewish living.

The Art of Judaism

The Enchantments of Judaism—Rites of Transformation from Birth Through Death, by Jacob Neusner (New York: Basic Books, 1987), explains how Jewish rituals function as artistic experiences, why some rituals no longer engage most Jews, and why the Jewish community should place more importance on the artistic expression of Judaism.

BASIC JUDAISM AND THE JEWISH HOME

For Children and for Families to Share

The Jewish Kids Catalog, written and illustrated by Chaya M. Burstein (Philadelphia: Jewish Publication Society, 1983, for ages 8–12, is a fun guide to Jewish history, heritage, and practices, filled with drawings and photographs. A wonderful book for every Jewish child.

Basic Judaism for Young People, 3 vols. "Israel," "Torah," and "God," by Naomi Pasachoff (West Orange, NJ: Behrman House, 1986), for ages 9–13. This innovative series addresses basic Jewish concepts in an interdisciplinary fashion by exploring the deeper meaning of basic Jewish values vocabulary. A good choice for parents who want to read and learn together with their children. Includes color illustrations and photos. Teachers' guides available.

What Does Being Jewish Mean?, by Rabbi E. B. Freedman, Jan Greenberg, and Karen A. Katz (New York: Prentice Hall Press, 1991), for children ages 5–12 and their parents, is a collection of "read aloud responses to questions Jewish children ask about history, religion and culture." Useful for parents who would like some help in answering their children's questions about Judaism and Jewish life. Personalize by discussing the responses with your children or rephrasing them to reflect your personal beliefs.

Menorahs, Mezuzahs, and Other Jewish Symbols, by Miriam Chaikin, with illustrations by Erika Weihs (New York: Clarion, 1990), for ages 9 and up, is a guide to the meaning of basic Jewish symbols and observances. Another good choice for parent-child sharing.

My Very Own Jewish Home, by Andrew Goldstein, photos by Madeline Wikler (Rockville, MD: Kar-Ben Copies, 1979), for ages 3 to 8, is a child's-eye view of the Jewish home. Use this photo essay of a Jewish home as the starting point for a "Jewish home tour" with your child.

JEWISH PARENTING

To Raise a Jewish Child—a Guide for Parents, by Rabbi Hayim Halevy Donin (New York: Basic Books, Inc., 1977), offers spiritual and practical advice on raising and educating a Jewish child.

The Hadassah Magazine Jewish Parenting Book, edited by Roselyn Bell (New York: The Free Press, 1989), contains a collection of *Hadassah* magazine articles on a multitude of pertinent subjects related to contemporary Jewish family life.

The Jewish Family Book, by Sharon Strassfeld and Kathy Green (New York: Bantam, 1981), in-

cludes family anecdotes, resources, and creative ideas on Jewish education and family experiences, in the home and the community. With black-and-white photographs.

Raising Children to Care, by Miriam Adahan (Jerusalem: Feldheim, 1988), blends traditional Jewish sources with contemporary psychology. Written from a strictly Orthodox viewpoint.

Raising Your Child to Be a Mensch, by Neil Kurshan (New York: Ballantine, 1989), is a rabbi and father's personal sharing about the important priorities in family life.

PERIODICALS FOR JEWISH PARENTS

Jewish Family, produced by Alef Design Group, Torah Aura Productions, 4423 Fruitland Ave., Los Angeles, CA 90058, (800) BE-TORAH, (213) 585-7312, appears six times a year. Each newsletter includes features on such topics as holidays, parenting, grandparenting, health, travel, resources, and recipes.

The Jewish Calendar, Isaac Nathan Publishing Co., 7106 Owensmouth Ave., Canoga Park, CA 91303, (800) 6-JEWISH, (818) 346-1410. This journal is published four times a year. Each issue focuses on a major holiday and also includes topics such as ethics, parenting, genealogy, the arts, and humor.

The Jewish Parent Connection, published by the Parent Enrichment Program of Torah Umesorah, National Society for Hebrew Day Schools, 160 Broadway, New York, NY 10038, (212) 227-1000, provides educational perspectives and Jewish information to parents of children at traditionally oriented day schools.

THE CHANGING AMERICAN JEWISH FAMILY

For Adults

The Hadassah Magazine Jewish Parenting Book (listed earlier) has several useful articles on dealing with the changing patterns of Jewish family life.

Jewish Marital Status, a Hadassah study, edited by Carol Diament (Northvale, NJ: Jason Aronson, 1989), is a collection of articles ranging from academic to deeply personal, on changing Jewish marital patterns, in the following catagories: single, not quite married, widowed, abandoned, divorced, remarried, intermarried, gay or lesbian, childless.

Jewish and Female—A Guide and Sourcebook

for Today's Jewish Woman, by Susan Weidman Schneider (New York: Simon & Schuster, 1985), is packed with useful information and resource guides. This volume explores everything from ethnic stereotypes to ritual, legal, and family issues.

The William Petschek National Jewish Family Center of the American Jewish Committee (AJC), Institute of Human Relations, 165 E. 56th St., New York, NY 10022, publishes a number of studies and articles on contemporary issues affecting the Jewish family, including: Jewish identity, family size, dual-career families, divorce, and intermarriage.

Choosing Judaism, by Lydia Kukoff (New York: UAHC Press, 1981), is a warm personal account of the author's conversion to Judaism, as well as general advice for the Jew by Choice, focusing on the emotional adjustments.

Your People, My People, by Lena Romanoff with Lisa Hostein (Philadelphia: Jewish Publication Society, 1990), is a guide to "finding acceptance and fulfillment as a Jew by Choice," written by a counselor to thousands of converts who is herself a Jew by Choice. Includes advice on raising children in a conversionary marriage.

Mixed Blessings, by Paul Cowen with Rachel Cowen (New York: Doubleday, 1980), is a guide to "Overcoming the Stumbling Blocks in an Interfaith Marriage" that grew out of workshops conducted by the authors, an intermarried couple in which the wife converted to Judaism and has since become a rabbi. Includes examples of various resolutions achieved by interfaith couples.

The Intermarriage Handbook, by Judy Petsonk and Jim Remsen (New York: Quill, 1991), is a comprehensive and practical self-help guide for interfaith households. Deals with possible options for raising children within an intermarried household.

Teens—Adults

The Invisible Thread—A Portrait of Jewish American Women, interviews by Dianna Bletter, photographs by Lori Grinker (Philadelphia: Jewish Publication Society, 1989), includes black and white photographs and interviews with 60 women, who express the variety and intensity of contemporary Jewish life in the United States.

For Children

Mommy Never Went to Hebrew School, by Mindy Avra Portnoy, with illustrations by Shelly O. Haas (Rockville, MD: Kar-Ben Copies, 1989), for ages 4–8. A mother explains to her young son about her conversion to Judaism before his birth.

Who Will Lead Kiddush? by Barbara Pomerantz, with illustrations by Donna Ruff (New York: UAHC Press, 1985), for ages 5–9, is a sensitive treatment of divorce in a Jewish home. I felt sad to read it yet glad that such a book exists for Jewish children wondering about change and stability when parents divorce.

Ima on the Bima—My Mommy Is a Rabbi, by Rabbi Mindy Avra Portnoy, with illustrations by Steffi Karen Rubin (Rockville, MD: Kar-Ben Copies, 1986), for ages 3–8. The changing role of women in Judaism is reflected in this story about a rabbi's role, described from her rabbi's daughter's viewpoint.

WHERE TO OBTAIN JEWISH BOOKS

Patronize your local Jewish bookstore if you are fortunate enough to live in a community with such a resource. Your synagogue and public libraries can also be a good source for Jewish books. In addition, you can keep informed of the latest Jewish publications and purchase Jewish books for adults and children at discounted prices by joining:

The Jewish Book Club, P. O. Box 941, Northvale, NJ 07647, (800)-336-9606.

Other sources for Jewish books include:

Enjoy-A-Book Club, P. O. Box 101, Woodmere, NY 11598, (516) 569-0324. A book club especially for Jewish children.

"America's Jewish Bookstore," the mail-order division of Pinskers Judaica Center, 2028 Murray Avenue, Pittsburgh, PA 15217, (800)-JUDAISM (in Canada: 800-776-9545).

Ma'ayan Book Company, P. O. Box 3197, Framingham, MA 01701, (800) 262-2926.

(The latter two also offer extensive listings of juvenile selections.)

SOURCES FOR JUDAICA FOR THE HOME

Judaica Distributors

The following Judaica distributors provide either catalogs or extensive mail-order services. Don't forget to also explore these: local Judaica gift shops, synagogue gift shops, area bookshops and galleries, Jewish Community Center art fairs and exhibits, Jewish museum and university gift shops, area craftspeople, and exhibitors at conventions of Jewish organizations.

HaMakor Judaica, Inc.—"The Source for Everything Jewish," P. O. Box 48836, Niles, IL 60714, (800) 426-2567. Retail store: 4150 W. Dempster, Skokie, IL 60076, (708) 677-4150, offers a glossy color catalog with a wide array of ritual items, books, and gifts.

Galerie Robin, 6808 Pennywell Dr., Nashville, TN 37205, (800) 635-8279. The color catalog presents fine Judaic artwork and ritual items.

Shoshana by Mail, 45 S. Main St., New City, NY 10956, (800) 845-4484. A color catalog presents a selection of contemporary Judaic art and crafts.

Kolbo, 435–437 Harvard St., Brookline, MA 02146, (617) 731-8743. This well-known shop for Judaic arts and books will ship items and can send brochures and photos.

The Moment Collection, 3000 Connecticut Ave., NW, Suite 300, Washington, DC 20008, (800) 221-4644, is *Moment* magazine's mail-order gift service.

J. Levine Co., 5 West 30th St. (between Broadway and 5th Ave.), New York, NY 10001, (212) 695-6888, is the world's biggest Jewish book and gift store.

California Stitchery, 6015 Sunnyslope Ave., Van Nuys, CA 91401, (800) 345-3332, has a catalog of Judaic designs in stichery of all types.

The L'Chayim Gift Shop, 7450 Callaghan Rd., San Antonio, TX 78229, (210) 341-5045, ships Judaica items all over Texas, the Southwest, and Mexico.

Raanan Enterprises, 1096 Sparrow Rd., Jenkintown, PA 19046, has a catalog of Judaica for children, including books and toys.

Calligraphers

Avco Graphics, 3313 Shelburne Rd., Baltimore, MD 21203, features Abraham Cohen's artwork, religious documents, and greeting cards.

Betsy Platkin Teutsch, 629 W. Cliveden St., Philadelphia, PA 19119-3651, (215) 438-6834, limited serigraphed editions of calligraphic artistic works.

The Jewish Art and Calligraphy Studio, 17 E. 67th St., New York, NY 10021, (212) 744-4355, carries one-of-a-kind and limited editions of Jewish art and life-cycle documents by artist-scribe Neil H. Yerman.

Peggy H. Davis Calligraphy, CM7 Adamsville Rd., Colrain, MA 01340, (413) 624-3204, commis-

sions and prints of religious documents, invitations, and decorations.

DA Greetings, Calligrapher Denni-Ann Gershaw-Smith can be contacted at (602) 783-0501. She designs life-cycle certificates, banners, and decorative signs. She also has a line of greeting cards in English, Hebrew, Spanish, and other languages.

Art Cooperatives

Art Sites, 7531 Coddle Harbor Lane, Potomac, MD 20854, (301) 299-5526, Washington, DC, area artists' cooperative that specializes in Jewish arts and crafts, including calligraphy, pottery, fine arts, jewelry, woodwork, and more.

American Guild of Judaic Art, P. O. Box 1794, Murray Hill Station, New York, NY 10156, Fax (212) 889-7581, is a national organization dedicated to promoting awareness of fine art and craft objects. Contact them for information on many leading American Judaic artists who create art and ritual objects for home and synagogue.

Garments

Larosh, 18744 Parthenia, #1, Northridge, CA 91324, (818) 886-5021, produces *tallitot* and other ritual garments of hand-woven silk, which can be personalized with family heirloom items.

Roz Houseknecht, 12116 Hunters Lane, Rockville, MD 20852, (301) 231-5339, weaves one-of-a-kind *tallitot, hallah* covers, clothing, and other items.

Handwovens by Hannah, Hannah Margolis, 5606 Ponderosa, San Antonio, TX 78240, (210) 684-8018. Hannah weaves personalized *tallitot, hallah* covers, baby blankets, and other items.

Clothing Art Design by Shelley Silver Whizin, Sherman Oaks, CA, (818) 906-3119. Shelley designs unique hand-painted *kippot*.

Gabrieli, 12 Mazal Dagim Street (P. O. Box 8077), Old Jaffa 68036, Israel, (03) 823323, (Fax) 972-3-817602. Contact: Mr. Arik Gabrieli. Well-known line of hand-woven *tallitot* and other items.

Beged Ivri, 111 Agrippas St., Jerusalem, Israel, (02) 250655. Reuven Prager designs unique clothing and ritual garments, based on the biblical designs of ancient Israel.

Exhibition

The International Jewish Festival is an annual exhibition including kosher food products, Judaic art, books, crafts, music, religious articles, gifts, catering, travel, educational materials, jewelry, and Jewish service organizations. The exhibitions are held each February in New York City and also travel to other major Jewish population centers. Those who can't make it to the festival in person can purchase the show directory, which lists names, addresses, and brief descriptions of the exhibitors. For more information, contact: Aharon Unger, vice-president and show manager, Eventful Enterprises, Inc., 21 W. 38th St., New York, NY 10018, (800) 822-EXPO.

Publications and Directories on Judaica

Judaica News, P. O. Box 1130, Fair Lawn, NJ 07410, (201) 796-6151, is a quarterly publication devoted to Jewish art and culture. Includes information on shows, festivals, museum exhibits, artists, and conferences. An annual supplement, **The Judaica News Directory**, is a comprehensive guide to sources for Jewish art, crafts, rare books, and antiques.

The Jewish Folk Arts Society, 11710 Hunters Lane, Rockville, MD 20852, (301) 230-1369, publishes a resource directory of Judaic artists of all types in the Washington, DC, and Maryland area and sponsors Judaic arts festivals.

The New Jewish Yellow Pages by Mae Shafter Rockland (New York: SBS, 1980) is a guide to Judaic artists, craftspeople, dealers, and galleries. Some listings are out of date, but author Mae Rockland Tupa, 106 Francis St., Brookline, MA 02146, is available for professional consulting and teaching about Jewish art and celebration.

KOSHER COOKBOOKS AND BOOKS ABOUT FOOD

For Children

Fins and Scales—A Kosher Tale, by Deborah Uchille Miller and Karen Ostrove (Rockville, MD: Kar-Ben, 1992), is a comic rhyming tale that explains kosher practices.

Little Daniel and the Jewish Delicacies, by Smadar Shir Sidi, illustrated by Miriam Schaer (New York: Adama Books, 1988), for ages 3–8, is not a cookbook but a storybook about the meaning behind many holiday foods and customs. It's illustrated with colorful collage-style pictures.

The Children's Jewish Holiday Kitchen, by Joan Nathan (New York: Schocken, 1987), for ages 5–12 (with parents), is unique in offering instruc-

tions for precisely who does what when making the easy recipes as an adult-with-child activity. The book includes holiday menus, photographs, anecdotes, and crafts.

A First Jewish Holiday Cookbook, by Chaya Burstein (New York: Bonim Books, 1979), for ages 6–12, includes fun and unusual holiday recipes that children can make, along with Burstein's lively illustrations and personal anecdotes.

Matzah Meals, by Judy Tabs and Barbara Steinberg, illustrated by Chari R. McLean (Rockville, MD: Kar-Ben Copies, Inc., 1985), for ages 7–12, contains kosher for Passover recipes, including all kinds of snacks, rated from very easy to "adult supervision needed."

Miracles Meals—Eight Nights of Food 'n Fun for Chanukah, by Madeline Wikler and Judyth Groner, illustrated by Chari Radin (Rockville, MD: Kar-Ben Copies, Inc., 1987), for ages 9–12, includes lots of winter recipes and Hanukkah party ideas.

For Family Cooking

There are dozens of kosher cookbooks for adults that can also be used when cooking with children. Here are a few from which you may learn as you cook:

The Jewish Holiday Cookbook: An International Collection of Recipes and Customs, by Gloria Kauffer Greene (New York: Times Books, 1985), contains 250 recipes, personal anecdotes, and food lore from Jewish communities of the world. It includes many unusual and even whimsical recipes to make with or for children, such as Gingerbread Sukkah and braided sweet *hallah* crowns.

A Lexicon of Jewish Cooking, by Patti Shosteck (Chicago: Contemporary Books, Inc., 1981), is an inclusive collection of folklore, foodlore, history, customs, and recipes.

The Jewish Holiday Kitchen, by Joan Nathan (New York: Schocken, 1979). Along with special holiday recipes from a variety of Jewish communities, this book supplies stories and anecdotes that take the reader to a variety of wonderful Jewish kitchens around the world.

From My Grandmother's Kitchen—A Sephardic Cookbook, by Viviane Alchech Miner with Linda Krinn (Gainesville, FL: Triad Publishing Co., 1984), combines Sephardic recipes with Miner's memoirs and photos of a Sephardic childhood in Geneva. Many of the recipes are based on fresh produce.

The Garden of Eden Cookbook—Recipes in the Biblical Tradition, by Devorah Emmet Wigoder (New York: Harper & Row, 1988). Along with produce-based recipes and plant lore, this cookbook tells the story of Wigoder's *aliyah* to the new State of Israel, where she started an organic biblical garden.

Something Different for Passover, by Zell J. Schulman (Gainesville, FL: Triad Publishing Company, Inc., 1986), provides creative and unusual Passover dishes, including *seder* menus.

Love and Best Dishes—Kosher Recipes from the Kitchens of the Agudas Achim Sisterhood (San Antonio: Agudas Achim Sisterhood, 1977), available from Congregation Agudas Achim, 1201 Donaldson, San Antonio, TX 78228, (210) 736-4216, has uncommonly easy and good basic recipes for Shabbat, holidays, Tex-Mex dishes, and everyday kosher cooking.

Magazines

The Kosher Gourmet and Jewish Perspective, 21 W. 38th St., Suite 1200, New York, NY 10018, (212) 302-6677, appears six times per year. It's a glossy, full-color magazine that includes gourmet kosher recipes and articles on contemporary Jewish culture and life-styles.

Jewish Vegetarianism (For Adults)

Judaism and Vegetarianism by Richard H. Schwartz (Marblehead, MA: Micah Pub., 1988), provides a Jewish approach to vegetarianism, short biographies of famous Jewish vegetarians, a guide to organizations, and some recipes.

FAMILY HISTORY

For Adults

From Generation to Generation—How to Trace Your Jewish Genealogy and Personal History, by Arthur Kurzweil (New York: Schocken, 1980), dispels the myths that say it's impossible to trace Jewish genealogies. In addition, Kurzweil's own inspiring story of discovering his roots will motivate you to do it for your family.

Reflections—A Jewish Grandparent's Gift of Memories, by Ronald H. Isaacs and Leora W. Isaacs (Northvale, NJ: Jason Aronson, 1987), is a book for grandparents to complete and give to their grandchildren. In it, they record their history,

memories, and ideas, along with family stories and photographs.

For Teens

My Generations: A Course in Jewish Family History, by Arthur Kurzweil (West Orange, NJ: Behrman House, 1983), enables the teen, alone or with parents, to research and record family history.

For Children

My Backyard History Book, by David Weitzman (Boston: Little, Brown & Company, 1975), for ages 8 to 12, is a fun book to read and inspire family record keeping for children as well as for adults.

The Castle on Hester Street, written and illustrated by Linda Heller (Philadelphia: Jewish Publication Society, 1990), for ages 4 to 9, is an award-winning book about grandparents who tell tales of their childhoods. Grandpa recalls marvelous adventures, while Grandma recalls the way it really was.

The Keeping Quilt, written and illustrated by Patricia Pallaco (New York: Simon & Schuster, 1988), for ages 4 to 9, is an award-winning story about a family quilt and the people who hand it from generation to generation.

Leaving for America, by Roslyn Bresnick-Perry, illustrated by Mira Reisberg (Emeryville, CA: Children's Book Press, 1992), for ages 5 and up, tells about a young girl's experience as she prepares to leave the shtetl behind. The detailed painting-collage illustrations are great conversation starters.

RESOURCES ON CREATING COMMUNITY

For Adults

Learning Together—A Sourcebook on Jewish Family Education, edited by Janice Alper (Denver, CO: Alternatives in Religious Education, 1987). The chapter "How to Start a Synagogue Havurah Program," pp. 41–54, by Sally Weber, gives specific guidelines on why and how to start a congregational *havurah* program.

The Third Jewish Catalog, edited by Sharon Strassfeld and Michael Strassfeld (Philadelphia: Jewish Publication Society, 1980), focuses on the theme of "community" and offers extensive practical advice for developing a variety of Jewish fellowships, both within and independent of synagogues.

The National Havurah Committee, P. O. Box 2621, Bala Cynwyd, PA 19004, is a national organization of *havurot* that offers publications and annual gatherings.

In addition to the preceding, the Reconstructionist, Reform, and Conservative movements have each produced materials and resources related to congregational *havurot*. Contact your congregation for details. The Federation of Reconstructionist Congregations and Havurot, Church Road and Greenwood Avenue, Wyncote, PA 19092, (215) 887-1988, allows the affiliation of independent *havurot*.

For Children

The Old Synagogue, written and illustrated by Richard Rosenblum (Philadelphia: Jewish Publication Society, 1989), for ages 5 to 8, is an award-winning story that shows the decline and revitalization of an old synagogue and the Jewish community surrounding it.

RESOURCE GUIDE FOR JEWISH LEARNING

RESOURCES FOR JEWISH STORYTELLING

Anthologies

There are many marvelous collections of Jewish stories available. Some lend themselves more to reading aloud to children, while others are more useful for adult reading, perhaps to be retold to children. Here are a few particularly comprehensive and readable editions to get you started:

For All Ages

The Classic Tales: 4000 Years of Jewish Lore, by Ellen Frankel (Northvale, NJ: Jason Aronson, 1989), is a comprehensive collection of Jewish stories from biblical to hasidic times, with a contemporary sensitivity to addressing the role played by women. Included are stories from the *Midrash*, the Talmud, Sephardic and other folk traditions, and more.

Jewish Stories One Generation Tells Another, retold by Peninnah Schram (Northvale, NJ: Jason

Aronson, 1987), is a collection of captivating Jewish folktales for all ages, retold by one of America's most famous Jewish storytellers. The stories have male and female protagonists who exhibit wisdom and goodness as much as bravery and beauty.

Tales of Elijah the Prophet, by Peninnah Schram (Northvale, NJ: Jason Aronson, 1991), contains 36 classic stories of Elijah the Prophet in his many folkloric guises of miracle worker and *mensch*.

Time for My Soul: Jewish Stories for the Holy Days, by Eugene Labovitz and Annette Labovitz (Northvale, NJ: Jason Aronson, 1987). This collection, geared for adults and older children, includes stories for each major holiday and Shabbat, interspersed with inspirational "Torah thoughts." Most stories are set in a traditional European Jewish milieu.

A Touch of Heaven—Eternal Stories for Jewish Living, by Eugene Labovitz and Annette Labovitz (Northvale, NJ: Jason Aronson, 1990), includes more stories and "Torah thoughts," based on Jewish values such as joy, faith, hospitality, and acts of kindness.

Souled!—Books I & II, by Hanoch Teller (New York: NYC Publishing, 1986, distributed by Feldheim books), is two books in one. One is a collection of stranger-than-fiction and often deeply moving true stories for adults (some are suitable for mature children), and the other consists of Jewish legends and folktales for older children. His *Soul Survivors* (New York: NYC Publishing, 1985) contains stories of righteous men and women (*tzadikim*). Teller writes from a strictly Orthodox viewpoint.

Elijah's Violin & Other Jewish Fairy Tales, by Howard Schwartz (New York: Harper & Row, 1985), is a collection of charming Jewish fairy tales culled from Jewish communities around the world.

Sidrah Stories: A Torah Companion, by Steven M. Rosman (New York: UAHC Press, 1989), offers a story to coordinate with a key theme of each Torah portion, from a wide variety of sources. Discussion questions are included.

Anthologies for Children (ages 6–12)

A Child's Book of Midrash—52 Stories from the Sages, by Barbara Diamond Goldin (Northvale, NJ: Jason Aronson, 1990), retells ancient stories from the Talmud and Midrash in contemporary, readable language.

RESOURCES

Stories for Children, by Isaac Bashevis Singer, translated from the Yiddish by the author and others (New York: Farrar, Straus & Giroux, 1985), is a warm and wonderful collection of original stories from the Nobel laureate's pen.

My Grandmother's Stories: A Collection of Jewish Folktales, by Adéle Geras, with illustrations by Jael Jordan (New York: Knopf, 1990), is a diverse collection of Jewish stories, beautifully illustrated and presented in the context of a young girl's visits to her grandmother.

Family Stories of Sholom Aleichem, selected and translated by Aliza Shevrin (New York: Charles Scribners Sons, 1991), contains five favorite tales from the great Yiddish author.

The Diamond Tree—Jewish Tales from Around the World, selected and retold by Howard Schwartz and Barbara Rush and illustrated by Uri Shulevitz (New York: Harper Collins, 1991), includes 15 traditional Jewish stories from diverse locations, including such unusual characters as Katanya, the Jewish "Thumbelina."

OTHER LITERATURE

Read-aloud Favorites for Young Children

What the Moon Brought, by Sadie Rose Weilerstein, illustrated by Marilyn Hirsh (Philadelphia: Jewish Publication Society, 1970). Ruth and Debby celebrate the Jewish holidays—the same warm and delightful Jewish American classic many of us grew up with. For ages 5 to 8.

The Best of K'tonton, by Sadie Rose Weilerstein, illustrated by Marilyn Hirsh (Philadelphia: Jewish Publication Society, 1980), is another nostalgic classic by Weilerstein, this one the adventures of the irrepressible "Jewish Tom Thumb," K'tonton. For ages 5 to 8.

The Savta Simcha series, by Yaffa Ganz, illustrated by Bina Gewirtz (New York: Feldheim Books), for ages 6 to 10, relates the adventures of a Jewish "Mary Poppins" and young friends in America and throughout the land of Israel. Lively stories with bright illustrations convey Jewish facts and values from a traditional viewpoint.

Storybooks by author and illustrator Marilyn Hirsh from Holiday House, New York, include such favorites as: The Tower of Babel; Captain Jiri and Rabbi Jacob; The Rabbi and The Twenty-Nine Witches—A Talmudic Legend; and Could

Anything Be Worse. All have charming illustrations, drama, humor, and Jewish *tam* (flavor).

Read-to-Yourself: Fiction for Older Children

There are new books of Jewish fiction coming out all the time for older children and young teens, ages 9 to 14. Frequent perusal of Jewish bookstores, book clubs, and catalogs is recommended to keep abreast of the many new publications for this age group. Here are just a few favorites for starters.

All-of-a-Kind Family series, by Sidney Taylor (New York: Dell), is a series of five books about five sisters and their little brother, growing up on the Lower East Side of New York. Jewish traditions, warm family ties, and the second-generation immigrant experience are central to these juvenile classics.

David and Max (Philadelphia: Jewish Publication Society, 1988), and Good if It Goes (New York: Aladdin, 1990), both by Gary Provost and Gail Levine-Provost, focus on the life passages of David, including his coming to terms with his grandfather's past (in the first book) and dealing with the many conflicting pressures during his *bar mitzvah* (in the second).

The Christmas Revolution, The Orphan Game, and The Long Way Home, by Barbara Cohen (New York: Lothrop), all focus on the adventures—some funny, some life-and-death serious—of the twin Berg sisters.

Turning Thirteen, by Susan Beth Pfeffer (New York: Scholastic, 1988), is a preteen novel about a very real American Jewish girl approaching her *bat mitzvah*. Humorous and sometimes tongue-in-cheek, this book still manages to address several important contemporary Jewish issues.

Pink Slippers, Bat Mitzvah Blues, by Ferida Wolff (Philadelphia, Jewish Publication Society, 1989), is about Alyssa, who is much more interested in ballet than in confirmation class. But a turn of events helps her to reconcile the various aspects of her identity.

The Adventures of Emes Junior Interpol, various volumes, by Gershon Winkler and Miriam Zakon, and the Devora Doresh Mysteries, by Carol Korb Hubner (all from Judaica Press, New York), are two mystery-adventure series about junior Jewish detectives. They're sort of a Jewish "Hardy Boys" and "Nancy Drew." These books convey traditional Jewish values in a fun way.

Comics

Shaloman, by Al Weisner, Mark I Comics, P. O. Box 5097, Philadelphia, PA 19111, is a "golden age of comics" style series featuring the adventures of a Jewish superhero with a Hebrew letter *shin* emblazoned across his chest.

Jewish Storytellers

Enjoying a live performance by a professional storyteller can be an exciting experience for the entire family. A directory of Jewish storytellers, lists of recordings by Jewish storytellers, a bibliography of Jewish stories, a newsletter, and other resources are available from **The Jewish Storytelling Center** (director: Peninnah Schram), 92nd St. YM-YWHA, 1395 Lexington Ave., New York, NY 10128, (212) 415-5542.

Bibliographies: Helpful Resources for Selecting Books of Jewish Interest

The Jewish Book Council, c/o Jewish Community Centers Association, 15 E. 26th St., New York, NY 10010-1579, has compiled a number of useful bibliographies of adult and juvenile books.

The Jewish Materials Resource Guide for Families and Havurot, compiled and edited by Carolyn Starman Hessel (available from JESNA—Jewish Educational Service of North America, 730 Broadway, New York, NY 10003-9540), is a comprehensive guide to materials for informal Jewish educational programs, as well as an extensive listing of resources for the Jewish home library.

RESOURCE GUIDE TO JEWISH MUSIC

Distributors

Tara Publications, 29 Derby Ave., Cedarhurst, NY 11516, (516) 295-2290, Fax (516) 295-2291, is the ideal place to begin or enlarge your collection of Jewish music. Their catalog features an extensive list of cassettes, CD's, records, music, and songbooks (they also publish music books), book-and-tape sets, and musical miscellany. They carry a large selection of musical styles: Israeli (from folk-dance music with instructions to folk tunes and hit songs), cantorial, Yiddish, Sephardic/Ladino, *klezmer*, hasidic, holiday and Shabbat, children's music, and Jewish American contemporary, as well as recordings of Jewish stories.

Nefesh Ami, "Soul of My People," NA Distributors, Inc., P. O. Box 651, Hicksville, NY 11801, (516) 933-2660, Fax (516) 933-2196. Their catalog features a wide range of Jewish audio and video recordings, featuring contemporary, folk, Israeli, Yiddish, Sephardic, rock, cantorial, and even Jewish blue-grass styles. They also carry books, Israeli music videos, taped Hebrew courses, electronic Hebrew dictionaries, and self-teaching recordings for aspiring cantors.

Hataklit, 457 N. Fairfax Ave., Los Angeles, CA 90036, (800) HATAKLIT, carries a very large selection of Israeli and other Jewish music, including the latest Israeli hits as well as folk music, children's songs, video sing-alongs (with both Hebrew and transliterated lyrics appearing at the bottom of the screen), Middle Eastern- and hasidic-style cassettes, and even Israeli Brazilian-style music. They also carry books in Hebrew and English.

A.R.E. Publishing, 3945 South Oneida St., Denver, CO 80237, (303) 770-2020, is a Jewish educational publisher that also carries a nice selection of recordings for children about Jewish holidays, heroes, and practices.

(For specific suggestions for Shabbat and holiday recordings and songbooks, see the appropriate Resource Guides.)

Performing Artists

Jewish Artists Co-op, P. O. Box 6061-115, Sherman Oaks, CA 91423, can provide information about a number of contemporary performers and groups who entertain audiences throughout North America.

Books

Heritage of Music: The Music of the Jewish People Stirring Our People's Soul, by Judith Kaplan Eisenstein (Rockaway Beach, NY: The Reconstructionist Press, 1981), for all ages, includes more than 100 songs with easy arrangements for singing and playing, with historical background.

RESOURCE GUIDE FOR VIDEOTAPES

See also the Music Resource Guide; several distributors of Jewish audio recordings also carry a good selection of videos.

Ergo Media Video, P.O. Box 2037, Teaneck, NJ 07666, (800) 695-3746, (201) 692-0404, is considered one of the country's premier distributors of videotapes of Jewish interest. They offer about a hundred selections of what they consider the highest quality in Judaic video, including videos on the American Jewish experience, juvenile, cooking, holidays and traditions, life-cycle events, Yiddish and Hebrew films, Jewish life around the world, music and art, the Holocaust and Resistance, and Israel.

Sisu Home Entertainment, 20 W. 38th St., Suite #402, New York, NY 10018, (800) 223-SISU, (212) 768-2197, offers a catalog of Jewish and Israeli video and audio recordings for children and adults.

Classic Telepublishing, P.O. Box 426, West Simsbury, CT 06092-0426, (203) 651-5257, produces a delightful **Bubbe's Boarding House** Jewish holiday series. The Meshuga Puppeteers present stories about **Bubbe** (Grandma) and her relatives and boarders, which in turn convey the holiday stories, customs, and songs as well as related issues of concern for Jewish children. Classic also produces and distributes other videos of Jewish interest. Their videos are available from Hamakor Judaica (1-800-426-2567) and Jonathan David Co., 68-22 Eliot Ave., Middle Village, NY 11379, (718) 456-8611, as well as some Judaica stores and RKO Warner Video Stores.

(See the Israel Resource Guide for details on the Shalom Sesame video series.)

RESOURCES FOR JEWISH SOFTWARE

For a wide variety of Judaic software, obtain catalogs from the two companies listed below. Programs available for today's home computer include games, Judaic clipart, education and Torah study, Jewish calendars, and Hebrew word processing.

Darka Corporation, 7074 N. Western Ave., Chicago, IL 60645, (800) 621-8227, (312) 465-4070, Fax (312) 262-9298.

Kabbalah Software, 8 Price Dr., Edison, NJ 08817, (908) 572-0891, Fax (908) 572-0869.

RESOURCE GUIDE TO JEWISH TOYS AND GAMES

See also under Resource Guide for Judaica for the home (pp. 307–309). Many catalogs mentioned carry Jewish toys and games, including handcrafted wood and fabric items.

Doron LaYeled of Israel produces beautiful and sturdy wooden puzzles that display holiday symbols and scenes in varying levels of difficulty, as well as wooden dominoes and Lotto with colorful Jewish symbols. Their "Simhat Torah procession" puzzle is the only Judaic toy I have seen that depicts a child in a wheelchair as a happy participant in the scene. They are available in the United States through **LaYeled**, 2841 W. Estes, Chicago, IL 60645, (312) 743-2032 (which also carries wooden lacing cards in the form of Jewish symbols), and through Constructive Playthings (see the following).

Constructive Playthings, Main Office, 1227 E. 119th St., Grandview, MO 64030, (816) 761-5900, (800) 255-6124. Constructive Playthings' catalog "Materials for Jewish Education" includes a generous selection of the aforementioned Doron LaYeled puzzles, as well as Hebrew magnetic and foam-rubber letters, flannel boards, stencils, and transfers.

The Learning Plant, P.O. Box 17233, West Palm Beach, FL 33416, (407) 686-9456, is a fun company! Their catalog includes "innovative educational materials": toys and games such as Bible story and holiday flannel boards, educational card games, stickers, foam-rubber *alef-bet* stencils, kits to make historical reproductions, holiday crafts kits, soft-sculpture toys, sturdy lacing cards with Jewish symbols, coloring books, wooden puzzles including *Doron Layeled*, board games, peel-and-stick felt kits with Jewish symbols and Hebrew words that adhere to smooth surfaces. They also carry books, videos, records, and teaching materials.

A Touch of Torah, 570 Crown St., Brooklyn, NY 11213, (718) 774-3076, is the source for a vast array of Jewish soft-sculpture toys for preschoolers, including stuffed dreidls, candles, *kiddush* cups, "Torahs" of all sizes, squeaky Torahs for baby, *etrog* rattles, *seder* plates, soft-sculpture *shofars* that can really be blown, and much more.

The Kosher Gourmet & Jewish Toy Cellar, 1645 Warwick Ave., Suite 213, Warwick, RI 02889, (800) 428-3414, ships kosher foods, gifts, Jewish toys, books, tapes, videos, and "a full line of Jewish baby needs."

Pockets of Learning, 31 G. Union Ave., Sudbury, MA 01776, (800) 635-2994, is a general toy company that numbers among its interactive felt wall hangings displays of "Noah's Ark" (with removable animals) and an attractive *alef-bet* pocket wall display, with a pocket for each letter of the Hebrew *alef-bet*, each of which contains a small stuffed felt toy that begins with that Hebrew letter.

These are carried by "The Source for Everything Jewish" and "Shoshana by Mail" (see Home Resource Guide, p. 308).

Aviv Judaica, 4726 New Utrecht Ave., Brooklyn, NY 11219, (718) 435-6201/6216, is the source of a vast array of cute stickers for Jewish holidays, *berachah* charts, place mats, baby dishes, card games, and toddler toys. Carried by many Judaica shops and distributors.

"Enjoy-A-Book Club," P.O. Box 101, Woodmere, NY 11598, (516) 569-0830, is a Jewish children's book club that also carries a good variety of Jewish games and puzzles.

Rolnik Publishers—Something Different, 10 Dov Fridman St., Ramat-Gan, Israel (03)-751-0848, Fax: 972-3-751-0858, available in the United States through The Jewish National Fund Department of Education, 114 E. 32nd St., Suite 1501, New York, NY 10016, (212) 779-0310, produces unique posters, puzzles, and decorations for children's rooms.

Mitzvah Toys, 2329 Warrensville Ctr., University Hts, OH 44118, (216) 321-0477, is a line of bright plastic preschool toys with a traditional Jewish orientation.

Judaica Miniatures

(Collectors' miniatures are not recommended for small children because their size and materials could be hazardous.)

By Barb, from Barbara Schuckman, 7 Aron Ct., Bethpage, NY 11714, (516) 433-8389, is a collection of amazingly detailed, handmade Jewish miniatures for the collector.

In the Beginning, P.O. Box 4229, Bay Terrace, NY 11350-4229, (718) 428-8951, has a Judaic miniatures line of more than 200 items.

Educational Games

Torah Aura Productions, 4423 Fruitland Ave., Los Angeles, CA 90058, (800) BE-TORAH, (213) 585-7312, is a Jewish textbook publisher that also produces a number of educational games on Jewish values, holidays, and the synagogue.

Alternatives in Religious Education (ARE), 3945 S. Oneida St., Denver, CO 80237, (800) 346-7779 (in CO:(303) 363-7779). This publisher carries several Jewish games on holidays, Shabbat, and the life cycle.

Tradition, from JOPCO, Inc., P.O. Box 35126, Houston, TX 77235, (713) 776-3401, is a Jewish "trivia" game available in both adults and children's versions, for play by 2 to 4 individuals or teams.

Aliyah, from Contemporary Designs, P.O. Box 60, Gilbert, IL 50105, (515) 232-5188, is another popular Jewish knowledge game.

Buki, Ltd., distributed by Howard Fields and Associates, 8278 World Trade Center, P.O. Box 58198, Dallas, TX 75258, (214) 760-8408, is a colorful, Israeli-made puzzle-and-game series that includes giant floor puzzles with Hebrew words and a variety of games that teach simple Hebrew words.

Orda Industries, Ltd., of Kibbutz Malkia, D.N. Merom HaGalil, Israel 13845, (U.S. Distributor: Bemiss Jason Corp., 37600 Central Court, Newark, CA 94560, (414) 722-9000), makes educational games, including several that teach elements of easy Hebrew; Shabbat; Jewish festivals; Israeli geography, nature, and science.

Eligad Educational Enterprises, 19 Michal St., Tel-Aviv Brae 53261, (03) 289430, has a series of inexpensive "Jewish Heritage Edu-Kit" educational games about Israel, for ages 7 to adults.

Coloring and Activity Books

Can You Imagine?—Creative Drawing Adventures for the Jewish Holidays, by Marji Gold-Vukson, illustrated by Michael Gold-Vukson, from Kar-Ben Copies (800) 4-KARBEN, provides four dozen drawing activities on Shabbat, biblical, and holiday themes, in an "uncoloring" format. For ages 5 and up.

Benjy's Bible Trails, by Chaya Burstein, from Kar-Ben Copies, teaches 6- to 10-year-olds about Bible people through stories, activities, and pictures to color.

Simcha Coloring Books is a set of two coloring books for ages 4 to 7, from "The Enjoy-A-Book Club" (listed earlier). One book focuses on Jewish holidays, the other on Shabbat, Jewish values, and the *alef-bet*.

Dover Publications, Inc., 31 E. 2nd St., Nieola, NY 11501, carries a number of quality Jewish-themed coloring books, including minibooks with Jewish stencils and Jewish "stained glass" pictures to illuminate, and two educational coloring books by popular children's illustrator and author Chaya Burstein: one on the Jewish holidays and one that illustrates Hebrew words.

Contemporary Designs, P.O. Box 60, 213 Main St., Gilbert, IA 50105, (515) 232-5188, creates coloring and activity books with Jewish educational themes. **A Creative Jewish Coloring Book**, by Jeffrey S. Winter (1992), is an "uncoloring" book that encourages children to imagine and illustrate their own Jewish ideas.

Parshah by Parshah, by Laya Block, illustrated by Mina Kreiswirth, Gan-Gani Pub., 1059 William Street, London, Ontario N5Y 2T2, Canada, is a beautifully illustrated series of coloring and activity books designed to teach about the weekly Torah portions.

The Gozal Series consists of seven charmingly old-fashioned coloring books for young children based on the Hebrew *alef-bet*, from the Jewish National Fund Dept. of Education, (212) 879-9300.

RESOURCE GUIDE FOR JUDAICA ARTS & CRAFTS

Fast, Clean and Cheap, by Simon Kops (Los Angeles: Torah Aura Productions, 1988), explains "everything the Jewish teacher (or parent) needs to know about art." It contains many easy but elegant projects and gives full instructions (including where to find supplies) for the arts-and-crafts novice. It's illustrated with black-and-white photographs.

An Artist You Don't Have to Be, written and illustrated by Joann Magnus with Howard I. Bogot (New York: UAHC Press, 1990), contains easy yet very creative art activities related to Jewish topics such as history, values, holidays, and Shabbat. It includes a glossary of terminology and technical-assistance information.

Jewish Holiday Crafts and **Hanukkah Crafts**, by Joyce Becker (New York: Hebrew Publishing Co., 1977 and 1978), presents ingenious projects such as Hanukkah *menorahs* made from objects such as spools of thread, candies, and flowerpots.

Arts & Crafts—around the Jewish Calendar, vols. 1 & 2, by Shoshana Mermelstein and Chava Shapiro (New York: Torah Umesorah Publications, 1978), contains craft projects for all the holidays and Shabbat, including many varieties of Rosh HaShanah cards and honey dishes, Simhat Torah flags, Sukkot decorations, Shavuot flowers, and so on. The book is illustrated with line drawings and includes a diagram for Hebrew lettering.

For the More Advanced Artist and Craftsperson

The Hanukkah Book and **The Jewish Party Book**, both by Mae Shafter Rockland (New York:

Schocken, 1985 and 1987), offer a variety of more sophisticated crafts that involve techniques such as silk screening, paper cutting, homemade stamp-pad printing, quilting, ceramics, and metalwork. Some of these projects can be done with older children. Ms. Rockland is a noted authority on American Jewish folk art.

Crafts Kits

Kids Handiwork, Inc., P. O. Box 711313, Houston, TX 77271-1313, (713) 541-1975, has kits to make Jewish puppets, holiday decorations, mobiles, *matzah* cases, and sponge-art prints with holiday themes and the *alef-bet*.

Creativities Art Center, 184 Danbury Rd., New Milford, CT 06776, (203) 350-9050, sells art enrichment packets with Jewish themes, to make items of plastercraft, wood, fabric, stained glass, and beads.

All Night Media, Inc., San Rafael, CA 94901, has a wide variety of materials for rubber stamp art, including a set of six stamps with Jewish themes. Their stamp kits and inks are widely available at stationery stores.

Media Escape,™ Inc., P.O. Box 24107, Denver, CO 80224, (303) 758-8232, carries a line of Judaic rubber stamps that convey "a range of Jewish expression from reverence to pure silliness."

RESOURCE GUIDE FOR TORAH STUDY

There are myriad materials available for making traditional Jewish texts available to the lay reader. Any sort of comprehensive list would be beyond the scope of this book. What follows are some basic volumes that often contain bibliographies and guides to further study.

For Adults

Secularly well-educated adults who would like to explore traditional Jewish studies would do well to let Barry Holtz be their guide. His **Finding Our Way: Jewish Texts and the Lives We Lead Today** (New York: Schocken, 1990) shows contemporary readers how the great texts of the Jewish tradition can become living sources of insight into issues of perennial human concern, while **Back to the Sources**, which he edited (New York: Summit Books, 1984), introduces the intelligent reader with no prior background in Jewish texts or Hebrew to the classics of the Jewish tradition: Bible, Talmud, *midrashic* literature, legal codes, mystical texts, and the prayer book. Holtz also edited **The Schocken Guide to Jewish Books** (New York: Schocken, 1992), which directs the reader to books on a variety of Judaic subjects.

Learning Torah—A Self-Guided Journey through the Layers of Jewish Learning, by Joel Lurie Grishaver (New York: UAHC Press, 1990), is highly recommended for teen and adult learners. This hands-on presentation of Torah study skills enables the learner to "enter into dialogue with the rabbis, the medieval commentators, and modern biblical critics."

For Family Study

Torah with Love—a Guide for Strengthening Jewish Values within the Family, by David Epstein, an attorney, and Suzanne Singer Stutman, a clinical psychotherapist, both of Washington, DC (New York: Prentice Hall, 1986), is the basic guide to why and how to conduct weekly family Torah discussions in the home. It combines classical materials and contemporary techniques such as games, simulations, and role-playing. An overview of moral development and a guide to English Torah commentaries are also provided.

Teaching Torah—a Treasury of Insights and Activities, by Sorel Goldberg Loeb and Barbara Binder Kadden (Denver, CO: Alternatives in Religious Education, 1984), provides a synopsis of every Torah portion in addition to "insights from the tradition," strategies for analyzing, extending, and personalizing the text, guides to related resources, and ideas for involving the family. Very useful for home study of the Torah portion.

A Torah Commentary (in several volumes), by Harvey J. Fields, with illustrations by Giora Carmi (New York: UAHC Press), can be used by youngsters from the preteen years on and is an excellent resource for family Torah study. It includes an overview of the story of each portion, a detailed translation into the contemporary idiom, commentaries by the author, and a wide range of classic and modern interpreters. Also included are illustrations, a bibliography, and a glossary of commentaries.

An Outline and Interpretation of the Weekly Sidrot (in two volumes), by Dr. Louis Kaplan (Baltimore: Board of Jewish Education, 1988), outlines, explains, and provides discussion questions for every weekly Torah portion.

The Rabbi's Bible (3 volume series), by Solomon Simon and Morrison David Bial (New York: Behrman House, 1974), for ages 10 and up, includes translated biblical texts, selected Hebrew verses, and traditional Jewish commentaries on the Torah and prophets, teacher's guides, resource books, and workbooks available from Behrman House, (800) 221-2755.

Torah and Bible for the Family Bookshelf
Humash (Pentateuch, Five Books of Moses)

The Living Torah, by Aryeh Kaplan (New York: Maznaim, 1979), offers a fresh and readable new translation of the *Humash*, as well as traditionally based commentary, notations, maps, and diagrams. It is available in English or Hebrew-English version. The *haftarot* (prophetic readings) are included.

The Torah: A Modern Commentary, W. Gunther Plaut, general editor (New York: UAHC, 1981), includes the Hebrew text and English translation of the Torah, along with a contemporary commentary that combines historical perspective with ethical gleanings. The *haftarot* are included.

For Teaching Torah and *Tanach* (Bible) to Children

Torah Aura Productions, 4423 Fruitland Ave., Los Angeles, CA 90058, (800) BE-TORAH, (213) 585-7312, Fax (213) 585-0327, is a one-stop Torah study resource for family study as well as for religious schools. A whole series of books on Torah study for ages 5 to adult are developmentally appropriate, challenging, and entertaining. The books are illustrated with engaging cartoons, or in some cases, with black-and-white photographs. Parent or teacher guides are available to provide background information.

The Hebrew Bible

TANAKH—The Holy Scriptures (Philadelphia: Jewish Publication Society, 1985) is a new translation of the entire Jewish Bible (*TaNaKh* is a Hebrew acronym for *Torah*, the Five Books of Moses; *Nevi'im*, the Prophets; and *Ketuvim*, the Writings), representing collaboration between rabbis from all perspectives and utilizing the findings of modern scholarship and archeology.

The Hebrew Prophets—A Story Workbook, written and illus. by Chaya M. Burstein (New York: UAHC Press, 1990), for ages 8 to 11, combines historical fiction, illustrations, brief textual selections, and activities to teach about the biblical prophets.

A Child's Bible: Book 1: Lessons from the Torah and **Book 2: Lessons from the Prophets and Writings**, by Seymour Rossel (West Orange, NJ: Behrman House, 1988), is an attractive child's introduction to the Bible that goes beyond the stories by highlighting the classic moral and spiritual messages of the text: *peshat*—"what does it mean?" *derash*—"what does it teach?" and *remez*—"a lesson about Torah." The book includes full-color illustrations and photographs.

Exploring the Prophets and Writings, by Carl S. Erlich (Hoboken, NJ: Ktav, 1990), for ages 10 to 14, includes a contemporary translation of biblical selections with commentaries and enrichment materials. A workbook and teacher's guide are available.

RABBINIC LITERATURE

Pirke Avot: For Adults

Torah From our Sages, by Jacob Neusner (Dallas: Rossel Books, 1984), available from Behrman House, is a new translation and explanation of the Jewish ethical classic, from one of today's foremost scholars.

For Young People

When a Jew Seeks Wisdom—The Sayings of the Fathers, by Seymour Rossel with Hyman Chanover and Chaim Stern (New York: Behrman House, 1975), an interpretation of *Pirke Avot* for preteens and up, which highlights Jewish values. Teachers' guides and a student encounter book are available; the book has color illustrations.

Introductions to Rabbinic Literature

For Adults

The Talmud for Beginners, vol. 1, **Prayer,** and vol. 2, **Text,** by Judith Z. Abrams (Northvale, NJ: Jason Aronson, 1991, 1993). This readable series introduces the adult beginner to the study of the Talmud in translation while providing an overview of the central ideas and issues of various talmudic volumes.

The Essential Talmud, by Adin Steinsaltz, translated from the Hebrew by Chaya Galai (Northvale, NJ: Jason Aronson, 1992), gives a one-volume overview of the background structure and general contents of the Talmud. (Steinsaltz's English translation of the entire Talmud is being published in multiple volumes by Random House.)

Invitation to the Talmud and **Invitation to the Midrash**, both by Jacob Neusner (San Francisco: Harper & Row, 1989), are "teaching books" that carefully guide the adult learner through selected passages from these classic rabbinic texts, leading to an overview of the ethos and contemporary relevance of each.

For Young People

Meet Our Sages, Learn Mishnah, and Learn Talmud, all by Jacob Neusner (West Orange, NJ: Behrman House, 1980, 1978, 1979), (800) 221-2755, for preteens through adults, are particularly suited for parent-child or group study. Each book includes Hebrew texts with translations, study questions, and illustrations in a format that is enjoyable yet challenging. Neusner emphasizes the timeless values to be learned from these Jewish classics.

Torah Aura Rabbinics Curriculum, from Torah Aura Productions, Los Angeles (800) BE-TORAH, for ages 8 and up, includes a series of workbooks and minilessons that make rabbinic texts and Jewish law come alive. Many of these lend themselves to parent-child study.

HEBREW RESOURCES

Here is a sample of innovative Hebrew programs that are being used in Jewish schools.

Early Childhood

Aleph—a Hebrew Language Program for Early Childhood, from the Board of Jewish Education of Greater New York, is a complete one-year curriculum that makes spoken Hebrew fun and natural for children ages 4 to 6.

For the Supplementary Hebrew School

Ot La-Ba'ot, by Rabbi Yosi Gordon, illustrated by Jackie Urbanovic (Los Angeles: Torah Aura Productions), is a set of Hebrew primer booklets for grades 3 to 5. This primer puts Hebrew reading into the context of Hebrew culture and teaches Hebrew as a whole language. Torah Aura also has an excellent Hebrew reading-readiness program that includes a colorful preprimer, *Alef Bet Gimmel Dalet*, and resource kit for introducing the

Hebrew alef-bet within the context of Jewish culture and values. *Daber Ivrit* is their book of twenty instant lessons in conversational Hebrew.

The Pyramid Method, designed by Cara Albom Nesser, 4600 California St., San Francisco, CA 94118, is in use in a number of Hebrew schools. The three-year curriculum is designed to teach Hebrew to children in grades 5 and up, in supplementary schools, who can already read and write Hebrew script. The program focuses on comprehension, conversation, and composition and includes many games to heighten retention.

The New Siddur Program for Hebrew and Heritage, by Pearl and Norman Tarnor (West Orange, NJ: Behrman House), is a new multilevel program that places the study of Hebrew prayers in a broader language context through the introduction of simple Hebrew stories and dialogues. A separate curriculum is available that emphasizes modern language and is appropriate for day-school use.

For Intensive Supplementary Schools and for Day Schools

The Telem Series, by Tzvia Thier, 8 Still Lane, West Hartford, CT 06117, (203) 236-3405, is a creative series for beginning Hebrew that combines Hebrew and Judaica in a whole-language format. Children are encouraged to write Hebrew and to illustrate their own textbooks, which include adapted Bible stories and an interactive *Haggadah*.

Shy Publishing, 126 Dover St., Brooklyn, NY 11235, (718) 615-0027. Dr. Shahar and Dr. Rina Yonay have developed a series of grammar workbooks, *Yesodot HaLashon*, and readers *HaMikra'a Sheli*, which can be used in a variety of educational settings. These books are based on research on language acquisition in children.

Especially for Day Schools

The Tal Sela Hebrew Language Arts Curriculum, 5151 Cote St. Catherine Rd., Montreal, Quebec, Canada H3W 1M6, (514) 345-2610, is considered one of the most dynamic and progressive methods of teaching Hebrew in the elementary Jewish day school. It is used in more than 150 schools in North America, Europe, South Africa, and Australia. Materials include student readers, workbooks, and educational games; teachers' manuals and teaching aids; audiocassettes and supplementary readers.

Hebrew Courses for Teens–Adults

On One Foot, by Noah Golinkin, is a program designed to teach the basics of phonetic Hebrew reading in one day. Participants are expected to continue their Hebrew study for at least a six-week follow-up program. The course draws on the Hebrew vocabulary of Jewish life that most Jews are familiar with to teach the Hebrew *alef-bet* and sounding skills. It has been offered successfully in synagogues all over the United States. For information, contact: Rabbi Noah Golinkin, Hebrew Literacy Publications, 5639 Thunder Hill Rd., Columbia, MD 21045, (301) 964-ALEF/(301) 982-1121.

Hebrew—A Language Course, by Ora Band and Bella Bergman; series editors, Dr. Sheldon Dorph and Rabbi Joel Gordon; series consultant, Dr. Arnold J. Band (West Orange, NJ: Behrman House), is a complete series from beginner to fluency in four books. Can be used with young teens through adults. A prose-and-poetry reader for the upper levels is also available.

Self-study for Teens–Adults

How the Hebrew Language Grew, by Edward Horowitz (Hoboken, NJ: Ktav Publishing House, 1960). This simple yet enjoyable classic makes Hebrew grammar more understandable by tracing the development of the language since ancient times. For teen through adult readers who already have some basic Hebrew knowledge.

Reading and Understanding the Prayer Book

(See also Resources on Prayer and Spirituality, p. 321.)

EKS, Classical Hebrew Educational Materials (Oakland, CA), produces **Teach Yourself to Read Hebrew**, a set of tapes with a book that enables the adult learner to teach him or herself to read Hebrew. Their **Prayerbook Hebrew the Easy Way**, by Joseph Anderson, et al., is a book for those who can read the Hebrew prayers phonetically but want to understand what they are saying.

Everyday Hebrew, by Eliezer Tirkel, edited by J. A. Reif (Lincolnwood, IL: Passport Books, 1991), is a complete self-teaching Hebrew course that includes a book and four audio cassette tapes. It teaches the adult beginner or advanced beginner to read, write, understand, and speak modern Hebrew, with an emphasis on practical, everyday communication. It's excellent for classes or for individual study.

Shalom from Jerusalem, from Rolnik Publishers, Tel-Aviv, produced in cooperation with the Hebrew Language Division, Dept. of Education and Culture in the Diaspora, World Zionist Organization and the Israel Ministry of Education and Culture, available from Dept. of Education and Culture, WZO, 110 E. 59th St., New York, NY 10022, (212) 339-6000, has courses of cassettes and written lessons on four levels from absolute beginner through advanced students. It emphasizes Hebrew literature and Jewish and Israeli culture.

Everyday Hebrew for Tourists is a special seven-lesson program from Rolnik Publishers, Tel-Aviv, produced in cooperation with Israel's "Open University," consisting of a tape and booklet that introduce some basic conversational Hebrew, focusing on situations a tourist would be likely to face. It is available in the United States from *Hataklit*, (800) HATAKLIT.

Hebrew Enrichment Materials

Books

Gesher Leyaladim ("Bridge" for Children) are children's books in simplified Hebrew for the beginning and more advanced student, available from The World Zionist Organization, Dept. of Education and Culture (listed above). There is a more advanced Gesher series for teens and one for adult students with a vocabulary of 1,000–1,500 words.

Miloni Series, from Israel's Centre for Educational Technology (available from many American Jewish booksellers), is a series of beautifully illustrated hardcover Hebrew-English dictionaries for children. **Miloni HaKatan (My Little Dictionary)** is a picture dictionary of more than 500 words in full-color pictures for young children. **Miloni (My Dictionary)** is a colorful dictionary with more than 800 words and 40 group entries for the elementary pupil. **Miloni LeSefer Bereishit** is a Hebrew dictionary for children especially designed for studying the Book of Genesis.

Adama Books, distributed by Modan, P. O. Box 1202, Bellmore, NY 11710, (516) 679-1380, publishes a number of children's books in Hebrew, including translations of English classics such as the "Little Bear" books, **Goodnight Moon**, and **Curious George**. They range from easy to more difficult Hebrew.

Recordings

Israel books, cassette tapes, and Hebrew videos for children (at a variety of levels) can be purchased from a number of distributors in this country. Try *Hataklit*, 457 N. Fairfax Ave., Los Angeles, CA 90036, (800) 428-2554, or **Chemed Book and Co.**, 3709 13th Ave., Brooklyn, NY 11218, (718) 972-5440, which specializes in instructional materials that parallel the Israeli school system, for children who are native Hebrew speakers. See the music and video resource guides for more distributers of Hebrew recordings.

Learning Materials

Creative Learning Aids, from Arbit Books, 8050 N. Port Washington Rd., Milwaukee, WI 53217, include *alef-bet* foam puzzles, Hebrew stencils, a Hebrew label-maker machine, and the Hebrew version of Scrabble.

RESOURCE GUIDE FOR YIDDISH

See also the resources for Jewish music and videos. Many Yiddish songs are available in audio recordings and songbooks, and vintage Yiddish films are available on video.

Workmen's Circle, 45 E. 33rd St., New York, NY 10016, (800) WC-CALL US, (212) 889-6800, is a fraternal organization that provides, among other social-welfare activities, educational programs, including secularist Yiddish schools for children. They also underwrite Yiddish cultural, musical, and theatrical festivals and publish songbooks and cassette tapes with Yiddish songs. Workmen's Circle has a catalog that includes Yiddish textbooks, storybooks, and music.

Pripetshik Yiddish Immersion Program is a Sunday-morning Yiddish-language program in the New York area, for children ages 2 1/2 to 12. Children do arts and crafts, reading and writing, music and dramatics in Yiddish. They publish their own magazine with Yiddish stories. For information, contact Rukhl Schaechter, (212) 569-6281, or Tova Dobkin, (718) 268-1517.

RESOURCE GUIDE FOR SEPHARDIC LANGUAGES AND HERITAGE

See also the music and video resource guides for performances of Sephardic song and dance.

Sephardic House, Congregation Shearith Israel,

8 West 70th Street, New York, NY 10023, (212) 873-0300 teaches the Sephardic heritage (including Ladino) through programs, classes, exhibits, and cultural events. They also make a number of publications and recordings available by mail to their members. Selections include philosophical and historical works, a cookbook, a Sephardic *Haggadah*, and a Sephardic Shabbat kit with stories and a cassette tape of songs.

RESOURCE GUIDE FOR LEARNING ABOUT PRAYER AND JEWISH SPIRITUALITY

Theology and Spirituality for Adults

God in Search of Man: A Philosophy of Judaism, by Abraham Joshua Heschel (Northvale, NJ: Jason Aronson, 1982). Rabbi Heschel, one of the most influential Jewish theologians of this century, was the scion of a prestigious hasidic family who was deeply committed to traditional Judaism. At the same time, the prophetic tradition compelled him to be a social activist. Any of his books are inspiring reading for those who want to rediscover the spiritual power of traditional Judaism for contemporary life.

Sacred Fragments—Recovering Theology for the Modern Jew, by Neil Gillman (Philadelphia: Jewish Publication Society, 1990). Each chapter of this book addresses one of the perplexing issues of faith for contemporary Jews who can no longer completely accept every traditional belief but want to retain the "sacred fragments" of the traditional system, even as they reformulate it within the framework of modernity.

Seek My Face, Speak My Name—A Contemporary Jewish Theology, by Rabbi Arthur Green (Northvale, NJ: Jason Aronson, 1992), is a poetic, mystical, yet thoroughly contemporary presentation of Jewish theology by one of the leaders of the Reconstructionist movement.

Who Needs God, by Harold Kushner (New York: Summit Books, 1989), is a warm and inspiring book about the spiritual dimension of life. It addresses people of all religions even as it springs from Rabbi Kushner's committed Jewish background and orientation.

The Healer of Shattered Hearts—A Jewish View of God, by David J. Wolpe (New York: Henry Holt, 1990), written by a young Conservative rabbi who was once "an ardent atheist,"

reaches back into the Jewish textual tradition to show how God can still speak to us today in our moments of sorrow or joy and in our modern experience of alienation.

Jewish Mysticism and Meditation

For Adults

The Way of Splendor—Jewish Mysticism and Modern Psychology, by Edward Hoffman (Northvale, NJ: Jason Aronson, 1989), gives an introduction to Jewish mysticism by way of its applications to mental health and spiritual well-being, showing where kabbalistic insights intersect with psychological research.

God Was in This Place and I, i Did Not Know, by Lawrence Kushner (Woodstock, VT: Jewish Lights Publishing, 1991), like several other popular books by Rabbi Lawrence Kushner, is an authentic American Jewish mystical expression. One biblical verse becomes the starting place for a range of traditional and contemporary Jewish understandings about "finding self, spirituality, and ultimate meaning."

Jewish Meditation—A Practical Guide, by Aryeh Kaplan (New York: Schocken, 1985), is a step-by-step introduction to meditation and the Jewish practice of meditation in particular. The late, revered Aryeh Kaplan, a physicist turned rabbi and prolific Judaica author, taught that meditation of various types, as well as spontaneous prayer and "conversations with God," are all intrinsic to authentic Jewish spirituality.

Jewish Spiritual Practices, by Yitzhak Buxbaum (Northvale, NJ: Jason Aronson, 1990), is "a modern-style self-help book from the sages," a volume of practical spiritual advice gleaned from hundreds of Jewish religious texts.

Jewish Liturgy and Prayer

Service of the Heart—A Guide to the Jewish Prayer Book, by Evelyn Garfield (Northvale, NJ: Jason Aronson, 1989), is a recently republished classic that explains the history and meanings of the traditional Jewish liturgy.

Jewish Worship, by Abraham E. Millgram (Philadelphia: Jewish Publication Society, 1971), explains the origins, development, and meanings of the *siddur* as a whole, as well as explanations of individual prayers. It also explores all major aspects of Jewish worship and the related theology.

"Synagogue and Prayer," in **The Second Jewish Catalog**, eds. Sharon Strassfeld and Michael Strassfeld (Philadelphia: Jewish Publication Society, 1976, pp. 264–316, is a good general overview of synagogue practice, the traditional service, and how to participate in it. Rabbi Pinchas Peli's essay on "Prayer, Prayer Books and the Pray-er," focuses on the inward dimension of prayer.

Understanding the Prayer Book

(See also the Hebrew Language Resource Guide, pp. 318–320.)

Eyn Keloyeynu, by Rabbi Noah Golinkin (Shengold Publishers, 18 W. 45th St., New York, NY 10036), teaches comprehension of 18 prayers of the Shabbat-morning service. Aims at increasing reading fluency, understanding ideas, and basic vocabulary of prayers, learning synagogue rituals, and acquiring a basic vocabulary of Jewish life. Available in general or Orthodox version.

For Young People and Their Parents
Spirituality

When Children Ask About God, by Harold S. Kushner (New York: Schocken, 1989), helps parents to talk about God and theology with their children. Be sure to get the revised edition, which has a new preface by Rabbi Kushner.

The Book of Miracles—A Young Person's Guide to Jewish Spiritual Awareness, by Lawrence Kushner, illustrated by Devis Grebu (New York: UAHC Press, 1987), uses Jewish texts and stories to lead preteens and their parents to an understanding of the holiness, wonder, and spirituality of everyday life.

God's Paintbrush, by Sandy Eisenberg Sasso, illustrated by Annette Compton (Woodstock, VT: Jewish Lights Publishing, 1992), is a colorful discussion-starter for children ages 5 to 9 and their parents.

Together—A Parent Child Kit, created by Vicky Kelman with Joel Grishaver and Jane Golub (New York: Melton Research Center of the Jewish Theological Seminary of America, 1984), is a set of nine parent-child activity kits for third-grade children and their parents, designed for use over a school year. A leader's handbook is available. Seven of the kits deal with Jewish holidays and Shabbat, but one explores the meaning of *berachot* (blessings), and another is about finding God in our lives. The latter includes a booklet for parents on talking about God with children, an interactive mini-*siddur*, and a parent-child game, "Hide and Seek," which integrates Bible stories and personal sharing. The game includes a cassette tape of traditional Jewish stories narrated by Peninnah Schram, accompanied by the voices of real parents and children "talking God" together. "Together" is available from the Melton Research Center, 3080 Broadway, New York, NY 10027, (212) 678-8031.

Spirituality: For Teens

Test of Faith, by Roberta Louis Goodman (Los Angeles: Torah Aura Productions), for preteens through adults, is a six-page "instant lesson" that facilitates one's understanding of the nature of "faith." It invites learners to examine their values, beliefs, and priorities and to contrast their definitions of faith with those of the Jewish sage Maimonides and of Dr. James Fowler, a contemporary researcher in the field of moral and religious development.

Finding God—Ten Jewish Responses, by Rifat Sonsino and Daniel B. Syme (New York, UAHC, 1986), examines a broad spectrum of traditional and contemporary Jewish theological ideas to help young adults discover a personal understanding of God.

The Invisible Chariot, by Deborah Kerdeman and Rabbi Lawrence Kushner (Denver, CO: Alternatives in Religious Education, 1986), for ages 14 and up, is a workbook that provides "an introduction to Kabbalah and Jewish Spirituality." A leaderguide is available.

Learning about the Synagogue and Jewish Prayer: For Children–Teens

Let's Go to Synagogue, by Ceil and David Olivestone, illustrated by Arieh Zeldich (Englewood, NJ: SBS Publishing, 1981), for ages 2 to 5, takes preschoolers through a traditional Shabbat morning service, experienced from a child's viewpoint.

Prayer Is Reaching, by Howard I. Bogot and Daniel B. Syme, illustrated by Marlene Lobell Ruthen (New York: UAHC Press, 1982), for ages 4 to 8, introduces young children to the Jewish concept of prayer and develops the association between God and the wonders of the world.

When a Jew Prays, by Seymour Rossel with Eugene B. Borowitz and Hyman Chanover (West Orange, NJ: Behrman House, 1973), for ages 9 to 11, explains the nature of prayer and the content of the Jewish prayer service. It includes color illustrations by Erika Weihs.

The **Torah Aura Tefillah Curriculum**, from Torah Aura Productions, Los Angeles, (800) BE TORAH, is an in-depth, multiyear curriculum for teaching the *siddur* to children from kindergarten through high school. It would also be good for parents who want to learn with their children. There is a prayers and blessings activity book for grades K-2, followed by a *siddur* commentary for grades 2-4. The remaining texts in this two-track series combine study of the Hebrew language of the prayers, prayer concepts and structures, and major Jewish concepts, all in attractive, illustrated formats.

Bechol Levavcha—With All Your Heart, by Harvey J. Fields, illustrated by Leo Glueckselig (New York: UAHC, 1976), is a set of two volumes, an interactive Reform prayer book and a commentary text, designed to help young teens and their parents learn about the Shabbat liturgy through biblical, talmudic, and modern sources.

SIDDURIM (PRAYER BOOKS)

For Adults, Teens, and Older Children

Each Jewish movement has its own version of the *siddur*, but all are based on the traditional order of the prayers. I believe it is important to explore *siddurim* from denominations other than one's own to gather different perspectives on Jewish prayer. (The *mahzor* is a special holiday prayer book for the Days of Awe or the festivals. I have not listed these here, but they are available in a similar range of editions.)

Sim Shalom, is the new Conservative *siddur*. It combines a traditional format with some additional and alternative readings and changes in wording that reflect contemporary concerns and Conservative theology.

Orthodox Siddurim: There are many editions of the traditional or Orthodox prayer book. Widely used are **The Complete Artscroll Siddur** (Mesorah), a particularly comprehensive *siddur*; the **Daily Prayerbook**, with translation and notes by Philip Birnbaum (Hebrew Publishing Co.); **The Authorized Daily Prayerbook**, by Dr. Joseph H. Hertz (Bloch), which has extensive notes; the **Metsudah Siddur** series, edited and translated by Rabbi Avrohom Davis (Metsudah), which has a user-friendly contemporary linear translation; and the Lubavitch hasidic **Siddur Tehillat HaShem** (Merkos L'Inyonei Chinuch).

Kol HaNeshamah ("Every Soul") is the new Reconstructionist *siddur*, currently appearing in several volumes. The Shabbat eve prayer book includes an adaptation of the traditional service, as well as alternative prayers and meditations, a unique dual-language translation of "God," readings, commentary, transliterations, and musical notations. Calligraphy, decoration, and a special page on which to meditate were done by Betsy Platkin Teutsch.

Shirim Uvrachot (Songs and Blessings) is designed for home use and includes Shabbat and holiday blessings and rituals, table songs with musical notation (cassette tape available), and children's prayers. An educational guide, **Reaching Into Prayer**, is available to explain the Reconstructionist *siddur*.

Gates of Prayer—Sha'arei Tefillah is the Reform *siddur*. It offers a variety of services for Shabbat and includes reading selections on special themes and songs and hymns in the back (transliterated and translated). The "Gates of _____" titles form a series, including **Gates of the Home**, a prayer book that focuses on home prayers, ceremonies, and readings for many life passages, and **Gates of Understanding**, which is designed to explain the Reform prayer book.

Sephardic *siddurim* of the Middle Eastern Jews are indicated by the description "Minhag Sephardim." One example is **"Siddur HaHodesh"** (Sinai Publishing, Israel). Completely in Hebrew, it contains many kabbalistic references, hymns for midnight prayer-song sessions, a girl's naming ceremony (from a few centuries preceding the *havurah* movement), and other unusual gems.

VeTaher Libenu ("Purify Our Hearts") is a *siddur* written and published by Congregation Beth-El of Sudbury, MA. It contains a fairly traditional format but with nonsexist language ("he" and "she" are used interchangably as pronouns for God). Although not quite as inclusive as some of the larger *siddurim*, its English translations are unusually beautiful and compelling.

Sha'arei Tefillah ("Gates of Prayer"), from Adama Books, is not to be confused with the Reform movement's prayer book of the same name. This "Gates of Prayer" is thoroughly Orthodox. It is beautifully illustrated with color calligraphy and full-color nature photography from Israel. The Hebrew prayers are untranslated but include brief English commentaries.

Kabbalat Shabbat: The Sabbath Evening Service, translated with commentary by Chaim Raphael (Behrman House), is a new Friday-night

Prayer book that combines prayer and study by including an in-depth commentary about the traditional Shabbat liturgy.

Prayer Books for Children

Gates of Wonder, by Rabbis Howard Bogot, Robert Orkand, and Joyce Orkand, artwork by Neil Waldman (New York: CCAR, 1990), for preschoolers, includes very simple prayers and colorful pictures that convey the emotion of prayer.

My Little Siddur, by Rabbi Azriel Dvir and Mazal Mashat, and **My Little Machzor** (High Holiday prayer book), edited by Jacob Maor and Mazal Mashat-Pnini and translated by Rabbi Sidney Gold (New York: Adama Books, 1986), are a set of charming prayer books adapted from Israel *siddurim* for kindergartners. Each is illustrated with color photos of children praying and observing traditions and contains excerpts from the Hebrew prayers, with the simplest of English translations and commentaries.

Kol HaNeshamah: Shirim Uvrachot (Songs and Blessings), from the Reconstructionist Movement (see earlier full description), contains children's bedtime rituals, beautifully illustrated.

Blessed Are You—Traditional Everyday Hebrew Prayers, by Michelle Edwards (New York: Lothrop, Lee & Shepard, 1993), is a beautiful and colorful book of prayers, for ages 4 to 9, with selected traditional blessings and prayer verses.

Baruch Atah—Befi Hataf ("Blessed Are You—For Children"), by Ze'ev Lipman (Tel Aviv: Tzabar Books, no publication date given), for ages 5 to 9, illustrates a child's basic prayers and blessings (in Hebrew only), with quaintly old-fashioned color illustrations of life in Israel. This charming book is available in the United States through several book distributors.

Shabbat—A Family Service, by Rabbi Judith D. Abrams, illustrated by Katherine Kahn (Rockville, MD: Kar-Ben Copies, 1991), is a traditionally structured service for children ages 4 to 8 and their families, including full-color pictures and simple yet poetic language. For the music of prayer, see the Music Resource Guide. For ritual objects and garments, see the Home Resource Guide.

RESOURCE GUIDE FOR JEWISH HISTORY

(For books specifically on Israeli history, for adults and children, see Israel Resource Guide, p. 339.)

Popular Jewish Histories

For Adults

A History of the Jewish Experience, by Leo Trip (New York: Behrman House, 1973), stresses the beliefs and practices of Judaism and their historical development. It's illustrated with black-and-white photos.

Jews, God and History, by Max I. Dimont (New York: Signet, 1962), is one of the most entertaining and readable popular accounts of Jewish history. It includes reference tables of world and Jewish history.

Wanderings—Chaim Potok's History of the Jews (New York: Alfred A. Knopf, 1978). Potok surveys the sweep of Jewish history, including philosophical perspectives and personal anecdotes from his life and travels. This outsized volume contains many color photographs.

My People—The Story of the Jews, by Abba Eban (New York: Berhman House and Random House, 1968). The statesman-scholar offers an epic presentation of Jewish history and identity throughout the ages. It's illustrated with black-and-white photographs.

The Illustrated Atlas of Jewish Civilization, edited by Martin Gilbert (New York: Macmillan, 1990), contains 200 illustrations and 100 full-color maps that survey 4,000 years of Jewish history around the world.

Written Out of History—Our Jewish Foremothers, by Sondra Henry and Emily Taitz (Fresh Meadows, NY: Biblio Press, 1985), should be read by Jewish women and men seeking to understand the many and varied contributions of women to Jewish civilization. It includes black-and-white photographs.

The Jews in America—Four Centuries of an Uneasy Encounter: A History, by Arthur Hertzberg (New York: Simon & Schuster, 1989), is both a full guide to the American Jewish past (since 1654) and a challenging vision of the future.

The Road From Babylon—The Story of the Sephardic and Oriental Jews, by Chaim Raphael (New York: Harper & Row, 1985), with maps and photographs, tells the saga of the Sephardic experience from the world of the Patriarchs until modern Israel.

One People—The Story of the Eastern Jews, by Devora and Menachem Hacohen, introduction by Abba Eban (New York: Adama, 1986), depicts the cultures and histories of Sephardic and other African and Asian Jewish communities from Iraq to

Ethiopia. With many colorful photographs and tales of different customs, this will interest young people as well as adults.

For Children and Teens

Introduction to Jewish History (from Abraham to the Sages) (1981) and *Journey Through Jewish History* (The Age of Faith and the Age of Freedom) (1983), both by Seymour Rossel (West Orange, NJ: Behrman House), are well-written, visually appealing, illustrated history books for children in the upper elementary grades. Accompanying activity books and teacher guides are available.

Pass the Torah, Please: Jewish Leaders from Mattathias to Saadia, by Cheri Ellowitz Silver (Denver, CO: Alternatives in Religious Education, 1990), for ages 10 to 13, presents more than 20 male and female Jewish leaders from the formative years of classical Judaism, through first-person monologues and interactive activities. It's illustrated with line drawings. A workbook and leader guide are available.

The Mystery of Being Jewish, by Molly Cone (New York: UAHC, 1989), for ages 12 to 15, tells the life stories of 20 modern Jews and how their Jewish identities influenced their lives. With black-and-white photographs. A teacher's guide is available.

The Amazing Adventures of the Jewish People, by Max I. Dimont (New York: Behrman House, 1984), for high-school students, is a new adaptation of Dimont's popular Jewish history. It includes black-and-white photographs.

My People—Abba Eban's History of the Jews, 2 vols., adapted by David Bamberger (New York: Behrman, 1979), is an adaptation of Abba Eban's classic for the junior-high level. With full-color photos and illustrations.

You Are the Historian, by Robert Sugar, from the series, **Our Story, The Jews of Sepharad** (New York: CAJE, 1991), available from the Coalition for the Advancement of Jewish Education, 261 W. 35th St., Fl. 12A, New York, NY 10001. This illustrated textbook-journal lets middle-school students become historians as they learn about the history of the Jews in Spain.

The Jews in America—A Picture Album, by Milton Meltzer (Philadelphia: Jewish Publication Society, 1985), for ages 8 and up, includes more than 100 prints and photographs to trace the heritage of Jewish Americans.

The Young Reader's Encyclopedia of Jewish History, edited by Ilana Shamir and Dr. Shlomo Shavit (New York: Viking, 1987), for ages 10 and up, is a concise guide to Jewish history, illustrated with many full-color pictures and photographs.

Chronicle—News of the Past, edited by Israel Eldad and Moshe Aumann (Jerusalem: The Reubeni Foundation, published by the Arrow Company, 1977), for ages 12 to adult, is a unique three-volume series of bound mock newspapers, each of which conveys a different historical period, from the time of Abraham through the dawn of Zionism.

Picture Parade of Jewish History, by Morris Epstein, illustrated by Maurice del Bourgo and F. L. Blake (New York: Bloch, 1977), for ages 9 and up, is a collection of historical anecdotes in cartoon story-strip form from the now-defunct *World Over* magazine for children. I remember these educational cartoons as one of the highlights of Sunday school. Facing each cartoon page is a page of historical background.

Historical Fiction for Children

The Mystery of the Coins, written and illustrated by Chaya M. Burstein (New York: UAHC Press, 1988), for ages 8 to 12, uses the fictional story of children investigating a mysterious coin collection to introduce stories that show the entire sweep of Jewish history and migration. This book is a favorite of both children and parents.

The Do-It-Yourself Jewish Adventure series from UAHC Press, New York, by Kenneth Roseman, includes **The Cardinal's Snuffbox** (the Spanish Inquisition), **Escape from the Holocaust**, and **The Melting Pot—An Adventure in New York**. For ages 9 to 13. The reader creates his or her own exciting, educational, and sometimes hair-raising reading adventures by making choices that result in instructions to turn to different pages of the book and obtain different progressions and various possible endings to the story. Each book can be read several times with different plots.

History Game

Expulsion, by Cherie Koller-Fox, from Alternatives in Religious Education of Denver, is a board game for ages 9 and up that teaches about Jewish life in Spain as well as about Jewish values and mysticism.

History Video: For Children

Fliegel's Flight—A Bird's-Eye View of Jewish History, produced by Scopus Films, London, 1988, for ages 9 to 12, captures the drama and sweep of Jewish history while glossing over the details. The music and animation make it appealing to children.

For 1 to 6 players or teams.

RESOURCE GUIDE FOR TRAVEL

(For Guides to Israel, see pp. 339–340.)

World Guide for the Jewish Traveler (revised), by Warren Freedman (New York: E. P. Dutton, 1984), is a guide to Jewish historical sites, synagogues, museums, and memorials in more than 100 countries and regions, including an in-depth tour of Israel. It emphasizes Jewish history and meeting Jews around the world.

The Jewish Traveler, edited by Alan M. Tigay (Northvale, NJ: Jason Aronson, 1994), is *Hadassah* magazine's guide to the world's Jewish communities. It highlights 48 cities from Nairobi to Rio, including information on accommodations, kosher eating, synagogues, Jewish Community Centers, sights, Jewish history, and current Jewish culture.

American Jewish Congress World Travel, (800) 221-4694, (212) 879-4588, a service to members of the AJC, a Jewish-sponsored human and civil rights and community service organization, includes tours for the entire family all over the world. This includes many trips to sites of Jewish interest and a number of special programs in Israel, including introducing American Jewish tourists to Israelis in their own field, business, or special interest.

The Guide to Everything Jewish in New York, by Joy Levitt and Nancy Davis (New York: Adama, 1986), leads the tourist and native to everything Jewish in the city with the world's largest Jewish population.

Guide to Kosher Eating and Accommodation in North America, by Judith Korey Charles and Lila Teich Gold (Cold Spring, NY: Nightingale Resources, 1990), is a pocket-sized guide to kosher travel.

RESOURCE GUIDE FOR CURRENT EVENTS

PERIODICALS

For Adults

Your local Jewish community newspaper can be a valuable source of information about local Jewish happenings and usually features some national and world Jewish news as well. Jewish organizations such as Hadassah, B'nai B'rith, and others produce fine monthly magazines, while the various movements—Reconstructionist, Reform, Conservative, and Orthodox—have their own noteworthy journals. A complete listing of the many Jewish periodicals in the United States can be found in the annual **American Jewish Yearbook** (American Jewish Committees/JPS). (Israeli periodicals can be found in the Resource Guide on Israel, p. 345.)

Moment Magazine, 3000 Connecticut Ave. N.W., Suite 300, Washington, DC 20008, (800) 387-8888, is an independent glossy Jewish monthly with a wide range of feature stories, interviews, debates in the Jewish community, columns, and reviews. A favorite feature of mine is the frequent inclusion of resource guides to everything from artists to summer camps—a great way to stay in touch with the Jewish world.

The Forward, 45 E. 33rd St., New York, NY 10016, (800) 877-5419, was launched in 1990 "to carry to the next generation the traditions of the Yiddish *Forverts* that guided generations of Jews to a new life in America." This weekly newspaper is noted for its news coverage, editorials, and extensive coverage of books and the arts.

Tikkun, "a bimonthly Jewish critique of politics, culture, and society," is published by the nonprofit Institute for Labor and Mental Health, 5100 Leona St., Oakland, CA 94619, (415) 482-0805. Progressive and sometimes controversial intellectual journal that explores social issues and cultural trends.

The Jewish Spectator, 4391 Park Milano, Calabasas, CA 91302, (818) 591-7481, is an intellectual quarterly journal sponsored by the nonprofit American Friends of the Center for Jewish Living and values.

Lilith—The Jewish Women's Magazine, 250 W. 57th St., New York, NY 10107, (212) 757-0818, is a quarterly Jewish feminist publication that has features, interviews, and reviews on issues of concern to contemporary Jewish women.

Sh'ma, c/o CLAL, 47 W. 34th St., New York, NY 10001, (212) 279-2525, biweekly, except summer, this simple black and white newsletter has become an important vehicle for dialogue within the Jewish community.

Ultimate Issues, 10573 W. Pico Blvd., Los Angeles, CA 90232, (213) 558-3958, written and published by Dennis Prager, focuses on social commentary and religious and political issues, generally from a conservative perspective.

For Preteens—Teens

Inside Reform Judaism, formerly known as "Keeping Posted," published by the UAHC, 838

Fifth Ave., New York, NY 10021, (212) 249-0100, is now included (for an additional subscription fee) bound inside **Reform Judaism**, the UAHC's official magazine. It consists of 14 pages of illustrated articles by recognized authors on a single theme of interest to young Jewish adults, along with a two-page study guide. Formerly, "KP" was used widely for youth and adult studies in all branches of Judaism, and back issues on more than 90 subjects are available.

The Jewish Reader, 705 Foster Ave., Brooklyn, NY 11230, (718) 692-3900, by contrast, has a very traditional Orthodox outlook. It features contemporary stories, history, and historical fiction, Torah commentary, science, and Jewish news briefs. For middle-school ages.

N.O.W.—The Current Events Newspaper, Schaffzin & Schaffzin, P. O. Box 173, Merion Station, PA 19066-0173, (215) 642-8389, is a (nondenominational) Jewish newspaper for middle-school readers. It includes current events, photos, understanding journalism, and controversial issues; readers write in. It's published monthly October through May.

Jewish Current Events, P. O. Box 19637, San Diego, CA 92159, is a newspaper for Jewish preteens to teens, containing news, features, biographies, stories, and a *mitzvah* club. It appears semimonthly during the school year.

Jewish Sports and Fitness, P. O. Box 4549, Old Village Station, Great Neck, NY 11023, (516) 482-5550, for teens to adults, is published quarterly by the Jewish Sports Congress. This lively newspaper and its sponsoring organization encourage Jewish identity, solidarity, and values through sports and fitness. Editorials examine such areas as moral guidance through physical education.

For Elementary-School Children

Shofar, 43 Northcote Dr., Melville, NY 11747, (800) 484-1088, ext. 4598, for ages 8 to 12, is published six times yearly (during the school year). A glossy color magazine with real child appeal, *Shofar* includes interviews with Jewish celebrities, holiday plays and stories, games, cartoons ("Shaloman"), "this month in history," recipes, reviews, hobbies like stamp and coin collecting, and even an advice column that addresses the (sometimes eye-opening) concerns of contemporary Jewish kids. A family education guide is also available.

Noah's Ark, 8323 Southwest Freeway, Suite 250, Houston, TX 77074, (713) 771-7143, for ages 6 to 10, is a monthly newspaper for Jewish children that appears as a supplement in some Jewish community papers and can also be obtained by subscription. Articles, stories, Hebrew dictionary, contests, games, and penpals. **Noah's Ark** also produces a variety of activity books and games.

Olomeinu—Our World, 160 Broadway, New York, NY 10038, (212) 227-1000, for ages 9 to 12, appears monthly during the school year, published by Torah U'Mesorah National Society for Hebrew Day Schools. Traditionally Orthodox in outlook, this four-color magazine includes articles on religious role models, holiday practices and laws, Jewish history, as well as fiction, games, quizzes, historical cartoons, an "Israel diary" about daily life in Israel, and a Hebrew feature.

Levana Monthly, Schaffzin, & Schaffzin, P. O. Box 173, Merion Station, PA 19066-0173, (215) 642-8389, for grades 3 to 5 (and their families), is a two-color holiday newspaper, eight issues per year, very inexpensive but available only in multiples of ten.

Child-Written Newspapers

The Kid's Page Packet, Barbara S. Goldman, 1140 McCabe St., Pittsburgh, PA 15201, (412) 781-4814, is a kit for those wishing to start child-written newspapers in their own community or school (it is modeled on Goldman's creation, the successful "Kid's Page" feature in the **Pittsburgh Jewish Chronicle**).

JEWISH MUSEUMS

There are many Jewish museums in North America. Here are some of the most well known:

Yeshiva University Museum—2520 Amsterdam Ave., New York City

The Jewish Museum—1109 Fifth Ave., New York City

The National Museum of Jewish History—55 N. 5th St., Independence Mall East, Philadelphia

B'nai B'rith Klutznick National Jewish Museum—1640 Rhode Island Ave, NW, Washington, D C

Spertus Museum of Judaica—618 S. Michigan Ave., Chicago

The Temple Museum of Religious Art—1855 Ansel Rd., Cleveland

Hebrew Union College Skirball Museum—3077 University Ave., Los Angeles

The Council of American Jewish Museums, under the auspices of the National Foundation for Jewish Culture, 330 Seventh Ave., 21st floor., New York,

NY 10001, publishes a directory of over forty member museums.

Of special interest to families with children: **Dolores Kohl Education Foundation**, 165 Green Bay Rd., Wilmette, IL 60091, (708) 251-6950. This noted Chicago-area resource center features a celebrated Jewish children's museum. Traveling exhibits are available. **Jewish Discovery Room**, Rita Kopin, director, Board of Jewish Education of Greater Washington, 11710 Hunter's Lane, Rockville, MD 20852, (301) 984-4455, is a one-room children's museum with hands-on exhibits and educational programs.

RESOURCE GUIDE FOR THE HOLOCAUST AND ANTI-SEMITISM

Scores of books about the Holocaust, including many new books for young readers, have been published in recent years. What follows are just a few selections with the ages for which they are most appropriate.

For Adults

A Holocaust Reader, edited by Lucy S. Dawidowicz (West Orange, NJ: Behrman House, 1976), is a collection of source documents, both official and personal, that show the Holocaust through both Jewish and German eyes.

The War Against the Jews, by Lucy S. Dawidowicz (New York: Bantam, 1986), is a full account of the Holocaust that presents Dawidowicz's view that the extermination of the Jews was central to Hitler's policy, to the subordination of all other elements.

Genocide: Critical Issues of the Holocaust, edited by Alex Grobman, Daniel Landes, and Sybil Milton (West Orange, NJ: Behrman House/Rossel Books), is a collection of brief essays describing the Holocaust and its impact on the modern world that are arranged for college-level and adult study groups.

While Six Million Died: A Chronicle of American Apathy, by Arthur D. Morse (New York: Overlook Press, 1985), documents American and British obstructions to the rescue of European Jews.

Night, Dawn, Day, by Elie Wiesel (Northvale, NJ: Jason Aronson, 1985), are three masterworks that convey the agony of the Holocaust and its aftermath in prose.

For Ages 7–9

The Number on My Grandfather's Arm, by David A. Adler, photographs by Rose Eichenbaum (New York: UAHC Press, 1987), is an age-appropriate story-in-photographs of a young girl and her grandfather, a survivor.

For Ages 8–12

The Yanov Torah, by Erwin and Agnes Herman with illustrations by Katherine Kahn (Rockville, MD: Kan Ben, 1985), is the stirring, true story of a Torah scroll rescued from the Nazis, piece by piece, and its ultimate journey from Russia to America.

Number the Stars, by Lois Lowry (New York: Dell, 1990), is a Newbery Award Medal Winner. It is a thrilling and touching tale based on the rescue of Danish Jewry by righteous Danish Christians.

For Ages 10–14

A Nightmare in History: The Holocaust 1933–1945, by Miriam Chaikin (New York: Clarion, 1982), is a clear, historically accurate and frank overview of the Holocaust. This is a widely praised volume.

We Remember the Holocaust, by David Adler (New York: Henry Holt, 1989), is a critically acclaimed collection of first-person memories of survivors, with photographs.

The Devil's Arithmetic, by Jane Yolen (New York, Penguin, 1988), is a celebrated fictional story of contemporary Jewish children who find themselves transported back to the time of the Holocaust.

Anne Frank: The Diary of a Young Girl (New York, Doubleday, 1967), is the famous diary of the teenager who has come to symbolize all the innocent children who died in the Holocaust.

Alan and Naomi, by Myron Levoy (New York: Harper & Row, 1987), is a well-written fictional story in which an American, Alan, tries to befriend Naomi, a young French immigrant girl who has been traumatized by Nazi brutality. It has now been made into a feature-length film.

The Upstairs Room, by Johanna Reiss (New York: Bantam, 1973), is the popular, personal story of a young girl who, hidden by righteous Christians, survived the Nazi period.

In the Mouth of the Wolf, by Rose Zar (Philadelphia: JPS, 1983), is the stirring personal account of a young girl who survives the Nazi era by pretending to be a non-Jew. (For adult readers too.)

I Never Saw Another Butterfly: Children's Drawings and Poems from Terezin Concentration Camp, edited by Hana Volavkova (New York: Schocken, 1978), is the artistic legacy of the children who died in Terezin. This is a book for older children and adults to share.

Rooftop Secrets and Other Stories of Anti-Semitism, by Lawrence Bush, with commentaries by Albert Vorspan and illustrations by Martin Lemelman (New York: UAHC, 1986), is a collection of eight short stories that span five centuries of Jewish history and confrontation with prejudice. Although from the title one would expect this to be a rather depressing book, it actually offers positive explorations of Jewish values.

The Endless Steppe: A Girl in Exile, by Esther Hautzig (New York: Scholastic, 1968), is the true story of a girl and her family who were exiled to Siberia by the Russians during World War II.

For Ages 13 and Up

All But My Life, by Gerda Weissmann Klein (New York: Hill and Wang, 1971), is the memoir of a Holocaust survivor who lost everyone she'd loved in the camps but lived to rebuild her life and rediscover hope and love.

My Enemy, My Brother, by James Forman (New York: Scholastic, 1969), is the powerful fictional story of a young survivor of Nazi torture who arrives in Palestine only to face new dilemmas in the conflict between Arabs and Jews.

They Fought Back: The Story of the Jewish Resistance in Nazi Europe, by Yuri Suhl (New York: Schocken, 1987), chronicles the story of the Jewish Resistance in the ghettos, and even in the concentration camps. Also by Suhl is **Uncle Misha's Partisans** (New York: Four Winds Press, 1973), a suspenseful story of Jewish Resistance fighters, based on historic events.

Hannah Senesh: Her Life and Diary (New York: Schocken, 1973) is a collection of the personal writings of Hannah Senesh, who immigrated to Israel and parachuted into occupied Europe to rescue Jews, only to be tortured and murdered by the Nazis.

Hitler's War Against the Jews—The Holocaust, by David A. Altshuler (West Orange, NJ: Behrman House, 1978), for grades 8 to 10, is a young reader's version of Dawidowicz's **The War Against the Jews**. A teacher's guide is available.

Never to Forget: The Jews of the Holocaust, by Milton Meltzer (New York: Dell, 1972), is a complete history of the Holocaust for young people, including personal testimonies. A teacher's guide is available.

RESOURCE GUIDE FOR JEWISH CAMPS AND YOUTH GROUPS

Check with your local synagogue or JCC for information about local activities and regional camps, or contact these national organizations about chapters in your area or for information on how to start your own.

Association of Jewish Sponsored Camps, Inc., 130 E. 59th St, New York, NY 10022, provides a brochure that offers basic information about dozens of member camps (of all Jewish denominations and philosophies) on the eastern seaboard and helps individuals to locate the camp best suited to their needs and desires.

B'nai Akiva of North America, 25 W. 26th St., New York, NY 10010, (212) 889-5260, is a religious Zionist youth movement seeking to interest youth in *aliyah* to Israel and social justice through pioneering as an integral part of their religious observance. It sponsors summer camps, leadership training, work-study programs at religious Israeli *kibbutzim*, tours to Israel, and college groups.

B'nai B'rith Youth Organization, 1640 Rhode Island Ave., NW, Washington, DC 20036, (202) 857-6633, has youth groups for Jewish teens that focus on service, learning, and Jewish religion and culture. They have national camp institutes and Israel programs and publications.

Brandeis-Bardin Institute, 1101 Peppertree Lane, Brandeis, CA 93064, (818) 348-7201, has nondenominational, pluralistic Jewish camp programs and Shabbat weekends for both adults and children, including Camp Alonim, a Jewish camp for children ages 8 to 16.

National Ramah Commission, 3080 Broadway, New York, NY 10027, (212) 678-8881, sponsors seven summer camps in the United States and Canada with an emphasis on Hebrew as a spoken language and Jewish living in the Conservative Jewish tradition. They also offer special seminars for youth in the United States and Israel, as well as educational tours to Israel for Jewish community high schools.

Hashachar/Young Judaea, 50 W. 58th St., New York, NY 10019, (212) 355-7900, Hadassah-sponsored movement seeks to educate Jewish youth in Jewish and Zionist values and active participation in and commitment to the American and Israel Jewish communities. They also maintain regional and national summer camps as well as summer and year programs in Israel. For a brochure of Young Judaea camps and Israel programs, call (800) 362-CAMP.

Merkos L'Inyonei Chinuch, Inc. (The Central Organization for Jewish Education), 770 Eastern Parkway, Brooklyn, NY 11213, is the educational arm of the Lubavitcher hasidic movement. They sponsor educational programs, publications, schools, and summer day camps for Jewish children.

Young Israel Youth, 3 W. 16th St., New York, NY 10011, (212) 929-1525, has Orthodox Jewish spiritual, cultural, social, and communal activities for youth, including study programs in Israel.

North American Federation of Temple Youth (NFTY), 838 Fifth Ave., New York, NY 10021, (212) 249-0100, seeks to educate Reform Jewish teens in Jewish values and their application to community service. They sponsor a network of youth groups, summer camps, educational, social action, and leadership programs in the United States and Israel.

National Conference of Synagogue Youth (NCSY), 333 Seventh Ave., New York, NY 10001, (212) 563-4000, is the central body for youth groups of Orthodox congregations, providing educational guidance, Torah study groups, scholarships, national and regional events, and study tours in Israel and the United States. They also have "Our Way" programs for the Jewish deaf and "Yachad" for the developmentally disabled.

United Synagogue Youth (USY), 155 Fifth Ave., New York, NY 10010, (212) 353-9439, seeks to strengthen identification with Conservative Judaism, based on the needs and interests of adolescents, through youth groups, tours of North America and Israel, and programming in a *mitzvah* framework.

Jewish Community Centers Association, 15 E. 26th St., New York, NY 10010-1579, (212) 532-4949, is the leadership agency for the North American network of Jewish Community Centers (which provide many youth programs and day camps; contact your local center for more information), YM-YWHAs, and camps. They publish a directory of approximately 200 Jewish resident summer camps throughout the United States and Canada.

National Jewish Committee on Scouting (Boy Scouts of America), 1325 Walnut Hill Lane, Irving, TX 75015-2079, (214) 580-2059, works with local Jewish committees to establish Cub and Boy Scout troops and coed Explorer posts in synagogues, JCCs, day schools, and other institutions.

National Jewish Girl Scout Committee, Synagogue Council of America, 327 Lexington Ave, New York, NY 10016, (212) 686-8670, promotes Jewish award programs, religious services, cultural exchanges with Israeli scouts, and assistance to local councils in organizing Girl Scout troops and Jewish Girl Scout committees.

American Zionist Youth Foundation, 110 E. 59th St., New York, NY 10022, (800)-27-ISRAE(L), (212) 339-6916, sponsors a wide variety of summer programs in Israel, for high-school and college students. The foundation also sponsors fields workers on campus and in summer camps, and publishes guides to educational and programming materials and to programs in Israel.

Jewish Sports Congress, P. O. Box 4549, Old Village Station, Great Neck, NY 11023, (516) 482-5550, promotes Jewish identity, unity, and values through sports and fitness. They sponsor publications, special events, and programs in the United States and Israel.

JEWISH FAMILY CAMPING

At a lecture on "alternative travel and recreation" with travel *mayven* Arthur Frommer, I was amazed to learn that the Unitarian Church had purchased 50 out-of-business children's camps and turned them into flourishing adult "summer camps" resorts with thematic programs, including a number specifically geared to family recreation and education. With all the concern in the Jewish community about the importance of the family unit, informal education, and the development of quality family educational programs, it would seem wise for the Jewish community to learn from this example.

Although the Jewish community has far to go in creating this type of family retreat environment, there are some fine programs available. Inquire through your synagogue, Jewish Community Center, or the regional camp of your Jewish denomination or movement: many of these sponsor weekend retreats or even longer camping programs for families. Here are four well-known programs, two on each coast, in which Jewish families can participate in camping or other forms of informal education. Call or write for details; in general, these are short programs of less than a week in duration.

Ramah Family Camp, Camp Ramah, 15600 Mulholland Dr., Los Angeles, CA 90077, (213) 476-8571 (camp is in Ojai, California), is noted for its flagship family camping program. The program aims to strengthen family life, Jewish life, and the Jewish life of the family through a combination of carefully planned Judaic activities (adult study sessions with scholars in residence, Jewish celebration, and worship), along with traditional "camp stuff" (sports, games, arts programs). Programs for adults, for children, and for adults and kids to do together. Families are housed together.

Brandeis-Bardin Family Camp, Brandeis, CA 93064, (818) 348-7201, (805) 526-1131. The family camp session at this well-known institute for Jewish life combines youth programs and child care for preschoolers with adult lectures, workshops, and discussions. There are also family activities: recreational, educational, and religious. Children from age 5 and up are housed with other campers their age.

The National Havurah Committee Annual Summer Institute, National Havurah Committee, P. O. Box 2621, Bala Cynwyd, PA 19004-6621, (215) 843-1470, is a week-long gathering for intensive Jewish study, discussion, celebration, and communal living, held at a college campus, attended by about 200 adults and 50 children. A full children's educational program is available, as well as a teen program. Recreational sports also available. There are regional retreats in between the national event.

P'nai Or Kallah, c/o ALEPH: Alliance for Jewish Renewal, 7318 Germantown Ave., Philadelphia, PA 19119, (215) 242-4074. This international avant garde religious network dedicated to Jewish renewal and the "building of inclusive community" holds a family camp every other summer. Four hundred adults and children gather for intensive Jewish learning and educational programming.

For those seeking to create a Jewish family retreat program in their own community, a new guidebook is available, produced by the Melton Research Center for Jewish Education of the Jewish Theological Seminary and the Whizin Institute for Jewish Family Life at the University of Judaism.

Jewish Family Retreats: A Handbook, by Vicky Kelman, is available from the Melton Research Center, 3080 Broadway, New York, NY 10027, (212) 678-8031.

RESOURCE GUIDE FOR JEWISH EDUCATION

Books

What We Know About Jewish Education, edited by Dr. Stuart L. Kelman (Los Angeles: Torah Aura, 1992), is a readable handbook of the latest research into the current state of Jewish education in North America. It includes articles by experts in such fields as the day and supplementary school, early childhood, family education, faith development, funding, communal planning, and changing Jewish schools.

Organizations

One of the most significant ways I know of to make a difference in Jewish education is to become a member and supporter of the **Coalition for the Advancement of Jewish Education (CAJE)**, 261 W. 35th St., floor 12A, New York, NY 10001, (212) 268-4210. CAJE is the largest Jewish–educator membership organization in North America and the premier grass-roots movement for the advancement of Jewish education. Jews from all over North America and the world, of every ideological peruasion, meet open-mindedly and respectfully through CAJE.

CAJE is most famous for its yearly Conference on Alternatives in Jewish Education, which is held at a college campus in a different American city each summer, and has also been held in Jerusalem. At each CAJE conference, some 2,000 Jewish educators– including teachers, administrators, rabbis, cantors, journalists, and writers, parents and community leaders—all get together "to learn and to teach." In addition to the scores of classes, there are exhibits of the latest in Jewish books and learning materials; resource centers; and entertainment by top Jewish musicians, storytellers, and other performers. There is always a special program for lay leaders, who are also encouraged to attend any of the regular programs. Whole families can participate; there is a full range of day-camp and day-care programs for children, as well as a teen program.

CAJE also sponsors networks to bring together educators with special interests of all types (including family education); a curriculum bank with hundreds of resources created by members; publications, regional mini-conferences, and more. Parents who care about their children's Jewish education will find these resources of great benefit.

They can help to connect you (and your school or other educational program) with experienced educators in your area or anywhere in the country.

The Jewish Education Service of North America (JESNA), 730 Broadway, New York, NY 10003, (212) 529-2000, is the coordinating, planning, and service agency for Jewish education in boards or bureaus of Jewish education and Jewish federations. Among other things, JESNA provides educational consulting, conferences, periodicals, research, placement services, fellowships, and a National Educational Resource Center. It makes your local Jewish community into part of a national and international movement for the enhancement of Jewish education at all levels. For those who wish to become more intensely involved in Jewish education, lay leadership in JESNA is an important avenue.

JESNA also provides a number of resource materials of interest to the individual Jewish family, *havurah*, or school, such as a Jewish Education Directory, bibliographies for Jewish study, and several publications about the latest trends and research in Jewish education. Jewish family education has become an increasingly important concern for JESNA, and they can provide consultation and support in this area as well.

FAMILY EDUCATION

See also CAJE and JESNA, listed earlier. Both have networks and resources devoted to Jewish family education. If you live in or near a major Jewish community, check with your Board of Jewish Education. Training programs, grants, and other initiatives in Jewish family education are proliferating rapidly.

Training Programs

Whizin Institute for Jewish Family Life, University of Judaism, 15600 Mulholland Dr., Los Angeles, CA 90077, (213) 476-9777, Ron Wolfson, director), is the site of an annual week-long intensive seminar for educators, rabbis, and lay leaders who want their Jewish communities to become involved in family education. Participants learn about the social, psychological, spiritual, and practical aspects of family education. The Whizin faculty also provides training and consultation to local Jewish communities.

The Cleveland Fellows Program, Cleveland College of Jewish Studies, 26500 Shaker Blvd.,

Beachwood, OH 44122, (216) 464-4050. This program offers master's degree level training in Jewish family education.

Books on Jewish Family Education

Learning Together—A Sourcebook on Jewish Family Education, edited by Janice P. Alpter (Denver, CO: Alternatives in Religious Education, 1987), describes many family education programs from around the United States and gives addresses for contacting Jewish family educators who might serve as consultants. A full bibliography is included.

The Jewish Family—Authority and Tradition in Modern Perspective, by Norman Linzer (New York: Human Sciences Press, 1984), is written by a professor at the Wurzweiler School of Social Work of Yeshiva University who offers a theoretical and philosophical model for Jewish family education, as well as some general ideas for future directions it could take.

Jewish Family Education Programs

Note: These outstanding programs can provide models for Jewish Family Education in other communities.

Jewish Experiences for Families (JEFF), Fresh Air Society, 6600 W. Maple Road, West Bloomfield, MI 48322, (313) 661-0600 (Harlene Appleman, coordinator), is one of the most extensive Jewish family education ventures in the country. Programs include holiday celebrations, family retreats, *havurot*, workshops, seminars, and special events. JEFF has also produced inexpensive materials such as family guides to various holidays (available in English or Russian).

P.A.C.E. (Parents and Children for Education), c/o Jo Kay, Religious School Director, Congregation Rodeph Shalom, 7 West 83rd St., New York, NY 10024, (212) 362-5880, is a religious-school program for children and their parents. The program includes adult-level classes, student classes, and family classes that parallel the regular school curriculum.

Harvard Hillel Children's School, 89 Abbotsford, Brookline, MA 02146 (Cherie Koller-Fox, director), is a unique school community with a flagship family education program that involves the entire family in programs for the Jewish holidays, *tzedakah* activities, and life-cycle events.

Temple Shalom, 175 Temple St., West Newton, MA 02165, (617) 969-3518, Julie Vanek, Temple

Educator, designs and runs exceptionally creative family education programs of all types, including congregation-wide "extravaganzas" for hundreds of participants.

MATERIALS FOR JEWISH FAMILY EDUCATION

Together, by Vicky Kellman, et al., from the Melton Research Center for Jewish Education, 3080 Broadway, New York, NY 10027, (212) 678-8031, consists of two programs, "Together: A Parent-Child Kit," for 8- to 9-year olds and their parents, and "Windows: Together 2," for 11- to 12-year-olds and their parents. The former series deals with holidays, Shabbat, prayers, and beliefs, while the latter is designed to make the *bat* or *bar mitzvah* year more meaningful.

Building Jewish Life, by Joel Lurie Grishaver, et al., from Torah Aura Productions, 4423 Fruitland Ave., Los Angeles, CA 90058, (800) BE-TORAH, is a series of innovative books on the holidays, synagogue, and other topics, each of which includes components for the child, parent, and Jewish school. Another product from Torah Aura is JET (Jewish Experiences Together), which includes packets of cards with suggested Jewish home activities.

The Art of Jewish Living series, by Ron Wolfson with Joel Lurie Grishaver, is a project of the Federation of Jewish Men's Club, 475 Riverside Dr., New York, NY, 10015, and the University of Judaism, Los Angeles. Books, tapes, and other materials provide Jewish parents with the background, skills, and creative ideas for holding a Passover *seder*, Shabbat dinner, or Hanukkah observance at home.

The Parent Connection, from the Bureau of Jewish Education of Greater Boston, 333 Nahanton St., Newton, MA 02159, (617) 965-7350, includes materials to set up a reading program for Jewish schools and libraries, especially for parents and children in kindergarten through second grade.

EARLY CHILDHOOD EDUCATION

The Board of Jewish Education of Greater New York, 426 W. 58th St., New York, NY 10019, (212) 245-8200, has developed many creative materials for early childhood education, including special materials for Hebrew language.

Mishpacha ("family") is their family education program, designed for nursery school children and their families.

Alternatives in Religious Education (A.R.S.) Publishing, 3945 S. Oneida St., Denver, CO 80237, (303) 363-7779, produces a wide variety of teaching materials for early childhood education, including **The Jewish Preschool Teachers Handbook (revised edition)**, by Sandy Furfine Wolf and Nancy Cohen Nowak, which is recommended for teachers and parents of Jewish children from ages 3 to 5, and **Head Start on Holidays: Jewish Programs for Preschoolers and Parents**, by Robert Louis Goodman and Andy Honigman Zell, which contains three years' worth of family programs for early childhood.

JEWISH SPECIAL EDUCATION

Organizations

(CAJE, listed earlier, has a Special Needs Network. A number of national youth groups, particularly those connected with the religious movements, have programs for children with special learning needs and physical challenges.)

P'tach (Parents for Torah for All Children), 4612 13th Ave., Brooklyn, NY 11219, (718) 854-8600, is a parents' advocacy group to provide traditional Jewish education to children with special needs. They have programs in several major Jewish communities in the United States, as well as in Israel.

The Jewish Braille Institute of America, 110 East 30th St., New York, NY 10016, (212) 889-2525, provides free programs and materials for blind and visually impaired Jews of all ages.

Books and Materials

A Question in Search of an Answer, by Roberta M. Greene and Elaine Heavenrich, from the Union of American Hebrew Congregations (Reform), 838 Fifth Ave., New York, NY 10021, (212) 249-0100, is a practical handbook for anyone concerned about or involved in Jewish education for children with learning disabilities.

Learning Disabled and Special Education materials, from the United Synagogue Commission on Jewish Education (Conservative), Book Service, 155 Fifth Ave., New York, NY 10010, (212) 533-7800, include materials, books, and resource guides for Jewish special education.

Special Education publications, from Torah

Umesorah Publications (Orthodox), 5723 18th Ave., Brooklyn, NY 11204, (718) 259-1223, include guides to implementing programs for learning disabled children in the Orthodox Jewish day school.

The Board of Jewish Education of Greater New York, 426 W. 58th St., New York, NY 10019, (212) 245-8200, has developed a Hebrew-school curriculum for learning-disabled children.

RESOURCE GUIDE FOR JEWISH INTERPERSONAL VALUES

Books and Study Materials

For Adults and Families

Danny Siegel, known to many as the *"mitzvah man,"* has written a veritable library of books on the Jewish approach to interpersonal relationships and *tzedakah*. Particularly recommended for every home library are the following three books he authored:

Gym Shoes and Irises (Personalized Tzedakah) — Book Two (Spring Valley, NY: Town House Press, 1987) is the indispensable primer for interpersonal *mitzvot*, a "Jewish Catalog" of Jewish ethics, *tzedakah*, and *hesed*. It includes many practical suggestions, inspiring role models, addresses of organizations, and several essays of special interest to parents.

Munbaz II and Other Mitzvah Heroes (Spring Valley, NY: Town House Press, 1988) tells the inspiring stories of some little-known (and a few famous) contemporary *mitzvah* role models, both Jewish and of other faiths. Addresses and suggestions are included so that the reader can get involved.

Where Heaven and Earth Touch (Northvale, NJ: Jason Aronson, 1989), an anthology of thought-provoking selections from classical Jewish source material on "Torah and Life-Values." This collection is good for family group discussion.

Traditional Texts

For Adults

The Dynamics of Tzedakah (Part One: essay; Part Two: educator's guide and sources), from the Shalom Hartman Institute for Advanced Judaic Studies (available from American Friends of the Shalom Hartman Institute, 1029 Teaneck Rd., Tea

neck, NJ 07666, (201) 837-0887, provides classic source materials (English and Hebrew) and contemporary perspectives on the Jewish ideal of *tzedakah*. It is excellent for study groups, adolescent to adult.

Ahavat Chesed ("The Love of Kindness as Required by God"), by the Chafetz Chaim (Rabbi Yisrael Meir Kahan), translated by Leonard Oschry (New York: Feldheim, 1976), is a major Jewish ethical text that explains the halachic aspects of the interpersonal *mitzvot* and their importance in Judaism.

For Young People

JEM — The Society for Justice-Ethics-Morality, c/o Rebecca Katz, P.O. Box 1012, Netanya, Israel 42110, produces publications for various ages designed to facilitate cognitive moral development using traditional Judaic sources and values. Their publications are available in English or Hebrew.

Jewish Values Vocabulary

For Adults

The Language of Judaism, by Simon Glustrom (Northvale, NJ: Jason Aronson, 1988), reveals the richness of Jewish values vocabulary, by providing in-depth explanations of 186 Hebrew words and expressions.

For Children

The Alef-Bet of Jewish Values, by Lenore C. Kipper and Howard I. Bogot, illustrated by Jana Paiss (New York: UAHC Press, 1985), explains one Hebrew values concept for each letter of the Hebrew alphabet.

BOOKS ON *TZEDAKAH* AND *HESED*

For Children

Ages 3–6

The Very Best Place for a Penny, by Dina Herman Rosenfeld, illustrated by Leonid Pinchevsky and Eliyahu Meshchaninov (Brooklyn, NY: Merkos Lalnyanei Hinuch, 1984), imaginative illustrations of a penny's many adventures before he finds his happy home in a *tzedakah* box.

Ages 5–9

Mitzvot, by Amye Rosenberg (West Orange, NJ: Behrman House, 1984), is a creative and attractive activity book that introduces young children to a number of the interpersonal *mitzvot*, such as honoring parents, hospitality, and kindness to animals.

Partners, by Deborah Shayne Syme, illustrated by Jeffrey Weiner (New York: UAHC Press, 1990), is a new release about two young boys who learn what it means to be "partners in making God's world a better place" by helping the homeless.

My First Book of Mitzvos, by Ruth Schild Karlinsky with photographs by Isaiah Karlinsky (New York: Feldheim Publishers, 1986), integrates both "interpersonal" *mitzvot* (honoring the elderly, returning lost property, etc.) and "ritual sphere" *mitzvot* (such as prayer and *kashrut*, with a traditional orientation). The text is written from the child's viewpoint and is accompanied by charming black-and-white photographs, apparently taken in Israel, which are good discussion starters.

My Special Friend, by Floreva G. Cohen, with photographs by George Ancona (New York: Board of Jewish Education of Greater New York, 1986), is the upbeat story of two young friends, one with Down's syndrome, and their interaction within a supportive synagogue setting. Some things are easier for Doron and some things are easier for Jonathan. It is fully illustrated with black-and-white photographs.

Yaffa Ganz's short-story books, published variously by Feldheim (New York) and Mesorah (Brooklyn), for ages 5 to 9, include **The Terrible Wonderful Day**, **The Story of Mimmy and Simmy**, **Shuki's Upside-Down Dream**, and others, each of which tells a story that illustrates a traditional Jewish value or *middah* (desirable character trait), in a nonpreachy and engaging fashion. Her books contain cheerful color pictures (illustrators vary).

Greening the Holidays, by Ellen Bernstein and Honey Vizer (Wyncote, PA: Shomrei Adamah, 1989), for ages 8 and up, available from Shomrei Adamah (Guardians of the Earth), Church Rd. and Greenwood Ave., Wyncote, PA 19095, is an illustrated guide to conservation projects that are built around the Jewish holidays.

JET (Jewish Experiences Together) 3: The Environment, by Tamar and Bruce Raff, from Torah Aura Productions, 4423 Fruitland Ave., Los Angeles, CA 90058, (800) BE-TORAH, (213) 585-7312, for children ages 7 to 10 and their parents, is a packet of 32 activity cards that suggest environmental and conservation projects that are based on Jewish values.

My Time: A Jewish Human Calendar for Children, Micah Publications, 255 Humphrey St., Marblehead, MA 01945, ages 5 to 9, includes coloring and activities to teach young children about the Jewish calendar and animal life.

Rachel and Mischa, by Steven and Ilene Bayar, illustrated by Marlene Lobell Ruthen, and photographs by Joanne Strauss (Rockville, MD: Kar-Ben, 1988), for ages 5 to 9, describes the unique problems of Jewish children in the former Soviet Union.

Falasha No More, by Arlene Kushner (New York: Shapolsky, 1986), for ages 7 to 10, tells the story of a young Ethiopian Jewish boy's adjustment to life in Israel. Highlights the beauties of the Ethiopian culture that the family chooses to preserve.

Tzedakah and Tikkun Olam Curricula, from Torah Aura Productions, 4423 Fruitland Ave., Los Angeles, CA 90058, (800) BE -TORAH, (213) 585-7312, includes a *tzedakah* workbook, instant lesson packets, *tzedakah* and values games, and media to teach about Jewish interpersonal values from grades one through adults.

For Preteens and Teens

Emma Ansky-Levine and Her Mitzvah Machine, by Lawrence Bush, illustrated by Joel Iskowitz (New York: UAHC Press, 1991), for ages 9 to 12, is a novel about a 12-year-old girl who discovers Jewish values and identity with the help of a mysterious *mitzvah* machine.

Monday in Odessa, by Eileen Bluestone Sherman (Philadelphia: Jewish Publication Society, 1986), for ages 10 to 14, is an award-winning story of a Jewish girl and her family attempting to leave the Soviet Union.

Tzedakah, Gemilut Chasadim, and Ahavah—A Manual for World Repair, by Joel Lurie Grishaver and Beth Huppin (Denver, CO: Alternatives in Religious Education, 1982), for ages 12 and up, is a workbook that combines ancient and modern texts, practical action projects, and space to record feelings and experiences in a detailed analysis of several interpersonal *mitzvot*. A leader guide is available.

The Return, by Sonya Levitan (New York: Fawcett Books, 1987), for ages 12 to 16. This award-winning young-adult novel tells the story of an Ethiopian girl's dangerous and difficult journey to reach the Promised Land.

Fear No Evil, by Natan Scharansky (New York: Random House, 1988), for adults and older teens, is the stirring autobiography of the most famous Prisoner of Zion in the former Soviet Union.

SOME SPECIAL *MITZVAH* ORGANIZATIONS

The number of worthy organizations is staggering; obviously the scope of this book prevents anything approaching a comprehensive list. Following is a limited selection of some special organizations, mostly Jewish-sponsored but including some major nondenominational organizations Jews may wish to support as an expression of major Jewish values. (Most of the following are tax-deductible; inquire of each.)

"The needy of your city first," wrote Maimonides (*Mishneh Torah* 7:13). Readers are obviously urged to support their local Jewish and general *tzedakah* organizations.

Ziv Tzedakah Fund, 263 Congressional Lane, Suite 708, Rockville, MD 20852, (301) 468-0060, is Danny Siegel's *tzedakah* fund, which started when he collected a few dollars to distribute on a trip to Israel; he now collects hundreds of thousands. The money goes to a number of grass-roots groups in Israel and the United States, the type that tend to be overlooked by the big funds. A regular newsletter keeps contributors updated on these groups. Siegel himself is the *tzedakah* resource person par excellence, known for his ability to inspire and motivate people about personalized *tzedakah*, values, and Jewish ethical behavior.

New Israel Fund, 1101 15th St. NW, Suite 304, Washington, DC 20005, (202) 223-3333, in partnership with Israelis, supports well over 100 Israeli voluntary organizations in such areas as civil rights, pluralism, and intergroup cooperation. For more information, see the section on Israel.

Jewish Fund for Justice, 920 Broadway, Suite 605, New York, NY 10010, (212) 677-7080, is a national Jewish grant-giving organization that provides "seed money" to community-based efforts to change the circumstances that breed poverty and injustice in the United States.

Mazon, 2940 Westwood Blvd., Suite 7, Los Angeles, CA 90064, (213) 470-7769. Mazon ("sustenance") urges Jews to contribute 3 percent of the cost of all *simchas* to their fund, which is distributed in grants to organizations that feed the hungry in the United States and around the world. Mazon is also involved in issues of national agricultural and food policy.

National Coalition for the Homeless, 1439 Rhode Island Ave. NW, Washington, DC 20005, (202) 659-3310, is a national, nonsectarian federation of agencies and organizations working to address and end homelessness.

The American Jewish World Service, 15 W. 26th St., 9th Floor, New York, NY 10010, (212) 683-1161, works to help people in third-world countries to feed themselves and become self-sustaining, sometimes incorporting Israeli agricultural technology. They can help "concretize" *tzedakah* for children by providing such information as the price of plows and livestock.

The Jewish Braille Institute of America, 110 East 30th St., New York, NY 10016, (212) 889-2525, provides extensive programs and materials for blind and visually impaired Jews of all ages in the United States and Israel—free of charge. Their recorded Judaica textbooks also help sighted children with reading disabilities. "Read-a-thon" enables Jewish children to use their sight to help the blind.

National Institute for Jewish Hospice, 6363 Wilshire Blvd., Suite 126, Los Angeles, CA 90048, (800) 446-4448, in California: 1-213-HOSPICE, provides information, training, referrals, and educational publications for families and professionals involved in the care of the Jewish terminally ill.

Friends of Yad Sarah, 1 Parker Plaza, Fort Lee, NJ 07024, (201) 944-7920, supports Yad Sarah, Israel's largest volunteer organization, which provides free loan of medical equipment.

Honor the Elderly

American Friends of Life Line for the Old in Israel, 1450 Broadway, New York, NY 10018, (212) 221-6050, is an all-volunteer organization that supports Lifeline for the Old (*Yad LaKashish*) located at 14 Shivte Yisrael Street in Jerusalem. LifeLine provides a wide array of services to seniors in Jerusalem, particularly a series of workshops where elderly Jews, Moslems, and Christians can rediscover a sense of dignity. Ask for information on purchasing products from the LifeLine workshops, visiting their Israeli facility, intergenerational programs, educational programs for your children, Jewish school, and tapes by *Beged Kefet*, a delightful musical group that donates all proceeds from its concerts and tape sales to LifeLine.

DOROT ("Generations"), 262 West 91st St., New York, NY 10024, (212) 769-2850, provides regular volunteer visitors and holiday supplies to elderly Jews living alone in Manhattan and a shelter to care for and relocate homeless senior citizens.

Project Ezra, c/o Misha Avramoff, 197 E. Broadway, Room U-3, New York, NY 10012, (212) 982-3700, provides help for elderly and disabled Jews on the city's Lower East Side.

National Association for the Jewish Poor, 1163 Manor Ave., Bronx, NY 10472, (212) 378-5865, was founded by Gary Moskowitz, an observant Jew and New York police officer who gets young people involved in helping New York's elderly (and other) Jewish poor.

Pikuah Nefesh: Saving Lives

Amnesty International USA, 322 8th Ave., New York, NY 10001, has played a significant international role in combating political imprisonment and torture, two of the greatest assaults on humanity in the image of God. They have chapters worldwide, including Israel.

Save the Children, 50 Wilton Road, Westport, CT 06880, (800) 767-1600, is the original, nonsectarian child sponsorship agency that enables people to sponsor a needy child in many countries around the world, not through direct handouts but by helping the children's communities through development projects and human services.

US Committee for Unicef (United Nations Children's Fund), 331 E. 38th St., New York, NY 10016, (212) 686-5522, saves the lives of children in developing nations who would die of malnutrition or easily preventable diseases. Five million children die each year from dehydration that could be prevented by simple "oral rehydration salts" that cost less than ten cents a dose.

LIFE-SAVERS Foundation of America, (800) 999-8822, screens individuals and groups with a simple blood test to determine match-ups for lifesaving bone-marrow donation. Various ethnic groups, including Jews of various ethnic backgrounds, are often needed as more likely sources of donors for individuals of the same ethnic origins. Set up a testing program in your area; write government representatives asking for adequate funding for these needs.

Other Groups Mentioned in This Section

Foundation to Sustain Righteous Christians, 823 United Nations Plaza, 10th floor, New York, NY 10017, helps to support righteous Christians who risked their lives to save Jews during the Holocaust but who now live in poverty.

The Rabbanit Bracha Kapach, 12 Lod St., Jerusalem, (02) 249-296: donate used wedding dresses, for loan to needy brides, on your next trip to Israel, or support the Rabbanit, a delightful Yemenite "distinguished citizen of Jerusalem" in her extensive personalized *tzedakah* for the city's poor, including thousands of dollars in Passover supplies each year.

Jewish War Veterans of the United States of America, 1811 R St. NW, Washington, DC 20009, (202) 265-6280, promotes American democratic values, combats bigotry and anti-Semitism, and educates the public about the Jewish contribution to American military service through a national memorial museum at this address.

Friends of the Israel Defense Forces, 15 E. 26th St., New York, NY 10010, (212) 684-0669, supports Israel's version of the USO.

Evaluating Charities

National Charities Information Bureau, 19 Union Square West, New York, NY 10003, (212) 929-6300, or the **Council of Better Business Bureaus' Philanthropic Advisory Service**, 4200 Wilson Blvd., Suite 800, Arlington, VA 22203, (703) 276-0100, both monitor national not-for-profit organizations and provide information about compliance with their voluntary ethical standards.

Pidyon Shevuyim: Rescuing

Ethiopian Jews

American Association for Ethiopian Jews (AAEJ), 1505 22nd St. NW, #300, Washington, DC 20037, (212) 223-6838, works to bring Ethiopian Jews to Israel, resettle them, and reunite families.

North American Conference on Ethiopian Jewry, 165 E. 56th St., New York, NY 10022, (212) 752-6340, helps to save and care for Ethiopian Jewish families still in Ethiopia and to bring them to Israel, resettle them, and aid in preserving their culture.

Russian Jews

Union of Councils for Soviet Jews, 1819 H St. NW, Suite 410, Washington, DC 20006, (202) 775-9770, is a confederation of 45 grass-roots organizations that support the rescue of Soviet Jewry through all manner of political, educational, and religious activities.

Israel Free Loan Association (IFLA), 1 Metudela St., P. O. Box 4171, Jerusalem 91041, Israel, (02) 669-405, provides emergency interest-free loans to new immigrants from Ethiopia and Russia.

As the gates of former Soviet emigration have now opened, the major task ahead will be to resettle Soviet Jewish refugees and help them to rebuild their Jewish identity after years of Soviet bans on Jewish resources and education. Local Jewish Federations have been mounting massive fund-raising drives for the United Jewish Appeal to help resettle these Jews in Israel and the United States, while local Jewish Family Service Agencies and synagogues often need individual and family volunteers to work with and welcome Russian immigrants and businesses to hire them and re-train them where necessary. Informal person-to-person interaction is crucial as well. Many local Jewish community relations councils, as well as national organizations, are sponsoring drives to provide such materials to Jews in the former Soviet Union and at local levels.

Central America

Border Support Group, P. O. Box 55245, Madison, WI 53705, (608) 256-2510: contact for information on Jewish/general involvement in amnesty for Central American refugees. Such a short time ago, Jews were denied sanctuary in this country. It's our turn to speak out for others.

SHALOM ORGANIZATIONS AND RESOURCES

Shelom Bayit: Dealing with Jewish Domestic Violence

Inquire with local Jewish family service agencies if counselors are specifically trained in dealing with family violence issues. This issue has been receiving more attention on the local and national level of Jewish communal organization. See "Domestic Violence: An NCJW Response," from the **National Council of Jewish Women**, 15 E. 26th St., New York, NY 10010, a booklet with resources, programming suggestions, and a bibliography on the subject of family violence. The Jewish Family Service of Greater Los Angeles has a particularly well-developed program, as well as materials that may be of interest to other communities.

Shalom: Children and the Future

Children's Defense Fund, 122 C St. NW, Washington, DC 20001, (202) 628-8787, is nonsectarian and works for better lives for our nation's most vulnerable citizens—its children—particularly the poor, minority, and handicapped. There are 13 million impoverished children in America—a staggering 20 percent of our children's peers. Publications on issues involving children and teens are available.

Stop War Toys Campaign, Box 1093, Norwich, CT 06360, (203) 889-5337, opposes toys that glorify violence and conflict. They have interesting educational materials to get children thinking.

Shalom: World Peace

The Shalom Center, 7318 Germantown Ave., Philadelphia, PA 19119, (215) 247-9700, urges members to commit to one action a month for world peace. The center is the source of political activism, **The Shalom Report** publication, and many educational materials, including a Shalom songbook and cassette of Jewish peace songs, peace curriculum (see the preceding), and special projects for Jewish holidays such as Passover and Sukkot. The center is also highly active in environmental issues.

ENVIRONMENT, CONSERVATION, AND ANIMAL WELFARE ORGANIZATIONS

Organizations and Resources

Shomrei Adamah—Guardians of the Earth (SAGE), a project of The Federation of Reconstructionist Congregations and Havurot, Church Road and Greenwood Ave., Wyncote, PA 19095, (215) 887-1988, works for a renewal of the traditional Jewish ties to nature in facing the pressing environmental challenges of the present. They develop resource materials on Jewish festivals (including a holiday booklet for children and families, **"Greening the Holidays"**) and "how to" conservation materials, work as a "voice for the Jewish community" in alliances with other ecologically concerned groups, and create Jewish educational materials. SAGE promotes the adoption of Tu BiShvat as a major environmental holiday for all people.

Society for the Protection of Nature in Israel (SPNI), 330 Seventh Ave., New York, NY 10001, (212) 947-2820 (13 Helena Hamalka St., Jerusalem [02] 222-357), is the Israeli version of the Sierra Club, involved with conservation, nature education, and interesting programs in Israel. Their quarterly English publication is available to foreign members.

Concern for Helping Animals in Israel (CHAI), P. O. Box 3341, Alexandria, VA 22302, (703) 698-0825, is the much-needed Israeli equivalent of the Humane Society or SPCA.

Micah Publications, the publishing arm of **Jews for Animal Rights**, 255 Humphrey St., Marblehead, MA 01945, (617) 631-7601, has a free catalog on Jewish animal rights and vegetarian publications.

Sierra Club, 730 Polk St., San Francisco, CA 94109, (415) 776-2211, promotes conservation of the natural environment through local and national activism. They have publications and outdoor activities for families. Their Legal Defense Fund (2044 Fillmore St., San Francisco, CA 94115), takes on legal battles for conservation.

Cousteau Society, 930 W. 21st St., Norfolk, VA 23517, promotes environmental issues, particularly marine-related issues, and has publications about marine life. Family membership includes magazines of special interest to families with children.

National Wildlife Federation, 1400 16th St. NW, Washington, DC 20036-2266, is a major conservation group that has clubs and publications for children ("My Big Backyard," "Ranger Rick") as well as adults.

Community-Supported Agriculture (CSA) is where members "adopt a farm" and share organic produce. For information on CSA contact the BioDynamic Farming and Gardening Association, P. O. Box 550, Kimberton, PA 19422, (215) 935-7797.

RESOURCE GUIDE FOR ISRAEL

For materials for learning Hebrew, see pp. 318–320. Books on general Jewish history, holidays, texts, folktales, and so on will often include material on Israel. Consult the appropriate sections.

PICTURE BOOKS AND GUIDEBOOKS FOR FAMILIES TO ENJOY AND PLAN FROM

Note: It may seem odd to list guidebooks and picture books first, but I'm convinced that Jewish children need vivid and colorful introductions to Israel. Today's children are visually oriented, accustomed to having the world delivered to their living room in full color. At the same time, guidebooks are essential, since Jews should learn about Israel with the orientation of actually spending time there!

Guidebooks

Insight Guides—Israel and **Insight Cityguides—Jerusalem** are more than simply guidebooks; they are the ideal one-volume introductions to Israel and to Jerusalem, respectively. **Insight Guides** are a series of widely available guidebooks from APA productions, Singapore (updated annually). They offer beautiful full-color photographs along with well-written and balanced texts that provide an overview of Israel's (or Jerusalem's) history, population, culture, and historical sights. The usual guidebook information about practical matters such as lodging, restaurants and entertainment is reserved for a section at the back.

Kids Love Israel—Israel Loves Kids: A Travel Guide for Families, by Barbara Sofer (Rockville, MD: Kar-Ben, 1988), is indispensable for anyone who is contemplating a visit to the Jewish homeland with children. This book includes everything from camps and pen pals to where the best playgrounds and zoos are to be found. Black-and-white photographs of children in action and simple maps are included. It is written by a mother of five.

The Heart of Jerusalem, by Arlynn Nellhaus (Santa Fe, NM: John Muir, Publisher, 1988, available from The Jewish Book Club), is an unusual combination guidebook and personal memoir. It conveys the atmosphere of living in Jerusalem and offers insider information for tourists or those who wish to spend extended time there, including tips for long-term visitors with children.

Frommer's Israel on $40 a Day (Englewood Cliffs, NJ: Prentice Hall, updated annually, is one of my favorites. This book is packed with useful information and written in a witty and entertaining fashion. It's almost like having your own private tour guide. Be careful, though, as the dollar estimates given may be misleading if you don't keep in mind that they refer to *per person* expenses (including children), and that inflation is always at work in Israel.

The Museums of Israel, by Joy Ungerleider-Mayerson and Nitza Rosovsky (New York: Harry N. Abrams, 1989), is a fun-to-read guide to Israel's 120 museums, accompanied by many beautiful color photographs.

Off the Beaten Track in Israel—A Guide to

Beautiful Places, by Ori Devir (New York: Adama, 1985), is a color-photo and guidebook to unusual, out-of-the-way sites in Israel. Maps are included.

Special Books for Learning Israel's History as a Family

Israel—The First Forty Years, by Abba Eban (New York: Scribners, 1987), tells the story of modern Israel entirely through photographs (black and white), with a running narrative by Eban. It's excellent for family look-and-learn sessions.

Front Page Israel, published by **The Jerusalem Post** (Jerusalem, 1986), presents the major events of modern Israel's history through reproductions of the front pages of the **Post** from 1932, when it was still **The Palestine Post**, into the 1980s.

More Picture Books for the Family to Enjoy Together

Israel, by Roger Baker, photography by Richard Novitz (New York: Crescent, 1988), is an oversized book with stunning color photographs by a popular British photojournalist.

All Israel—A Catalog of Everything Israeli, edited by Josephine Bacon (Secaucus, NJ: Chartwell Books, 1988), gives a basic overview of Israeli life, history, and cultures, with many color and black-and-white photographs.

The Israelis—Photographs of a Day in May, by Amos Elon and 55 photographers (Keter Publishing House, Jerusalem/Harry N. Abrams, New York, 1985), is the result of one day's worth of candid photography by 55 top photojournalists. It captures the diversity, dynamism, pathos, and whimsy of daily life in Israel.

History of Modern Israel

For Adults

(See also Resource Guide to Jewish History.)

The Siege, by Conor Cruise O'Brien (New York: Simon & Schuster, 1986), is a thorough history of a century of the Zionist enterprise. O'Brien, an Irish diplomat, first became interested in the Middle East when alphabetical order placed him precisely between Israel and Iraq at the United Nations General Assembly. His account is intended "neither to indict or to flatter modern Israel, or to exhort or admonish it," but to help the reader understand "how Israel came to be what and where it is, and why it cannot be other than what it is."

Life in Israel

For Adults

Heroes and Hustlers, Hard Hats and Holy Men—Inside the New Israel, by Ze'ev Chafetz (New York: William Morrow and Company, 1986), is a witty account of social trends in contemporary Israel. Americans who have lived in Israel find themselves saying, "I know these people he's writing about. . . ."

A Purity of Arms: An American in the Israeli Army, by Aaron Wolfe (New York: Doubleday, 1989), is an American immigrant's firsthand account of service in the Israel Defense Forces in today's complex political and moral climate. Of interest to teens as well as adults.

A Walker in Jerusalem, by Samuel Hellman (New York: Summit Books, 1986), is a book in which the author, part social anthropologist, part pilgrims, explores the many layers of Jerusalem's history.

For Children

Even though Jewish publications are burgeoning, there is a definite shortage of quality books on Israel written for Jewish children. We need many more really beautiful, colorful picture and photography books, more novels (there are nearly none) about Israeli youngsters with whom American children can identify, and storybooks about children's daily life in Israel. Here are a few that are available today—I hope that more will be on the way.

A Kid's Catalog of Israel, written and illustrated by Chaya M. Burstein (Philadelphia: Jewish Publication Society, 1988), for ages 8 to 9 and up, is without a doubt the finest book on Israel for youngsters and should be in every Jewish child's home library along with Burstein's **Jewish Kid's Catalog**, which is full of pictures, photographs, activities, and information about Israel's history, people, culture, and daily life.

Israel Is, by Susan Remick Topek, illustrated by Kathy Kahn (Rockville, MD: Kar-Ben), for ages 2 to 5, presents the sights and people of Israel in a colorful board book format.

Hurry—Friday's a Short Day and **Just a Week to Go**, both by Yeshara Gold, with photographs by Yaacov Harlap (Brooklyn, NY: Mesorah Pub.), for ages 4 to 8, present the experiences of a young Orthodox boy in Jerusalem's Old City as he and his family prepare for Shabbat and Pesah, respectively. The color photographs are delightful.

What's an Israel?, written and illustrated by Chaya Burstein (Rockville, MD: Kar-Ben, 1983) for ages 4 to 9 takes children on a "tour" of Israel that includes stories, puzzles, maps, and games.

Our Jerusalem, by Yaffa Ganza, with photographs by Zev Radovan, Shmuel Schwartz, and Richard Nowitz, and artwork by Alice Kresse (West Orange, NJ: Berhman House), for ages 5 to 7, is a set of eight folders that teach children about Jerusalem through a simple text and activities. It includes beautiful color photographs. However, the subject matter—the city of Jerusalem—would have been more appropriate for children a few years older.

I Live in Israel, by Max Frankel and Judy Hoffman (West Orange, NJ: Behrman House, 1979), for ages 8 to 10, takes children on a "tour" of Israel through the eyes of Israeli boys and girls. Activities are included.

Aviva's Piano, by Miriam Chaikin (New York: Clarion, 1986), for ages 6 to 9, one of the few books to convey a story about children's experiences in Israel, chronicles the difficulties of new immigrant Aviva in getting her piano into her new apartment at the *kibbutz*.

The Secret Grove, by Barbara Cohen, illustrated by Michael J. Deraney (New York: UAHC Press, 1985), for ages 7 to 12, is an example of the kind of high-quality book that should be coming out about Israel. It is based on a true incident in which an Israeli Jewish boy and Palestinian boy from Jordanian territory happen to meet in an orange grove prior to the Six-Day War. The characters and illustrations are realistic and appealing, the story emotional and engrossing to youngsters.

Alina: A Russian Girl Comes to Israel, by Mira Meir, translated by Zeva Shapiro, with photographs by Yael Rozen (Philadelphia: Jewish Publication Society, 1982), for ages 7 to 12, is the touching story in "photo-essay" form of a young Russian immigrant to Israel as she makes the difficult adjustment to life in her new home. This book is a family favorite in our home.

"Older" Readers

A Kid's Catalog of Israel, by Chaya Burstein (Philadelphia: Jewish Publication Society, 1982). See listing above. **Journey with the State of Israel**, by Levana Moshone and Shimon Yanav (Jewish National Fund Dept. of Education, 1989), for ages 9 and up, conveys key chapters in the history of modern Israel through stories based on actual events. This is one of the better books on Israel. It presents stories of well-known Israelis ranging from Abie Natan to Ida Nudel and Yonatan Netanyahu, as well as ordinary citizens. This book

doesn't hesitate to depict the difficulties of Israel's social challenges, such as the integration of various immigrant groups. Several episodes deal with the human dimension of the country's wars and security problems, and one deals rather sketchily with the human dimensions of the Palestinian–Israeli conflict. It is illustrated with black-and-white photographs. This book is also available in a Hebrew edition. **Theodor Herzl: The Road to Israel**, by Miriam Gurko, illustrated by Erika Weihs (Philadelphia: Jewish Publication Society, 1985), balances the personal and the historical aspects to tell the inspiring story of the founder of modern Zionism, for ages 8 to 12.

Hannah Szenes—A Song of Light, by Maxine Schur (Philadelphia: Jewish Publication Society, 1985), for ages 9 to 13, is the biography of the young Israeli heroine who lost her life after parachuting into Nazi-occupied Europe in 1943.

Our Golda—The Story of Golda Meir, by David A. Adler, illustrated by Donna Ruff (New York: Puffin Books, 1984), for ages 8 to 11, is a short biography of Israel's first woman prime minister, with special attention to her childhood years.

One More River, by Lynne Reid Banks (New York: William Morrow and Company, 1992), for ages 10 and up, is a rare treat—an exciting work of juvenile fiction, set in Israel. It's 1967, and 14-year-old Lesley is miserable when her parents take her from a comfortable Canadian existence to life on a border *kibbutz*, but adventure and self-discovery await her there.

MUSIC OF ISRAEL

See Music Resources, p. 313.

VIDEO

Shalom Sesame is a growing series of Israel videos for American children, produced by the "Sesame Street" folks. It's available from any of the distributers listed under Video Resources, pp. 313–314, or from Shalom Sesame, P.O. Box 2284, South Burlington, VT 05407, (800) 428-9920. Combined segments of travelogue, animation (which introduces some Hebrew letters and phrases), Muppets in Hebrew and English, and American and Israeli television and entertainment personalities. The original five took audiences to tour and meet "The Land of Israel," "Tel Aviv," "Kibbutz," "The People of Israel," and "Jerusalem," and a number of additional shows on special topics continue to be brought out—including "Sing Around the Seasons," "The Aleph-Bet Telethon," "Kids of Israel," and "Tales of the Desert."

Making Friends

(See section on pen pals, p. 131.)

GesherNet ("gesher" means "bridge") is a new education telecommunications network that links students, educators, and community groups in the United States and other countries with those in Israel. In Israel, the network fosters computer communication between children of many religious and ethnic backgrounds (Orthodox and secular, Arab and Jewish, and so forth) who might otherwise never meet. All that is needed to access the network is a computer, a modem, and a telephone (and money to pay the bills!). For information, contact Judy Eber c/o 63 Maybrooke Rd., Rochester, NY 14618, or call Network and World information, Customer Service, (800) 669-4463, or (203) 249-7221, and request a GesherNet account.

POSTERS

Sometimes you can get free posters from:

EL Al Israel Airlines, 850 Third Ave., New York, NY 10022, (212) 940-0708.

Israel Government Tourist Office, 350 Fifth Ave., 19th Floor, New York, NY 10118, (212) 560-0650.

Israel Office of Information, Jewish Agency, 515 Park Ave., New York, NY 10022, (212) 752-0600.

Inexpensive, attractive posters are available from Jewish National Fund, Dept. of Education, 114 E. 32nd St., New York, NY 10016, (212) 779-0310, has "seven varieties" of Israeli produce that are beautiful color-photo posters and are also available as postcards. They make ideal decorations for a *sukkah* (when laminated) or for a Tu BiShvat *seder*.

Board of Jewish Education of Greater New York, 426 W. 58th St., New York, NY 10019, among others, carries a lovely set of nature posters from the Society for the Protection of Nature in Israel. (My mother had these hanging in her apartment in Jerusalem when she lived there for a year.)

Rolnick Publishers, 10 Dov Fridman St., Ramat Gan, Ramat Gan, Israel, FAX 972-3-751-0858, in addition to posters, carries calendars, greeting cards, and puzzles with scenes of Israel. Many of their products are available from the Jewish National Fund mentioned earlier.

Sapir Jewish Heritage Center, 1 Hatupim St., P. O. Box 979, Old City, Jerusalem, Israel 91009, (02) 286-121, produces a series of beautiful posters for the Jewish holidays. These posters are nice when laminated for the *sukkah* or as home decor.

STAMPS AND COINS

Society of Israel Philatalists, 27436 Aberdeen, Southfield, MI 48076, (313) 557-0887, can be contacted for information on Israeli stamp collecting.

Israel Stamp Agency in North America, One Unicover Center, Cheyenne, WY 82008-0006, (800) 443-3232, distributes postal issues of Israeli stamps by subscription.

Israel Coins and Medals Corp., Ltd., 350 Fifth Ave., New York, NY 10118, (212) 560-0690, is a source for coins and commemorative medals of the Israeli mint. These include medallions, jewelry, and coins for life-cycle events.

IMPORTANT ADDRESSES

Zionism: Education and *Aliyah*

The Jewish National Fund (JNF), education address listed under "Posters." The folks who plant trees in Israel also carry educational kits for collecting Israeli stamps and coins as well as a wide variety of educational materials (ranging from charmingly quaint to state of the art) on Israel, ecology, and trees, the Bible, and Hebrew. For information on planting trees, contact their other office: 42 E. 69th St., New York, NY 10021, (212) 879-9300.

Zionist Organization of America (ZOA), ZOA House, 4 E. 34th St., New York, NY 10016, (212) 481-1500, is a general American Zionist organization that works in support of Israel and Zionist ideals.

World Zionist Organization—American Section, 110 E. 59th St., New York, NY 10022, (212) 339-6000, is the American section of the worldwide Zionist body. The WZO works to foster *aliyah* and support of Israel through education, youth programs, publications, and so forth. At the same address:

WZO Department of Education and Culture offers publications on Hebrew language and literature, Israeli life, and Zionism.

American Zionist Youth Foundation (AZYF), (800)-27-ISRAE(L) or (212) 339-6916, coordinates and provides information on a wide variety of educational programs and Israel tours for high school and college-age young adults.

North American Aliyah Movement (NAAM), (212) 339-6060, sponsors tours, programs, groups, and publications that foster *aliyah* to Israel from North America. Once actually in Israel, the complementary organization is:

Association for Americans and Canadians in Israel (AACI), Jerusalem area office: 6 Rehov Mane, (02) 636-932, is a "home away from home" for North American immigrants to Israel who are in need of social networks, counseling, advice, and even some material assistance like loans.

Investment

State of Israel Bonds, 215 Park Ave. South, New York, NY 10003, (212) 677-9650, offers bonds for the support of Israel's economic development.

AMPAL—American Israel Corporation, 10 Rockefeller Plaza, New York, NY 10020, (212) 586-3232, invests in Israeli economic enterprises.

PEC Israel Economic Corporation, 511 Fifth Ave., New York, NY 10017, (212) 687-2400, organizes, finances, and administers enterprises located in, or affiliated with, enterprises in Israel.

Tzedakah

See the resource guide to Jewish interpersonal values, pp. 336–339, which includes a number of specific listings of charitable organizations in Israel.

New Israel Fund, 1101 15th St. NW, Suite 304, Washington, DC 20005, (202) 223-3333, supports grass-roots and citizens' action efforts of Israelis working to achieve social justice and to protect and strengthen the democratic process in Israel. The NIF seeks to enrich the quality of relationships between Israelis and North American Jews through fellowships, educational programs, and cooperative goals. It contributes to organizations large and small in areas such as Jewish–Arab cooperation, religious pluralism, women's rights, interethnic (Sephardic–Ashkenazic) relations, and civil rights. The NIF offers tours of beneficiary organizations for visitors to Israel.

United Jewish Appeal, Inc. (UJA), 99 Park Ave., New York, NY 10016, (212) 818-9100 (or contact your local Jewish Federation in the unlikely event that they don't call you first!), through local Jewish Federation/UJA annual campaigns, raises money for Israel: for Jewish social welfare, cultural, and education agencies in local communities, and for social welfare and educational services

to Jewish communities in 33 other countries through the Joint Distribution Committee. In Israel, through the Jewish Agency, funds go to the settlement and education of new immigrants, building villages and farms in rural areas, programs for disadvantaged and troubled youth, and the revitalization of distressed urban neighborhoods ("Project Renewal"). While the cumbersome bureaucracy of the Jewish Agency has come under criticism over the years, UJA campaigns remain a major source for support to Israel.

"Family Missions to Israel," sponsored by the UJA, provides families with a fast-paced, emotional, in-depth, and generally fairly luxurious tour of Israel, which is still geared to the particular needs of the children and teenagers in the group. These tours may be partially subsidized but usually require a substantial monetary pledge to the local Federation/UJA campaign. Inquire through your local Jewish Federation for details.

General Touring

See earlier listings for "Israel Government Tourist Office" (there are branches in other major U.S. cities) and for EL Al Airlines, or speak to your travel agent.

PROGRAMS IN ISRAEL

A vast array of Israel programs are available, both commercially run and nonprofit. There are many more programs for teens and young adults than those especially designed for families. The following organizationally based programs for families are not run for profit and thus are generally reasonably priced, and all strive to give their participants a feeling for life in Israel.

LEVI—Living Experience in Israel, sponsored by the B'nai B'rith Israel Commission, 1640 Rhode Island Ave. NW, Washington, DC 20036, (202) 857-6580, is a three-week (with optional extension) work-study program for families with children in grades 1 to 12. One parent must be a B'nai B'rith member or must join prior to the program. Families live in a hotel near the beach in the seaside resort city of Nahariyah, just north of Haifa. Adults and teenagers volunteer in JNF forests, hospitals, and archeological digs, while children spend time at day camp. Afternoons are spent learning Hebrew, discussing Israel and Jewish history, socializing, and in the evenings, there are special discussions and cultural programs. Guided tours to Jerusalem, the Negev, and the Galilee are included.

Melitz Centers for Jewish Zionist Education, 19 Yishai St., Abu Tor, Jerusalem; U.S. address: 730 Broadway, New York, NY 10003, (212) 529-2000, runs highly respected Israel seminars, retreats, and study tours, including special family study tours that focus on Jewish identity, Jewish values, and Zionism, from a standpoint of pluralism and tolerance. Hospitality and interactive programs with Israelis are available. Melitz also designs intensive study/values/activism-oriented tours for American groups such as synagogues.

"Taste of Israel" Programs, sponsored by the Eretz Yisrael Movement, 15 E. 26th St., Suite 1303, New York, NY 10010, (212) 684-7370, is a group that claims its sole aim is to bring Jews to visit Israel and to encourage *aliyah*.

Their programs include family-oriented programming (including programs for families with infants and preschoolers), such as the "Inside Israel" 20-day touring program, based at a four-star hotel in Jerusalem, as well as service-oriented programs and consultation and planning assistance for those interested in spending longer periods in Israel. My friends who have tried these programs for a couple of summers recommended them.

NAAM Israel Programs—NAAM is the North American Aliyah Movement, part of the World Zionist Organization, 110 E. 59th St., New York, NY 10022, (212) 339-6060. For families and includes an International 3½-week Family *Ulpan* (Hebrew course) in Jerusalem, as well as 2-week "Family Experience" tour, and two-week Israel fact-finding tours for those considering *aliyah*.

Hebrew Programs

All the organizations listed here have at some time offered programs that involved an *Ulpan* (intensive Hebrew language study component). Inquire through each for details about future plans. In addition, when it comes to *Ulpan*, the "ultimate" is:

Ulpan Akiva—International Hebrew Study Center, Green Beach Hotel, P. O. Box 6086, Netanya, Israel 42160, (53) 52312. This widely acclaimed language school offers a wide range of lengths and levels of Hebrew courses, as well as courses in conversational Arabic, for an international clientele of individuals and families. Residents stay at a pleasant yet simple resort on the Mediterranean beach and enrich their Hebrew studies with classes on Judaic and Israeli issues, as well as cultural events. Their Shabbat programs are reminiscent of summer camp. My mother

spent a summer there and gives it her hearty endorsement.

Nature Tours

While in Israel, it's worthwhile to take a tour with the Society for the Protection of Nature in Israel (SPNI), the Israeli counterpart to the Sierra Club. There are tours in English and family-oriented tours. One can join from the United States and receive their English-language quarterly by contacting SPNI, 330 Seventh Ave., New York, NY 10001, (212) 947-2820. In Israel, the main office is located at 13 Helena Hamalka St., Jerusalem, 02-222357.

Guides to Programs and Resources in Israel

The Directory of Jewish Educational Resources in Israel, edited by Dr. David Resnick (JESNA— Jewish Educational Service of North America, 730 Broadway, New York, NY 10003-9540), is an extensive listing of educational materials, services, and information about educational resources in Israel, useful for the family interested in educational programs and products as well as for the professional educator.

The Committee for Programs in Israel, at the Jewish Federation Council of Greater Los Angeles, 6505 Wilshire Blvd., Los Angeles, CA 90048, (213) 852-1234, ext. 2415, publishes a comprehensive yearly directory of programs in Israel that lists general programs as well as those organized specifically by California communities.

Summer Camps and *Bat/Bar Mitzvah* Arrangements

Many family tours make a *bar/bat mitzvah* celebration in Israel available. **Kids Love Israel, Israel Loves Kids**, by Barbara Sofer (Rockville, MD: Kar-Ben, 1988), (800) 4KAR-BEN, provides information on *bat/bar mitzvah* in Israel, as well as an extensive listing of programs in Israel for children, including day camps.

Denominational Movements

Religiously oriented Jews planning to visit Israel for an extended period, or to make *aliyah*, will often want to continue to participate in the kind of religious environment they had back home. Although Israeli Jews tend to view religion as a choice between Orthodoxy (actually several varieties thereof), "traditionalism," or secularism, most American Jews are comfortable with a range of religious denominations.

Reform, Conservative, and a wide range of Orthodox groups all have synagogues, settlements, schools, and institutions of higher learning in Israel (the Reconstructionist Movement, while smaller, also has activities in Israel). Your synagogue can direct you to *aliyah* activities and Israeli institutions sponsored by your denomination.

Programs for Teenagers

There are many quality programs in Israel for teenagers and young adults. Fine programs are run by the major Jewish youth groups, such as NFTY, NCSY, USY, Ramah Camps, Young Judaea, B'nai Akiva, and others as well as by local Jewish communities. Some communities have savings-incentives programs designed to help youngsters participate in Israel programs; some are heavily subsidized. AZYF (see earlier listing under "World Zionist Organization") coordinates and catalogs a number of short- and long-term Israel tours and study programs for teens.

Dr. Perry London of Rutgers, one of the nation's leading authorities on Jewish identity development, has pointed out the unique potential of the "Israel experience" in enhancing a young person's Jewish identity. He emphasizes that there is much more that could be done to extend the educational follow-up to many of these experiences.

Without detracting from any of the other fine Israel programs for young people, I can't resist mentioning a couple of my personal favorites here, programs that I believe have exceptional educational content in addition to unique transformative potential:

Nesiya—National Seminar in Israel for Young Artists (Nesiya means "a journey"). American office: c/o JCC of Cleveland, 26001 South Woodland Blvd., Cleveland, OH 44122, (216) 831-0700, ext. 357 or 359. Exceptional program for artistically involved teenagers and young adults that synthesizes touring the land of Israel and encountering Jewish texts with artistic expression in a wide variety of media, including writing, visual arts, dance, video, photography, theater, and music. Participants also meet with Israeli artists and performers.

Alexander Muss High School in Israel Program, American office: 3950 Biscayne Blvd., Miami, FL 33137, (800) 327-5980, (305) 576-3286, is an 8-week high school program that is offered year around to tenth and eleventh graders. They have

campuses in Israel at Hod Hasharon and Hadassim Youth Village. This program is an "educational adventure" of discovering Jewish history and heritage through extensive touring and study with a top-level staff. In addition, students keep up with their high school subjects, as general American high school subjects are also taught during the program (credits are transferable), and there is a full sports, recreational, and social agenda.

PERIODICALS

The Jerusalem Report, P. O. Box 580, Mount Morris, IL 61054, (800) 827-1119, is a glossy bi-weekly magazine that includes a full range of news, features, and editorials on life in Israel and the Jewish world.

The Jerusalem Post International Edition, P.O. Box 282, Brewster, NY 10509, (914) 878-9522. This noted weekly newspaper offers a wide range of articles on what's happening in Israel.

ERETZ Magazine, P. O. Box 11286, Gilo Post Office, Jerusalem, Israel 94268, published quarterly, explores Israel's land, culture, history, and society.

Israel—Land and Nature is an English-language quarterly about nature and conservation in Israel, available to members of the Society for the Protection of Nature in Israel (see p. 344).

RESOURCE GUIDE FOR SHABBAT

Adults/Teens

The Art of Jewish Living—The Shabbat Seder, by Dr. Ron Wolfson (New York: The Federation of Jewish Men's Clubs, 1985). A detailed, step-by-step practical guide for holding a Shabbat evening ritual in the home. Delightful photographs and anecdotes from contemporary families are included in this softcover book, giving the feeling that a group of friends are welcoming your family into Shabbat observance. Includes full texts of prayers and songs. A companion tape is available with all the Shabbat prayers and melodies, sung slowly, as well as a prayer-song book (*bencher*) that includes the same photos and the Hebrew-translation-transliteration laid out in an easy-to-follow column format (excellent for adult beginners as well as young people).

The Sabbath by Abraham Joshua Heschel (New York: Farrar, Straus & Giroux, 1951). A classic presentation of the meaning of Shabbat for modernity, including the holiness of time and Shabbat as a "sanctuary in time." I am one of the many readers who was deeply influenced, indeed transformed, by this book.

Shabbat Shalom: A Renewed Encounter with the Sabbath, by Pinchas Peli (Washington DC: B'nai B'rith Books, 1989). Delves into the historical, legal, philosophical, and literary sources of Judaism to explore and interpret the Sabbath anew.

The Jewish Way—Living the Holidays, by Irving Greenberg (New York: Summit Books, 1988), offers a philosophical guide to the Shabbat and holy days. Although Greenberg is a modern Orthodox rabbi, he presents (in addition to his interpretation of the traditional Shabbat) his vision of "a pluralistic Shabbat experience," with input from liberal Rabbi Haskell Bernat.

Sabbath—The Day of Delight, by Abraham E. Millgram (Philadelphia: Jewish Publication Society, 1965). An anthology of source material, customs, and stories related to Shabbat. Good resources for study and discussion sessions.

The First Jewish Catalog, edited by Richard Siegel, Michael Strassfeld, and Sharon Strassfeld (Philadelphia: Jewish Publication Society, 1973). "Shabbat," pp.103–115 by Murray Schaum, the editors, and Rabbi Zalman Schachter, captures the mood and enchantments of the Shabbat experience, particularly the table of mystical and philosophical associations of each period of the Shabbat day.

How to Run a Traditional Jewish Household, by Blu Greenberg (Northvale, NJ: Jason Aronson, 1989). "Shabbat," pp. 25–94, offers warm, personal, and extremely practical Shabbat instructions from a Modern-Orthodox perspective.

Gates of Shabbat, written and edited by Mark Dov Shapiro (New York: CCAR, 1991), includes the ceremonies and rituals of Shabbat in the spirit of Reform Judaism.

For Children and Families

For Tots

Shabbat Shalom (Rockville, MD: Kar-Ben, 1989) is a wordless board book with pictures by Yaffa of preparations for and welcoming Shabbat.

Shai's Shabbat Walk, by Ellie Gellman, illustrated by Chai McLean (Rockville, MD: Kar-Ben, 1985), is a board book with an interesting approach to Shabbat. Rather than focusing on the ritual items like candles and *hallah*, the book tries to capture the spirit of the Sabbath as a day for resting, singing, and sharing.

For Ages 4–9

A Sense of Shabbat, by Faige Kobre (Los Angeles: Torah Aura, 1989), tells the story of a family Shabbat through black-and-white photographs. The emphasis is on a small child's viewpoint of the sensory experiences of the Sabbath.

Shabbat Delight—A Celebration in Stories, Games and Songs, by Rabbi Ron Isaacs (available from the American Jewish Committee, 165 E. 56th St., New York, NY 10022). A "kit" of games, cassette tapes, storybook, and guide to the Sabbath, for families with young children.

Shabbat Can Be, by Rabbi Raymond A. Zwein and Audrey Friedman Marcus (New York: UAHC Press, 1979). Large, colorful illustrations, good for discussion, convey the spirit of Shabbat to young children, through about grade 2. Parent/teacher guide available.

Before Shabbat Begins, by Floreva G. Cohen, illustrated by Jill A. Lustig (New York: Board of Jewish Education, 1985). Preschoolers are captivated by this story of Shira, who can't wait to show off her Shabbat dress but soon learns that caring for others is even more important.

Mrs. Moskowitz and the Sabbath Candlesticks, written and illustrated by Amy Schwartz (Philadelphia: Jewish Publication Society, 1991). Mrs. Moskowitz just doesn't feel that her cramped new apartment is a home until she and her cat Fred discover her Sabbath candlesticks and start to *make* it into home for Shabbat.

Hurry, Friday's a Short Day—One Boy's Erev Shabbat in Jerusalem's Old City, by Yeshara Gold (Brooklyn, NY: Mesorah Publications, 1986). Beautiful full-color photographs show how a five-year-old boy in the Jewish quarter of Jerusalem's Old City prepares for Shabbat with his family.

A Thousand Guests for Shabbos, by Yaffa Gottlieb, illustrated by Aidel Backman (Brooklyn, NY: Aura Publication Co, 1984). A young boy's fantasy about the huge Shabbat dinners he will host someday really appeals to children. Although some of the slightly forced rhymes may elicit groans, the story conveys explanations of many traditional Sabbath customs as well as elements from classic Jewish tales.

Poppy Seeds, Too—A Twisted Tale for Shabbat, by Deborah Miller, illustrated by Ken Ostrove (Rockville, MD: Kar-Ben, 1982), is a lighthearted and silly rhyming tale that reminds me of some of my early ventures into *hallah* baking.

For Ages 8–12

Shabbat: A Peaceful Island, by Malka Drucker (New York: Holiday House, 1983). A general overview of Shabbat includes activities and recipes.

The Seventh Day: The Story of the Jewish Sabbath, by Miriam Chaikin (Garden City, NY: Doubleday and Co., 1980), tells the story of the origins and meaning of Shabbat.

The Shabbat Catalogue, by Ruth Brin (New York: Ktav, 1978), is a collection of stories, activities, crafts, recipes, plays, and songs for Shabbat.

See also the Holiday Resource Guide (p. 348) for parent–child learning programs ("Building Jewish Life," "Together," and so forth), and other general holiday books that include Shabbat materials.

MUSICAL RECORDINGS

For Children and Families

The following are all available from Tara Publications. (See Music Resources, p. 313.)

Because We Love Shabbat, audiocassette and songbook by Leah Abrams (L. A. Records/Board of Jewish Education of Greater New York). This collection of original and traditional Shabbat songs (mostly English; Hebrew integrated well so that children without much Hebrew background can follow) is one of our family's favorites. ("Gotta Get Ready by Sundown" has actually been known to motivate my children to put away their toys and start cleaning!) The tape follows the Shabbat experience from preparation through *Havdalah*. High quality of both music and educational value. The companion book, by Tara Publications, contains the lyrics and some additional songs as well as suggested activities for classroom or home use.

The Seventh Day, audiocassette by Fran Avni and Jacki Cytrnbaum (Lemonstone), is a creative and enjoyable musical experience that takes the listener through a full Shabbat experience through song and story. More sophisticated appeal will hold the interest of slightly older, kindergarten to elementary-age, children.

Shabbat Songs, by Adi Sulkin, a leading Israeli music educator (Sulkin-Vardit Productions), includes a book with texts of the Hebrew songs and activity instructions in Hebrew and English. For classroom or home use.

Shabbat Shalom, performed and produced by Cindy Paley, is a cassette and booklet of 20 delightfully arranged songs that celebrate Shabbat. Combines Hebrew and English. The booklet includes complete texts, translations, and transliterations. Good for learning songs from as well as listening or moving to.

Celebrate with Us—Shabbat, various artists (Jewish Family Productions), teaches the traditional melodies, prayers, and traditions for Shabbat to young children through story, song, and games, performed by the "Celebrate with Us Family."

SONGBOOKS AND ANTHOLOGIES

For Adults and Families

The **Harvard Hillel Sabbath Songbook** includes background, translations, transliterations, and musical notations to nearly a hundred songs and prayers for the Shabbat table.

The Book of Songs and Blessings, from the United Jewish Appeal (UJA), is a useful song booklet that includes Hebrew, phonetic transliterations, and English translations. Particularly noteworthy is the way in which this book integrates contemporary sentiments while maintaining the traditional forms of classic prayers such as the Grace after Meals (*Birkat HaMazon*).

Kol HaNeshamah: Shirim Uvrachot (Songs and Blessings), edited by David Tentsch (Wyncote, PA: The Reconstructionist Press, 1991), includes songs and prayers for home Shabbat rituals from a Reconstructionist approach. Musical notation is included, and a cassette tape of the songs and a companion table booklet are available.

The following songbooks are all from Tara Publications (see p. 313):

Shabbat Melodies, a songbook edited by Velvel Pasternak; the **Z'mirot Anthology**, a songbook edited by Neil Levin (over 150 selections including vocal line, chords, texts, sources, translations, and transliterations); and the **Z'mirot and Birkat HaMazon**, a handbook of traditional Shabbat songs and the Grace after Meals, which—unlike most such booklets—includes music notation along with the Hebrew texts and transliterations. A cassette recording of the traditional **Z'mirot—Shabbat Songs for the Home**, sung by Velvel Pasternak, is also available from Tara, including the melodic sections of the Grace after Meals.

See the Music Section (pp. 313) for more musical resources that can enhance Shabbat.

Israeli Music for Shabbat

Shabbat Shalom—"A Treasure of Songs Israel Sings on Shabbat" (The Israeli BOOKASSETTE series) includes traditional and more modern Israeli songs for Shabbat. Includes a hardcover songbook with lyrics in Hebrew, phonetic transliteration, and English translation. It's available from most of the music distributers listed on p. 313.

RITUAL OBJECTS FOR THE SABBATH

See pp. 307–308 for Resource Guide to catalogs of ritual objects and Judaica.

RESOURCE GUIDE FOR THE JEWISH HOLIDAYS

There is an abundance of literature on the Jewish holidays. Refer also to **Resources on Basic Judaism**, pp. 305–306, where general guidebooks on Jewish life (for adults or children) contain material about the holidays. Resource guides to cookbooks, music, videos, softwear, crafts, and Judaica for the home will also include items for the Jewish holidays.

General Holidays

For Adults

The Jewish Way—Living the Holidays, By Rabbi Irving Greenberg (New York: Summit Books, 1988), reveals much of Rabbi Greenberg's philosophy of Judaism by using the holidays and Shabbat, in their development through history to our day, as a vehicle for understanding the Jewish ethos.

The Jewish Holidays—A Guide and Commentary, by Michael Strassfeld, illustrated by Betsy Platkin Teutsch (New York: Harper & Row, 1985). Strassfeld, co-editor of the famous "Jewish Catalogs," combines historical material and practical guidelines with a creative and often original philosophical look at the themes of the Jewish holidays. A unique feature of this book are the commentaries by five contemporary Jewish thinkers, in the fashion of traditional Jewish texts with their commentary-filled margins.

Seasons of Our Joy—A Handbook of Jewish Festivals, by Arthur I. Waskow (New York: Summit Books, 1982). Waskow, a social activist and creative Jewish thinker, offers background and traditional practices (including recipes) for the holidays, as well as contemporary implications and innovative possibilities for observing the holidays today. The book emphasizes nature and the cyclical character of Jewish observance.

The Wheels of Observance—A Growth Guide to the Jewish Holidays, by Rabbi Anson Laytner (CLAL—47 W. 34th St., New York NY 10001, (212) 714-9500), is an inexpensive booklet with a nondenominational approach to enhancing one's personal Jewish observance through the Shabbat and holidays. For each holiday, observances are listed that draw the individual closer to the Jewish cultural core through ritual, study, and relationships. Use this guide either with a more complete holiday book, or better yet, with a rabbi or teacher and a friend. It's excellent for *havurot* and study groups.

For Families

Jewish Family Celebrations, by Arlene Rossen Cardozo (New York: St. Martin's, 1982), is the ideal introductory handbook for families who want to celebrate the Jewish holidays and Shabbat with beauty and understanding. The book offers historical background, warm personal recollections, practical guidelines, blessings, songs (with musical notation), and recipes.

The Complete Family Guide to Jewish Holidays, by Dalia Hardof Renberg (New York: Adama, 1985), is an attractive and informative guide to the holidays, with emphasis on celebrating them with children. It includes historical background, practical information, crafts, recipes, illustrations, and many black-and-white photographs.

Celebration—The Book of Jewish Festivals, edited by Naomi Black (Middle Village, NY: Jonathan David, 1989), features six major Jewish festivals in an attractive format with color photographs. Holiday background is included, as well as poems, songs, stories, clever crafts ideas, and recipes.

The Jewish Party Book, by Mae Shafter Rockland (New York: Schocken, 1978), is a contemporary guide to customs, creative folk arts, and unusual recipes for holidays as well as life-cycle events. The book includes black-and-white photographs.

Family Guides for the Holidays Series, from the Baltimore Board of Jewish Education, 5800 Park Heights Ave., Baltimore, MD 21215, is a set of small pamphlets packed with information and ideas for observing several of the major Jewish holidays at home. Each includes home ceremonies and readings, recipes, crafts, and illustrations.

Home Reference Sets for the Holidays

The Book of Our Heritage (3 vol. set), by Eliyahu Kitov, translated by N. Bulman and Ruth Royde (New York: Feldheim, 1978), is an encyclopedic yet readable set of books on every aspect of the traditional Jewish year.

Jewish Publication Society Holiday Anthologies series, by Phillip Goodman, from the Jewish Publication Society, Philadelphia, is a series of seven thick volumes (Rosh HaShanah, Yom Kippur, Sukkot and Simhat Torah, Hanukkah, Purim, Passover, and Shavuot), which anthologize holiday selections from the Bible, Talmud, and *Midrash*, along with historical essays, fiction, and poetry. Also included are children's stories, crafts, recipes, songs (with musical notations), and prayers. Some black-and-white illustrations and photos are included. (There is also a Sabbath anthology by Abraham E. Millgram; see the Shabbat Resource Guide, p. 345.)

Books for Parents and Children Together

The Building Jewish Life Series, from Torah Aura Productions, 4423 Fruitland Ave., Los Angeles, CA 90058, (800) BE-TORAH, by Joel Lurie Grishaver, photos by Grishaver, Jane Golub, and Alan Rowe, is a series of holiday and Judaica books, each of which includes a text for children, background material for parents, read-aloud holiday stories, and religious-school lesson plans. There are two levels, covering kindergarten through third grade. This series takes a fresh and thoughtful approach to teaching the holidays. The books are illustrated with contemporary photographs and cartoonlike drawings.

Together: A Child-Parent Kit, from the Melton Research Center, 3080 Broadway, New York, NY 10027, created by Vicky Kelman, with Joel Grishaver and Jane Golub, designed for third-graders and their parents, is a series of nine magazinelike kits, each of which includes activities and readings for the children, readings for the parents, and activities to do together. They must be purchased as a set. Six kits have holiday or seasonal themes, while three deal with Shabbat, blessings, and theology, respectively. The activities include games, puzzles, stories, cutouts, recipes, craft projects, reading materials, and even correspondence with the Melton Center (children write in and receive a small prize). The kits are illustrated with photographs and cartoonlike drawings.

General Holiday Books

For Children

For Toddlers to Age 9:

Very First Board Books Series, from Kar-Ben Copies, 6800 Tildenwood Lane, Rockville, MD 20852, (800) 4-KARBEN, includes a number of holiday titles, available separately or in sets, done by various authors and illustrators. Now even tots can have their own attractive Jewish library.

My Body Is Something Special, by Howard I. Bogot and David B. Syme, photos by Gay Block (New York: UAHC Press, 1982), for ages 3 to 6, is a charming book illustrated with photographs that shows young children performing different holiday activities with different parts of their bodies.

The Home Start Program, general editor Dr. Hyman Chanover from Behrman House, West Orange, NJ, 07052, (800) 221-2755, is a series (purchased in one package for a year) in two levels, for nursery school to kindergarten, or for grades 1 and 2. It includes color picture booklets, activity magazines or books, a parent handbook, and cassette tapes with songs and stories.

Chag Sameach, by Patricia Schaffer (Berkeley, CA: Tabor Sarah Books, 1985), includes black-and-white holiday photos of a variety of American Jewish families, including adopted children of various races and children with handicaps.

My Very Own Jewish Library, created by Judyth Sypol and Madeline Wickler, from Kar-Ben Copies, Rockville, MD 20852, for ages 5 to 10, is a series of eight illustrated holiday books available separately or as a set. The books introduce the major Jewish holidays through narrative, stories, words, and music to holiday blessings and songs. Some include coloring, crafts, and recipes.

Jewish Days and Holidays, by Greer Fay Cashman, illustrated by Alona Frankel (New York: Adamah Books, 1986), for ages 5 to 8, is a full-color, illustrated guide to the major Jewish holidays and Shabbat, that emphasizes holiday background and symbols. It includes Israeli Independence Day and Tisha B'Av. This is one of the few holiday books for children that has appeared in both Israeli and American editions.

Danny Loves a Holiday, by Sydney Taylor,

illustrated by Gail Owens (New York: C. P. Dutton, 1980), ages 5 to 8, seven holiday stories about Danny, a realistic young boy in a Jewish school.

For Ages 8–12:

Follow the Moon—A Journey Through the Jewish Year, by Yaffa Ganz, illustrated by Harvey Klineman (New York: Feldheim, 1984), for ages 8 to 11, is a colorfully illustrated guide to each Hebrew month and its important dates.

The Book of Jewish Holidays, by Ruth Kozodoy (West Orange, NJ: Behrman, 1981), for ages 8 and up, is a thorough and attractive guide to holiday history and observance. Full-color illustrations and photographs make this a nice family or child's book.

Holiday books by Miriam Chaikin, from Clarion Books, New York, for ages 8 to 11, include **Sound the Shofar** (High Holidays), **Light Another Candle** (Hanukkah), **Shake a Palm Branch** (Sukkot), **Make Noise, Make Merry** (Purim), and **Ask Another Question** (Passover). They include the stories, history, and customs of each holiday.

Holiday books by Malka Drucker, in several volumes published by Holiday House, New York, include **Sukkot: Time to Rejoice; Hanukah: Eight Nights, Eight Lights; Passover: A Season of Freedom**. For ages 9 to 12, each book includes holiday background, themes, crafts, food, games, and music.

Jewish Holidays and Festivals, by Dr. Isidor Margolis and Rabbi Sidney L. Markowitz (Secaucus, NJ: Citadel, 1974), is an unassuming yet useful little paperback that's been around for years. Written for ages 9 to 12, but useful as a general family book, it contains quick summaries of holiday background and customs, stories for every holiday, and holiday quizzes.

INDIVIDUAL HOLIDAYS

There are so many materials currently available on the Jewish holidays that the following can provide only a sampling. The various series, such as **Building Jewish Life, Together,** and **My Very Own Jewish Library** (all described earlier), include books for several individual holidays. Music, videos, and software selections related to the Jewish holidays can be found from the suppliers noted in the appropriate resource guides, pp. 313–314.

The Days of Awe

For Adults and Families

Days of Awe: A Treasury of Legends and Learned Commentaries Concerning Rosh Hashanah, Yom Kippur, and the Days in Between, by S. Y. Agnon (New York: Schocken, 1982). Israel's Nobel laureate compiled this extensive collection of source materials, laws, customs, and stories for every period of the High Holidays.

Moments of Transcendence—Inspirational Readings for Rosh Hashanah, and **Moments of Transcendence—Inspirational Readings for Yom Kippur**, both edited by Rabbi Dov Peretz Elkins (Northvale, NJ: Jason Aronson, 1992), contain hundreds of inspiring and thought-provoking readings to correspond to each element of the traditional High Holiday liturgy.

For Children

My Little Machzor, edited by Mazal Mashat-Pnini, translated by Rabbi Sidney Gold (New York: Adama Books, 1986), for ages 4 to 7, is a young child's first holiday prayer book, with color photographs of traditional holiday observances in Israel.

Building Jewish Life: Rosh Ha-Shanah and Yom Kippur Mahzorim (Los Angeles: Torah Aura Productions, 1987) are for children ages 5 to 8 and their families. They're complete with stories, photos, illustrations, and key prayers in Hebrew and English.

Family Services, for Selichot, Rosh Hashanah, and Yom Kippur, by Judith Z. Abrams, designed and illustrated by Katherine Janus Kahn, from Kar-Ben Copies of Rockville, MD 20852, are for families with children ages 4 to 7. An accompanying tape is available.

A Rosh Hashanah Walk, by Carol Levin, illustrated by Katherine Janus Kahn (Rockville, MD: Kar-Ben, 1987), for ages 3 to 7, is a story in rhyme about a *tashlich* walk.

Sneakers to Shul, by Floreva G. Cohen (New York: Board of Jewish Education, 1978), for ages 4 to 7. Young Noah wants to know why everyone wears sneakers to synagogue on Yom Kippur.

First Fast, by Barbara Cohen (New York: UAHC Press, 1982), for ages 8 to 11, tells the story of a wager between two boys one Yom Kippur several decades ago.

Days of Awe—Stories for Rosh Hashanah and Yom Kippur, by Eric A. Kimmel, illustrated by Erika Weihs (New York: Viking, 1991), gives an overview of the Days of Awe, followed by retellings of three traditional stories that illustrate the seasonal themes of charity, prayer, and repentance.

Sukkot

For Children

Leo and Blossom's Sukkah, written and illustrated by Jane Breskin Zalben (New York: Henry Holt, 1990), for ages 3 to 7, is a charming story about anthropomorphic bear-children and their Sukkah holiday. They even have a *lulav* and an *etrog*.

The Big Sukkah, by Peninnah Schram, illustrated by Jacqueline Kahane (Rockville, MD: Kar-Ben, 1986), for ages 4 to 8. Berl wishes he had a bigger house to which to invite his relatives. But he builds the biggest *sukkah* in town.

The House on the Roof, by David Adler, illustrated by Marilyn Hirsh (Rockville, MD: Kar-Ben, 1976), for ages 5 to 9, is a story about an elderly man who builds a *sukkah* on the roof, to the consternation of the landlady.

A Tale of Three Wishes, by Isaac Bashevis Singer, illustrated by Irene Lieblich (New York: Farrar, Straus & Giroux, 1976). Singer's enchanting tale captures the mystery of Hoshanah Rabbah, a night when the gates of heaven open and one's wishes may come true.

Hanukkah

For Adults and Families

Haneirot Halalu—These Lights Are Holy: A Home Celebration of Chanuka, edited by Rabbi Elyse Frishman, illustrated by Leonard Baskin (New York: CCAR, 1989), published by the Reform movement but wonderful for Jewish homes of any "denomination," this is a beautifully illustrated handbook to a home celebration of Hanukkah.

The Art of Jewish Living: Hanukkah, by Ron Wolfson (New York: Federation of Jewish Men's Clubs and the University of Judaism, 1985), contains detailed explanations of Hanukkah's history and rituals, along with photographs and interviews of contemporary families sharing their Hanukkah experiences.

The Hanukkah Book, by Mae Shafter Rockland (New York: Schocken, 1975), includes historical background, games, party ideas, advanced folk arts and crafts, recipes, and gift ideas for the holiday. It's illustrated with drawings and black-and-white photographs.

For Children

A Hanukkiyah for Dina, by Floreva G. Cohen (New York: Board of Jewish Education, 1980), for ages 3 to 6, is the perfect Hanukkah story for preschoolers. Dina longs to have a Hanukkah menorah like everyone else in the family, but she is "too little"—until her loving Grandpa thinks of a plan. (The book is also available in simple Hebrew.)

Beni's First Chanukah, written and illustrated by Jane Breskin Zalben (New York: Henry Holt, 1988), for ages 3 to 7, is another picture book of the fantasy bear world celebrating the festival of lights.

Malke's Secret Recipe, by David A. Adler, illustrated by Joan Halpern (Rockville, MD: Kar-Ben, 1989), for ages 4 to 8, is an amusing story of Hanukkah in Chelm.

Potato Pancakes All Around, written and illustrated by Marilyn Hirsch (Philadelphia: Jewish Publication Society, 1978), for ages 5 to 9, is a humorous "stone soup" type of story, with potato *latkes*, rather than soup, as the magic recipe. The charming illustrations glow in gold and brown, like an old photograph.

Hanukkah Cat, written and illustrated by Chaya Burstein (Rockville, MD: Kar-Ben, 1985), for ages 3 to 8, is a children's favorite about a stray cat who comes to stay on Hanukkah. It's suitable for reading one section aloud each night of the holiday. There's a cassette tape available, recorded by Cherie Karo Schwartz.

Just Enough Is Plenty, by Barbara Diamond Goldin, illustrated by Seymour Schwartz (New York: Viking Child Books, 1988), for ages 6 to 10, is an award-winning story of Hanukkah in the *shtetl* that emphasizes the importance of sharing. It's illustrated with colorful primitive-style pictures.

The Odd Potato, by Eileen Sherman, illustrated by Katherine Kahn (Rockville, MD: Kar-Ben, 1984), for ages 7 to 10, is about a girl who has lost her mother and now decides to make Hanukkah for her family.

All the Lights in the Night, by Arthur A. Levine, illustrated by James E. Ransome (New York: Morrow, 1991), for ages 7 and up, is the inspiring, fact-based story of two brothers' Hannukkah celebrations during their journey to freedom from czarist Russia.

The Power of Light, by Isaac Bashevis Singer, illustrated by Irene Lieblich (New York: Farrar,

Straus & Giroux, 1980), for ages 8 and up, contains eight engrossing Hanukkah stories from the Nobel laureate's pen, one for each night of the holiday, with lovely color illustrations.

The Christmas Revolution, by Barbara Cohen, illustrated by Diane DeGroat (New York: Lothrop, Lee & Shepard Books, 1987), for ages 8 to 11, is a realistic children's novel about some Jewish children's adventures in public school at Christmas and Hanukkah time.

The Hanukkah Book, by Marilyn Burns, illustrations by Martha Weston (New York: Four Winds Press, 1981), for ages 9 to 13, explains the holiday's story and rituals. It also includes illustrated recipes, crafts, and games as well as a chapter on the Hebrew calendar and a section about dealing with Christmas.

Tu BiShvat

For Children

A Tree Full of Mitzvos, by Dina Herman, illustrated by Yoel Kenny (Brooklyn, NY: Merkos L'inyonei Chinuch, 1985), for ages 3 to 7. A tree growing outside a traditional Jewish home learns that the kindness he can do for other living creatures is a very worthy *mitzvah* indeed.

The Gift That Grew, by Yaffa Ganz, illustrated by Harvey Klineman (New York: Feldheim, 1986), for ages 4 to 8. Young Elisha learns how to appreciate and care for a tree, God's gift of nature.

Alina, A Russian Girl Comes to Israel, by Mira Meir, photos by Yael Rozen (Philadelphia: Jewish Publication Society, 1982), for ages 5 to 10, is the story of a young immigrant's adjustment to Israel, illustrated with black-and-white photographs. Alina learns to put down roots, much like the little tree that she plants for her first Tu BiShvat in Israel.

Honi and His Magic Circle, by Phillis Gershator, illustrated by Shay Rieger (Philadelphia; Jewish Publication Society, 1979), for ages 5 and up, is a charming presentation of the legendary figure Honi, who wandered the land of Israel planting carob trees for coming generations. A Jewish antecedent of Johnny Appleseed and Rip Van Winkle, Honi sleeps for 70 years and awakens to find his trees grown.

Seders for Tu BiShvat

For All Ages

A Seder for Tu Bishvat, by Harlene Appelman and Jane Shapiro, illustrated by Chari R. McLean (Rockville, MD: Kar-Ben Copies, 1985). Especially for children and their families, this educational and appealing *seder* format includes history, stories, songs, planting, and other activities.

Seder Tu Bishvat—The Festival of Trees, written and edited by Adam Fisher (New York: CCAR, 1984). Another contribution to *Clal Yisrael* (all Jewry) from the Reform movement is this beautiful guidebook for a Tu BiShvat *seder*. It includes two programs, one for mixed groups and one for young children.

Tu BiShvat Materials for All Ages

The Jewish National Fund (JNF), Department of Education, 114 E. 32nd St., Suite 1501, New York, NY 10016, (212) 779-0310. The Jewish National Fund plants trees in Israel on Tu BiShvat and throughout the year. Their education department's catalog has many interesting items on trees, nature, Zionism, and Israel. For example, the book **Ecology in the Bible**, by Nogah Hareuveni with Helen Frenkly (Kiryat Ono: Neot Kedumim, 1974), has beautiful color photos of Israel's natural beauty as well as intriguing explanations of the ties between nature and Jewish symbols and teachings. (For example, did you know that there's a *menorah* plant?)

Purim

For Children

Do-It-Yourself Megillah, text by Joel Lurie Grishaver, design by Lisa Rachwerger (Los Angeles: Torah Aura Productions, 1988), for ages 5 to 8, is a book that transforms into an illustrated scroll of Esther.

A Purim Album, by Raymond A. Zwerin and Audrey Friedman Marcus, illustrated by Marlene Lobell Ruthen (New York: UAHC, 1981), for ages 5 to 8, retells the traditional Purim story through the experiences of a young girl who plays the part of Esther in her school play.

Goldie's Purim, written and illustrated by Jane Breskin Zalben (New York: Henry Holt, 1991), for ages 5 to 7. The cute bear adventures continue when Goldie dresses up as Queen Esther.

Megillahs for All Ages

The Whole Megillah, by Shoshana Silberman, illustrated by Katherine Kahn (Rockville, MD: Kar-

Ben, 1990), for ages 5 to adult, is a fully illustrated abridged *megillah* for home, school, and synagogue. It includes commentary, songs, discussion questions, activities, and crafts.

The Family Megillah, by Rabbi Meir Zlotowitz and Rabbi Nosson Scherman (Brooklyn, NY: Mesorah Publications, 1987), is a handy Hebrew-English text of the complete Book of Esther, with traditionally oriented commentaries.

Passover

For Adults

The Art of Jewish Living: The Passover Seder, by Dr. Ron Wolfson (New York: Federation of Jewish Men's Clubs and the University of Judaism, available from Torah Aura Productions, 4423 Fruitland Ave., Los Angeles, CA 90058). This is the ultimate guidebook for *seder* leaders. The historical background and structure of the *seder* is fully explained, and rituals and activities for each section are offered. Texts of the key prayers are given in Hebrew, English, and transliteration. Contemporary families share their traditions and experiences, illustrated with black-and-white photographs. It also shows how to prepare for the holiday. An accompanying workbook and tape of the prayers is available from United Synagogue of America. The book is also available in Russian.

A Feast of History, by Chaim Raphael (New York: Gallery Books, 1972), teaches the history and meaning of Passover, with illustrations throughout.

For Children

Happy Passover Rosie, written and illustrated by Jane Breskin Zalben (New York: Henry Holt, 1990), for ages 3 to 7. It's *seder* time in fantasy bearland. The pictures are full of cute holiday details.

Just a Week to Go, by Yeshara Gold, photographs by Yaacov Harlap (Brooklyn, NY: Mesorah, 1987), for ages 5 to 9, includes color photographs of the beauties of traditional Passover preparations in the Jewish quarter of the Old City of Jerusalem, as five-year-old Raffi gets ready for the *seder*.

Everything's Changing—It's Pesach, by Julie Auerbach, illustrated by Chari Radin (Rockville, MD: Kar-Ben, 1986), for ages 3 to 8, is a clever rhyming tale about how grown-ups' expectations seem to change in the spirit of Passover.

Only Nine Chairs—A Tall Tale for Passover, by Deborah Miller, illustrated by Karen Ostrove (Rockville, MD: Kar-Ben, 1982), for ages 3 to 8, is a fun rhymed story of trying to fit in too many Passover guests.

The Passover Parrot, by Evelyn Zusman, illustrated by Katherine Kahn (Rockville, MD: Kar-Ben, 1983), for ages 4 to 8. Adventure ensues when a parrot learns the four questions.

But This Night Is Different—A Seder Experience, by Audrey Friedman Marcus and Raymond A. Zwerin, illustrated by Judith Gwyn Brown (New York: UAHC, 1980), for ages 5 to 8, is a lively and thoughtful presentation of the uniqueness of the *seder* experience.

Dayenu—Or How Uncle Murray Saved the Seder, by Rosalind Schilder, illustrated by Katherine J. Kahn (Rockville, MD: Kar-Ben, 1988), for ages 4 to 9. At first, Uncle Murray and Aunt Helene decide that a *seder* is too much work. But soon a funny and joyful celebration is underway.

A Family Passover, by Anne, Jonathan, and Norma Rosen, photos by Laurence Salzmann (Philadelphia: Jewish Publication Society, 1980), ages 5 to 9. A contemporary family prepares for Passover, and each step of the way is documented in black-and-white photographs by an outstanding photographer.

Videos for Children

My Exodus (Los Angeles, CA: Torah Aura Productions, 1985), for ages 8 to 11. Child performers share their memories of leaving Egypt in an appealing production that teaches traditional texts and fulfills the Passover injunction, "in each generation, every person should view him or herself as if he or she personally went out of Egypt."

Passover *Haggadahs*

There are dozens upon dozens of *Haggadahs* available today. Here are a few popular editions:

For Adults and Families

Passover Haggadah: The Feast of Freedom, edited by Rachel Rabinowicz, illustrated by Dan Reissinger (New York: Rabbinical Assembly, 1982), is the Conservative movement's official *Haggadah*. It has a clear translation, attractive graphics, and commentaries that bring the text alive. A song cassette and a children's coloring book are also available.

The New Union Haggadah, edited by Herbert Bronstein, drawings by Leonard Baskin (New York: CCAR, 1985), is the Reform movement's

RESOURCES

Haggadah, with beautiful artwork and both traditional and contemporary texts.

The Family Haggadah, edited by Rabbi Nosson Scherman and Rabbi Avie Gold (Brooklyn, NY: Mesorah, 1981), is the complete traditional text of the *Haggadah* with facing Hebrew and English pages, along with instructions and marginal comments.

On Wings of Freedom, edited and translated by Rabbi Richard N. Levy (Hoboken, NJ: Ktav Publishing and B'nai B'rith Hillel Foundation, 1989), is the Hillel *Haggadah* for the Nights of Passover, with a thought-provoking blend of the traditional texts and contemporary interpretations. A leader's handbook is available, with additional discussion topics.

A Family Haggadah, by Shoshana Silberman, illustrated by Katherine Kahn (Rockville, MD: Kar-Ben, 1987). This family-oriented *Haggadah* blends tradition and innovation, text and commentary. An accompanying tape is available: "Songs for a Family Seder," sung by Cantor Robert Freedman and students of the Princeton Jewish Center Religious School.

For Use with Young Children

My Very Own Haggadah, by Judyth Saypol and Madeline Wikler, illustrated by Chaya Burstein (Rockville, MD: Kar-Ben, 1983), for ages 3 to 7, includes songs, recipes, crafts, and pictures to color.

Building Jewish Life Haggadah by Joel Lurie Grishaver, et al. (Los Angeles: Torah Aura Productions, 1989), for ages 5 and up, has a simplified text, clear instructions, attractive black-and-white photographs, and cartoonlike illustrations. It's ideal for model *seders*, for young children to use at the regular *seder*, and even for a very simplified home *seder*.

Mah Nishtanah?—A Passover Haggadah for Young Children, edited by Shaul Meizlish (Tel Aviv: Shai Publishers, 1985), for ages 5 to 9, shows each step of the *seder*, illustrated with color pictures and color photos of a family *seder* in Israel.

Artscroll Youth Haggadah, edited by Rabbi Nosson Scherman and Rabbi Meir Zlotowitz (Brooklyn: Mesorah, 1987), for ages 8 and up, contains the entire traditional *Haggadah* text, with simplified translations and comments, fully illustrated in color.

The Animated Haggadah, by Ronny Orgen and Uri Shinar (New York: Shapolsky, 1985), for ages 5 to 10, is a fun *Haggadah* for children. It has colorful "claymation" illustrations. An accompanying videocassette and activity book are also available.

We Tell It To Our Children: The Story of Passover, by Mary Ann Barrows Wark, illustrated by Craig Oskow (Mensch Makers Press, 1588 Northrop, St. Paul, MN 55108), involves young children in the *seder* experience through the use of puppets, pictures, and songs set to familiar folk tunes.

Yom HaShoah (Holocaust Memorial Day)

See Learning about the Holocaust, pp. 328–329.

Yom HaAtzma'ut (Israel Independence Day)

See Israel Resources, pp. 339–345.

Shavuot

Who Knows Ten?, by Molly Cone, illustrated by Uri Shulevitz (New York: UAHC, 1965), for ages 5 to 8, explains the biblical origins of the Ten Commandments, with a story to illustrate the application of each one.

God's Top Ten, by Roberta Louis Goodman (Los Angeles: Torah Aura Productions, 1992), for ages 9-12, is an interactive booklet that tells stories about and interprets the Ten Commandments. Excellent for parent-child learning.

When I Stood at Sinai, by Joel Lurie Grishaver, et al. (Los Angeles: Torah Aura Productions, 1992), for ages 11 and up (also recommended for family study sessions), is "an interactive Midrashic fantasy" that combines traditional sources and commentaries by a Hebrew-school class.

MUSIC FOR THE JEWISH HOLIDAYS

See Music Resource Guide, p. 313, for distributers of cassettes, CDs, records, and songbooks that include many holiday titles. Here's some sample selections of particular appeal to young families:

"Apples on Holidays and Other Days," by music educator Leah Abrams (LA Records), contains 24 original activity songs, chants, and riddles for holidays and everyday, for very young children. Songbook available.

Fran Avni and Jackie Cytrnbaum have created three popular cassettes for the holidays and Shabbat, from Lemonstone. Holiday titles are "Latkes

354

and Hamentashen" (Hanukkah and Purim) and "Mostly Matzah" (Passover). A combination of songs, stories, and instrumentals creates a listening treat.

Cindy Paley's Shabbat & holiday recordings feature "classic" and contemporary Jewish song in Hebrew, English, and Yiddish. They come with song booklets with translations and transliterations. Her holiday selections include "A Singing Seder" and "Hanukkah, a Joyous Celebration in Song."

Adi Sulkin's "Let's Sing" bookcassettes are a series of 15 bookcassettes for the Jewish family created by a leading Israeli music educator and produced in Israel. The booklet includes English and Hebrew texts and instructions for movement and other activities.

Song and music books from Tara Publications (see listing under music resources, p. 313) that feature holiday songs include **Hebrew Songs for All Seasons**, by Susan Searles, 91 songs with vocal lines, guitar chords, and the lyrics in Hebrew, transliteration and translation; **Holidays in Song**, edited by Velvel Pasternak, with more than 100 holiday favorites with vocal line, chords, Hebrew texts, transliterations, and translations; **The New Children's Songbook**, edited and arranged by V. Pasternak, is a comprehensive collection of 110 Jewish children's songs for holidays and many other occasions, which includes vocal line, guitar chords, Hebrew texts, activity suggestions, and singable English settings; **Hebrew Festival Melodies**, by Albert Rozin (Century) includes 22 holiday songs arranged for the elementary pianist (guitar chords included).

RESOURCE GUIDE FOR SPECIAL TIMES OF LIFE

General

For Adults

How to Run a Traditional Jewish Household, by Blu Greenberg (Northvale, NJ: Jason Aronson, 1989). The section on "Special Stages of Life" explains the Orthodox requirements as well as the human and humorous side of Jewish life-cycle ceremonies. Another chapter discusses the *mikveh* laws.

The Jewish Party Book, by Mae Shafter Rockland (New York: Schocken, 1978), is a contemporary guide to customs, folk crafts, and foods, for life-cycle events as well as for holidays. It includes

directions for how to make your own wimpel, baby quilt, invitations, party decorations, and much more. There's also a chapter on family reunions. With black-and-white photographs.

Jewish and Female, by Susan Weidman Schneider (New York: Touchstone, 1985). The section on "Rhythms and Cycles" contains a number of ideas for new and old ceremonies that celebrate a woman's life-cycle events and rites of passage. The book also offers a feminist perspective on the *mikveh*.

The Rhythms of Jewish Living—A Sephardic Approach, by Marc D. Angel (New York: Sepher-Hermon Press, 1986), presents a Sephardic outlook on the natural rhythms and passages of life, from birth to death.

For Children and Teens

The Life Cycle Workbook, by Joel Lurie Grishaver (Denver, CO: Alternatives in Religious Education, 1978), for ages 9 and up, teaches about Jewish life-cycle observances, including relevant vocabulary and source materials. The companion "Jewish Life Cycle Game," by Nachama Skolnik Moskowitz, teaches children ages 9 to 13 about the Jewish life cycle.

Birth, Covenant Ceremonies, and Hebrew Names

For Adults

The Jewish Baby Book by Anita Diamant (New York: Summit Books, 1988), is a complete guide to Jewish traditions and innovations surrounding pregnancy, ceremonies for daughters and sons, naming, holding a *simhah* (joyful party), birth announcements, adoption, and more.

The Jewish Women's Resource Center of the National Council of Jewish Women, 9 E. 69th St., New York, NY 10021, (212) 535-5900, offers collections of original naming ceremonies for baby girls, weaning prayers, and creative rituals for female life-cycle events. They also welcome donations of original poems and ceremonies.

Daughters of the King: Women and the Synagogue, edited by Susan Grossman and Rivka Haut (Philadelphia: Jewish Publication Society, 1992), includes personal vignettes by Susan Grossman and Tikva Frymer-Kensky on suggested new rituals for dealing with miscarriage (pp. 284–290) and for affirming pregnancy (pp. 290–296), respectively.

Learning Together—A Source Book for Jewish Family Education, edited by Janice P. Alper (Denver CO: Alternatives in Religious Education, 1987). This handbook to Jewish family education offers suggestions for Jewish childbirth classes, wimpel and heirloom-making workshops, and more.

And Hannah Wept: Infertility, Adoption and the Jewish Couple, by Michael Gold (Philadelphia: Jewish Publication Society, 1988), is an outstanding resource for those who are concerned with infertility, pregnancy loss, genetic diseases, adoption, and related issues. Rabbi Gold, himself an adoptive parent, speaks to the individual families as well as the Jewish community.

The Jewish Family Book, edited by Sharon Strassfeld and Kathy Green (New York: Bantam, 1981), includes a number of personal anecdotes by parents who share their feelings and experiences surrounding *brit milah* and naming their children.

The Complete Book of Hebrew Baby Names, by Smadar Shir Sidi (San Francisco: Harper & Row, 1989), lists and defines more than 5,000 Hebrew names and includes suggestions on naming.

Welcome to the World: Jewish Baby's Record Book, by Selma Weintraub and Elaine Ravich (New York: Women's League for Conservative Judaism, 1985), is a Jewish baby book with an attractive format, including quotations from traditional Jewish sources.

Music

Where Dreams Are Born: Jewish Lullabies, available from Sheera Recordings, P.O. Box 19414, Portland, OR 97219, (800) 541-9904, is a recording of favorite lullabies performed by Margie Rosenthal and Ilene Safyan in Yiddish, Hebrew, Ladino, and English. It won the Parents' Choice Honor Award for 1992.

Video

Brit Milah, (800) BABY-BOY, is a toll-free telephone number for contacting Rabbi Yehoshua Krohn, certified *mohel*, who has produced a well-received video program on the significance of the traditional *brit milah*.

Benai Mitzvah

For the Parents

Putting God on the Guest List, by Rabbi Jeffrey K. Salkin (Woodstock, VT: Jewish Lights Publishing, 1992), explains "how to reclaim the spiritual meaning of your child's *bar or bat mitzvah*." It emphasizes the Jewish values that can be realized in the context of the *mitzvah* experience and encourages parent-child interaction and discussion.

The Bar/Bat Mitzvah Planbook, by Jane Lewitt and Ellen Epstein (Lanham, MD: Scarborough House, 1991), is a step-by-step practical guide to planning your child's *mitzvah* celebration and making it a special and meaningful event.

For the Bat or Bar Mitzvah

Mitzvah, by Jacob Neusner (West Orange, NJ: Behrman House, 1981), explains the meaning of *bar* and *bat mitzvah* through primary sources and values-oriented discussions.

Your Bar/Bat Mitzvah, from UAHC Press, New York, is a series of individual pamphlets that include the Hebrew and English of each Torah and *haftarah* portion (with cantillation marks), along with commentaries that teach Jewish history, *Midrash*, and contemporary applications.

Media

Mitzvah Vision, P.O. Box 1331, Mercer Island, WA 98040, (206) 232-6544, (800) 544-9543, is a video series that helps youngsters prepare for *bat* or *bar mitzvah*. One general videocassette teaches basic prayers and cantillation, while a second is specific to each individual portion.

For Parents and Children Together

Windows: Together 2, developed by Victoria Kelman and Joel Grishaver, from The Melton Research Center, 3080 Broadway, New York, NY 10027, is a series of four booklets and leader's guide, designed to be used in a series of family programs for *b'nai mitzvah* youngsters and their parents. The themes of "Becoming" (*bat* and *bar mitzvah*), "Being" (laws and ethics), "Believing" (theology), and "Belonging" (community) are explored through drama, text study, simulations, writing, and discussions.

The Teen Years

Books for Teens

How Do I Decide?, by Roland B. Gittelsohn (West Orange, NJ: Behrman House, 1989). Rabbi Gittelsohn offers frank discussion of the many difficult issues that face today's teens. He uses fictional case studies, traditional texts, and contemporary observations to help young people develop Jewish values and a sense of responsibility. Illustrated with black-and-white photographs.

Love in Your Life—A Jewish View of Teenage Sexuality, by Roland B. Gittelsohn (New York: UAHC Press, 1991), provides a modern Jewish perspective on teenage love and sex, drawing on rabbinic literature, social scientific surveys, and the experiences of teens the author has counseled.

When Living Hurts, by Sol Gordon (New York, UAHC Press, 1985), provides encouragement and help to teens and young adults who are feeling lonely or depressed.

Discussing Sex with Children

For Adults

Does God Belong in the Bedroom?, by Rabbi Michael Gold (Philadelphia: Jewish Publication Society, 1992), explores contemporary sexual ethics based on the wisdom of classical Jewish sources.

"Jewish Silence on Sexuality," by Rabbi Harold M. Schulweis, in **Jewish Marital Status—A Hadassah Study**, edited by Carol Diament (Northvale, NJ: Jason Aronson, 1989), is a good starting point for reconsidering the Jewish attitude toward sexuality. Another recommended article on the Jewish sexual ethos is "Sexuality—The Pleasure Principle," in chapter 5 of **Jewish Female**, by Susan Weidman Schneider (see earlier listing).

Discussing Death with Children

For Teens and Adults

What Happens After I Die?—Jewish Views of Life After Death, by Rifat Sonsino and Daniel B. Syme (New York: UAHC Press, 1990), offers a variety of traditional and contemporary Jewish opinions on the subject of what happens after death.

For Children

Bubbe, Me, and Memories, by Barbara Pomerantz, photographs by Leon Lurie (New York: UAHC, 1983), for ages 5 to 8, is an award-winning book about how a child's memories of her grandmother help her to deal with the grandmother's death. It's illustrated with black-and-white photos.

Zeydeh, by Moshe Halevi Spero, illustrated by Madeline Hirsch (Lawrence, NY: Semcha Publishing, 1984), tells a story about a child's reaction to the death of his beloved grandfather. It includes descriptions of traditional practices and beliefs. An introduction for parents and teachers provides a Jewish perspective to help in answering a child's questions.

INDEX

INDEX

INDEX

About the Author

Julie Hilton Danan is the head of Judaic Studies at the Jonathan Netanyahu Academy and the religious program director for Congregation Beth Am, both in San Antonio, Texas. A popular educator and speaker, she has written articles on Jewish education, Israel, and Jewish parenting and family life for many periodicals, including *Hadassah Magazine*, the *Baltimore Jewish Times*, and the *Philadelphia Jewish Exponent*. She currently lives in San Antonio, Texas, with her husband and five children.